MARK TWAIN'S TALE OF TODAY

Halley's Comet Returns–The Celebrated Author Critiques American Politics

DONALD TIFFANY BLISS

80-8980-89

Hale & Northam LLC

Copyright 2012 Donald Tiffany Bliss

Second Printing 2017

Donald Tiffany Bliss
ISBN: 147740502X

ISBN 13: 9781477405024

Library of Congress Control Number: 2012908198

CreateSpace Independent Publishing Platform
North Charleston, South Carolina

**To Evan Bliss, who lit up the world with
his music, poetry, humor, thoughtfulness and love**

Also by Donald Tiffany Bliss

The Law of Airline Customer Relations, Stability, Security, Safety and Service
Counsel for the Situation: Shaping the Law to Realize America's Promise
(coauthor of the memoirs of the Honorable William T. Coleman Jr.)

What the Reviewers have said –

"Bliss is exceptionally well qualified to write a book on Twain and politics… An expertly guided tour for the reader who seeks a unified theory of Twain's politics." *Kevin MacDonnell, Twain Scholar*

"Bliss writes with a clarity and intelligence that are captivating… What he has to say about the life and legacy of Twain struck me as new and valuable." *James Broderick,* ***BookPleasures.com***

"Well written and so full of facts and figures that you will be in awe of the detail of research…All-in-all this is an amazing story that makes you think twice about what you thought you knew about Mark Twain." *Dad of Divas," A Great Book,"* ***Top 500 Reviewer***

"Destined to become a major source for anyone researching Twain's political views and writings…Bliss the barrister proves his case beyond a reasonable doubt that politics is just as wicked and human an enterprise now as it was in Twain's day, rendering Twain's political observations timeless." *Kevin MacDonnell,* ***Mark Twain Forum***

Table of Contents

Illustrations

> *Sam Clemens, Holder Of Patents*
> *Sam Clemens and His Nevada Friends*
> *Offices of the Virginia City Territorial Enterprise*
> *Senator William Stewart*
> *The Willard Hotel*
> *General "Black Jack" Logan*
> *Clemens Covering The Impeachment Debate*
> *Elisha Bliss, Jr.*
> *Walter and Arlene Bliss*
> *Mark Twain House, Hartford*
> *Charles Dudley Warner*
> *J. Keppler 1880 Cartoon*
> *Senator Dilworthy*
> *Mark Twain and John Raymond*
> *Mark Twain, Author of The Gilded Age*
> *Manuscript from The Gilded Age*
> *Inauguration of President Grant*
> *William Dean Howells*
> *The Clemens Family in Their Hartford Home*
> *Minneapolis Tribune Cartoon*
> *For President—Cleveland/Stevenson*
> *Thomas Nast Cartoon*
> *Mark Twain and Helen Keller*
> *Sam Clemens/Mark Twain Writing in Bed*
> *Halley's Comet*

MARK TWAIN'S TALE OF TODAY

Halley's Comet Returns–The Celebrated Author Critiques American Politics

Preface: A Tale of Today

"I came in with Halley's Comet in 1835. It is coming again next year, and I expect to go out with it. It will be the greatest disappointment of my life if I don't go out with Halley's Comet. The Almighty has said, no doubt: Now here go these two unaccountable freaks; they came in together; they must go out together."

— MARK TWAIN, 1909

On November 30, 1835, Halley's Comet graced the sky above the hamlet of Florida, Missouri. Samuel Langhorne Clemens was born prematurely—a sickly child whose parents doubted he would survive. Sam says he once asked his mother, "Were you afraid I wouldn't survive?" She replied, "No. I was afraid you would."

In 1909 the famed author, humorist, lecturer, and public commentator Mark Twain predicted his own death. And when Halley's Comet returned on its seventy-five-year cycle, Mark Twain died on April 21, 1910. By the time of his passing, he had become America's first private citizen global celebrity.

Robed in a white suit, white cravat and white shoes, crowned with unruly white hair and smoking an ever-present cigar, he was an astute observer and much sought-after commentator on American politics. His insightful commentary retains an uncanny relevance to the challenges facing contemporary America. His views are as fresh and provocative as those of any contemporary cable TV "talking head," Sunday morning roundtable debater, political blogger, or radio talk show host. As Twain reportedly said, "History does not repeat itself; it rhymes."

Mark Twain remains today among the most quoted of public figures. His aphorisms are cited to support almost any proposition—often inconsistent and contradictory positions. With a handy maxim for most any occasion, he is fondly quoted by Tea Party and Occupy Wall Street activists, union leaders, and liberal and conservative commentators. After all Samuel L. Clemens was not a political scientist or philosopher who expounded a concrete, coherent theory of governance. He was an equal opportunity satirist, ridiculing the dogmas, shibboleths, and platitudes that characterize the conventional wisdom, regardless of ideological bearings.

One of Twain's favorite techniques was to show the absurdity of a position or policy by making people laugh at it as he argued for it with the most exaggerated and lurid reasoning. Sometimes his less-than-subtle readers missed the point. In the process his true opinion was never actually revealed.

The progenitor of American political satire, Twain's progeny include, to cite but a few, H.L. Menken, Will Rogers, Christopher Buckley, Jon Stewart, Stephen Colbert, Bill Maher, George Carlin, the Capitol Steps, Second City, and the annual Gridiron dinner at which politicians and the press poke fun at themselves and each other. Indeed, most successful politicians appreciate the value of humor in getting their message across and easing the tensions of democracy. And when it is absent, progress often stalls and partisanship prevails.

With passionate faith in the Republic's potential, despite the corrupting nature of political power, Twain believed that satire and story-telling are among the most effective instruments of reform. In one of his last, most philosophical stories, not published until after his death, Twain reveals how he combats what he sees as humankind's inherent venality: "Power, Money, Persuasion, Persecution– These can lift at a colossal humbug– push a little– crowd a little– weal in a little, century by century: but only laughter can blow it to rags and atoms at a blast. *Against the assault of laughter nothing can stand.*"[1]

Through humor and fiction Twain unveils his reformist agenda. In fiction like *A Connecticut Yankee in King Arthur's Court* and *Huckleberry Finn*, he imparts his faith in representative democracy in which individuals are free to innovate in a merit-based society and to act on their conscience, rejecting stale conventions and prejudices. In *The Gilded Age* and *Pudd'nhead Wilson*, he exposes the darker side – the corrupting influence of political and economic power exercised by flawed human beings.

Given the breadth and turbulence of his experience, it was inevitable that Clemens's views would evolve and mature as he traveled through the phases of life. Not surprisingly, two excellent books about his social and economic positions depict very different portraits. Philip Foner, in *Mark Twain: Social Critic* (1958), stresses Twain's "burning hatred of all forms of intolerance, tyranny and injustice, an abhorrence of cant and pretension," as well as his crusade against corruption and support for the working person, women's rights, and honest and efficient democracy.[2] Louis Budd, in *Mark Twain: Social Philosopher* (1962), does not disagree with these statements but emphasizes Clemens's faith in the free-enterprise system, pragmatic involvement in politics, skepticism of bureaucracy, defense of property rights, and pursuit of wealth through innovation and invention.[3] Both portraits accurately reflect dimensions of this complex and anguished icon. Attempts to pin labels on him such as liberal or conservative are not only fruitless—they contradict the very iconoclastic independence from labels and doctrine that characterized his outlook. He once wrote in his *Notebook*, "The radical of one century is the conservative of the next. The radical invents the views. When he has worn them out the conservative adopts them."[4] In his mature years, Twain would have been called a nineteenth century liberal who places his faith in individual achievement, responsible free enterprise, administering to the poor through voluntary associations, and minimal government intrusion into the lives of citizens. A strong advocate of representative democracy, he believed that educated voters should elect honest, independent-thinking individuals who put public interest above political and personal aggrandizement, overseeing a limited government that gives each person—regardless of birth status, race, or gender—"*a fair chance and no favor.*"[5]

Twain took on government, business, and labor leaders during a period in American history that has many parallels with the twenty-first century—economic cycles of boom and bust, rapid technological and cultural change, risky financial innovation and speculation, corporate misfeasance, global integration, the triumph of "rugged individualism" over community values, the influence of money in politics and the lobby in Congress, the growing disparity between the rich and middle class, polarized political parties and stalemated government, and US military intervention in faraway lands. With his acerbic wit, Twain commanded public attention and demanded that Americans rise up, exercise their democratic powers, and hold their leaders accountable. For a fresh look at the possibilities, it's well worth revisiting his advice and commentary in the context of contemporary society. As Twain said in 1908, "history repeats itself: whatever has been the rule in history may be depended upon to remain the rule."[6] He called it the "Law of Periodical Repetition, everything which has happened once must happen again and again and again—not capriciously, but at regular periods"—like the return of Halley's Comet.[7]

During the economic boom of 1869–73, Twain wrote his first novel in collaboration with Charles Dudley Warner, an editor of the *Hartford Courant*. The title of the book, *The Gilded Age: A Tale of To-day*, gave its name to the era it describes. This provocative tale about Americans' obsession with getting rich—greed and speculation in the financial markets and the influence of money and lobbyists in Congress—remains a *Tale of Today*.* Contemporary commentators are drawing parallels between our age and the Gilded Age.[8] In *Divided Heart*, E. J. Dionne posits that in the twenty-first century, "we are now confronting the reemergence of radical individualism and our own version of

---

* When "Gilded Age" is not italicized, it refers generally to the historical period from after the Civil War through the turn of the century. When italicized it refers to Mark Twain's controversial book.

the Gilded Age."[9] Nobel prize-winning political economist, Paul Krugman, puts it more bluntly: "we live in a second Gilded Age, as the middle-class society of the postwar era rapidly vanishes."[10]

After the Civil War, a network of debt-financed, federally subsidized railroads united east and west in a powerful commercial union. Large corporations—like the Pennsylvania Railroad, the Union Pacific, Carnegie Steel, Western Union, Standard Oil, and the emerging consolidated giant "trusts" in beef, tobacco, and sugar—dominated the national economy. Wall Street secured its role as America's financial epicenter as it invented new ways to make money from transactions in stocks and bonds—some legitimate, some not so. Railroad speculators sought to develop the vast expanses of land now accessible by rail, inflating real estate prices. Immigration surged to meet the demand for workers in the industrialized cities, sparking sometimes violent ethnic strife and labor unrest. Captains of industry and finance—frequently targets of Twain's acerbic satire—like Jay Gould, Cornelius Vanderbilt, John D. Rockefeller, Andrew Carnegie, and J. P. Morgan—amassed great fortunes amidst the squalid conditions of the working urban and rural poor. Income disparity reached an all-time high as the pursuit of the almighty dollar became the predominant cultural value. The evolving system of corporate organization enabled a small minority of very wealthy men to exercise enormous power over commerce and government.[11]

In the nation's capital, the federal government had grown in size and importance during the Civil War. In 1867 thirty-two-year-old Sam Clemens arrived in Washington and served briefly as a senator's aide and capital reporter. From his ringside seat, he watched representatives of the railroads, Wall Street, mining, agriculture, and manufacturing flood the corridors of power seeking special favors. Contrary to the conventional wisdom, entrepreneurs did not compete solely in unregulated free markets; they competed in Congress, fiercely lobbying for funding, land grants, and special-interest legislation. Congress picked winners and losers, and money co-opted the legislative process. Clemens became a lifelong observer and critic of American democracy at work. In volume 1 of his unexpurgated *Autobiography*, published in 2010– one hundred years after his death as he had stipulated– Twain did not mince words in describing what Congress does "*so faithfully and with such enthusiasm for our lawless railway corporations, our rotten beef trusts, our vast robber dens of insurance magnates; in a word, for each and all of our multimillionaires and their industries—protect them, take watchful care of them, preserve them from harm like a Providence, and secure their prosperity, and increase it.*"[12]

Drawing on his "gold mine" of Washington experience, Twain began writing *The Gilded Age*. As he wrote, the sleepy press awoke and exposed the multifarious scandals that erupted during President Grant's administration. In a thinly disguised tale of politicians, speculators, and corruption, the coauthors describe a Congress overrun by lobbyists, consumed by self-dealing, and fueled by railroad and Wall Street money.

By the time *The Gilded Age* was published in November 1873, the speculative bubble had burst. In September 1873 the nation's premier investment bank—Jay Cooke & Co., which had financed the Union victory—collapsed. It had made too many risky loans for overvalued real estate and underutilized railroads. The country entered what was then called the Great Depression. The economy shrank for sixty-five straight months—still an unbroken record. By 1876 half the nation's railroads were bankrupt, and half the iron and steel foundries were closed. Three years later wholesale prices were down 30 percent.[13] *The Gilded Age* conveys a powerful message about the perils of a culture obsessed with getting rich, a free market driven by risky speculation, and a government subservient to moneyed interests.

A hundred years after the book's publication, history began repeating itself. Starting in the mid-1970s, the modern era of speculative finance brought a flurry of mergers and acquisitions, leveraged buyouts, the savings and loan crisis, the dot.com bubble, a plague of large corporate scandals and bankruptcies, risky investment vehicles—like junk bonds, securitized mortgages, and credit default swaps—and the bailout of financial institutions and corporations too big to fail. It's no coincidence that by 2007 financial and insurance institutions accounted for 40 percent of US corporate profits compared to only 10 percent in the 1970s.[14]

The rich grew richer and the middle class poorer. According to a study by the Congressional Budget Office, in 1970 the wealthiest *1 percent* of families took in 9 percent of the total national income, but by 2007 they accounted for 23.5 percent—as much income each year as the bottom 60 percent of Americans. And the top 1 percent possessed as much wealth as the bottom 90 percent.[15] By 2009, the top twenty-five hedge fund managers averaged a billion dollars each in income that was taxed at a lower rate than their secretaries, as Warren Buffet is fond of saying. By 2012 the average CEO compensation of a major corporation was 350 percent of their workers' wages—a ratio that exceeded almost all other developed nations.

For the average American, the latest census in 2010 brought bad news. Since peaking in 1999, median family income had declined 7.1 percent. With the loss of manufacturing jobs and the erosion of unions, the typical male worker's income in 2010 fell to the 1978 level. With the decline in housing values, the net worth of American families plunged even more. A June 2012 Federal Reserve survey found that the median net worth of American families declined 39 percent in the three years since the 2007 recession began.[16] Income disparity reached levels not seen since 1911.

A significant difference between the Gilded Age and today is the global reach of modern multinational corporations, transcending national regulatory jurisdictions and impacting the world's economic fortunes. In the Gilded Age, corporations imported cheap labor from China and Ireland, but in recent decades US-based corporations easily move capital and jobs to emerging markets with lower wages and taxes. US multinationals earned more profits abroad than in the United States, and from 1999 to 2008, they cut their domestic workforces by 1.9 million jobs while increasing employment overseas by 2.4 million.[17] Avoiding a 35 percent corporate tax rate, US companies kept more than two trillion dollars overseas, and their investment in the US domestic economy fell precipitously. It was a self-defeating strategy as middle class families accumulated mounds of debt to maintain their standard of living, and— encouraged by government policies—they purchased homes beyond their means to use as ATM machines. When their borrowing power was saturated, consumer demand fell and the economy stalled.

In The Gilded Age, Twain focused on the influence of the lobby and money in Congress. Despite numerous regulatory restrictions and campaign finance reforms, these influences continue unabated. More than twelve thousand active, registered lobbyists—many of them former members of Congress or congressional aides—raise campaign funds and draft legislation. The power of the fourth branch is as great as ever. In the *Buckley v. Valeo, SpeechNow.org,* and *Citizens United* decisions, the courts opened the sluices to unlimited independent expenditures by wealthy individuals, corporations, unions, and advocacy organizations in support of candidates for public office, decimating statutory attempts to limit the influence of money in politics by capping campaign contributions. The cost of election campaigns has skyrocketed. Members of Congress running for reelection in the now perpetual campaign devote endless hours to fund-raising, diverting them from the legislative business, which is delegated to staff and lobbyists.[18] In 2016, the cost of senate races in Florida and Pennsylvania each exceeded $50 million.

Mostly remembered today as the "Lincoln of our literature," Clemens was an astute observer of the political process, a caustic commentator on contemporary social and economic issues, and an unrelenting critic of phony patriotism and jingoistic foreign policy. He implores Americans and their elected representatives to reject platitudes, platforms, pledges, and petty partisanship and instead to think and act independently, relying only on their conscience. His insightful commentary about corporate lobbying, the corrupting influence of money in the legislative process, an overtly political media, parliamentary gamesmanship, an arrogant foreign policy, and a lethargic, uniformed voting public remains relevant today. The snares and traps that threaten

American democracy are not new. It's worthwhile to revisit what America's first "talking head" had to say about them. That is the purpose of this story.

Samuel Langhorne Clemens spoke with authority. His life-long interest in politics dated back to his father's Whig-affiliated political activity and financial speculation that left the family penurious. After his father died, Sam dropped out of school at twelve and continued his education as a printer's devil for his brother's newspapers and later as a journalist sparring with the Nevada territorial legislature. He learned early on that in speaking truth to power, the medicine goes down a lot easier with a heavy dose of humor. *"History has tried hard to teach us that we can't have good government under politicians,"* he quipped, *"Now to go and stick one at the head of government couldn't be wise."*[19] Twain was an early master of the sound bite, but beneath the surface of a pithy epigram was a fundamental irony: the talent and tactics required to campaign for public office are not necessarily the skills needed to govern effectively.

After Nevada senator William Stewart dismissed his young legislative aide in 1868, Clemens became a reporter covering Congress during the hapless Andrew Johnson administration. That his Senate boss chaired the Pacific Railroad Committee while on the dole of the Central Pacific Railroad was simply the way Washington did business. Twain's oft-quoted comment—*"It could probably be shown by facts and figures that there is no distinctly native American criminal class except Congress"*[20]—was not such a stretch given the bribery and vote-buying that pervaded Congress, as well as its practice of passing legislation that enriched its sponsors. *"I am a moralist in disguise,"* he confessed, *"it gets me into heaps of trouble when I go thrashing around in political questions."*[21] As Clemens the journalist covered the congressional debates on postwar reconstruction of the South and President Johnson's impeachment proceedings, he witnessed partisan party warfare at its worst—but he also saw Congress at its best. Monumental civil rights legislation and constitutional amendments were debated and passed, perfecting the flawed Constitution by abolishing slavery and establishing equal protection and voting rights for freedmen—rights mostly to be ignored in the decades that followed.

After Clemens became a celebrated author, he frequently visited Washington to lecture, lobby, advise presidents, and testify before Congress. Eschewing political parties and public office, the mature Twain campaigned for and against candidates based on their character and record of integrity. "I simply want to see the right man at the helm," he said, "I don't care what his party creed is."[22]

As he grew in public stature, Clemens became a sought-after commentator. He bitterly attacked America's imperialist engagement in unjust wars and its occupation of foreign lands. He strongly advocated social and racial justice and passionately promoted civic education. He feared the American experiment would fail unless educated and informed voters elected competent representatives who acted with courage and independence, instead of reciting "thread-bare platitudes and 'give-me-liberty-or-give-me-death' buncombe," as he put it.[23] Invoking burlesque buffoonery, sardonic satire, irreverent irony, and poignant pathos, Twain's only guide was his conscience—free of blind allegiance to any political or religious institution or conventional wisdom. In his many books, articles, newspaper reports, unpublished dictations, letters, lectures, and essays, he spoke caustically, critically, and insightfully about the American political system.

How were Clemens's views formed? Like the Mississippi River Valley from which he came, Clemens drew sustenance from many streams of America. His empathy for the human predicament and diverse exposure to the American experience shaped his views on politics. He grew up poor in a border slave state where he was at the epicenter of the great slavery debate. He gained confidence as a river pilot, tasted the freedom and rugged individualism of a frontier miner, lived many years abroad, and lectured around the world. As a son, sibling, loving husband, and father, he experienced heartbreaking tragedy. Clemens once said that "the secret source of Humor itself is not joy but sorrow."[24] He had a deep well from which to draw. Beneath the acerbic wit was a fearless assault on the greed and corruption that threatened American self-government and free enterprise.

Clemens views evolved and changed (sometimes 180 degrees) through the years. In a speech entitled "Consistency," he wrote: "What then is the true gospel of consistency? Change. Who is the really consistent man? The man who changes. Since change is the law of his being; he cannot be consistent if he is stuck in a rut." He mocked the average man who "has turned the right and wrongs of things entirely around and is proud to be 'consistent,' unchanging, immovable, fossilized."[25] This writer's conundrum is when to refer to Clemens and when to refer to Twain. I prefer to ascribe experiences, actions, and attitudes to the man Samuel Clemens rather than to the pseudonym Mark Twain, even though it was Twain whom the public came to revere as America's first authentic author and global icon. When quoting or paraphrasing what he wrote or spoke as Mark Twain, I identify the source as Twain. When was Twain really speaking for Clemens the man? That question will never be fully answered.

This book is not a biography. There are many fascinating biographies of Samuel Clemens/Mark Twain, as well as his three-volume autobiography, a paragon of scholarship, published by the Mark Twain Project in Berkeley, which was completed in 2015. Some biographical information is necessary in the following six chapters to illustrate how his life experiences and early writings shaped and foreshadowed his views about American politics. Chapters seven through nine discuss *The Gilded Age: A Tale of To-day*, which addresses the state of American politics in ways that speak boldly to contemporary conditions. I have sought to differentiate between Clemens's views and my own views about how his commentary remains relevant today. I do not mean to speculate as to what Clemens would have thought about American politics today that even his most vivid of imaginations could scarcely have predicted. I assume complete responsibility for my own interpretations and fully appreciate that Twain's commentary is often susceptible of multiple interpretations. Chapters ten and eleven recount Clemens's involvement in politics during the last three decades of the nineteenth century, his relationships with presidents and Congress, and his growing disillusionment with political campaigns and corrupt government. Chapters twelve through fifteen take a different tack and focus on Clemens's evolving views of the significant issues of his time: civil rights, women's suffrage, church and state, the role of government, laissez-faire economics, and so forth. Chapters sixteen through eighteen discuss Clemens's foreign policy activism, culminating after the turn of the century in his bitter criticism of President Theodore Roosevelt and his fervent opposition to all manifestations of colonialism and oppression. The final chapter attempts to sum up Clemens's views on politics and governance—contradictions and all—and offers a few of my own suggestions about how we might still take into account his cogent commentary. To paraphrase Santayana, if we do not learn from history, we are destined to repeat it.

This book merges two lifelong interests. My great-grandfather Elisha Bliss Jr., president of the American Publishing Company of Hartford, published six of Twain's early books, among them his best-selling *The Innocents Abroad: A New Pilgrim's Progress*; his tales of his western experiences, *Roughing It*; *The Gilded Age: A Tale of To-day*; and the American classic, *The Adventures of Tom Sawyer*. Although Clemens stayed with Bliss until Elisha's death in 1880, he does not remember him fondly in his *Autobiography*— and that is an understatement! Yet, to publish several of his last books, Clemens returned to the American Publishing Company, then run by Elisha's sons, Frank and Walter—my grandfather— whom he remembers more fondly.

My other interest arises from over forty years working in Washington, DC, for the federal government and in the private practice of law. I've had a ringside seat for the workings of government and politics and their interaction with American capitalism in the nation's capital. Having worked as a registered lobbyist, testified before Congress, drafted regulations and legislation, directed a political action committee, and advised private clients on the mysterious workings of the federal bureaucracy, I periodically return, like Halley's Comet, to Mark Twain's words: *"It cannot be well or safe to let the present political conditions continue indefinitely. They can be improved, and American citizenship should rise up from its disheartenment and see that it is done.*"[26]

This second printing of Mark Twain's Tale of Today incorporates certain corrections provided by readers and an index. Some but not all of the statistics have been updated, but the flaws in American politics insightfully articulated by Mark Twain remain essentially unchanged.

As this second printing goes to press, we have witnessed the inauguration of President Donald J. Trump after an extraordinary presidential campaign that seemed to defy all political conventions. While there are many interpretations of Trump's surprising victory, it is not a stretch to assume that some of Clemens' well-honed observations during the Gilded Age may have been contributing factors– a Congress and federal bureaucracy that had lost touch with the American people, rising income inequality that leaves too many working families behind, the corrupting effect of money in politics, and a general skepticism of professional politicians. The 2016 campaign revealed the pent-up frustrations of many Americans with the uneven impact of globalization and brought into question America's global responsibilities in a world beset with proliferating terrorism and ethnic and religious conflict. Echoes of "America First" resonated with the majority vote in the electoral college. A 2017 report showed that the eight richest people in the world, six of them Americans, have as much wealth as the poorest one-half of the world's population– is this really sustainable? We do not know what the future will bring. It is a pity that Mark Twain is no longer around to comment on it– or at least ease our anxieties in a troubled world with a heavy dose of humor.

Donald T. Bliss
Washington, D.C.
March 2017

Prologue: A Flying Trip To Washington

"If you were a member of Congress (no offense). "

— MARK TWAIN

Raised in the river town of Hannibal, Missouri, seventeen-year-old Sam Clemens grew restless. His work as a printer's devil and budding writer on his brother's local newspaper had piqued his interest in faraway places and the world beyond his parochial upbringing. He fantasized about visiting the glittering Crystal Palace, the huge glass dome being constructed on Fifth Avenue for the 1853 New York World's Fair. Sam traveled to St. Louis in June 1853 to live with his sister and brother-in-law for a couple months.

The gateway to the frontier—the largest city west of the Mississippi with a population exceeding one hundred thousand—St. Louis bustled with immigrants, slave traders, river merchants, and speculators eyeing the riches of the western territories. There Sam planned a trip to the nation's birthplace and the financial centers of the Northeast. It was his first venture out of the Midwest, and it launched him on a life of adventure and personal growth that seemed utterly unimaginable for a poor Missouri boy with little formal schooling.

After living and working as an itinerant printer in New York and Philadelphia, Sam decided to take what he described as a "flying trip" to the nation's capital. He boarded a night train in Philadelphia and arrived at the Baltimore and Ohio station in Washington on the morning of Thursday, February 16, 1854.[1]

Just north of the Senate wing of the Capitol, the Italianate building was not far from where Union Station, designed by Daniel Burnham and completed in 1907, sits today. The snow was "falling so thickly," Sam wrote, that he "could scarcely see across the street," which was probably a good thing. As the snow melted, the city turned into rivers of mud swirling through mostly unpaved streets. Livestock roamed freely among the fewer than sixty thousand inhabitants, including slaves and freed blacks.

Sam Clemens could never abide the Washington weather, which he thought was a perfect metaphor for its politics—fickle, unpredictable, and shifting between extremes of hot and cold. This may explain why, though he visited the capital city often, he rarely stayed long. As he later wrote: "If you were posted on politics, you are posted on weather. I can't manage either; when I go out with an umbrella, the sun shines, if I go without it, it rains; if I have my overcoat with me, I am bound to roast—if I haven't, I am bound to freeze. Some people like Washington weather. I don't. Some people prefer mixed weather; I prefer to take mine 'straight.'"[2]

In 1854 Washington was only beginning to take the shape envisioned by Pierre L'Enfant's 1790 plan. With little funding available, the many squares, triangles, and circles on the map awaited paved streets, landscaping, and the monuments to history that would eventually grace the city.[3]

Scattered throughout the town, among the mostly unattractive "cheap little brick houses" and wooden residences, were a few magnificent government buildings of neoclassic white architecture of which Sam took note—the Treasury, the Post Office and the Patent Office. He thought the Treasury Building, with its long row of columns, was a "pretty edifice" that, he later wrote, "would command respect in any capital."[4] Still under construction, the General Post Office Department was planned to house the Tariffs Commission and Samuel F. B. Morse's first telegraph office as well as the Post Office headquarters. The Patent Office Building, north of Pennsylvania Avenue between Fifth and Ninth Streets in the heart of Penn Quarter, was constructed in 1839 on land that L'Enfant had reserved for a nondenominational cathedral. In the American spirit of innovation and invention,

a Patent Office seemed a more suitable shrine. It was the inspi-
rational highlight of Sam's short visit, and he would return to it
often in the future. It also housed the Department of the Interior
and a national museum. (The building remains today one of
Washington's finest, the home of the National Portrait Gallery
and the Smithsonian Museum of American Art.) Climbing the
front steps, Sam caught a panoramic view of the neighborhood.

Sam then visited the Mall. Andrew Jackson Downing had
begun to landscape the northern part of the Mall, but coal and
lumber yards filled much of the rest as it sloped toward the
swampy Potomac flats. Sam entered the Smithsonian Institute,
which looked "half-church and half castle," designed in the
Norman style like the Trinity Church he had visited in New York
City. It contained a library of thirty-two thousand volumes and a
lecture hall seating two thousand. That evening Benjamin Park, a
noted editor, critic, poet, and popular lecturer, recited his poem
"Fashions," ridiculing the clothing styles and fads of the day.[5]

Built by slave labor, the president's house was constructed with
Aquia Creek sandstone, whitewashed to create what Sam called
a great "white barn" surrounded by muddy farmland. Burned
by the British during the War of 1812, the reconstructed house
resembled a plantation, befitting a city known for its southern
efficiency. The grief-stricken, recently elected President Franklin
Pierce, an ancestor of Barbara Bush, resided there. Two months
before his March 1853 inauguration, he and his wife had seen
their eleven-year-old son decapitated in a train wreck, the last
of their three children to die before he became president. Jane
Pierce was despondent, writing letters to her dead son, but the
president had to muster the will to lead a nation increasingly
divided over slavery.

North of the president's house, Lafayette Square foreshadowed the city's elegant future. At its center stood Clark Mill's
statue of General Andrew Jackson at the Battle of New Orleans,
sitting astride his rearing horse in a magical display of eques-
trian prowess.[6] It was erected the year before, a precursor to the
myriad statutes that festoon the town with war heroes from many
battles—past and future. Sam thought the statue was "a beautiful
thing, and well worth a long walk on a stormy day to see."[7]

Jackson was president the year Sam was born, but the more he learned about him, the less he respected him, especially for his abusive spoils system—filling government posts with incompetent supporters. In later years Sam was to muse: What if there had been a cable informing General Jackson that the War of 1812 was over before he fought the superfluous Battle of New Orleans? The nation probably would have been spared his presidency. "We have gotten over the harms done us by the war of 1812, but not over some of those done us by Jackson's presidency," he wrote in *Life on the Mississippi*.[8]

Stately homes clustered around Lafayette Square, including the mansion of William Corcoran, a wealthy banker and philanthropist, who entertained lavishly and later gave his extensive art collection to the Corcoran Gallery. Aristocratic southerners were the elite of Washington society.

L'Enfant's plan provided for a wide avenue between the White House and the Capitol. Pennsylvania Avenue was the city's spine, a thriving central market under construction along the south side, with churches, restaurants, hotels, and shops to the north.[9]

Sam rose early on Friday morning and headed for Jenkins Hill, upon which L'Enfant's "Congress House" was constructed. "Sinking ankle deep in the mud and snow," he traipsed around the Capitol grounds until Congress came into session at about eleven o'clock. Construction had begun to expand the neoclassical Capitol building to accommodate the increased membership of the House and Senate as western territories became states. Years later the wooden dome was replaced by the much larger cast-iron dome that sits there today. Sam would later call the completed building "the most exquisitely beautiful edifice that exists on earth...There are many buildings that are grander and statelier, and a half a dozen times as large, but if there is one that is so symmetrical, so graceful, so fascinating to my eye, I have not heard of it." He could no more get tired of looking at the Capitol than he could "tire of sunset in the mountains or moonlight on the sea," except for the frescos inside the dome, to be avoided as the "delirium tremens of art."[10]

When the session began during his 1854 visit, Sam sat in the Senate gallery, observing that the senators dressed "very plainly, as they should," avoiding garish "display" as they gave "the people the benefit of their wisdom and learning for a little glory and eight dollars a day." With a precocious adolescent's sense of history, Sam wrote to his family for publication in his brother's new newspaper, the *Muscatine Journal*: "The Senate is now composed of a different material from what it once was. Its glory hath departed. Its halls no longer echo the words of a Clay, or Webster, or Calhoun.* They have played their parts and retired from the stage; and though they are still occupied by others, the void is felt." He naively wrote that the senators "did not speak unless they had something to say" but quickly added, the same "cannot be said of the Representatives."[11]

Although 1854 was a period of relative calm, the turbulence of slavery was bubbling up below the surface. Congress was debating a critical issue: whether to allow slavery in the western territories. As the territories became either slave or free states, they would shift the delicate balance in Congress and influence federal policy on slavery—the seismic fracture in nation's constitutional foundation could not be neglected much longer.

Sam took notes on the senators. Senator Lewis Cass, Democrat of Michigan, is "a fine looking old man."[12] Cass, a former general and lawyer, had lost the presidential election of 1848 to Zachary Taylor, but he later became secretary of state under the ineffectual president James Buchanan. Cass was an advocate of the popular sovereignty doctrine under which the people in each territory that achieved statehood could choose for themselves whether the new state would be slave or free.

Senator William H. Seward, a Whig of New York, is "a slim, dark, boney individual" who looked "like a respectable wind would blow him out of the country."[13] A former governor of New

---

* Aware of the founding fathers' vision of the Senate as a great deliberative body in which the important issues of the day are debated, Sam eagerly looked forward to his first of many visits to the Capitol. Daniel Webster's eloquent March 7, 1850, three-hour soliloquy in defense of the Union had referred to the Senate as "a body to which the country looks, with confidence, for wise, moderate, patriotic, and healing counsels" (Senate Historical Office, March 7, 1850). Sam's initial impressions of Congress fell far short of this ideal, and he became increasingly disillusioned with the institution despite his friendships with many of its members.

5

York and outspoken opponent of slavery, he later joined a new political party, the Republicans. Much to his surprise, he lost the 1860 Republican presidential nomination to a little-known country lawyer, Abraham Lincoln. He reluctantly agreed to serve as Lincoln's secretary of state as the president assembled his team of rivals. On that day in 1854, Sam listened from the gallery to a portion of Senator Seward's three-hour oration in support of retaining the Missouri Compromise of 1820, which prohibited slavery in the western territories north of the 36°30' parallel of latitude, except for Sam's home state—Missouri.

This tenuous agreement was threatened by the Kansas-Nebraska bill, which in addition to creating the new states of Kansas and Nebraska, would repeal the Missouri Compromise. Under the bill, introduced just a month before Sam's visit, the western territories, as they achieved statehood, could decide for themselves whether they wished to be slave or free states. The act passed in May, unraveling the fragile compromise on slavery and inciting a rush of southerners and northerners to Kansas, seeking to control the outcome of the plebiscite, among them a fiery abolitionist preacher from the Adirondacks named John Brown. Their violent encounters, which gave the territory the name Bleeding Kansas, were the prelude to the Civil War.

Sam's eyes shifted toward the "Little Giant," fidgeting impatiently as he waited his turn to speak. Standing five feet four, Stephen A. Douglas, Democrat of Illinois, who was sponsoring the Kansas-Nebraska legislation, looked like "a lawyer's clerk."[14] A great orator and dominant figure in the Senate, he had lost the 1852 presidential race despite popular support from the "Young America" faction of the Democratic Party. In 1858 he defeated Lincoln for the Illinois Senate seat, only to lose to him in the 1860 presidential election.

Having heard enough Senate oratory, Sam trudged through the mud over to the House. He was not moved by the "moving" speeches he heard, as the eighteen-year-old wrote for the *Muscatine Journal*—a half a dozen representatives appeared to have "something weighing on [their minds] on which the salvation of the Republic depended." Anxious to relieve themselves of this weighty responsibility, they yelled, "Mr. Chairman, Mr.

Chairman," their pleas echoing throughout the chamber.[15] Fourteen years later, Mark Twain remembered "perfectly well" the House debate on the Kansas-Nebraska Act, recalling that the members "seemed to be a mob of empty headed whipper snappers that had only come to Congress to make incessant motions, propose eternal amendments, and rise to everlasting points of order." He wrote, "They glanced at the galleries oftener than they looked at the Speaker, they put their feet on their desks as if they were in a beer mill; they made more racket than a rookery, and let on to know more than any body of men ever did know or ever could know by any possibility whatsoever."[16]

Amid the loquacious congressmen, Sam's eyes came to rest on the stately Thomas Hart Benton. The ancient Benton had been a senator for the first thirty years of Missouri statehood, then suffered an election defeat and returned to the House for one final term. Sam had idolized Benton ever since the senator had visited Hannibal on October 26, 1849, when Sam was almost fourteen. As an adult, Twain later put his impressions into the words of Tom Sawyer, recalling that the "greatest man in the world...proved an overwhelming disappointment—for he was not twenty-five feet high, nor even anywhere in the neighborhood of it."[17] As Benton tirelessly, thanklessly, and unsuccessfully fought to resolve the slavery issue, his eloquence was undiminished. Clemens watched Benton as he sat "silent and gloomy in the midst of the din, like a lion imprisoned in a cage of monkeys."[18]

This was not the lofty debating society envisioned by the founding fathers, where the elected elite would grapple with the great issues of the day. The visit made a lasting impression on the young tourist. Nearly two decades later, Mark Twain revisited the scene in *The Gilded Age*: "A dreary member was speaking; the presiding officer was nodding; here and there little knots of members stood in the aisles, whispering together; all about the House others sat in all the various attitudes that express weariness; some, tilted back, had one or more legs disposed upon their desks; some sharpened pencils indolently; some scribbled aimlessly, some yawned and stretched; a great many lay upon their breasts upon the desks, sound asleep and gently snoring...

Hardly a sound disturbed the stillness, save the monotonous eloquence of the gentleman who occupied the floor."[19]*

As Congress concluded its business for the week, Sam took in a play on Friday night at the National Theatre. Edwin Forrest was starring in *Othello*. Clemens had a lifelong fascination with theatre—on the stage and in politics. Over the weekend he walked around the fledgling city, his clothing caked with mud. He was puzzled by the unfinished Washington Monument, later describing how a "skeleton of a decaying scaffolding lingers about its summit."[20] Construction began in 1847 but stalled at 156 feet the following year due to lack of funds and interest. He later described the unpleasing stump rising out of "mud—sacred soil is the customary term." Twain wrote: "The memorial Chimney stands in a quiet pastoral locality that is full of reposeful expression. With a glass you can see the cow-sheds about its base, and the contented sheep nibbling pebbles in the desert solitudes that surround it, and the tired pigs dozing in the holy calm of its protecting shadow." The Potomac River threatened to lap at its base, and just to the north was the Washington Canal, built in 1815. (Touted to tourists as Venetian, the canal was an open sewer, not to be filled in until the construction of Constitution Avenue in 1911.) Clemens hoped one day the Washington Monument would be finished, symbolizing the "nation's veneration" for a man who would by then be known as the "Great-Great-Grandfather of his Country."[21] In fact construction resumed in 1879, and the monument was dedicated in 1885—the tallest masonry structure in the world.

On Saturday Sam spent four hours in the Patent Office. The first floor housed models of inventions submitted for patents. The second story was the national museum, containing thousands of antiquities. There Sam saw the original Declaration of Independence,

---

* Not much has changed today except for the introduction of technology. A visitor to the gallery might notice a few back-benchers awaiting their turn to speak as a solitary member drones on, but now it is before a C-SPAN camera providing a news feed for the locals back home. And as of a 2011 change to the House rules, back-benchers may bring their Blackberries and iPhones onto the floor and alleviate their boredom by tweeting their constituents.

the clothes George Washington wore when he resigned his commission as commander in chief, Washington's sword and camping equipment, and the coat Andrew Jackson wore at the Battle of New Orleans. The teenager was intrigued by the Peruvian mummies. Their hair was perfectly plaited but their bodies were "black, dry and crisp," and their faces "a shapeless mass of skin and flesh." The highlight of his visit was seeing Benjamin Franklin's 120-year-old printing press, which was capable of printing 125 sheets an hour. He marveled at the "vast progress" that had been made in the art of printing. "Hoe's great machine," he wrote, could throw off "twenty thousand sheets in the same space of time."[22] As a printer's devil, Sam had witnessed the revolutionary change in printing and publishing as newspapers flourished and reached an increasingly literate public. As a writer he greatly benefited from these changes, but as an investor in printing technologies he suffered untold losses.

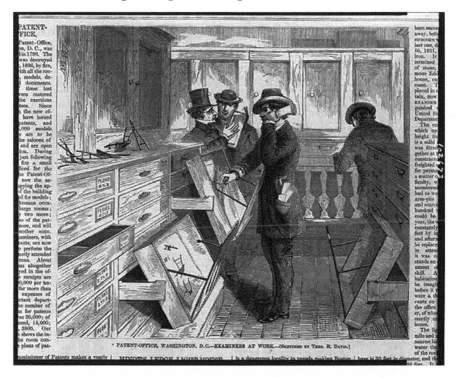

Sam Clemens, holder of three patents, visited the patent office in Washington D.C. many times. Courtesy: Library of Congress

As Sam plodded along the capital's unpaved streets, the inquisitive adolescent displayed his innate observational talents. The public buildings, he wrote for the newspaper, are "fine specimens of architecture" that "would add greatly to the embellishment of such a city as New York." Signaling the satiric wit that would characterize his view of the nation's capital in later years, the eighteen-year-old added that in Washington, "they are sadly out of place; looking like so many palaces in a Hottentot village." He described the rest of the city as consisting almost invariably of very poor two- and three-story brick houses "strewed about in clusters" as though "they might have been emptied out of a sack by some Brobdignagian gentleman, and, when falling, been scattered abroad by the winds."[23]

The following Thursday, Sam returned to Philadelphia. He stayed there a couple weeks, then headed back to New York and on to Keokuk, Iowa, where Orion and his mother were then living. Sam would not return to the capital—that "grand old benevolent National Asylum for the Helpless"—until 1867 as a young man of thirty-two.[24] By that time the arrival of westerners with the Lincoln administration, the exodus of the southern aristocracy, the accretion of federal power during the Civil War, and the influx of legions of job-seeking veterans greatly changed the character of Washington. But one thing did not change: the business of Washington remained politics. Sam's first impressions of Congress were not favorable, and they did not improve as time went on. He later wrote that "fleas can be taught nearly everything that a Congressman can."[25] He likened members of Congress to the chameleon that "whirls one eye rearwards and the other forwards—which gives him a most Congressional expression (one eye on the constituency and one on the swag)."[26]

PART I

Political Apprenticeship

"Don't let schooling interfere with your education."

MARK TWAIN

CHAPTER ONE

Shaping Sam's Views Of Democracy

"I laugh because I must not cry."

— Abraham Lincoln

Four-year-old Sam Clemens honed his ear for dialogue and storytelling at the feet of Aunt Hannah and Uncle Dan'l, slaves at his uncle John Quarles's Missouri farm. Sam and his Quarles cousins played with Uncle Dan'l's countless children. They sat together in the kitchen in the slave quarters "with the fire light playing on their faces and shadows flickering upon the walls," as they listened to the "Golden Arm" and other tales passed down through the slave community. Uncle Dan'l was to become the primary voice of the slave Jim, companion of Huckleberry Finn as they drift down the Mississippi River. Sam recalls his encounter with a young slave boy named Sandy whose singing, whistling, and laughing all day long began to irritate him. When Sam complained, his mother, Jane, teared up and said that the poor boy sang to forget that he would "never see his mother" again having been separated from his family. Sam wrote in his *Autobiography*, "Sandy's noise was not a trouble to me any more." His mother, Sam said, "never used large words" but "had a natural gift for making small ones do effective work."[1]

Sam had little patience with institutions of learning—schools and churches. His favorite course was truancy. His insatiable curiosity was nurtured by experience, human contact, and a life-long addiction to reading. His enormous capacity for friendship; his fascination with human beings of all kinds, castes, and colors; and a peripatetic search for new frontiers of experience could not be wholly satisfied in the rural Midwest of his day. As Sam's career evolved into Mark Twain's, he found his voice through storytelling. His acute commentary on American society was best expressed in parables. According to Wilson Carey McWilliams, "In Twain's political teaching it is the storytellers who lay the foundation of politics—and especially of Republican political life and virtue."[2] Twain thought that truth was often best expressed through fiction. In 1905 Twain summed up his approach in a speech on the "Russian Sufferers":

> I am going to tell a story; and there is this advantage about a story, anyway, that whatever moral or valuable thing you put into a speech, why, it gets diffused among those involuted sentences and possibly your audience goes away without finding out what that valuable thing was that you were trying to confer upon it; but, dear me, you put the same jewel into a story and it becomes the keystone of that story, and you are bound to get it—it flashes, it flames, it is the jewel in the toad's head—you don't overlook that.[3]

As a child Sam experienced firsthand the pain of poverty, the false promises of "get-rich schemes," and the self-destructive impulses of speculative capitalism. His father, John Marshall Clemens, was born in the Virginia Piedmont (now West Virginia). At a time when fathers often named their sons after revered icons,

John Clemens was named after the eminent Chief Justice of the United States, Virginia Federalist John Marshall. Clemens traveled to Kentucky where he bought an unfertile farm, studied law, and was licensed to practice it. He married the vivacious and witty twenty-year-old Jane Lampton. When his farm failed, the Clemens family moved to Tennessee where he opened a general store in Jamestown, helped build the court house, and was elected clerk of the circuit court. In Tennessee he purchased more than seventy-five thousand acres of virgin yellow pine forest, believing there was coal, copper, and iron underneath. John Clemens lost his general store in the financial crash of 1834, precipitated by President Andrew Jackson's attack on the Second Bank of the United States, which dried up credit for local businesses. To his dying day—indeed on his deathbed—John Clemens espoused the dream that the undeveloped Tennessee land would one day make the family rich.[4] It never did.[*]

His brother-in-law, John Quarles, wrote John Clemens urging him to come to Missouri, a land of new and promising opportunities. Clemens could not resist such a call, and so it was that in Florida, Missouri, Sam was prematurely born. He was a sickly child, bedridden for his first four years.[5] His father began to speculate in business ventures, such as the Salt River Navigation Project intended to link the town of Florida to the Mississippi River. The project cratered when Congress failed to fund it.

A non-churchgoing deist, John Clemens was also an active member of the Whig Party. Founded by Henry Clay and John Quincy Adams, the Whigs were a counter to the agrarian and egalitarian Democrats inspired by Jefferson and Jackson. John Clemens believed in a more refined democracy in which an educated aristocracy ruled over a stratified society, at the bottom of which were the slaves. For twenty years the Whigs promoted commerce, property rights, and cooperation between business and government to spur economic growth. They distrusted the majority rule of the uneducated masses and placed confidence in an elitist judiciary.

---

[*] After the land was finally sold by the Clemens family many years later to pay off property taxes, oil was discovered underneath it.

On November 6, 1837, John Clemens was sworn in as a judge, presiding over jury trials at the Monroe County Court House for two dollars a day.[6] Although his term ended on August 8, 1838, he proudly called himself "Judge" for the rest of his life.

The financial panic of 1837 hit the Clemenses hard, and in November 1839, the family (including four-year-old Sam) moved to Hannibal, which grew over the next decade from a sleepy village of 150 people to a town of more than twenty-five hundred. The principal river port in northeastern Missouri, it was the jumping-off point to the frontier. By the time Sam left Hannibal in 1853, the town had half a dozen churches, five newspapers, four general stores, four saloons, several private schools, saw mills, two hotels, two pork slaughterhouses, a tobacco manufacturer, a hemp factory, a distillery, and Marion College, which failed when its president was exposed as an abolitionist.[7]

As the northernmost slave state, Missouri was fertile ground for the despised abolitionists who ferried escaped slaves across the river to freedom in Illinois. In 1841 John Clemens sat on a jury that sent three abolitionists to state prison for twelve years.[8] He continued to speculate in land, navigation, and railroads—and grew deeper in debt. Despite his business failures, he remained a respected, leading member of Hannibal's southern aristocracy, launching the town library and promoting road, water, and rail transportation projects. Embracing the Whig philosophy that the elite should serve the public, John Clemens was elected justice of the peace and a delegate to the Missouri State Whig Convention. He worked unsuccessfully to establish an educational institution, the Florida Academy, as his debts mounted.

As Twain's official biographer, Albert Bigelow Paine, said about Judge Clemens, in words that would prove genetically prophetic about Sam as well: "With all his ability and industry, and with the best of intentions, John Clemens would seem to have an unerring faculty for making business mistakes."[9] By 1847 Clemens had sold his remaining slave, his house, his furniture, his eating utensils, and the family cow. The next year he filed for election as clerk of the county circuit court. Returning from the county seat on horseback in a sleet storm, "Judge" Clemens caught pneumonia and died at the age of forty-nine. Sam dropped out of school and went to work ostensibly to help support his family.[10]

Sam's mother, Jane, was the strength of the family. She was smart, funny, and unconventional. Trapped in a loveless marriage, she doted on her children and took a great interest in their education and character development. Jane was curious about everything and exhibited a deep compassion for all humans and animals. She exposed Sam to organized religion— the Methodists at first, the Presbyterians later—and at times to alternative belief systems, including the supernatural and folk superstitions. According to her grandchildren, in later life Jane was not a regular churchgoer or Bible reader. She was curious about the varieties of religious expression and occasionally attended a Jewish synagogue.[11]

Sam was a handful—rebellious, gifted, and fidgety. Sam's rebellion reflected an internal turmoil wrought by the conflict between his personal experience and what he was taught by the established institutions—the schools, the churches, and the political institutions—especially about slavery. "The local papers said nothing against it; the local pulpit taught us that God approved it, that it was a holy thing and that the doubter need only look in the Bible if he wished to settle his mind."[12] It would take him years to reconcile the opposing forces, and he expressed that reconciliation poetically in *Huckleberry Finn*.[13]

Much has been written about Sam's immersion in the Calvinist doctrines of personal guilt, predestination, and the salvation of the select few with hell's fire and brimstone for all others, but Sam was exposed to conflicting currents of religious thought, including his father's deism and his uncle John Quarles's Universalism. Quarles, whom he admired more than his father, believed that all humankind (regardless of belief systems) is saved. Quarles's influence ultimately resurfaced in the mature Twain's passionate conviction that all humans should be treated with respect regardless of their religious tradition.

Although his politics would evolve, Sam adopted his father's patrician view that the educated, propertied, wealthy, and cultured class would make better choices and govern more effectively than the uneducated and uninformed masses. As he witnessed the corruption, greed, and political influence of the financial buccaneers during the Gilded Age, he realized that education and civic participation, not *wealth*, were the critical factors in a workable democracy. For the mature Clemens, the one constant was character. Personal integrity was more important than party ideology. Democracy meant intelligent people of good faith working for the common good. Human nature being what it is, democracy's greatest flaw is the ascendance of self-interest over the public interest. His views about voting rights for women and African Americans changed over the years, but he held firm to the conviction that educated and informed voters, regardless of race or gender, were essential to elect honest and competent public officials.

The youthful Sam was also shaped by family tragedy—tragedy that would revisit him as a husband and father. John and Jane Clemens had seven children, four of whom reached adulthood: Orion (1825–1897), Pamela (1827–1904), Sam, and Henry, who barely reached maturity (1838–1858). Others were Pleasant Hannibal, born in 1829, who lived only three months; Margaret (1830–39); and Benjamin (1832–1842). Sam's relationship with his older brother Orion was complex; he loved, pitied, supported, and ridiculed him through the years. Orion gave Sam an important start on several of his "careers." On several occasions Sam attempted unsuccessfully to give Orion a jump start when his career waned and collapsed. Sam was close to his sister Pamela (sometimes Pamelia), who was married to William Moffett—a successful St. Louis businessman—until his untimely death at thirty-eight. Sam bore a sense of personal guilt in the circumstances surrounding the deaths of his older sister Margaret, his older brother Ben and his father, all of whom died before he was twelve. The ghosts of his deceased father and siblings would haunt him throughout his life, and his embellishment of the stories no doubt reflects the stifling burden of guilt that sprouted from his Missouri roots. He tells how he spied on an autopsy of his father that Jane had ordered to determine whether he had syphilis. His mother allegedly made the feisty youth kiss his father's dead body and promise to be good. When his sister Margaret was ill with bilious fever, Sam sleepwalked into her room and, as witnessed by Orion, pulled back the cover on her bed—replicating an old rural folktale called "plucking at the coverlet," a sign of impending death. When Margaret died a few days later, Mother Jane thought that Sam had supernatural powers. In 1842 his brother Ben died, also of bilious fever. Jane made Sammy kneel by the side of his dead brother while tears cascaded down her checks, causing him to feel responsible.

Most bizarre and cursed of all, however, was his brother Henry's death in a steamboat accident for which Sam (unjustifiably) held himself responsible. In 1858 Sam had gotten his unsettled younger and closest brother, Henry, a job as a mud clerk on the Mississippi River steamboat the *Pennsylvania,* on which Sam was a pilot apprentice. Defending his brother, Sam got into a heated argument with the boat's pilot—the ill-tempered William Brown—which ended with Sam crashing a stool over the pilot's head as the unmanned vessel veered off course. Sam was forced to leave the steamboat for another assignment. Henry remained on board for the return trip upriver. Sam then had a dream in which Henry appeared in a metal casket wearing Sam's clothes. On his breast was a bouquet of white roses with a red rose in the center. The *Pennsylvania* exploded in one of the worst disasters in river history. Henry was badly burned trying to save some passengers. Sam reached his makeshift hospital bed in the Memphis Exchange and lingered bedside until, to ease Henry's pain, he summoned a young intern in the middle of the night who administered a morphine overdose. When Henry's metal casket arrived in St. Louis, Henry was dressed in Sam's clothes with white roses encircling a red rose on his chest. Sam's lingering Christian faith probably dissipated that evening. He engaged in séances to communicate with his departed brother.[14]

The tragedy of his early years returned in his adult life as he experienced the premature deaths of his eighteen-month-old son, two of his three daughters in their twenties, and his beloved wife, Livy. He once told an Australian journalist that he "could never be a humorist until he could feel the springs of pathos."[15]

How did Clemens's childhood shape his views about government and society? His affection for the slaves on his uncle's farm would spark skepticism about the hypocrisy of established institutions. His love for their storytelling culture taught him a powerful way of communicating values and ideas. His mother taught him to cherish independence, explore new frontiers of thought and place, and laugh at the unfortunate predicaments of human experience. From his father he learned the precision of language, the value of political participation by the elite, and—most importantly—the financial distress caused by unfettered capitalism. His parents' unfulfilled aristocratic aspirations nurtured a hunger for social acceptance, despite his professed disdain for social pretense.[16] His exposure to conflicting strains of religious thought caused him to dismiss dogma but search for and convey universal moral values. Pervasive tragedy, especially the deaths of his siblings, caused him to reject authority—whether divine or human—empathize with human vulnerability, and embark on a relentless quest for meaning and purpose.

Throughout a lifetime of diverse experiences and global travel, Clemens drew deeply from his Missouri roots. As a lecturer, river pilot, journalist, author, and activist, he was at heart a moralist who wanted to share the lessons of his life experience. Humor and fiction were the tools he chose to convey his sense of the truth of each situation.[17]

CHAPTER TWO

The Education Of A Printer, Pilot, And Political Reporter

"A printer's shop is a poor boy's college."

— ABRAHAM LINCOLN

After his father's death, Sam attempted unsatisfying jobs in a grocery, an apothecary, a blacksmith shop, and a bookstore. He even studied law but gave it up "because it was so prosy and tiresome."[1] Twelve-year-old Sam was then hired as a printer's devil, or apprentice, by twenty-four-year-old Joseph P. Ament, owner of the vehemently Democratic *Missouri Courier*, which purchased the *Hannibal Gazette* and merged the papers. In the mid-nineteenth century, newspapers were intensely partisan, with editors often active in political parties. They also were a primary source of entertainment, offering community information, opinion, humor, gossip, and literary filler. And, like today, they reported the unsavory news of the day and the political schisms that were especially intense in the border state of Missouri. Sam undoubtedly set the type for stories about the lynching of escaped slaves and slaves accused of rape or murder. He read reports about the northern abolitionists across the river who refused to comply with the Fugitive Slave laws that compelled the return of runaway slaves. Sam detested those "infernal abolitionists."

In 1850 Orion acquired the *Hannibal Western Union,* a worthless weekly Whig-oriented newspaper. A few months later, he purchased the *Hannibal Journal* and merged the two papers. Fifteen-year-old Sam went to work for his older brother at a salary of $3.50 a week, which was rarely paid.[2] He began as a printer and editorial assistant, but was soon contributing comical sketches and reporting news from the more comfortable Whig perspective, displaying his ripening political convictions. While the rote learning of his school days had sparked truancy, Sam's practical work in the newspaper office sparked curiosity—knowledge was imparted through political banter among competitive newspapers and excerpts from great authors and thinkers that served as filler. Sam's exposure to Shakespeare, Milton, Dumas, Dickens, Carlyle, Cicero, and Greek mythology whetted his appetite for classic literature.[3] He became a voracious reader, for, as he once said, a person who won't read has no advantage over a person who can't read. Capturing the news arriving by telegraph, Sam reported on the Mexican war. A first-term congressman from Illinois was a solitary voice protesting the "unconstitutional" war, and it may have cost Abraham Lincoln his reelection to the House.

When Orion was out of town, Sam tried out his satirical skills, often targeting political opponents or incompetent officials. Although crude and sophomoric, Sam's humor hit a chord with the readers. The *Journal* became a daily, and Sam wrote a regular column, making fun of everything from corruption in the Missouri legislature to Queen Victoria and the British monarchy. To his mother's chagrin, he quipped that the newly enacted whiskey tax made it a patriotic duty to drink.[4] In a letter to the

Hannibal Western Union, fifteen-year-old Sam ridiculed a municipal ordinance forcing farmers to sell their eggs in the local market (a "most eggscellent, eggs-plicit, eggs-travagent, eggs-trordinary ordinance").[5] He squabbled with the newspapers in neighboring towns about railroad routes and ridiculed Democratic politicians. In his September 16, 1852, column, "Blabbing Government Secrets," Sam lampooned Missouri's Democratic governor Austin Augustus King and the Democrat-controlled state legislature for spending all their time passing special-interest bills to reward their friends. In his satire the legislature calls a special session to change Sam's pseudo-name from Perkins to Blab "all at a cost of *only a few thousand dollars to the State*—these Democratic legislators work cheap, don't they, Editor?" Sam wrote that a relative was "hung last week for his rascality, and I'm glad of it; for he was a Democrat and ought to have been hung long ago."[6]

In "Editorial Agility," Sam satirized his former boss—*Missouri Courier* editor Joe Ament, "a soft-soaper of Democratic rascality"— over the presidential campaign between the New Hampshire Democrat Franklin Pierce and the Whig general Winfield Scott.[7] Pierce won. In his "Assistant's Column," he wrote scathingly about women's suffrage—an issue he would revisit many times over the years: "On Saturday night Mr. Jacques got drunk and proceeded to show his utter contempt for such new-fangled humbugs as 'woman's rights,' and his own peculiar exalted ideas of 'Man's rights' by unmercifully beating and maltreating his wife and children."[8]

Sam's passion and skill as a writer was forged in the newspaper print shop. Like Ben Franklin, he learned to edit copy, set type, fit narrative into space-limited columns, and operate the presses. He also learned to clean up the messy, ink-permeated print room. The tedious typesetting process and space-constrained columns gave him an appreciation for the power of words concisely used. Gratification was immediate in a community where the readers were neighbors and friends.[9] If Sam had not spent most of his adolescent years in the newspaper printing business, there never would have been a Mark Twain. His use of pseudonyms arose from the need of a small-town newspaper to preserve the writer's anonymity on certain controversial articles and to delude readers into thinking there was a variety of contributing reporters whom the paper could ill-afford.*

By 1853, to Orion's great disappointment, Sam caught the reporter's bug—his curiosity could not be quenched in Hannibal—and in June he moved to St. Louis. He stayed with Pamela until August, when he set off for New York City, traveling by Mississippi River paddle boat, train, stagecoach, Lake Erie steamer, and Hudson River keel boat. Arriving in New York City, Sam went to work for John A. Gray's printing shop, along with two hundred other employees.[10]

Sam's letters to his family were published in the *Hannibal Journal* and later in the *Muscatine Journal.* In September 1853 after the Hannibal paper failed, Orion, his wife Mollie, and Jane moved to Muscatine, Iowa, on the Mississippi River about 310 miles north of St. Louis, where Orion started a new newspaper.

After two months in New York, Sam headed to Philadelphia to work as a substitute typesetter for the *Inquirer.* He visited Ben Franklin's gravesite at Christ Church, the cracked Liberty Bell, Carpenter's Hall, and the old State House on Chestnut Street, where the Declaration of Independence had been adopted. As Sam entered the east room of the first story, he was overcome with "an unaccountable feeling of awe and reverence" as though he was "treading on sacred ground." In Germantown he visited the Chew House (or Cliveden)—where General Washington attacked the British billet in the 1777 battle of Germantown—and the house of Lydia Darrah. As Sam recounts to the *Muscatine Journal,* Lydia informed "Gen. Washington of the intended attack of the British upon his camp; and her heroic conduct defeated the plans of the red-coats and saved the Americans." She deserves a "monument," Sam wrote, but instead, "as one might almost guess, her old mansion is now occupied by a Jew, as a clothing store."[11] Sam then visited the old slate-roof house that had been

---

* Sam used bogus bylines such as "Rambler," "Grumbler," "A Son of Hannibal," "Saveron," and "Josh." In his frontier reporting in later years, he would use such names as "Thomas Jefferson Snodgrass," "Soleleather," "Sargent Fat hom," "W. Epaminodas Drastic," and "Blab" before settling on "Mark Twain."

occupied by William Penn, John Adams, John Hancock, and other icons of America's brief history. Resting on a pine bench where Washington and Franklin once sat, Sam wrote that the Philadelphia assembly room, where the Congress had first met, was now an auction mart: "Alas! That these old buildings, so intimately connected with the principal scenes in our country, should be so profaned." Anticipating the historic preservation movement, the precocious seventeen-year-old asks: "Why do not those who make such magnificent donations to our colleges and other institutions, give a mite toward their preservation of these monuments of the past?"[12]

How many seventeen-year-old school dropouts today would visit these historic sites on a solo first trip to Philadelphia? Sam's letters home tell volumes about his love of history, his hopes for the young nation's democratic experiment, and his passion for preserving the legacy Americans inherited from their founders—all lifelong obsessions.

While living in Philadelphia, Sam took a few days off to make his "flying trip" to Washington, DC. Disenchanted with the legislators' vacuous rhetoric and procedural maneuvering, he later quipped that a "Congressman is the trivialest distinction for a full-grown man."[13]

In April 1854 Sam returned to the Midwest and was employed as a typesetter for the *St. Louis Evening News*. He continued to write about local matters, attacking the police and an Irish bookkeeper who embezzled funds from the local Democratic Party, venting his Hannibal-grown prejudices against Catholics and immigrants. Industrialization, Catholic immigration from Germany, Ireland, and Italy; and the acrimonious slavery debate were converging in the proverbial perfect storm. St. Louis was about to erupt. On August 7, 1854, there were riots. The virulently anti-immigration "Know Nothings" attacked the immigrant neighborhoods. As Sam later told the story, he briefly joined the militia to quell the uprising, but as the threat of bloodshed loomed, Sam handed his musket to a friend and retired for a drink before heading home. It was not the last time he would avoid armed conflict.

Having grown up with a southern Whig bias, Sam and Orion were sympathetic to the Know Nothing Party's anti-immigration fervor. They backed the Know Nothing candidate, Millard Fillmore, for the presidency in 1856.[14] Fillmore ran against frontier hero General John C. Fremont—the nominee of the new Republican Party—and James Buchanan, Democrat of Pennsylvania. Several southern states threatened to secede if the staunchly antislavery Fremont won, and the unavailing Buchanan prevailed.

In February 1857 Sam moved to Cincinnati. Having read about the cocoa riches in the Amazon headwaters, he boarded a packet, the *Paul Jones*, and headed to New Orleans intending to catch a ship to Brazil. Sam's wanderlust was the source of his creative inspiration and the curse of his reckless speculation. Fortunately there was no ship from New Orleans to Brazil. Instead Sam signed up as an apprentice to the legendary river pilot Horace Bixby and embarked for St. Louis. Clemens worked as a cub until he received his pilot's license on April 9, 1859.

Over a four-year period, Clemens would make 120 trips on as many as nineteen steamboats, covering the twelve hundred miles of the Mississippi between New Orleans and St. Louis. Comparing river piloting to his other vocational experiences, he tellingly displays the value he placed on freedom of thought and action—a value that permeates so much of his writing and his views on economic and social issues:

> A pilot, in those days, was the only unfettered and entirely independent human being that lived in the earth. Kings are but the pampered servants of parliament and people; parliaments sit in chains forged by their constituency; the editor of a newspaper cannot be independent, but must work with one hand tied behind him by party and patrons, and be content to utter only half or two thirds of his mind; no clergyman is a free man and may speak the whole truth, regardless of his parish's opinions; writers of all kinds are manacled servants of the public. We write frankly and fearlessly, but then we "modify" before we print.[15]

Clemens kept a notebook on the river—a practice that developed his keen observational skills. A pilot must know from memory every sandbar and eddy in the constantly changing river. He "got acquainted" with "all the different types of human nature that are to be found in fiction, biography or history." There was not a character he ever wrote about that he hadn't known "on the river."[16]

If it had not been for a cannon ball that burst the smokestack of the *Nebraska* and a Union blockade at Memphis, Clemens might never have become an author. He took his nom de plume from the river. Mark Twain is the second mark on a line lowered from a boat into the water to check its depth, indicating twelve feet, which meant the muddy waters were safe to navigate. During his years on the river, Clemens grew in self-confidence and fine-tuned his leadership skills, leading a raucous team of hard-living men.

While on the river, Clemens read Suetonius, Pepys, Malory, Carlyle, Cervantes, Plutarch, Darwin, Macaulay, Shakespeare, and the Bible. A favorite was Thomas Paine, whose *Common Sense* had inspired the American Revolution and whose *Age of Reason* provided the intellectual underpinning for Sam's growing skepticism of institutionalized religion.

As Clemens cruised the Mississippi, which divided east and west, the tectonic plates of North and South were quickly separating. The unresolved issue of slavery—the singularly silent sin of the imperfect Constitution—was about to boil over. In St. Louis a slave, Dred Scott, who had lived and married in a free state and territory, had sued for his freedom. Exhausting his appeals, he petitioned the Supreme Court. Two days after James Buchanan's inauguration, the nation's highest court issued the infamous *Dred Scott* decision, which declared slaves the property of their masters and denied citizenship and the right to sue in court to all African Americans whether free or a slave. Plummeting to the nadir of Supreme Court decision-making, Chief Justice Roger Taney wrote:

> It is too clear for dispute, that the enslaved African race were not intended to be included and formed no part of the people who framed and adopted...the Declaration of Independence....They knew that it would not in any part of

27

the civilized world be supposed to embrace the negro race, which by common consent, had been excluded from civilized Governments and the family of nations, and doomed to slavery....The unhappy black race were separated from the white by indelible marks and laws long before established, and were never thought of or spoken of except as property.[17]

For Clemens the river was a sanctuary between conflicting cultures enabling him to ignore the conflict that churned within. He had cohorts who were zealous proponents and opponents of slavery. Now twenty-two, he wrote letters to newspapers along the river, occasionally venturing into politics. He supported Stephen A. Douglas over Abraham Lincoln in the 1858 Illinois senatorial election after their famous debate in Alton, Illinois. Douglas was the more accomplished orator whose position on slavery was more equivocal than Lincoln's. Sam debated the issues with his fellow pilots and chastised his old friend Will Bowen for favoring secession. Sam favored compromising on slavery to save the Union and once rescued a Union flag from a secessionist gang.

In 1860 Clemens supported the Constitutional Union Party and its candidates, John Bell of Tennessee for president and Edward Everett of Massachusetts for vice president. They campaigned on a platform of preserving the Union by compromising on slavery. The new party consisted of mostly southern Whigs and Know Nothings; it did not survive the 1860 election.

Orion moved in a different direction. He had studied law in St. Louis under Edward Bates, a former slaveholder who opposed slavery's expansion into the territories. Born on a Virginia plantation, Bates represented Missouri in Congress as a Whig before losing a Senate race to Democrat Thomas Hart Benton. When the Whigs dissolved, he joined the Republican Party and was one of four principal contenders for the presidential nomination in 1860, losing to Lincoln, who appointed him attorney general in his cabinet of rivals. In that position Bates wrote a courageous opinion, defying the Supreme Court's *Dred Scott* decision by holding that a Negro is a citizen of the United States and therefore may serve as captain of a US merchant ship.[18]

Schooled by Bates in law and politics, Orion set up an unsuccessful law practice in 1860. Twain once said that Orion was so balanced in his presentations to a jury that it was never clear who he was representing. In the hostile territory of northern Missouri, Bates and Orion dauntlessly campaigned for Lincoln. Missouri was the only state to go for Lincoln's northern Democrat opponent, Stephen Douglas.

Meanwhile Sam's brother-in-law, William Moffett, had been elected president of the St. Louis Merchants Exchange. His business success was in contrast to his friend in the office next door. There the unassuming and bored Ulysses S. Grant spent more time hobnobbing with William than tending to his failing bill-collecting business. Grant returned to his home town of Galena, Illinois, and then, after Lincoln's election and the secession of southern states, found more suitable employment.

Clemens's loyalties, like those of many Missourians, were complex; he vacillated between preserving the Union at all costs and defending the South from northern intrusions. He had friends and mentors who were strong unionists and others who were passionate secessionists. In referring to the river battle over Memphis in *Life on the Mississippi*, Twain later wrote: "Two men whom I had served under, in my river days, took part in that fight: Mr. Bixby, head pilot of the Union fleet, and Montgomery, Commodore of the Confederate fleet."[19]

Lured by boyhood friends, he signed up with the Missouri state militia, which was resisting the federal troops' occupation of the capital, Jefferson City. Clemens joined an outfit called the Marion Rangers, and was sworn in as a second lieutenant of the Ralls County unit by Colonel John Ralls, a hero of the Mexican war. Rolls gave a rousing, bombastic induction speech exhorting the bedraggled group of bungling misfits to "drive all invaders from the State of Missouri."[20] The flowery speech was in the tradition of Sir Walter Scott, who Clemens grew to detest and blame for much of the contorted chivalry of southern culture.[21]

According to Clemens, the Marion Rangers specialized in retreats, and when their retreat reached his birthplace of Florida, Missouri, Clemens did the only honorable thing– he deserted.

He explained years later that he was "incapacitated by fatigue through persistent retreating."[22] He said he could have been a good soldier, having "learned more about retreating than the man that invented retreating."[23] He "claimed, though he did not know at the time, that an Illinois regiment, led by Colonel Ulysses S. Grant, was in hot pursuit.[24]

Clemens documented his brief Civil War experience in an 1885 short story, "The Private History of a Campaign that Failed." What starts out as a burlesque satire shifts subtly into an anguished moral "epitome of war; that all war must be just that—the killing of strangers against whom you feel no personal animosity; strangers whom, in other circumstances, you would help if you found them in trouble, and who would help you if you needed it."[25] The story had been solicited by *Century Magazine* as part of its Civil War series intended to help heal the wounds of war by showing the nobility of battle and heroism of both sides. Not surprisingly, Clemens's contribution was omitted from the four-volume publication, *Battle Leaders of the Civil War.* The short story about the campaign that failed foreshadowed Twain's later, darker writings on "unjust wars".

By the age of twenty-five, Clemens had been a typesetter, tourist, river pilot, erstwhile soldier, and journalist. He had visited the cradle of liberty and the nation's capital. He had observed the hypocrisy of established institutions—schools, churches, and government. He was witness to a nation about to be torn apart by slavery, the emergence of the industrial age, and the immigration surge. As a printer's devil, reporter, and rapacious reader, he had "unlearned" his rote formal education. He had worked with role models like pilots Horace Bixby and George Ealer, who could spew Shakespeare as he navigated the treacherous river shoals. He had seen a variety of the American experience—democracy from the grass roots up, the people who nourished it, and the petty parochial prejudices that threatened to destroy it. Growing up in a border state and cruising the river north and south, he had been battered by conflicting arguments and opinions from which he learned to listen to and appreciate the many sides of an issue. He had dabbled in politics and war and decided that if he could not be a pilot forever, then he was more suited to be a detached observer than a player in the nation's unfolding events.

CHAPTER THREE

Frontier Politics

*"Everyone is a moon & has a dark side
which he never shows to anybody."*

— MARK TWAIN

In the fall of 1859, the Comstock Lode, rich in silver and gold, was discovered in a mountain range about thirty miles east of the Sierra Nevada Mountains. After the army and frontiersmen fought off the Indians, miners flooded into the territorial towns. In March 1861 the arriving hoards in search of bountiful silver treasures caused Congress to establish the Nevada Territory, which it split off from the Utah Territory. Nevada silver would influence the national political debate over monetary policy in the decades to come, pitting the bimetallists of the West and South against the Wall Street "gold bugs" who insisted on a currency based only on the gold standard.

As a reward for his campaigning for Lincoln, Orion was appointed secretary of the new territory. Having failed in his newspaper business and law practice, the penurious Orion was to make $1,800 a year. After deserting the Marion Rangers, Sam was persona non grata to the Union and Confederate causes. Orion offered a way out. Sam accompanied his brother as an unpaid, unofficial aide and, from his bountiful earnings as a pilot, paid Orion's way out west.

The brothers set out on the two-thousand-mile trek from St. Louis on the steamboat *Sioux City* up the Missouri River to St. Joseph and then by Overland Stage to Carson City, Nevada. On the way to Carson, Clemens had his first of several unpleasant encounters with American Indians, who were shooing away vultures to carry off carrion. It took a long time for Sam to overcome his prejudice against American Indians.

Orion's boss was Governor James Warren Nye, who had been New York City police commissioner and chairman of William Seward's presidential campaign. With flowing white hair, the lean and loquacious Nye "was a seasoned politician, not statesman." His "deep lustrous brown eyes," according to Sam, "could talk as a native language the tongue of every feeling, every passion, every emotion."[1]

The Clemens brothers were responsible for setting up the territorial legislature and preparing the budget. Nye, schooled by the Tammany Hall political machine, had little interest in procedures and spending accountability. When he tried to get Orion to set up slush fund accounts, the straitlaced Orion refused. They clashed continually, and Sam came vigorously to his brother's defense.

Displaying his father's entrepreneurial genes, Sam entered the lumber business to supply the fast-growing demand for housing. He staked out a yellow pine forest but left his campfire unattended. After the lumber venture went up in flames, he tried his hand and pick at prospecting, accumulating a large number of worthless wildcat mining stakes and going heavily into debt. By June 1862 he admitted defeat. Though he did not know it at the time, Sam had accumulated great wealth—not through mining silver, but through mining a variety of fascinating stories about the new frontier. They were to be retold in stories, lectures, and a best-selling book, *Roughing It.* Yielding to his true talent, Clemens became a reporter for the Virginia City *Territorial Enterprise* at six dollars a day.

By the time Sam arrived in Virginia City, nestled on the eastern slope of Mount Davidson close to the Comstock Silver Lode and Gold Hill, it was the liveliest town "America had ever produced," as he later wrote in *Roughing It.* It was cluttered with "hurdy-gurdy houses," "wide-open gambling palaces," a large police force, "a dozen breweries, and a half a dozen jails and station-houses in full operation." The streets were jammed with quartz wagons and freight teams, and buggies would sometimes have to wait half an hour to cross C Street, the main road through the town. With a population 90 percent male, there were "street fights, murders, inquests, riots and a whiskey-mill every fifteen steps."[2] On average there were about four murders a week, but no one was ever convicted. Cain's murder of Abel would "rank as eminently justifiable homicide,"[3] Sam wrote. Amid the chaos and sprawl, a real urban community was struggling to emerge—banks, hotels, theatres, hospitals, schools, libraries, competing newspapers, a French restaurant frequented by Clemens, and "some talk of building a church."[4]

Of the newspapers, the *Territorial Enterprise* was the most respected, allied with the Union Party that supported Nevada's statehood. As Copperheads (Southern sympathizers) and avid unionists did battle in the press, Clemens avoided national issues, immersing himself in local politics. He was viewed as a southerner who kept his private views closely guarded. The *Enterprise*'s twenty-three-year-old editor in chief, Joe Goodman, instructed his young reporter: "Never say we learn so and so...Or that it is rumored, or that we understand so and so," but get the "absolute facts" and "say it *is* so and so." "You are pretty certain to be shot," he added, but "you will preserve the public confidence."[5] Goodman's readers were not intellectual giants, and he encouraged his reporters to write burlesque, satire, and humor that would entertain as well as inform. Initially Clemens covered conventional news—crime, lawsuits, inquests, bullion prices, city council resolutions, and mining claims.[6]

Mark Twain and his Nevada friends.
Courtesy. The Mark Twain House & Museum, Hartford, CT

Office of the Virginia City *Territorial Enterprise,* where Samuel Clemens
covered the Nevada Territorial Legislature.
Courtesy Library of Congress

Covering mining litigation, Clemens had his first encounter with a formidable trial attorney, William Morris Stewart, a multi-millionaire who would later serve as Nevada's first senator and in 1867 as Sam's boss in Washington, DC. In a clash between two mining companies, Stewart successfully argued that a surface claim included "all dips, angles, spurs and variations thereof." On October 20, 1862, Clemens reported on the "great wrong" perpetrated by California-transplanted judge Gordon S. Mott and jury by ejecting a mining company from an underground ledge below the surface claim of Stewart's client. He wrote that Judge Mott's original decision "clinches my ancient opinion that hell is peopled with honester men than California."[7] The lawsuit lingered through the appellate process until 1865 when the companies merged. The Nevada judiciary was infested with corruption, bribery, and political influence, and Stewart's tenacious pursuit of his client's interest led to the resignation of the whole judicial branch, including Nevada's chief justice George Turner, a Lincoln appointee.

Clemens surreptitiously mocked Stewart's legal acumen by using a device he often employed, attributing his own comments to another character—in this case the "Unreliable," his good friend Clement Rice of the competing *Daily Union*. Describing how "Bullyragging Bill" would take on a losing case that no other lawyer would touch, the Unreliable says that Bill Stewart will "worry the witnesses, and bullyrag the Judge, and buy up the jury and pay for 'em; and he'll prove things that never existed."[8]

Clemens pleaded with Goodman to be assigned to cover the second session of the Territorial Legislature in Carson City. Reporters received a seven-dollar-a-day bonus for covering the sessions, which provided the official record. As a serious, disciplined journalist, Sam's reporting on the mundane legislative session was fair and straightforward but not noteworthy. On February 3, 1863, he signed an article "Mark Twain," the first known use of the alias.[9] He used the pseudonym when he wanted to introduce humor, opinion, and colorful commentary. The legislators, who "enlivened their deliberations with horseplay and champagne," gave Mark Twain leeway as the "court jester" but would not countenance satire or criticism in the straight news reports of Sam Clemens.[10]

In *Roughing It* Twain mocked the legislators' penchant for handing out private toll road franchises to their supporters and friends. He pointed out that "every citizen owned about three franchises." Unless Congress gave Nevada "another degree of longitude" there would not be enough territory to accommodate all the toll roads, "the ends of them were hanging over the boundary-line everywhere like a fringe."[11]

Clemens loved to exercise journalistic power: "I was there every day in the legislature to distribute compliment and censure with evenly balanced justice and spread the same over half a page of the *Enterprise* every morning; consequently I was an influence."[12] He wrote his mother on August 19, 1863: "I was a mighty heavy wire-puller at the last Legislature. I passed every bill I worked for, & on a bet, I killed a bill by a three-fourths vote in the House." He bragged that "a reporter in the Legislature can swing more votes than any member of the body."[13] Clemens claimed credit for the passage of a law requiring every corporation to file its complete charter with the secretary of the territory—Orion—"which netted fees of about $1000 a month."[14]

At the urging of Goodman, Clemens advocated transferring the state capital from Carson City to Virginia City. He attacked the Carson City politicians and their "stream of iniquitous private franchises." Clemens argued that if the legislature were in Virginia City, vigorous press oversight would subject such dealings to public scrutiny. The bill to remove the capital to Virginia City resulted in a tie vote, which effectively killed it.[15] The Carson City legislators got even—they eliminated the per diem bonus to legislative reporters.[16]

When Governor Nye traveled east to visit his wife and family, Orion served as acting governor for as long as six months. He was popular with the legislature. Although the legislators couldn't "trust each other, nor anybody else," Sam wrote in his *Autobiography*, "they could trust him." Orion was respected for his honesty, "but it didn't do him any good in a pecuniary way, because he had no talent for either persuading or scaring legislators."[17]

In February 1863 shots were fired along the California-Nevada border. The two jurisdictions readied for war over disputed mining territory. Were the valuable Aurora mines in Mono, California, or Esmeralda, Nevada? Acting governor Orion Clemens stepped in and negotiated a diplomatic settlement with California's not-so-bright governor Leland Stanford. Nevada retained the mines. In a letter to his sister, Sam was less diplomatic: "How I *hate* everything that looks, or tastes, or smells like California!– And how I hate everybody that loves the cursed State!"[18]

In October 1863 Nevada called a constitutional convention in Carson City to prepare for statehood. Praised for his skill in avoiding war with California, Orion was unanimously elected secretary of state. Stewart had drafted the proposed state constitution and lobbied for it—until a provision was added to tax undeveloped mines. Ever the clever lawyer, Stewart initially construed the tax to mean "nothing in particular," arguing that "a mere hole in the ground was not a mine" and not taxable. Under Stewart's interpretation, Sam argued, a year from now, there will not be a mine left in the Territory.[19] Worried about the tax provision, Stewart decided to switch sides and oppose ratification of the constitution he had drafted. Although Sam initially supported the constitution, he also switched sides. Doing Orion no favors, Twain wrote for the *New York Sunday Mercury* about "the secret history" of the convention authorizing the state constitution, which involved payoffs to various interests. According to Twain, the bill reported out of the committee had "a lot of blanks in it," including the "amount of money appropriated to defray expenses of the Convention, etc." Both houses passed the bill without filling in the blanks; it was duly enrolled and signed by the presiding officers. What Twain called a "worthless, meaningless, and intentionally powerless instrument" was transmitted to Governor Nye for his signature—at night. "And lo! a miracle. When the bill reached the Governor, there was not a solitary blank in it! Who filled them, is—is a great moral question." Twain wrote: "The bill was a fraud; the convention created by it was a fraud, the fruit of the convention was an illegitimate infant constitution and a dead one at that."[20] Under mounting media pressure, the courts declared the constitution and elections invalid.

Nevada was finally admitted to the Union as the thirty-sixth state on October 31, 1864, just before Lincoln's reelection. The president wanted Nevada's support in adopting the constitutional amendments to abolish slavery and grant citizenship rights to freed blacks. Stewart and Nye were elected senators, with Stewart gaining seniority and a six-year term by a drawing.[21] Orion again was a shoo-in for election as secretary of state. Always the puritan, Orion abruptly decided to campaign for prohibition. Twain wrote in his *Autobiography* that Orion would "change his religion [and his views on temperance] with his shirt."[22] Foolishly campaigning for prohibition in a state where drinking, along with gambling, was a favorite avocation, Orion did not receive a single vote. Although he served briefly in the state legislature, his career in politics was over. With the death of his vibrant young daughter, Jeannie, in February 1864, Orion began a downward spiral and never regained his footing.

Twain's celebrity status was on the rise. He was elected "governor" of the Third House of the Territorial Legislature, a parody of Nevada politics, which the legislators called the Play House. Liquor flowed freely as legislators and reporters lampooned Nevada politics with crude frontier humor that would make a Washington press corps Gridiron dinner seem like a prayer meeting. Ironically funds raised during Twain's mock gubernatorial address were used to construct a Presbyterian church in Carson City.[23]

Presiding over the mock legislature, Twain dispensed with the opening prayers as "merely ornamental and entirely unnecessary." When Assemblyman Young rose to question the decision, Twain responded, "You have been sitting there for thirty days, like a bump on a log, and you never rightly understand anything. Take your seat, Sir. You are out of order." He mocked Governor Nye, senator-elect Stewart, and Stewart's domineering wife. Twain complained that in the legislature Stewart "gave the same infernal speech for the last thirty days," attacking the

proposed tax on mines "with all the insistence of a stuck phonograph record."[24] His voice rising, Twain feigned frustration:
"I am not going to sit here and listen to that same old song over
and over again. When I want it, I will repeat it myself—I know it
by heart, anyhow." It has become "a sort of nightmare to me." He
urged Stewart to "say it backwards, or sing it to a new tune." He
then accused Stewart of shedding false tears for the "poor miners."[25] (Stewart later returned the criticism from the floor of the
Capitol.) Twain adjourned the session for an hour on account
of his cold and "ordered up a galleon of gin and a spoonful of
molasses for use of the president."[26]

Twain's mock performance mirrored his view of legislative
reality. "Each member," he wrote, "rode his own hobby, and policy was often determined by whim or rhetoric rather than intelligence."[27] In his closing remarks to the legislators, Twain's humor
barely disguised his disdain for the legislative process: "You have
spoken on every subject but the one before the house, and voted
without knowing what you were voting on or having any idea
what would be the general result of your action."[28*]

Clemens wrote his mother: "Everybody knows me, and I fare
like a prince wherever I go," and, "I am proud to say I am the
most conceited ass in the Territory."[29] Stewart agreed. Clemens
"went around stirring up trouble," he wrote in his memoirs.[30]

Through parody Clemens vented his unvarnished opinion of
the legislators' "small minds and selfish souls." They were "for
sale or rent on the mildest possible terms." In a short story called
"Those Bastard Children," he mocked the legislators through
the eyes of their children.[31] In "Concerning Notaries" he made
fun of the surplus of notaries spawned to pay off political supporters. There were 1,742 Notary applications, he observed,
alleging that Chief Justice Turner and Stewart, among others,
had plied him with liquor seeking his support for appointment
to one of these political plums.[32] Clemens decried the hypocrisy

---

* The tradition of legislative parody continues to this day. Unfortunately legislators continue to provide ample material for the satirists as they rarely have
the time to read thousand-page bills, and thus, in the words of Twain, they
"vote without knowing what" they are "voting on or having any idea of what
would be the general result" of their actions.

of stump oratory with grand phrases like "the voice of the people" or "the public welfare," as the orators lined their pockets with the income from their business interests.[33] In 1865 Twain wrote the "Story of the Bad Little Boy" who grew up to become "wealthy by all manner of cheating and rascality; and now he is the infernalest wickedest scoundrel in his native village, and is universally respected, and *belongs to the Legislature*."[34]

Twain's colorful commentary sometimes overshot the mark. He wrote a parody about a father's grisly axe murders of his wife and nine children. The father had lost all his savings in the purchase of worthless stock in the San Francisco Spring Valley Water Company. Having cut his own throat ear to ear, the father rode to Carson City on horseback carrying the scalp of his red-haired wife dripping blood. The ghastly murders were fantasy, but the story was widely reprinted as straight news.

The tale drew angry protests from readers for it horrific content. Clemens defended the parody as an exposé of fraud by the San Francisco Spring Water Company, which had borrowed money to pay dividends concealing its failing finances. He argued that because of interlocking connections between the newspapers and financial institutions, no San Francisco newspaper would expose the corruption. When the readers realized they had been duped, they were not appeased. Seeking to expose the greed, corruption, and excesses of capitalism run rampant, Twain had overstepped the boundaries of responsible journalism with his "massacre" parable. He was not deterred.

In another story, written in a drunken stupor and accidentally published by a copy editor looking for filler, Clemens alleged that the revered US Sanitary Commission, the precursor to the American Red Cross,* was diverting local funds to a society promoting miscegenation—an explosive topic, as Lincoln had issued the Emancipation Proclamation the previous year. The readers' outrage led to several vitriolic attacks and counterattacks

---

* The US Sanitary Commission raised funds and supplies for the relief of union soldiers. Its prestigious board included Clara Barton and Frederick Law Olmsted, the famed landscape architect who planned New York's Central Park. Clemens's sister-in-law Mollie was active in local fundraising and was greatly embarrassed by the article.

between rival newspapers, culminating in Clemens challenging a rival editor to a duel. As in his brief tenure with the Marion Rangers, Clemens left town before the bullets started flying. He was off to San Francisco to avoid indictment under a Nevada antidueling statute.

Observing skillful politicians maneuvering for advantage, Clemens had become an expert on legislative procedures. He witnessed the influence of lobbyists, vote trading, patronage, and bribe taking as the modus operandi of the legislative process. These lessons would accelerate his learning curve when he later served briefly in the nation's capital and provide abundant material for his political satires.

Making a fresh start in San Francisco, Clemens was hired by the *Morning Call* where he covered local news, crimes and courts, and the election campaign. Knowing Clemens satirical propensities, the staunchly pro-Lincoln *Call* editors assigned him to cover the Democratic rallies and state convention. The Copperheads were stirring up trouble and some feared a civil war might break out in California. Clemens reported on a rash of stagecoach robberies by Confederate guerillas seeking to raise funds for the South. In "A Stage Robber Among Us," Clemens identified the robbers as Constitutional Democrats sympathetic with the Confederacy, and in another article he described a court room scene in which an intoxicated robbery defendant, J.F. Dolan, heaped "curses on anything pertaining to the Union cause [and] declare[d] himself a strong Jeff. Davis man." In his campaign for a second term, Lincoln faced opposition from the commanding general he had discharged for unwillingness to fight, George McClellan, and Clemens covered the state convention, ridiculing the chairman, C.L.Weller as "troubled with Alcatraz on the brain," and suggesting that another speaker "can't vote for McClellan because he belongs in Jeff. Davis' cabinet."[35]

The *Call* editors were willing to overlook Clemens' "literary inventions," and colorful slanting of the facts against the Democrats, but his instinct for targeting injustice brought trouble. He wrote about the stoning of a Chinese man by some teenage thugs while the police stood by enjoying the spectacle, thereby exposing endemic San Francisco racism against the Chinese. Worried about offending the paper's mostly Irish readership, the editors rejected the article. Clemens was furious. With the editor's encouragement, he resigned. Clemens said he didn't much care for the *Call's* readership anyway—the Irish immigrants who didn't "own much city property" or "pay any taxes."[36]

Clemens then free-lanced for the upscale *Californian,* publishing nine articles. In "An Unbiased Criticism," he wrote about a Calaveras County election in which the opponents fabricated an issue over the merits of rival sewing machines as they hurled mud at each other. For the *Golden Era,* he wrote in 1863 "The Great Prize Fight," a farce about a fierce California Republican gubernatorial nominating convention between the blustering incumbent governor Leland Stanford and his successful challenger, Ferdinand Low, invoking images of a bloody boxing match to depict the ruthless game of politics untethered to the people's concerns. In the short story, Stewart is the lawyer for one of the candidates. The contest is resolved by a secret deal between the contestants about which the electorate had no clue.[37] In these stories Twain shows how rhetorical invective and phony trumped-up issues in political campaigns enable politicians to avoid taking a stand on the tough issues presented by governing. The articles caught the attention of coeditors Bret Harte and Charles Henry Webb. Harte, a few years younger but an ascending writer of frontier fiction, hired Clemens to write for the *Californian.*[38]

Back east General Lee surrendered to General Grant at Appomattox, President Lincoln died at the hand of an assassin five days later, and the Radical Reconstructionists in Congress waged war with his successor, Andrew Johnson of Tennessee. The frontier reporter seemed oblivious to these earth-shattering events as the nation entered a period of hysteria over the martyred president.

As discussed in Joe Fulton's recent book *The Reconstruction of Mark Twain,* Clemens had not completely severed his southern roots. He avoided Civil War politics, but could not resist satirizing the maudlin, sentimental war stories popularized in

Harper's Weekly. In "Lucretia Smith's Soldier," published in the *Californian*, he mocked the shallow patriotism and romanticizing of war, foreshadowing the fierce antiwar polemics he would write after the turn of the century. Lucretia has been nursing her wounded soldier lover for three weeks, but when the bandages are removed from his face, she discovers she has been "snuffling and slobbering over the wrong soldier."[39] For the *Alta California*, he wrote a burlesque attributing the biblical language of Job to the tribulations of an Ohio volunteer infantryman. Mocking wounded soldiers who served the Union cause may seem outrageous, but Clemens outdid himself when he wrote a series of columns, "Answers to Correspondents," in the *Californian*, deriding the hysteria—"waiving the bloody shirt"—that followed Lincoln's assassination. He ridiculed the drunken John Wilkes Booth's exaggerated theatricality and the comparisons of Lincoln to Caesar or Christ. In the *Alta California*, Clemens published on April 17, 1867, a parody of a popular maudlin poem by Fritz Smith called "The Martyr." Twain's version reads "Gone! Gone! Gone! Forever and forever...Gone! Gone! Gone! Gone to his endeavor!"[40]

In writing about a San Francisco Fourth of July celebration for the *Enterprise*, Clemens mocked superficial patriotism, expressed in "cheap flags" and "large medallion portraits of Lincoln and Washington—apparently executed in white wash, mud, and brickdust, with a mop."[41] Crudely commenting on the lineup of blacks in the Independence Day parade, Clemens wrote in "Mark Twain and the Colored Man" that the lighter-skinned blacks marched at the front, followed by "nicely graduated shades of darkness to the fell and dismal blackness of undefiled and unalloyed niggerness." Anticipating the theme of his 1894 novel *Pudd'nhead Wilson*, he quipped, "No man could tell where the white folks left off and the niggers began."[42]

After a barroom brawl, Clemens vacated San Francisco and holed up for three months in the wilderness at Angel's Camp and Jackass Hill with prospectors and other itinerant lowlifes, drinking, gambling, and exchanging tall tales. From one of the tales,

Twain came up with an idea for a story about a champion jumping frog, surreptitiously filled with buckshot and left despondent at the starting gate as his upstart challenger jumps off with the sweepstakes. Ignoring the politics of the day, he completed his short story "Jim Smiley and his Celebrated Jumping Frog," later called "The Celebrated Jumping Frog of Calaveras County."[43] He made clear that he "should never be expected to write editorials about politics or eastern news. I take no sort of interest in those matters."[44] He did name the frog "Dan'l Webster" after the revered Whig orator. In a later version of the story, he renamed the narrator Horace Greeley, *The New York Tribune* publisher and presidential candidate in the 1872 election.

When the frog story first appeared in the New York *Saturday Press*, it evoked laughter and curiosity about this unconventional new voice from the West. As it was widely reprinted, Twain's fame penetrated the East. No less an icon of the eastern literary establishment than James Russell Lowell called it "the finest piece of humorous writing yet produced in America."[45]

Clemens wrote hundreds of articles for the *Golden Era*, the *Sacramento Union*, the *San Francisco Bulletin*, and—still—the *Territorial Enterprise* (which always took pleasure in criticizing San Francisco officialdom). He supported the Taxpayer Party, which advocated greater efficiency in the San Francisco city government as it coped with a population growth surge. He attacked the monopolistic practices of the Bank of California in buying up mines, urged the Internal Revenue Service to end special privileges for a lawyers' group, and campaigned for well-paid fire departments to replace voluntary organizations.[46] He approached economic issues with political common sense, calling for easing the credit crunch by issuing "greenbacks"—paper money—and arguing against local protectionism.

Nevada had proposed a law requiring any company owning a mine to have its headquarters in the state. Clemens objected, arguing that the law would "roll back the tide of eastern capital which is now setting so steadily toward Nevada...You can make those mines flourish and you can make money like smoke out of them, and open up a vast field for well-paid labor and a profitable commerce if you take pains to make the road straight and passage easy for eastern capital."[47]

Twain had the dual reputation of "Moralist of the Main" and "Wild Humorist of the Sagebrush Hills." On the Pacific Coast, he was first a moralist and secondarily a humorist.[48] Throughout his writing career, he was concerned with message. Plot, narrative, character, climax, and structure all yielded to the message he wished to convey. He was usually the rebel, embodying the struggle of individual conscience against society's oppressive conventions, hypocrisies, and corruptions. His books were rarely reviewed as great literature. He claimed he wanted to be a preacher of the gospel, and ministers were among his closest friends, but he could not subscribe to the necessary stock in trade, i.e., religion.[49]

A favorite local target was the San Francisco police and its Irish Democratic chief, Martin G. Burke, whose force he accused of racism, brutality, graft, having ties to organized crime, and hiring political incompetents. Twain's edgy commentary probably landed him in jail one night for drunkenness. Ever fearless, his satirical diatribe against the chief in "A Remarkable Dream" may have hastened Clemens's departure from the city. In a February 15, 1866, article for the *Enterprise* about the police chief's mishandling of officer misconduct, he wrote, "Chief Burke's Star Chamber Board of Police Commissioners is the funniest…theatrical exhibition in San Francisco." When a policeman is charged with misconduct, "you would imagine that fearful Commission was really going to raise the very devil. But it is all humbug, display, fuss, and feathers. The Chief brings his policeman out as sinless as an angel, unless the testimony be heavy enough, almost, to hang an ordinary culprit, in which case a penalty of four or five days' suspension is awarded."[50] In "What Have the Police Been Doing?" Clemens reported that the police had denied medical attention to a man whose skull they had split like an apple. The detainee had been caught stealing four flour sacks. He "died with the calm serenity which is peculiar to men whose heads have been canned with a club."[51] The police chief brought a libel suit against the *Enterprise,* which caused a spike in circulation and enhanced Twain's rising reputation. Police incompetence and corruption are recurring themes throughout his writing. "The Stolen White Elephant" and "A Double-Barreled Detective Story" are conventional mysteries that display police graft and stupidity.

In 1866 Clemens sailed for the Sandwich Islands (as Hawaii was then known), commissioned to write a series of articles for the *Sacramento Union*. Fortuitously he was in Honolulu when reports came in about the arrival of a lifeboat with the captain and fourteen crewmembers of the *Hornet*, which had been burned and sunk off the coast of South America forty-three days earlier. With the assistance of Anson Burlingame, the respected US minister to China who was in Hawaii at the time, Clemens garnered an exclusive interview with the survivors. Clemens and Ambassador Burlingame, one of the founders of the new Republican Party, became lifelong friends. The ambassador's benevolent diplomacy and respect for foreign cultures planted the seeds that later sprouted in Clemens's virulent anti-imperialism. Twain called him "one of the ablest diplomats America has produced, and his works proved it."[52] Clemens's grisly *Hornet* story was shipped off on the next boat to California, where it was widely reprinted. He later wrote versions of the tale for articles in *Harper's* and the *Century* magazines.[53]

The lifeboat story anchored a set of esoteric experiences in Hawaii involving conflicts among native cultures, meddling missionaries, and American diplomats. Clemens met the thirty-four-year-old King Kamehameha V and covered the local political scene. He praised the king's edict limiting voting rights to propertied males. He gently ridiculed the "threadbare platitudes" of the Hawaiian legislators[54] and mocked the legislator who proposed a bill to construct a suspension bridge from Oahu to the island of Hawaii (a distance of 150 miles) so the natives wouldn't get seasick.[55] Clemens's opinion of the Hawaiian Assembly was like his opinion of the Territorial Legislature and his future opinion of Congress: "A wooden-head gets up and proposes an utterly absurd something or other, and a half a dozen other wooden-heads discuss it with windy vehemence for an hour, the remainder of the house sitting in silent patience the while, and then a sensible man—a man of weight—a big gun—gets up and shows the foolishness of the matter in five sentences. A vote is taken and the thing is tabled." It was no wonder, Clemens concluded, that "few men of first class ability can afford to let their affairs go to ruin while they fool away their time in legislatures...But your chattering one-horse village lawyer likes it, and your solemn ass from the cow counties, who don't know the Constitution from the Lord's Prayer, enjoys it, and these you will find in the assembly."[56] He enjoyed recalling the words of the Wisconsin legislator who rose to address a bill setting penalties for arson: "They ought to either hang him or make him marry the girl!"[57]

Clemens then visited the Haleakala Volcano on Maui and the Kilauea Volcano on the big island, which erupted during his stay. He poked fun at native feudal practices[58] and contemporary customs,[59] later incorporating material on Hawaiian superstitions into *A Connecticut Yankee in King Arthur's Court* in describing sixth-century English feudal society.[60] After closely observing the taciturn native aristocrats, he concluded that "the nobles are able, educated, fine-looking men, who do not talk often, but when they do, they generally say something," which was not the case of "their white associates."[61] In his first exposure to a foreign culture, Clemens began to appreciate how people of diverse backgrounds and traditions contribute to America's cultural mainstream, discarding the archaic customs that have held back the older cultures from which they came.[62]

The rich material acquired during his four months and a day in Hawaii supplied twenty-five articles for the *Sacramento Union* and launched Twain's career as a lecturer. Facing a crowd of two thousand at San Francisco's Maguire Academy of Music, Twain's knees wobbled. He momentarily lost his voice but recovered. With his self-deprecating Missouri twang, punctuated by pregnant pauses, he mesmerized his audience.[63] He was to become a phenomenon that would permeate American culture in the century to come and beyond, for good or for bad—a global celebrity.

Riding high on his West Coast fame, Twain bucked the trend of manifest destiny. He headed east to cultivate the notoriety sparked by the lead-laden champion amphibian. He made arrangements to be the "Travelling Correspondent" of the *Alta California*, filing reports from whatever port to which his wanderlust brought him. On December 15, 1866, the thirty-one-year-old journalist departed on the *America*, sailing through the Golden Gate and down the Californian and Mexican coasts. He traversed Nicaragua by land, lake, and river; survived cholera epidemics; visited exotic foreign ports; and sailed up the Eastern Seaboard. He arrived in New York on January 12, 1867.

There, after several failed attempts to publish a book on the Sandwich Islands, he was persuaded by publisher Charles Henry Webb to compile a collection of short stories anchored by the celebrated frog. Clemens left the details to Webb, and the poorly compiled and printed book sold only a few thousand copies.

After a brief trip to St. Louis to visit family and a stunning lecture at the famed Cooper Union in New York, Clemens made plans to join a planned excursion that was then making news in the city: the steamship *Quaker City* tour to Europe and the Holy Land. The trip would greatly enrich and complement Clemens's growing inventory of adventures to write about. He was disappointed when General Tecumseh Sherman, who had signed up for the voyage, backed out to fight the Indian wars, and when the noted preacher Henry Ward Beecher ("the most famous man in America") decided to write a novel and bailed out of the excursion along with forty members of his congregation.

Before leaving on the *Quaker City* on Saturday, June 8, 1867, along with sixty-four other passengers, Clemens corresponded with his old foil Senator Stewart of Nevada. Clemens would accept a position as the senator's private secretary (and legislative clerk) beginning in the winter of 1867 after the ship returned to New York. On board, Clemens met Mary Mason Fairbanks, the wife of a part owner of *The Cleveland Herald*, who would become a literary mentor and confidante. Charlie Langdon, the brother of his future wife, was also a passenger. Clemens filled the gap created by Sherman and Beecher's bailout and became the shipboard celebrity, entertaining the younger, more tolerant set and offending some of the older, more sanctimonious cruisers, including the pious captain Charles C. Duncan.

He filled his notebook with none-too-flattering sketches of his fellow passengers, places visited, and observations about a variety of cultures and forms of government. For the young reporter, the tradition-bound monarchies, stratified class structures, and paternalistic bureaucracies contrasted sharply with the frontier democracy he had experienced in Carson City. In addition to his fifty-two reports to the *Alta*, he also sent letters to Horace Greeley's *New York Tribune* and *The New York Herald*—fierce competitors that were later to merge. The readers, accustomed to dry renderings of far-off places and reverent descriptions of religious shrines, were treated to candid, conversational, unpretentious, and sometimes irreverent prose. Comparing the privileges of the wealthy in America and Italy, he wrote: "if a man be rich, he is very greatly honored, and can become a legislator, a governor, a general, a senator, no matter how ignorant an ass he is—just as in our beloved Italy the nobles hold all of the great places, even though sometimes they are born noble idiots."[64] He marveled at how the bankrupt Italian government could build such palatial edifices and how in each city the church had built a magnificent cathedral "while starving half her citizens to accomplish it."[65] Some readers were deeply offended. Others, including some Washington power brokers, laughed uproariously.

PART II

Political Engagement

History rhymes

CHAPTER FOUR

Sam Clemens's
Short Government Career

"It could probably be shown by facts or figures that there is no distinctively native American criminal class except Congress."

— MARK TWAIN

As the *Quaker City* excursion progressed, a *New York Tribune* reader chuckled at the witty and irreverent descriptions of foreign shrines.* His name was Elisha Bliss Jr. of the American

---

* Instead of writing in awe of the magnificent Italian cathedrals as was the practice in previous travelogues, Twain, for example, made fun of the relics in the churches: "We find a piece of the true cross in every church we go into, and some of the nails that held it together.... I think we have seen as much as a keg of these nails.... And as for the bones of St. Denis, I feel certain we have seen enough of them to duplicate him, if necessary" (IA, 165). See Bibliography and End Notes References for complete citations.

Publishing Company in Hartford, Connecticut, a subscription publishing house of travelogues and religious tracts. Spotting an extraordinary talent, he noted an editorial comment that the writer—Mark Twain—ought to publish a book of his travels abroad. Bliss quickly penned a letter on November 21, 1867, to Samuel L. Clemens, addressed to the *Tribune* bureau in New York, where it lay unattended for about ten days.

The *Quaker City* returned to New York Harbor on November 19, 1867. Two days later, after a dinner with *The New York Herald's* editorial board, Clemens took the overnight train to Washington, DC, arriving on Friday morning. November 1867 was an extraordinary time in the nation's history. The Civil War was over, Abraham Lincoln had been assassinated, and the overwhelmingly Republican Congress was at war with his recalcitrant and ineffectual successor, Andrew Johnson of Tennessee, who had gotten off to a bad start when he showed up drunk for his vice presidential inauguration in the Senate chamber. The dominant issue was reconstruction— under what terms the defeated states of the Confederacy should be readmitted into the Union. With frequent use of his veto pen, Johnson resisted mightily the efforts of the Radical Republicans to protect the freed slaves from southern retribution and bring them into the mainstream of the reconstructed southern economy. In 1866 he vetoed the Freedman's Bureau Bill, then the civil rights acts. In his veto messages, Johnson proclaimed: "Of all the dangers which our nation has yet encountered, none are equal to those which must result from the success of the effort...to Africanize the half of our country," for "everyone would, and must admit, that the white race was superior to the black."[1]

In the words of Charles Dickens, whose New York lecture Clemens attended, this was "the best of times and the worst of times."[2] For the first time, Congress overrode presidential vetoes and passed civil rights and reconstruction legislation. Between 1865 and 1870, Congress passed and the states ratified constitutional amendments that abolished slavery, created equal rights under the law, and prohibited voting discrimination based on race. The amendments potentially extended the promise of the Declaration of Independence that "all men are created equal" to all male citizens regardless of race; women would have to wait another fifty years.

This was also a time of widespread political and corporate corruption. The capital was caught up in the postwar frenzy of the industrial age, the westward expansion into the seemingly limitless frontier with its infinite supply of natural resources, the immigration surge, and the rise of the rapacious robber barons. Freed of the class constraints and stale traditions of old Europe, the rootless Americans struggled for success under the prevailing philosophies of laissez-faire and "survival of the fittest." Industrial and financial tycoons amassed great fortunes while working men, women, and children struggled under oppressive conditions. As the railroads opened up the West, their representatives—along with the agents of mining, agriculture, timber, banking, and the financial markets—crowded the Capitol's corridors seeking legislative favors.

Fourteen years earlier Clemens had arrived in a city covered with freshly fallen snow. Now Washington was a mammoth mud hole. The unpaved streets had been devastated by heavy army wagons. Clemens ridiculed the shortsightedness of the city's fathers for not diluting the mud and creating a system of canals. A trip from the Capitol to the White House could take one or two hours as hacks—one-horse carriages for hire—would get stuck in the mud. There were few sidewalks. Freed black men carried boards on their shoulders and, for a tip, would help pedestrians walk across muddy streets or from a shop or restaurant to a carriage. Hundreds of freedmen seeking the protection of the federal government crowded into slums with names like "Murder Bay." The stench of rotting mule carcasses rose from the Mall, and tree stumps jutted out everywhere—reminders of the Union troops who had camped out in the city, chopping down trees for firewood during the preceding winters. Washington's resident population of 75,000 ballooned to 130,000 as veterans flooded the city looking for jobs.

Clemens marveled at the new House and Senate wings and the Capitol dome, crowned by sculptor Thomas Crawford's *Freedom* statue, symbolizing the power amassed by the federal government as it fought to preserve the Union. Through pensions, war claims, patronage, railroad charters, mining and timber rights, patents, military contracts, agriculture, and mail delivery, the federal government was irreversibly involved in the lives of most Americans. In 1829 there were only 625 federal civilian employees; forty years later the workforce had grown tenfold. And as Clemens later wrote in *The Gilded Age*, every "individual in public employment, from the highest bureau chief, clear down to the maid who scrubs Department halls…represents Political Influence…Mere merit, fitness and capability, are useless baggage to you without 'influence.'" [3]

Just as his literary and lecturing career was taking off, Clemens's decision to take a job in Washington seemed like an odd change of course. He was undoubtedly lured by a steady source of income (six dollars a day) as he hobnobbed with the influential and powerful—people who could help him build a career of fame and fortune, or at least provide good material for future satires. He also hoped to travel to China and believed his Washington contacts would prepare him for that journey. Finally, he was concerned about his jobless brother, Orion. He bragged to his mother about his prospective employment—"I believe it can be made one of the best paying berths in Washington"—and added: "Say nothing of this. At least I can get an office for Orion, if he or the President will modify their politics."[4] Although he lobbied for Orion's appointment as a clerk in the Patent Office, Orion never did get a government job.

Clemens recalled in fiction the scene of his arrival at the B&O railroad station, where he was "assailed by a long rank of hackmen" driving decrepit carriages that belonged in a museum and shaking their whips in his face.[5] He went directly to a weather-beaten old boarding house at 224 F Street NW, at the northwest corner of the intersection with Fourteenth Street, to meet with his new boss, Senator William Stewart.* In his memoirs published forty years later, Stewart described Clemens's arrival with vindictive hyperbole:

I was seated at my window one morning when a very disreputable-looking person slouched into the room. He was

---

* In subsequent years a classy department store, Garfinkles, and then a Borders bookstore occupied the site. It is now a music venue and restaurant, Hamilton's.

arrayed in a seedy suit, which hung upon his lean frame in bunches with no style worth mentioning. A sheaf of scraggy black hair leaked out of a battered old slouch hat, like stuffing from an ancient Colonial sofa, and an evil-smelling cigar butt, very much frazzled, protruded from the corner of his mouth. He had a very sinister appearance. He was a man I had known around the Nevada mining camps several years before, and his name was Samuel L. Clemens.[6]

The senator called Clemens "the most lovable scamp and nuisance who ever blighted Nevada"—a reporter for the "otherwise" very reputable *Territorial Enterprise.* Stewart admired Orion, who "was a respectable young gentleman and well liked," but Clemens was "not popular" in Nevada, he wrote. Clemens "did not care whether the things he wrote were true or not" as long as they were funny.[7] When Clemens wrote a satirical article "without the slightest foundation in fact," Stewart confronted him: "You are getting worse every day. Why can't you be congenial like your brother Orion? You ought to be hung for what you have published this morning."* According to Stewart, Clemens replied, "I must make a living…My employers demand it, and I am helpless."[8] Stewart warned his new secretary during the interview: "If you put anything in the paper about me I'll sue you for libel."[9]

Why did the senator hire this unlikely candidate as his private secretary? He claimed he hired Clemens to subsidize the writing of a book on the *Quaker City* excursion. As Stewart tells the story with gleeful embellishment, Clemens announced as he arrived, "Senator, I've come to see you on important business. I am just back from the Holy Land."

---

* Clemens admitted that "in my earlier writings, my sole ideal was to make comic capital out of everything I saw and heard. My object was not to tell the truth, but to make people laugh" (Carter, 156; Henderson, 99). But gradually "a remarkable transformation" took place as "the genial humorist" became "a reformer of the vigorous kind" (Carter 158).

A strong supporter of western railroads and mining, Republican Nevada Senator Stewart hired Clemens in 1867, but does not remember him fondly in his memoirs. Courtesy: Leonard Wainstein and Neale Publishing

The senator replied: "That's a mean thing to say of the Holy Land when it isn't here to defend itself. But maybe you didn't get all the *advantages*. You ought to go back and take a post-graduate course. Did you walk home?"

"I have a proposition," said the unruffled Clemens. "There's millions in it. All I need is a little case stake.... I've started the book already, and it's a wonder." He handed a few pages of the manuscript to the senator, who read them and found them "bully."[10]

With this awkward beginning, Clemens started his new job. He repaid his boss by praising Stewart's legislative work in frequent reports to the *Territorial Enterprise*.[11] Clemens performed specified clerical duties but had plenty of time to pursue his writing—a common practice in Clemens's day that today would likely be an ethical breach. (Walt Whitman had similar arrangements as a lowly clerk in the Department of the Interior, but was fired when he was found to be the author of a "dirty book"—*Leaves of Grass*.)[12] James Henry Riley was clerk to a congressional mining committee and political correspondent for the *Alta California*. He and Clemens became close friends.

To save money Clemens moved into a large front room in the senator's second-floor apartment, opposite the old Ebbitt House where several congressmen were quartered; it was a block north of the Willard Hotel. Miss Virginia Wells—a seventy-year-old aristocratic Virginian with smooth plastered white hair who had lost everything in the war—managed the lodging house.[13] Clemens took his meals and socialized at the Round Robin bar at the Willard. A block to the east stood the president's house.

The Willard was a favorite watering hole of Washington power brokers. Favor-seekers would seek out the president and other officeholders in the hotel lobby, hoping to persuade them of the righteousness of their cause. The term "lobbyist" is often attributed to the Willard Hotel lobby,* although it in fact originated from the lobbies outside the Senate and House chambers, to which the doorkeepers would allow selective admission for a gratuity.[14]

Clemens and the senator were an odd couple, but they had more in common than either would have cared to admit. They shared a rugged individualism shaped by the frontier and an unbridled ambition to succeed and reap the material rewards of success. Born in rural upstate New York, Stewart dropped out of Yale in 1850 to prospect for California gold. Well before Clemens's arrival on the Overland Stage, Stewart was the epitome of the western pioneer—fighting Indians and bandits, facing down gunslingers, and administering frontier justice. Having failed to make his fortune at prospecting, he studied law and served briefly in 1854 as California attorney general. In 1860 he moved to Nevada, lured by the Comstock discoveries. He made a fortune—not in mining but in mining litigation.

---

* The 1892 *Dictionary of American Politics* defined a lobby as a collective group of men called lobbyists in the "business of corruptly influencing legislators." They usually accomplish their purposes by "means of money paid to the members" or "any other means that is considered feasible" (Jacob, 5).

"The Willard Hotel in 1867 as seen from the boarding house apartment shared by Sam Clemens and Nevada Senator William Stewart. Sam had his meals at the Willard.
Courtesy: Library of Congress

As a Republican and Nevada's first senator, Stewart arrived in Washington in 1865 and called upon President Lincoln, whose countenance he described as "the saddest I ever saw," except when he greeted a visitor from whom he wanted something. Then his "face would overflow with genial good humor; and he would usually tell an anecdote which would illustrate the situation and invariably induce the visitor to agree with him."[15]

President Lincoln took the senator by both hands and said, by Stewart's own account, "I am glad to see you here. We need as many loyal States as we can get, and, in addition to that, the gold and silver in the region you represent has made it possible for the Government to maintain sufficient credit to continue this terrible war for the Union."[16]

Stewart was smart, articulate, and ruthless. More than six feet tall, with a long, flowing beard and piercing eyes, he was more feared than liked. He was admired for his political skill, mastery of detail, and tenacious pursuit of his objectives. At first he was a moderate in the Lincoln vein, supporting the reentry of the southern states to the Union on reasonable terms. He called Lincoln "the greatest man this hemisphere has produced."[17] Stewart was the first senator to support both universal amnesty for the confederates and suffrage for the freedmen. He proposed a resolution that prohibited racial discrimination, anticipating the Fourteenth and Fifteenth Amendments. He was one of only three persons present at the emergency swearing in of President Johnson, and he supported Johnson's veto of the freedman's bill because he thought the power it gave the commission to acquire land was prone to abuse. But when Johnson reneged on his promise not to veto civil rights legislation, Stewart was furious. He detested Johnson and joined the Radical Reconstructionists. He voted for the president's impeachment, describing Johnson as "the most untruthful, treacherous, and cruel person who ever held place of power in the United States."[18]

Stewart served in the Senate from 1865 through 1875 and again from 1893 to 1905. He was the author of the 1872 National Mining Act, which established the primacy of local mining laws and free access by miners and mining companies to the public domain. He also claimed to have turned down President Grant's offer of a Supreme Court appointment. The senator was a principal author of the Fifteenth Amendment, which declares that the right to vote shall not be denied on the grounds of race, color, or previous condition of servitude. He claimed personally to have obtained president-elect Grant's support for the amendment, which was ratified on February 3, 1870. Nevada was the first state to ratify it.

Stewart had a darker side.[19] While chair of the Senate Pacific Railroad Committee, he was on the dole of the Central Pacific Railroad and its founding partners, Collis P. Huntington, Leland Stanford, Mark Hopkins, and Charles Crocker. The Central Pacific spent hundreds of thousands of dollars to bribe members of Congress; in return the railroad got nine million acres of free land (larger than the state of Maryland) and $24 million in government bonds. Altogether the railroads received 131,230,358 acres of land from the US government or the equivalent in size of the third-largest state behind Alaska and Texas. Of Stewart, Huntington wrote: "[He is] peculiar, but thoroughly honest, and will bear no dictation, but I know he must live, and we must fix it so that he can make one or two hundred thousand dollars. It is in our interests and I think his right." For his efforts, Stewart was generously rewarded fifty thousand acres of fertile San Joaquin farmland disguised as a dummy trust. Nevada's other senator, James Nye, was promised an ownership stake in the new township of Lake's Crossing. When the Central Pacific began operations, linking with the Union Pacific to form the first transcontinental railroad, Lake's Crossing became Reno, Nevada.[20]

While Stewart had run for office as the defender of "the honest miner," he grew rich as an advocate of mining and railroad interests, and he shipped his family off to Paris for the winter. Even his admirers admitted he was "a money-hoarding, cold-blooded pirate of high finance" with a "highly developed instinct" for "money-making." At heart he was "a romantic adventurer" who played "the game of speculation for the game itself, and not for the spoils." As his friend George Rothwell Brown put it, "Probably no man in the United States has won and lost more fortunes."[21]

Clemens claimed to have served as the senator's proxy on some of the powerful Senate committees on which Stewart sat: Judiciary, Public Lands, Pacific Railroads, and Mines and Mining. Sam said he voted to accept or reject committee reports, although there is no official record of it.[22]

As a legislative clerk, Clemens observed both houses of Congress in action. In his journal he noted that "the Senate is a fine body of men, and averages well in the matter of brains." He thought the two Nevada senators—Stewart and Nye—were "the handsomest men...in Congress." Despite his personal disagreements with his employer, he praised Stewart's introduction of a bill to establish a national mining school that "will be an excellent thing for the whole mining community from Pike's Peak to the Pacific and from the northern gold fields, clear down to Mexico."[23] The bill would have phased out, over several years, the federal government's tax on bullion, one-fifth of which was collected from Nevada. In the initial years, the tax revenues would be used to purchase securities to fund an endowment, with the interest paying for the operating expenses of the tuition-free mining school. Although the bill was not enacted in its original form, the Nevada School of Mines was established in 1888. The senator also sponsored legislation establishing the Stewart Indian School in 1880 in Carson City.

Clemens also worked with the House of Representatives, "composed chiefly of grave, dignified men beyond the middle age," looking "worthy of their high position."[24] He joked that members "pay only questionable attention when the chaplain is on duty, but they never catch flies when he is praying."[25] Clemens jotted in his ever-present notebooks his impressions of public figures, their physical characteristics, abilities, strengths, weaknesses, and achievements. He thought the fighting politician Major General Nathaniel P. Banks of Waltham, Massachusetts, chair of the Foreign Relations Committee and the Republican Caucus, was the most handsome House member. Congressman Allison of Iowa was also handsome, but was "essentially ornamental," standing "around where women can see him."[26] The homeliest was Banks's Massachusetts colleague from Lowell, General Benjamin F. Butler. Clemens's notes read: "Forward part of his bald skull looks raised like a water blister...Butler is dismally & drearily homely, & when he smiles it is like the breaking up of winter."[27] Butler managed the impeachment fight against President Johnson as pugnaciously as he had occupied New Orleans during the Civil War, where he had earned the nickname "the Beast."

Among the most capable in the House were John Armor Bingham of Ohio (a "ready debater" who "commands attention"), the future president James Garfield of Ohio ("young, able and scholarly"), John Denison Baldwin of Massachusetts ("unblemished character, one of the best read men"), Horace Maynard of Tennessee ("one of the purest men in Congress"), and two influential African American leaders, A. H. Galloway and M. Harris of North Carolina, elected during the Reconstruction period.[28]

Clemens reflected on President Johnson's December 3, 1867, third annual message to Congress. The tin-eared president gratuitously justified his flurry of civil rights vetoes, opining that "negroes have shown less capacity for government than any other race of people."[29] He continued to taunt his Republican opponents: "No independent government of any form has ever been successful in their hands," but has ended in a "relapse into barbarism."[30] Clemens wrote in his notebook that "the President's Message is making a howl among the Republicans" who "say it is insolent to Congress." In contrast, "the Democrats say it is a mild, sweet document, free from guile." Of one thing Clemens was sure: "The message has weakened the president. Impeachment was dead, day before yesterday. It would rise up and make a strong fight to-day if it were pushed with energy and tact."[31]

The Republicans were incensed when they learned that the presidential message had been secretly sold to selected members of the press before it was delivered to Congress. Representative Charles Drake of Missouri offered a resolution condemning "the tone & language of the message," arguing that it was "calculated to incite insubordination, if not violent resistance to laws."[32] Congressman John A. Logan, a general who had fought in the Battle of Bull Run while serving in Congress, facetiously introduced a resolution to deter a "violent collision" between Congress and the president. Recognizing that the Congress's enforcement powers were negligible compared to the commander in chief, he proposed abolishing the "corps of pages that now constitute the military force of the House" in order "to avoid civil conflict."[33] Clemens thought that "Black Jack" Logan, so named for his piercing black eyes, was "better suited to war than making jokes."[34] Logan became one of the House managers of Johnson's impeachment trial.

As Congress adjourned for the holidays, Clemens summed up the session for the *Territorial Enterprise* with his signature sarcasm:

"I don't know whether they have done anything or not. I don't think they have...they have eased up on some of the thousands of millions of debt—they have smitten the Goliath of gold with a pebble—they have saved the country."[35]

On December 22 in *Mark Twain's Letters from Washington, Number 1,* for the *Territorial Enterprise,* he invokes a favorite metaphor comparing the fickle, unpredictable Washington weather to the political climate:

> Scurrilous Weather...There is too much weather...As politics goes, so goes the weather...To-day it is a Democrat, tomorrow a Radical, the next day neither one thing nor the other. If a Johnson man goes over to the other side, it rains; if a Radical deserts to the Administration, it snows; if New York goes Democratic, it blows—naturally enough; if Grant expresses an opinion between two whiffs of smoke, it spits a little sleet uneasily; if all is quiet on the Potomac of politics, one sees only the soft haze of Indian summer from the Capitol windows; if the President is quiet, the sun comes out; if he touches the tender gold market, it turns up cold and freezes out the speculators; if he hints at foreign troubles, it hails; if he threatens Congress, it thunders; if treason and impeachment are broached, lo, there is an earthquake![36]

Clemens bragged to his mother: "Am pretty well known, now—intend to be better known. Am hob-nobbing with these old Generals & Senators & and other humbugs for no good purpose."[37] Although Clemens worked closely with legislators and government officials, he preferred the company of newsmen at the *Tribune* bureau. He later wrote of congressmen, "They carry themselves high, and as prudent men; and though they are fools, yet would seem to be teachers."[38] By forging Stewart's signature, Clemens used the congressional "franking privilege" of free postage in letters to friends and family. Because of negative publicity rising from its widespread abuse, Clemens wrote to a friend that he "trembled to think they may abolish the franking privilege."[39] It was abolished in 1873, but reinstated in 1895 under tighter controls.

GENERAL JOHN A. LOGAN.

"Sam wrote for the *Territorial Enterprise* that Major General and Congressman John A Logan complained that members of Congress were wasting the taxpayers money by publishing remarks in the *Congressional Globe* that were written by lobbyist and never delivered on the House Floor."
Courtesy: Library of Congress.

Stewart was not impressed with his bohemian staffer. The senator complained that his roommate helped himself freely to whiskey and cigars, took over the hall bedroom and tormented the landlady by lurching drunkenly in the halls and smoking in bed.[40] He threatened to give Clemens a thrashing. When Stewart turned down his request for a loan, Clemens felt no further loyalty to his boss. As he later put it in his fanciful account of his tenure with Stewart, he held the secretarial position for "two months in security and great cheerfulness of spirit." But one day the exasperated senator bellowed, "Leave the House. Leave it forever and forever, too." Clemens "regarded that as sort of a covert intimation that my services could be dispensed with and so I resigned."[41] He was replaced by E. A. Pretois of Staunton, Virginia, and Sacramento.

Whatever the truth of this anecdote, the record shows that although he was on the payroll for over a month, Clemens's official duties lasted only from Monday, November 25, through Monday, December 2, when Congress adjourned for the session.[42] He informed the readers of the *Territorial Enterprise* and the *Tribune* of his resignation, declaring "I could no longer hold office and retain my self respect."[43]

Freed of his clerical responsibilities, Clemens poked fun at the institution from which he resigned. In "The Facts Concerning the Recent Resignation," he announces his resignation as clerk to the "Senate Committee on Conchology" and takes aim at a variety of Washington practices. He lampoons taxpayer-financed government junkets abroad, ridiculing Admiral David Farragut's European "pleasure excursion as too expensive." If he has no fighting to do, he should bring his fleet home, and if he wants a pleasure excursion, it would be more economical for him to "go down the Mississippi on a raft." Clemens targets unjustified military aggression, deriding the secretary of war's inept Indian campaigns. He mocks the proliferation of superfluous government reports, noting "the extravagant length" and deadly bureaucratic prose of the treasury secretary's report that "nobody would read." He suggests adding poetry and conundrums to liven it up. He attacks political patronage, lampooning the hiring of incompetent clerks who had nothing to do except pad their expense reports."[44] He boasts having submitted a bill to the government requesting $2,800 in compensation for "mileage to and from Jerusalem via Egypt, Algiers, Gibraltar, and Cadiz, fourteen thousand miles at twenty cents a mile."[45]

In a follow-up piece, "The Facts Concerning the Recent Important Resignation," he took on members of Congress directly, satirizing their "offensive personalities" as well as their whiskey-drinking during committee sessions: "They carry their whiskey into committee rooms in demijohns and carry it out as demagogues."[46]

In a burlesque on Congress, "The Facts in the Case of the Senate Doorkeeper," published in the *New York Citizen*, Twain imagines that he is called back into service as the Senate doorkeeper. He locks all the doors and charges fifty cents admission for senators to enter the chamber. He graciously allows Senate president Ben Wade to enter for free since he is "the ring master of the circus." He introduces a bill entitled "An Act Entitled an Act Supplementary to an Act Amending of an Act to Confer Universal Suffrage upon Women." He blocks a bill granting US citizenship to Giuseppe Garibaldi, the unifier of Italy,* and is impeached for violating Senate rules. In the "Articles of Impeachment," he is charged with "disrupting and disorganizing the Senate time and again," materially retarding its "reconstruction at the period of its most promising progress."[47] In one short satire, Clemens manages to mock superfluous legislative language, women's suffrage, the reconstruction debate, the Johnson impeachment, special-interest legislation, the inordinate power of congressional staff, and the practice of charging lobbyists a fee to access the Senate and House lobbies.

---

* Garibaldi also fought successfully for Latin American independence, and, at a time when the Union forces were suffering successive defeats, there were discussions to hire the acclaimed military leader as a general in the Union Army. Garibaldi offered to command the Union armies on the condition that President Lincoln declare that the purpose of the Civil War was to abolish slavery, an action that Lincoln believed he had no constitutional authority to take. Garibaldi lived briefly in the United States and applied for US citizenship. The Masons, of which he was a member, lobbied hard and unsuccessfully to make this global hero a US citizen.

Clemens also focused on inefficiency and incompetence in the federal bureaucracy.[48] In "Concerning the Great Beef Contract," he traces a government contractor's claim for payment for thirty barrels of beef to have been delivered to General Sherman's army. After an Indian attack on the supply train, only one barrel was actually delivered. The claimant recounts his visits to the White House; the Departments of State, Navy, Interior, and Agriculture; the postmaster general; and the patent office, each of which denies responsibility and misdirects him to another bureaucracy. In the Treasury Department, he is bounced from first auditor to sixth comptroller, to commissioner of odds and ends to the corn beef bureau, and on to the dead reckoning division, where he encounters the fourth assistant junior clerk reading newspapers and sixteen beautiful women writing books. He finally locates a clerk who informs him that the government might possibly pay for the one barrel if he can get special relief legislation through Congress. Through this experience the claimant learns that he could "trace a thing through the Circumlocution Office of Washington, and find out after much labor and trouble and delay, that which he could find out on the first day if the Circumlocution Office was as ingeniously systematized as it would be if it were a great private mercantile institution."[49]

"The Great Beef Contract" also pokes fun at the surplus of incompetent federal patronage employees with nothing of consequence to do. "The Clerkship business in Washington seems to me to be the chief wonder of this metropolis," Clemens reported to the *Alta California*. "The heads of Departments are harassed by Congressmen to give clerkships to their constituents until they are fairly obliged to consent to get a little peace."[50] Clemens overheard one cabinet officer say that "he could transact the business of his department infinitely better" if he "dared dismiss one-third of his clerical force." "These Departments are crowded with clerks and other small Government fish," Clemens wrote in his notebook, "Illinois heads the list, she furnished 450 of them!" After Illinois, according to this list, Pennsylvania, Ohio, Massachusetts, and New York furnished the most patronage. Rhode Island provided more than the entire Pacific Coast. Mr. Newcomb introduced a resolution inquiring "how many clerks are employed in the various federal departments, how long they have held their offices, what salaries they get, and what congressional Districts they were recommended from.... This will create quite a stir." Clemens suggested adding "an inquiry" about "how much these clerks do" and "how much they don't do," which would make "the stir" an "absolute flutter."[51]

Commenting on the constant turnover in personnel, Clemens reported to the *Alta*, "When a representative of ours learns, after long experience, how to conduct the affairs of his office, we discharge him and hire somebody that [doesn't] know anything about it."[52] Clemens became a strong advocate for hiring and retaining competent expertise for the federal government through the creation of a civil service. He campaigned for the Pendleton Civil Service Reform Act and applauded its enactment in 1883.

In the series of satires shortly after his government employment, Clemens also took on the legislative lobby, a subject he would return to in his first novel. In "The Facts in the Case of George Fisher, Deceased," Twain describes a claimant and his heirs who, through succeeding generations, perpetuate an "unrelenting swindle" of the US government by lobbying successive Congresses over fifty-seven years (with a short break to fight for the Confederacy) to increase sevenfold their frivolous claim for crops destroyed by Indians. Clemens predicts that future generations will "make pilgrimages to Washington, from the swamps of Florida, to plead for a little more cash" as they "drag their vampire schemes before Congress."[53]

In an article on "My Late Senatorial Secretaryship," Clemens shows why his Senate aide career was so short. He mocks the venerable senatorial practice of responding to constituent mail. Senator Nye receives a letter from a constituent seeking a post office for a Nevada town. The senator tells Clemens to answer it "ingeniously" with "arguments that there was no real necessity for an office at that place." Clemens answers the letter for the senator: "Don't bother about a post-office in your camp. I have your best interests at heart, and feel that it would only be an ornamental folly. What you want is a nice jail, you know—a nice substantial jail and a free school." Replying to another letter from constituents who wished to incorporate a Methodist church, Clemens wrote that their idea was "ridiculous" because Congress knew nothing about religion.[54]

In less than a month, Clemens had mastered the arcane Senate rules and procedures, which he put to good use in his satirical renderings, starting with an 1868 piece entitled "Cannibalism in the Cars." Stranded on a train in a snowstorm, a starving group of travelers is forced to decide who among them should be eaten to ensure the survival of the others. They approach the dilemma with the decorum of the US Congress, engaging in heated but respectful debate, invoking parliamentary procedures—motions, amendments, nominations, committee referrals, and reports. The debate devolves from personal qualities of leadership into the tastiness of particular travelers.[55] Mr. Halliday of Virginia rises to amend the report by substitution: "Bulk is what we desire—substance, weight, bulk. These are the supreme requisites now—not talent, not genius, not education."[56]

The superficiality of Washington society was another favorite target to which Twain would return in his first novel. The southern aristocracy that had graced the city's social life prior to the Civil War was gone. There were no roots or social traditions other than the exercise of political power. The only business of Washington was politics; the only thing manufactured was political scandal. Socializing consisted of using one hand for a friendly slap on the back of a competitor and the other for a stab in the back. In *The American Claimant*, Twain wrote that "when a man comes to Washington, I don't care if it is from heaven... it's because he wants something."[57] He went on: "Washington gathered its people from the four winds of heaven, and so the manners, the faces, and the fashions there, presented a variety that was infinite."[58] It was a "microcosm, and one can suit himself with any sort of society within a radius of a mile."[59] In an anonymous column, Clemens noted the "eccentricities" of congressmen when it came to morals. Many "prefer to have their families remain at home that they may better enjoy their freedom here," for "Washington is a free and easy place, and never more so when Congress is in session."[60]

In politics it was not what you knew but who you knew. In Washington titles were everything. It was not so much your roots, your character, your experience, your wisdom, or even your wealth; rather, it was the position you held—or once held. Toward the end of his life, Twain wrote in his *Autobiography* that "titles of honor and dignity once acquired in a democracy, even by accident and properly usable for only forty-eight hours, are as permanent as eternity is in heaven."[61] Recalling his father's clinging to the title "judge" to assume a dignity that his poverty might otherwise have denied him, he wrote, "Once a justice of the peace for a week, always 'judge' afterward." It is "our democratic privilege," he said, to "adore titles and heredities in our hearts and ridicule them with our mouths."[62] We inherited this propensity for titles from the monarchies, people "without title and a long pedigree, whether they had great natural gifts and acquirements or hadn't, were creatures of no more consideration than so many animals, bugs, insects."[63] And once obtained, titles were passed along to spouses and future generations. Nepotism was endemic. Clemens ridiculed "the masquerade in the peacock shams of inherited dignities and unearned titles."[64]

Clemens's brief career as a federal employee reinforced the "low opinion" of politicians he had formed on the frontier. "The government of my country shuns honest simplicity, but fondles artistic villainy," he said, "and I think I might have developed into a very capable pickpocket if I had remained in the public service for a year or two."[65] He wrote for the *Chicago Republican*: "Congress is the most interesting body I have found yet. It does more crazy things, and it does them with graver earnestness, than any State legislature."[66] Admonishing burglars who broke into his last home at Stormfield, the aging widower Clemens said, "They'll send you from here down to Bridgeport jail, and the next thing you know, you'll be in the United States Senate."[67]

Having covered the Nevada Territorial Legislature for two sessions and Congress for one, Clemens fully understood the legislators' skill at manipulating parliamentary procedures for self-advancement and self-dealing.[68] An experienced legislative reporter, he had an instinct for scandal and chicanery.

Clemens's tools of satire and ridicule were effective in exposing the flaws—and not the achievements—of the legislative process. Yet despite pervasive corruption during this period, Congress actually rose to the occasion, proposing the postbellum constitutional amendments, enacting civil rights legislation, and working with passion and skill to eradicate the vestiges of slavery. Congress laid the foundation for realizing the true promise of the founding charters, even though this constitutional framework would mostly lay dormant, ignored by the courts, Congress, and the executive for decades as the nation slipped into the Gilded Age and greeted the new century with retrograde policies of racial segregation. With Clemens's acute observational skills, he mastered the complexity and subtlety of the human-parliamentary interaction in legislation. Could he have missed the forest for the trees? If so, it is a perspective that has been shared by many Americans during much of our history. It is often difficult to recognize and appreciate monumental events until they are viewed from the vantage of historical hindsight.

In a 1906 interview with *The Washington Post*, Clemens said that he "could write a book on my discoveries and not enumerate all of them. I have learned that legislation is a much more complicated proposition than I ever dreamed it to be. It looked very simple and easy at a distance, but a closer view gave me quite a different impression."[69]

A Tale of Today

Twain's early satires on government resonate today. Admiral Farragut's "junket" to Europe, recounted in "The Facts Concerning the Recent Resignation," is replicated in hundreds of congressional fact-finding missions abroad to such foreign policy trouble spots as St. Andrews in Scotland and Prague in the springtime.* And those "superfluous," lengthy government reports that "nobody" reads have increased in geometric proportions. Congress has mandated by statute thousands of reports—so many that is impossible to get an accurate count. Who reads these reports and what action is taken on them? The State Department's inspector general found that in 2010, US embassies alone spent fourteen hundred person hours every year writing over three hundred reports mandated by Congress. Eliminating the duplication and waste in unnecessary embassy reporting would save $50 million a year.** In "The Facts in the Case of the Senate Doorkeeper," Twain charges a fee to enter the Senate and House lobbies. Today no such fees are charged,

---

* Congressional delegations abroad (CODELS) are so common that the *Washington Post* had a regular columnist who delighted in poking fun at them. (E.g., Al Kamen, "In the Loop," May 13, 2011, A14c6—"Don't forget! There's still time to pack for that fine congressional delegation trip led by Dan Burton (Rep-Ind.)...leaving Saturday for Dublin and Prague....Spring in Prague? Too good.") The House Friends of Scotland Congressional Caucus was planning a mid-August fact-finding trip with spouses and golf clubs via military jet to St Andrews, Scotland—"Ah, CODELS, the last great bipartisan conspiracy" (Kamen, July 8, 2011, A12cs2-3).

** Small embassies complain that the constant demand for detailed reports "imposes unduly heavy demands on limited personnel resources" (State Department Inspector General Report, November 9, 2010, quoted in Al Kamen, "In the Loop," *Washington Post*, November 10, 2010, A17cs3-4). Secretary Gates was so annoyed by the huge amounts of time spent by the defense department in preparing congressionally mandated reports that no one read that he required a sticker be placed on each report stating the cost of preparing the report. A 2012 report on Afghanistan cost $1,605 a page (see Kamen, "In the Loop," Washington Post, May 3, 2012, A15cs1-3).

*but access is facilitated for lobbyists who contribute generously to a senator's campaign. With remarkable prescience, Twain targets the enormous power of congressional staff, the misman-agement of Senate time, and votes on superfluous legislation, such as the "message votes" taken in recent years—bills with-out any prospect of enactment intended solely to send a mes-sage to the opposition and the media, such as the 60 House votes to repeal "Obama care" while Obama was still president. Minority Leader Mitch McConnell called them a "show vote designed to fail."[70] Clemens once vented his frustration with wasted voting in a February 1884 letter to Laurence Hutton, proposing "a **permanent** committee of one or two faithful hard workers…to canvass the delegations, & never allow the bill to come to a vote in either house, 'till a sure majority has been SECURED."[71]*

In "Concerning the Great Beef Contract," Twain sati-rizes the bureaucratic "passing-the-buck" phenomenon—the lack of private-sector incentives in a sprawling bureaucracy to establish accountability and measure efficiency. In the cen-tury since Clemens's short government career, the size and complexity of the federal bureaucracy has grown beyond what even Clemens's vivid imagination could have envisioned— the proliferation of federal programs, employees, departments, agencies, bureaus, and offices, and extensive federal involve-ment in the private sector through regulations, grants, entitle-ments, contracts, outsourcing, and tax incentives.

While the federal government provides excellent and essen-tial services that improve the nation's quality of life,[72] the ever-expanding bureaucratic maze also creates inefficiencies, redun-dancies, conflicts, market distortions, lack of accountability, and opportunities for fraud and waste. Is it necessary to have fifteen agencies overseeing food safety laws, twenty programs to help the homeless, or eighty programs to promote economic development? If Clemens were looking for material today, he might start with the *federal response to the September 11, 2001, terrorist attacks on the World Trade Center in New York. In 2010 a **Washington Post** study found that 1,271 government organizations and 1,931 private companies work on programs related to counterterrorism, that 854,000 people hold "top secret" security clearances, that thirty-three building complexes have been built or are under construction since September 2001 to house intelligence work (the equivalent of twenty-two Capitol buildings), that many security and intelligence agencies do the same work, and that fifty thousand intelligence reports are published each year.[73] Is it any wonder that a lone terrorist occasionally slips through the bureaucratic cracks, only to be subdued by an alert passenger, flight attendant, or citizen?*

Bureaucracies spend inordinate amounts of time talking to each other, resolving inter-agency conflicts, and lobbying to expand their programs. Profit-making institutions face frustration in finding accountable decision makers who can resolve issues expeditiously. Companies face conflicting regulatory demands, redundant reporting requirements, and constantly changing tax and regulatory policies that deter long-term planning and investment.

In "The Great Beef Contract," Twain also targets the hiring of incompetent patronage employees, an issue partially addressed by the Pendleton Civil Service Reform Act of 1883, which he strongly supported. The Civil Service Reform Act of 1978 and subsequent legislation have further strengthened the cadre of federal employees who are selected on merit and not patronage. Today political appointees constitute a small percentage of the federal workforce—fewer than ten thousand out of a workforce of over 2.7 million. Nonetheless political appointees occupy most of the high-level strategic, policy, and management positions. And this presents legitimate concerns. There are questions about the experience and competence of campaign supporters and lobbyists who are hired to direct major federal programs or are appointed to political ambassadorships. There are concerns about unfilled positions during transitions between administrations, the lengthy gap between nomination and confirmation, and the rapid turnover of high-level political appointments, whose tenure averages about eighteen months—hardly long enough for on-the-job training. Concerns also are raised about the proliferation of inexperienced aides in the White House who insulate the leadership from the institutional wisdom of career experts and the lack of opportunities for outstanding career employees to rise to top-level positions.

In "The Facts in the Case of George Fisher, Deceased," Twain previewed an issue about which he would have more to say in **The Gilded Age**—lobbying for special legislation that enriches particular individuals or institutions. During the Gilded Age, the railroad lobbyists competed for land grants and bond financing, and in recent years thousands of registered lobbyists have lobbied for all kinds of special legislation, festooning thousand-page bills with hundreds of special provisions, earmarking appropriations for specific projects, and providing more than $1 trillion in annual "tax expenditures"—special deductions or credits that benefit specific businesses or economic sectors.

Twain also captured enduring Senate traditions. His comedic replies on behalf of a senator to constituent mail explain why his career as an aide was so brief. Anyone who has written a senator only to receive a form response that politely avoids taking any controversial position can readily appreciate the travesty of his candor. Twain's satire on congressional protocol in his story on cannibalism also hit the mark. With the advent of C-SPAN, television viewers can now observe how congressional debates, conducted with decorous deference, *can quickly devolve into a kind of political cannibalism as members rhetorically attempt to eat their opponents alive. In his 1989 farewell address to the House, ousted speaker Jim Wright bemoaned the "mindless cannibalism" that consumes Congress.*[74]

The low regard with which the public appears to hold Congress in recent years, as shown by opinion polls, no doubt reflects the complexity and messiness of legislative sausage making. A July 2016 Gallup poll showed that only 13 percent of the public approved of Congress, down from 42 percent in 1973. Out of the horse trading, political posturing, and petty wrangling, however, great things occasionally happen.

CHAPTER FIVE

A Capitol Reporter

"Reader, suppose you were an idiot. And suppose you were a member of Congress. But I repeat myself."

— MARK TWAIN

After Clemens left Senator Stewart's apartment, he moved five times in three months. He rented a room at 356 C Street and then moved to 76 Indiana Avenue, where he had a little back room with a sheet-iron stove, a cheap and musty carpet, a perpetually unmade bed, and a couple of chairs. A visiting friend described the foul smell of tobacco smoke. The floor was littered with newspaper clippings and torn pages of discarded manuscript. Partially dressed, Clemens paced the floor in slippers, smoking and swearing. When he finally settled down to work, he was a "steam engine at full head."[1] Clemens wrote that his *Alta California* colleague James Henry Riley and he "lodged together in many places in Washington during the winter of '67-'8, moving comfortably from place to place, and attracting attention by paying our board—a course which cannot fail to make a person conspicuous in Washington."[2] In "Riley—Newspaper Correspondent," Clemens describes his friend as "the most entertaining company" he ever met. As Clemens told the story, Riley once served as a Chinese court interpreter, but was dismissed because "his translations were too free." He didn't speak Chinese. He was replaced by a Chinese man who "did not know any English."[3]

Clemens also roomed with the hard-drinking William Swinton, whose brother was chief of *The New York Times* editorial staff. The two men wrote two letters a week for twelve obscure newspapers around the country and were paid a dollar for each. In his *Autobiography*, Twain claims they were "the fathers and originators of what is a common feature in the newspaper world now, the syndicate." The tall, red-haired Swinton, whom Twain described as "a brilliant creature, highly educated, accomplished," had been a special correspondent for the *Times* during the Civil War.[4] His accurate reporting of Union troop movements had gotten him into trouble. General Ambrose E. Burnside ordered him shot, but General Grant intervened, sparing his life but banishing him from the front.[5]

In December 1867 Clemens met General Ulysses S. Grant at a Washington reception. After shaking hands Clemens retreated to a side wall and watched Grant intensely for an hour or so as he greeted visitors in the seemingly endless reception line. The General looked "poor, modest and unhappy" as he gave each hand a "single shake and threw a quick look-out for the next."[6] It was the inauspicious beginning of an extraordinary relationship. Given his deep-welled cynicism about public figures, Clemens picked his heroes selectively. Grant would rise to the top of the list.

A few weeks later, Clemens and Bill Swinton called at Grant's Washington home seeking an interview. The general was out at a dinner. His wife, Julia, promised to keep him at home one Sunday evening, but there is no record that an interview ever took place, despite Clemens's bravado letter to his Mother: "Swinton & I are going to get the old man into a private room at Willard's & start his tongue with a whiskey punch. He will tell everything he knows & twice as much as he supposes." Clemens planned to use the information "as coming from a high authority" so as not "to betray the old man." He promised his mother not to print anything that "would give [the general] pain," only "to tickle his vanity." Perhaps because he never got his interview, Clemens later wrote fictitious interviews, one probably in *The New York Times* and one in the December 1868 *New York Tribune* in which he peppered the taciturn Grant with insensitive questions to which the then president-elect responded with his trademark silence or by reciting his campaign slogan, "Let us have Peace."[7] Capturing Grant's laconic personality, the spoof, much like a *Saturday Night Live* skit, mocked the evasive spin and nonanswers that characterize so many political interviews.

Freed from his Capitol Hill desk job, Clemens was enjoying life to the fullest, reliving his western vagabond days. It was one of the last times in his life he could be a completely free spirit. He was "quite a lion," his biographer Paine wrote, a "bachelor, faultless in taste, whose snowy vest [was] suggestive of endless quarrels with Washington washerwomen."[8] The coming holidays would introduce Clemens to some respectable folk who would domesticate the fun-loving frontiersman.

On December 25, 1867, Clemens traveled to New York and took a room at the Westminster Hotel. The next night he moved in with Dan Slote, his *Quaker City* roommate. They hosted a reunion "blow out" of *Quaker City* friends. Among the guests was Charlie Langdon, who extended a Langdon family invitation for dinner at the St. Nicholas Hotel on December 27. At the dinner Clemens met his future wife, Charlie's sister Olivia Langdon, known as Livia to her family and Livy to her friends. Clemens joined the Langdon family on New Year's Eve to hear Charles Dickens read *David Copperfield.* Dickens, wearing a black velvet coat with a fiery "red flower in his button hole," acted out the storm scene from Copperfield "with great force and animation."[9]

Sam cherished the evening with Livy but later gave the lecture mixed reviews.[10]

On New Year's Day, Clemens attended a party at the home of Thomas Berry at 115 West Forty-Fourth Street, where he spent the day and evening charming Livy and her friend Alice Hooker, who was visiting from Hartford, Connecticut. On Sunday, Clemens attended Plymouth Church in Brooklyn as the guest of the famed preacher Henry Ward Beecher. At dinner with the Beechers after church, he met a woman he greatly admired—Harriet Beecher Stowe, author of *Uncle Tom's Cabin* and a resident of Nook Farm. On the same visit, he renewed his acquaintance with Emma Beach, a woman whose company he enjoyed on the *Quaker City* trip.

On January 6, Clemens took the train back to Washington in a confused state. He had been exposed to fundamentally disparate societies—moneyed eastern progressives, frontier bohemians, and philistine power brokers in the capital. Where did he belong? What path should he take? Clemens had options. He was in demand as a journalist. He had offers to lecture and a proposal to write a book. He had been recommended for government posts, including a mission to the Sandwich Islands, a consul post in China, and a delegation to Europe led by his diplomatic friend Anson Burlingame. Clemens was unsure of which path to take and was reluctant to relinquish his freedom.

Clemens had accepted a two-night speaking engagement in Washington on January 9 and 10, 1868, apparently arranged without his knowledge by a less-than-sober friend. He drew a large crowd to hear his lecture on "The Frozen Truth," an account of the *Quaker City* tour. Playing up to the local audience, he said, no doubt with satirical relish, that "no quarter of the old world has *such* a monument as the Washington Monument," and "no officials there are more efficient, patriotic or collect their salaries more promptly than our members of Congress."[11] Clemens canceled the second night when the *Evening Star* carried a synopsis of the first. Twain's success as a lecturer was in part due to his dramatic use of the pause, which ended in a surprise, often self-deprecating, witticism—a technique he believed would not work if the audience had already read the script.[12]

Now a full-time Washington reporter, Clemens turned down an offer to give eighteen lectures around the country for one hundred dollars apiece, having "solemnly yielded up my liberty for a whole session of Congress."[13] The famed cartoonist Thomas Nast tried but failed to get Clemens to join him on a combination speaking and drawing tour.

Clemens hobnobbed with the staff of the *Tribune's* Washington Bureau at 470 Fourteenth Street NW, across the street from the Willard Hotel. He was paid about forty dollars for a column of print. He also wrote for the *Alta California*, the *Enterprise*, the *Chicago Tribune* and *Republican*, the Washington *Evening Star*, *The New York Citizen*, and the *Galaxy* magazine. When *The New York Herald* tried to steal him from the *Tribune*, Clemens agreed to cover Washington for the *Herald* without a byline, writing to his brother that he planned "to abuse people right & left...There are a lot of folks in Washington who need vilifying. This is the place to get a poor opinion of everybody in. There are more pitiful intellects in this Congress."[14]

Washington was bustling with hard-charging war reporters who had stayed on in the capital to cover the growing federal bureaucracy and the congressional battles between the Radical Republicans and the southern sympathizers. They were smart, educated men (and a few women) who holed up on newspaper row, stretching between the Willard hotel on Pennsylvania Avenue and along the 500 block of Fourteenth Street. Leading political figures would drop by to talk politics, exchange gossip, and offer up information on their accomplishments to be reported to their constituents. To supplement their meager income, reporters took on government clerkships, accepted pay from lobbyists to write stories in support of corporate clients—like the Northern Pacific and the New India Mining Company—traded inside information, wrote speeches, and worked for political campaigns. The ethical lines were fuzzy.

From his days covering the Nevada legislature, Clemens was a skillful reporter who rewarded his sources with favorable stories and employed his satirical pen to send shivers through those he disdained. Far from a saint, he was more independent and scrupulous than most. The press had an essential role in democratic self-government in supplying accurate information to the public and holding their elected leaders accountable, and Clemens thought the media, failing in its responsibilities, was a silent partner in the corruption that pervaded Washington.

In "How I Edited an Agricultural Paper," Twain ridiculed the editorial arrogance of journalists who feigned understanding of issues about which they were ignorant. When criticized for nonsensical reporting on turnips growing on trees and the guano bird, the editor defended himself: "I have been in the editorial business going on fourteen years, and it is the first time I ever heard of a man's having to know anything in order to edit a newspaper."[15]

In his *Sketch Book*, Twain wrote in 1870 that "the *liberty* of the Press is called the Palladium of Freedom, which means, in these days, the liberty of being deceived, swindled, and humbugged by the Press and paying hugely for the deception."[16] In 1873 Clemens told the Hartford Monday Evening Club that the press had excused or defended so many corrupt officials that it condoned a Senate "whose members are incapable of determining what crime against law *is*, they are so morally blind." The press had created a "Congress which contracts to work for a certain sum and then deliberately steals additional wages out of the public pocket."[17] Clemens bemoaned the proliferation of newspapers reporting through the prism of party partisanship, substituting opinion for fact. As the numbers "increase, our morals decline." If there is "one newspaper that does good, I think we have fifty that do harm." Clemens complained that the "free press...is licensed to say any infamous thing it chooses...and advocate any outrageous doctrine it pleases." It should be held "in bounds" by public opinion, but "the trouble is that the stupid people—who constitute the grand overwhelming majority of this and other nations—do believe and are molded and convinced by what they get out of newspapers."[18]

On Saturday evening, January 11, 1868, Clemens answered a toast from the Washington Newspaper Correspondents' Club at Welcker's, Washington's top-ranked restaurant. His topic was "Women: The Pride of the Professions and the Jewel of Ours."[19] In remarks before his all-male audience, he praised the beauty of Eve in the Garden of Eden, "particularly before the fashions changed."[20] Clemens bragged to his mother that Speaker of the House Schuyler Colfax said "it was the best dinner-table speech he ever heard at a banquet."[21]

When Anson Burlingame resigned as minister to China to represent the Chinese government, California senator John Conness wanted Clemens to replace him. Conness also recommended Clemens for the prestigious San Francisco postmaster position.[22] When Conness retired from the Senate, Clemens commended him for his hard work on behalf of the West Coast, describing him as "one of the pleasantest men, socially, and one of the best hearted that exists."[23] Signaling his evolving political pragmatism, Clemens asked whether his successor Senator Casserly's view of democracy is "of the political stripe, as set forth in bombastic platforms, or is it of the practical stripe that looks to the most goods to the greatest numbers?"[24]

Clemens claims he turned down both positions—San Francisco postmaster and Minister to China—to avoid the nomination and confirmation process and to concentrate on writing his book on the *Quaker City* tour. He knew it would take "an angel" to please both the president and the Senate during a time of open warfare on appointments.[25]

Clemens had no scruples about asking a former legislator from his California days—then Supreme Court justice Stephen J. Field—to intervene with the president on behalf of his political recommendations.[26] A strong unionist, Field had returned to the Democratic fold after the war. He supported President Johnson's lenient policies toward the South. Field had thoroughly enjoyed Twain's letters to the *Tribune* from Naples about what the Pompeii ruins told us about the Romans: "Sodom was clean and Gomorrah was pure, compared with Pompeii."[27] A master at cultivating powerful people, Clemens, like today's successful journalists, rewarded his sources with accolades. He wrote for the *Enterprise*. "On the Democratic side of the fence, Judge Field, of California, is talked of more and more every day in connection with the presidency of the United States...[The Democrats] must have a man whose record as a Union man is unblemished; whose record as a war man is spotless; and one whose conservatism cannot be gainsaid. Thus far, Judge Field is the only man they have found who fills this bill."[28]

Clemens thought the Democrats would need a strong candidate to run against the likely Republican nominee, Ulysses S. Grant. "Flaws that were merely damaging in the days of Pierce and Polk would be dismissing now," he said.[29] Clemens also advised Nevada readers that Senator Nye should be high on the list for the Republican vice presidential nomination, but his political advice was ignored. In 1868 the Democrats nominated Governor Horatio Seymour of New York, who lost handily to Grant, who had selected Colfax of Indiana as his running mate. Justice Field remained on the Supreme Court for another thirty years, a strong proponent of laissez-faire and limited government.[30]

Of the three independent and equal branches of government, Clemens held the Supreme Court in the highest regard—it consisted of educated, elitist men in whose hands the Republic is protected from the tyranny of the majority. Clemens thought "disgraceful" that members of Congress would "question the honor and virtue of the highest tribunal of our country."[31] He believed that the justices jettisoned their party affiliation when assuming the bench: "The Judges have the Constitution for their guidance; they have no right to any politics save the politics of rigid right and justice when they are sitting in judgment on the great matters that come before them." He added: "When we become capable of believing that our Supreme Judges can so belittle themselves and their great office so as to read the Constitution of the United States through blurring and distorting political spectacles, it will be time for us to put on sackcloth and ashes."[32]

In reporting for the *Territorial Enterprise* from December 1867 through April 1868, Clemens praised the legislative skill of

Nevada's congressional delegation.[33] He extolled his estranged employer's floor speech on Pacific Coast mining as "by far the best and ablest effort of its kind," but it would not help Stewart with the voters. Clemens "never knew a man to do his constituents a great service, or to do his whole duty by them honestly and well, that they didn't put him on the shelf and send some ass to represent them that was of no use whatsoever." The exasperated reporter proclaimed: "If I were in Nevada next fall, I would take the stump for Stewart."[34] Clemens also settled old scores[35] and continued to ridicule the partisan pettiness that consumed so much of Congress's time. When the Senate cut off stationery supplies for its members, he called it "the cheapest fraud I have ever heard of."[36]

On January 11 Clemens advocated ratification of a treaty with Hawaii that would prevent the English and French from occupying the islands and benefit the sugar planters and West Coast processors by eliminating heavy import duties.[37] The treaty failed because many senators saw it as a precursor to annexation. Initially a booster of the West Coast sugar business, Clemens later reversed course and opposed annexation.

On January 30 Clemens took on the Treasury Department, "rotten with swindling and rascality." Whiskey and cotton frauds were cheating the government out of two hundred million dollars a year, and some senators were beginning to speak out lest the public think they were in on the game. Congress had established a procedure to allow persons whose cotton or other crops had been unlawfully seized during the war to seek redress though a court of claims. Clemens condemned treasury secretary Hugh McCullough for putting himself "above the supreme law of the land" by awarding ten million dollars to claimants who said they were union supporters without any adjudication of their claims. Moreover, the secretary's excessive expenses had increased business taxes "at a time when the industrial interests of the country are not able to bear the increased pressures it entails."[38] Clemens wrote that Stewart declared "war against the Secretary of the Treasury with more vim and spirit than any other Senator" and lauded Nye's remarks on the floor charging a conspiracy between the secretary and the New York banks to contract the currency in paying down war debt, to the detriment of the western states.[39]

In a February 13 article for the *Tribune*, Clemens poked fun at a legislative practice that continues to this day. Drawing from the *Globe* (predecessor to the *Congressional Record*), he described a floor speech by Representative Logan. General Logan complained that Illinois Democrat Samuel Scot Marshall had inserted "revised and extended" remarks in the record that he had "never actually made." Marshall protested Logan's attempt to "censor" him, but Logan urged that the practice of injecting "speeches never made" into the record be "abolished." "It is infamous," he argued, "that the people should be taxed dollar after dollar to pay for speeches that are written by lawyers in this city." Drawing laughter, he referred to two congressmen from Ohio who recorded the same speech on the House floor, one a few days after the other, written by a lobbyist.[40]

The acrimonious political debate of the day was Reconstruction. The founding fathers' failure to resolve the slavery issue led to the Civil War, but now the war was over and critical questions remained unanswered. On what terms should the former rebel states rejoin the Union? How should they be governed? How should freedmen be protected from retribution and racial violence? How should their right to vote for representatives who would advance their interests be assured? Members of Congress and the president had very different ideas about what the Constitution commanded (or permitted). The Radical Republicans sought to disqualify the leaders of the rebellion from holding state office and to reorganize southern institutions and traditions, even redistributing plantation lands to freedmen. As conquered territory, the federal government could do with the South as it saw fit, without any constitutional limits. Union loyalists (carpetbaggers) should govern the rebel states, and Union troops should remain in the South to protect the rights of blacks. Ten southern states were not represented in Congress, but some moderate Republicans and southern Democrats argued that because the Constitution was created by sovereign states, Congress had no power to reconstruct the rebel states. They should be returned to home rule, their representatives should be elected to Congress, and Union troops should be withdrawn. Clemens wrote for the *Enterprise* that when Senator Garrett Davis of Kentucky argued that the Reconstruction bill would give the Negro "the power to rule over the white man," Stewart rose to respond. It was a matter of simple math, he said: one Negro cannot "dictate to ten white men" as long as the two colors are divided in that proportion in the country.[41]

Applying an ill-chosen metaphor, Johnson argued that federal military rule of white southerners "binds them hand and foot as absolute *slavery*, and subjects them to a strange and hostile power, more unlimited and more likely to be abused than any other now known among civilized men." He complained that granting the black man the vote was "clothing the negro race with political privileges torn from white men!" Aware that the southerner Johnson had been a tailor, Twain quipped in his news report that a southern congressman he had encountered seems well-attired despite having his clothes torn from him.[42]

In his February 13 *Tribune* article, Clemens wrote a parody about the Reconstruction debate. Two-term representative Samuel Beach Axtell of California had asked him, the reporter, "to act in his stead in Congress for a few days."* In the satire the Pacific delegation thought that if Twain threw the weight of his wisdom into it, he "could settle this Reconstruction business." But the surrogate congressman's attempts to gain the floor to speak on "the great question of Reconstruction" were "always forestalled by one driveling idiot or another." Mocking the flowery platitudes arising from the House floor, Twain sat silently during the "nauseating tirade" of Mr. Lipservice, Mr. Muscle, Mr. Ananias, and a dozen others who "have failed to extinguish the sacred fountain of my patriotism, or befoul its pure fires with the wrathful deluges they have exhaled from the Aegean stables of their degraded souls" He finally gained the floor from the speaker to make his inaugural

---

* Axtell would later serve as governor of both the Utah and New Mexico Territories and then chief justice of the latter, where he gained a well-earned reputation for corruption. While a member of Congress, he was on the payroll of the Central Pacific as a confidential attorney (Kaiser, 85).

speech as a surrogate congressman. "When the proud bird of freedom spreads its broad pinions," he began before he was repeatedly interrupted and shouted down, promising to take the floor the next morning "at which time I shall be ready with a speech in their atrocious dialect."[43]

Twain never did get to make his floor speech. Instead he was called before the Newspaper Correspondents Association that evening and "found guilty" by its chair "of conduct unbecoming a respectable member" of the press—that is, "descending to the rank of a common Congressman." As the chair explained, "Pause and reflect on the style of men these people are. They are sent here by a confiding people, to carry out in an honorable and dignified manner, the behests of a great nation...How do they show their appreciation of their great office? By utter[ly] offensive personalities—slang—inferior wit—and unnecessary and procrastinating speeches upon unimportant matters." Of course this was not true of all members, but the majority by their silence are "accessories to the wrong."[44]

On February 15 the Reconstruction bill finally passed the House 123–45.[45] On February 18 Twain let loose under the headline "The Political Stink-Pots Opened." Congress was debating, amending, and maneuvering on Reconstruction legislation "with unprecedented energy, even for their tribe," and "awful is the smell thereof." They "foul the air with their corrupt and suffocating breath." The more Congress reconstructs, he wrote, "the more the South goes to pieces." Referring to Jesus's parable of a house built on sand, Clemens complained that Congress is building Reconstruction on sand; there is "not enough Constitution under her." Congress worried that the Supreme Court might find the Reconstruction Acts unconstitutional and the South would revert to its prewar traditions. Clemens thought the issue should be decided by the Supreme Court. If the Reconstruction Acts are constitutional, then the Supreme Court will sustain them, he wrote, but "if they are not we ought to hope they will annul them."

The Radicals's leader, Thaddeus Stevens, argued that the Reconstruction Acts are "outside the Constitution," and "that the conquered rebels have no right to dictate to the victors—no right to say under what terms they will come in." Clemens wrote mockingly of the Radicals's logic. If the president vetoes the legislation, then the veto must be overridden. If the Supreme Court "obstructs the regeneration of rebeldom," then the Supreme Court must go too. "The political cauldron boils," Clemens wrote. "Let her boil."[46]

As the war between Congress and President Johnson continued, the impeachment debate heated up. Johnson was the ultimate champion of states' rights, and he directed the return of the rebel states to home rule without consulting Congress. When Congress passed laws to the contrary, the president vetoed the legislation.[47] But Johnson's multiple vetoes of Republican-passed legislation were an exercise of his constitutional authority, even though when Congress overrode his vetoes, he defaulted on execution. Early attempts to impeach Johnson over political differences in handling the rebel states failed.

Congress "has never given up on its impeachment scheme," wrote Twain; "foiled in one attempt, it straightway essays another."[48] When an impeachment resolution stalled, a frustrated Congress deteriorated into petty partisan politics. It stripped the president of funding for his clerical staff. Clemens depicted Johnson using the metaphor of a sick patient attended by congressional physicians and nurses; they were female impersonations of key figures such as nurse Mrs. Stevens—known as Thad—Mrs. Boutwell, Mrs. Bingham, and Mrs. Brooks. He wrote: "Retrenchment breeds strange legislation. Or rather, the weak things that are done in its name breed it. They could not impeach the president because—as Mr. Stevens says—they were afraid. But what of it? They have triumphed anyhow. They have won a dazzling victory. They have taken away his private secretaries. It was a wonderful strategy. He cannot write any more letters to General Grant now. He cannot spin out any more interminable messages to Congress." Clemens was disdainful: "It does not become Congress that it has been battling with the colossal artillery of impeachment to descend to throwing mud. Such conduct is neither royal, republican, nor democratic. It is simply boy's play." Taking away the president's clerical staff "is an unworthy and an ungrateful little spite," by which Congress "descend[s] to scratching and hair pulling." Congress represents the American nation and this "is not a nation that fights in this way."[49]

Then when the president attempted to fire war secretary and Lincoln-holdover Edwin M. Stanton, Congress seized the opportunity. The smart but irascible, stubborn, and generally disliked Stanton refused to resign and barricaded himself in the War Department, and Stewart—his close ally—joined him in the office for a night or two. Congress had passed over Johnson's veto the Tenure in Office Act requiring Senate consent to remove a cabinet officer.

In the House a Bill of Impeachment was drawn up, and Twain wrote in "Lazarus Impeachment Comes Forth" that "out of the midst of the political gloom, IMPEACHMENT, that dead corpse, rose up and walked forth again."[50] The House impeachment resolution presented a new and complex set of political issues. The Tenure in Office Act was of doubtful constitutionality and in 1926 the high court deemed it invalid. But Johnson had clumsily violated the statute by trying to replace Stanton. Clemens described the scene: "On Friday the nation was electrified by the president's last and boldest effort to dislodge Mr. Stanton. The wild excitement that pervaded the capital that night has not had its parallel here since the murder of Mr. Lincoln. The air was thick with rumors of dreadful import." Otherwise tranquil citizens fear "anarchy, rebellion, bloody revolution!"[51]

Clemens wrote a satirical piece for the *Washington Evening Star*. In "A New Cabinet Regulator," he suggested using a barrel of gunpowder to blast Stanton from the War Department. He thought such a plan would be "expeditious, unostentatious, and singularly effective," although he recommended placing the powder above him to "blow him downwind" because blowing him up might "elevate him" and "excite envy."[52]

When Johnson sent the avuncular Army Adjutant General Lorenzo Thomas in his dress uniform over to the War Department to evict Stanton and serve as interim secretary, Clemens wrote that "it was an open defiance of Congress—a kingly contempt for long settled forms and customs—a reckless disregard of the law itself!!"[53]

Taking a break from the congressional fireworks, on February 22 Twain lectured on the Sandwich Islands to the Ladies Union Benevolent Society in Forrest Hall in Georgetown. According to the *Washington Morning Chronicle,* he offered to show the audience "how the cannibals eat their food if some lady would hand him a baby."

The audience, "including many of the most prominent persons of Georgetown,…was in almost continuous roars of laughter."[54]

The other news of that day—George Washington's birth date—was no laughing matter. The House of Representatives voted to impeach Johnson.* According to Clemens, the city went berserk. "The excitement was intense…Hotels and saloons were crowded with men, who moved restlessly about, talking vehemently and accompanying their words with emphatic gestures." The Senate galleries were overflowing. Influential dignitaries could not gain access and threatened to discharge the doorkeepers. Stevens, "the haggard, cadaverous old man, dragged himself to his place and sat down. There was a soul in his sunken eyes, but otherwise he was a corpse that was ready for a shroud. He held his precious impeachment papers in his hand signed at last. In the eleventh hour, his coveted triumph had come." Stevens "rose up and in a voice that was feeble but yet distinctly audible because of the breathless stillness that hung over the great audience like a spell, he read the resolution that was to make plain the way for impeachment of the president of the United States."[55]

Clemens respected the aging, decrepit Stevens. Clubfooted, his "whole face sunken & sharp" with "*very* deep eyes" and "unshaven cheeks," Stevens "belongs to another age," Clemens wrote. Over Johnson's veto, Stevens had pushed through Congress several postwar civil rights acts and the Fourteenth Amendment granting due process and equal protection to all citizens, regardless of race. A lifelong bachelor, the irascible Stevens was a dark knight. Historians have never given "the bravest old ironclad in the Capitol," as Clemens called him, the credit he deserves for perfecting the promise of the founding fathers.[56] Stevens was too ill to prosecute the impeachment. Instead, the fearless, polarizing Massachusetts congressman Ben Butler led the House floor managers of the Senate impeachment trial. Butler was smart, articulate, and hardworking, generating a charisma among his colleagues that overcame his unpleasing physical appearance.

---

* Under the Constitution, the House votes to impeach and the Senate conducts a trial, presided over by the chief justice, to determine by a two-thirds vote whether to remove the president from office.

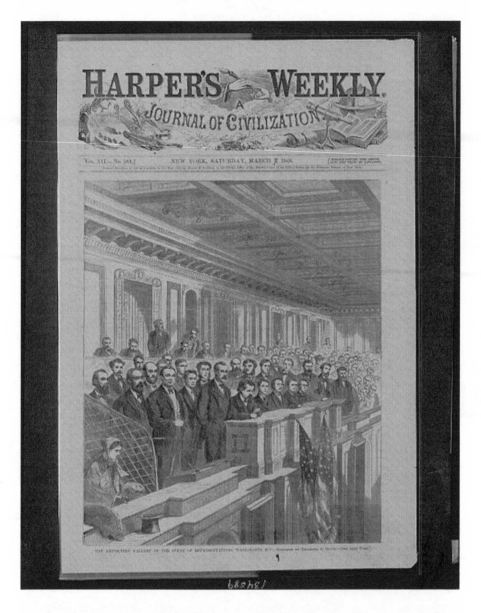

Sam Clemens covering the debate on the impeachment of President Andrew Johnson from the reporters' gallery of the U.S. House of Representatives. Courtesy: Library of Congress

With the capital consumed by the Senate trial over the next several months, Clemens handicapped the odds on impeachment as the political crosscurrents ebbed and flowed. If Johnson were impeached, he would have been succeeded by Senate president Ben Wade, who had his detractors and competitors. The competitors, Salmon Chase and Speaker Colfax, did not wish to see another Republican elevated to the presidency with a head start on the next election. General Grant's supporters shared the sentiment, although the reticent, humble Grant was more inscrutable, suggesting that the flamboyant General Phillip Sheridan, who Johnson was trying to remove as military commander of the reconstructed Louisiana, would make a good candidate.

In "Mr. Welles and His Marines," Clemens satirized President Johnson's supporters. He depicted Navy Secretary Gideon Welles leading a rescue team to the beleaguered president armed with whiskey jugs.[57] Clemens's reports of the impeachment trial were generally balanced and gave Johnson a fair rendering. After meeting Johnson at a White House reception, he felt sympathy for him as a "plain simple good natured old farmer" who "seemed friendless and forsaken." He thought that Maryland senator Reverdy Johnson, a "constitutional lawyer, worked very effectively against the impeachment." He continued to heap praise on Stewart, quoting at length from the senator's floor speech defending Reconstruction and noting that the North too had made great sacrifices during the war.[58]

Despite the prevailing wisdom that Johnson would be impeached, Clemens astutely predicted on March 7 that the impeachment would fail: "Nobody's prophecies concerning Washington matters ever come out right. Isaiah himself would be a failure here."[59] Stevens "fought hard for impeachment even when he saw that it would not succeed." Calling Congress a "whole tribe of Damn Cowards," Stevens gave "the finest word painting on a Congressional topic produced this session."[60] Sleuthing about the shenanigans that simmered beneath the surface—the promised payoffs and bribes—Clemens wrote that "right here in this heart and home and fountain-head of law—in this great factory where are forged those rules that create good order and compel virtue and honesty in the other communities of the land, rascality achieves its highest perfection." In Congress "rewards are conferred for conniving at dishonesty but never for exposing it."[61] In May the Senate was one vote short of the two-thirds needed for conviction, and Johnson was acquitted.[62] By that time, however, Clemens was long gone to San Francisco.[63]

After Clemens left Washington, he wrote less about politics but continued to follow it closely. With the election of President Grant in 1868, he wrote a devastating apocryphal critique of Johnson's last cabinet meeting. Submitted to the *Tribune,* "The White House Funeral" skewered the president for "nursing anarchy and rebellion," Secretary Seward for buying "all the icebergs and volcanoes that were for sale on earth" (mocking Alaska's purchase as "Seward's Folly"), and the other cabinet officers for disloyalty to the Republican cause.[64] The article was set in type but withdrawn at the last minute as wire reports came in that Johnson was near death. It was not published until after Clemens's death.

Restless and ambitious, Clemens had grown tired of the Washington scene. "Surely government pap must be nauseating food for a man—a man whom God has enabled to saw wood & be independent," he wrote Orion in February 1868.[65] While his stay in Washington was less than four months, his experiences in the nation's capital would inform his work as a writer, reporter, lecturer, social commentator, reformer, and, yes, even as a lobbyist. In *The Gilded Age,* his first novel, written five years later, he would describe Washington as "a feverish, unhealthy atmosphere in which lunacy would be easily developed...Everybody attached to himself an exaggerated importance from the fact of being in the nation's capital, the center of political influence, the foundation of patronage, preferment, jobs and opportunities...There was always some exciting topic at the Capitol, or some huge slander was rising up like miasmatic exhalation from the Potomac."[66]

Clemens had added to his reservoir of anecdotes—a reservoir that included tales from the Mississippi Valley, the frontier, the Pacific Islands, Europe, and the Holy Land. He now had a bundle of insights from the nation's capital that would nurture his growing skepticism about human nature and the exercise of political power—the gap between publicly professed morality and private greed. He wrote that "the Prince of Darkness could start a branch hell in the District of Columbia (if he has not already done it), and carry it on unimpeached by the Congress of the United States, even though the Constitution were bristling with articles forbidding hells in this country."[67]

Clemens was ready to move on. Elisha Bliss's letter had opened the way. Clemens would complete the book based on the fifty-two letters he had written on the *Quaker City* tour for the *Alta California*, about half of which had been published. First he had to head out to San Francisco to negotiate the rights to use the letters. On March 10, 1868, he left for New York. The next day he took the steamer *Henry Chauncey* bound for San Francisco. He had carried with him a deep skepticism of the democratic process, disgust at the pettiness of partisan politics that paralyzed relations between Congress and the executive branch, and a notebook full of tales of pompous legislators and their vote-buying, self-dealing habits that would be fodder for *The Gilded Age*.

Years later in an interview with *The New York Herald*, Clemens was asked why he did not remain in Washington. His reply invoked the memory of his last days of unfettered freedom before he decided to pursue his craft with discipline. He said, "Washington is no doubt the best town in the country for a man who wants to get all the pleasure he can in any given number of months. But I wasn't built that way. I don't want the earth at one gulp." He admitted that leaving Washington had "saved his life." He could now "go to bed early and keep out of the social excitements and behave myself. You can't do that in Washington." And so he "ran off to San Francisco; there I got elbow room and quiet."[68]

A Tale of Today

In Clemens's time rabidly partisan newspapers were the primary sources of information—information distorted by a political agenda, short on facts and long on opinion. There are fewer newspapers today and a greater variety of media outlets—networks, cable TV, radio talk shows, the blogosphere, and Twitter, to name a few. But it is not self-evident that Clemens would retract his comment that for every one that does good, there are "fifty that do harm." Given the global impact of today's media, Twain's rendition of the old proverb may be prophetic: "A lie can travel half way around the world while the truth is putting on its shoes.[69] Efforts by a few responsible journalists to fact-check erroneous statements made during the heat of an election campaign only serve to show how falsehoods repeated with Gatling-gun rapidity capture media time and shape voter opinions.

In his essay "Interviewing the Interviewer," Twain mocked the journalistic practice of making up falsehoods to create a sensation that attracts readers, a practice in which he not infrequently indulged.[70] Today, the Internet is a breeding ground for fake news fictitiously and falsely vilifying political figures. Falsehoods permeate the airwaves to such a degree that there is no commonly accepted fact base upon which voters can debate the issues. Perversely, the practice of manufacturing fake news invites mischievous interference by foreign entities in the democratic election process.

Recommended for San Francisco postmaster and minister to China, Clemens said he was unwilling to undergo the tortuous confirmation process during a time of partisan bickering between Congress and the executive branch, subjecting himself to salacious scrutiny as he waited in limbo, suspended between the warring branches of government.[71] Many talented prospective presidential appointees today would empathize with this sentiment. As **The Wall Street Journal** editorialized, "One reason fewer good people want to serve in government is that so many of them become fodder for Congressional bullies."[72]

Many legal scholars today would agree with Clemens's sentiment that justices should shed their politics upon assuming the bench, administering justice on the basis of established precedent. Even if not always followed, it remains a worthy goal of judicial review.

*Twain's amusing story on the abuse of revised and extended remarks in the **Congressional Globe** (now **Record**) was based on an actual colloquy on the House floor in which Congressman Logan charged that two members had read the same speech in consecutive days drafted by a lobbyist lawyer. Only two? In 2009 **The New York Times** reported that forty-two congressmen from both parties had used the same speech prepared by a company lawyer on pending health care legislation either on the House floor or in extended remarks in the **Congressional Record**.[73]*

In his satire on Reconstruction legislation, Clemens ridiculed the flowery rhetoric and insipid banalities that spurt forth like geysers in congressional debates. Instead of meaningful discussion that would enlighten the public on the issues, legislators invoke emotionally charged platitudes to pander to their constituents' biases. Today fiercely competitive media in search of ratings and advertising revenues escalate trivial matters to apocalyptic proportions while ignoring complex matters of substance. Space-limited new multimedia sources from cable television to Twitter place a premium on shrill and provocative sound bites that provoke needless conflict, mischaracterize an opponent's position, and displace rational analysis, civilized discourse, and a search for common ground. Masters at crafting ambiguity, politicians send subliminal code words to motivate their activist (often extremist) base while avoiding any quest for pragmatic solutions lest this be deemed weakness. Serious problems fester unattended while repetitious banalities soak up precious legislative floor time. Under the Clemens standard, contemporary House debates, in which fast-talking members compress party-distributed talking points into one-minute time allotments before the C-SPAN cameras, are a waste of time.

In his reports from the capital, Clemens offered unvarnished insights into the stress points that threatened the American democratic experiment—insights upon which he would elaborate in the next phase of his career as an author and sought-after commentator.

CHAPTER SIX

A Blissful Encounter

"The people's author."

— ELISHA BLISS JR.

In early December 1867, while living with Stewart at F and Fourteenth Streets, Clemens opened the November 21, 1867, letter from Elisha Bliss Jr., the Hartford publisher. It read: "We are desirous of obtaining from you a work of some kind, perhaps compiled from your letters from the East &c, with such interesting additions as may be proper." Bliss explained that the American Publishing Company was in the subscription publishing business and "can give an author as favorable terms and do as full justice to his productions as any other house in the country." Bliss concluded: "If you have any thought of writing a book, or could be induced to do so, we should be pleased to see you, and shall do so."[1]

Founded just three years prior, the American Publishing Company was located at 148 Asylum Street in Hartford, Connecticut. Subscription publishers sold their books through traveling agents—often disabled Civil War veterans, school teachers, and ministers—who wanted a second income. They went door to door, reaching both city dwellers and rural residents who rarely visited a retail book store. Customers were shown a prospectus of a religious tract, encyclopedic text, travelogue, or biography of a Civil War general, bound with a cloth book cover with sample pages and illustrations. The publisher would begin printing only when a sufficient number of orders were in hand. Subscription books were more expensive than books sold in retail stores: $3.50 for the cloth (two days wages for the working man), five dollars for the leather binding, and up to eight dollars for the full Turkey morocco. They often sold more copies than retail books.

With a population of about forty thousand, Hartford, the center of the subscription business, was a thriving and prosperous New England city—a little Boston without all the big city problems. In August 1868 Clemens described Hartford as "the handsomest city in the Union, in summer." As the home of the insurance industry, "there is quite a spirit of speculative enterprise there."[2]

ELISHA BLISS JR.
BORN 1821
DIED SEPT 25 1880

President of the
AMERICAN PUB. Co 1867-1880

Until he died in 1880, Elisha Bliss, Jr., President of the American Publishing Company, published and marketed Mark Twain's books, including *The Innocents Abroad*, *The Gilded Age*, and *Tom Sawyer*. In his *Autobiography*, Twain does not remember Bliss fondly. Nonetheless, after the failure of his own publishing company, Twain returned to the American Publishing Company, then run by Frank and Walter Bliss, at the end of his career. **Courtesy: Mark Twain House & Museum, Hartford, CT.**

Walter and Arlene Bliss, the author's grandparents. Walter served as treasurer and secretary of the American Publishing Company and wrote Twainiana Notes. Courtesy: Author's Collection

There were some twelve to fourteen subscription publishing companies in Hartford that sent out over ten thousand agents to sell more than thirty books a year.[3] They posed a perceived threat to the retail trade publishers, who argued that the product was inferior from a literary and production standpoint and that their sales force engaged in unsavory tactics. Defending his product, Bliss wrote to the *Tribune* that a lot of farmers, workers, and rural families were introduced to the world of literature through the subscription business.[4] But was this the path forward for Mark Twain?

Clemens was disappointed that his first collection of short stories had sold only a few thousand copies, and he was impressed that Bliss's company had sold one hundred thousand copies of *The Secret Service, the Field, the Dungeon and the Escape,* a work by his *Tribune* colleague Albert Deane Richardson.[5] (Richardson was killed two years later by his wife's former suitor who was acquitted on an insanity plea, reinforcing Clemens's lifelong aversion to the jury system and the insanity defense, which he attacked in multiple satiric forms.) In his December 2 reply to Bliss, Clemens pointedly asked how much money he would make from the book, explaining that this question "had a great deal of importance" for him.[6] He was concerned that writing a book would divert him from more profitable journalistic and public speaking ventures. Bliss had offered a flat fee of $10,000, but Clemens negotiated a royalty of 5 percent, exceeding Richardson's royalty of 4 percent.[7] This was one of the few truly astute business decisions Clemens ever made. To tide him over as he wrote the six-hundred-page travelogue, he asked for a $1,000 advance, which Bliss accommodated.

If becoming a great literary figure had been his ambition, Clemens might have pursued an established trade publisher like Harper & Brothers, Houghton Mifflin, or Macmillan, all of which published his contemporary Henry James (who sold but a fraction of books that Mark Twain did; Twain's worst-selling book did better than *Daisy Miller,* James's bestseller). Twain's rough-edged, vernacular style of journalistic prose probably would not have excited retail trade publishers or, for that matter, any known publisher. He did not write the plebeian prose of the travelogues and heroic histories favored by subscription publishers. Nor did he write in the high-toned, structured English tradition of other American novelists of that era. It would take a new kind of publisher to appreciate the distinctly American voices that Twain would capture. Although neither Clemens nor Bliss could foresee it at the time (as they each had more pecuniary interests in mind), the American Publishing Company's customer base provided an ideal platform for launching the first truly American author—the Thomas Jefferson of the literary world, declaring his independence from the British Empire of literature, reflecting the cultural roots of American democracy.

To meet Bliss's commercial specifications, Clemens added filler, along with diversionary and extraneous subplots, that degraded his literary product. But in 1868 he had made a choice. Twain would not only become the greatest author ever introduced through subscription publishing, but he would also transform the nature of American literature. As biographer John Lauber has said, "Subscription publishing made him literally the people's author; his career and his work are unimaginable without it."[8]

To cut short protracted negotiations by correspondence, Clemens left Washington by train and arrived in Hartford on January 24, 1868. He stayed with friends of the Langdons—John and Isabella Hooker. John was a sixth-generation descendant of the Reverend Thomas Hooker, who founded Hartford in 1636.* John's wife, Isabella Beecher Hooker, was the sister of Harriet Beecher Stowe and the famous Brooklyn preacher Henry Ward Beecher. At the Hookers' home, Clemens witnessed no swearing, tobacco chewing, or drunkenness. As he later explained in an *Alta* letter: "I have to smoke surreptitiously when all are in bed, to save my reputation, and then draw suspicion upon the cat when the family detect the unfamiliar odor. I never was so absurdly proper in the broad light of day in my life as I have been for the last day or two. So far, I am safe, but I am sorry to say that the cat has lost caste."[9]

---

* Among the original congregants of Reverend Hooker's Congregational Church in the settling of Hartford were two of Elisha Bliss's antecedents, Thomas and George Bliss.

Clemens met with Bliss, and after agreeing to a "splendid" contract, he boasted to a Hannibal boyhood friend that he had made "a tip top contract...with the heaviest publishing house in America & I get the best terms they have ever offered any man except one."[10] Lauber declares that "for the only time in his life, he was thoroughly satisfied with a publisher and told him so."[11] Clemens's enthusiasm for Bliss would last for several years. On January 28, 1870, he wrote from Elmira, "I'll back you against any publisher in America, Bliss— or elsewhere."[12] Their roller coaster relationship deteriorated over time and grew increasingly contentious, but Elisha Bliss remained Twain's publisher until Bliss's death ten years later.[13]

With a signed contract, Clemens turned to the task at hand— to write a book based on the *Quaker City* expedition drawing from the fifty-two letters he had sent to the *Alta California*, which provided only about half of the six hundred pages he had contracted to supply. He would have to add new narrative and create a structured, coherent book with a consistent style and characters. He made progress during his two-month stay in San Francisco where his friend Bret Harte gave him an editorial hand.

Clemens returned to Hartford and stayed in an upper room at Bliss's home where he received additional guidance on how to structure the book, advice on what to discard, and editorial polish. Over the course of seven months, Bliss persuaded Clemens to delete certain stories and add additional material from the *Alta* letters.[14] The publisher's second wife, Amelia Crosby Bliss, did not find Clemens a gracious house guest. He swore at the maids and burned holes in the sheets as he smoked cigars while writing in bed all night. Each morning the Blisses' ten-year-old son Walter picked up the cigar butts Clemens had tossed out the window during the night.[15] At a social gathering one evening, Clemens made a joke about "the Church of the Holy Speculators," referring to Hartford's prestigious and well-heeled Asylum Hill Congregational Church. As Clemens described it later, Amelia Bliss cautioned him that the minister was standing right behind him. Clemens whirled around and was introduced to the Reverend Joseph Hopkins Twichell, who was to become his closest friend.

The tall, athletic Twichell had been a chaplain for three years of the Civil War. He preached a kind of social gospel—similar to many modern mainstream Protestant churches—sidestepping impenetrable theology by espousing "good works."[16] During long walks in the woods, the skeptical, worldly Clemens and the idealistic, if naïve, minister talked about politics and social policy. Clemens attended Twichell's church regularly but never became a member.[17]

When Twain completed the *Quaker City* manuscript, Bliss circulated it to the company's directors. Several reacted in shock. They were appalled at the satire of religious institutions and practices. Such burlesque blasphemy made a mockery of the publishing house's high standards and threatened to destroy its credibility with it pious customer base. Mocking the Christianizing of Europe, Twain contrasted the barbarism of the Roman Coliseum, where wild beasts tore the Christians from limb to limb, with the "pleasant Inquisition" that persuaded the people to honor the Blessed Redeemer "by nipping their flesh with pincers—red hot ones...then by skinning them alive a little, and finally by roasting them in public.... There is a great difference between feeding parties to wild beasts and stirring up their finer feelings in an Inquisition."[18] One company director, Sidney Drake, took Clemens on a buggy ride and pleaded with him to release the company from its contract.[19] Clemens was furious. Having written to Clemens suggesting a "*humorous* work," Bliss was committed to expanding the company's literary reservoir to include "a work *humorously inclined*."[20] Bliss sensed he had a groundbreaking best seller on his hands. He confronted the board. If the board disapproved the publication, Bliss would take the book elsewhere and go with it. The directors backed down.

The Innocents Abroad, or the New Pilgrim's Progress was published on July 20, 1869. The reviewers had never seen anything like it. They raved about the raw style and populist prose, and the book sold fifty thousand copies the first year.[21] For the first time, an American writer viewed our European heritage not with the awe of a grateful stepchild but from the perspective of a common-sense democrat who could distinguish between stale tradition and high art. Shedding English pretensions, this original American author wrote with a transparency, openness, honesty, and simplicity that was without precedent. Among the glowing reviews was that of William Dean Howells, writing anonymously for the prestigious *Atlantic Monthly*. When Clemens visited the editorial offices in Boston to thank the editor, he was introduced to Howells, who became a lifelong friend and literary mentor.[22] Howells would later call Twain "the Lincoln of our literature."[23] *The Innocents Abroad* reflected Clemens's firsthand exposure to Old World cultures embedded with monarchical traditions, stratified class structures, paternalistic bureaucracies, and stifling state churches. Amid the irreverent humor and conversational prose, Twain's admiration for American-style democracy shone forth. Unlike Europeans, Americans, he wrote, "even have the effrontery to complain if they are not properly governed, and to take hold and help conduct the government themselves."[24] The contrast of Europe with the fledgling frontier democracy—to be reflected in his next book—could not have been greater.

On May 10, 1869, the Central Pacific and Union Pacific Railroads were joined at Promontory, Utah. Two months later Mark Twain published *Innocents Abroad*. Faster printing processes, speedy distribution systems, cheaper paper, and a more literate public all contributed to a surge in readership and demand for books. Twain rode the crest of the publishing surge. In the first five years, *Innocents Abroad* would sell over 250,000 copies—a phenomenal record, given that the US population was only forty million. By comparison in 1826 James Fennimore Cooper's best-selling novel *The Last of the Mohicans* sold fifty-seven hundred copies.[25]

The flow of sizable royalty checks facilitated Clemens's transformation from freelance journalist to Mark Twain the author—from frontier vagabond to eastern socialite. He also was beginning another transition—from a conservative southerner to a progressive New Englander. Clemens arduously courted and won over Livy Langdon and gained the consent of her father, Jervis Langdon, a wealthy and politically progressive businessman. Jervis and his wife, Olivia, had been active in the Underground Railroad. Among many others, they had aided the escape of a Baltimore ship caulker who became their friend and an outspoken abolitionist—Frederick Douglass.

Sam wooed Livy with 184 love letters* crafted over a seven-teen-month period with prose that equaled the best of a romance novel:

> [You] lifted the clouds from my firmament & made it glad with sunshine...I <u>must</u> offer a prayer for the dear heart that first taught my lips to pray. I must take [you] in my arms...& swear to love, honor & cherish [you] through joy & sorrow, through pleasure & pain, through sun & storm, & toil & scheme & labor for [you], with hand & brain, by day & night, all the years of my life, till the shadows of that evening, whose sun rises only in eternity, shall close around me, & thicken into the long night of death. God shield you, & love you & bless you always, my darling![26]

About to be assimilated into a prominent family, Clemens sought respectable employment as he pursued his writing career. After negotiations with newspapers in Hartford and Cleveland waned, Jervis Langdon loaned his daughter's fiancé $25,000 to establish him as a one-third owner and managing editor of the staunchly Republican *Buffalo Express*.[27]

On February 2, 1870, in the Langdon's' parlor, it took two ministers—Twichell and Thomas K. Beecher (yet another Beecher sibling)—to marry the curious couple of seeming opposites. Beecher was the quirky pastor of the Park Church in Elmira, founded and financed by the Langdons when their Presbyterian Church balked at their antislavery activism. As a wedding present, Jervis surprised the young couple when their carriage arrived at their new home at 472 Delaware Avenue, Buffalo, New York. Clemens wrote editorials and columns for the *Express*, initially promising to stay clear of politics. "We have a political editor who is already excellent," he said, "and needs only to serve a term in the penitentiary to be perfect."[28]

---

* Livy's count. Sam's count was 189, about half of which have been recovered (compare Powers 245, 280). See *The Love Letters of Mark Twain*, ed. Dixon Wecter (1949).

Having married into the Langdon family, Clemens's lingering ambivalence on matters of race disolved in favor of his earliest childhood instincts. In November 1869 he met Frederick Douglass, also on a lecture tour. Douglass told Clemens about how in 1848 he had enrolled his nine-year-old daughter, Rosetta, in an all-white female academy in Rochester, New York. His daughter was sent home after a white parent objected. Douglass asked the principal to let the children vote on the issue. They unanimously voted to bring Rosetta back to school.[29]

Clemens was deeply moved by the story. It brought back memories of his halcyon childhood days, sitting with the slave children as Uncle Dan'l passed along the tales from one generation to the next. As a southerner, Clemens had criticized the interference of northern abolitionists and written articles and letters with disparaging comments about Negroes, occasionally invoking a less formal appellation. He had been suspicious of Lincoln's antislavery platform, fearing his election in 1860 would precipitate a civil war—as it indeed did. The Langdons' northern progressive Republicanism brought out the better angels of his nature. His affection and admiration for his abolitionist father-in-law helped him discard old prejudices and nurture a growing passion for social justice.

Despite his comfortable new life, tragedy revisited. Livy's beloved father died of stomach cancer on April 6, 1870, and her best friend, Emma Nye, died of typhoid fever on September 29 while staying in their home. In November their first child, Langdon, was born a month prematurely, and the young parents feared the sickly child would not survive. Then in early 1871, Livy contracted typhoid herself; she never fully regained her health.

Clemens continued to cultivate his capital-city contacts. After his father-in-law was diagnosed with stomach cancer, Clemens made several trips to Washington to lobby for a bill that would benefit the Langdons' Tennessee business interests. Clemens bragged to Livy that he was more effective than an obscure Washington lobbyist because legislators were indebted to him for his favorable reporting on their accomplishments. He said "he could get any man's ear for a few moments, & also his polite attention & respectful hearing." With the help of Senator Stewart, Clemens buttonholed the Tennessee delegation and corralled enough members of the Senate Judiciary Committee to report the bill favorably, which he deemed a "big success." He sought mightily to impress his wife and ailing father-in-law with his legislative prowess, but the bill did not pass the Senate.[30]

While in Washington, Clemens was invited by Stewart to a reception with President Grant. They shook hands but each became tongue-tied. After an awkward pause, Clemens said, "Mr. President, I...I am embarrassed. Are you?" Grant said "Yes," and Clemens moved on. Twain wrote a satirical fantasy of this experience for the *Buffalo Express* claiming he had held up a receiving line of fifteen hundred people as he chatted with the president about life in Nevada and its smooth-talking governor, by then Senator Nye, until Twain was evicted by a Secret Service officer.[31] (Ten years later Clemens was again introduced to Grant at a Chicago event. Without missing a beat, the stone-faced Grant said, "Mr. Clemens, I am not embarrassed, are you?")[32]

On July 8, 1870, Clemens sat for the Civil War photographer, Matthew Brady. The photograph was among the last of Brady's widely distributed portraits of famous people before he sunk into poverty, alcoholism, and blindness.[33] Clemens then walked over to the House and Senate galleries and watched the lawmakers engage in parliamentary maneuvers. In the Senate they debated Chinese immigration and citizenship. Senator Stewart was filibustering against an amendment to the Naturalization Act sponsored by Senator Charles Sumner of Massachusetts to prohibit discrimination against the Chinese. To Clemens's chagrin, the author of the Fifteenth Amendment unabashedly opposed Sumner's amendment, arguing that the Chinese coolies were pagan imperialists incapable of functioning in a Christian democracy. After the debate, Clemens dined with the sanctimonious Senator Samuel Clarke Pomeroy of Kansas and Hannibal Hamlin of Maine. Hamlin had returned to the Senate after serving as the Republican Party's first vice president until he was unfortunately replaced by War Democrat Andrew Johnson when Lincoln ran for a second term on the National Union Party.[34] At night in his hotel, he wrote Livy, "Oh, I have gathered enough material for a whole book! This is a perfect gold mine."[35]

On February 2, 1871, Clemens returned to Washington on another lobbying mission for the Langdon Company's coal mining interests, staying at the Ebbitt House. Samuel Sullivan (Sunset) Cox, an eloquent and highly respected Democratic member of Congress, hosted a dinner for him that evening at Welcker's Restaurant. Back at his hotel that night, he received a telegram that Livy was seriously ill with typhoid fever. Clemens took the next train back to Buffalo,[36] returning to Washington on September 7 and 8, 1871, to secure a patent for one of his several inventions—an elastic garment strap.[37] On October 23 he returned again to give the "Artemus Ward" lecture in Lincoln Hall, attracting a crowd of two thousand. The reviews were mixed. Twain's efforts to revive the humor of his deceased friend and predecessor—Ward had been Lincoln's favorite funnyman—mostly fell flat.[38]

The Mark Twain House in Nook Farm, Hartford. Courtesy: Mark Twain House & Museum, Hartford, CT

As Twain's book sales increased, he grew tired of his job at the *Buffalo Express*. It was time for a change of venue—time to move to Nook Farm,* which was Hartford's most affluent western

---

* John Hooker had developed Nook Farm with his brother in-law Francis Gillette, briefly a US senator from Connecticut. Francis Gillette's son William was an actor, noted for his portrayal of Sherlock Holmes. He made a recording of his impersonation of Mark Twain's speaking voice which some consider the closest surviving replication of his authentic voice since no recordings of Twain's voice have been found.

suburb, shaded by sycamores and chestnuts and settled by a mix of intermarried Puritan descendants, writers, artists, and progressive reformers.[39] The Clemenses rented from the Hookers while their eccentric gingerbread house, planned by Livy and designed by the architect Edward Tuckerman Potter, was being constructed. On September 19, 1874, they moved into their High Victorian Gothic mansion at 351 Farmington Avenue, where the Clemenses were to spend the happiest years of their lives.

Despite his newfound success, tragedy was never far behind. Taking out his firstborn for a stroll one windy April day, Clemens became lost in thought and forgot to cover the young boy from the elements. The nineteen-month-old Langdon became ill and died in his mother's arms on June 2, 1872, of diphtheria—unrelated to the cold he caught in April. As with the death of his siblings, Clemens felt responsible for his young son's death.[40]

Bliss urged Clemens to write a second book, based on articles and short stories about his mining and reporting days in Nevada and California and his trip to the Sandwich Islands. Bliss gave the book the title *Roughing It*, and it was published on January 30, 1872. Although it did not sell as well as *Innocents Abroad*, Clemens thought it was better written.

Clemens finally succeeded in getting his forty-five-year-old brother a job. Bliss hired Orion as editor of the monthly circular, the *American Publisher*, an organ advertising subscription books. But as with all his jobs since Nevada, Orion's employment came to an unhappy conclusion. Orion confronted Bliss about his accounting practices, claiming his brother was denied half the profits of *Roughing It*. Clemens, by then a director of the company, asked to see the books, and Bliss complied, but he could find no discrepancies. Bliss fired Orion. Clemens wrote his sister on April 28, 1873: "Orion did a thing which was utterly inexcusable—it was the act of a half-witted child, and I could not say a word when he was discharged.[41] Nonetheless, the seeds of distrust between Clemens and Bliss were planted. The blissful encounter turned sour.

Clemens complained that Bliss did not reward him sufficiently for the revenues and fame he brought to the company.

He began to "interpret as dishonesty Elisha Bliss's astute profit-making."[42] In his *Autobiography* Twain does not remember Bliss fondly. He writes that "when it came to lying Bliss could over-shadow and blot out a whole continent,"[43] and that "Bliss told the truth once, to see how it would taste, but it overstrained him and he died."[44] The cantankerous aging Twain refers to Bliss as "a tall, lean, skinny, yellow, toothless, bald-headed, rat-eyed professional liar and scoundrel,"[45] a "repulsive creature," and a "bastard monkey" with "the intense earnestness and eagerness of a circular-saw" and the "gibbering laugh of an idiot."[46] Yet the kindly aging Twain had "only compassion for him" and would "send him a fan" if he could.[47] In his biography, Paine, well-aware of Clemens's propensity to vilify those whom he thought had done him wrong, described their contractual relationship in more generous terms. "Bliss," he wrote, "was a shrewd, capable publisher, who made as good a contract as he could; yet, he was square in his dealings, and the contract which Clemens held most bitterly against him—that of *Roughing It*—had been made in good faith and in accordance with the conditions of that period."[48]

Clemens remained with Bliss until Elisha's death in 1880. After his disappointment with other publishers and the failure of his own publishing company, he came back to the American Publishing Company near the end of his book-writing career for the publication of *Pudd'nhead Wilson, Following the Equator,* and his complete works. The company was then managed by Elisha's sons, Frank and Walter, toward whom Clemens apparently had no animosity. For as Clemens wrote George Cable in 1883, "If I were to advise you to issue through a Hartford house, I would say, every time, go to my former publisher, the American Publishing Company, 284 Asylum St. They swindled me out of huge sums but they do know how to publish a book and besides I think they are honest people now."[49]

CHAPTER SEVEN

An American Novelist Is Born

"The Father of American Literature."
— WILLIAM FAULKNER

Clemens was hitting his stride—a celebrated author, popular lecturer, man of means, and member of the social elite. What was next? The answer came at a dinner party in Nook Farm one snowy December evening in 1872. Charles Dudley Warner—a journalist and author of a well-known humorous commentary on life using one summer in his garden as a frame—and his wife, Susan, were among the guests, along with Sam and Livy.

The elegant and erudite Warner, with wavy graying hair, a trim goatee, and mustache, was well-traveled and knowledgeable about world affairs. Born in Plainfield, Massachusetts, Warner— six years older than Clemens—studied law at the University of Pennsylvania and worked as a railroad surveyor in Missouri in

1853–54. He moved to Hartford to become associate editor of the *Evening Press*, which then merged with the staunchly Republican *Courant*. The vivacious Susan, an accomplished pianist, loved to accompany Clemens as he sang the spirituals and jubilee songs of his Mississippi River days. During the after-dinner banter, Warner and Clemens began chiding their wives about the lightweight novels they were reading. According to Paine, the women retorted with a challenge: "If you think the books we are reading are so bad, why don't you write a better one?" Warner and Clemens looked at each other and accepted the challenge. They made a pact to write a novel together—as partners. The critic Bryant Morey French, author of a study of the book that emerged from that evening, suggests that they decided to write a burlesque of the contemporary dime-store novels their wives were reading.

Bliss was intrigued. Subscription houses did not publish fiction, and neither Warner nor Clemens had written a novel. Collaboration offered each of them some assurance. Warner was a meticulous if somewhat prosaic author, and Twain had demonstrated his boundless capacity for imagination and satire. They each were acute observers of the Washington scene and shared a healthy skepticism of politics. Combining Warner's discipline with Twain's inventiveness could take Bliss's company in a lucrative new direction. The project was shrouded in secrecy lest a competitor get wind of the idea and beat them to the market. Clemens harbored his own trademark insecurities: Could he succeed in this new medium? "When a man starts out in a new role," he worried, "the public always says he is a fool and won't succeed."[1]

In January 1873 Clemens began writing with a vengeance, completing the first eleven chapters (399 pages of manuscript) in a few weeks. Drawing upon his experiences with his mother's Missouri cousin, James Lampton—an inveterate schemer, dreamer, and promoter—Clemens spun an autobiographical yarn about his roots in rural America. He wrote his sister asking her to collect secretly all the gossip she could generate about Lampton. Twain depicted life in a small town, Obedstown, in eastern Tennessee.

**Charles Dudley Warner, an editor of the *Hartford Courant*,
co-authored *The Gilded Age* with Mark Twain. It was their first novel.
Courtesy: The Mark Twain House & Museum, Hartford CT.**

At Warner's suggestion, Lampton became Colonel Eschol Sellers, though the name was changed to Beriah and then Mulberry in later editions after a real Eschol Sellers emerged from Bowlesville, Illinois, threatening a lawsuit. Clemens's father became Si Hawkins, family patriarch. Like John Marshall Clemens, Hawkins was the owner of undeveloped Tennessee land that he hoped would reap the family a fortune. Clemens's brother Orion was the inspiration for the character Washington Hawkins, the naïve, always hopeful and optimistic believer—a frontier Candide.[2]

Then on the morning of January 31, Clemens picked up *The New York Tribune.** The headline on page one propelled him in a new direction. The pharisaic Senator Pomeroy, whom Clemens as a Senate staffer had detested, paid a $7,000 bribe to a Kansas state legislator to support his bid for reelection to a third term.*** The state senator promptly delivered the cash to a legislative clerk, denouncing Pomeroy publicly for bribery.[3] This was the Washington Clemens remembered, and he was reminded of each day as scandals erupting from the capital lit up the press: the backroom deals, the powerful lobbies, bribery and vote-buying, self-dealing legislation, and the hypocrisy of public pontification and private perfidy. It was called "The Great Barbeque." Clemens created the character Senator Abner Dillworthy after Pomeroy.

Washington reflected the nation as a whole, and the nation Clemens knew was deep in the grimy, clamorous, turbulent industrial age in which powerful bankers, manufacturers, and railroad tycoons co-opted the corridors of power, and impoverished rural inhabitants dreamed of making it rich as they watched their dreams evaporate into despair. Clemens's notebook was filled with material from his times in Missouri, Nevada, and Washington. Now he would tap that "gold mine."[4]

---

* The *Tribune* also contained a negative review of *Roughing It*, which irritated Clemens no end. (A second review in the paper a few weeks later was favorable.)

** Until the Seventeenth Amendment to the Constitution was ratified on April 8, 1913, senators were elected by their state legislatures, not by popular vote.

After the sacrifice of the Civil War, the epoch of greed had arrived. Wall Street financiers and corporate monopolists amassed enormous wealth as the working classes struggled under oppressive conditions. The cultural premise of American democracy was challenged as the gap between rich and poor widened to an unprecedented degree, and the rich infiltrated the political process. The press awakened from a deep sleep. Each morning the papers revealed new scandals confirming the nefarious alliances between the robber barons, elected politicians, and appointed officials at all levels of government: Credit Mobilier, the Whiskey Ring, Black Friday, the Salary Grab, the Belknap Affair, the Sanborn Contracts, the Emma Mine Swindle, the Pacific Mail Contract, and the Indian Ring. As president, the great war hero Ulysses S. Grant sat despondently in the White House while his friends, appointees, and supporters conspired with the tycoons to raid the Treasury. It was an age of riches emblazoned on a frayed social fabric like gilt paint on rotten wood—a Gilded Age, in the brilliant name Clemens and Warner hit on for the title of their book. The authors got the name from Shakespeare's *King John*: "To gild refined gold, to paint the lily…is wasteful and ridiculous excess."

Daily disclosures of scandals provided shape and content to the coauthors' roman à clef (scandalous fiction involving real persons). In a series of articles, *The New York Sun* exposed how Congressman Oakes Ames of Massachusetts, a large shareholder in the Union Pacific and brother of its president, established the corporation Credit Mobilier as the contractor to complete the construction of the last six hundred miles of the transcontinental railroad. Credit Mobilier distributed discounted and free stock to members of Congress, who in turn passed excessive appropriations to fund the construction. Lavish dividends were paid, mostly from federal appropriations. Allegations of corruption implicated vice president Colfax, House leader James A. Garfield (later president), and James G. Blaine (speaker of the house and three-time candidate for president).

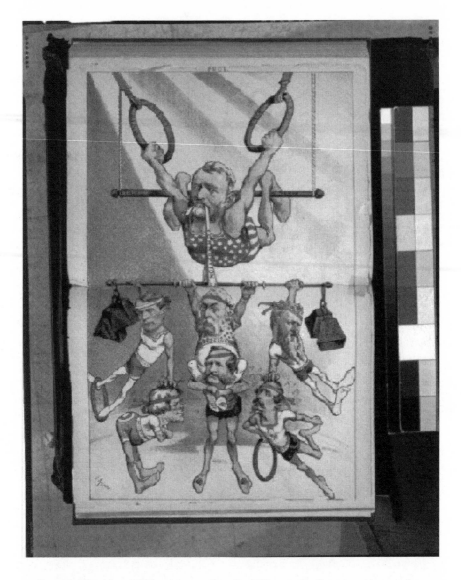

Joseph Keppler 1880 cartoon showing Ulysses S. Grant as an acrobat, on trapeze "third term," holding on to the "whiskey ring," "navy ring," with strap "corruption" holding up acrobats Belknap, Babcock and others. Courtesy Library of Congress

In the Whiskey Ring, more than a hundred federal officials were convicted of taking bribes to dole out stamps to whiskey distillers, avoiding high federal taxes to pay off Civil War debts.[5] Grant's secretary of war, William W. Belknap, channeled bribes for trade licenses on Indian reservations into Republican Party coffers.[6] On Black Friday in 1869, Jim Fisk and Jay Gould's failed attempt to corner the gold market sent the price plummeting, and thousands of investors sustained huge losses—except Fisk and Gould who refused to honor their obligations.[7] Finally, the Salary Grab Act of March 3, 1873, doubled the president's salary and surreptitiously increased congressional pay by 50 percent for the previous two years—a bonus for the good work they felt they had accomplished. After the public outcry, the retroactive raise was rescinded.*

Clemens's notebooks are filled with references to these and other developing scandals, which pervaded every level of government. New York's notorious Tammany Hall was the archetype of local politics.[8] The speculative shenanigans of rural small town life, big city political machines, and Capitol Hill drew sustenance from the same well of greed. The novel became a political and social satire. Scholars have shown how closely the story line tracked daily press reports in the *Tribune,* the *Congressional Globe,* and Senate investigative reports.[9] According to French in *Mark Twain and the Gilded Age,* the satire's characters are thinly disguised stand-ins for contemporary legislators and political figures caught up in the unfolding scandals described in the book's Washington narrative.[10] Applying his well-honed journalistic instincts, Clemens masters the facts as corruption is exposed. He is as concerned with the authenticity of the narrative as he is with its dramatic development. He once told Rudyard Kipling that he didn't "care for fiction and story books"; it was the facts that he read about. "Get your facts first," he said to Kipling, "then you

---

* In 1990 Congress was more sophisticated, enacting automatic annual cost-of-living pay increases that can be rescinded only by a vote of Congress. Instead of voting itself a pay raise, Congress gets to curry public favor by rescinding an automatic pay raise, which it has done seven times since the law was passed, allowing silent pay raises to go into effect thirteen times. More importantly, congressional salary increases do not become entangled in the routine legislative constipation or political posturing that characterize its other constitutional duties, such as appropriating funds for the executive branch.

can distort 'em as much as you please."[11] His mastery of the legislative process and firsthand experience with how it is manipulated for selfish ends enables Clemens to illustrate in dramatic form the way power corrupts, despite the checks and balances of democracy. In *The Gilded Age*, he comes as close to a documentary as fiction can get.[12]

A barely disguised Pomeroy became Senator Dilworthy, living in an elegant mansion adjacent to Lafayette Park. According to French, "The entire episode of the Dilworthy exposure and investigation was drawn, down to the minutest detail, from published reports of the Pomeroy case."[13] Twain paints an accurate portrait, which "far from being overdrawn, is a surprisingly exact copy."[14] That the illustration of Dilworthy in the book so closely resembles the pious, bearded Pomeroy is proof of the authors' faith in their First Amendment's protections.

Twain transparently depicts the handsome former Nevada governor Nye as Senator Balloon, who knows the scripture better than any man, but milks the Indians for all they are worth.[15] In a Senate ethics investigation requested by Dilworthy (Pomeroy), Balloon (Nye) defends Dilworthy's reelection bribery by attacking his accuser for threatening the "ancient dignity" of the Senate.[16]

Senator Balaam is based on Senator James Harlan of Iowa, the former secretary of the interior who had fired Walt Whitman for writing "a dirty book." Harlan, like Pomeroy, was among the group tagged "Christian Statesmen." Their "comedy of temperance and religion" was not taken seriously by their colleagues, who recoiled from their "odor of sanctity." Harlan was notorious for his role in swindling the Indians by diverting large sums appropriated for their food and clothing. In 1868 he was charged with profiting from the illegal sale of Cherokee lands.[17] Of the major characters dominating the news of the day, only President Grant, who makes a cameo appearance, is spared the satire.

SENATOR DILWORTHY ADDRESSING SUNDAY SCHOOL
Illustration of Senator Dilworthy in first edition of *The Gilded Age* by
Augustus Hoppin (1828-1896) closely resembling Senator Samuel Clarke
Pomeroy, whose vote-buying scandal broke as the authors wrote the novel.
Courtesy: Augustus Hoppin, Illustrator for The American Publishing
Company.

Warner's assignment was to write a parallel story recounting the fortunes of two young Philadelphians who travel to Missouri and get caught up with Hawkins and Sellers. Together, Twain and Warner developed the character Laura Hawkins, the beautiful, charming, and sophisticated Washington lobbyist who becomes the protagonist. Clemens was fascinated by the plethora of female lobbyists in the capital, and Laura is drawn from the high end of the scale.

Although the two authors wrote separate chapters and story lines, they collaborated closely, exchanged ideas, and reworked each other's material. As Clemens put it, "Warner had worked up the fiction [and] I hurled in the facts."[18] The two authors read the manuscripts out loud to their wives in the evenings, accepting critical comments, toning down the mockery of religion, and correcting misstatements of etiquette in describing Washington society. Twain's chapters are livelier and better written, but Warner brought organization to the project, sequencing the chapters. The final product is an amalgamation that makes the book hard to categorize: Is it a roman à clef, a melodramatic burlesque of modern romance novels, an autobiographical tale of the rural Midwest, an exposé of corruption in government and business, a satire of the judicial and legislative systems, or a reformist's take on American democracy? The reviewers were confused.

In the sixty-three chapters and 161,000 words of *The Gilded Age*, the authors tell a complex set of interrelated tales. Twain's story begins autobiographically around 1840 as Colonel Sellers (James Lampton) persuades Si Hawkins (John Marshall Clemens) to move to Hawkeye, Missouri, to pursue "the biggest scheme on earth."[19] On the way to Missouri, Hawkins adopts two children, Clay and Laura, and the family becomes entangled in a steamboat race between hyper-competitive captains, resulting in a fatal collision and explosion—twenty-two dead, ninety-six missing. An inquest results in the "inevitable American verdict—'NOBODY TO BLAME.'"[20] After arriving in Missouri, Judge Hawkins and Colonel Sellers have "made and lost two or three moderate fortunes" and are "pinched by poverty."[21] Hawkins resists Sellers's pleas to sell the seventy-five thousand acres of undeveloped Tennessee land.

Drawing on his experiences as a young bachelor, Warner writes about two eligible young Philadelphians, Harry Brierly and Philip Sterling, who travel to Missouri to work on a railroad survey. They hope to get rich by buying up the land adjacent to the planned railroad. The young men meet Colonel Sellers, who is promoting a river/railroad development scheme—the Salt Lick Navigation Project. Sellers also lobbies Dilworthy on the project when the senator visits Hawkeye. The senator is a "good man," the Colonel explains, "He's only been in Congress a few years, and he must be worth a million."[22] Sellers and Hawkins naively bank on Senator Dilworthy's sponsorship of an appropriation, unaware that Wall Street financiers backing the project have set up the dummy Columbus River Slackwater Navigation Company to soak up $200,000 in federal appropriations with hidden commissions, capital assessments, and congressional bribes. None of the appropriated funds are left to pay for the project costs incurred by Sellers, who proudly likens himself to the speculator who remarked, "I wasn't worth a cent two years ago, and now I owe two millions of dollars."[23] Sellers and Hawkins go deeply into debt, replicating John Marshall Clemens's financial failure when Congress failed to fund his Salt River navigation project, forcing the family's move to Hannibal.

In an unrelated subplot, a hardworking, industrious young man named Philip Sterling falls in love with a headstrong, rebellious Quaker lady, Ruth Bolton, who wants to go to medical school. Philip plans to earn his fortune the hard way, but seems dull compared to the operative Harry Brierly, whose charm easily ingratiates him with social and political society. Harry knows everybody from the governor to hotel waiters and, as an enthusiastic capitalist, he has mastered the "Wall Street slang at his tongue's end" as he engages in "the land and railway schemes with which the air is thick."[24]

Meanwhile, the beautiful Laura Hawkins marries a sleazy former Confederate officer and bigamist, Colonel Selby, who crudely abandons her. Si Hawkins dies in poverty, bequeathing only the hope that someday the Tennessee land will reap riches for the family. The hardworking pragmatist Clay becomes the family provider.

Facing a financial catastrophe, Colonel Sellers moves his scheming to the nation's capital. He persuades Laura to accompany him to lobby for a congressional appropriation to purchase the Tennessee land at an inflated price, ostensibly in order to build an industrial school for freed slaves. The Colonel explains Washington to Laura: "It doesn't need a crowbar to break your way into society there as it does in Philadelphia. It's democratic, Washington is. Money or beauty will open any door. If I were a handsome woman, I shouldn't want any better place than the capital to pick up a prince or a fortune."[25] Washington Hawkins moves to the capital to serve as Senator Dilworthy's private secretary and secretary to the committee, and Harry Brierly and Laura become lobbyists working to pass the appropriations. They all become entwined in the web of greed, corruption, and Washington social pretenses as they advance their earmark appropriation—the Knobs Industrial University Bill—that will fund the purchase of the Tennessee land. With her beauty and charm, Laura masters the Kabuki card-calling rituals that are the keys to entry into the three distinct Washington aristocracies: the Antiques, the high-bred old families who trace their ancestry to the nation's founders; the Parvenues, who have held official positions if only for a fleeting moment, often accompanied by great wealth and "a pleasant little spice of illegality;" and the Middle Ground, families of educated public men of character from nearly every state who work conscientiously in the executive and legislative branches on behalf of the American public.[26] Soon Laura is the center attraction at Washington social events and the confidant of committee chairs.

And then Colonel Selby reappears. When Laura fails to reignite their romance, she follows him to New York and shoots him dead in a hotel lobby. Over the next year she becomes a cause célèbre in the national media as she awaits her murder trial. The authors move from legislative corruption to a satire on the judicial system.

Clemens was influenced by a story he had heard out west. A spurned lover named Laura Fair confronted her ex-boyfriend on the Oakland to San Francisco ferry and shot him dead in front of his wife. Fair was acquitted by a jury on her defense lawyer's novel theory of "emotional insanity." The story was "emblazoned in American headlines from coast to coast."[27]Clemens was appalled by the verdict, which reinforced his growing skepticism of the jury system. Fair had been involved in an earlier, nonfatal shooting in Virginia City, and Clemens knew that she had been convicted in a first trial in the Oakland ferry murder, which was overturned on appeal on a technicality.[28] In *The Gilded Age*, however, he dealt only with the second trial, and Warner's legal training proved helpful in describing trial tactics.

In a Fourth of July speech at a gathering of Americans in London in 1872, Clemens explained his skepticism: "We have a criminal jury system which is superior to any in the world; and its efficiency is only marred by the difficulty of finding twelve men who don't know anything and can't read. And...we have an insanity plea that would have saved Cain."[29] Clemens was reflecting widespread criticism of jury selection from the pools of vagabonds who hung around the courthouses hoping to collect $1.50 a day. He also recalled his experience with frontier justice, having written bluntly in *Roughing It*: "The jury system puts a ban on intelligence and honesty, and a premium upon ignorance, stupidity and perjury. It is a shame we must continue to use a worthless system because it *was* good a thousand years ago."[30] In a discarded draft dedication for *Roughing It*, Twain had written: "To the late Cain...out of mere human commiseration for him that it was his misfortune to live in a dark age that knew not the beneficent Insanity Plea."[31] Reflecting his Whig-rooted elitist bias, Twain suggested "tamper[ing] with the jury law" to put a "premium on intelligence and character" and closing the "jury-box against idiots, blacklegs, and people who do not read newspapers."[32]

At her trial in *The Gilded Age*, Laura Hawkins is represented by an unscrupulous attorney named Braham. He is a parody of John Graham, the lawyer for Tammany Hall, who defended Boss

William Tweed before friendly Irish-American judges and weak-kneed juries who succumbed to his emotional, teary-eyed tirades. According to the prestigious *North American Review*, "Most of the Judges [installed by the Tammany Ring] in charge of criminal business in New York are coarse, profane, uneducated men."[33] Judge O'Shaunnessy, who presides over Laura's trial, is modeled after Judge John McCunn, a Ring protégé who emigrated from Ireland at the age of sixteen and learned the law as a messenger in a law office. McCunn was "notoriously corrupt, treacherous, and vain." He had accumulated a fortune of a million and a half dollars through fraud and speculation.[34]

Corruption at all levels of government permeates *The Gilded Age*, as power not character is the overriding virtue that commands public veneration. Mayor William M. Weed (Boss Tweed) and his crooked contractors "had stolen $20 million from the city and was a man so envied, so honored, so adored, indeed, that when the sheriff went to his office to arrest him as a felon, that sheriff blushed and apologized" for the "offense of an arrest" of "so exalted a personage as Mr. Weed." The public expresses its outrage by repeatedly electing Weed and his crony contractors to the state legislature.[35]

As Laura's trial consumes the media, the Tennessee land appropriations bill is stalled in Congress. Then the reelection bribery of its sponsor, Dilworthy, is revealed. Exposed to the sunlight, the senator's supporters desert him like a herd of gazelles being stalked by a cheetah. In a climactic scene, Congress unanimously rejects the land bill as Laura is acquitted by the jury on grounds of "emotional insanity."

The tale's end was much discussed. Clemens and Warner agreed that a jury would acquit Laura of the murder charge. But what then? Warner wrote the final chapter with a happy ending: Laura would marry and disappear into the sunset. Clemens had a different idea: Laura would take her story on the lecture circuit, where she would be hissed and booed and driven from the stage by an angry mob hurling stones and curses. Retreating to her hotel room, she would suffer a heart attack and die. The wives debated the alternative endings and voted for Clemens's.

It was a strange resolution. Was Clemens venting his insecurities on the lecture circuit?

Clemens had proposed that the cartoonist Thomas Nast do the illustrations for the book, but Bliss chose to collect illustrations from less costly sources. When the manuscript was finished, the authors requested J. Hammond Trumbull, Hartford's most erudite man, to provide "mottoes" for each of the chapter headings in forty-two different languages, including Arawak, Basque, Chinese, Sanskrit, Sindhi, Sioux, and Yoruba. The quotes, relating to the chapter content, are intended "to take in the whole world."[36]

The New York Tribune disclosed the title of the book on April 23, 1873, as "a name which gives the best promise of the wealth of satire and observation which is easy to expect from two such authors."[37] In promoting the book, Bliss shrewdly stressed Twain's early chapters, recounting Colonel Sellers's escapades and the steamboat race and explosion. Although the prospectus referred to "satire directed against prominent persons and things," there was no mention of the chapters on Washington politics or the chapters written by Warner. Bliss touted Twain as "the people's author" and thought the story about small-town America would resonate best among his mostly rural subscription readers. The political satire drawn from Clemens's Washington experience reflected the small-town culture of pretension, speculation, scheming, corruption, and hypocrisy on a grander scale.

Reviews of the book were mixed. Compare the *Boston Evening Transcript,* which said the book "shines...with a genuine and intrinsic radiance" and contains "some of the most vivid and natural characterizations of any book recently published in the United States" with the *Hartford Times*: "A very odd piece of architecture...a trifle jerky and jolty."[38] Many newspapers, especially outside the major cities, were favorable, relying heavily on Bliss's promotional materials. The large-city press and literary journals were mostly critical, sometimes vituperative: the *Chicago Tribune* ("a fraud to the reading public," a "trashy book, so utterly bald, so puerile, so vicious"), the *Boston Advertiser* ("a distortion"), and the *New York Daily Graphic* ("an incoherent series of sketches").[39]

The Republican-oriented newspapers were undoubtedly defensive about the thinly disguised satire of the corrupt Grant era. Even Twain's close friend, mentor, and literary booster, William Dean Howells, a staunch Republican, could not bring himself to write a review for the *Atlantic Monthly*. The critics complained that the Twain and Warner stories did not flow together into a cohesive narrative. Mostly they were unable to fathom such an extraordinary departure from conventional literature—a baldly transparent political satire that mocked the idealized vision of the grand American experiment. *The New York Herald* admitted that "something unusual has been produced, something unusually clever, too—only it is not, strictly speaking, a tale."[40] *The New York World* called it "a severe, truthful and painful satire," and the *Cincinnati Daily Times* "a cruel, unflinching dissection of our moral and social condition."[41] Thoughtful commentators did not judge the book as a conventional novel but, as the *Herald* said, as "a story with a purpose as much as 'The Pilgrim's Progress.' It is written to expose speculators, lobbyists, and corrupt legislators.... There is great power in the book, and of an uncommon kind."[42] The optimistic *Boston Transcript* believed that the book would "help on the reforming tendency in the politics of the day."[43]

Among literary scholars, Bernard DeVoto wrote that "something memorable has happened in American literature." The opening chapters, he thought, were "on a higher level of realism than American literature had ever obtained."[44] Maxwell Geismar found the book impossible to "evaluate by ordinary critical standards" because it is "hardly a novel at all in technical terms...it is a unique chronicle in the national letters; and without it our literature would be immensely impoverished."[45] Arthur Hobson Quinn called it "the prose epic of the age" but "more interesting as a social study than as a novel."[46] Philip Foner thought it was "one of the few important novels produced in America in the last quarter of the nineteenth century."[47]

Although *The Gilded Age* was published too late for the holiday shopping season and after the September 1873 Panic sent the economy into a tailspin, book sales remained strong until the end of the century. The book may have helped readers understand why their government seemed unable to redress the crippled economy. Over the long term, the book did not sell as well as Twain's first two subscription books.

Viewing the book from a contemporary perspective, Pulitzer Prize-winning political historian Garry Wills wrote a *New York Times* essay in 1976 entitled "Mark Twain has been gone one hundred years but his political wisdom endures." Wills wrote that as a history lesson, it is "Our Best Political Novel," which "grows with every reading."[48]

Seven years later Henry Adams, descendant of two presidents, anonymously published *Democracy*, which like *The Gilded Age* was a thinly disguised account of political corruption in the lobby-infested capital. The main character, Senator Silas Ratliffe, is a stand-in for James Blaine. Adams, who like Clemens would suffer family tragedy (the suicide of his wife Clover) and bankruptcy, wrote despairingly of the nation's political system but with less wit and hope for reform than Clemens.[49]

The Gilded Age had a second life as a play. Clemens loved the theater and was an ardent theatergoer, critic, playwright, and booster; he was friends with actors, writers, and producers. He loved being center stage as a lecturer, a singer, and an actor in family entertainment.[50] His ear for dialogue and farce was honed by Uncle Dan'l, by the traveling Mississippi River troupes whose performances ran from mutilated Shakespeare to blatantly racist minstrel shows, and by the frontier touring companies' staple of romance and burlesque. Clemens viewed politicians as mediocre actors—like Jacques in Shakespeare's *As You Like It*: "they have their exits and their entrances," and in their time, "play many parts."

In May 1875 Clemens learned that an old colleague, the drama critic of the *Golden Era*, Gilbert B. Densmore, had pirated the Twain stories from *The Gilded Age* for a stage play in San Francisco. Instead of bringing suit, Clemens bought the play and expanded it as his own dramatic adaptation of the novel. While Livy was pregnant with their second daughter, Clara, who was born on June 8, 1875, joining her two-year-old sister Susy,

Clemens worked on the play. *Colonel Sellers* opened at the Opera House in Rochester, New York, on August 31.

From the San Francisco play, Clemens recruited John T. Raymond, a Falstaff-type character actor who brought Colonel Sellers to life on stage. The play previewed in Buffalo before opening at the Park Theatre on Broadway, where it ran for 119 nights and was warmly received by the audience, including on one occasion President Grant who laughed uproariously without the slightest discomfiture. Backstage after the performance, the president warmly congratulated Raymond.[51]

The play went on tour, traveling to both large and small venues, and earned the author substantial revenues—an incentive for Clemens to continue his playwriting. Unfortunately he was never able to replicate the commercial success of *Colonel Sellers*.

The reviews of the *Colonel Sellers* were mixed. Raymond's acting was universally praised, but Twain's deficiencies as a novice playwright were duly noted. He had little sense of structure or plot development. Clemens admitted to the city editor of the *New York World* that it wasn't "a good play. It's a bad play, a damned bad play. I couldn't write a good play. But it has a good character, and that character is the best I can do."[52] A similar criticism has been made of his novels, beginning with *The Gilded Age*—that they lacked structure and progressive plot development. Twain states forthrightly at the opening of *Huckleberry Finn*: "Anyone attempting to find a plot will be shot." Novels are a more forgiving medium than plays.

Many theatrical and cinematic productions of Twain's novels and characters have been performed through the years. Twain himself wrote or collaborated on several more plays. It was only with the initial production of *Colonel Sellers*—the symbol of American excess and greed in *The Gilded Age*—that Twain was able to achieve a modicum of success in the theater he so loved.[53]

The Gilded Age was the first novel ever published by a subscription house as well as Twain's first novel. Upon finishing it, he began work on the next one, which he would write by himself: *The Adventures of Tom Sawyer*.

The Gilded Age introduced a new genre—political satire that exposed the stress points and fractures in American-style democracy and capitalism. The genre would find expression in literature and theater over the ensuing decades and then later in film and television. The Gilded Age has become the generic name for the historic era that spanned the mature Twain's lifetime. Krugman defines the "Long Gilded Age" as "the entire period from the end of Reconstruction in the 1870's to the coming of the New Deal in the 1930's..., a period defined above all by persistently high levels of economic inequality."[54] It is more than a label of an historical period. It is a reminder of how fragile a democratic free society is and how easily government can be co-opted by the rich and powerful. The label comes up again whenever the nation seems to be veering off course as it lurches toward that "more perfect union."

Mark Twain and John Raymond, who played Colonel Sellers in the successful Broadway production. Courtesy: Kevin MacDonnell and the Mark Twain House, Hartford, CT and Bridgeman Art Library

Sam Clemens in Brighton, England on September 12, 1872. After the death of his son, Clemens left for England to gather material for a new book and meet with the British publishers of The Gilded Age. Courtesy: Mark Twain Project, The Bancroft Library University of California, Berkeley

CHAPTER EIGHT

The Gilded Age: A Tale Of Congress Today?

> *"In a free country like ours, where any man can run for*
> *Congress and anybody can vote for him, you can't expect*
> *immortal purity all the time...Even in these days when people*
> *growl so much and the newspapers are so out of patience, there*
> *is still a very respectable minority of honest men in Congress."*
>
> — COLONEL SELLERS, THE GILDED AGE

*T*he Gilded Age was subtitled *A Tale of To-day,* and so it is.
Clemens's cogent observations about the influence of money
in Congress retain an uncanny relevance to contemporary
politics. In the ensuing century, after the enactment of thousands
of pages of statutes and regulations, progress undoubtedly has
been made—with stops and starts and backsliding along the way.
Yet much work remains to create an ethical, just, and egalitarian
republic. In *The Gilded Age,* Twain illustrates in excruciating detail
the means by which speculators, financiers, and corporations

139

achieve their legislative goals. Their methods may differ today, but they are no less successful in influencing the legislative process for their benefit. The challenges facing American democracy are not new, and as Twain admonished, continued progress will depend on informed and engaged citizens who speak out and demand accountable government.

The Lobby

The Gilded Age portrays how lobbyists work closely with members of Congress and their staffs in shaping the legislative product to advance their clients' interests. At the heart of the tale are the cozy relationships among Senator Dilworthy; the senator's secretary, Washington Hawkins; the lobbyist Laura Hawkins; Laura's love-struck admirer and co-lobbyist, Harry Brierly; and the developer-schemer Colonel Sellers. The synergistic relationship between legislator and lobbyist enriches both senator and speculator.

The beautiful, beguiling Laura is a sophisticated practitioner of the lobbying trade as she persuades senators and representatives to support Dilworthy's legislation to appropriate funds to buy the Tennessee land. Invoking personal charm and coquetry, she offers financial incentives and threatens blackmail. She charms House Appropriations Committee chairman Buckstone, who becomes infatuated with her, and she skillfully entraps the bill's most ardent opponent, Congressman Trollop. Laura writes a stirring floor speech on pension legislation for Trollop and then extorts his vote by threatening to reveal its author. She reminds Trollop that he had received stock for his vote for the National Internal Improvements Relief Measure, Twain's thinly disguised reference to Credit Mobilier. In those days large commercial projects funded by Congress were known as internal improvements.[1] Laura then offers Trollop's brother-in-law either a paid position or a board of trustee's membership with the proposed Knobs Industrial University. The congressman prefers the nonpaying board membership—which has oversight over millions in federal appropriations.[2]

Laura represents a new phenomenon in the postbellum period—the female lobbyist. Women had lobbied for such noble causes as suffrage and equal rights, but there also were the "lobbyesses" who worked the halls of Congress for land grants, subsidies, patents, government contracts, pensions, and patronage.[3] Iowa congressman Grenville Dodge described them as "unscrupulous thieves" and "pretty women with flashing diamonds" whose skill was "to handle and influence men." The writer Emily Briggs described the lobbyess working for Gould and fellow railroad tycoon Collis Huntington as "a luscious, mellow banana; a juicy, melting peach; a golden pippin ripened to the very core." Her "silk, satin, velvet, feathers, and laces prove what a railroad can do when its funds are applied in the right direction."[4] George Townsend described yet another type of lobbyess—one who traded sex for votes.[5] They were seen everywhere, "making the streets and hotels disreputably gay." A "female rascal could work a bribe with all her might." Some were "highly paid prostitutes." The Hartford-based Colt Arms Company allegedly "maintained a whore house on C Street."[6] With Livy's guiding editorial pen, Twain was not about to dredge up his characters from the gutter. Laura's tactics were more sophisticated.

Women comprised but a small fraction of the lobby corps invading Capitol Hill, which was a fierce battleground for competing railroad tycoons and their corporate empires. Independent lobbyists—known as strikers—became a Third House of Congress. They were hired to seek government favors for their clients and deny favors to their competitors. Contrary to the fantasy of some contemporary politicians that industrialization was spawned solely by brilliant entrepreneurs free of government restraint, Congress was deeply involved in choosing winners and losers. Railroad lobbyists competed for congressional land grants and bond subsidies. A former congressman from upstate New York, Richard Franchot, gave up his seat on the House railroad committee to earn five times the salary as Central Pacific's lobbyist. By 1876 he was lobbying for or against thirty-five bills in the Senate and House. The Texas Pacific Railroad hired over two hundred lobbyists, many of them former members of the Senate and House, to protect the company's interests against legislation advanced by their competitors, shipper advocates, and government reformers.[7] In her fascinating book *King of the Lobby*, Kathryn Allamong Jacob recounts the long career of Sam Ward, the preeminent Gilded Age lobbyist, a consummate connoisseur whose lavish dinner parties set the standard. Among his clients was the Pacific Mail Steamship Company, which was accused of paying $120,000 in bribes to secure a subsidy to carry the mail to China.[8] A former Civil War general, chief engineer for the Union Pacific, and single-term Iowa congressman, Grenville Dodge was a lobbyist for the Union Pacific and the Texas Pacific Railroads. He originated grassroots lobbying, persuading newspapers to editorialize and prominent citizens to write in support of legislation. Because few people were living in the expansive West served by the transcontinental railroads, Dodge's method of ginning up support is facetiously called Astroturf lobbying.

When like a wake of vultures, the press corps descended on the Grant administration's scandal epidemic, the influx of lobbyists was a favorite target. Unscrupulous lobbyists engaged in bribery, blackmail, extortion, and seduction. To appease the reformers, there were mild efforts to rein in the abuses. Republican Massachusetts senator George Boutwell introduced a bill to organize a bar of the Senate and House, establishing ethical standards for lobbyists based on the British practice of accrediting lawyers who advocated before parliament. The bill gained no traction. Republican congressman Ellis Roberts introduced a bill that would have required lobbyists to register with and report their expenditures to the clerks of the House and Senate and the committees that they lobbied. The bill passed the House on March 3, 1875, the last day of the session, but died in the Senate. A year later a more modest proposal by Republican George Frisbie Hoar was adopted by resolution for the House only. Before it expired at the year's end, clients were required to file the names of agents representing them with the House.[9]

Although a law requiring the registration of lobbyists would not be enacted until 1946, these initial proposals implicitly recognized that the lobby played a significant role as the power and complexity of the federal government grew. Lobbying abuses would have to be curtailed if democracy was to function properly, but lobbying was here to stay.

A Tale of Today

And stayed it has, and that's not all bad. Washington lobbyists can and should play a constructive role as brokers between private and public interests. The right to petition the government, embedded in the First Amendment, entitles citizens to hire experts in the byzantine legislative and administrative processes. In a regulated market economy, government officials require information from the private sector to understand how to meet their statutory responsibilities efficiently and avoid unintended consequences and market distortions. Lobbyists and Washington lawyers (of which there are more per capita than any other city in the world) can be honest brokers in facilitating good government decision-making.[10]

Since Mark Twain's Gilded Age, federal regulation of the private sector has become increasingly comprehensive. In 1914 Congress passed an eight-page Federal Trade Act, and in 1935 Social Security was chartered in a twenty-eight-page law. By 2010, however, financial reform legislation (the Dodd-Frank Bill) ran 2,319 pages, surpassing the 1990-page comprehensive health care reform bill (the Patient Protection and Affordable Care Act) that preceded it. The granddaddy of them all, of course, is the 3,387-page Internal Revenue Code and the twenty volumes of regulations interpreting it. Members of Congress cannot become sufficiently expert in the complexities of financial services, health care, the tax code, or energy resources.* They must get help from experts who can explain the consequences—whether intended or not—for a particular economic sector or business. Lobbyists can provide critical information to lawmakers, and many of them specialize in specific provisions of the tax code that incentivize businesses to—among other things—invest in research and create jobs.

---

* Lobbyists with competing interests contribute to the complexity of legislation as they seek advantage for their clients, advocating the opening or closing of loopholes, exceptions, thresholds, and deferred effective dates.

Due to the vagueness of the lobbying registration requirement, it is impossible to tell exactly how many lobbyists there actually are. In 2011 there were 12,633 active registered lobbyists, spending $3.3 billion on lobbying—that's more than six million per member of Congress.[11] And this is a gross understatement. As many as 90,000 "strategic advisors," "historians," and legislative advocates claim they do not meet the registration threshold. Because of the bad rap lobbyists have received in recent years, there were 2,214 fewer registered lobbyists in 2011 than in 2010. Some people who had registered out of caution recalculated their time spent influencing government decision-making to be less than 20 percent of the time spent for a client, and they decided they no longer needed to register.[12]*

*Like Laura Hawkins, many lobbyists today function like adjunct congressional staff. Laura wrote one floor speech for Congressman Trollop, but when health care legislation was pending in 2009, twenty-two Republicans and twenty Democrats in the House used the same language in remarks ghostwritten by a Washington lobbyist for a global biotechnology company. The company's political action committee had made campaign contributions to many of these congressmen. When asked about the "coincidence," the lobbyist responded: "This happens all the time. There is nothing nefarious about it."[13] **The New York Times** disagreed, calling it a "depressing example of how members of Congress can be spoon-fed views and even the exact words of high-powered law firms." The editorial concluded that "it is disturbing that the industry was able to so easily shape the official record*

---

* A lobbyist is required to register only if he or she meets three criteria: (1) two or more contacts with a member, congressional staff, or administration official on behalf of a client, except for scheduling or status inquiries; (2) at least 20 percent of time spent for a single client is spent on lobbying; and (3) the client pays at least $3000 to the lobbyist in a quarter. Such former members as Tom Daschle and Newt Gingrich have not registered, claiming that they provide strategic advice and do not lobby.

to its liking. It is even more disturbing that so many members of Congress were willing to parrot the industry talking points."[14] Lobbyists frequently provide lawmakers with draft language to insert in bills. If they fail to get the language in the statute or the committee report, they persuade a couple of friendly legislators to engage in a colloquy on the Senate or House floor interpreting the law in a favorable fashion; it then becomes part of the legislative history that some judges will rely upon in construing the statute.

As in the Gilded Age, the "revolving door" between government and the private sector spins at a dizzying pace as members of Congress, congressional staff, and federal agency employees leave government to become lobbyists. Public officials capitalize on their time in office to gain expertise and contacts that can be converted into private-sector profits. Knowing how the game is played, they help each other out until it is time to switch chairs. According to Shelia Krumholz, executive director of the Center for Responsive Politics, "Companies pay a premium for lobbyists who've spun through the revolving door because it can be a small price relative to the payoff if they can shape legislation."[15] David Arkush, director of Public Citizen's Congress Watch adds: "Wall Street hires former members of Congress and their staffs... because they have personal relationships with current members... and it's hard to say no to your friends."[16]

Between 1999 and 2008, the financial industry spent $2.7 billion in reported federal lobbying expenses and $1 billion in political action committee contributions to advocate successfully for a series of legislative and administrative deregulatory actions limiting oversight and enabling risky innovation.[17] The consequences are well known: the financial markets nearly collapsed in 2008 as the proliferation of risky home mortgages to feed the demand for mortgage-backed securities led to the burst of the housing bubble. Billions of dollars of treasury and federal reserve *funds were used to rescue financial institutions too big to fail and government sponsored enterprises implicitly guaranteeing the loans. As a result, big banks gobbled up their weaker competitors and became even bigger. The infusion of liquidity did little to ease the housing foreclosure epidemic or supply credit to small and mid-size businesses, the economy's job-creating engine.*

Since the start of 2009 when Congress debated legislation to enhance federal oversight of financial institutions and prevent a future near-collapse, "more than fourteen hundred former members of Congress, Capitol Hill staffers or federal executive branch employees registered as lobbyists on behalf of the financial services sector."[18] That's right—more than one thousand four hundred! Among them, according to Dan Eggen of the Washington Post, were seventy-three former members of Congress, 148 former staffers of the House and Senate banking committees, and more than forty former Treasury Department employees.[19]

On July 22, 2010, Dan Eggen and Kimberly Kindy reported that three out of four lobbyists representing the oil and gas industry had previously worked in the federal government. Among the six hundred registered lobbyists were eighteen former members of Congress, dozens of former presidential appointees, and two former directors of the Minerals Management Service (the agency renamed after the media criticized its lax regulation preceding the massive 2010 BP oil spill in the Gulf of Mexico).[20]

The revolving door also operates counterclockwise. With the election of a new Congress every two years, there is a surge of lobbyists leaving their K Street offices for jobs on Capitol Hill. After the 2010 midterm election, at least 150 former lobbyists were hired in top policy positions for members of

Congress.[21] *While there are ethics regulations restricting lobbying by former federal employees, there are few rules restricting lobbyists hired by Congress. They often take a pay cut to work on Capitol Hill. Or do they? Sometimes companies see an advantage in placing their employees in key congressional staff positions and find ways to soften any income loss. A **Wall Street Journal** sampling of financial disclosure forms in 2009 revealed that 250 congressional staffers earned a total of $13 million that year from their former employers or other outside jobs, including deferred compensation, stock grants, bonus payments, and inflated home purchases.*[22]

In today's complex regulatory environment, private sector participation in government policymaking is essential, and abuses of the "revolving door" cannot be allowed to distort the need for effective communication between government and the private sector. As a successful author, frustrated with the inadequacy of copyright protection, Clemens tirelessly lobbied Congress for reforms. He complained that there were no writers or artists in Congress who understood their business. The Democratic speaker of the House Champ Clark genuinely appreciated Clemens's expertise on the issue and credited his persistence in bringing about enhanced protections. Clemens told Livy that lobbying for a good cause in the public interest is a responsibility of good citizenship: "One must not refuse an office of that kind when asked—a man who prides himself on his citizenship *can't* refuse it."[23]

Money Talks

In *The Gilded Age*, money greases the lobbyist's influence, assuring access and the legislator's attention and cooperation. As Brierly and Senator Dilworthy talk strategy on the appropriation for the Salt Lick Extension of the Pacific Railroad, Brierly asks for an appropriation of a million dollars, which he estimates would reap the land speculators two million. "You'd better begin," the senator cautions, "by asking only for two or three hundred thousand, the usual way. You can begin to sell town lots on that appropriation." A portion of the appropriation will be "for necessary expenses," and "there are members who will have to be seen." Once the seed money is appropriated, however, and the senators begin to reap their rewards, subsequent appropriations will follow with ease. The cynical reporter Hicks tells Colonel Sellers: "To be sure, you can buy now and then a Senator or a Representative; but they do not know it is wrong, and so they are not ashamed of it. They are gentle, and confiding and childlike, and in my opinion these are qualities that ennoble them far more than any amount of sinful sagacity could." And Sellers replies: "We would have to go without the services of some of our ablest men, sir, if the country were opposed to—to—bribery. It is a harsh term. I do not like to use it."[24]

The Wall Street financiers behind Sellers's scheme are more blunt. "A congressional appropriation costs money": the sums needed are $40,000 for a majority vote of the House Committee and the same for the Senate, an extra $10,000 for each of the chairmen, $3,000 each for seven male lobbyists and $10,000 for one female, $3,000 for ten "high moral" senators and congressmen who will give "tone to a measure," and $500 a piece for twenty "small fry country members who won't vote for anything…without pay."[25] Mr. Bigler of Pennypacker, Bigler & Small complains to Ruth Bolton's father: "The price is raised so high on a United States Senator now, that it affects the whole market; you can't get any public improvement through on reasonable terms."[26] Twain summed it up: "I think I can say, and say with pride, that we have some legislatures that bring in higher prices than any in the world." And in a quote often attributed to him: "We have the best government that money can buy."[27]

A Tale of Today

In today's legislative environment, a member of Congress would have to be an idiot to accept a bribe, though Clemens would not be surprised if a few idiots remained. He once dictated for his **Autobiography,** *"All Congresses and Parliaments have a kindly feeling for idiots, and a compassion for them, on account of personal experience and heredity."[28] With the enactment of campaign finance reforms in 1973 and 1974, there are many legal avenues available for members of Congress to supplement their incomes, enhance their lifestyles, and assure their reelection. Campaign finance reform placed limits on individual contributions but authorized the creation of political action committees (PACs), enabling corporations, unions, and interest groups to pool the contributions of their employees, shareholders, and members and funnel contributions to grateful politicians. In 1974 608 PACs contributed $12.5 million to House and Senate candidates, and in 2016, PACs raised over $2 billion.[29]*

Like Haydn's variations on a theme by Brahms, all kinds of innovative variations have evolved from the statutory goal of capping and disclosing campaign contributions. These include PACs connected to corporations, unions, and trade associations; ideologically oriented or single-issue PACs; leadership PACs, and super ("independent expenditure") PACs. However well-intended, PACs have had several unintended consequences. First, they advantage incumbents—especially powerful committee and subcommittee chairs—who as the largest recipients of "special-interest" money are in the best position to advance the contributor's cause. Second, PACs contribute to the skyrocketing cost of election campaigns. In 1974 the spending for all House and Senate races was $77 million. Four elections later, the combined total was $343 million, and by 2010 it was

$1.8 billion—twenty-three times what is was before campaign finance reform.[30] A close Senate race went from a few hundred thousand to more than $50 million for each of the 2016 Florida and Pennsylvania Senate races. By limiting the amount of individual and PAC contributions at a time of escalating campaign costs, incumbents have to devote increasing amounts of time to raising money from a larger pool of donors. Many have learned that money can be raised faster by appealing to ideological extremists and single-issue zealots. Legislators without private fortunes spend as much as 50 to 70 percent of their time dialing for dollars, attending fundraisers, and courting high rollers—time that cannot be spent on reading proposed legislation, committee oversight, and constituent service. Incumbents increasingly delegate the day-to-day legislative business to ever-expanding staffs. House committee and member staff more than tripled from 3,000 in 1960 to 9,300 in 1980. The Senate staff grew from about 2,700 in 1959 to about 7,000 in the 1970s.[31] Third, the lengthening campaign cycle detracts from the camaraderie that used to characterize the congressional club. Instead of bipartisan social interaction and cooperation, incumbents engage in aggressive year-round fundraising that too often calls for demonizing the opposition. Fourth, for party leaders and incumbents in safe seats, PACs enable lawmakers to burnish their lifestyle, employ friends and relatives, and purchase the loyalty of less senior members. Fifth, PACs greatly facilitate the work of lobbyists, who raise money for incumbents in a position to advance their clients' interests. *

---

* It is not uncommon for a lobbyist or company representative, after a meeting with a member of Congress, to receive a phone call in the next couple of days from the congressperson or a fundraiser asking for a contribution.

*The perception of corruption arises when lobbyists contribute to election campaigns and are given special access in return. As lobbyists combine fundraising with legislative influence, the tale of **The Gilded Age** becomes the tale of today. **Washington Post** editor and author Robert G. Kaiser quotes former Kentucky Democratic congressman Romano Mazzoli: "People who contribute get the ear of the member. They have access, and access is it. Access is power. Access is clout."[32] Replicating the Gilded Age practices of Mark Hana, who extorted corporate contributions to elect William McKinley in 1896, both Republican and Democratic congressional leaders have favored lobbyists from their own party from whom they may extort contributions.[33] Then a series of scandals drew media attention to lobbying abuses, including Jack Abramoff's representation of Indian tribes for which he was well compensated—some $82 million. Abramoff hosted private-jet Scottish golf excursions for members of Congress, lavished on them expensive gifts and meals, and invited them to his luxury skyboxes at sports events. After congressional and Justice Department investigations, Abramoff and several colleagues went to prison.[34] According to Kaiser, Abramoff used to tell friends, "I was participating in a system of legalized bribery. All of it is bribery, every bit of it."[35] In a 60 Minutes interview, he described how he got a committee chairman—a frequent guest at his Signatures Restaurant bar—to drop some esoteric language in a pending bill.* The chairman, who later went to jail, admitted he didn't "know what it was for" and "didn't care." The language granted a backdoor license to an Indian casino client.[36] In his mea culpa memoirs, Abramoff*

---

* Abramoff told *60 Minutes* interviewer Leslie Stahl that he "was actually thinking of writing a book, *The Idiot's Guide to Buying a Congressman*," but admitted that most congressmen don't feel they're being bought; in their own minds they justify the system.

151

writes, "*Members swim in a swamp of corruption and thrive on it.*"[37] *Kaiser also quotes former member of Congress and secretary of defense Leon Panetta: "Legalized bribery has been part of the culture of how this place operates." Panetta complains that members of Congress rarely legislate because "their spending more and more time dialing for dollars... The only place they have to turn is to lobbyists... It has become an addiction they just can't break."*[38] *As former Senate Finance Committee chair Robert Dole told the **Wall Street Journal**'s Al Hunt, "When these political action committees give money, they expect something in return other than good government. It's making it much more difficult to legislate. We may reach the point where if everybody is buying something with PAC money, we can't get anything done."*[39]

*Protected by the First Amendment, lobbying performs a useful role in shaping effective policy, but when lobbying is combined with fundraising, it is prone to abuse. As a first step to foster transparency, Congress passed the toothless 1946 Federal Regulation of Lobbying Act that required filing and financial disclosure for lobbyists who met a vague threshold. In the Lobbying Disclosure Act of 1995 and the 2007 Honest Leadership and Open Government Act, Congress strengthened oversight and extended regulation to those lobbying the executive branch. But Congress has not directly focused on the nexus between lobbying and fundraising. In **Time Magazine**, Steven Brill proposed prohibiting legislators from accepting campaign contributions from persons and firms who lobby them.*[40] *A bipartisan American Bar Association Task Force has recommended doing away with the 20 percent threshold, imposing additional reporting requirements, and limiting fundraising by lobbyists.*[41] *In his January 2012 State of the Union address, President Obama proposed prohibiting lobbyists from fund-raising for federal candidates they had lobbied* *within the previous two years and prohibiting fundraisers from becoming lobbyists during the same period. He also proposed limits on all lobbyists' contributions to federal candidates, parties, and PACs.[42] A chastened Abramoff would go even further banning all lobbyists, government contractors, and persons who benefit from federal funds from making political contributions. He also advocates a lifetime ban on lobbying for all former members of Congress and staff.[43]*

Senator Boutwell's proposal in 1875 to establish a bar of qualified, licensed legislative representatives—subject to an enforceable ethics code—also has merit. It would help define lobbying with greater clarity and provide for on-the-record communications between lobbyists and members of Congress. There would be fewer opportunities for special-interest interventions if Congress enacted shorter, simpler, more general legislation and delegated the details to the executive branch to implement through statutorily prescribed, transparent, on-the-record administrative proceedings.

In addition to feeble attempts at lobbying reform, campaign finance reforms have been less than effective. The emerging PAC industry, like a surging river, always finds new channels to raise cash. A popular innovation is the "leadership" PAC, ostensibly to enable leading senators and representatives to help their fellow lawmakers win elections. According to federal election commission reports, leadership PACs raised over $46 million in the 2008 election cycle. Reports filed on some of these PACs disclosed that up to two-thirds of the funds raised did not go to other candidates at all but were expended for administrative costs to raise money. These costs included gourmet meals and private jet trips to luxurious resorts where members mingled with high-roller donors. Among the reported expenditures were $70,403 to the Ritz Carlton in Naples, Florida, $60,000 for a Beverly

Hills party, $223,000 for a golfing event, $30,000 at Disney resorts, $6,285 for private jets, $39,600 on steaks at Charlie Palmer's, $9,800 on limousines and entertainment, and $2,094 on ski lift tickets. According to Meredith McGehee, policy director of the nonprofit Campaign Legal Center, these leadership PACs enable members to fund their "personal life style, so you really don't have to pay for anything yourself. It's where the special-interest money flows." Top donors include union and corporate PACs in telecommunications, aviation, insurance, banking, real estate, and defense. Some thirty Democrats and seventeen Republicans collected $1.07 million without spending a cent on other candidates. One Louisiana congressman spent two-thirds of the funds raised on Mardi Gras balls. In another case, consulting fees were paid to a congressman's nephew.44 When leadership PAC funds are actually spent on another candidate's campaign, it is often to garner support for and loyalty from junior members for the leader's agenda.

Not only does money talk, but such talk is protected free speech according to a series of judicial decisions, beginning with **Buckley v. Valeo.** *These decisions opened up the sluice gates for corporate and other "independent" funding of election campaigns. In a 2010 Supreme Court decision,* **Citizens United v. Federal Election Commission,** *the Court held 5–4 that the First Amendment prohibits statutory limits on corporate and union funding of independent political broadcasts. The Court struck down a provision of the Bipartisan Campaign Reform Act of 2002 prohibiting corporations and unions from electioneering communications naming a candidate within thirty days of a primary or sixty days of the general election. 45* **The New York Times** *editorialized that* *"a lobbyist can now tell any elected official: if you vote wrong, my company, labor union, or interest group will spend unlimited sums explicitly advertising against your election." Affirming* **Citizens United**, *the Court on June 26, 2012 invalidated a 1912 Montana statute that for one hundred years had banned corporate campaign contributions. It was enacted to end the corrupt control of state politics by the copper barons during the Gilded Age.46*

With the escalating competition for cash in each new presidential campaign, innovative ways are created to skirt Congress's failed attempts to limit individual political contributions and encourage federal funding of general elections. With his amazing internet fund-raising skill, candidate Obama in 2008 reversed course and rejected federal matching funds, condemning to obsolescence public campaign financing that had been used since 1976 to fund general presidential elections, enabling candidates like Reagan, the Bushes, Carter, and Clinton to mount their fall campaigns without raising a dime. But in the 2008 election the two major parties raised a whopping $1.5 billion and that was without a potent new vehicle that has since emerged—the super PAC.

In the 2012 campaign (which began in earnest when the 2010 campaign ended), super PACs rose unlimited funds from wealthy individuals, corporations, unions, and special-interest organizations in support of particular candidates. In the early 2012 primaries, these super PACs swamped the airways with negative advertising, targeting opponents, breeding cynicism about politicians and distracting voters from the pressing policy choices that face the nation. Subject to far fewer restrictions than regular PACs, campaigns, or political parties, super PACs are supposed to be independent of campaigns and parties, but they are usually run by the candidates' former staffers or close friends.

They may even contribute limited amounts directly to a candidate's campaign.

Contrary to initial concerns that corporate money (especially foreign corporate money) would unduly influence presidential elections, most of the millions that began flowing into super PACs has come from a handful of billionaires with strong ideological convictions and their privately held companies. Large publicly traded corporations have generally avoided funding super PACs lest they offend shareholders or customers. According to one report, in the 2016 election ten individuals funded 30 per cent of total PAC funding, including two individuals who contributed more than $80 million each one to Democratic and the other to Republican candidates.47 Of 310 million Americans, fewer than 200 contributed over 80 percent of super PAC funding. Ever innovative, some super PACs were recreated as section 501(c)4 (social welfare nonprofits), like Crossroads GPS, which are not required to disclose their donors. They can run issue ads criticizing the President and other incumbents without reference to any candidate.

Another variation is the creation of individual customized super PACs where a relative or close friend of a candidate creates a vehicle to bypass the cap on individual contributions. The money flowing through these new vehicles makes current "limits on campaign contributions a mere fig leaf."48 Statutory limits on individual and traditional PAC campaign contributions are meaningless if an individual can give millions to a super PAC acting on behalf of a candidate and managed by a close colleague of the candidate. Is America returning to the plutocracy of the Gilded Age when a handful of tycoons could bankroll a candidate? In the words attributed to William McKinley's super fundraiser, Mark Hanna, "There are two things that are *important in politics. The first is money and I can't remember what the second one is."*

If experience with the super PAC and new non-profit vehicles proves to be as distortive as some critics have suggested, it may take a constitutional amendment to curtail them. At a minimum Congress could define what constitutes an independent expenditure and restrict the close ties between super PACs and the candidates by forbidding the hiring of political associates, the exchange of donor lists, the use of common pollsters and media consultants, candidate appearances at fundraisers, and the sharing of strategies. Congress should prohibit the abuse of section 501(c)4 vehicles and require that all contributors to election-related issue ads be disclosed promptly. A bill to do some of this– DISCLOSE– was defeated in 2010. 59 senate Democratic votes were insufficient to break the filibuster. It was blocked again in 2012.

It is possible that the egregious consequences of the super PAC phenomenon will be self-correcting. Candidates in both parties are discovering that false or embellished negative advertising can backfire, creating a voter backlash and putting the candidate on the defensive. About $7 billion was spent on federal 2016 elections, and it is perhaps instructive that the presidential candidate who challenged the pernicious effects of super PACs and spent the least money won a majority of the electoral college.

The Quid Pro Quo

To secure the necessary votes for the Knobs Industrial University, Colonel Sellers says that "members will have to be seen." The Wall Street financiers are more blunt, calculating the dollar cost of each vote for a committee chair, committee members, rank and file members of Congress, etc. In return, the members receive the quid pro quo, legislation benefiting their clients. In a play on words that resonate today, Sellers complains to Phillip, "Our public men are too timid. What we want is more money...Talk about basing the currency on gold; you might as well base it on **pork**."[49]

A Tale of Today

When lobbyists raise money for legislators, they expect something in return, like modern-day "pork"—the congressional earmark. In the words of former Oklahoma Republican senator, Tom Coburn, "Thousands of instances exist where appropriations are leveraged for fundraising dollars or political capital."[50] Usually behind closed doors as committees mark-up appropriation bills, powerful lawmakers insert line item provisions that benefit their state or district, and legislative leaders dole them out to corral recalcitrant party members into supporting the party's agenda.

The federal Office of Management and Budget defines earmarks as "funds by the Congress for projects, programs, or grants where the purported congressional direction (whether in statutory text, report language, or other communication) circumvents otherwise applicable merit-based or competitive allocation processes, or specifies the location or recipient, or otherwise curtails the ability of the executive branch to manage its statutory and constitutional responsibilities pertaining to the funds allocation process."[51] While this definition is quite devastating, congressional reformers often use pithier language—"pork" or "pork barrel projects"—to describe earmarks that benefit some other state or district. In the **Congressional Pig Book***, the nonpartisan organization Citizens Against Government Waste reported $16.5 billion in earmarks in 2010.[52] Using less restrictive criteria,* **The Washington Post** *reported 11,320 earmarks totaling $32 billion.[53] There were the celebrated cases: the $223 million Alaska "bridge to nowhere" connecting a mainland town of fourteen thousand to an island with only fifty residents, the nearly $200 million to expand a Pennsylvania airport serving only three* *commercial flights a day, the National Cowgirl Hall of Fame, and $100,000 for a single stop light in Canoga Park, California.[54] Responding to public pressures, in 2007 lawmakers were required to attach their names to the earmarks they sponsored.*

*In 2008 earmarks became a campaign issue, precipitating a public backlash, mostly for the wrong reason—to reduce federal spending. Abolishing earmarks would have a marginal effect on escalating deficits and debt and is no substitute for terminating failed programs, entitlement reform, and revenue enhancements. The most egregious abuse of earmarks is how they are used to reward lobbyists' campaign contributions, as Senator John McCain has called them, "the gateway drug to corruption." In 2009 **The Washington Post** disclosed allegations of corporate influence-peddling in awarding defense contracts involving more than thirty lawmakers.[55] A purloined secret memo described how a K street lobbying firm had raised more than $6.2 million in campaign contributions for the reelection of seven members of Congress in mostly safe seats, who in turn had allegedly steered $200 million in earmarked defense contracts to clients of the lobbying firm. For their efforts, the lobbying firm received $114 million in lobbying fees from the defense contractors.[56] The revelations surprised no one. This seems to be more the rule than the exception.*

Sometimes members of Congress receive a deferred payment for sponsoring earmarks. A former Senate Majority leader, for example, directed $1.6 million to a defense contractor in 2007 and resigned later that year (just beating the effective date of new ethics rules) to become a registered lobbyist for the contractor with a $50,000 monthly retainer.[57]

Belatedly responding to the public outcry, members of Congress pushed through reforms banning earmarks. In 2011 Congress passed a two-year moratorium on earmarks, which the Senate extended for another year. Efforts to legislate a permanent *ban have drawn little support. It remains to be seen whether an earmark ban will curtail money's influence in obtaining special-interest legislation, or whether earmarks will rise from the ashes, reincarnated in a new form.* Indeed, in 2017, a Congressional movement is underway to reinstate earmarks.*

In December 2011 a six-month study of the defense authori-zation bill, directed by Senator Claire McCaskill, identified 115 spending proposals as the equivalent of earmarks—worth $834 million—that passed the supposedly earmark-free House. Many of them were sponsored by newly elected members who had cam-paigned against earmarks. Avoiding earmark terminology, the amendments were written as line-item appropriations targeted to specific projects in the members' districts. McCaskill scrubbed the earmarks from the Senate bill, which passed Congress earmark-free.[58] Like a giant sponge, whenever the government presses down on certain abuses, alternative approaches pop up to replace them. New terms have popped up like "member-directed spend-ing," "plus-ups," "budget enhancements," "additions," or "pro-grammatic adjustments." An earmark ban does not prevent a member from incorporating language provided by a lobbyist in legislation regulating an industry, authorizing a program that benefits home-town businesses, making a line-item appropriation, reducing tariffs on items imported by constituents' companies, or providing a tax break for the benefit of campaign contributors. It does not prevent a powerful lawmaker with a hand on the purse

---

* Many members of Congress believe that earmarks are a proper exercise of Congress's constitutional appropriations powers and that they fund worthwhile projects that may be neglected by the executive branch, especially if it is controlled by the opposite party. Former Speaker Boehner admitted that it is a lot harder for the leadership to marshal votes in support of the party's legislative agenda if he cannot reward members who vote for legislation their constituents do not like. In past years, passing the 2011 deficit reduction legislation, he claimed, would have required $20–40 billion in earmarks to entice renegades to support the party's agenda.

from calling up a department official to urge her or him to fund a specific project.

Earmarks pale in impact to some 180 specific "tax expenditures" *—credits, deductions, and loopholes—that total 1.08 trillion dollars annually, nearly equal to the $1.09 trillion in tax revenues actually received by the federal government. It is a lot easier for politicians to support tax breaks than direct federal spending. To use a favorite lobbyist phrase, tax expenditures are a "win-win." They give constituents a government benefit and lower their taxes at the same time, deferring the cost to nonvoting future generations. Many anti-tax conservatives, most of whom have signed a pledge not to raise taxes, regard the elimination of tax expenditures to be a tax hike. In 2012 all but four House Republicans and six Senate Republicans had signed the Taxpayer Protection Pledge. The number of tax expenditures has nearly doubled in the past twenty-five years as lobbyists work with the House Ways and Means Committee to pick winners and losers and incentivize private sector activity such as home ownership, private pension contributions, housing construction, employer-provided health insurance benefits, energy exploration, corporate aircraft, and green technology. According to the 2010 Commission on Fiscal Responsibility and Reform (the Simpson-Bowles Commission), most of these tax expenditures benefit corporations, the upper middle class and wealthy individuals, who itemize their deductions. These tax preferences explain why one fourth of millionaires pay taxes at a lower rate than their employees.[59]

---

* No one knows how many tax breaks there really are. The actual number differs depending upon the definition. The congressional Joint Committee on Taxation counts three hundred while the Treasury Department lists 172. The 2010 Commission on Fiscal Responsibility and Reform (known as Simpson-Bowles) counted 180.

> *Harvard law professor Lawrence Lessig contends that corporations lobby for tax expenditures because there is a quantifiable payoff. He cites a study showing how "a firm spending an average of $779,945 on lobbying a year, an increase of 1 percent in lobbying expenditures, produced a tax benefit of between $4.8 million to $16 million. That's a 600 percent to 2,000 percent return—not bad for government work!"[60] In order to disguise the projected long term effect on the budget deficit, many targeted tax benefits are temporary, but these so-called "tax extenders" serve another purpose—filling the campaign coffers. They are routinely extended after a flurry of lobbying and fundraising activity every two years (when members of the prestigious House Ways and Means Committee run for reelection).[61]*

Congressional Self-Dealing

The Gilded Age illustrates how members of Congress serve their constituents' interests in ways that bring personal financial reward and assure reelection. Twain captured the sophisticated self-dealing, packaged as the public good, which too often characterizes the legislative product.

The Knobs University scheme was dressed up as a noble venture to teach freed slaves vocational skills. In the Reconstruction Congress, it is hard to imagine a greater public purpose than preparing freedmen for economic livelihood. As the "one principle" and "guide" in his "public life," Dilworthy gratuitously imparts to Laura, "I never push a private interest if it is not justified and ennobled by some larger public good."[62] In reality they planned to profit personally from the government's purchase of the land.* Dilworthy's earmark could have been modeled after a dozen bills passed during the Gilded Age which were

---

* Clemens undoubtedly recalled that when the Freedmen's Bureau bill, sponsored by the Judiciary Committee chair, Illinois senator Lyman Trumbull, was being debated in the Senate, Stewart had criticized "the unlimited power given the commissary to purchase land for educational purposes." The bill passed unchanged over President Johnson's veto.

clothed in a public purpose, like Credit Mobilier (completion of the transcontinental railroad) and the Northern Pacific legislation providing for the inflated purchase of railroad property. The Cooke brothers, Henry and Jay, had worked closely with House Speaker James Blaine to get that "bill in shape for passage."[63] In persuading Congressman Trollop to vote for the Tennessee land bill, Laura reminds him that he has accepted free stock in his brother-in-law's name in exchange for his vote for the Steamship Subsidy Act—another not so subtle parody of Credit Mobilier,[64] or perhaps the subsidy for the Pacific Mail Steamship Company, which had repeatedly failed to pass Congress until the company spent a whopping $900,000 on lobbyists and newspaper editors to promote the bill. It was finally enacted on June 1, 1872.[65]

As the transcontinental railroads opened up the West, the Indians residing there were besieged by cavalry attacks and congressional corruption. Senators Stewart, Nye, and Pomeroy* all benefited from the displacement of Americans Indians.[66] In *The Gilded Age*, the reporter Hicks chats with Colonel Sellers about how Senator Balloon is advancing the public good, a colloquy inspired by former Nevada governor, then-senator Nye's bilking of the Indians:

> **Hicks**: Balloon has had a good deal of public experience...He was governor of one of the territories a while, and was very satisfactory...He was an ex-officio Indian agent, too. Many a man would have taken the Indian appropriation and devoted the money to feeding and clothing the helpless savages, whose land had been taken from them by the white man in the interests of civilization; but Balloon knew their needs better. He built a government saw-mill on the reservation

---

* Clemens may have recalled how Senator Pomeroy had inserted a railroad purchase clause in the Kickapoo Treaty of 1862, providing for the sale of "surplus" Kickapoo lands for $1.25 an acre to the Atchison, Topeka & Pike Railroad, in which Pomeroy held a controlling interest. The Kickapoo protested that a tribal interpreter had been bribed and only one leader had signed the document, but despite an investigation into the matter, no action was taken.

with the money, and the lumber sold for enormous prices—a relative of his did all the work free of charge—that is to say he charged nothing more than the lumber would bring.

Sellers: But the poor Injuns—not that I care much for Injuns—what did he do for them?

Hicks: Gave them the outside slabs to fence in the reservation with. Governor Balloon was nothing less than a father to the poor Indians. But Balloon was not alone, we have many truly noble statesmen in our country's service like Balloon. The Senate is full of them.[67]

Hicks describes how the clever senator abused the congressional franking privilege by shipping "seven huge boxes of old clothes…a ton of second hand rubbish, old books, pantaloons and what not through the mails as registered matter." Hicks applauds Balloon's "ingenuity," remarking, "Can you picture Jefferson, or Washington, or Adams franking their wardrobes through the mails?"[68] He then speciously laments, "Statesmen were dull creatures in those days." Sellers chimes in that Balloon was being considered for the post of Minister to China or Austria and what "a good example of the national character" he would be: "John Jay and Benjamin Franklin were well enough in their day, but the nation has made progress since then."[69]

During the Gilded Age, it was standard practice for members of Congress to reap financial benefit from projects they were promoting. The nation's preeminent banker, Jay Cooke, declared that if a member of Congress was anybody at all, he would be interested in investing in an enterprise that came before Congress.[70] In Credit Mobilier, dozens of legislators invested in a company that was a creature of congressional appropriations.

A Tale of Today

Today strict conflict-of-interest rules apply to the executive branch and government contractors and grantees, but far more permissive rules apply to the first branch of government. Congress appropriates billions of dollars for industry bailouts and subsidies, stimulus projects, and infrastructure development. Congress oversees financial institutions, insurance companies, the housing sector, and automobile manufacturers. Congress chooses winners and losers in the tax code, health care reform, and the rescue and regulation of financial institutions. Through appropriations, taxation, and regulatory mandates, Congress significantly impacts the profitability of private companies.

In an excellent series of investigative reports, **The Washington Post** detailed how members of Congress applied the Dilworthy principle—ennobling private gain with some larger public purpose. Comparing public records on congressional holdings to earmark appropriations, the reporters identified thirty-three members from both parties who earmarked $300 million for dozens of projects that enhanced the value of their own properties. To cite a few examples, an Alabama senator directed more than $100 million to renovate downtown Tuscaloosa near a commercial building he owned (this was before the devastating tornado hit the city). A Georgia congressman earmarked $6.3 million to replenish a beach nine hundred feet from his vacation cottage. The Kentucky chairman of the House Appropriations Committee targeted $7 million in federal funds to revitalize his home town of Somerset, which included such improvements to the street on which he lived as narrowing the street to control traffic, burying overhead utilities, rebuilding sidewalks, constructing new driveway aprons, and installing decorative street lamps.[71] Conflicts aside, why is the federal government funding the installation of decorative street lamps and constructing driveway aprons?

*The **Post** investigation also identified sixteen members of Congress of both parties who have directly funded organizations where their family members are employed. A South Dakota senator on the Appropriations Committee directed $4 million to a Pentagon program for which his wife was a contract employee. An Arizona congressman on the House Appropriations Committee obtained a one-million-dollar grant for a scholarship program for high-risk students headed by his daughter. The **Post** found a pattern of targeting funds to colleges where relatives were employed or served as trustees. For example, a Texas congresswoman secured millions in appropriations for the University of Houston where her husband was an administrator, and an Ohio congressman earmarked $2.3 million for Bowling Green State University where his wife was a senior vice president.*[72]

*Each of these projects may have served a noble purpose, and the **Post** dutifully reported the justifications offered by lawmakers who protested that the institutions should not be punished simply because they employed relatives of members of Congress. Nonetheless congressional disclosure and ethical requirements, which differ between the House and Senate, need tightening if they are come close to what Congress requires of the executive branch.*

These trends parallel a substantial rise in stock ownership by members of Congress over the past decade. According to the Center for Responsible Politics, in 2010 more than half the members of Congress owned stock in individual companies, up from ninety-one in 2001.[72] *Not surprisingly, the legislators' investment returns were more successful than the general public's. One study showed that from 1985 to 2006, congressional portfolios outperformed the market by 55 percent. According to Harvard professor Dennis F. Thompson, "No one else has this kind of success, not even mutual fund or hedge fund managers."*[74]

Members of Congress and their staffs determine the content, prospects, and timing of pending legislation and its effect on business sectors and companies. They receive confidential information from the executive branch and private parties about economic developments and proposed federal actions. Legislators vote on bills that affect their finances and this raises the appearance of conflict, regardless of their motivation. On June 24, 2012, the lead story in **The Washington Post** *revealed that one hundred and thirty members of Congress or their families had made 5,531 trades in stocks or bonds worth $218 million in 323 companies registered to lobby before committees on which they served.[75] Professor Thompson, author of a book on conflicts of interest, says, "Stronger regulation of financial conflicts is necessary not so much to prevent quid pro quo deals, but to check the erosion of trust in government." In his view, "The problem is structural," and "it is time for Congress to take a fresh look at the financial conflict-of-interest rules, and how they should be enforced. It is not surprising that between 1984 and 2009, a period during which American household wealth declined, the medium net worth of a member of the House more than doubled and that 44 percent of members of Congress were millionaires.[76]*

On the November 13, 2011, broadcast of 60 Minutes, Steve Kroft did a segment on how members of Congress accumulate great wealth while in office by investing in securities and real estate, the value of which is affected by pending legislation or information obtained from confidential government sources. In the interview, Kroft described how a former speaker of the house reaped millions from land that he had purchased adjacent to a proposed highway that he later earmarked for construction and how a committee chair traded in health care stocks as he marked up comprehensive health care reform legislation.[77]

Prior to the 60 Minutes exposé, congressional "insider trading" legislation languished for six years, quietly ignored. But after the program aired, President Obama in his January 2012 State of the Union address urged Congress to send him a bill banning insider trading by members of Congress, promising to sign it the next day. One hundred forty members of Congress rushed to co-sponsor the Stop Trading on Congressional Knowledge Act ("Stock Act") that would make it illegal for members of Congress and their staffs to buy or sell securities based on nonpublic information relating to pending legislation and would require them to report trades in securities of more than $1000 monthly to the clerk of the House or secretary of the Senate. The legislation passed both houses of Congress and was signed by the President in March 2012. The bill appears to be narrower than insider trading felony laws already on the books and enforced in the private sector.[78] The speedy enactment of the Stock Act attests to the power of the media to influence legislation; however, it is doubtful that any of the stock or bond trades referred to above would have violated the STOCK Act which requires the knowing use of insider information. Unlike rules applicable to the executive branch, the STOCK Act does not prohibit members from investing in companies they oversee or influence. In 2017, the president's nominee for Secretary of Health and Human Services will doubtless face questions during his confirmation hearing about his profitable trades in health care company stocks while sponsoring legislation that would affect these companies.

While statutory ethics standards apply to executive branch employees, they do not apply to the President, although the President is subject to the "emoluments" clause of the US Constitution, prohibiting compensation or gifts of value from foreign governments. Moreover, the President sets an example for his employees, and

> *potential conflicts receive substantial media and congressional scrutiny. As this second edition goes to press, substantial questions have arisen concerning the disentanglement of President-elect Trump's family businesses. It remains to be seen how these issues will be addressed.*

Parliamentary Gamesmanship

In *The Gilded Age*, Twain demonstrated his mastery of Congress's arcane rules and procedures. Ward Just writes in his introduction to the Oxford edition: "It's remarkable how much he knew about how things worked...how a bill got from here to there in the American legislature."[79] Twain takes the reader through an all-night filibuster on the House floor.* As the dawn arrives, the exhausted Tennessee land bill sponsor, Chairman Buckstone, rises to speak and with an "injured look" states, in reference to a time-honored filibuster tradition, "It was evident that the opponents of the bill were merely talking against time, hoping in this unbecoming way to tire out the friends of the measure, and so defeat it." Buckstone finds such conduct "out of place in so august an assemblage as the House of Representatives."[80] With the majority on his side, he pushes the legislation through to final passage, cleverly leaving blank the amount of funds to be appropriated for the purchase of the Tennessee

---

* The filibuster is invoked unsuccessfully in *The Gilded Age* to prevent the enactment of corrupt legislation. Supporters of the filibuster argue that it enables the minority to block bad legislation and that it is consistent with framers' intent to devise checks and balances that slow the process of expanding federal power. In the words of nineteenth century Yale professor William Graham Sumner, a friend of Clemens, "Nearly all the machinery of Congress is an elaborate mechanism for preventing anything from being done, and although it stops many measures which a great many of us think it very advisable to pass, we cheerfully do without them lest some of the others should get though likewise" (quoted in Grant, 124). And so the filibuster or the threat thereof has been invoked to block civil rights, environmental, and health care legislation, among others.

land.* Opponents' consecutive motions to fill in the blanks with appropriations of $2.50 and twenty-five cents, respectively, were roundly defeated. With $3 million inserted in the blank, the Knobs bill passes the House. It must still pass the Senate.

According to Senator Dilworthy, "Providence sometimes acts differently in the two Houses." But "there is an *esprit de corps* in the Senate...[that makes] the members more complaisant towards the projects of each other...extend[ing] a mutual aid which in a more vulgar body would be called 'log-rolling.'"[81] Senator Dilworthy and Laura prepare for the Senate vote. In the end, they fail because they each become enmeshed in scandal. Their supporters desert them like ducks scattering after the first shot from behind the blind.

As a legislative aide, Clemens quickly learned how parliamentary rules can be manipulated for partisan advantage, for example, by invoking the threat of a filibuster. In drafting the Constitution, the framers—skeptical of human nature and the abuse of power—built in checks and balances.** In a short and mostly generally phrased document, they were quite explicit when more than a majority vote is required to take specific kinds of actions. A law must pass both houses of Congress by a majority vote, and the president may sign or veto it. Congress may override a presidential veto by a two-thirds vote in each house. The Constitution expressly requires a two-thirds vote of the Senate to consent to the ratification of treaties, to remove the president or other officials from office following their impeachment by the House, and to expel its own members. A two-thirds vote of both houses is required to propose an amendment to the Constitution. Of course, the Constitution allows each house to "determine the Rules of its Proceedings," but when more than a majority vote is required, the Constitution is uncommonly explicit.

---

* Twain undoubtedly recalled the Nevada's legislature's attempt to push through a state constitution with special funding blanks mysteriously filled in after the floor debate.

** Once a law is passed, it is the president's responsibility to execute it. Congress exercises oversight, but it cannot interfere with the constitutional responsibilities of the executive branch by, for example, retaining a one-house veto over executive action.

A Tale of Today

Apparently the Senate is not satisfied with the framers' handiwork. Its rules require unanimous consent, the agreement of all one hundred senators, for many procedural actions. One senator can block legislation or a judicial nomination from coming to the floor for a vote. In the absence of unanimous agreement, sixty votes are required to begin a debate and sixty votes to end a debate. These rules bestow enormous power on a single senator from a sparsely populated state. Although the framers gave the states with smaller populations disproportionate power—each state has two senators regardless of population—the Senate apparently considers this inadequate. When the Constitution was ratified, the ratio of the most populous to the least populous state was 20:1; today it is 70:1. About 17 percent of the US population can elect the Senate majority, which makes the Senate among the least representative of legislative bodies in working democracies—especially for racial and ethnic minorities who tend to cluster in a few large states. Although there are slightly fewer people in Alaska than South Central Los Angeles, the Alaskans have two senators looking out for their interests, which may explain why Alaska receives the most federal aid per capita of any state and unemployment in South Central exceeds 11 percent.

*In their excellent book about a dysfunctional Congress, **The Broken Branch**, Thomas Mann of the Brookings Institute and Norman Ornstein of the American Enterprise Institute—two of the most respected Congress watchers—point out that the Senate was established to temper the exuberance of the people's House. When Thomas Jefferson asked George Washington why he had consented to the creation of the Senate, Washington allegedly responded, "Why did you poor that coffee into your saucer?" "To cool it," Jefferson replied. "Even so," said Washington, "we pour legislation into the senatorial saucer to cool it."[82] One hundred years later when the senate blocked a passage of a bill to arm US* merchant ships on the eve of World War I, a frustrated Woodrow Wilson complained: "The Senate of the United States is the only legislative body in the world that cannot act when its majority is ready for action. A little group of willful men, representing no opinion but their own, have rendered the great government of the United States helpless and contemptible."[83] Yet the founding fathers warned of minority obstructionism. In Federalist Paper #22, Alexander Hamilton was remarkably prophetic:

> What at first sight may seem a remedy is, in reality, a poison. To give a minority a negative upon the majority (which is always the case where more than a majority is requisite to a decision), is...to subject the sense of the greater number to that of the lesser... If a pertinacious minority can control the opinion of the majority...the majority, in order that something may be done, must conform to the views of the minority...and thus the smaller will overrule that of the greater. Hence, tedious delays; continual negotiation and intrigue; contemptible compromises of the public good...upon some occasions things will not admit of accommodation; and then the measures of government must be injuriously suspended, or fatally defeated. It is often, by the impracticality of obtaining the concurrence of the necessary number of votes, kept in a state of inaction. Its situation must always savor of weakness, sometimes border upon anarchy.[84]

The trouble began inadvertently in 1806 when Vice President Aaron Burr recommended that the Senate simplify its rules by eliminating the motion to call for a vote ("moving the previous question"), leaving no way to end a debate. In 1917 the Senate adopted Rule XXII requiring a two-thirds majority of those present to end debate, enabling a minority to occupy the floor and prevent a bill from coming to a vote. Historically the filibuster was invoked on rare occasions to protect the interest of a regional minority (e.g., southern opposition to civil rights legislation), usually requiring a few all-nighters. Advocates of the filibuster point out that it is a safeguard against frequent changes in federal law and policy that create havoc in the private sector. As the majority in Congress shifts from one election to the next, laws can be enacted and then repealed with a suddenness that disrupts family and business planning.

In 1975 the Senate amended the rule to require 60 votes in the form of a cloture motion to end debate and bring a bill to the floor for a vote. The majority must muster 60 votes, regardless of the number of senators present. Today the mere threat of a filibuster is enough to prevent a bill from coming to a vote. The minority party has invoked the rule to frustrate the will of the majority, resulting in stalemate.[85] Each session dozens of bills that pass the House die in the Senate. Political scientist Barbara Sinclair found that since 2000 about 70 percent of major bills have been filibustered compared to about 8 percent in the 1960s.[86] Mann and Ornstein show how three noncontroversial bills in the 111th Congress that eventually passed the Senate by more than 90 votes were nonetheless subject to lengthy filibuster delays, obstructing the work of the Senate and wasting twenty days of valuable floor time with "mind-numbing" repetitive roll calls.[87]

Equally as egregious, a single senator can put a hold on legislation or the confirmation of an appointment (even for reasons unrelated to the qualifications of the nominee). A rule that was adopted as a courtesy to senators in the days of horse travel, enabling them to delay a vote until they could arrive at the Capitol and question an appointee, has become a common partisan blocking procedure. A single senator can block the *appointment of a judge or a cabinet or subcabinet officer and frustrate the president's constitutional responsibility to execute the laws and the Senate's responsibility to "advise and consent" to presidential appointments.[88] The plethora of presidentially appointed positions offer low hanging fruit for partisan mischief. At the end of President Obama's first year in office, only 64.4 percent of presidential nominees had been confirmed, compared to 80 percent under during his predecessor's first year.[89] By what twisted logic does the opposition party contend that it can hold the president accountable for his job performance when it blocks the appointment of key officials to implement his policies? The domestic, foreign policy, and national security challenges facing the federal government are too complex, and global conditions too precarious, to permit a drift in leadership where key jobs remain unfilled for months, even years. The system cripples the ability of an elected president to carry out his or her mandate. [90]**

Although Congress is beginning to implement procedural reforms,[91] it is still far from the deliberative body envisioned by the framers when formalities fill mostly empty chambers for days on end, when many bills are introduced simply for public relations messaging, when committee hearings turn into festivals of haranguing sound-bites, and when staff and lobbyists write thousand page bills that senators have no time to read. Mann and Ornstein ask: Where is the deliberative body envisioned by the framers "that would attract people of ability to work for the common good?"[92]

---

* The Senate has modified its rules to expedite the confirmation process for many presidential appointees; however, the Senate Republican majority's refusal in 2016 to conduct hearings on Supreme Court nominee Merrick Garland after the death of Justice Scalia left the Supreme Court for months with only eight justices, affecting its decisions on several significant issues before it.

> *Some of the inefficiencies and frustrations in Congress are due to divided government, which the voters too often prefer in times of economic stress. In 2017 the Republicans will have the majority of both houses of Congress and the presidency. Perhaps this will present an opportunity to restore the fundamental responsibilities of Congress as envisioned by the Framers, such as timely confirmations and appropriations.*

Partisan Trench Warfare

Clemens worked on Capitol Hill during one of the most divisive times in American history as Republicans and Democrats squabbled over matters consequential (Reconstruction and impeachment) and inconsequential (cutting off stationary supplies and defunding the president's secretary). Disgusted with the games-playing between the parties, he wrote: "There is not any kind of wisdom in this kind of warfare. These parties stand for the United States. They represent the American nation, and it is not a nation that fights in that way."[93] Years later, as a public figure whose endorsement was sought after, he became increasingly disenchanted with the party system. He saw how little political rhetoric has to do with policy making and governance, how campaign promises scatter like ashes in the shifting breezes of public opinion, how the campaign trail's pious platitudes and ringing rhetoric yield to cynical and corrupting influences in the exercise of power, and how negative campaigning and character assassination enables candidates to avoid confronting the real issues of concern to voters. Twain became convinced that loyalty to party too often displaces loyalty to country and that party loyalists sacrifice the public good for partisan advantage.

A Tale of Today

With the influx of campaign money over the past few decades, formidable industries have evolved that thrive on partisan politics—sophisticated polling, campaign consulting, political advertising, and innovative fund-raising through mass mailings, Internet marketing, "bundling" of big donors, super PACs, and 501(c)4's. Raising money and attracting media attention are the keys to political success. It is safer, easier and more effective to purchase advertising that demonizes an opponent than to take a stand on a controversial public policy issue that may alienate a block of voters. Former president Gerald Ford, who came from the old school of a more personal, bipartisan politics, spoke candidly in the old Senate Chamber in 2001 about the value of "authenticity as much as ideology, especially in this age when so much of what passes for public life consists of little more than candidates without ideas hiring consultants without convictions to stage campaigns without content."[94] In the perpetual campaign cycle, maneuvering for partisan advantage has infected the end-goal of legislating and governing.

In most mature democracies, election campaigns are condensed into a manageable few months. In a satirical exchange with French novelist Paul Bourget, Clemens conceded that France "can teach us how to elect a President in a sane way; and also how to do it without throwing the country into earthquakes and convulsions that cripple and embarrass business, stir up party hatred in the hearts of men, and make peaceful people wish the term extended to thirty years."[95] In the United States, the perpetual campaign leaves little time or reward for quiet backroom compromise in pursuit of effective public policy. Electioneering displaces the hard work of overseeing and managing federal programs.

Partisanship threatens to paralyze public policy. Pragmatic politicians are squeezed out through state legislative gerrymandering. Thirty years ago centrists in both parties (moderate Republicans and conservative or Blue Dog Democrats) were the catalyst for compromise. Today they are a diminishing breed with little influence, and legislative battles too often end in stalemate. In most states, after the census is complete, the party in control of the state legislature redraws the congressional districts to assure the reelection of their party's incumbents. In place of cohesive populations entitled to representation, they gerrymander oddly shaped districts of rural, suburban, and urban precincts that have in common only the voters (or race) that ensures the election of the party's candidate.* Creating these safe havens discourages contested elections in which candidates are held accountable to their constituency and must appeal to independent voters. The party primary becomes the decisive factor, and the threat of a primary challenge keeps incumbents from deviating from the strict party line. Stephen Moore's Club for Growth, Grover Norquist's Americans for Tax Reform, and other conservative entities are eager to fund a conservative primary alternative to a mainstream Republican who strays too far from the herd and becomes a RINO (Republican-in-name-only). Well-funded primary campaigns– relying heavily on out-of-state money– can even punish senior, respected, conservative statesmen like Indiana senator Richard Lugar who was ousted because he worked too closely with then-senator Obama on nuclear non-proliferation.

---

* Gerrymandering is named after the salamander district contours established by Massachusetts governor Elbridge Gerry in 1812.

The call for reform is beginning to be heard. Fifteen states—including the largest, California—have established bipartisan or nonpartisan redistricting commissions, and two additional states have created advisory commissions to propose plans that create cohesive districts and foster competitive elections. Comparing California redistricting after the 2000 and 2010 census is instructive. After the 2000 census, the state legislature drew enclaves so protective of incumbents that only one of the state's fifty-three congressional districts changed parties in the ensuing decade. In contrast after the 2010 census, a fourteen-member Citizens Redistricting Commission, consisting of five Republicans, five Democrats, and four technical independents, held hearings and agreed upon a transparent redistricting process that shook up the congressional districts, causing at least eight incumbents to retire rather than face another incumbent of the same party or an influx of voters from the opposite party. Iowa may have devised an even better system, relying on nonpartisan experts to redraw the lines.[96] Establishing competitive congressional districts in which candidates are forced to appeal to a broader cross-section of voters will not automatically reverse party polarization and partisan gridlock, but it will help over the long term.

During turbulent times voters tend to prefer divided government. In the fifteen elections between 1870 and 1900, the majority party in the House changed six times; in eighteen of those years, different parties held the presidency and at least one house of Congress. Between 1995 and 2017, control of Congress changed as many times as it had in the previous fifty years.[97] Conditioned by the media to expect instant results, voters have no patience for long term strategies. If the ship of state cannot turn on a dime in two years, the disillusioned voter swings to the other party. As the parties maneuver against each other, competition

*for power replaces legislating in the common interest. Voter vola-
tility leads to stalemate and gridlock.*

*Like competing teams in the National Football League, the
polarized parties in Congress plot for tactical advantage. Coached
by pollsters and party consultants, they huddle in caucuses and,
with extraordinary team discipline, devise plays to focus media
attention on their agenda and block their opponent's offensive
strategy. Much of Congress's time is wasted by invoking parliamentary procedures for political advantage, calling for votes not
to pass legislation but to send a message to the media or embarrass the opposition, and seeking to hurt or help the president and
his party's reelection prospects. Unfortunately, the media message
being skillfully conveyed by the parties—like Twain's short stories "An Unbiased Criticism" and "The Great Prize Fight"—
often masks the pressing challenges facing the public.[98] The hard
choices are ignored and phony battles manufactured as the issues
are distorted through the prism of the perpetual campaign. The
challenger on the attack has the advantage because complex,
intractable economic and social problems that require bipartisan
cooperation to address and time to implement become media targets for incumbent failures.*

*There is probably not a single member of Congress who would
not privately concede that current entitlements (Social Security,
Medicare and Medicaid) are a run-away-train, that the tax code
is an abomination, that the mounting deficit is a threat to the
global economy, and that both parties are to blame for the current state of affairs. Yet as the parties throw rocks at each other,
Congress continues (to invoke appropriate clichés) to "kick the
can down the road."*

*As Clemens had witnessed, there have been historical periods
of great partisan acrimony, especially over the slavery issue. In
May 1856, for example, South Carolina congressman Preston*

Brooks *viciously assaulted Massachusetts abolitionist senator Charles Sumner with his cane. Sumner collapsed on the Senate floor and was carried out, not to return for four years. During other periods—the 1960s through the 80s—members from opposing parties socialized together, developed strong bonds of friendship and produced bipartisan legislation. With bipartisan majorities Congress passed monumental legislation on civil rights, education, clean water and air, worker safety, consumer protection, Medicare, Medicaid, and tax reform.*

With the 1994 election of the Republican majority in the House and the ascendency of Speaker Newt Gingrich, the most recent era of bipartisan cooperation began to fade. The now infamous memo issued by Gingrich's GOPAC, entitled "Language, A Key Mechanism of Control," provided a thesaurus of epithets that Republicans were encouraged to use to demonize the opposition: "corrupt," "destructive," "radical," "intolerant," "traitors." Sensitive to the new media's thirst for sound bites, choir director Newt offered platitudes that Republicans were urged to invoke in their speeches and interviews: "principled," "courage," "vision," "passionate," "prosperity."[99] Legislative business was crammed into Tuesday afternoon through Thursday morning so members could return to their districts to bond with their supporters, raise money for reelection and visit their families who were encouraged to remain at home. Consequently, today there is little interaction—official or social—between the parties. The era of bipartisan cooperation is over.

The spirit of compromise has deteriorated so badly that the dean of the House, John Dingell, felt compelled to speak out in a **Washington Post** *guest column on September 9, 2011. Dingell, who was elected to the House in 1955, taking the seat of his father who had served since 1933, wrote that the public is "angry and frustrated" that Congress is failing "to do its constitutional* *duty...in favor of partisan squabbling and partisan political games." Noting that public approval of Congress had fallen to a record low of 12 percent, he said, "I am ashamed of our performance—of us all, on both sides of the aisle."[100] He wrote: "We in Congress are tearing our country apart and weakening the foundation established by great leaders before us. Is anyone in Congress truly proud that we have not produced a budget? That we caused the downgrading of US government securities, as well as appalling disorder and confusion in financial markets? Or that this situation caused the lack of job creation and economic growth that has contributed to the hopelessness and misfortune of millions of Americans?"[101]*

*Major legislative achievements in past decades have been facilitated by centrist lawmakers who worked across the aisle to forge compromises. The unsung heroes of the 1960s civil rights legislation were the Republicans who worked with northern Democrats and President Lyndon Johnson to overcome southern obstruction. Today the centrists have all but disappeared, succumbing to primary challenges or election loses in the few remaining competitive districts where independent voters still hold sway. Others have retired, frustrated by the party leadership's unwillingness to compromise, punished by loss of seniority privileges for veering from the party line or driven to the opposite party. The polarizing parties are achieving unprecedented ideological purity that reflects increasing cultural polarity in the nation at large. In its study of roll-call votes in the 111th Congress, the **National Journal** found that the most liberal Republican is now more conservative than the most conservative Democrat.[102] The premature retirement of two respected moderate senators, one from each party, tells the story in op-ed pieces they published explaining their reasons for leaving a dysfunctional Senate, encased in gridlock. Indiana senator Evan Bayh wrote in **The New York***

Times: *"There are many causes for the dysfunction: strident partisanship, unyielding ideology, a corrosive system of campaign financing, gerrymandering of House districts, endless filibusters, holds on executive appointees in the Senate, dwindling social interaction between senators of opposing parties and a caucus system that promotes party unity at the expense of bipartisan consensus."*[103] *Maine senator Olympia Snowe wrote for* **The Washington Post** *that she had decided not to seek another Senate term (after forty years in public office) because of the dysfunction and polarization in the institution. "Simply put, the Senate is not living up to what the Founding Fathers envisioned. The greatest deliberative living body is not living up to its billing. The Senate of today routinely jettisons regular order, as evidenced by its failure to pass a budget for more than one thousand days; serially legislates political brinksmanship...and habitually eschews full debate and an open amendment processmin favor of competing, up-or-down, take-it-or-leave-it proposals...Everyone simply votes with his or her party and those in charge employ every possible tactic to block the other side. But that is not what America is all about, and it's not what the founders intended....*

"The great challenge is to create a system that gives our elected officials reasons to look past their differences and find common ground if their initial party positions fail to garner sufficient support. In a politically diverse nation, only by finding that common ground can we achieve results for the common good. That is not happening today, and frankly, I do not see it happenings in the near future."[104]

Preoccupied with partisan trench warfare and the continuous election cycle, Congress neglects its constitutional responsibilities. It fails to establish and adhere to a budget that provides for revenues to cover the costs of federal programs. It funds undeclared *wars on borrowed money.* Congress fails to reauthorize essential programs, and rarely does it timely appropriate funds to implement the laws. Instead, funding authority for nonmilitary programs is usually passed in the form of temporary continuing resolutions and bundled up in an omnibus bill at the end of the fiscal year with little or no debate. All too frequently, intense partisanship threatens a government shut-down. As the precipice is approached, legislators aim their rhetorical excesses at the TV cameras and government productivity grinds to a halt. Without authorizing legislation and timely appropriations, the executive agencies and their contractors and grantees cannot efficiently plan and execute their programs.*

The lack of disciplined congressional appropriations based on program evaluation, oversight, and substantive debate has resulted in deficit spending, spiraling debt, bloated bureaucracies, and unsustainable entitlements like Social Security, Medicare, and Medicaid, which threaten to engulf the entire federal budget.

Instead of using congressional oversight to score partisan points, Congress should evaluate the effectiveness of federal programs, eliminate duplication and conflict among the hundreds of programs it has created, terminate the thousands of pages of laws that have either achieved their objectives or failed to achieve them, eliminate or fund state mandates that are crushing state budgets, and fine-tune and improve the reauthorization of essential federal programs—like highway and bridge construction, environmental protection, and clean energy development. Only short term stopgap measures keep these programs going at all. It took more than five years of stalemate, twenty-three stopgap extensions, and a two-week partial shutdown of the Federal Aviation Administration before Congress in February 2012

---

* Congress has not declared war since World War II. Most recently, it has avoided its responsibility to debate and authorize the military response to ISIS.

finally reauthorized the expired programs that regulate airline safety, upgrade airports, and transition to a far more energy and environmentally efficient satellite-based air navigation system. This is no way to run a railroad—or an aviation system. Since expiring in 2009, surface transportation reauthorization was subject to repeated temporary extensions as highways, bridges, and city transit systems continue to deteriorate. When Congress finally passed a two-year reauthorization in June 2012, it failed to provide sufficient revenues by, for example, increasing the gas tax, leaving a projected shortfall of $85-$115 billion in funding required to meet the next decade's transportation infrastructure needs.

It is not enough, of course, simply to restore a veneer of bipartisanship—cooperation across the aisle in pursuit of compromise—if the effect is agreement on the lowest common denominator least likely to offend any constituency. In past eras, bipartisanship has too often resulted in undisciplined acquiescence in the status quo, logrolling, and mutual self-promotion and corruption. Effective bipartisanship means courageous cooperation in making tough decisions. This type of leadership has too often been lacking even in the halcyon days of bipartisan cooperation.

With rational discourse and long-term planning, these challenges are solvable today, but while political parties play the blame game, changing demographics—an older population and a declining middle class—will make the solution all the more painful as time passes. But few Democrats are willing to advocate serious entitlement reform, preferring to attack the Republicans for endangering Medicare and Social Security, and the Republican no-tax pledgers refuse to agree to revenue enhancements, preferring to castigate the Democrats as the tax and spend party. The American public understands that the current path is not sustainable, yet political institutions seem incapable of formulating responsible solutions.

In a democracy ideological differences and debate among alternative visions are critical to establish the contours in which pragmatic solutions can be designed, implemented, and fairly evaluated. Neither party has a monopoly on ideas, and progress is usually made by drawing on the best ideas from along the political spectrum. Where ideological differences degenerate into partisan bickering, however, there is no time for civil discourse, analytical open-mindedness, and respect for opposing points of view that are critical to fashioning workable solutions that generate successful results. Can Congress put aside partisan sparring long enough to come together to address out-of-control deficits and debt, unsustainable entitlements and state mandates, comprehensive tax reform, job creation in a transformational economy, an educated workforce, international competition, fair and affordable health care, a deteriorating infrastructure, climate-change, a cost-effective global response to the threat of terrorism, a fair immigration policy, rising income inequality, and other urgent priorities?

CHAPTER NINE

A Gilded Tale Of Human Nature In Politics, The Media, And Business

"It is a civilization which has destroyed the simplicity and repose of life; replaced its contentment, its poetry, its soft romantic-dreams and visions with the money fever, sordid ideals, vulgar ambitions, and the sleep which does not refresh; it has invented a thousand useless luxuries, and turned them into necessities, and satisfied none of them; it has dethroned God and set up a shekel in His place."

— Mark Twain

*T*he *Gilded Age* is a tale of human vulnerability—of Americans' obsession with getting rich, of the conflict between public and private morality, of the failures of representative democracy and its guardian the press in the hands of flawed human beings, and of the tension between government and the free-enterprise system. It is also a morality play, subtly suggesting that incessant greed and hollow speculation ultimately crash and integrity, innovation, and conscientious endeavor prevail over the long run.

Twain appreciated that many members of Congress and business leaders were individuals of intelligence, broad experience, and integrity in their private lives but not in the exercise of power in the institutions they led. Many voters seem to agree; they admire their elected representatives and bosses personally but view Congress as dysfunctional and business as mercenary. In Twain's day senators like Stewart and Pomeroy and businessmen like John D. Rockefellers and John Wanamaker were devout Christians advocating high moral and ethical standards, except in the context of the institutions in which they thrived. In modern psychological terms, they applied different moral standards in different cognitive frameworks. In Twain's words, "Morals consist of political morals, commercial morals, ecclesiastical morals, and morals."[1] In his view, "The political and commercial morals of the United States are not merely food for laughter, they are an entire banquet."[2] He elaborated: "Our Congress consists of Christians. In their private life they are true to every obligation of honor; yet in every session they violate them all, and do it without shame; because honor to party is above honor to themselves. It is an accepted law of public life that in it a man may soil his honor in the interest of party expediency—*must* do it when party expediency requires it...By vote they do wrongful things every day, in the party interest, which they could not be persuaded to do in private life."[3]

Twain explained that members of Congress who would never steal their neighbor's money would misappropriate the taxpayer's money to buy votes and "take care of the party." He argued, "They would not dream of committing these strange crimes in private life."[4] Nonetheless, sometimes the aphrodisiac of power and perceived invincibility at the pinnacle of political and corporate life causes the "public morality" to spill over into private lives.

Fallen Angels

In *The Gilded Age*, we see pompous and pious senators succumb to moral and financial turpitude. Dilworthy returns to Kansas to campaign for reelection by the state legislature. The senator makes the rounds of the churches, leading prayer meetings, preaching from the pulpit and teaching Sunday school. He meets with the temperance societies and visits the ladies' sewing circle, where he "even took a needle now and then and made a stitch or two upon a calico shirt for some poor Bibleless pagan of the South Seas."[5] And then, to ensure his successful reelection, he slips $7,000 in bank bills to a skeptical state legislator, who is but one of fifty legislative recipients of Dilworthy's largess.

A Tale of Today

Senator Dilworthy's fall from grace is a story often retold in the nation's capital. Like thunderstorms, Washington scandals intermittently recur, upsetting the natural order. They provide the "exciting topic" of the capital's social life, say the authors of **The Gilded Age**, "rising up like a miasmatic exaltation from the Potomac."[6] Law and order conservatives and deficit hawks—who preach against corruption, excessive spending, and government waste and abuse—serve prison time for accepting gratuities from government contractors, tax evasion, and conspiring to commit bribery. Churchgoing, Bible-quoting, prayer-breakfast devotees who advance the legislative agenda of the religious right become ensnarled in alleged payoffs to silence adulterous relationships, show up on the elite client list of sophisticated prostitutes, engage in adulterous affairs with staffers, harass pages of either sex, or play footsie in airport men's rooms. Neither party is free from media-hyped scandals. The gap between publicly professed and privately practiced morality has been a favorite topic of writers from Chaucer (with his hypocritical Pardoner) to Moliere (in Tartuffe). Sinclair Lewis's Elmer Gantry in 1927 captured the American cultural rendition of the "gift that keeps on giving."[7]

Congress Investigates its Own

In *The Gilded Age,* Congress shows its inability to judge its own. Having been publicly shamed for his attempted bribery, Dilworthy seeks to salvage his reputation by calling for a congressional investigation. No mind that a Kansas inquiry has already found him guilty of bribery and his reelection to a third term has failed. Quoting a fictional press report, Twain writes: "Under the guise of appointing a committee to investigate the late Mr. Dilworthy, the Senate yesterday appointed a committee yesterday to *investigate his accuser.*" For as Twain wrote, an investigation in the hands of the Senate "simply becomes a matter for derision—...amusing but not useful."[8]

In a thinly veiled satire of the congressional investigation of Credit Mobilier, Colonel Sellers explains to the skeptical Washington Hawkins how Congress investigates its own: "In a free country like ours, where any man can run for Congress and anybody can vote for him, you can't expect immortal purity all the time...Sixty or eighty or a hundred and fifty people are bound to get in who are not angels in disguise...but still it is a very good average...There is still a very respectable minority of honest men in Congress."[9] Sellers concedes that Congress never actually "punish[es] anybody for villainous practices. But good God we *try* them don't we!"

Hawkins is not impressed: "Do you think a Congress of ours could convict the devil of anything?"

Sellers tells him not to be so hard on Congress, pointing out that when sworn witnesses and his own confessions proved Congressman Fairoak's (Ames') guilt, Congress "hurled a resolution at him declaring that they disapproved of his conduct!"[10] According to French, an earlier draft of the manuscript made specific reference to Credit Mobilier with Sellers explaining, "All they need is some examples—just a sort of sop you know to throw to the press & the people & keep them quiet."[11] Of all the members implicated in Credit Mobilier, only the arrogant Republican Ames and the Democratic floor leader, the elegant James Brooks of New York, were singled out in a resolution condemning their acts. On matters of ethics, Congress displays rare bipartisanship.

A Tale of Today

In 2010 the House Ethics Committee was embarrassed by the leak of a memo concerning the investigation of thirty members of Congress for earmarking funds for the clients of lobbyists who had contributed to their campaigns. The committee rushed out a 305-page report exonerating the members. Campaign contributions, lobbying fees, and earmarked appropriations were all legal. Despite coincidences in timing and allegedly "incriminating" e-mails, any connection among them was speculative.[12]

In response to persistent press disclosures, Congress has taken its ethics self-policing more seriously. In both houses there has been greater transparency in conducting hearings and hiring ethics investigators. In an initial step toward reform, on March 11, 2008, the House passed Resolution 895 by a vote of 229–182, creating the Office of Congressional Ethics, an independent bipartisan panel of six nonlawmakers to review and investigate possible ethics violations by House members. Its findings were made public and referred to the House Ethics Committee, consisting of House members from both parties.13 As its first act in 2017, the House, upset with the airing of too much dirty laundry, secretly voted to abolish the independent Ethics Office. A few hours later, fa of mwergersollowing the public outcry after the secret vote leaked to the press, the House reversed itself.

The Failure of the Fourth Branch

As a journalist and political reporter, Clemens understood the value of the press as the fourth branch of government. The fictional reporters in *The Gilded Age* enjoyed gossiping about congressional corruption but had little interest in investigating it and reporting the facts. In an 1873 article, "The License of the Press," Twain argued that because American journalism is too beholden to corporate and political interests, it lacks objectivity and independence.[14] He wrote facetiously in 1888, "Take the most important function of a journal in any country, and what is it? To furnish the news? No, that is secondary. Its first function is the guiding and molding of public opinion."[15]

In *The Gilded Age*, Twain colorfully captures congressional interaction with the press. He describes how members leak confidential information to reporters to embarrass their opponents and cultivate favorable stories and how they use the press to shape public opinion on pending legislation. When at the invitation of the speaker, Chairman Buckstone rises to introduce the bill "To Found and Incorporate the Knobs Industrial University," there are mildly negative press reports. Senator Dilworthy predicts that during the course of the debate, the New York papers will editorialize against the bill in increasingly strident terms. "It is just what we want," he says to Laura. "Persecution is the one thing needful now" because even though it will scare off some weak supporters, it will turn strong supporters "into stubborn ones." It will gradually turn "the tide of public opinion" as "the great putty-hearted public loves to 'gush' and there is no such darling opportunity to gush as a case of persecution affords."[16] Dilworthy then explains that wavering congressmen will desert the bill as negative press reports come in, but then, as "public sentiment" begins to change, they will again become staunch advocates of the legislation. As the bill's prospects ebb and flow, legislators react to changing public opinion as shaped by newspaper reports.

Journalism became more vigilant and independent during Clemens's lifetime as "muckrakers" like Nellie Bly, Ida Tarbell, Lincoln Steffens, and Henry Watterson launched investigative reporting. Clemens grew to respect the press when it demonstrated a lack of reverence for autocratic authority, declaring that "irreverence is the champion of liberty, and its only sure defense." He wrote in 1888, the press's "frank and cheerful irreverence is by all odds the most valuable quality it possesses." Annoyed by British critic Mathew Arnold's condescending comments about the American press, Twain complained that the English press keeps the public "diligently diverted from the fact that all [the glories of England are] for the enrichment and aggrandizement of the petted and privileged few, at the cost of the blood and sweat and poverty of the unconsidered masses." In contrast, he wrote, "our press does not reverence kings, it does not reverence so-called nobilities, it does not reverence established ecclesiastical slaveries, it does not reverence laws which rob a younger son to fatten an elder one, it does not reverence any fraud or sham or infamy, howsoever old or rotten or holy, which sets one citizen above his neighbor by accident of birth... To my mind a discriminating irreverence is the creator and protector of human liberty... Our irreverent press [has] made us the only really free people that has yet existed on the earth; and I believe we shall remain free, utterly free and unassailably free, until some alien critic with sugared speech shall persuade our journalism to forsake its scoffing ways and serve itself up on the innocuous European plan."[17]

A Tale of Today

For many media outlets today, irreverence takes on a highly partisan flavor. Members of Congress select friendly media outlets to shape public perceptions and pander to their constituents' biases. Too often the media are co-conspirators, distorting the facts to mold public opinion.

Much has been written about the billions flowing into election coffers, but less scrutiny has been given to the growing industry of corporate, trade association, and advocacy group media campaigns to shape public opinion and influence pending legislation. The effectiveness of the "Harry and Louise" commercials in opposing the Clinton administration's health care initiative launched an era of legislation-focused advertising. Today, media campaigns are often focused on specific markets where vulnerable legislators are sitting on the fence and employ targeted local advertising, emails, and robocalls designed to marshal voter opinion and influence a legislator's vote.

Elected officials then cite opinion polls to explain, rationalize, or validate their positions. As Twain said, "Public Opinion... settles everything. Some think it is the Voice of God."[18]

Clemens understood that the public has little knowledge of the arcane legislative process—replete with traps and hurdles. What the public sees and hears from the press during the long, drawn-out process of legislating, they do not like. They express their disdain in consistently low approval ratings. In 2011 by some polls voter approval of Congress fell to as low as 8 percent.[19]

Today, despite the many sources of expression, the trends are not promising. With more than 600 cable TV outlets, 13,000 radio stations, 255 million websites, and 26 million blogs, the consumer is deluged with fast-breaking not-always accurate information and sound-bite opinions tailored for an ever-narrowing attention span.[20] The plethora of internet outlets increasingly becomes a breeding ground for fake news, some of it coming from foreign sources. Internet vulnerability enables foreign governments to intervene in the US democratic processes in ways that fuel partisan media obsession. Like the newspapers of Clemens's day, many of the new outlets—cable pundits, radio talk show hosts, the blogosphere, Twitter—tend to be overtly partisan. The hyper-competitive media fan the flames of partisanship and polarize public opinion. There are lots of opinions and little fact-investigation. The more negative and sensational the opinion, the higher the ratings and advertising revenues. The race to the bottom in objectivity, fairness, and accuracy is fully protected by the First Amendment. Twain's admonition of newspaper editors sweeps a wider swath today: "The less a man knows, the bigger noise he makes and the higher salary he commands."[21] As he wrote in 1870, "the first great end and aim of journalism is to make a sensation. Never let your paper go to the press without a sensation. If you have none, make one. Seize upon the prominent events of the day and clamor about them with a maniacal fury that shall compel attention. Vilify everything that is unpopular– harry it, hunt it, abuse it, without rhyme or reason, so that you can get a sensation out of it. "[22]

Cost-cutting in the print media has compromised fact-based in-depth reporting and investigative journalism. Unable to compete with the visual media in bringing breaking news to the public, newspapers perform as essential role as an the investigative watchdog on government corruption and incompetence and as an independent source of fact-checking. Yet due to plummeting circulation, some respected newspapers have failed and others have laid off investigative staff. When the media fails to report the facts fairly based on independent investigation, public policy issues cannot be debated on a common factual foundation. When the public and their elected representatives cannot agree on the basic facts, there is little hope for bipartisan cooperation in crafting solutions.[23]

All forms of media can play a more constructive role in establishing a common factual basis and holding public officials accountable in the pursuit of good public policy. But will the people listen? As politics increasingly becomes a competitive sport, is the public interested in facts and analyses or simply cheerleaders who reinforce their innate biases? Does the cacophony of new communications technologies drown out the voices of reason and moderation and leave no time for listening to other points of view or reflective thinking?

Responsible Free Enterprise

In *The Gilded Age*, Twain contrasts the destructive impulses of speculation and get-rich scheming with the rewards of hard work, innovation, and productivity in a dynamic free-market economy unconstrained by European-style class stratification or bureaucratic stultification.

The fast-talking Colonel Sellers is a burlesque rendition of the consummate speculator and schemer. He dreams up schemes to export slaves to Alabama, raise mules for the southern markets, purchase wildcat Midwestern banks, market a solution for sore eyes, and develop a new town at the conjunction of a river and railroad. In each case, Sellers squanders whatever fortune he can amass and ends up poorer than before. To retain the pretense of success, he hides his poverty. Washington Hawkins shivers with cold as he visits Sellers's modest home. The Colonel begins "to tell about the enormous speculation… which some London bankers had been over to consult with him about—and soon he was building glittering pyramids of coin, and Washington was presently growing opulent under the magic of his eloquence. But at the same time Washington was not able to ignore the cold altogether." When Hawkins accidently knocks off the door to the word-burning stove and sees only a lighted candle, Sellers explains that the stove cures rheumatism by giving the appearance of heat. When Washington is served a scrumptious diner of turnips, cornbread, and fresh water, Sellers explains that the menu cures rheumatism.[24] Maintaining the perception of wealth is critical to the art of speculation.

Given the disastrous effect of Clemens's own speculation on his family's finances, his aphorism in "Pudd'nhead Wilson's New Calendar" seems apt: "There are two times in a man's life when he should not speculate: when he can't afford it, and when he can."[25]

By comparison Clay Hawkins is without pretense as he accumulates wealth through hard work in Australia and becomes the family provider. Warner's story of Philip Sterling's hard-earned success is even more compelling. Philip struggles with multiple career choices, but he eventually gains wealth by eschewing a career in law and politics and pursuing engineering. These men live at a time, the coauthors muse, when young men of prominent families "have really been educated for nothing and have let themselves drift, in the hope that they will find somehow, and by some sudden turn of good luck, the golden rod to fortune." Philip "was not idle or lazy, he had energy and a disposition to carve his own way. But he was born into a time when all young men of his age caught the fever of speculation, and expected to get on in the world by the omission of some of the regular processes which have been appointed from of old." Among his contemporaries there were plenty of examples. Philip "saw people, all around him, poor yesterday, rich to-day, who had come into sudden opulence by some means which they could not have classified among any of the regular occupations of life." Philip might have been a "rail road man," a "politician," a "land speculator," or "one of those mysterious people who travel free on all the rail roads and steamboats, and are continually crossing and re-crossing the Atlantic, driven day and night about nobody knows what, and make a great deal of money by so doing."[26] The authors could well be describing the world of finance today—peopled by "financial engineers" who fly around the globe dreaming up new moneymaking schemes.[27]

Manuscript page from The Gilded Age. "Raw Turnips" is substituted for "dried apples" as the meal served by the impoverished Colonel Sellers to Washington Hawkins which Sellers claims cures rheumatism.
Courtesy: Author's Collection

When Alice Bolton (Ruth's sister) urges Philip to become a lawyer and run for Congress, he responds, "The chances are that a man cannot get into congress now without resorting to arts and means that should render him unfit to go there." He continues, "I could not go into politics if I were a lawyer, without losing standing somewhat in my profession, and without raising at least a suspicion of my intentions."[28] Philip applies his engineering and geological talents to the coal mining business. He treats his employees with dignity and respect, but success eludes him and he is forced to lay them off. On the precipice of bankruptcy, he literally tunnels his way, a solitary figure with pick and drill, to a valuable seven foot thick coal vein that will make him a wealthy man.[29]

The Gilded Age is a morality play. It contrasts the abuses and excesses of capitalism with the rewards of diligent endeavor. The astute Clemens and Warner did not condemn all speculation as bad. They understood that risk-taking is essential to economic growth and productivity—and Clemens did more than his share of risk-taking. In the to the British edition of *The Gilded Age*, the authors wrote that "in America, nearly every man has his pet scheme, whereby he is to advance himself socially and pecuniarily." This gives rise to speculation: "It is a characteristic which is both bad and good for both the individual and the nation. Good, because it allows neither to stand still, but drives both forever on, toward some point or another which is ahead.... Bad, because the chosen point is often badly chosen, and the individual is then wrecked; the aggregation of such cases affects the nation."[30]

Speculation, in Clemens's view, was "good" if it involved taking risks to develop new products and services, "contribut[ing] to the world's wealth."[31] The Gilded Age was the age of unparalleled invention and innovation in industry, transportation, and the home. Clemens applauded his father-in-law's coal mining empire, Andrew Carnegie's revolutionary steel-making processes, and the entrepreneurship of inventors like Thomas Edison, Nikola Tesla, and Alexander Graham Bell because they improved the quality of life and added value to the economy, and he rationalized his own failed investments in the Paige typesetter because they were intended to improve productivity. He once said that inventors "were the creators of the world, after God," and "an inventor is a poet—a true poet [which] marks him as one not beholden to the caprices of politics but endowed with greatness in his own right."[32] Hank Morgan counseled in Connecticut Yankee that the first thing you want in a new country is a patent office. "A country without a patent office and good patent laws was just a crab, and couldn't travel anyways but sideways or backwards."[33] In 1871 Clemens patented his self-pasting scrapbook from which he earned more revenues that year than from his books.[34]

Speculation was "bad," however, if it sought simply to make the rich richer by manipulating financial markets, crushing smaller competitors, and exploiting the workforce and consumers. Clemens abhorred the tactics of Jay Gould, Jim Fisk, and Commodore Vanderbilt because they accumulated enormous personal wealth through corruption and the abuse of consumers, workers, and competitors. In *Connecticut Yankee*, Hank Morgan dismisses the money-making potential of knight-errantry: "No sound and legitimate business can be established on the basis of speculation…You're rich– yes– suddenly rich– for about a day, maybe a week: then somebody corners the market on *you*, and down goes your bucket-shop."[35]

Having experienced boom and bust economies triggered by speculative scheming, innovative forms of financing like stock watering, and corrupt practices in business and politics, Clemens faith in the free market was based on innovation in products, not financial instruments, and he condemned illegitimate profits from financial manipulation.[36]

A Tale of Today

A hundred years after the Gilded Age, Wall Street reinvented itself, initiating an era of mergers and acquisitions, leveraged buyouts, junk-bond financing, petrodollar recycling, massive bankruptcies, the dot-com bubble, arbitrage, and derivatives.[37]

Spurred by advances in technology, government deregulation, and innovative financial engineering, a multi-trillion dollar market in mortgage-backed securities, collateralized debt obligations, and credit default swaps, grew without oversight. In 1980 close to 100 percent of all financial instruments were regulated, but by 2008, 90 percent were exempt from regulation.[38] As in 1873, the boom went bust, and global financial institutions were brought to the brink of collapse in 2008.[39] Americans lost nearly $13 trillion in the value of their houses, retirement plans, and investments. Controversial federal interventions by the Treasury Department and the Federal Reserve bailed out large investment houses, banks, and insurance and automobile companies, and federal stimulus spending probably averted another great depression. Some speculators lost fortunes but many were able to recover and enhance their wealth as the brunt of the economic downturn hit the middle class and the poor. The gap between the rich and poor rose to levels not seen since before the Great Depression. Was history repeating itself?

****

Did the ever-skeptical satirist Mark Twain grossly overstate the flaws of the Gilded Age? Did he exaggerate the corruption and incompetence of Washington politicians, the malevolence of the robber barons? There is nary a word in *The Gilded Age* about the unsung heroes of the postbellum era, inventors who revolutionized the quality of life and statesmen who provided the legal framework under which all Americans, regardless of race or gender, would one day enjoy the unfulfilled promise of America's grand democratic experiment.

As a satirist and humorist, Clemens exposed democracy's soft underbelly. He gave birth to a long line of political satire. Satiric negativity undoubtedly contributes to the low opinion polls of Congress and government in general. But then comics need material, and Congress supplies it. Yet there are periods during which Congress rises to the occasion. Ironically, Clemens brief

201

tour of government duty was during such a period. He took little notice—that was not the job of the satirist or skeptical reporter. For democracy to work, the electorate cannot listen only to the satirist. Well-educated citizens—the kind Clemens espoused—must demand concrete achievement and accountable government. Responding to an educated citizenry's nobler expectations, Congress has enacted laws establishing social security, civil rights, Medicare, financial oversight, clean air and water, worker safety, universal health care and welfare reform, to name a few of its milestone accomplishments. A healthy partnership between government and the private sector has spawned the Internet, satellite-based global communication, flat screen television, and revolutionary (if costly) health care.

CHAPTER TEN

Mark Twain Among The Republicans

*"You are right. I am a moralist in disguise; it gets me into
trouble whenever I go thrashing around in political questions."*

— MARK TWAIN

In his youth Clemens had flirted with three political parties: the
Whigs, the Know Nothings (also known as the American Party),
and the Constitutional Union Party, all of which disappeared
after the War between the States. In the pivotal election of 1860,
the critical issue was the extension of slavery into the territories,
which split the political system into four parties. The Republican
ticket of Lincoln and Hannibal Hamlin of Maine swept the
populous northern states and won the election with less than
40 percent of the popular vote. Still a southerner at heart and
struggling with his ambivalence about slavery and the North-
South conflict, Clemens did not vote for Lincoln.

Instead, in 1860 Clemens supported the Constitutional Union Party, composed of former Whigs and Know Nothings. Its slogan was "The Union as it is; the Constitution as it is." Heading the ticket was John Bell of Tennessee, who had defeated former Texas governor Sam Houston for the presidential nomination at the Baltimore convention. The vice presidential nominee was Edward Everett of Massachusetts, who had been president of Harvard University and secretary of state in the Fillmore administration. Clemens's party came in third. The southern Democrats, who came in second, nominated John C. Breckinridge of Kentucky and Joseph Lane of Oregon. As the sitting vice president, the youngest ever to be elected, thirty-five-year-old Breckinridge was the only candidate to support slavery and secession. He became the confederacy's secretary of war. The Northern Democrats' Stephen A. Douglas of Illinois and Herschel Johnson of Georgia came in last. The only state they won was Missouri.

When Clemens arrived in Carson with his brother—a Lincoln appointee—he found himself in the company of a host of Republican officeholders. They were not spared his satiric pen, not even Orion ("the strangest compound that ever got mixed in a human mold")[1], or the staunchly Republican Nevada Supreme Court. He mocked the "exceedingly flowery style" of Chief Justice George Turner, whom he tagged "Professor Personal Pronoun."[2]Associate Justice Horatio Jones was the "bastard offspring of an emasculated Governor and four impotent legislators."[3] Attorney General Benjamin E. Bunker was "the densest intellect." Bunker became the target of a practical joke in which Clemens sought his legal advice on property rights in a valuable ranch that was covered by a fictitious avalanche.[4] Governor Nye, of course, was to become Senator Balloon in *The Gilded Age*.[5] Years later, when Nye was asked why he failed to show up to introduce Clemens at his Cooper Union lecture, he remembered Clemens from Nevada days as a "damn secessionist."[6]

Clemens's views about Lincoln began to change when the president expressed strong support for Nevada statehood. On March 21, 1864, Lincoln signed legislation enabling Nevada's admission into the Union. When Clemens moved to San Francisco, he covered Lincoln's 1864 reelection for the pro-Republican *Call*. Clemens savored Lincoln's comment that his Democratic opponent, General George B. McClellan, was "h___l" on "dress parade" but of "no account in action."[7] An admirer of simplicity of expression, Clemens was impressed with Lincoln's Gettysburg Address and his Second Inaugural Address. He wrote in his *Notebook* in 1866, "Eloquent Simplicity—Lincoln's 'With malice toward none, with charity for all, & doing the right as God gives us to see the right, all may yet be well—very simple & beautiful."[8]

In Washington in 1867–68, Clemens worked for the Republican majority in Congress, and as a Capitol reporter he wrote primarily for Republican-oriented newspapers. With his February 2, 1870, marriage into the Langdon family, he joined the society of northern progressive Republicans. In those days the policies of the two major parties were in some respects the mirror reverse of today. The Republican Party, in the tradition of Alexander Hamilton, supported an activist federal government that protected the industrial base with high revenue-raising tariffs, enforced the voting rights of African American males, maintained a strong navy, assured a stable dollar, advocated civil service reform, and expanded the national transportation system. Republicans were nineteenth century liberals who valued free enterprise, rugged individualism, and volunteerism in caring for the less fortunate. The Democratic Party, in the Jeffersonian tradition, advocated limited federal government, a laissez-faire economic policy, and states' rights. They criticized the high taxes on consumers extracted by protective tariffs and argued that federal surpluses should be returned to taxpayers. They criticized the waste and extravagance of federal programs and objected to federal intrusion into state voting practices.

Uprooted from his southern heritage and increasingly comfortable in his associations with Republican officeholders, newspapers, neighbors, and family, Clemens gradually overcame his anti-abolitionist resentments and, like other former Whigs, felt more at home with the elitist style of governing advocated by the Republican Party. He privately expressed support for General Ulysses S. Grant's Republican ticket in 1868 but avoided taking a public stance. As an owner/editor of the Republican-oriented *Buffalo Express*, Clemens supported the party's economic positions, advocating a sound monetary policy and the recall of the inflationary "greenback" paper currency issued during the Civil War.[9]

Clemens's respect for the martyred Lincoln grew throughout his lifetime. He expressed it with humor and eloquence at a Carnegie Hall celebration of Lincoln's ninety-second birthday on February 12, 1901. After joking about how he had intended to drive General Grant into the Pacific Ocean during his two-week stint as a Marion Ranger, Clemens and the audience turned serious as he explained his conversion in personal terms. As Southerners during the Civil War, he said, "we believed in those days we were fighting for the right—and it was a noble fight, for we were fighting for our sweethearts, our homes, and our lives." Speaking for himself, he added, "Today we no longer regret the result, today we are glad it came out as it did." Of Lincoln he said, "We are here to honor the noblest and the best man after Washington that this land, or any other land, has yet produced." At this time, "The old wounds are healed, and you of the North and we of the South are brothers yet."[10] More poignantly, Clemens told the American Society in London on July 4, 1907, that Lincoln's Emancipation "not only set the black slaves free, but set the white man free also."[11]

As Clemens forged friendships with his Nook Farm neighbors, he socialized among the founders of the Connecticut Republican Party. The Hawleys, the Warners, the Stowes, and the Hookers viewed the Democratic Party as tainted by the legacy of slavery, contaminated by corrupt political machines like Tammany Hall, infiltrated by uneducated immigrants and factory workers, and antagonistic to manufacturing and a stable currency. Local elections were hard fought as candidates endorsed by the Republican *Courant* exchanged vituperative charges with those supported by the Democratic *Hartford Times*. For Clemens's friends and associates, any departure from the Republican line was heresy.

Inauguration of President Ulysses S. Grant in 1869. Chief Justice Salmon P. Chase holds the Bible.
Courtesy. Library of Congress

Twain conceded that he "had been accustomed to vote for Republicans more frequently than for Democrats" and that "in the community" he was regarded as a Republican. Nonetheless, he confessed that since as early as 1865 he had not regarded himself as Republican or Democrat.[12] He claimed to have been "converted to a no-party independence by the wisdom of a rabid Republican," George Hearst, "the father of William R. Hearst...and grandfather of Yellow Journalism—that calamity of calamities."[13] The elder Hearst was a home-schooled Missourian who walked all the way to California to prospect for gold. Investing in the Comstock Lode, Nevada's Ophir Mine and other mining ventures, he presided over the nation's largest private mining company. He bought the *San Francisco Examiner,* launching the Hearst publishing empire.

In 1865 Clemens ran into Hearst at the Lick House in San Francisco, and Hearst offered him the following advice that helped shape Clemens's political views:

> I am a Republican. I expect to remain a Republican always. It is my purpose, and I am not a changeable person. But look at the condition of things. The Republican party goes right along, from year to year, scoring triumph after triumph, until it has come to think that the political power of the United States is its property, and that it is a sort of insolence for any other party to aspire to any part of that power. Nothing can be worse for a country than this...The parties ought to be so nearly equal in strength as to make it necessary for the leaders on both sides to choose the very best men they can find. Democratic fathers ought to divide up their sons between the two parties if they can, and do their best in this way to equalize the powers. I have only one son. He is a little boy, but I am already instructing him, persuading him, to vote against me when he comes of age, let me be on whichever side I may. He is already a good Democrat, and I want him to remain a good Democrat—until I become a Democrat myself. Then I shall shift him to the other party if I can.[14]

Relying on this "wise" advice from a self-made "unlettered man," Clemens claimed he had "never voted a straight ticket from that day to this" and that he had "never belonged to any party" or "any church from that day to this," remaining "absolutely free" in these matters. In this independence," he said, he "found a spiritual comfort and peace of mind quite above price."[15] George Hearst followed his own advice. He ran unsuccessfully for governor of California as a Democrat in 1882 and became California's Democratic senator in 1886, serving until his death in 1891.

Despite the good advice, Clemens stuck mostly with Republican candidates until 1884. In the 1872 election Grant's opponent was *Tribune* editor Horace Greeley, who had left the Republican Party over differences with Grant to run as a Liberal Republican, endorsed by the Democrats. A frequent contributor to the *Tribune*, Clemens claims he met Greeley only once, an unpleasant encounter when he mistakenly stumbled into the *Tribune* editor's office and was told to "clear out!" Clemens was appalled by Greeley's about-face on the issues, questioning the Emancipation, advocating leniency for the rebel leaders and equivocating on women's suffrage. He had criticized Greeley's signing of Jefferson Davis's bail bond in 1867. Like most politicians, Greeley was a master at skillful obfuscation and ambiguity, which Twain satirized by mocking his notoriously illegible handwriting, suggesting that where the language could not be deciphered, the proof readers simply substitute the words "reconstruction" or "universal suffrage."[16] According to Clemens, Greeley complained that women's suffrage advocates Elizabeth Stanton and Susan B. Anthony "had done more than any open enemy to thwart the triumph of women's rights."[17] Under the pseudonym of Ujjain Unyembembe, Clemens wrote a pointed satire during the 1872 campaign, claiming that the famed explorer Dr. Livingston decided to remain in Africa when he learns that Greeley has converted to the Democratic Party and that the Ku Klux Klan "swing their hats and whoop for him."[18] General John A. Logan, whom Clemens had satirized during his capital reporting days, was nominated for vice president on the ticket. Clemens was in London on November 5, 1872, when Grant won a second term. Greeley died three weeks after the election from a brain inflammation, the day before Clemens's thirty-seventh birthday. After Grant's victory, Clemens wrote Thomas Nast, the famed cartoonist whose constant lampooning in *Harper's Weekly* of Greeley's eccentricities and political capriciousness may have turned the election: "Nast you, more than any other man, have won a prodigious victory for Grant—I mean, rather, for Civilization and progress."[19]

Grant's second term went badly, tarnished by scandal, the continuing battle over Reconstruction, and economic recession. On September 15, 1873, the president was Jay Cooke's guest at his Ogontz estate, where the man who won the war feasted with the man who financed it. Three days later, Jay Cooke's bank failed, precipitating the Panic of 1873. The stock market shut down for ten days. Bankruptcies doubled over the next five years, including eighty-nine of the nation's 364 railroads. In 1874 the Republicans lost control of Congress. As Grant's term came to an end, real wages had fallen by 25 percent and forty-three thousand businesses had failed.[20]

Clemens regretted that Grant's record of accomplishments was largely overlooked—his humane and Lincolnian views on southern rehabilitation, his progressive policies on race and civil rights, his sound fiscal and monetary policies, his conservation initiatives, and his advocacy of peaceful resolution of conflicts through international arbitration. The first national park—Yellowstone—was established during his administration. Clemens especially respected Grant's balanced approach to the South. While the president had signed the Amnesty Act of 1872 absolving former confederates, he also signed legislation promoting black voting rights and prosecuted Ku Klux Klan leaders. He shepherded through the Fifteenth Amendment and signed the Civil Rights Act of 1875, mandating equal treatment in public accommodations and jury selection, and he created the Department of Justice under the Attorney General with enhanced powers to enforce civil rights laws.

Yet these accomplishments were overshadowed by the record of scandals and economic reversal. In his final message to Congress, Grant apologized for the state of affairs. In control of the House, the Democrats launched thirty-seven investigations and eagerly anticipated capturing the presidency after a twenty-year hiatus as they hurled charges of corruption. The

Republicans countered by "waiving the bloody shirt," associating the Democrats with slavery and the Civil War. Passions ran high in the hotly contested presidential campaign.

Clemens abhorred the mudslinging that dominated political campaigns. Why would a person of character be willing to endure such malicious demagoguery? Through satire, Clemens showed how the whirligig of politics and media speculation can destroy a candidate's reputation. In an article for the *Galaxy* magazine, "Running for Governor," he wrote that he had decided to become a candidate with a completely clean record because all his opponents were tainted by crime. Upon entering the race, he was immediately attacked falsely for fabricated heinous crimes and immoral acts: perjury in China and thievery in Montana, places he had never been; the slander of his opponent's grandfather, whom he had never heard of; and intoxication, though he was a teetotaler. His reputation was permanently scarred because no one was interested in the facts or paid any attention to his explanations. He withdrew from the gubernatorial race as one "who was once a decent man."[21]

In an article in the *New York Evening Post*, "Mark Twain, a Presidential Candidate," he announced his intention to run as a candidate who "cannot be injured by investigation of his past history." He would reveal everything: how "with heartless brutality" he ran his rheumatic grandfather up a tree "in his night shirt at the point of a shotgun" because he snored; how he ran from the battle of Gettysburg because he preferred to let others save the country; how he buried his aunt under a grapevine that needed fertilizing, dedicating her to this high purpose; and how he planned to make poor people into sausages to feed "the natives of cannibal islands," improving "our export trade." With this open record of his wickedness, let a congressional committee "prowl around my biography in the hope of discovering any dark & deadly deed that I have secreted."[22]

As the 1876 campaign began, the nation celebrated its one hundredth birthday in Philadelphia. The population had grown from 2.5 million to 46.1 million. Despite the economic setback, 76,808 miles of railroad track created a national commerce, and steel production had grown twenty-five fold in the ten years since Clemens had served as senator's aide—from 19,643 tons to 533,191 tons.[23] But industrialization came at a cost. Americans worked the farms and factories from dawn to sunset, six or seven days a week. Child labor was common and the workplace dangerous. Immigrants arrived from Europe in search of jobs, but attempts to organize labor faltered in the recessionary environment. Civil War wounds festered as southerners resisted the carpetbaggers' occupation of the rebel states. Uprooted from the plantations, freedmen roamed the South in search of scattered families and a new livelihood. Attempts to enforce the rights guaranteed by the constitutional amendments were frustrated as southern whites imposed obstacles to voting, Black Code laws were enacted,* and violence against blacks escalated. On the positive side, primary public education was widespread (though absenteeism was high) and 80 percent of the population was literate (only 20 percent of blacks). There were almost a thousand daily newspapers with a combined circulation of 3.6 million, and more than two thousand books were published annually.[24]

As the presidential election approached, Howells urged Clemens to campaign for the Republican candidate Rutherford B. Hayes, his wife Elinor's cousin. A former Ohio governor, Hayes was the kind of courageous leader and intellectual elitist that Clemens could support.** Quitting his Cincinnati law practice in April 1861, Hayes volunteered for the Union army. He was wounded five times (once severely in the left arm at South Mountain in the Antietam campaign). Gallantly leading the Twenty-Third Ohio infantry, Hayes rose to the rank of Major General. While serving in the military he was elected to Congress but would not travel to Washington until the war was over. In Congress, he detested President Johnson and supported the Radical Republicans' Reconstruction legislation.

---

* Laws in southern states after the Civil War restricting the ability of freed slaves to own land, conduct business, move freely in public spaces and, in some cases, establishing vagrancy laws, forced labor, and denying education.

** Hayes was the only Harvard Law School graduate to move into the White House until January 20, 2009, when two graduates—Barack Obama, class of 1991, and Michelle Obama, class of 1988—moved in together.

He considered his greatest achievements the ratification of the Fifteenth Amendment and the establishment of Ohio State as a land-grant university under the Morrill Act. Although he later migrated toward reconciliation with the former rebel states, he insisted that "home rule" for the South be accompanied by a guarantee of equal rights for blacks.   Hayes

At the 1876 Republican Convention in Cincinnati, there was a battle for the soul of Lincoln's party, which Frederick Douglass had described as the "sheet anchor of the colored man's political hopes and the ark of his safety." The power of the abolitionists and Radical Reconstructionists was fading. A new power base had emerged—the financiers, industrialists, and tycoons of the Gilded Age. But reformers and activists were fighting for control. They were led by former Treasury secretary Benjamin H. Bristow, who irritated Grant by launching an investigation of the Whiskey Ring during his administration, and by the radical Indiana senator Oliver P. Morton. House Speaker James Blaine, dubbed by cartoonist Thomas Nast as "the Plumed Knight," and New York senator Roscoe Conkling, arch enemies, represented the emerging power base.

In 1876. William Dean Howells persuaded Clemens to campaign for his wife Elinor's cousin. Rutherford B. Hayes. Howells was Twain's literary mentor and called him the "Lincoln of our Literature."
Courtesy: Library of Congress

Blaine was tainted by railroad scandals and Conklin by ties to Tammany Hall. Hayes was a "dark horse" candidate who came in fifth on the first ballot behind the leader Blaine. Realizing that Bristow, with Grant's opposition, could not prevail, and that Morton was too extreme and in failing health, the reformers shifted their votes to Hayes as a compromise candidate whose reputation for integrity and advocacy of civil service reform made him an attractive if less zealous alternative.

Clemens replied cautiously to Howells's request that he campaign for Hayes, saying he did not think Hayes's defeat was possible, but he wanted the "victory to be sweeping." He added: "It seems odd to find myself interested in an election. I never was before."[25] Clemens should have known that Hayes's victory was far from assured, given the recession and voter disenchantment with the Grant administration's scandals. There was not much difference between the candidates. The Democrat, New York governor Samuel J. Tilden, was a reformer who had defeated the Tammany Ring and sent Boss Tweed to prison. Clemens thought Hayes had a better chance of achieving reforms than the Democrats with their ties to big city machines. Hayes advocated replacing patronage with a merit-based civil service system, federal support for nonsectarian public education (but not parochial schools), a single presidential term (precluding reelection politics), repayment of the national debt, the establishment of honest and capable local government in the South, and the protection of the constitutional rights of *all* citizens.

As was the custom of the day, the candidates did not campaign themselves; it was considered undignified to toot one's own horn. Surrogates campaigned for them. Unable to secure the appointment of his Ohio confidant, Edward F. Noyes, as chairman of the Republican National Committee, Hayes acquiesced in Grant's and Blaine's choice of former Interior secretary Zachariah Chandler to coordinate Hayes's state party campaigns. As chair, Chandler continued the unsavory practice of assessing a portion of each civil servant's salary to finance the campaign (and firing those who would not pay).

Clemens played a limited role in the campaign, supporting Hayes's positions on civil service reform, a single presidential term, enforcement of the post-Civil War constitutional amendments, the repayment of the national debt, and protecting the public schools against sectarian interference. He gave a tepid interview to *The New York Herald* arguing that "the solid men in both parties were equally good and equally well meaning," but when elected both would "shamelessly ignore their platforms" as the Democrats had done when they were "powerless to save us from the ravages of the Tweed gang." He conceded that if Charles Francis Adams, the grandson and great grandson of presidents—"a pure man" and a "proven statesman"—were the Democratic candidate, he "would vote for him in a minute," but that given the choice, he thought Hayes would "appoint none but honest and capable men to office."[26]

In a September 30 Hartford campaign speech after a noisy torchlight parade, Clemens extolled Hayes's plan to fill federal jobs on the basis of "worth and capacity" rather than through "party dirty work."[27] He complained that the "present civil System, born of General Jackson, and the Democratic party, is so idiotic, so contemptible, so grotesque, that it would make the very savages of Dahomey jeer and the very gods of solemnity laugh."[28] Replacing political hacks with competent civil servants was critical to Clemens's concept of a workable democracy.[29] Clemens argued that no one would "hire a blacksmith who never lifted a sledge" or "hire a school teacher who does not know the alphabet." To the roaring, inebriated crowd, he quipped, "We even require a plumber to know something about his business;" he should "at least know which side of a pipe is the inside." After his signature pause, he concluded, "But when you come to our civil service, we serenely fill great numbers of our minor public offices with ignoramuses." Having warmed up the crowd, he continued, "We put the vast business of a Customhouse in the hands of a flathead who does not know a bill of lading from a transit of Venus…Under a Treasury appointment we pour oceans of money, and accompanying statistics, through the hands and brains of an ignorant villager who never before could wrestle with a two week wash bill…Under our consular system we send creatures all over the world who speak no language but their own…mutilated parts of speech."[30] In "The Coming Man," Twain had complained about the poor quality of political ambassadors.[31] Clemens's solution—sever government service from politics and apply the same rigorous standards of education, training, competence, and promotion that are applied in the military service.

Indulging in the negative campaigning he consistently condemned, Clemens created an attack ad against Tilden. The ad depicted a volume the size of a postage stamp, titled "What Tilden has Done for his Country," which would be posted on a larger page entitled, "What Mr. Tilden Has Done For Himself." Clemens also campaigned for the Republican Joseph R. Hawley, who was then running for Congress from Connecticut. Over his distinguished career, this Nook Farmer served as a Civil War major general, governor, senator, three-term congressman from Connecticut, editor of the *Hartford Courant,* and president of the United States Centennial Commission. As a "square, true, honest man in politics," Hawley was occupying "a mighty lonesome position," Clemens wrote.[32] Hawley won. As Clemens later conceded to Howells, "I can't seem to get over my repugnance to reading or thinking about politics, yet. But in truth, I care little about any party's politics—the man behind it is the important thing."[33]

In November Hayes lost the popular vote to Tilden and went to bed election night assuming defeat. Twichell's former commanding general, Daniel E. Sickles of New York, was not so sure. He calculated that if Hayes won the West Coast states and South Carolina, Louisiana and Florida, he would have 185 votes needed to win the Electoral College by one vote. There was sufficient evidence of fraud and suppression of black votes in the southern states to warrant a recount, and the carpetbagger Republicans controlled the state governments. Florida, for example, was so close that if the votes of two precincts were thrown out, Hayes would carry the state by forty-one votes. Disputed ballots in Florida would determine the presidency in 1876 as they would again in 2000. The qualification of one Oregon elector was also in dispute. Although the constitutional path was unclear, Sickles rushed over to awaken the sleeping chairman of the Republican National Committee who cabled the southern states, where the Republican officeholders eventually certified Hayes the winner, although the Florida Supreme Court reversed the governor's certification. The matter was thrown before Congress where the

Democrats controlled the House and the Republicans controlled the Senate. Some members argued the issue should be resolved by the Supreme Court, but instead a Commission of eight Republicans and seven Democrats was established to sort out the vote counts. By an 8–7 vote, the Commission decided to accept the certification of the southern governors and not require a recount, making Hayes the winner.* Southern Democrats in the House threatened to filibuster ratification of the decision, and a flurry of negotiations began between party functionaries as the candidates remained aloof. The Republicans made numerous proposals to the southern Democrats to establish home rule and withdraw the federal troops stationed in southern states. Hayes naively insisted that a condition of home rule was the guarantee of equal rights for freedmen.

Clemens eventually came to view the negotiated settlement as an expedient reversal of Republican principles, which reinforced his growing disillusionment with party politics. Thirty years later in his *Autobiography,* he described "the stealing of the presidential chair" after Tilden had won the 1876 election as "one of the Republican Party's most cold-blooded swindles of the American people."[34] He rationalized, "I was an ardent Hayes man but that was natural, for I was pretty young at the time. I have since convinced myself that the political opinions of the nation are of next to no value."[35]

Despite his autobiographical reflections, Clemens acknowledged that the new president mirrored his own views of good government. Like Clemens, Hayes kept a journal in which he expressed his Whig-rooted philosophy that "the intelligence of any country ought to govern it."[36] In his Inaugural Address, Hayes stressed that "universal suffrage should rest upon universal education," which required "liberal and permanent provision for the support of free schools by the state governments, and, if need be, supplemented by legitimate aid from national authority."[37] Hayes

---

* Like the Supreme Court in *Bush v. Gore,* 531 US 98 (2000), the Commission by a one-vote majority rejected the decision of the Florida Supreme Court, rejected calls for a recount or revote, and upheld the certification of the state Republican officeholders. Was history repeating itself?

called for "thorough, radical, and complete reform" of the civil service, "returning to the principles and practice of the founders of government."[38] Like Clemens, Hayes believed that "he serves the party best who serves the country best."[39] His appointment of Carl Schurz as secretary of the interior and William Evarts as secretary of state bolstered the president's standing with reformers to the displeasure of Blaine and Conkling.

Although Hayes later conceded that his strategy of southern reconciliation did not succeed, he was adamant about using federal power to enforce the constitutional rights of all citizens, especially the right of blacks to vote in the South. He repeatedly vetoed "riders" on appropriations bills by southern congressmen seeking to defund the federal marshals or strip the federal government of voting enforcement powers. The military served seven months without pay because Hayes would not sign appropriations bills with riders restricting his enforcement authority.

After the first state dinner, the First Lady (Hayes coined the term)—Lucy Webb Hayes ("Lemonade Lucy")—decided not to serve alcohol in the executive mansion.* The temperance movement was in full swing, although the president did not support prohibition. When Lucy sought celebrity support for the Illinois Temperance Society, Clemens wrote for the record: "Mrs. President Hayes, Total abstinence is so excellent a thing that it cannot be carried to too great an extreme. In my passion for it, I even carry it so far as to totally abstain from Total Abstinence itself."[40] Like Clemens, Hayes attended his wife's church but never joined any religion. A devotee of Emerson's transcendentalism, he privately considered himself agnostic.

Clemens's disdain for Washington politics never dissuaded him from lobbying for an appointment or legislation that served his interest. On April 27, 1877, he visited Washington to attend a rehearsal at the Ford Theatre of his (ultimately unsuccessful) play *Ah Sin*, which he co-wrote with Bret Harte, although Clemens complained that Harte failed to uphold his part of the

---

* At various times in history, the president's home has been known as "The President's Palace," "The President's House," and the "Executive Mansion." President Theodore Roosevelt officially named it "The White House" in 1901.

partnership as their relationship spiraled downward. During his twenty-four-hour stay, Clemens attempted to get an appointment with President Hayes, bringing with him a letter of recommendation from Howells for the appointment of his frontier friend, Charles Warren Stoddard, to a consular post. Before the election, Clemens had written Stoddard, touting "Hayes' strong literary taste and appreciation,"[41] suggesting that his friend write Howells seeking help in securing a consulship somewhere—a practice that provided authors a steady income with the time to write. The meeting with Hayes was blocked by a White House aide, Colonel W. K. Rodgers, a man of mediocre talent.** Stoddard did not get the appointment.[42] Hayes was circumspect in dealing with favors asked by campaign supporters.[43] He even rejected his wife's request that he appoint her well-qualified brother as Surgeon-General of the Marine Hospital Service, vowing never to engage in nepotism.[44] Unlike his predecessors (and most successors), Hayes kept current officeholders in place until he could nominate someone eminently qualified to replace them.

Clemens was more successful in blocking Bret Harte's attempt to secure a consulship at Nice. The president contacted Howells privately asking his opinion about Harte after he had received two letters from Clemens alleging "sinister things about him." Howells replied that he had heard the same from Mark Twain. Hayes's oldest son, Birchard, wrote Elinor that his father had read the letters and "there is no danger of [Harte's] appointment."[45]

Hayes and Clemens's mutual regard continued after Hayes refused to be drafted for a second term and returned to Fremont, Ohio. Hayes's personal library included *The Innocents Abroad, The Prince and the Pauper,* and *A Connecticut Yankee in King Arthur's Court.*[46] In several journal references to *Connecticut Yankee,* Hayes found it "instructive" but "not equal to Prince and Pauper."[47] He thought it was "Sound on the question of wealth and poverty.

---

* In those days there was no National Security Council, Office of Management and Budget, and a host of "czars" (White House special assistants) shadowing the executive departments. To head his nine-person staff, Hayes selected as his private secretary a man who had failed in the ministry, law, and business and managed to antagonize the press and the public. Of greater assistance was Hayes's twenty-one-year-old son, Webb.

No rule, just and wise, except the rule of the whole people. Our danger is the rule of the few wealthy. These are the serious points of the book."[48] Still troubled by the book's message, he wrote a month later that the story tends "to show the wrong and evils of the money-piling tendency of our country, which is changing laws, government, and morals and giving all power to the rich and bringing in pauperism and its attendant crimes and wretchedness like a flood. Lincoln was for a government of the people. The new tendency is '*a government of the rich, by the rich and for the rich*'" (italics added).[49]

Faced with a severe recession and several devastating strikes during his administration, Hayes conceded he had failed to address "the giant evil and danger in this country—the danger which transcends all others— is the vast wealth, owned or controlled by a few persons."[50] In later years, he became an advocate of government policies "that would prevent the accumulation of vast fortunes." He warned of the dangers of monopolies and lauded the enactment of the Sherman Anti-trust Act, which, though vague and crude, was "beneficent in its results."[51]

As Hayes refused a second term, Clemens joined an ill-advised movement to draft Grant for a third term as president. Grant's supporters, known as "the Stalwarts," organized a major event to drum up popular support for the war hero—a reunion of the Army of the Tennessee in Chicago in November 1879. Twain was invited to be the last of many speakers. He sat on the platform with distinguished generals Sherman, Sheridan, Pope and others. After hours of platitudinous patriotism and flag-waving, a bit of humor was in order. That was Twain's job. His chosen topic—"The Babies: As They Comfort Us in Our Sorrows, Let Us Not Forget Them in Our Festivities"—was a big hit with the president, who sat "like a statute of iron and listened without the faintest suggestion of emotion to fourteen speeches." Twain wrote Howells that when he took the podium after two in the morning, "I shook him up like dynamite & and he sat there...& laughed and cried like the mortalist of mortals."[52]

The heavy burden of Grant's scandal-ridden years in the White House quickly sank the campaign. James Garfield, a congressman from Ohio and Republican floor leader was nominated. Garfield had been a canal boat driver, preacher, school teacher and principal, college professor and president, lawyer, and major general in the Union Army. He had won several early Union victories in eastern Kentucky. Overlooking his involvement in the Credit Mobilier scandal, Clemens wrote Howells that Garfield "suits me thoroughly & exactly."[53] He campaigned tepidly and hypocritically for Garfield at the Hartford Opera House on October 26, 1880, attacking the Democratic Party and its candidate, war hero General Winfield Scott Hancock, for proposing to repeal the high Republican tariffs. He praised Grant for his patriotic willingness to serve again if called upon, and pitched legislation to restore the financially strapped ex-president's army pension, which had been forfeited when he ran for president. Clemens celebrated Garfield's victory at the Opera House on November 2, with somber remarks entitled "Funeral Oration over the Democratic Party." He summarized the Republican sweep in Connecticut with a law and order comment that would become a central Republican Party plank: "The most important part of the victory was the election of Republican sheriffs in seven counties out of eight. That is as it should be. Have officers and criminals on opposite sides."[54] He then wrote the president-elect, asking him to retain his "personal friend" Fred Douglass* as Marshal of the District of Columbia.[55]

In June 1881 Clemens joined Sherman and Secretary of War Robert Lincoln on a milk train winding its way toward West Point. Sherman and Lincoln addressed the gathered crowds at each station stop while Clemens relaxed in the private car smoking cigars. Needling him, Sherman asked whether Clemens had

---

* Douglass had asked Clemens to petition president-elect Garfield to retain him as marshal of Washington, DC, noting sardonically that "it will put the President in good humor in any case and that is very important." Clemens wrote to Garfield: "I offer this petition with peculiar pleasure and strong desire, because I so honor this man's high and blemishless character and so admire his brave, long crusade for the liberties and elevation of his race. He is a personal friend of mine, but that is nothing to the point—his history would move me to say these things without that. And to feel them, too." As US marshal, Douglass presided over Garfield's inauguration and was then appointed as the first African-American recorder of deeds for the District of Colombia.

paid his train fare. When Clemens said no, Sherman cajoled him into earning his fare by joining the celebrities in addressing the assembled crowds. The three men took turns revving up the townspeople.[56]

Like Lincoln, Garfield was born in a log cabin. Like Lincoln, his only prior elective office had been in the US House. And sadly, like Lincoln he was assassinated. On July 2, 1881, while walking through the Baltimore & Potomac Railroad Station at Sixth Street NW (currently the site of the National Gallery of Art), President Garfield was shot by Charles Guiteau, who had been rejected for federal employment. Garfield lingered on through the summer and died on September 19, 1881, likely due to medical malpractice rather than the initial gunshot wound.

Despondent over Garfield's assassination, Clemens resumed his torrent of satire about the "thieves" and "pauper intellects" who controlled Congress and the free railroad passes they received for their generous appropriations. He scribbled in his notebook possible dialogue for a story as he often did: "Papa's been in the legislature. There now! That ain't anything. I've got an uncle in hell."[57] Clemens blamed the pernicious practice of patronage for creating the false expectations that led to the assassination. He stepped up his advocacy for an informed citizenry, favoring the Republican plank of federal aid to education, especially for freed blacks and immigrants, so they could participate responsibly in a democracy. Congress consistently blocked such proposals lest they facilitate the exercise by African Americans of their Fifteenth Amendment voting rights despite the obstacles of literary tests, poll taxes, and grandfather clauses in state voting laws.

Garfield was succeeded by Chester A. Arthur, whom Clemens called "an excellent gentleman with a weakness for his friends."[58] Arthur had been the Republican machine-picked collector of the port of New York, the nation's most powerful federal office, which received 70 percent of the customs' revenues and provided a patronage bonanza of 1,262 jobs. Hayes had tried unsuccessfully to prohibit patronage and campaign assessments at the Custom house and replace Arthur with Theodore

Roosevelt Sr., a reformer. Eventually, Hayes did replace Arthur with a professional surveyor, Edward A. Merit, ironically setting Arthur on a path to the presidency as the machine-picked vice presidential nominee.[59] Arthur's shady patronage practices had earned him Clemens's distrust. Recognizing the climate of suspicion that greeted him after the assassination, President Arthur declared his independence from the fighting factions within the Republican Party. His greatest achievement was the enactment of the Pendleton Civil Service Reform Act, a bipartisan measure sponsored by Democratic senator George A. Pendleton of Ohio. The Act created the Civil Service Commission and provided that federal employees should be selected on their merits after a competitive exam and not hired, promoted, or fired for political reasons.

On November 24 and 25, 1884, Twain and his lecture partner, George Washington Cable, gave readings at the Congregational Church in Washington to enthusiastic audiences. Billed as the "Twins of Genius," they had met in 1881 and, at Cable's suggestion, had begun lecturing together in 1884. After the performance, visitors to the dressing room included Arthur and Douglass. Cable, a Creole from New Orleans, was thrilled to witness the chance meeting of the president of the United States and "a runaway slave."[60] The lecture partners repeated their successful performance at the same church venue on February 28 of the following year.[61] On March 2, Sam wrote Livy from Washington, again invoking his favorite weather metaphor:

> Similarity between Washington and other cities probably doesn't exist. The differences are almost innumerable. The city is big; it is also small; it is broad; it is narrow. It is sometimes wet, sometimes it is clouded with dust. The sun rises early without a smile, thinly veiled and cold; later it burns like Hell; still later the clouds rise up, and suddenly you find yourself engulfed in darkness, wet through the rain—and, as a consequence—your moral state quite probably upset. Before you can open your umbrella, the bad weather has again vanished and everything lies in bright sunshine. You shut your

eyes, deliver a solemn "Thank God," open your eyes again, and holy Moses, its snowing.[62]

During this period Clemens was working with the seriously ill former president Grant on his memoirs. Clemens's publishing company, Charles L. Webster & Co., had contracted to publish the two-volume *Personal Reminiscences.* Dying from throat cancer, the courageous General struggled to complete the book, hoping to leave his wife, Julia, and family an inheritance that the financial failure of his Wall Street brokerage firm, Grant & Ward, would otherwise have precluded. Having resigned his commission and forfeited his pension when he ran for president, Grant was essentially bankrupt. In the last day of the Arthur presidency, Congress passed a bill reinstating Grant's commission and pension.

General Sherman had lobbied hard for the bill. Securing its passage in the House seemed doubtful as the session drew to its mandatory close at noon March 4, but the Democratic speaker Samuel Randall, an admirer of Grant, reconvened the House on Inauguration Day and instructed the clerk to backdate the paperwork. He then urged the senators to reconvene, but it was already a few minutes past noon when a senate clerk climbed up to the clock and turned it back twenty minutes, allowing time for the bill to pass. Sam wrote Livy, "We were at General Grant's at noon when the telegram arrived" and "was put in his hand." It "was like raising the dead." The incoming president Grover Cleveland signed Grant's commission of reinstatement.[63]

To assuage Grant's insecurity about his writing ability, Clemens told him his autobiography was of the "same high level" as Caesar's *Commentaries* in its "clarity of statement, directness, simplicity, unpretentiousness, manifest truthfulness, fairness and justice toward friend and foe alike, soldierly candor and frankness and soldierly avoidance of flowery speech."[64] History has validated Clemens's praise. The 1,215-page autobiography remains in print and is considered among the best memoirs ever written. Sitting upright in a chair all night in his upstate New York cottage, Grant finished volume II and died three days later.

The clear and concise prose of the unassuming hero was an instant success. As Clemens had promised, the best seller more than amply provided for his heirs. Thanks to Clemens's generous contract terms, Julia received nearly $450,000 from book sales.

From their tongue-tied encounter in the White House receiving line in 1870 until Grant's death on July 23, 1885, Clemens and Grant's seemed an unlikely friendship. The antiwar deserter, loquacious self-promoter, and caustic critic of the Gilded Age, Sam Clemens, bonded with the nation's most revered war hero, the taciturn, self-effacing "Sam" Grant, who presided over one of the most corrupt administrations in history. How could this be?

The two men came from middle America and were shaped by the Mississippi River. Grant had lived in the river town of Galena, Illinois, and followed the river south during the war. After several failed attempts, he captured Vicksburg, which led to his command of the Union armies, the preservation of the Union and the abolition of slavery. *Huckleberry Finn,* Twain's greatest work, went on sale the same year as Grant's memoirs, and Grant's courageous completion of his manuscript in the face of insufferable pain and imminent death may well have spurred Twain on to complete his own classic, in which he makes his most eloquent statement on slavery.[65]

For Twain, Grant was the antithesis of the bombastic politicians whose soaring rhetoric belies their menial accomplishments. Grant was a man of few words whose accomplishments spoke for themselves. In Grant, Twain saw a man of character— a humble steward of the nation—whose Achilles' heel was his loyalty and trust of friends who betrayed him, a flaw with which Twain empathized.

Perhaps blinded by his personal and professional admiration for Grant, Clemens viewed the general as above the political fray and a naive victim of the corrupt political system. Increasingly disillusioned with the negativity of partisan politics, Clemens was about to declare his independence from the conventional politics of his Nook Farm neighbors.

A Tale of Today

Twain's observations during his "Republican" period offer valuable insights on contemporary politics. His complaint that negative advertising diverts voter attention from the fundamental issues facing the nation, tarnishes reputations without remedy, and discourages good people from running for office, remains valid in this era of increasingly negative campaigning. In past elections, commercials dramatizing murderer Willie Horton's release from prison, intended to denigrate presidential candidate Michael Dukakis's stance on crime,* and the commercial by the "Swift Boat Veterans for Truth" attacking candidate John Kerry's Vietnam service illustrate how negative advertising can be used to shape the perception of character in ways that are hard to rebut. Negative advertising works. Personal attacks on political opponents are on the upswing in both political parties. In the 2012 presidential campaign, millions of dollars were expended seeking to define the opposing candidate in negative terms. With the victor, go the spoils—increasing public disillusionment with their elected representatives. Both candidates in the 2016 presidential campaign spent much of their time denigrating their opponent in harshly negatives terms, supplemented by the rising phenomenon of fake news and conspiracy theories circulating in the internet as well as leaked emails by foreign interests dominating media time. As a result candidate disapproval ratings reached historic heights.

---

* In 1986 convicted murderer and rapist Willie Horton had been given a forty-eight-hour furlough under a Dukakis Massachusetts program. He disappeared and was recaptured ten months later after terrorizing a Maryland couple. The commercial, portraying a menacing bearded black man, was roundly criticized for its not-so-subtle subtext.

In his letter to Thomas Nast acknowledging the power of his cartoons in election campaigns, Clemens appreciates how humor—whether expressed in cartoons or late-night comedy—can affect the outcome of an election. Many young voters claim that their most trusted news sources are the television comedy satires like those of Jon Stewart and Stephen Colbert. Political campaigns capsulize the "ten thousand high-grade comicalities which exist in the world."[66] Clemens demonstrates how humor can pierce through political spin, holding up vacuous promises and hyperbole to ridicule and reducing a campaign to its pragmatic essence.

Although he later criticized the Republicans for stealing the 1876 election, Clemens's admiration for Hayes's presidency is instructive. Hayes strongly supported the appointment of federal employees based on merit, including political appointees of either party, rejecting appointments solely to reward friends and supporters. Upon taking office, Hayes kept on incumbents who were doing a good job, avoiding a turbulent transition in which high level jobs remain vacant for months.

Hayes stuck by his promise not to seek a second term because he felt that a president could not run for reelection without compromising his ability to put the national interest above party interest. Hayes's proposal for a single six-year presidential term would enable the president to focus on governing during a sustained period of time without the distraction of the perpetual campaign and the public skepticism as to whether his proposals are what is best for the nation or what best promotes his or her reelection.

In Hayes's day presidential candidates rarely left their front porch to campaign, leaving it to surrogates to lead the attack. This preserved a sense of dignity that is too often lacking in presidential politics today. Indeed, it seems that with each succeeding *election campaign, civil discourse plummets further in a barrage of negativity, incivility, and outright crudeness.*

Clemens also admired Hayes's toughness in repeatedly vetoing appropriations bills with riders added by southern legislators that would defund voting rights enforcement in the South. Standoffs between Congress and the president on appropriations riders, with the prospect of an impasse shutting down the government, are not a new phenomenon.* Finally, Hayes warned of the danger of rising income disparity in which the wealthy few are able to co-opt the legislative process to perpetuate their advantage.

---

* Over the years, the president and Congress have fought over appropriations riders—amendments attached to funding bills—that seek to curb executive authority in such areas as environmental regulation, Planned Parenthood, or the enforcement of minority voting rights. If the president vetoes the bills he risks defunding the program or shutting down the government.

The Clemens Family in their Hartford home in 1884. Clara, Livy, Jean, Sam and Susy. Courtesy: The Mark Twain House & Museum Hartford, CT

CHAPTER ELEVEN

Mark Twain The Mugwump

"I simply want to see the right man at the helm.
I don't care what his party creed is."

— MARK TWAIN

I n the 1884 election, Clemens practiced what he preached—character trumps party politics, or "May the best man win." With the nomination of James Blaine, he complained that the "Republican Party has deserted us and deserted itself," even though Clemens claimed that he had not deserted the "Republican Code of principles."[1]

Blaine had been a three-term speaker of the house where he was a forceful leader for a moderate (Lincolnian) approach to rehabilitating the former Confederate states. He supported impartial suffrage and the Fourteenth Amendment. He had ably served as secretary of state under Garfield and briefly under Arthur.

Blaine's policies and experience qualified him for the presidency. But there were persistent allegations of corruption. He had been accused by his opponents of sponsoring legislation funding the Little Rock & Fort Smith Railway and the Northern Pacific Railway, profiting from the sale of bonds he held in each company, and lying about his involvement. They coined the ditty, "Blaine, Blaine, James G. Blaine / the continental liar from the State of Maine."

Clemens was indulging in his favorite pastime—playing billiards, smoking cigars, and discussing politics with four friends on the top floor of his Hartford home—as the Republican Party convention was meeting at Exposition Hall in Chicago. His four Hartford Republican guests were opposed to Blaine and not "seriously expecting" his nomination. Backed up with the deadly facts, the "*Hartford Courant* had been holding Blaine up to scorn and contumely...denouncing him daily" and "criticizing his political conduct."[2] Avid disciples of the Republican *Courant,* Clemens and his colleagues believed that a coalition of supporters of incumbent president Chester Arthur and Senator George Edmunds of Vermont would be able to marshal the votes to defeat Blaine and avoid block defections from the party. Although Clemens had expected little from the New York machine politician who succeeded the assassinated Garfield, he was pleasantly surprised by Arthur's presidency, especially the enactment of the Pendleton Civil Service Reform Act. He said it "would be hard to better President Arthur's administration," but wanted to hear from the rest of the 55 million Americans on the subject.[3] George Griffin, the Clemens's butler and a former slave, stood by the telephone in the kitchen, to receive reports from the convention. He relayed the message up to the billiard room through a speaking tube. Then came the "paralyzing surprise"—the convention nominated Blaine. "The butts of the billiard cues came down on the floor with a bump," Clemens recalled, "and for a while the players were dumb." Henry Robinson broke the silence and said sorrowfully that it "was hard luck to have to vote for that man." Clemens piped up, "We *don't* have to vote for him."

Robinson was appalled: "Do you mean to say that you are not going to vote for him?" "Yes," Clemens replied, "I am not going to vote for him." The men were in shock. When the party chooses a man, they all sang in unison, "That ends it." Loyal party members must vote for the party's nominee.[4]

Clemens had supported Republican candidates for sixteen years: Grant, despite eight years of scandal; Hayes, only to see his agents negotiate away his party's principles to steal the presidency; and Garfield, despite Credit Mobilier allegations and his protectionist platform. Given his longstanding aversion to corrupt politics, Clemens could not take it anymore. He was "bitter with rage against the corruption of Lincoln's once great party," he wrote to a friend.[5] Yet Clemens's Nook Farm associates and literary mentors like Howells were unwavering Republicans. "People seem to think," he grumbled, "they are citizens of the Republican Party and that that is patriotism and sufficiently good patriotism."[6] Clemens argued with his billiard partners, saying that "no party held the privilege of dictating to me how I should vote." If "loyalty is a form of patriotism," he said, "I was no patriot." He added, "I didn't think I was much of a patriot, anyway, for oftener than otherwise what the general body of Americans regarded as the patriotic course was not in accordance with my views." Clemens argued that the difference between patriotism in the American democracy and in a monarchy ought to be "that the American could decide for himself what is patriotic and what isn't; whereas the King could dictate the monarchist's patriotism for him."[7]

Clemens "made no converts." His billiard partners admitted they didn't want to vote for Blaine, but felt compelled to do so. They were confident Clemens would "come around" by Election Day.[8]

Clemens wrote to Howells, who remained adamant in his support of the Republican candidate: "Certainly a man's first duty is to his own conscience & honor—the party and the country come second to that, & never first." He urged Howells to refrain from voting rather than "soil" himself by voting for Blaine.[9] He wrote another friend, advocating that Senator Edmunds run as an independent.[10]

In the voice of Hank Morgan in *A Connecticut Yankee,* Twain later explained that his "kind of loyalty was loyalty to one's country, not to its institutions or its office-holders." He wrote that "institutions are extraneous, they are mere clothing, and clothing can wear out...become ragged." "To be loyal to rags," he argued, "is a loyalty of unreason, it is pure animal; it belongs to monarchy, was invented by monarchy."[11] More pointedly, he declared that partisans were taught that "the only true freedom of thought is to think as the party thinks...that patriotism, duty, citizenship, devotion to country, loyalty to the flag, are all summed up in loyalty to the party."[12]

The *Courant,* which had been making a "tar baby" of Blaine, had an "uncomfortable time" determining what to do. Its editor, General Joseph R. Hawley, was then serving in Congress, and after nine hours of telegraphing back and forth between editors in Hartford and Washington, "at midnight the pill was swallowed." The *Courant* decided to praise what "it had so long censured." It "never recovered its virtue entirely." An active editor, Charles Dudley Warner "could not stomach the new conditions." Clemens reported that Warner "decided to retire his pen altogether" and "kept his vote in his pocket on Election Day."[13]

Clemens was amazed at how quickly Blaine's harshest critics became his staunchest admirers. Within two weeks James G. Batterson, the president of the Travelers Insurance Company, rescinded his vehement denunciations and presided over rallies in support of the party's nominee. The American member of a board of scholars revising the New Testament applied his facility in revising biblical texts. Having repeatedly condemned Blaine's immorality, "it took him only a few days to revise" his position—he now commended the party's "good fortune to secure an archangel as its nominee." Clemens tended to equate religion and party politics. Both demanded blind-faith loyalty, suppressing independent judgment and common sense. For this reason, Clemens proudly proclaimed that he had never joined an organized party or church.[14] The shock of Blaine's nomination solidified Clemens's evolving conviction that political parties like institutionalized religion thwart progress by covering up malfeasance and substituting slogans for the search for solutions.

With the exception of Johnson, the Republican Party held the White House from 1860 through 1884. Reflecting on George Hearst's admonition in 1865, Clemens wrote: "There is a President of the Republican Party, but there has been only one President of the United States since the country lost Mr. Lincoln forty-two years ago. The highest duty of the President of the Republican Party is to watch diligently over his party's interest, urgently promoting all measures, good or bad, which may procure votes for it, and as urgently obstructing all, good or bad, which might bring its rule into disfavor."[15]

In Clemens's opinion, "to lodge all power in one party, and keep it there, is to insure bad government, and the *sure and gradual deterioration of the public morals*."[16] In "the interest of party expediency" politicians by their votes "do wrongful things every day."[17] In his autobiographical dictations, he said: "For fifty years our country has been a constitutional monarchy, with the Republican Party sitting on the throne...Ours is not only a monarchy but a hereditary monarchy—in the one political family. It passes from heir to heir as regularly and as surely—and as unpreventably as does any throne."[18]

In a 1901 speech to the New York City Club, Clemens recounted his boyhood experience with the "Anti-Donut Party." He explained that in electing officers of the local society of the Ancient Order of United Farmers, modeled after the Freemasons, some members were willing to sell their votes for donuts. When he and a few colleagues protested against such corrupt practices, they were dubbed the "Anti-Donut Party." Clemens conceded that he and the other dissenters may well have had their price, but they really didn't like donuts. The "Anti-Donut Party" put up a candidate, who lost the election badly. From this Clemens drew a lesson: "We decided never again to nominate anybody for anything. We decided to simply force the other two parties in the society to nominate their very best men...The next time we had an election, we told both the other parties that we'd beat any candidate put up by one of them of whom we didn't approve. In that election, we did business. We got the man we wanted."[19]

In a more serious vein, Clemens prepared a plan for a "Casting Vote Party" that would force political parties to nominate their best people. He proposed that the "balance of power shall be lodged in a permanent third party with no candidates of its own and no function but to cast its whole vote for the best man put forward by the Republicans and Democrats."[20] The system would force the major parties to nominate candidates of impeccable character with broad-base appeal. He never published the plan, perhaps because the Mugwumps came along in 1884 with a similar intention.

As Paine put it, "if we except the Civil War period, there never has been a more raucous political warfare then that waged between the parties of James G. Blaine and Grover Cleveland in 1884."[21] A frustrated Clemens joined the Independent Republicans—the Mugwumps—an Algonquin word meaning "Big Chief." The Mugwumps did not support any party or platform and did not put up a candidate. They simply voted for the candidate who had the strongest record of acting with courage, integrity and independence. As Clemens put it: "Our principles were high and very definite. We were not a party; we had no candidates; we had no axes to grind…When voting, it was our duty to vote for the best man, regardless of his party name. We had no other creed."[22]

In his exuberance, Clemens claimed as Mugwumps others who defied convention: "Washington, Garrison, Galileo, Luther and Christ." Clemens's identification with the Mugwumps was deeply rooted in his personal experience. During this time, he was writing *Huckleberry Finn,* struggling with his youthful ambivalence about northern interference with southern society and his rejection of slavery– reflecting two unyielding political positions that led to civil war and the ultimate failure of political factionalism. "Loyalty to petrified opinions never yet broke a chain or freed a human soul in this world—and never will," he later said.[23]

Clemens's skepticism about political parties echoed a minority voice from the nation's past. In his farewell address, George Washington warned against creating political parties. He predicted that they would "serve to organize faction, to give it an artificial and extraordinary force; to put, in the place of the delegated will of the nation the will of a party, often a small but artful and enterprising minority of the community." Washington worried that political parties would "become potent engines, by which cunning, ambitious, and unprincipled men will be enabled to subvert the power of the people, and to usurp for themselves the reins of government."[24]

Clemens had witnessed how unscrupulous political bosses in smoke-filled rooms selected candidates whose loyalty was to the party machine. In the general election, the voters were faced with a choice between two inferior candidates, neither of whom was prepared to govern in the public interest. In *The Gilded Age,* as a pattern of bribery is revealed, Twain describes the consequences of a detached, disinterested electorate that yields political power to corrupt and ambitious men of mediocre talents:* "Perhaps it did not occur to the nation of good and worthy people that while they continued to sit comfortably at home and leave the true source of our political power (the 'primaries') in the hands of the saloon-keepers, dog-fanciers and hod-carriers, they could go on expecting 'another' case of this kind, and even dozens and hundreds of them and not be disappointed."[25]

Edmund Yates, a thoughtful English observer of American politics, described Clemens's views: "Mark Twain sees plainly the gravity of the present and future in the United States and accordingly has very little patience with the spread-eagleism and cheap declamations of contending politicians. Probably his political creed is not very different from that of the Independents, a new and still unorganized party, which is daily growing among the citizens of the great Republic."[26]

---

* Twain elaborated in *The Gilded Age:* "In our country it is always our first care to see that our people have the opportunity of voting for their choice of men to represent and govern them....We hold it safest to elect our judges and everyone else. In our cities, the ward meetings elect delegates to the nominating conventions and instruct them whom to nominate. The publicans and their retainers rule the ward meetings (for everybody else hates the worry of politics and stays at home); the delegates from the ward meetings organize as a nominating convention and make up a list of candidates—one convention offering a democratic and another a republican list of—incorruptibles; and then the great meek public come forward at the proper time and make an unhampered choice and bless Heaven that they live in a free land where no form of despotism can ever intrude" (GA, 530–31).

In a November 12, 1905, interview with *The New York Herald*, Twain said: "If you ask me what I suggest as a remedy for the present conditions, I'll tell you that some one, a man of great executive ability...will have to enlist all the energies in the formation of a permanent third party...The sole reason for the existence of this new third party must be to elect the candidate of either the democratic or the republican party who is believed to be best fitted for the office for which he is nominated."[27] Faced with a choice between Blaine and Grover Cleveland on Election Day, Clemens "consummated" his "hellish design" in a public polling place where, in those days, "any spectator could see how a man was voting." Soon his "double crime," not voting for a Republican and voting for a Democrat, was "known to the whole community."[28] As Twain later wrote, "Actually voting for the Democratic candidate was criminal to a degree for which there was no adequate language discoverable in the dictionary."[29]

Applying the Mugwump standard, Cleveland was the stronger candidate—an independent thinker and actor with a record of common-sense liberalism. He was not without blemish. He had paid a Polish immigrant to serve in his stead in the Civil War and had fathered an illegitimate child a decade earlier, but his public record was that of an honest politician who had fought corruption. As mayor of Buffalo, he had successfully taken on the political machine that awarded city contracts to bidders with friends in high places. As New York governor, he fought Tammany Hall, rejected railroad fare hikes, called for an income tax, vetoed "pork barrel" legislation and rejected mediocre patronage appointments. To Clemens delight, Cleveland insisted that government "conduct its affairs with the same efficiency and effectiveness as a private business." He supported laws protecting workers' bargaining rights and regulating worker hours and child labor. He proposed the regulation of the financial markets to protect minority shareholders, complaining that "immense salaries are paid to officers; transactions are consummated by which the directors make money while the rank and file among the stockholders lose it; the honest investor waits for dividends and the directors grow rich."[30]

LIABLE TO GET HURT.

From MINNEAPOLIS TRIBUNE, 14 February 1901.
Bottom caption:"Better quit your foolin', Mark, and go back and work at your trade."

When confronted with allegations concerning his illegitimate child during the campaign—"Ma, Ma, where's my Pa?" the Republicans chanted—he instructed his staff simply to "tell the truth." For Clemens, the paramount issue was integrity in public office, not private indiscretions that did not affect his ability to govern. He wrote Howells: "To see grown men, apparently in their right mind, seriously arguing against a bachelor's fitness for President because he has had private intercourse with a consenting widow! These grown men know what the bachelor's other alternative was—& tacitly they seem to prefer that to the widow. Isn't human nature the most consummate sham & lie that was ever invented?"[31]

When Cleveland won the election in a squeaker, Clemens bragged that the Mugwumps had "elected him." Cleveland's supporters answered the "Ma, Ma, where's my Pa?" chant with one of their own: "Gone to the White House, Ha Ha Ha!" The Cleveland administration did not disappoint. To Clemens's delight, the president declared in his inaugural addresses that he would "limit public expenditures to the actual needs of government economically administered," and would reform the management of government by "the application of business principles to public affairs."[32] The uncharismatic, overweight Cleveland was all business; he refused to cultivate the press, attend their annual Gridiron dinner, or attend baseball games despite his love of the sport. He had been unable to afford a college education, but nonetheless rejected an honorary degree from Harvard. His executive actions lived up to his words. He rejected the spoils appointments system, retained Republican officeholders who were doing a good job, and refused to make appointments based on political service. He canceled Navy construction contracts that resulted in inferior ships and recaptured lands from railroads that had breached their agreements, transferring the land to legitimate settlers. Cleveland vetoed 414 bills in his first term, second only to Franklin Roosevelt's 635 vetoes over his multiple terms—Cleveland vetoed private pension relief bills and legislation to purchase seed grain for Texas farmers. He opposed Democratic populists who wanted to go off the gold standard and Republicans who wanted to raise tariffs. He reappointed the Republican Frederick Douglass as the District of Columbia's Recorder of Deeds, but did little to advance civil rights. On foreign policy, he opposed American expansionism and imperialism.

In his final message to Congress on December 8, 1888, Cleveland expressed concerns about economic trends: "The fortunes realized" by our corporations "are no longer solely the reward of sturdy industry and enlightened forethought" but "result from the discriminating favor of the Government and are largely built upon undue extractions from the masses of people." Like President Hayes before him, he worried: "The gulf between employers and the employed is constantly widening and classes are rapidly forming, one comprising the very rich while in another are the toiling poor."[33]

On September 23, 1885, Clemens wrote to President Cleveland somewhat obsequiously, as he was prone to do with people in power from whom he wanted something: "Every one of us in this town who voted for you last fall would vote for you again today. And would be glad to do it, too, glad to testify that the good intentions, which they saw in you have been ratified by your acts; glad to testify that they believe in you, rest in you, stand by you, & are day by day increasingly proud of you & grateful that you are where you are."[34]

President Cleveland replied thanking Clemens for his "kind sensible, hard-headed words." In unusually candid language, Cleveland acknowledged that he wanted "to do some good in the cause of reform and better government." He thought his "back was stiff enough to withstand the palatable pressure and cursing; but I have every day to guard against my *temper*, lest by an explosion aimed at certain provoking hunters after mice, I should injure a good cause." Concerned about overreacting to the troglodytes opposing reform, Cleveland said he would not want to "injure a vase in an effort to whack a mosquito."[35]

On November 19, 1885, Clemens traveled to Washington to meet with the president. He urged Cleveland to make international copyright "the child of his administration, & nurse it & raise it."[36] Cleveland became a strong advocate of copyright reform.**

---

* The Clevelands had five children, including Baby Ruth, who died of diphtheria at the age of thirteen and for whom the candy bar is named. As a Mugwump who eschewed trading political favors for votes, Clemens could not appropriately seek a patronage appointment from the president, and so on several occasions he wrote to Baby Ruth asking her to discuss some important matter with her father, such as retaining in office a friend who was a Republican consul in Frankfort. President Cleveland would graciously respond on behalf of his one-year-old firstborn, granting the request (MT *Autobiography* 1, 604–05).

In January 1886 Clemens returned to Washington to testify before the Senate Committee on Patents. That afternoon he visited the home of John M. Hay, Lincoln's former private secretary, who later served as secretary of state under Presidents McKinley and Theodore Roosevelt. Hay exemplified the elite man of character and experience that Clemens, like his devoted Whig father, thought should be entrusted with leadership: "When such men come forward, it has a good influence, for it emboldens other men of like stamp to do likewise."[37] Hay introduced Clemens to Henry Adams, the historian, novelist, and journalist, whose anonymously written book *Democracy,* like *The Gilded Age,* boldly displayed the corruption that infested American politics. While Clemens continued to praise Hay publicly, he later was privately distressed by Hay's imperialist policies as secretary of state. Clemens confided in Twichell, "I am sorry for John Hay; sorry and ashamed. And yet I know he couldn't help it. He wears the collar & he had to pay the penalty." Hay took no pleasure in "distorting history, concealing facts, propagating immoralities, & appealing to the sordid side of human nature," but what could he do? "He was his party's property."[38]

That November evening in 1886, Clemens joined a "prodigious crowd" at a reception in the home of General John A. Logan.[39] Logan had been Blaine's running mate. Although Clemens had opposed the ticket, he wanted to publish Logan's memoirs. Clemens was taking a breather from writing and lecturing and focusing on his publishing company, Charles L. Webster & Co. He hoped to replicate the successful publication of Grant's memoirs by contracting for the memoirs of other popular Civil War generals. On December 6, 1886, *The New York Times* announced the publication of *McClellan's Own Story, the War for the Union* by Webster & Co. General George B. McClellan's self-justifying memoirs did not sell as well as Grant's.[40] Clemens was unable to contract for Logan's memoir because the general died on December 26, 1886.[41]

Despite Clemens's less-than-stellar war record, he enjoyed the company of generals. He loved to visit West Point to speak to the cadets, always a lively audience. He continued to cultivate his associations with politicians of all political stripes, although his acerbic wit was neither intimidated nor deterred. At a banquet in New York City on December 5, 1886, he gave a speech that evoked much laughter. He was followed to the podium by the eminent New York senator William M. Evarts. A distinguished Harvard Law School graduate, Evarts had successfully defended Johnson at his Senate impeachment trial and was rewarded with the post of attorney general.* He served as secretary of state under President Hayes. Evarts enjoyed scoring points against fellow speakers, but his "put down" of Twain (according to *The New York Times*) boomeranged. As Clemens returned to his seat, Evarts stood up and thrust both of his hands into his trouser pockets, as was his habit, and dryly remarked, "Doesn't it strike this company as a little unusual that a professional humorist should be funny?" Clemens waited until the laughter subsided and allegedly called out from his seat, "Doesn't it strike this company as a little unusual that a lawyer should have his hands in his *own* pockets?"[42]

In March 1888 Clemens traveled to DC in a push for copyright legislation. He spoke to the House Judiciary Committee, participated in readings by several noted authors that were attended by President Cleveland and the First Lady, and was invited to a White House reception. Clemens also gave a reading at the Old Soldiers Home. Now a global celebrity whose opinions were much sought after, Clemens's schedule of appointments included art patrons, literary societies, newspaper publishers, scientists, explorers, and politicians. He met with the two senators from Colorado, Thomas Mead Bowen and Adair Wilson; Illinois congressman Robert Hitt; Ohio congressman Sunset Cox, then chairman of the Banking and Currency Committee; and the secretary of the Navy, William Collins Whitney. He returned to Washington again on January 31, 1889, to lobby for the copyright bill and spoke to the Norwood Ladies Literary Association on "New Laws and Old Yarns."[43]

---

* Evarts's great-grandson was Archibald Cox, the special prosecutor whose firing during the 1973 Saturday Night Massacre led to the articles of impeachment brought against President Nixon.

Given Cleveland's feisty independence, disdain for patronage, and vetoes of special-interest legislation, he not surprisingly lost his bid for a second term to Republican Benjamin Harrison, an Ohio-born and educated Indianapolis lawyer and Civil War veteran. Cleveland won the popular vote but lost the Electoral College after Tammany Hall got revenge, defeating him in his home state. Harrison's great-grandfather had signed the Declaration of Independence and his grandfather, William Henry Harrison, had been president of the United States for one month, having contracted pneumonia while giving his inaugural address. Having run on a protectionist, high tariff platform, Benjamin Harrison signed the McKinley Act (named after the future Republican president then serving in the House) which raised tariffs on consumer goods, including food products, clothing, and crockery. A 48 percent tariff on imports caused a spike in prices and a surge of consumer complaints. He also signed the nation's first antitrust legislation, the Sherman Anti-Trust Act—intended to rein in the growing monopolies—and the Sherman Silver Purchase Act of 1890, requiring the government to purchase silver for certificates that could be redeemed for silver or gold. Passed to ease the farmers' debt burden, the Silver Purchase Act sparked inflation and led to the financial panic of 1893.

An August 14, 1890, trip to Washington was aborted when Clemens received word that his eighty-seven-year-old mother had suffered a stroke. He left the capital by train for Keokuk, Iowa. He was back in DC by August 23, seeking investments for his Paige typesetting machine from Senator John P. Jones, chairman of the Finance Committee, and others.[44] Jones turned him down, preferring to invest in the Mergenthaler Linotype.[45] On October 28 he endured another forty-eight-hour train trip to Hannibal to attend his mother's funeral.

The failure of the Paige Compositor and his publishing company, among other unsuccessful investments, led to Clemens's bankruptcy and humiliation. With the financial advice of Standard Oil industrialist Henry Huttleston Rogers, and at the insistence of Livy, Clemens planned a global lecture tour and another travel book, *Following the Equator*, in order eventually to repay his debtors one hundred cents on the dollar.[46]

In 1892, running on his reputation for independence and integrity, Cleveland won his party's nomination over a Tammany Hall-supported Democratic senator from New York, David B. Hill. Cleveland selected Adlai E. Stevenson of Illinois as his running mate. The 1892 election was a rematch between Harrison and Cleveland. It was the cleanest, most courteous, and least contentious campaign since George Washington ran unopposed. Harrison did not campaign, remaining at the bedside of his wife, Caroline, who was dying of tuberculosis. Cleveland graciously reciprocated, declining to capitalize on his opponent's misfortune. Cleveland won by a wide margin, in part because the people protested the rising cost of imports resulting from the Republicans' high tariffs.

Mark Twain supported the Democratic ticket of Grover Cleveland and Adlai Stevenson in 1892. Courtesy: Library of Congress

The first and only president ever to serve two nonconsecutive terms, Cleveland likely did not enjoy the second round as much. He was confronted with the stock market panic of 1893, a deep recession, labor unrest, an Hawaiian crisis, and cancer of the mouth. On a yacht in New York Harbor in the summer of 1893, his entire upper jaw was secretly replaced with an artificial device. He survived all these setbacks without compromising his integrity, but he had no interest in seeking a third term. Clemens's respect for the president did not carry over to Congress's Democratic majority, which Clemens said "was made up of cowards." Failing to address the economic crisis, these "blockheads & poltroons" left the country "in a state of intolerable commercial congestion."[47]

For Clemens, Cleveland's two terms validated his evolving theory of politics: choose character and integrity over platform and party. Cleveland's moderate views of limited government, fiscal responsibility, monetary stability, noninterventionist foreign policy and corruption-free administration were consistent with Clemens's "limited democracy" views. Neither party had a monopoly on good governance by well-qualified, responsible public servants. In his *Autobiography*, Twain tells of writing to Cleveland after his retirement from public office:

> HONORED SIR:—Your patriotic virtues have won for you the homage of half the nation and the enmity of the other half. This places your character as a citizen upon a summit as high as Washington's...Where the votes are all in a man's favor the verdict is against him. It is sand and history will wash it away. But the verdict for you is rock and will stand.[48]

The letter displays another presidential virtue as Clemens saw it—courage. Effective leadership means taking courageous stands on issues even though they are unpopular with a large segment of the population. A leader who holds up his finger to test the shifting breezes of fickle public opinion lacks the requisite character for governance. On occasion presidents must risk public disapproval, even anger. Cleveland sacrificed his first bid for reelection, but his courageous leadership was ultimately vindicated.

Clemens's support of Cleveland did not convert him to the Democratic Party, as the 1896 and 1900 elections would show. The populists' "free silver" wing captured the Party with the candidacy of William Jennings Bryan. The big business, imperialist, expansionist wing of the Republican Party nominated William McKinley. The bitterly contested all-out battle of 1896 was the polar opposite of the 1892 campaign. Clemens was out of the country for most of 1896, following the equator on his lecture tour to pay off his bad business bets. This offered a convenient excuse for sidestepping a campaign in which he disliked both candidates.

Tragedy struck again on August 18, 1896, when he learned while in England that his favorite daughter Susy had died of spinal meningitis at the age of twenty-four. Depressed and blaming himself for his long absence when Susy was in need, Clemens wondered how a parent can "receive a thunder-stroke like that and live."[49] He lost what little interest he had in the forthcoming election and McKinley's victory.

The 1900 election was a rematch between McKinley and Bryan. Invoking the Mugwump principle, Clemens detested both candidates. Bryan's free silver, populist policies were unsafe. McKinley's military excursion into the Philippines was naked imperialism. McKinley rode easily to victory, riding on the improved economy and the US victory in the Spanish-American war with the youthful Teddy Roosevelt on the ticket. Clemens told the City Club of New York in a January 4, 1901, speech on municipal corruption that "I just didn't vote for anybody." He said he had kept the vote, and kept it "clean, ready to deposit at some other election." He wasn't about to cast his vote "for any wildcat financial theories, and it wasn't cast to support the man who sends our boys as volunteers out into the Philippines to get shot down under a polluted flag."[50] He wrote a friend that if he had been in the country two months before the election, he "would have gone on the stump against *both* candidates." He wished "the public would lynch both of those frauds."[51]

Clemens had had it with political parties. Shrilly proclaiming platitudes to reinforce voter prejudices, the parties exaggerated and exacerbated their differences, painting their principles as true and good and their opponents as false and evil. By failing to listen to, respect, or even tolerate their opponent's positions, they forced policy into extreme positions that inhibited pragmatic compromises designed to draw the best from political debate. Parties substituted dogma for genuine inquiry, fostering a herd mentality. Twain wrote:

> It is desire to be in the swim that makes successful political parties. There is no higher motive involved…The average citizen is not a student of party doctrines, and quite right; neither he nor I would ever be able to understand them. If you should ask him to *explain*– in intelligible detail– why he preferred one of the coin-standards to the other, his attempt to do so would be disgraceful. The same with the tariff. The same with any other large political doctrine; for all large political doctrines are rich in difficult problems– problems that are quite above the average citizen's reach. And that is not strange, since they are also above the reach of the ablest minds in the country; after all the fuss and all the talk, not one of those doctrines has been conclusively proven to be the right one and the best.
>
> When a man joins a party, he is likely to stay in it. If he changes his opinion– his feeling, I mean, his sentiments– he is likely to stay anyway; his friends are of that party.[52]

In frustrated hyperbole, Twain summed up his Mugwump views in 1907: "All Democrats are *insane,* but not one of them knows it; none but the Republicans and Mugwumps know it. All the Republicans are *insane,* but only the Democrats and Mugwumps can perceive it. The rule is perfect; *in all matters of opinion our adversaries are insane.*"[53]

From time to time, there were rumors that Clemens would be drafted for public office, perhaps inspired by his satirical essays about running for governor or president. On July 27, 1876, *The*

Chicago Times reported that Clemens was being considered as an independent candidate for mayor of Hartford and had intimated he would accept the nomination. The paper opined that as a substantial "property owner," he would provide a "decent police force," and would "not be the tool of any caucus or set of politicians."[54] In January 1878 *The New York Sun* ran two bogus interviews alleging that Twain had become editor of the *Courant* and planned to run for governor of Connecticut. In 1880 a rumor was widely circulated in the newspapers that he was contemplating a run for Congress. Despite the urging of John Hay and Mary Fairbanks, his Cleveland mentor from *Quaker City* days, an annoyed Clemens vehemently denied any interest in public office, preferring "to call the plays from the sidelines." He wrote Fairbanks, "I have never yet coveted a seat in Congress—or in any other place where one must be always servant & never master."[55] The press continued to speculate, suggesting growing support for the aging Clemens as a presidential candidate, to which he replied: "No matter how healthy a man's morals may be when he enters the White House, he comes out again with a pock-marked soul."[56]

On the other hand, when a reporter suggested that he run for governor of New York, he replied, "I am the real man. I am sure I would make a great Governor."[57] When *The New York Herald* wrote in 1906 that if either of the New York senators were to resign, Twain would be a possible successor, Clemens called this "the most gigantic compliment I ever received."[58] These statements seemed inconsistent with his remark the following January that "We have lately sent a United States Senator to the penitentiary, but I am quite well aware that of those that have escaped this promotion there are several who are in some regards guiltless of crime—not guiltless of all crimes, for that cannot be said of any United States Senator, but guiltless of some kinds of crimes."[59] In *The Gilded Age*, Twain described a notorious burglar who took offense at a statement that "he had served one term in the penitentiary and also one in the US Senate," complaining that the "latter statement is untrue and does me great injustice."[60]

Throughout his life Clemens's condemnation of political corruption was at war with his need to be liked and respected by powerful lawmakers and to have influence over them. In January 1907 he was dragooned into attending a dinner at the Union League Club in honor of the notoriously corrupt Montana senator William Andrews Clark. The sixty-eight-year-old "copper king" made his fortune through ruthless business tactics and bribed his way into the US Senate—"I never bought a man who wasn't for sale," he rationalized. Considering Clark about "as rotten a human being" as can be found "anywhere under the flag," and the "most disgusting creature that the republic has produced since Tweed's time," Clemens sat silently fuming, trapped at the head table while the pompous senator smilingly absorbed the praise heaped upon him. Twain conceded in his autobiographical dictations that he was "willing to waive moral rank and associate with the moderately criminal of the Senators," but he had "to draw the line" with Clark. Unable to vent his frustration publicly lest he risk his influence among the well-connected, Clemens, as he so often did, took revenge in his dictations, which he would ban from publication until well after his death. He wrote that the jailbird's radiant smile as his worshipers broke out in grateful applause would serve him well "when Satan gives him a Sunday vacation in the cold storage vault."[61]

At an early age, Clemens had become intrigued by the human dimensions of politics. He would judge political leaders not by what they promised and proclaimed but by what they did—what they accomplished and how they did it. Speaking in parables, as in story of the anti-donut party, Clemens laid out his political philosophy: The greatest threat to representative democracy is corruption, which can take many forms, and therefore in politics character is everything. The purpose of politics is to address issues and solve problems in the public interest, not for personal aggrandizement or to advance party prospects, principles, or platforms. As he said in his New York City Club speech, "Principles aren't of much account anyway, except at election-time. After that you hang them up to let them season."[62] Promises made to garner votes in the heat of a campaign are worthless compared to a consistent record of candor, courage, and integrity.

A Tale of Today

Clemens admired the Democrat Cleveland because of his record of fighting political machines and corrupt legislatures. While the Republicans focused on his peccadillos, Cleveland focused on the issues of responsible governance. As president, Cleveland courageously bucked his party's leaders and public opinion, vetoing hundreds of special-interest bills and eschewing patronage to appoint qualified officials of either party. It cost him his reelection. Undervalued by historians, in Clemens view, Cleveland epitomized the quality of courageous, independent leadership that places governing above politics—a quality that seems all too rare in this age of the perpetual campaign.

Clemens's idealized view of the legislature in a representative democracy consists of accomplished men who thoughtfully debate the issues of the day, applying their practical experience and knowledge of history, as they forge consensus in the public interest—a vision he believed was shared by the founders. His mature, expanded vision embraced thoughtful men of color and women. He once said that "if women could vote, each party would feel compelled to put up the best candidate it could or take the risk of being voted down by the women."[63]

Clemens detested elected representatives who put "loyalty to party above loyalty to country," who manipulated parliamentary procedures for tactical advantage, and who suppressed their conscience to advance a political agenda by parroting party platitudes. The problem with such legislators and the voters who elect them, he complained is "that the only true freedom of thought is to think as the party thinks; that the only true freedom of speech is to speak as the party dictates; that the only righteous toleration is toleration of what the party approves; that patriotism, duty, citizenship, devotion to country, loyalty to flag, are all summed up in loyalty to party."[64]

What would Clemens think of candidates for Congress today who sign pledges solicited by special-interest organizations (e.g., the Taxpayer Protection Pledge, the Pro-Life Presidential Leadership Pledge, or the Family Leaders' Fourteen-Point Promise)? Why would an elected representative tether his or her conscience to a platitude, relinquishing the right to engage in thoughtful inquiry, analysis, and independent action and the ability to compromise—the pulse of a vibrant democracy?

Blaine's nomination in 1884 simply reaffirmed Clemens's long-held view that when the political bosses choose the party's candidates, the voters are often presented with inferior candidates selected for their party loyalty rather than their ability to govern. Election campaigns, like the great prize fight, are contests in which negative blows are hurled and fundamental issues ignored.

Joining the Mugwumps, Clemens advocated an independent voting bloc that would examine the record, experience, and character of the nominees and throw its support to the candidate with the superior ability to govern in the public interest. Over time the parties would get the message and nominate stronger candidates. This does not mean that issues were unimportant to Clemens. They were vitally important. But Clemens thought that because political campaigns and party platforms trivialized and distorted the issues, a candidate's record was a far better indicator of how he would govern.

In today's perpetual campaign, the parties—advised by consultants and pollsters—seek to portray a nation at a perilous crossroads: Will America return to the halcyon days of dynamic free enterprise unfettered by the heavy bureaucratic hand, or will America refashion itself on the static model of European states? While perhaps making for good drama, this debate does little to address the real issues of economic growth and job creation in an interconnected, intensely competitive and increasingly automated global economy, the burden of out-of-control budgets and burgeoning federal debt, protecting the nation's security cost-effectively through global cooperation, and a Congress captive to moneyed interests. Yet these are the issues that concern the American people and are reflected in grassroots movements from the Tea Party to Occupy Wall Street.

Instead of addressing these issues, the long and drawn out, party-focused primary process polarizes the nation, empowers the more extreme activists within each party, and rewards loyalty to party principles over pragmatic problem solving and consensus building. Low voter turnout during the primaries often results in the nomination of candidates who reflect the extreme views of a small minority of voters.

*Reflecting on recent "toxic levels of hyper-partisanship and legislative dysfunction gripping American politics," **New York Times** op-ed contributor Phil Keisling has suggested abolishing party primary elections.[65] He argues that primaries are characterized by "abysmal voter turnout, incessant waves of shrill, partisan invective; and legions of pandering politicians making blatant appeals to party extremists." Although primaries were intended as a reform, replacing the smoke-filled backrooms in which candidates were anointed, they have had the unintended consequence of giving small, vocal minorities in the extreme wings of both political parties inordinate power in selecting candidates for public office. In the 2006 New York State primary, for example, only 5 percent of those who were registered voted. Keisling proposed a national, fully open primary in which all candidates of all parties would run. The general election would be a runoff of the top two. In 2010, 54 percent of California voters adopted Proposition 14, which requires, effective in 2012, that all candidates for federal and state office, other than the presidency, run* *in a single, open primary. The top two vote-getters will meet in a runoff election, regardless of political party. Louisiana and Washington State have similar top-two primary systems.*

American voter frustration with both major parties is reflected in the growing number of voters who consider themselves independent, which increased from 29 percent in 2000 to 42 percent in 2016. Yet in thirty-one states, one or both party primaries are restricted to party members. If independents were able to vote in either party primary, candidates might broaden their message to reach a larger constituency, better preparing them to serve their entire district if elected rather than an ideological minority. Some states allow cross-over voting (Democrats may vote in the Republican primary and vice versa), but this could cause mischief as members of one party in an uncontested primary could cross over and vote for the weakest candidate in the opposition party.

Finally there is always the third-party option—of which Americans Elect is a recent example—offering all registered voters an opportunity to shape the platform and select candidates online in a virtual convention in cyberspace. Another group called No Labels, which is supported by Starbucks CEO Howard Schultz, discourages contributions to parties and candidates and promotes ideology-free cooperative problem-solving across party lines.[66] In this respect it is like the Mugwumps.

Twain's emphasis on character and record over campaign rhetoric and party platforms may naively ignore the diverging visions of the political parties, which reflect a substantial cultural divide. While it may be difficult to predict how a candidate will actually govern midst the campaign haze of negativity, fake news and prevarication, there can be no doubt today that elections have consequences. The surprise victory of Donald Trump in 2016 reflects to some extent the frustration of working men and women who felt left behind by globalization and ignored by a dysfunctional Congress and an out of touch federal bureaucracy. The fact that voters in the rust belt turned to a nonpolitician businessman also reflects, as documented by many opinion polls, dissatisfaction with politicians generally. A number of voters who had voted for Obama in 2008, hoping for change in the status quo, voted for Trump in 2016 as their expectations faltered. In his willingness to take on the establishment in both parties, Trump may well be the first "independent" candidate in modern history to win a presidential election. It remains to be seen how Trump will deliver on his promise to restore good paying domestic jobs and "drain the Washington swamp."

CHAPTER TWELVE

The Seeds Of Democracy

"Its name is Public Opinion. It is held in reverence. It settles everything. Some think it is the Voice of God."

— Mark Twain

As the most peripatetic writer of his time, Clemens's views of democracy were shaped in the hundreds of cities, towns, and hamlets he visited or lived in throughout the United States and abroad. He wrote his mother on June 1, 1867, "All I do know or feel, is, that I am wild with impatience to move—move—Move!"[1] An acute observer of human nature with an ear for the vernacular, he observed the American democratic experiment—its promise and its flaws—from the grass roots to the corridors of power. He could compare American culture, society, and politics to Europe, Asia, and other continents.

Twain's legacy is a stronger and more tolerant democracy. As a writer and lecturer, he gave voice to the silent aspirations of a pluralistic populace. As a satirist he pierced through pious platitudes and patriotic slogans to the essence of the Republic—to its enduring values and unfulfilled potential. As a humorist he laughed at the icons and traditions that Americans hold so dear lest we all take ourselves too seriously and forget that we are a work in progress, plodding toward a blurry vision of a more perfect nation. As a commentator, he challenged the myth of American exceptionalism, our self-image as the shining city on the hill, morally superior to other nations and cultures. America had to earn its greatness by responsible participation in democratic self-government and the world community.

No national hero or creed was off-limits. In "A New Biography of Washington," he skewered the myth that young George could not tell a lie. Washington sets a bad example, Twain complained, as all boys learn to lie at an early age.[2] Could democracy function if elected officials from diverse regions with polarized opinions always spoke the unvarnished truth? And Ben Franklin, of course, did many great things to honor his country around the world, but in "The Late Benjamin Franklin," Twain lampoons how Ben "prostituted his talents to the invention of maxims and aphorisms calculated to inflict suffering upon the rising generation of all subsequent ages." What teenager does not bemoan his mother's recitation of "early to bed, early to rise...?"[3]

In a Fourth of July speech in London in 1872, Twain praised America as "a great and glorious land": "A land which has developed a Washington, a Franklin, a William M. Tweed, a Longfellow, a Motley, a Jay Gould, a Samuel C. Pomeroy, a recent Congress which has never had its equal—(in some respects) and a United States Army which conquered sixty Indians in eight months by tiring them out—which is much better than uncivilized slaughter, God knows."[4]

The juxtaposition of the revered and tainted was a more honest rendering of American history than is usually recounted at

July Fourth celebrations.* Speaking in a similar vein in December 1881 to the New England Society of Philadelphia, a group of Puritan descendants, Twain questioned why we should celebrate the *Mayflower* tribe. After all, he complained, they had "skinned alive" his Indian ancestor. He then claimed as ancestors the Quakers, the Salem witches, and the African slaves, all of whom had been exiled, murdered, or enslaved by the Society's ancestors. Typical of his backhanded praise, he said, "Your ancestors broke forever the chains of political slavery and gave the vote to every man in this wide land, excluding none!—except those who didn't go to the orthodox church." Contrasting the Society's Puritan descendants to the multiethnic society America had become, Twain boldly suggested that Plymouth Rock be sold and the Society disbanded.[5] The speech was an insightful allegory of a nation in transition in the late nineteenth century. America was growing out of its Calvinist roots, dominated by white Anglo-Saxon Protestant males, to embrace immigrant populations and freedmen. In the last half of the twentieth century it would become more of a meritocracy—under the law all races and genders would potentially have an equal opportunity to succeed. By 2040 it is expected to become a pluralistic collage of minorities— Americans of European heritage no longer in the majority.

Clemens readily acknowledged that American democracy did not spring full-grown from the founding fathers' vision. Our self-styled grand republic was deeply rooted in English history, with a common language, law, and literature. He called the Magna Carta the first Fourth of July. In fact he thought there were five July Fourths, the others being the Petition of Right, the colonial protest of no taxation without representation, the Declaration of Independence, and the Emancipation Proclamation. All but the

---

* An exception is Frederick Douglass's speech on July 5, 1852, in Rochester, New York, "The Meaning of the Fourth for the Negro," where after paying due respect to the founding fathers, he describes what Independence Day means to a slave: "to him your celebration is a sham; your boasted liberty an unholy license; your national greatness, swelling vanity; your sounds of rejoicing are empty and heartless; your denunciation of tyrants, brass-fronted impudence...There is not a nation on earth guilty of practices more shocking and bloody than are the people of the United States at this very hour."

last were made by British subjects. He considered it important that immigrant populations accept the common bonds and values that evolved from our English heritage.[6]

Through fiction Twain expresses most eloquently the philosophy that underlies his political views. In *Tom Sawyer* and *Huckleberry Finn,* he extols freedom of individual conscience and action– regardless of pedigree or education– expressed in irreverence for conventional wisdom and established institutions. In *The Prince and the Pauper* and *Pudd'nhead Wilson,* he illustrates the injustice of distinctions based on class and race. In each case, he ultimately acknowledges that freedom of conscience and the protection of the rights of minorities and dissenters depends upon a framework of just laws.

Twain's most powerful exposition of democratic values is found in *A Connecticut Yankee in King Arthur's Court,* published in 1889. Twain provides a fictionalized account of efforts to create a democratic republic out of the English feudal system. In selecting Thomas Mallory's *Le Morte d'Arthur* and Camelot as his destination, Twain targets the mythical foundation of the British Empire from which arises the divine right of kings, nobility, chivalry, and colonialism. With biting satire, he condemns a clueless inherited aristocracy, an oppressive established church, a docile peasantry, and unjust laws that incarcerate prisoners indefinitely without trial for trivial "offenses." Twain's alter-ego Hank Morgan time-travels from nineteenth century Connecticut to sixth century England, introducing guns, the telegraph, the telephone, newspapers, railroads, and soap. As King Arthur's sidekick, known as the "Boss," he sees democracy and capitalism as integrally interrelated. He naively believes that technology will prepare the way for democratic government. By introducing newspapers and communications technology, he attempts to empower the common people who are oppressed like "the French before the memorable and blessed Revolution which swept a thousand years of such villainy away in one swift tidal wave of blood." More than a century before the Internet, Clemens understood the power of technologies to break down autocratic barriers that stifle the competition of ideas. Morgan believes the suppressed masses will become informed citizens, elect their own leaders, organize the workers and participate in a healthy democracy and competitive free market. Twain's medieval "spring awakening" comes to a disturbing end. The people of the sixth century are not ready for democratic self-government. Technology alone cannot change human nature. Infected with the speculative fever of modern markets, the economy crashes. Armed with the weaponry of modern technology, civilization is crushed.[7]

Clemens's passion for the revolt of the oppressed masses against the monarchy dated back to Hannibal when he found a leaf from a book on Joan of Arc floating along the street. He read Thomas Carlyle's *French Revolution* at least eight times. "One of the greatest creations that ever flowed from a pen," he wrote his friend Mary Fairbanks,[8] as he filled its margins with critical notations. Another favorite was Thomas Paine's *Rights of Man.* Responding to a letter from Howells complimenting *A Connecticut Yankee,* Clemens wrote: "I am glad you approve of what I say about the French Revolution. Few people will. It is odd that even to this day Americans still observe that immortal benefaction through English and other monarchical eyes...Next to the 4th of July and its results, it is the noblest and holiest thing and the most precious that has ever happened on this earth."[9] While he didn't like the French and their culture, he applauded their rejection of monarchy. Clemens admitted to Howells that when he read the *French Revolution* in 1871, he was a Girondin, but as he reread the book through the years, he became a Jacobin, and then a Marat Sans-culotte. The innate rebel within the young Clemens who empathized with society's underdogs was maturing into the radical voice of the senior Twain, champion of the oppressed.**

Although he never hesitated to criticize its imperfections, Clemens remained an ardent supporter of American democracy,

---

* The Girondins were moderate bourgeois revolutionaries who were overthrown by the Jacobins instigating the reign of terror. Jean-Paul Marat was a fiery defender of the radical sans-culottes, the lower classes of urban workers and peasants. Clemens's aversion to monarchies permeates his writings from the Duke and the Dauphin in *Huckleberry Finn* to *Joan of Arc* and his soliloquies on Czar Nicholas and King Leopold. When Emperor Dom Pedro II of Brazil abdicated in 1889, he wrote Howells: "These are immense days! Republics & rumors of republics, from everywhere on earth" (Howells Letters, 290).

especially against foreign critics. Effective democracy requires an informed, involved electorate. For Clemens, this means more than simply a passive knowledge of the issues and the candidates qualifications for public office. It requires active engagement in the political process, citizen advocacy for accountable government and corporate responsibility, and a willingness to challenge political banalities, party pressures, and bureaucratic arrogance and incompetence.

Skeptical of universal suffrage, Clemens thought impoverished and uneducated voters could too easily be bought—a distrust of majority rule based on his experiences with corruption at all levels of government. He feared that uninformed voters would be manipulated and oppressed by political machines, elect scoundrels to public office, and be swayed by empty slogans and demagoguery, acquiescing in policies and practices that were not in the public interest or for that matter, in their own interest.[10] He was amazed how uneducated poor people often voted against their own self-interest. In *Connecticut Yankee* he compared the feudal serfs to the "poor whites" in the antebellum South "who were always despised and frequently insulted by the slave-lords around them," and yet "were ready to side with the slave-lords in all political moves." Even though only 5 percent of southern whites owned slaves, the other 95 percent shouldered their "muskets and pour[ed] out their lives" to prevent the destruction of slavery, "the very institution that degraded them."[11]

In England in 1874, Clemens praised the London plan to limit the franchise to taxpayers, noting that "there is no law here which gives a useless idler the privilege of disposing of public moneys furnished by other people."[12] "Ignorance, intolerance, egotism, self-assertion, opaque perception, dense and pitiful chuckle-headedness—and an almost unconsciousness of it all," Twain wrote, "it is of this...that voters are made. And such is the primal source of our government! A man hardly knows whether to swear or cry over it."[13]

Voters need to speak out intelligently; otherwise the corrupt or noisy fringes will dominate the news and distort the perception of public opinion. The vast majority, occupying the mainstream of the political spectrum, too often acquiesces in the "silent-assertion lie that no wrong was being done [to the] persecuted and unoffending." Clemens wrote that "the universal conspiracy of the silent-assertion lie [is] hard at work always and everywhere." Silence keeps alive "despotisms and aristocracies and chattel slaveries, and military slaveries, and religious slaveries."[14] Twain lamented, "It is by the goodness of God that in our country we have those three unspeakably precious things: freedom of speech, freedom of conscience, and the prudence never to practice either of them."[15] For free speech in America "ranks with the privilege of committing murder: we may exercise it if we are willing to take the consequences....Murder is sometimes punished, free speech always– when committed."[16]

Traveling in and living throughout the United States and abroad made Clemens a better citizen, enabling him to rise above the parochial confines of his rural Midwest upbringing. His familiarity with other cultures instilled in him a deep appreciation for America's potential and impatience with its stubborn failure to realize it. He railed against provincialism, prejudice, and ignorance that characterized the majority of voters, noting that "you never saw a bigoted, opinionated, stubborn, narrow-minded, self-conceited, almighty mean man in your life but he had [been] stuck in one place since he was born."[17] Clemens argued that "broad, wholesome, charitable views of men and things cannot be acquired by vegetating in one little corner of the earth all one's lifetime."[18] He recognized from his own experience that "travel is fatal to prejudice, bigotry, and narrow-mindedness, and many of our people need it sorely on these accounts."[19] It is unrealistic of course to expect all citizens to become self-educated, as Clemens had, through global wanderings.

A citizen's education in a democracy is a lifelong venture in passionate curiosity. The habitual truant and school dropout was skeptical of higher education. Twain once wrote, "Education consists mainly in what we have unlearned"; or more to the point, "Don't let schooling interfere with your education."[20] On Walt Whitman's seventieth birthday, he observed to the poet, a fellow school dropout, that the telephone, electric light, and other innovations had been invented by people like them.[21] Brilliance and creativity were not derived from formal education. Clemens praised the lyceum movement, in which working-class people became self-educated experts and shared their knowledge on the lecture circuit.

The curiosity that underpins good citizenship was not innate; it required education and training. "A little citizenship ought to be taught at the mother's knee and in the nursery," he said in a speech to the YMCA in 1906.[22] In another speech in 1908, he exhorted the City College of New York alumni that "citizenship should be placed above everything else, even learning."

> Have you ever thought about this? Is there a college in the whole country where there is a chair of good citizenship? There is a kind of bad citizenship which is taught in the schools, but no real good citizenship taught.
>
> You can begin that chair of citizenship in the College of the City of New York. You can place it above mathematics and literature, and that is where it belongs ...
>
> Good citizenship would teach accuracy of thinking and accuracy of statement.[23]

Clemens was careful to distinguish good citizenship—as an essential ingredient of democratic self-government—from patriotism, the fuel that sustains nationalism and autocracy. He argued: "There are some which teach insane citizenship, bastard citizenship, but that is all. Patriotism! Yes; but patriotism is usually the refuge of the scoundrel. He is the man who talks the loudest."[24]

In today's terms true patriotism is not saluting the flag, wearing a flag pin, "supporting the troops," or reciting the pledge of allegiance (as important as symbols may be). It is not forfeiting independence of thought and action by signing pledges to special-interest organizations. True patriotism requires respect for the values embedded in the nation's charters—respect for free speech and the ideas of others, respect for freedom of religion and tolerance for other faiths (or nonfaiths), and respect for the equal treatment under law of all Americans, regardless of race, gender, ethnicity, or birth status. True patriotism requires engaged, informed citizens working through their democratic institutions and demanding integrity, competence, and accountability from their elected representatives. This is the kind of patriotism that Clemens believed would vitalize American democracy. In its multi-layered complexity, American democracy offers an almost infinite number of access points for the engaged, informed citizen to debate and shape public policy: Federalism (there are more than 90,000 governments), separation of powers (bicameral legislatures, executive rulemaking and judicial review) and elections (more than half a million elected officials).

Clemens's later writings reflected a darker philosophy of determinism. Humans were shaped by heredity and the environment, he believed, without an independent capacity to chart their own course or effectuate change. This philosophy influenced his views on public policy and progress, although he was consistently inconsistent in applying it. He accepted Darwinian evolution and castigated religious fanatics who rejected it. In *Personal Recollections of Joan of Arc*, he referred to the children who "became properly stocked with narrowness and prejudices got at second hand from their elders, and adopted without reserve, and without examination. It goes without saying. Their religion was inherited and their politics the same."[25] In *Is Shakespeare Dead?* Twain expressed his frustration with how democracy functions given mankind's deterministic nature:

When even the brightest mind in our world has been trained up from childhood in a superstition of any kind, it will never be possible for that mind, in its maturity, to examine sincerely, dispassionately, and conscientiously any evidence or any circumstance which shall seem to cast a doubt upon the validity of that superstition. I doubt if I could do it myself. We always get at second hand our notions about systems of government; and high tariff and low tariff; and prohibition and anti-prohibition; and the holiness of peace and the glories of war; and codes of honor and codes of morals;...and our preferences in matter of religious and political parties...We get them all at second-hand, we reason none of them out for ourselves. It is the way we are made.[26]

Yet Clemens believed that since humans are products of their environment, it is possible to improve them through education, training, and better environmental circumstances. He believed that democracy's root failure was the educational system. Reflecting his own boyhood frustration, he wrote in *The Gilded Age* that school was "a place where tender young humanity devoted itself for eight or ten hours to learning incomprehensible rubbish by heart out of books and reciting it by rote, like parrots; so that a finished education consisted simply of a permanent headache."[27] Education failed to take into consideration the individual talents, aspirations, and capabilities of the student. Classical education neglected skills training that would prepare children for useful, dignified occupations in the trades and crafts. In *Following the Equator,* he complained that schools in India made "handicrafts distasteful to boys who would have been willing to make a living at trades and agriculture."[28] In *The American Claimant,* he satirized the Englishman who had "excelled at Oxford, come to America," assumed he was set for life, but "mighty near starved because he had learned no useful trade."[29] A productive society needed both intellectuals and skilled workers who would enhance productivity through practical inventiveness. From his own experience, Clemens's curiosity was ignited when he learned the printer's trade and became a self-educated reader. He strongly supported educational reform tailored to the latent talents of children, preparing them for a productive life as contributing participants in a dynamic economy. "Out of the public school," he wrote, "grows the greatness of a nation."[30] The key was schooling that stimulated latent talent rather than bored the student with cookie-cutter curricula.

Secular education reform meant that schools must teach students to think for themselves and not simply accept the precepts of the established institutions, unlike the "good-hearted" and obedient children he describes in *Joan of Arc*. Education "can turn bad morals into good, good morals to bad: it can destroy principles, it can recreate them; it can debase angels to men and lift men to angelship."[31] In the end "a man can seldom…fight a winning fight against his training."[32]

Instead of teaching good citizenship, "we teach the boys to atrophy their independence. We teach them to take their patriotism second-hand; to shout with the largest crowd without examining the right or wrong of the matter—exactly as boys under monarchy are taught."[33] Even worse, we teach our children "to regard as traitors" those who "do not shout with the crowd." This is "most foreign" to our democracy—"the delivery of our political conscience into somebody else's keeping."[34] "I would teach patriotism in the schools," he said, as reported by *The New York Times* in 1901, "and teach it this way: I would throw out the old maxim, 'My country right or wrong, &c.,' and instead I would say, 'My country when she is right.' I would not take patriotism from my neighbor or from Congress. I should teach the children in the schools that there are certain ideals, and one of them is that all men are created free and equal. Another is that the proper government is that which exists by the consent of the governed."[35] In his *Notebook*, Clemens wrote, "We have thrown away the most valuable asset we have—the individual right to oppose both flag and country when he (just he by himself) believes them to be wrong."[36]

Clemens argued that teaching children American literature was one way to instill "that love of country and reverence for the flag which is Patriotism."[37] While this may sound like a commercial for his books, wrapping *Tom Sawyer* in the flag, it was a fairly bold statement. Consider the kind of love of country that *Huckleberry Finn* instills—love for diversity, love for the underdog, and freedom to challenge conventional institutions and seek a more humane society. The Concord City officials disagreed, banning the book from the public library.

With his lifelong love of theatre, Clemens believed that a children's theater provided by the Educational Alliance of New York City was "a valuable adjunct for any educational institution."[38] He was deeply moved by the school children's production of *The Prince and the Pauper* in April 1907, recalling his own children's rendition twenty-two years earlier. As president of the East Side Children's Theatre, Clemens praised its "ingenuity" in teaching lessons not "wearily by books and by dreary homily, but by visible and enthusing action" that goes "straight to the heart."[39] Clemens proposed that New York establish forty children's theatres that would "make better citizens, honest citizens," upgrade the "educational level" and create a "real republic."[40]

A Tale of Today

Twain repeatedly stressed that human nature inevitably drifts towards monarchy as ignorant or apathetic voters seek social acceptance in like-minded communities. Fueled by this herd mentality, blind patriotism and media-reinforced biases, autocratic power arises, whether in the form of a dominant political party or a charismatic leader. Only informed citizen engagement and independent thinking can check the corrupting influence of unrestrained power and ensure a workable representative democracy.

Yet, little, if any, progress has been made in educating engaged and informed citizens over the past century. According to international surveys, the educational level of American school children today is only about average among developed nations, ranking below countries in Asia and Europe in sciences and mathematics. Most disturbing, schools are dropping courses on civics. Less than one-third of school districts now offer them.[41] According to a 2011 report, the National Assessment of Educational Progress, American youths scored lowest on US history among all disciplines. Only 2 percent of high school seniors *know what **Brown v. Board of Education** is about, and fewer than 10 percent have a basic understanding of the Constitution and the Bill of Rights.[42] In 2015, US college graduation rates ranked 19th out of 28 countries studied by the OECD.*

In 1875 Twain bluntly expressed his views about limited democracy in an *Atlantic Monthly* story, "The Curious Republic of Gondour." In this allegory universal suffrage has delivered "all power into the hands of the ignorant, nontax paying classes; and of necessity the responsible offices were filled from these classes also." As the country deteriorates from mismanagement by poor and ignorant office-holders, the Gondourians devise a solution. Additional votes are given to educated and wealthy people. As a result, "for once,—and for the first time in the history of the republic,—property, character, and intellect were able to wield a political influence; for once money, virtue, and intelligence took a vital and united interest in a political question...; for once the best men in the nation were put forward as candidates."[43]

The views of Huck Finn's father, Pap, illustrate poignantly the threat to democracy that Twain saw in according the vote to ignorant, backward, and superstitious people. Pap ridiculed Huck's attempt to learn to read and write as "hifalut'n foolishness." Pap was on his way to vote, "if I warn't too drunk to get there." Pap had heard about a mulatto "p'fessor" who "could talk all kinds of languages and knowed everything." Pap was outraged that this "prowling, thieving, infernal white-shirted free nigger" could vote. Pap thought he ought to be sold back into slavery. As Huck explained, "Whenever his liquor begun to work, he most always went for the govment."[44] Pap's internal anger at his station in life was redirected toward the government. This displacement phenomenon recurs periodically in American political history, especially when the economy is struggling, although sometimes today it is fueled by tea rather than liquor.

Like Churchill, Clemens disparaged democracy except in comparison to all other forms of government. Although a work in progress, America, as the oldest continuous constitutional democracy, established a model that other nations have sought to emulate. In the twenty-first century, advances in communications technology, rippling through the Internet, have galvanized protest movements against oppressive regimes, demanding democratic self-government. As the conclusion of *A Connecticut Yankee* prophetically shows, the path toward genuine democratic reform is a long one that requires the development of strong institutions and an educated and engaged populace. Reaching a desired outcome takes decades and strong support from like-minded nations. Democracy is hard work; it offers the potential for equality of opportunity, but it demands responsible, informed participation. Success in a meritocracy requires individual initiative and persistence. Too often the ideological enthusiasm that fuels the overthrow of a dictator like a Mubarak or Gaddafi turns to disillusionment as the people realize that democracies are far from efficient in creating jobs, reducing income disparity or engendering tolerance for diverse ethnicities and religions. Indeed, removing the iron hand of a Tito or Saddam Hussein may give birth to ethnic strife or even civil war. Perhaps *Connecticut Yankee* should be required reading for National Security Council staffers charged with assessing the uncertain prospects of the 2011 "Arab Spring" and other technology-inspired protest movements against corrupt and oppressive regimes.*

In 1897 Twain addressed the issue of democratic egalitarianism in "The Quarrel in a Strong Box," ostensibly about the national debate on the gold standard. In the story, various coins argue about their relative rights and privileges, with the penny claiming primacy. A judge rules that they are all *"free and equal."* He continues: "The meaning of the phrase is curiously misunderstood. It does not propose to set aside the law of Nature—which is, that her children are created unequal and of necessity *must* be. They are unequal in strength, health, stature, weight,

---

* History is replete with the failure of democratic revolutions—Kerensky was replaced by Lenin, the French revolution begat the Second Empire, the overthrow of the Shah of Iran resulted in the rule of the Mullahs, and Gorbachev and Yeltsin were succeeded by Putin, with the jury still out.

comeliness, complexion, intellect, and so on. The Constitution cannot alter that and has not tried to. It only makes all equal in one way; it gives each an equal right with his neighbor to exercise his talent, whatever it may be, thus making free to all, many roads to profit and honor which were once arbitrarily restricted to a few."[45]

In his *Notebook* Twain writes that America is the only society "that does not degrade many to exalt the few." Nonetheless, he recognizes that although "we all have music and poetry in our soul; some of us simply are able to get it out better than others."[46] In the words of the English rebel in *The American Claimant*, who wishes to shed all the advantages of "hereditary lordships and privilege" in order to prove his self-worth: "I will go to America, where all men are equal and all have an equal chance; I will live or die...as just a man."[47] And Sally Sellers (the Colonel's daughter), contrasting America and Siberia, proclaims that in America "no man is better than his neighbor, by the Grace of God, but only by his own merit."[48]

In *Connecticut Yankee*, Hank Morgan was repulsed by the monarchy and established church that in "two or three centuries" had "converted a nation of men to a nation of worms," creating a "seventh-rate" aristocracy which "would have achieved only poverty and obscurity if left, like their betters, to their own exertions." He proudly boasted that he was from Connecticut, where the Constitution provides that "all political power is inherent in the people, and all free governments are founded on their authority, and instituted for their benefit; and that they have *at all times* an undeniable and indefeasible right to *alter their form of government* in such a manner as they may think expedient."[49]

What made democracy—despite its many flaws—better than any other system was the fact that when everything went terribly wrong the people could change their government. Following a New York state election when the Tammany Democrats were swept from office, Clemens wrote enthusiastically to Livy: "*Now* you understand why our system of government is the *only* rational one that was ever invented. When we are not satisfied, we can *change* things."[50]

PART III

Policies And Positions

"What then is the true Gospel of consistency? Change."

MARK TWAIN

CHAPTER THIRTEEN

Mark Twain The Social Activist

"I have no race prejudices, and I think I have no color prejudices or creed prejudices. All that I care to know is that a man is a human being—that is enough for me; he can do no worse."

— MARK TWAIN

Although Clemens grew up in a slave-owning, Calvinist community with deeply ingrained mores and traditions, there were many contradictory influences that shaped his views of public policy. There were his Methodist and Presbyterian Sunday school teachers, his mother's brand of liberal Calvinism, his father's free-thinking deism, and his uncle John Quarles's Universalism. There were his friendships with the slave children and his rebellious Hannibal comrades, an occasional inspiring school teacher, his exposure to the raunchy river culture of a port town, and his education as a printer's devil. There were his father's Whig-rooted political views and his abolitionist brother Orion's conversion to the new Republican Party.

Young Clemens fantasized about joining the ministry. He loved to convey a moral message; it was religious doctrine that troubled him. Throughout his life, he enjoyed the company of ministers of many faiths. Paine wrote, "Ministers always loved Mark Twain. They did not always approve of him, but they adored him."[1]

In Cincinnati in 1856, Clemens lived with a Scot named Macfarlane who espoused a dark determinism—humans were an evolutionary aberration capable, unlike their cousins in the animal kingdom, of malice, enslavement, and brutality.[2] During his piloting days, Clemens read Tom Paine, absorbing his skepticism of organized religion. In his visit to the Sandwich Islands in 1866, Clemens witnessed non-Christian religious traditions and the influence of the Christian missionaries.[3] He became a master mason in the Ancient Free and Accepted Masons, whose deism viewed all religions as distorted versions of a universal truth.[4]

The Clemens family also flirted with telepathy, spiritualism, mental science, and Christian Science. His surviving daughter, Clara, embraced Christian Science.[5] Twain's trip to India in 1896 piqued his interest in Hindu cosmology, which is reflected in his later writings, such as "No. 44, The Mysterious Stranger."[6]

As he traveled broadly—occupationally, geographically, and intellectually—Clemens's views of the vexing issues of the day evolved. Over a lifespan many of the inconsistencies in his positions can be explained as a natural progression, a maturing that reflected an inquisitive mind and a life fully lived. But not in every case. Inconsistencies and internal contradictions persisted.

As a political reporter, fiction writer, commentator, and satirist, Clemens's views on the issues were not always easy to pin down. Was he making a serious point or simply mocking some public policy or official? Newspaper editors would sometimes accompany a humorous article with an message to readers to take seriously the points he raised. This chapter briefly recounts the evolution of Clemens's views on church and state, race and prejudice, women's suffrage, and social policy. The following chapter discusses his views about the role of government, and chapter fifteen traces his views on economic issues such as capitalism and labor, copyright protection, and international trade.[7]

Church and State

Given the diversity and evolution of his religious experience, Clemens inevitably became a strong advocate for religious pluralism and the separation of church and state. His moral compass, aversion to hypocrisy, and passion for justice were not rooted in theocratic dogma. His religious philosophy was quilted together from many sources and shaped his views on politics and public policy. Having witnessed the church's embracing of slavery in the South and its oppression of the masses in Europe, he was fearful of the domination of an established church and its stifling impact on participatory democracy.

Clemens wrote in his *Notebook*, "Faith is believing what you know ain't so."[8] Given the importance of religion to Livy (although in the end she drifted more to his view than he to hers) and his friendship with Twichell, in 1880 Clemens attempted to distill a moral code in which he could believe. He decided that he believed in an Almighty God, but that the Bible was "imagined & written by man" and was not authorized or inspired by God, and that "the universe is governed by strict & immutable laws" with which God "does not interfere." He was uncertain and indifferent as to whether there was a "hereafter" but he was sure that he would neither be rewarded nor punished for deeds done on earth. "Moral laws," he once wrote, "are the outcome of the world's experience."* They need "no God to come down out of heaven to tell men that murder and theft and the other immoralities were bad, both for the individual who commits them and for society which suffers from them."[9] He was vague about "the other immoralities."[10] Law and public policy are derived from human experience, not divine authority. Of one thing he was certain: government should not impede through censorship

---

* In his marked-up copy of William Lecky's *History of European Morals*, he had written "sound and true" by Lecky's endorsement of the utilitarian view that all morality is a product of experience.

or theocratic regulation the individual's freedom to pursue the religious vision and lifestyle that best accommodates his or her spiritual quest.

With Livy as his censor, Twain's writings are mostly devoid of erotica and sexual fantasy. A notable exception is his pornographic short story "1601"—written in 1876 but hidden from his wife and daughters—in which in early English dialogue, Queen Elizabeth interrogates her court to identify who has "broken wind," invoking crude scatology and references to genitalia that would make Shakespeare and Chaucer blush.[11] After Livy's death, Clemens met the English author, Elinor Glyn, at his favorite New York restaurant, Delmonico's, on Fifth Avenue. She had written a best-selling novel, *Three Weeks*, about an adulterous affair between a young man and an older woman, which had provoked the wrath of Victorian critics. In candid conversations with Glyn, Clemens privately agreed with the book's premise "that the laws of Nature are paramount and properly take precedent over the interfering and impertinent restrictions obtruded upon man's life by man's statutes."[12] Clemens, however, was not prepared to repudiate all conventions publicly because they "furnish us peace, fairly good government, and stability." He thus declined Glyn's appeal to support publicly her "free love" agenda, but he conceded in unpublished autobiographical dictations that man "cannot escape obedience to the laws of passion" and is "beset by traps which he cannot possibly avoid and which compel him to commit what are called sins."[13] What distinguished man from the animals was his misguided "moral sense," creating rules that divide right from wrong. Knowing not right from wrong, the angels, he said, are "wholly pure and sinless."[14] Paine quotes Twain as saying, "we have no *real* morals, but only artificial ones—morals created and preserved by the forced suppression of natural & healthy instincts." Clemens thought that "the moral idea was undergoing constant change, that what was considered unjustifiable in an earlier day was regarded as highly moral now."[15] Because morals were based on human experience, Clemens understood that laws embracing moral conventions would change and evolve over time.

"There are a million rules in the world," Clemens observed, "and this makes a million standards to be looked out for." In India he noted the shock of the high-caste veiled ladies that Englishwomen would walk around with bare faces, while the Victorian ladies were appalled that the Indian women exposed their bare thighs. From such conflicts, Clemens concluded "All human rules are more or less idiotic, I suppose."[16]

Clemens's religious philosophy grew darker in his later years.[17] He repudiated the conventional Victorian theology (still prevalent today) that man is the noblest work of God. After rehearsing the trials and errors of evolutionary progression, Twain renounced his "allegiance to the Darwinian theory of the Ascent of Man from the lower animals...in favor of a new and truer one...the Descent of Man from the Higher Animals."[18]

Twain accepted the usefulness of organized religion to the extent it encouraged human beings to live lives of compassion, integrity, and selflessness. He applauded the good works of men of the cloth—the Catholic missionaries in Hawaii,[19] the Dominican friars of Italy who risked (and lost) their lives helping the sick during a cholera epidemic,[20] and the participation in the Underground Railroad by the members of the Langdon's Park Church.[21] He could not countenance religious dogma that defied common sense and scientific knowledge or religious hypocrites—like the corrupt Senator Pomeroy and the Sunday school teachers John D. Rockefeller Sr. and John Wanamaker, whose business practices belied their pious pronouncements.[22]

Most troubling to Clemens was the historical record of institutionalized religion in obstructing progress—whether in the science of astronomy, the suppression of free inquiry, or the abolition of slavery. Only when the march of history proved the church dead wrong did the pendulum swing and religion suddenly become the champion of change, the advocate of reform. In London he scribbled in his *Notebook* that "the Church here rests under the usual charge—an obstructer and fighter of progress; until progress arrives, then she takes the credit."[23] History emphatically taught, Clemens thought, that established religion was antithetical to democratic self-government. Clemens understood that the American democratic experiment was unique, not because of free elections, separation of powers or even free speech. All this had been tried before. What was novel about American democracy, reflecting the writings of Sir Francis Bacon, John Locke, and Thomas Jefferson, was the separation of church and state—the lack of an established religion providing divine authority for the work of government, the system of laws, or the conscience of the people.[24]

Twain's criticism of established religion permeates his writing. In *The Innocents Abroad*, he contrasts poverty in Italy with the grand cathedrals and aristocratic priest craft: "She is to-day one vast museum of magnificence and misery."[25] Twain wondered why the people tolerated the Catholic Church as the largest landowner in Italy. He wrote in his *Notebook*: "The priesthood and church impoverishes a people by propagating ignorance, superstition & slavery among them, & then godifies itself for its fine and noble work in furnishing crumbs of relief, procured by begging—not from its own coffers but from the pockets of the paupers it has created."[26]

Twain's acerbic criticism of the Catholic hierarchy was undoubtedly well-received by his overwhelmingly Protestant readership given the prevalent anti-Roman bias of the day.[27] In *A Connecticut Yankee*, Twain describes an established church that indoctrinates the masses with feudal superstitions, suppresses freedom of thought and speech and relegates the people to a state of poverty and ignorance, asserting that only the "after life" really matters. The Yankee, Hank Morgan, is convinced that "any Established Church is an established crime" and must be assailed "in any way or with any weapon."[28] Morgan explains to his sixth century comrades that religion has its purpose, but to minimize its threat to the state, a wide variety of religions should be encouraged. Echoing Thomas Paine's *Age of Reason*, that "concentration of power in a political machine is bad and an Established Church is only a political machine," Morgan warns that when a United Church "gets itself into selfish hands, as it is always bound to do, it means death to human liberty, and paralysis to human thought."[29]

Hank proposes establishing a Protestant church to provide religious competition and separating education in the schools from the churches. He "confined public religious teaching to the churches and the Sunday-Schools, permitting nothing of it in my other educational buildings."[30] Hank rejects substituting his own Presbyterian Church for the Catholic Church as the established religion, even though the Presbyterians are a more democratic sort. "You never see any of us Presbyterians getting into a sweat about religion and trying to massacre the neighbors," Clemens wrote to Howells.[31] Morgan reasoned that "a man is only at his best, morally, when he is equipped with the religious garment whose color and shape and size most nicely accommodate themselves to the spiritual complexion, angularities and stature of the individual who wears it."[32] Religion can coexist with democracy only in "a split-up and scattered condition."[33] King Arthur's subjects found this all quite puzzling as they had never conceived of a nation in which the people actually had a say in their government. Hank told them that he "had seen one—and that it would last until it had an Established Church."[34]

Having lived in Berlin and Munich, Clemens was critical of the German government's subsidies of its two principal religions—Catholic and Lutheran—and their schools. Other churches were taxed to support these preferred religions. Equally as "infamous," he asserted, was the practice in the United States of providing tax exemptions for church property. "The infidel and the atheist and the man without religion are taxed to make up the deficit in the public income."[35] Clemens even drafted a petition demanding that New York give equal status to all "Sabbaths" or eliminate the blue laws that gave special status to Sundays. With such pronouncements, Clemens could have been a charter member of the Americans United for Separation of Church and State.

In November 1907, on the advice of the artist Augustus Saint-Gaudens—who designed the ten- and twenty-dollar gold coins—President Theodore Roosevelt ordered the words "In God We Trust" deleted from the coins. Rather than accept the artist's view that the words marred the design, Roosevelt declared that placing the motto on money was a "sacrilegious association of God and Mammon." He was widely ridiculed, mostly by cleric advocates of retaining the motto. Clemens, who thought Roosevelt "was very much in the habit of furnishing a poor reason for his acts when there was an excellent reason staring him in the face," had a different idea about the ensuing controversy. He thought the motto "was a lie."[36] Speaking at 11:00 p.m. to a raucous, well-liquefied crowd of City College alumni and faculty at the Waldorf Hotel on "Education and Citizenship," Twain veered off the subject matter to address the coin controversy. In so doing he spoke about religion with a candor he usually reserved for his unpublished autobiographical dictations:

> We used to trust in God. I think it was in 1863 that some genius suggested that it be put upon the gold and silver coins which circulated among the rich. They didn't put it on the nickels and coppers because they didn't think the poor folks had any trust in God...
>
> Now, that motto on the coin is an overstatement. Those Congressmen had no right to commit this whole country to a theological doctrine. But since they did, Congress ought to state what our creed should be.
>
> There was never a nation in the world that put its whole trust in God. It is a statement made on insufficient evidence.[37]

Responding to the outcry from the nation's pulpits, Congress did what it does best—it pandered to the politically-active clergy and mandated "In God We Trust" on all coins, humiliating the president.* That December Twain dictated for his unpublished autobiography: "It is not proper to brag and boast that America is a Christian country when we all know with certainty five-sixth of our population could not enter in at the narrow gate." Indeed, he added, hell must be "the only really prominent Christian community in any of the worlds."[38] Not that Twain had anything against hell. He once told the story of the clergyman

---

* Supporting the theory that no issue is ever finally resolved, in 2011 atheist Michael Newdow vowed to continue his fight to remove "In God We Trust" from all US currency after the Supreme Court denied his petition for review.

who asked a parishioner where he wanted to go in the afterlife. "Heaven for climate," the parishioner responded, "and Hell for society."[39]

In the last book he published, *Extract from Captain Stormfield's Visit to Heaven,* Twain described heaven as populated with people of all races, creeds, and colors—American Indians, Negroes, Chinese, Jews, Mohammedans, and a small minority of white Christians—a description taken from a page of his uncle John Quarles's Universalism.[40] Despite a religion's claim of a single pathway to salvation, Clemens ultimately concluded, religious affiliation didn't make any difference because "it is not the ability to reason that makes the Presbyterian, or the Baptist, or the Methodist, or the Catholic, or the Mohammedan, or the Buddhist, or the Mormon, it is the environment."[41] Or more succinctly, "the religious folly you are born in you will *die* in."[42] And more sarcastically, "What God lacks is convictions—stability of character. He ought to be a Presbyterian or a Catholic or *something*—not try to be everything."[43]

A Tale of Today

Clemens's admonition that democracies must guard against attempts to introduce theocratic dogma into the legislative process is worth remembering today. The continuing assaults on the First Amendment's prohibition on the enactment of any law respecting an establishment of religion or prohibiting the free exercise thereof are subtle, varied, and persistent. A healthy democracy, according to Clemens, requires religious pluralism under which alternative belief systems coexist in an environment of mutual toleration, if not respect. As Pudd'nhead Wilson put it, "True irreverence is disrespect for another man's god."[44] Government should remain neutral and not pick winners and losers by codifying morality.

> *Yet today members of Congress seek to incorporate their religious convictions into government policy on health care, education, and the public welfare. They introduce legislation to defund Planned Parenthood, to allow employers to deny health services that are contrary to their religious beliefs, to provide backdoor financial assistance to parochial schools, to allow prayer in schools and the Ten Commandments in public buildings, and to determine when life begins, what constitutes marriage, and how life should end. Maintaining the wall between "free exercise" and "establishment" and resisting the intrusion of religion into politics and public policy requires, as Clemens's warned, constant vigilance.*

Race and Prejudice

As Clemens traveled—geographically and psychologically—out of the southern cultural traditions in which he was raised, he gradually shed his ingrained prejudices and became an advocate and activist for racial and ethnic equality of opportunity. His enlightenment was uneven, and for some minorities it came slowly. He was most eloquent in advancing the rights of African Americans and the Chinese, but more ambivalent about American Indians and certain immigrant groups and religious minorities.

African Americans. Having grown up in a slave-owning community, young Clemens simply accepted slavery as a given in the natural order of things. He was "not aware that there was anything wrong about it, " and was taught "that God approved it."[45] On a more instinctive level, he enjoyed his friendships with the thirty slaves on his uncle's farm: "All the negros were friends of ours, and with those of our own age we were in effect comrades... We were comrades; color and condition interposed a subtle line which both parties were conscious of and which rendered complete fusion impossible."[46]

Ingrained racism occasionally surfaced in Clemens's early years. In his trip east in 1853, he was appalled by the cockiness of northern blacks, writing his mother, "I reckon I had better black my face, for in these Eastern States niggers are considerably better than white people."* He longed for a "good old-fashioned negro."[47]

As he got older, he had friends on all sides of the slavery issue, especially during his river piloting days. Clemens was ambivalent. For a man who in his older years was rarely hesitant about lunging into the most controversial topics, young Clemens sidestepped the central issue of the time. He was not alone. Most of the founding fathers opposed slavery, but to secure ratification by the southern colonies, they compromised in drafting the Constitution. They included several provisions allowing the slave trade until 1808, counting slaves as three-fifths of a person for representational and tax apportionment purposes, and requiring the return of fugitive slaves—all without actually mentioning the word "slavery." The singular sin of slavery was silently passed on to subsequent generations.

At the time of Clemens's birth, five of the seven presidents of the United States had been slave owners. When Sam was fifteen, Congress enacted the Fugitive Slave Act requiring the free states to capture and return escaped slaves to the South. On March 4, 1857, twenty-one-year-old Sam left New Orleans

---

* A master of realism in language, Twain while working in Washington in 1868 ridiculed a brutal Confederate officer, Colonel Jay Hawkins, who "lost heavily in the war ... an uncle, a nigger, a watch, and thirty dollars in Confederate money" (Budd, 35). As a southerner, the young Clemens occasionally used the term "nigger," abhorrent by today's politically correct standards, but as he matured, when he was speaking for himself and not his characters, he used the term "Negro." Nonetheless in his writing he accurately and unabashedly reflected the language of the time, place, and person described. The use of any other term would have degraded the realism of the situation depicted. The term vividly displayed the savage condescension of the archaic southern culture. It lent pungency to the satire of unconscionable racism that pervaded American life. In his masterpiece, *Huckleberry Finn*, Twain used the term more than 219 times. For today's reader (and student) the word sends offensive shockwaves, as it should if it is accurately to represent the horror of the time and not sweep aside, as Americans are prone to do, the stains on its history.

on the *Colonel Crossman* piloted by Horace Bixby on his way to St. Louis where the slave Dred Scott had sued for his freedom. On March 6, the Supreme Court issued its notorious decision in *Dred Scott v. Sanford*. Reflecting the conventional wisdom that Negroes were an inferior race, the nation's highest Court held that neither slaves nor free blacks were entitled to the rights of citizenship—"the unhappy black race" was "doomed to slavery" and "never thought of or spoken of except as property."[48] Even Lincoln, though opposed to slavery, believed that blacks could not live harmoniously with whites.[49]

When the thirty-two-year-old Clemens worked in Washington, he could understand why when the Radical Republicans sought to integrate freedmen into the reconstructed southern economy, white southerners felt threatened.[50] As large bands of freed slaves roamed throughout the South searching for jobs and separated family members, fearful southern officials imposed Black Codes, restricting the blacks' mobility and denying their right to vote, carry guns, and hold certain jobs. Federal troops occupied the South to protect the blacks, carpetbaggers, and scalawags (southerners who supported the Union) from hostility and retribution.

When Clemens was forty-one, under the Hayes-Tilden compromise federal troops were removed from the South and reconstruction measures were phased out. Jim Crow laws launched an era of racial apartheid while Washington looked the other way. The Ku Klux Klan, the Knights of the Golden Circle, the White Leagues, the Red Shirts, and other supremacist groups stirred up racial hatred. There was an upsurge in lynchings.[51] This was the confused world of race relations in which Clemens's career unfolded. While America was regressing, Clemens was progressing.

Clemens's first mature reflections on the evils of slavery are in the dialect of a servant slave woman. In "A True Story, Repeated Word for Word As I Heard It," published in 1879, Aunt Rachel tells how her husband and seven children were placed on the "oction" block in Richmond, bound in chains, inspected, assaulted, and sold off to different masters. She never saw most of her family again. Her youngest son, however, escaped to the North, joined the Union army to search for his mother and found her twenty-two years later when his regiment took possession of the plantation on which she worked.[52] In an *Atlantic Monthly* review, Howells described the poignant tale as "by far the most perfect piece of work." It "leaves all other stories of slave life infinitely far behind" and reveals "the simple dramatic report of reality which we have seen equaled in no other American writer."[53] In a few pages, Twain capsulated the strength of African American familial love and loyalty, the brutality of slavery, the contribution of black soldiers to the Union victory, the postbellum searches to reunite scattered families, and the challenges facing freed but abandoned slaves after the war—all issues reverberating throughout the nation in the decades following the war.

Huckleberry Finn is Twain's most eloquent statement on the brutality and immorality of slavery. With an ear for the many dialects of time and place, Twain shows slavery from the male perspective as the runaway slave Jim—illiterate and superstitious—seeks freedom to reunite his family. He finds himself floating down the Mississippi River on a raft with Huck Finn.

In dramatic fiction Huck reflects the young Clemens's personal struggle to reconcile the deeply embedded conventions of the South with his personal experiences with African Americans. Endowed with little schooling, abject poverty, and a drunken, racist father from whom he is running away, Huck understands the seriousness of the crime he is committing—aiding and abetting a runaway slave. He is shocked to learn from Jim of his plans to buy the freedom of his wife and children, thus depriving other white masters of their property. This is not only a crime against the law laid down by Congress and the Supreme Court; it is an unpardonable sin against God. To do "the right thing," Huck composes a letter to Jim's owner, Miss Watson, telling her of the runaway slave's whereabouts. Then he faces Jim. He sees a courageous, loyal, grateful, and selfless friend who loves his family. With simple, heartfelt reasoning, he makes a decision not to send the letter: "All right then, I'll *go* to hell," he says to himself as he tears up the letter.[54]

Huck's epiphany reflects Clemens's conviction that individuals must have the courage to think and act upon their conscience even when contrary to conventional law and theology. It represents his mature view that human qualities of loyalty, selflessness, and friendship are universal and not the private preserve of any race, class, or religion. Yet as the novel unfolds, it is apparent that the inherent dignity and equality of all human beings must be embraced by religion and protected by law.

Twain addresses race from a female perspective in his 1894 book *Pudd'nhead Wilson*.[55] The heroine Roxy is one-sixteenth Negro. She gives birth to a baby boy on the same day as her master's wife, who dies within a week. Roxy takes care of the two babies, who look alike. She can tell them apart only by the clothes they wear. The master's son wears ruffed soft muslin with a coral necklace, and Roxy's son wears a coarse tow-linen shirt. Recognizing that her son, who is one-thirty-second Negro, is a slave and will be sold down the river, Roxy decides to switch the babies.[56] Twain mocks the American tradition that one drop of Negro blood "outvotes" the rest and condemns Roxy's son to slavery.[57]

Roxy's son is raised as her master's son. He acquires all the attributes of a brutal slave owner and treats his mother and his slave servant (the master's son) cruelly. He commits murder and is sentenced to life imprisonment. The truth comes out after the death of the master. The town lawyer, Pudd'nhead Wilson, had fingerprinted the babies at birth. Reversing roles, the master's son finds that he is ill-prepared to manage the estate, having acquired traits of inferiority from his days as a slave. Roxy's son is released from prison when the estate makes the plea that he is too valuable as a productive slave to keep in confinement.* By this last twist, Twain exposes slavery as simply a profit-making device by which white plantation owners extracted their wealth from uncompensated labor. He further illustrates the absurdity of distinctions based on race. The environment shapes each of

---

* Similarly, in *Huckleberry Finn* an inflamed mob backs off a call to lynch Jim when someone astutely asks who will pay his owner.

the boys. And the environment, distorted by the aberration of slavery and racial discrimination, misshapes each of them badly.[58]

Clemens understood that the abolition of slavery was only the beginning of a process that would have starts, stops, and reversals. He knew the South had regressed and that the citizenship accorded blacks was strictly second-class. Clemens believed that education was critical to enable blacks to assimilate into the economic mainstream. He anonymously paid tuition and board for several students to attend Lincoln University, the first institution of higher learning for African Americans in the country (and the alma mater of Thurgood Marshall). He introduced Booker T. Washington at a Carnegie Hall fundraiser for the Tuskegee Institute in Alabama.[59] He paid the Yale Law School tuition of a Negro student, Warner T. McGuinn, who, as Dean Frances Wayland wrote to Clemens, was "last year by examination considerably above the average of his class."[60] Upon graduation from Yale Law School, McGuinn became a successful attorney in Baltimore.* Clemens's passionate commitment to improving race relationships strengthened as the situation throughout the country deteriorated. Most horrific was the increase in lynchings, which Clemens studied with growing concern.

On August 26, 1869, Clemens published an editorial in the *Buffalo Express*, titled "Only a Nigger," about a Negro who had been lynched in Tennessee for committing rape and later found to be innocent. Clemens wrote: "Ah, well! Too bad, to be sure! A little blunder in the administration of justice by Southern mob-law; but nothing to speak of. Only a 'nigger' killed by mistake—that is all. Of course, every high-toned gentleman whose chivalric impulses were so unfortunately misled in this affair… is as sorry about it as a high-toned gentleman can be expected to be sorry about the unlucky fate of 'a nigger.' But mistakes

---

* After graduating from Howard University Law School, Thurgood Marshall worked in McGuinn's office before becoming counsel to the NAACP. Marshall was the first African-American (though he never liked the appellation) to serve as solicitor general of the United States and later justice of the Supreme Court.

will happen even in the conduct of the best regulated and high-toned mobs."[61]

In *Huckleberry Finn* Twain probes the cowardly crowd psyche that constitutes a lynch mob, a favorite theme of his. Standing on his porch roof, a shotgun in hand, Colonel Sherburn stands down a lynch mob: "If only a *half* a man shouts…'Lynch him, Lynch him!' you're afraid to back down—afraid you'll be found out to be what you are—*cowards*."[62] Twain believed that most people caught up in a lynch mob did not want to be there. They were afraid of resisting mob psychology.

Twain's essay "The United States of Lyncherdom" was provoked by an especially brutal 1901 lynching in Missouri. A young white woman on the way to church was murdered. In retaliation three African Americans (two of them quite elderly) were lynched, five homes were burned, and thirty families were driven into the woods. For Twain lynching was an extreme manifestation of the herd mentality, a defect in human nature that explains, among other things, party-centric voting patterns and the patriotic fervor that sustains unjust wars.

Lamenting the lack of courageous sheriffs and brave citizens to repel the herd mentality of a vigilante posse, Twain facetiously proposed bringing back the missionaries from China and putting them to work Christianizing the white supremacists. The missionaries "have the martyr spirit; nothing but the martyr spirit can brave a lynching mob, and cow it and scatter it."[63] He wrote:

Let us import missionaries from China, and send them into the lynching field. With 1,511 of them out there converting two Chinamen apiece per annum against an uphill birth rate of thirty-three thousand pagans per day, it will take upward of a million years to make the conversions balance the output and bring the Christianizing of the country in sight to the naked eye; therefore, if we can offer our missionaries just as rich a field at home…why shouldn't they find it fair and right to come back and give us a trial? The Chinese are universally conceded to be excellent people, honest, honorable, industrious, trustworthy, kind-hearted and all that—leave them alone, they are plenty good enough just as they are; and besides, almost every convert runs a risk of catching our civilization. We ought to be careful. We ought to think twice before we encourage a risk like that; for, *once civilized, China can never be uncivilized again.*[64]

Clemens never completed his plan to expand the essay into a book, *The History of Lynching in the United States,* and the suppressed essay was not published until 1923. Regretfully, it was still topical. According to a Tuskegee Institute study, nearly thirty-five hundred African Americans were lynched between 1882 and 1968. In 1909, the year before Clemens's death, race riots and multiple lynchings broke out in Lincoln's hometown of Springfield, Illinois. Yet despite intensive lobbying by the NAACP and its counsel Charles Houston and Thurgood Marshall, presidents from Theodore Roosevelt to William Howard Taft refused to support federal anti-lynching legislation. Even the socially progressive Franklin D. Roosevelt refused to support such legislation lest he offend the southern committee chairmen whose help was needed to enact New Deal legislation. Truman was the first president to support it, and it did not pass Congress until 1968, incorporated in the codified criminal code, as one of a series of civil rights laws enacted during President Lyndon Johnson's administration.

A Tale of Today

Since the 1954 **Brown** decision and the civil rights legislation of the 1960s, progress has been made in opening up opportunities for African Americans, many of whom have reached the pinnacle of professional achievement in science, education, government, business, sports, and entertainment. Yet the vestiges of 250 years of slavery remain. Many neighborhoods and schools remain de facto segregated. The unemployment rate for blacks is nearly double that of whites, and approaches 50 percent for black teenagers in some urban

> *areas. Racial discrimination in law enforcement on the street and in the prisons draws international scrutiny and protests. The median income of black families hovers around 60 percent of white families. The net worth of white families is about twelve times that of black families. According to the 2010 census, 40 percent of black children live in poverty. Much work remains to be done to create the nation that Clemens envisioned, which gives every citizen "the same legal right and privilege."*

Chinese-Americans. Clemens's awakening to the evils of racial discrimination did not begin with African Americans. It happened when he was a reporter in San Francisco covering local crime. He had previously written unflattering comments about the Chinese in Virginia City and New York. In San Francisco he observed blatant discrimination against Chinese immigrants, who were assaulted with impunity, subjected to police brutality, hauled into court on spurious charges, and denied the basic right to defend themselves. One day he saw a Chinese man carrying laundry being attacked by dogs while Irish-Americans stood by laughing. "A butcher increased the hilarity of the occasion by knocking some of the Chinaman's teeth down his throat with half a brick,"[65] Clemens wrote up the story for the *Morning Call*, but the editor refused to publish it lest he offend the paper's predominantly Irish-American readership. The spat cost Clemens his job at the paper, and it took him a while to overcome his prejudice against Irish-Americans.

After Clemens came east, he published a series of articles in the *Galaxy Magazine* about discriminatory laws and practices targeting the Chinese. In "Disgraceful Persecution of a Boy," Twain satirically defends a white boy who is prosecuted for stoning a Chinese man. Twain describes how the police keep constant watch on the "unsuspecting almond-eyed son of Confucius" and arrest him for his "suspicious manner," how discriminatory taxes and immigration fees are imposed on the Chinese, and how the

Chinese are hanged for misdemeanor offenses. Given the circumstances, it is understandable "how the boy, tripping along to Sunday school," says to himself, "Ah, there goes a Chinaman. God will not love me if I do not stone him." Twain concludes: "Everything conspired to teach him that it was a high and holy thing to stone a Chinaman, and yet he no sooner attempts to do his duty that he is punished *for* it."[66]

In "Goldsmith's Friend Abroad Again," a naïve Chinese man, Ah Song Hi, leaves Shanghai, "my oppressed and overburdened native land," to emigrate to America, "that noble realm where all are free and equal, and none reviled and abused—America! America, whose previous privilege it is to call herself the Land of the Free and the Home of the Brave."[67] In letters home, he downplays the mistreatment and brutalities to which he is subjected. His optimism fades as he loses his job, goes deeply in debt, becomes a pauper and lands in jail.

In "John the Chinaman in New York," Twain asks how "we, who prate so much about civilization and humanity, are content to degrade a fellow human being?" How do we reconcile our discriminatory policies against immigrants with the America that "has a broader hospitality for the exiled and oppressed," the America that is "always ready to help the unfortunate?"[68] Paraphrasing a line from the *Dred Scott* decision, "a Chinaman has no rights that any man was bound to respect," Twain contends that in the West, the Chinese were treated as badly as the African Americans in the South. As Philip Foner has said of Twain's sketches on Chinese-Americans, "No one has given us a more devastating portrayal of the contrast between the myth and reality of American democracy so far as the Chinese in this country were concerned."[69]

Clemens's friend from the Sandwich Island days, US Minister to China Anson Burlingame, negotiated a treaty establishing consular relations between the United States and China—a dramatic welcome of China into the community of nations surpassed only by the Nixon-Kissinger visit to Beijing over one hundred years later. Burlingame asked Twain to write an analysis of the historic treaty for *The New York Tribune*, a project Twain enthusiastically undertook. The Treaty provided for the appointment of Americans as Chinese consuls in various cities, empowered to protect the rights of Chinese living in the United States. Article 6 gave Chinese residents the same "privileges and immunities" granted "citizens or subjects of a most favored nation." The Treaty eliminated a discriminatory mining tax assessed only on the Chinese, and—Twain hoped—provided a pathway for eventual naturalized citizenship. Chinese were permitted to acquire real estate, to testify in court (even against a white person), to sit on juries, and to attend public schools. Twain claimed that the Treaty made "men out of beasts of burden."[70] He finally got to use some of the colorful prose from his rejected article for the *Morning Call*, declaring that they "can never set the dogs on the Chinamen anymore, nor "can some white brute break an unoffending Chinaman's head with a brick."[71]

Clemens was shocked when Burlingame, who represented the Chinese government after resigning his ministerial post, died unexpectedly in February 1870 at the age of forty-seven. "There isn't one man in Washington in civil office with the brains of Anson Burlingame," he wrote, "and I suppose if China had not seized and saved his greatest talents to the world, this government would have discarded him when his time was up."[72] In his eulogy, Twain aptly described what he himself would become. Burlingame "had outgrown the narrow citizenship of a state, and become a citizen of the world; and his charity was large enough and his great heart warm enough to feel for all its races and to labor for them."[73]

Clemens looked forward to the day when Chinese-Americans could become full citizens and elected officials, contributing their values of thrift, order, community solidarity, and hard work to American society. His optimism was premature. When the transcontinental railroad was completed, there was a surplus of "coolie labor" that threatened the "mechanics," the working classes. Discriminatory fervor and calls for deportation surged. President Arthur vetoed a Chinese exclusion bill in 1881, but signed a second version in 1882 that placed a ten year moratorium on immigration and barred the Chinese from US citizenship.

Immigration. Clemens's views on immigration swung 180 degrees during his lifetime. When he left Hannibal for St. Louis in 1853, he became enmeshed in the anti-Catholic, anti-foreign-born wave of prejudice as German and Irish immigrants clashed with native-born Americans. On his first trip east, he wrote home about the "mass of human vermin" in the immigrant neighborhoods of Philadelphia and New York. In *Roughing It* he was rough on the Irish. Over time these prejudices faded. In his mature years, beginning with his series of stories for the *Galaxy* on the Chinese, Clemens became a strong advocate for the assimilation of immigrant populations into the American mainstream.[74] He advocated opening up labor unions to immigrants and providing them with educational and skills training opportunities.

A Tale of Today

Whether it is building a wall on the Mexican border or excluding Muslim immigrants, the issue of immigration has become intensely politicized and will remain so until Congress addresses immigration law reform comprehensively. Meanwhile a flurry of state immigration laws (e.g., Arizona, Alabama, Georgia, Indiana, Colorado, South Carolina, and Utah) have attempted to fill the vacuum. In June 2012, the Supreme Court, inter alia, struck down provisions in the Arizona law that criminalized an alien's unauthorized application for work and failure to carry a registration document.[75] In 2017, the president issued an executive order denying funding to so-called Sanctuary Cities, in which local law enforcement fails to cooperate in the enforcement of federal immigration laws. What do we do about millions of undocumented immigrants, many of whom are productive members of their communities? Such concerns likely will continue until elected politicians tone down the supercharged rhetoric— like the congressional debates on Chinese exclusion in the late nineteenth century— and Congress acts on comprehensive immigration reform.

Anti-Semitism. Growing up in Hannibal, Clemens observed—and to a limited extent participated in—the anti-Semitic practices of the community. Two Jewish schoolmates, the Levin brothers, were harassed. In his early satires, there are crude references to Jewish stereotypes, which quickly faded from his writing. Clemens grew in respect for what he called, "the world's intellectual aristocracy."[76] After his only surviving daughter, Clara, married a Russian-Jewish pianist, Ossip Gabrilowitsch, he had many family conversations about ethnic prejudice and anti-Semitism. He told Ossip that anti-Semitism arose from "the swollen envy of pigmy minds."[77]

In 1898 while Clemens was living in Austria, street riots broke out over a dispute between Austria and Hungary. As a diversionary tactic, the Austrian government began attacking the Jews. Near the conclusion of an article in *Harper's* in March 1898, Twain mentioned the attacks on the Jewish people, and several readers wrote asking for further explanation.[78] Twain accommodated their request in the summer of 1898, by publishing "Concerning the Jews," and inadvertently setting off a storm of controversy.[79] By stressing the substantial contributions of Jews in commerce, science, art, and literature, he thought he was eradicating the "crafty pawnbroker" stereotype. In actuality he was substituting one stereotype for another—the "brilliant intellectual" who let others do the fighting and menial labor. Few issues are more fraught with subtle complexity, and Twain did not bring any expertise, experience, new data, or scientific research to the task. Some of his facts were just plain wrong. He took the criticism stoically and tried to correct the factual errors in a 1904 essay, "The American Jew as a Soldier."[80] Having abandoned his usual medium of satiric ambiguity and instead addressed a sensitive social issue as a serious commentator, Twain felt the full brunt of criticism from experts who had spent their whole lives studying (and living with) anti-Semitism.

American Indians. Clemens's writings are replete with crude references to American Indians as "savages." Schooled in the romanticized view of the noble savage through fiction, Clemens was shocked as he traveled on the Overland stage from St. Joseph to Carson City in 1861, to see Indians begging for food, sifting through garbage, and filching carrion from vultures and coyotes.[81] His encounter with the Goshutes, a tribe eking out a living in the harsh desert of eastern Nevada and Utah southwest of the Great Salt Lake, reinforced his disillusion, as he recounted in *Roughing It*:

> The nausea which the Goshoots [*sic*] gave me, an Indian worshiper, set me to examining authorities, to see if perchance I had been over-estimating the Red Man while viewing him through the mellow moonshine of romance. The revelations that came were disenchanting. It was curious to see how quickly the paint and tinsel fell away from him and left him treacherous, filthy and repulsive—and how quickly the evidences accumulated that whenever one finds an Indian tribe he has only found Goshoots more or less modified by circumstances and surroundings—but Goshoots after all. They deserve pity, poor creatures, and they can have mine—at this distance.[82]

In Twain's colorful use of the vernacular, it is difficult to distinguish prejudicial stereotyping from burlesque. Twain's criticism was aimed at the "noble savage" depicted in the novels of James Fennimore Cooper, Francis Parkman, and Bret Harte and was directed more to the writers' prose, mimicking the English romantic tradition of Sir Walter Scott, whom Twain detested.[83]

Clemens's views on American Indians matured more slowly than his stance on other racial minorities and retained a certain ambiguity. In *Life on the Mississippi* (1883), Twain criticized the French for taking the Louisiana territories from the Indians and selling it to the Americans. When La Salle set up his cross with the arms of France on it, he was "saving the savages; thus compensating them with possible possessions in heaven for the certain ones on earth which they had just been robbed of."[84]

Clemens was so incensed by the barbarous treatment of the Indians by private bounty hunters and the army out west that he wrote President Cleveland in 1885 urging him to take action to protect the Indians from the unsavory acts of government officials promoting abhorrent practices. He wrote: "You not only have the power to destroy scoundrelism of many kinds in this country, but you have amply proved that you have also the unwavering disposition and purpose to do it." To dramatize the point, he enclosed an official notice:

$250 REWARD
The above reward will be paid by the Board of County Commissioners of Grant County to any citizen of said county for each and every hostile renegade Apache killed by such citizen, on presentation to said board of the scalp of such Indian.
By Order of the Board, E. Stine, Clerk.[85]

The president ignored Clemens's plea. While Cleveland was sensitive to injustice, he also was passionate about restoring law and order in the West. The protection of life and property was an indispensable prerequisite to justice, and he was determined that Indians who "take to the sword shall perish by the sword." During Cleveland's administration, Captain Leonard Wood, who would later earn Clemens's scorn for his brutal response to the Philippine insurrections, scoured the border and upper Mexico in search of Geronimo and the renegade Apaches.[86]

More typically, as Clemens set off on the overland portion of his global lecture tour in 1895, he wrote in his *Notebook* about seeing a "flathead dude" on the reservation in Spokane, Washington, and "squaws prowling about back doors and windows begging and foraging—a nuisance once familiar to me."[87] In reporting on his global tour in *Following the Equator*, he vehemently criticized the Australian settlers' treatment of the aborigines, reducing the native population by 80 percent in twenty years, foreshadowing the anti-imperialist writings that were to come.[88] When in 1906 he condemned the Moro massacre of Muslims in the Philippines,[89] Twain remained strangely silent about similar atrocities against Indians on US soil.[90]

Women's Suffrage

Clemens's relationships with the women in his families—his mother, Jane; his sister, Pamela; Orion's wife, Mollie; his wife, Livy; and his daughters, Susy, Clara, and Jean—gave him comfort and support that sustained him through turbulent times and shaped him into a fuller, multidimensional human being and social activist. In his professional life, he sought affirmation and encouragement from Mary Fairbanks, and he developed an appreciation for the women's suffrage movement from his Nook Farm neighbor Isabella Hooker.

Clemens took note of the oppression of women in primitive societies during his Sandwich Island trip in 1866. In the old days, he wrote: "Woman was rigidly taught to know her place. Her place was to do all the work, take all the cuffs, provide all the food, and content herself with what was left over after her lord had finished his dinner. She was not only forbidden, by ancient law, and under penalty of death, to eat with her husband or enter a canoe, but was debarred under the same penalty, from eating bananas, pine-apples, oranges and other choice fruits at any time or any place."[91]

Noblewomen fared better, often having multiple husbands whom they rotated each month. In 1866 Hawaii was a matrilineal society. Nobility was determined through the female line, which Clemens recommended to the European aristocracy as "exceedingly sensible." "It is," he said, "easy to know who a man's mother was, but, etc., etc."[92]

Clemens was not always an advocate of women's rights. His early writings on women's suffrage were crude and disrespectful. In 1867 he ridiculed the Missouri women's campaign for a vote "along with us and the nigs."[93] He ruefully predicted the successful election of a woman for State Milner but worried that husbands would end up as nursemaids for "neglected children." As a court jester, he mocked "George Francis Train—the great Fenian Female Suffrage Ass,"[94] and in a prepared lecture, "An Appeal in Behalf of Extended Suffrage to the Boys," he ridiculed the suffragettes.[95] In March 1867 he wrote for the St. Louis *Missouri Democrat*:

I think I could write a pretty strong argument in favor of female suffrage, but I don't want to do it. I never want to see women voting, and gabbing about politics, and electioneering. There is something revolting in the thought. It would shock me inexpressibly for an angel to come down from above and ask me to take a drink with him (though I should doubtless consent), but it would shock me still more to see one of our blessed earthly angels peddling election tickets among a mob of shabby scoundrels she never saw before.

Women, go your ways! Seek not to beguile us of our imperial privileges. Content yourself with your little feminine trifles—your babies, your benevolent societies and your knitting—and let your natural bosses do the voting. Stand back—you will be wanting to go to war next. We will let you teach school as much as you want to, and we will pay you half ages for it too, but beware! We don't want you to crowd us too much.[96]

In 1867 Clemens attended a lecture by Anna Dickinson at the Cooper Institute. She made a strong case for opening up new career opportunities for women, who were then confined mostly to teaching and nursing. Clemens wrote to the *Alta California* that Dickinson "reasons well, and makes every point without fail." Her eloquence could move the audience and her satire "cuts to the quick." But he was not persuaded: "She used arguments that would not stand analysis."[97]

In a series of satires on the women's movement during this early period, Twain depicted a legislature in which elected women amended the "Common School System" to provide education "for remodeling and establishing fashions for ladies' bonnets."[98] In other articles he parroted arguments advanced by opponents of women's rights. Granting women the right to vote would demean their cherished status in society as they succumbed to the corrupting influence of the political system. The political machines would induce an uneducated, ignorant woman to "work, bribe and vote with all her might."[99] Twain did not want to take "the High Priestess we reverence at the sacred fireside and send her forth to electioneer for votes among a mangy mob who are unworthy to touch the hem of her garment."[100] Antifeminist editors advised their readers to take Twain's satires seriously, and Clemens himself said this was a "time for all good men to tremble for their country."[101]

When confronted by a woman calling herself "Cousin Jenney" who had taken offense at his satire, he promised to address the issue with "the gravity the occasion demands," conceding that capable women would perform better in government posts than many of the ward-heelers given patronage appointments. He admitted to Jenny that American women would vote with "fifty times the judgment and independence exercised by stupid, illiterate newcomers from foreign lands.[102] He conceded that justice was on the side of women's suffrage, and "that his task would have been easier if she hadn't all the arguments on her side."[103] But Clemens quickly retreated to more comfortable satire, worrying that if given the vote, women would ban drinking and cigar smoking—a fear not entirely unjustified given the linkage between the suffrage movement and the temperance crusade.

A March 1874 letter to the *London Standard* marks a turning point in his position. He defended the women's crusade against rum on the grounds that women are "voiceless in the making of laws & the election of officers to execute them. Born with brains, born in the country, educated, having large interests at stake, they find their tongues tied & their hands fettered while every ignorant whiskey-drinking foreign-born savage in the land may hold office." With characteristic hyperbolic ambiguity, he continued:

> I dearly want the women to be raised to the political altitude of the negro, the imported savage, & the pardoned thief, & allowed to vote. It is our last chance, I think. The women will be voting before long, & then if…the highest offices can continue to be occupied by perjurers & robbers; if another Congress (like the forty-second) consisting of fifteen honest men & 296 of the other kind can once more be created, it will

be the last time.... Both the great parties have failed. I wish we might have a woman's party now, & see how that would work. I feel persuaded that in extending suffrage to women this country could lose absolutely nothing and might gain a great deal.[104]

Clemens later dated his conversion to 1875 when he was forty and in Nook Farm socializing with Isabella Beecher Hooker, a staunch feminist. At her urging he began to speak out at public meetings in support of women's voting rights, denouncing the prejudice that blocks progress—prejudice that the "voter wear pantaloons instead of petticoats." Completing his about-face, he questioned whether America had a true democracy when half the population "was voiceless in the making of laws and the election of officers to execute them." By the turn of the century, he was proclaiming that "if women could vote they would vote on the side of morality...would not sit indolently at home as their husbands and brothers do now, but would...set up some candidates fit for decent human beings to vote for."[105]

Clemens was persuaded that the women's vote would have a leavening effect on politics, but he did not retreat from his conviction that educated and informed voters were essential to a workable democracy. When a group of conservative women defeated female suffrage legislation in Illinois in 1891, Clemens wrote in his *Notebook* that he breathed a sigh of relief, "for the ballot, which is useful only in the hand of the intelligent, could have gone into the hands of those very women." [106] In 1895 Clemens witnessed the success of women's movements in Australia and New Zealand. Although women could not serve in the legislature in New Zealand, they were granted the right to vote in 1893, and 85 percent of them did. "Do men ever turn out better than that—in America, or elsewhere?" he asked.[107]

In January 1901 he spoke with a touch of condescension on "Votes for Women" at the Hebrew Technical School for Girls at Temple Emmanuel in New York:

Referring to woman's sphere in life, I'll say that woman is always right. For twenty-five years I've been a woman's rights man. I have always believed, long before my mother died, that, with her gray hairs and admirable intellect, perhaps she knew as much as I did. Perhaps she knew as much about voting as I.

I should like to see the time come when women shall help to make the laws. I should like to see that whip-lash, the ballot, in the hands of women. As for this city's government, I don't want to say much, except that it is a shame—a shame... If women had the ballot to-day, the state of things in this town would not exist.

If all the women in this town had a vote to-day they would elect a mayor at the next election, and they would rise in their might and change the awful state of things now existing here.[108]

In an unpublished portion of his autobiography, Twain lauds the work of Isabella Hooker and the more prominent advocates of the suffrage movement, Susan B. Anthony, Elizabeth Cady Stanton, and Mary Livermore:

When these powerful sisters entered the field in 1848 woman was what she had always been in all countries and under all religions, all savageries, all civilizations—a slave, and under contempt. The laws affecting women were a disgrace to our statute-book. Those brave women besieged the legislatures of the land, year after year, suffering and enduring all manner of reproach, rebuke, scorn and obloquy, yet never surrendering, never sounding a retreat; their wonderful campaign lasted a great many years, and is the most wonderful in history, for it achieved a revolution—the only one achieved in history for the emancipation of a half a nation that cost not a drop of blood. They broke the chains of their sex and set it free.[109]

He wrote in *Following the Equator*, "Man has ruled the human race from the beginning," and "it was a dull world, and ignorant and stupid...It is not such a dull world now. This is woman's opportunity—she had none before. I wonder where man will be in another forty-seven years."[110] Although Clemens's declaration of gender emancipation was premature, he predicted in 1901 that if he lived another twenty-five years, he would see women "armed with the ballot." He did not live to see the ratification of the Nineteenth Amendment in 1920 prohibiting the denial of voting rights "on account of sex."[111]

A Tale of Today

Clemens's idealized view of women as the saviors of democracy has not yet come to pass. Yet, since 1964 more women than men have voted in presidential elections, and since 1980 the proportion of eligible female adults who vote has been greater than the proportion of eligible males. The women's vote has decided elections, and although women are not a monolithic voting bloc, pollsters have identified a gender gap suggesting that certain issues are important to women voters, and this has shaped the candidates' positions and federal policy. Women clearly made a difference in the election of President Obama in 2008, and the first bill he signed into law was the Lilly Ledbetter Act, reversing a 2007 Supreme Court decision that made it more difficult for women to initiate pay discrimination lawsuits. Other laws that reflect the power of the women's vote include the violence against women act, the family and medical leave act, and federal funding programs for family planning and childcare. The Trump campaign's progressive proposals on daycare, urged by his daughter Ivanka, show that neither party is immune from the concerns of women.

Our political system is stronger as women increasingly serve in elected positions at all levels of government. In 2016, there were 105 women in the House and 20 women in the

Senate– about 20 percent in each house of Congress. *In the Senate in particular, the women seem to have a bipartisan camaraderie and willingness to work across the aisle reminiscent of earlier times. For two hundred years the Supreme Court consisted entirely of men. At the end of 2016 three of the eight justices were women. Women serve as governors and CEOs. Barred from medical and law schools only a few decades ago, women make up a majority of many entering classes. While this represents genuine progress, it falls short of real equality, proportional to the nation's population. Substantial male majorities in legislatures can be insensitive to women's concerns, and pay disparity and pockets of discrimination linger in the public and private sectors.*

Prohibition. Although Clemens became a convert to women's suffrage, he did not buy into its cousin, the temperance movement.* As he wrote in his *Notebook* in 1895:

The manner in which these absurd liquor laws are broken breeds contempt for the law in general…. These laws give rise to smuggling, and informing and perjury…In the States and Canada they are often repealed on the very first opportunity…Why don't the temperance agitators remember Edmund Burke's words? Lawful indulgence is the only check on illicit gratification. Abolishing matrimony would not stamp out fornication. Well, marriage is to morality what properly conducted licensed liquor traffic is to sobriety. In either case a certain human propensity is regulated so as to be a blessing; while left to itself, or subjected to repressive efforts, it would be a curse.[112]

---

* For a short time when he was fourteen years old, Sam was a member of the Cadets of Temperance, a youth group, but he resigned after three months (MT *Autobiography* 1, 590).

Prohibition would only make drinking more tantalizing. In *Pudd'nhead Wilson*, he wrote, "Adam was but human. He did not want the apple for the apple's sake, he wanted it because it was forbidden. The mistake was in not forbidding the serpent, then he would have eaten the serpent."[113] In the famous fence white-washing scene in *Tom Sawyer*, when Tom gets all his friends to do his work for him, Tom has "discovered a great law of human action…that in order to make a man or a boy covet a thing, it is only necessary to make the thing difficult to attain."[114] And this is how Tom accumulates a piece of blue bottle-glass, a key that won't unlock anything, a couple of tadpoles and all manner of wealth—like the capitalist tycoons of the Gilded Age who acquired all manner of unnecessary possessions through trickery and deceit. Twain once quipped that "civilization is the limitless multiplication of unnecessary necessities."[115]

Clemens did not believe in legislating morality. Character was established in the face of adversity, not through statutory commands. His short story "The Man That Corrupted Hadleyburg" was his most eloquent portrayal of the weakness of human virtue untested "in the fire." The nineteen incorruptible leading citizens of the town profess a record of impeccable honesty, until they are confronted with, and gradually yield to, a temptation. For some, their guilt is alleviated when they believe no one else is aware of their transgression. Their true fear is not doing wrong but the disclosure of their deed.[116] For Clemens, true morality did not mean professing to live a virtuous life in a cloistered environment but rather seeking out adversity and temptation and dealing with them courageously and with integrity.

A Tale of Today

Clemens held strong libertarian convictions: an antipathy to legislating morality, resistance to government intrusion into the lives of citizens, and a view that morals reflect human experience and evolve over time. Preserving freedom, in Clemens's view, requires a pluralistic society in which the people tolerate alternative beliefs and lifestyles and seek to persuade others of their convictions through reasoning rather than legislative fiat. His contrarian application of these principles caused him to challenge conventional thinking and popular trends of his day from Sunday blue laws to temperance. Applying Twain's principles to societal issues today would raise some interesting questions about intractable problems that fester unresolved and divide the nation culturally: the legalization of marijuana and legislating reproductive health, to cite two examples.

Medical Care

Having faced the illness and death of family and friends (despite the intervention of physicians), Clemens was outspoken on issues of disease and health care.* During his lifetime there were many forms of medical treatment in competition for consumer attention. The Clemens family experimented with many of them, including hydrotherapy, osteopathy, electric shock, homeopathy, the rest cure, kinesipathy (curative muscle movements), starvation, health foods, patent medicines, mind cure, mental science, and Christian Science. Clemens opposed restrictions on medical care choices and lobbied against efforts by physicians to prohibit alternative approaches through licensure laws. He joined the campaign to legalize osteopathy in New York State.[117] He raised concerns about medical error, which he facetiously claimed was often caused by the illegibility of physician-prescribed prescriptions. He thought the family should be free to decide when and in what form medical care is needed. Clemens believed that during his century advances in medical practice came about because the patient took a strong interest in his or her own health care. He wrote about "the revolt of the patient

---

* Clemens's views on health care are fully explored in K. Patrick Ober's book *Mark Twain and Medicine*, Columbia: University of Missouri Press (2003).

against the physician. The patient fell to doctoring himself, and the physician's practice fell off. He modified his methodology to get back his trade."[118]

On paying for health care (admittedly during a much simpler time), Clemens thought medical professionals should be paid to maintain a family's health rather than to treat specific symptoms, which, in Clemens's view, encouraged excessive and unnecessary doctor visits. He wrote in his *Autobiography*:

> Consider the wisdom and righteousness of that old-time custom—the paying of the physician by the year. Consider what a safeguard it was, for both the physician's livelihood and self-respect, and the family's health. The physician had a regular and assured income, and that was an advantage to him; the family were safe from his invasions when nothing was the matter, and goodness knows that was an advantage to the family.
>
> Look at the difference in our day. What is the common, the universal, custom of the physician with a limited practice? It is this: to keep on coming and coming, long after the patient has ceased to need him—and charging for every visit.[119]

A Tale of Today

While medicine was more art than science during his lifetime, Clemens's views are remarkably prescient. Recent studies have shown that hospital errors may result in secondary illnesses or death for as many as one-third of hospital admissions. The soaring cost of medical malpractice insurance reflects the high number of medical malpractice claims. Mistakes in administering drugs or the interaction of drugs prescribed by different physicians often cause unintended consequences. Recent government and private sector efforts to reduce hospital and physician errors by the introduction of technologies that computerize and coordinate treatment information address concerns that Clemens raised more than one hundred years ago.

In recent years there also has been a resurgence of interest in alternative forms of health care. In 1999 Congress created the Center for Complementary and Alternative Medicine in the National Institutes of Health to evaluate alternatives from a scientific perspective. Having been disappointed with the effectiveness of some of the alternative treatments he explored, Clemens would likely have welcomed objective scientific analysis of alternative approaches.

Given the spiraling cost of health care today, it is noteworthy that Clemens warned about the excessive use, abuse, and fraud that could result when payments are made for the treatment of symptoms, as is common under Medicare, Medicaid, and private fee-for-service indemnity insurance plans. Instead of being paid for each poke, pinch, prod, probe, and pull, Clemens wisely advocated that doctors be paid on an annual basis to look after the health of the family.

Social Activist

Having overcome his ambivalence about race and gender, Clemens's childhood empathy for the underdog resurged in his final decades. He became a champion of many causes. At Helen Keller's request, he raised funds for programs that helped the blind find useful occupations. He supported the Anti-Child Slavery League and endorsed limited work-hour legislation.[120]

He wrote "A Dog's Tale" in support of an antivivisection law; he wrote "A Horse's Tale" at the request of the esteemed actress Minnie Maddern Fiske to protest bullfighting, which used old and crippled horses as animal fodder. In *A Horse's Tale*, Buffalo Bill's favorite horse, the aging Soldier Boy, is stolen and ends up in a bullring, succumbing to a most gory ending. Clemens criticized the needless killing of wildlife in Theodore Roosevelt's famed hunting expeditions, one of several festering conflicts in their tumultuous relationship. Clemens ridiculed these much-publicized events, comparing Roosevelt's cornering of a black bear in Louisiana aided by a pack of yapping hounds to shooting a cow in a pasture. Roosevelt's Boone & Crockett Club would stalk the largest male game—with giant antlers or tusks—for members' trophy walls. Clemens claimed with some scientific support that this selective hunting led to the weakening and decline of the species.[121]

CHAPTER FOURTEEN

Mark Twain The Government Skeptic

"There is great danger that our people will lose our independence of thought and action which is the cause of much of our greatness, and sink into the helplessness of the Frenchman or German who expects his government to feed him when hungry, clothe him when naked, to prescribe when his child may be born and when he may die, and, in the fine, to regulate every act of humanity from the cradle to the tomb, including the manner in which he may seek future admission to paradise."

— MARK TWAIN

Clemens's advocacy for racial justice, women's rights, peaceful diplomacy, and myriad social causes, and his scathing criticism of the abuses of legislative and executive power, won plaudits from the progressives. But when he questioned the federal government's ability to intervene fairly and effectively in domestic issues, he disappointed these same progressives. Any attempt to label Clemens as liberal or conservative, at least as those terms are bandied about today, would be a fruitless exercise. He remained deeply skeptical of government and the exercise of governmental power by flawed human beings—whether in the form of censorship, invasion of privacy, judicial autocracy, bureaucratic arrogance and incompetence, or the abuse of regulatory, taxing, and spending powers.

Speech and Censorship

As a writer Clemens opposed censorship. In an unfinished letter to the editor on the "Whitman Controversy," he criticized Boston district attorney Oliver Stevens's order to James R. Osgood and Company to withdraw Walt Whitman's *Leaves of Grass* from publication, alleging that it violated the Massachusetts's statute on "obscene literature."[1] Clemens compared the pornography of classic literature—the works of Boccaccio, Rabelais, Chaucer, and Shakespeare, read and revered by gentlemen scholars and students—to the less salacious passages targeted by the district attorney. He condemned the hypocrisy of banning less offensive "bad books" by contemporary writers like Whitman, Swinburne, and Wilde, but said he had no objection to censorship of erotic material as long as it was applied equally to the classics for "the effects produced by it are exactly the same, whether the writing was done yesterday or a thousand centuries ago."[2] The draft letter was not sent, possibly because Clemens had his own censor—Livy.

Crime and Punishment

Subtly revealing his growing skepticism about the death penalty, Clemens wrote a letter to *The New York Tribune* in 1871, signed Samuel Langhorne, about a famed linguist who was sentenced to death for an atrocious murder. He begins with a shrill defense of the death penalty: "I believe in capital punishment. I believe that when a murder has been done it should be answered for in blood." Referring to the low ratio of capital punishment convictions in England at the time, "Langhorne" concedes "that the death-law is rendered almost inoperative by its very severity," but he writes: "It is better to hang one murderer in sixteen... than not to hang any at all."[3] Realizing that the linguist's death would deprive the nation of a book he was writing on the unity of all languages, Langhorne suggests—completely undercutting his advocacy of capital punishment—that some stupid person be executed in place of the condemned.

Although he was reluctant to broach the issue in public, by 1879 he had written in his *Notebook* that he opposed capital punishment as barbaric and ineffective—an "anachronism" and "the opposite of a deterrent."[4] He abhorred the inequality of justice rendered as the wealthy and well-lawyered were spared death on some trumped-up insanity defense, and the poor were sent to the gallows. In "A New Crime," Twain described how the "very wealthy' Baldwin family got their son acquitted of several murder charges on the ground of fits of temporary insanity. He then compared other brutal murders in which the wealthy and politically influential were acquitted and the poor hanged. He concluded that "crime is dying out." "If you, having friends and money, kill a man," that "is *evidence* that you are a lunatic." What was needed is not laws against crime, "but a law against insanity."[5] More bluntly, in "Murder and Insanity" he wrote, "The use of the plea of insanity on all occasions is making every murder trial a farce."[6]

Twain's most dramatic narrative of the temporary insanity plea was Laura's trial in *The Gilded Age*, which led to her acquittal. But in 1908 Clemens applauded an insanity defense crafted by his billiard partner and across-the-street New York City neighbor, Martin Littleton, the defense attorney for Harry K. Thaw. In full view of the audience attending a musical at Madison Square Garden's rooftop cabaret, Thaw killed the famed architect Stanford White point blank with a bullet in the face. White had seduced Thaw's young bride, showgirl Evelyn Nesbit, when she was a single teenager. Despite a plea of temporary insanity, the first trial resulted in a hung jury. Littleton was retained for the retrial. He presented a compelling defense of insanity rooted in lifelong mental illness. Thaw was found not guilty by reason of insanity and sent to a mental institution. Clemens was fully sympathetic with the verdict and pleased that Littleton had rejected the "temporary insanity" gimmick and established a history of mental illness. Clemens thought White was a "remorseless seducer," and he condemned the voyeuristic media for unfairly tarnishing Nesbit's reputation.[7]

Clemens advocated replacing the death penalty with public humiliation, which he thought was a stronger deterrent to crime than capital punishment. He wrote in his *Notebook*: "Sense of ridicule is bitterer than death & more feared."[8] Instead of imprisonment, which provided a training ground for young criminals, he advocated shame as a motivating factor to reform behavior. Clemens also abhorred the popular tendency to make "a hero of a villain."[*] In his 1869 short piece "Lionizing Murderers," he makes fun of the benevolent Christian women and clergy who glorified condemned murderers as unfortunate victims of circumstances.[9]

Informed by his experiences with frontier justice, Twain's writings are permeated by his disdain for the judicial system—obdurate adherence to precedent despite changing circumstances, ignorant and pliant juries, arbitrary and autocratic judges, and corrupt and incompetent law enforcement. True justice, in Clemens's view, should not be influenced by wealth, political power, randomness of birth or the environment. For this reason, he was an early advocate of prison reform. Young offenders were simply products of their inheritance and upbringing. Incarceration "put the beginners in with the confirmed criminals," he wrote in *What is Man?*, fostering recidivism. Instead government should provide a stimulating, healthy, educational environment for youthful offenders.[10]

---

[*] There is a widely circulated, perhaps apocryphal story that Clemens once met Jesse James in a dry goods store in Missouri. James came up to him and said, "Well, I reckon we're about the best in our lines." Not recognizing him, Clemens asked, "from what throne of greatness" he had come, and Jesse replied, "Why I am Jesse James," and he scurried off.

A Tale of Today

Clemens's condemnation of the death penalty as inherently unequal and unjust is reflected today in the work of the NAACP Legal Defense and Educational Fund. It has made the elimination of the death penalty a litigation priority, viewing it in racial terms as the modern equivalent of lynching, which Clemens had so vigorously attacked. Days before he left office in January 2003, Illinois governor George Ryan commuted the death sentences of 156 prisoners, calling the Illinois death penalty system arbitrary, capricious, and immoral. In a state with a black population of 15 percent, 62 percent of the prisoners on death row were black. The governor found that more death row inmates had been exonerated through DNA testing or other new evidence than had been executed.[11] On July 11, 2011, Illinois governor Pat Quinn signed into law legislation ending the death penalty and commuted to life imprisonment without parole the sentences of the remaining fifteen men on death row.[12] During Clemens's lifetime, two states—Wisconsin and Maine—abolished the death penalty. In 2016, there are 19 states plus the District of Columbia which have abolished the death penalty, and there are a number of additional states which rarely invoke it.

Clemens's views about incarceration also resonate today. He believed that incarceration of juveniles prepared them for a life of crime and that prisons were the last refuge of the poor and the oppressed. Juvenile facilities today are filled with youngsters convicted of minor drug offenses, trespassing, shop-lifting and petty theft, where they are schooled by hardened gang members, resulting in a recidivism rate of nearly 80 percent in some states.[13] The United States has the largest prison population in the world (seven times the per capita *rate of Canada), and 40 percent of its prisoners are African American.[14] In 2003 black men were twelve times more likely to be sentenced to prison for drug offenses than white men,* even though impartial studies show that blacks and whites use and sell drugs at about the same rates.[15]*

The Expanding Federal Government

Clemens relished satirizing the expanding federal bureaucracy. He ridiculed Congress's corrupt practice of using Civil War veteran pensions for nonpartisan "vote-buying."[16] Explaining why a district attorney he supported was not elected, he quipped, "I am not a Congress, and I cannot distribute pensions, and I don't know any other legitimate way to buy a vote."[17] He compared the expansion of the federal pension program to the fall of Rome, whose "liberties were not auctioned off in a day, but were bought slowly, gradually furtively, little by little" first by providing corn to the poor and then to the middle class and finally to buy votes. Similarly, "at first we granted deserved pensions, righteously and with a clean and honorable motive, to the disabled soldiers of the Civil War," but then, solely to purchase votes, "amazing additions were made to the pension list." The corrupted program, he said, "dishonors the uniform."[18] Clemens was concerned that

---

* Why? Police tend to enforce the drug laws more vigorously in inner-city open-air drug markets or near school zones than in white suburbia; mandatory prison sentences for crack cocaine (used in the inner city) have been much higher than powered cocaine (the preferred choice of middle-class whites), though the effects are the same, and blacks are disproportionately subjected to arrest, search, and seizure based on suspicion of drug use. Another contributing factor is the powerful lobby of privatized prisons in some states. Private prisons consume a large share of state budgets and profit from crowded prison populations. Congress is currently debating legislation that would ameliorate but not eliminate the disparity in the treatment of offenses involving crack versus powered cocaine. In 2016, President Obama's attorney General, Loretta Lynch, announced the Justice Department's intention to eliminate privatized federal prisons.

the "stupendous wealth" doled out by Congress and "its inevitable corruptions and moral blight" would inevitably transform well-intended programs into massive instruments of autocratic power. Expanding federal power would "likely cause endless trouble."[19] He worried that the government's mania for meddling in the private affairs of its citizens would subvert the people's "independence of thought and action, which is the cause of much of our greatness."[20] Clemens feared that Americans would "sink into the helplessness of the Frenchman and German who expects his government to feed him when hungry, clothe him when naked, to prescribe when his child may be born and when he may die, and, in fine, to regulate every act of humanity from cradle to the tomb."[21]

Clemens also condemned inefficiency, waste, and corruption in federal programs, such as those assisting American Indians. He worried that as large corporations and wealthy individuals exerted control over the political process, a plutocracy would emerge to protect and enhance a privileged class. His skepticism of centralized government was rooted in his conviction that the human propensity was "to drift into monarchy." It is "in our blood and bones, and ineradicably, we carry the seeds out of which monarchies and aristocracies are grown: worship of gauds, titles, distinctions, power."[22]

It is "unavoidable and irresistible," Clemens wrote, that "circumstances will gradually take away the powers of the States and concentrate them in a central government."[23] He urged that "we obstruct these encroachments and steadily resist them."[24] He worried that "if the States continue to fail to do their duty as required by the people, *constructions of the Constitution will be found* to vest the power where it will be exercised—in the national government."[25] He doubted that Congress and the executive branch would handle the accretion of power responsibly. Isolated in a capital city, uprooted from the financial, commercial, cultural, and academic centers of the nation, Washington politicians and government officials were aloof, arrogant, and insulated.[26] Congress passes laws covering "some industry they know nothing about" which then begins "to confuse and hamper interested parties because they do not understand it." But this "has been provided for in a most curious way. Each public department in Washington keeps a minor asylum of salaried inmates whose business is to invent a meaning for laws that have no meaning; and to detect meanings where any exist, and distort and confuse them. The process is called 'interpreting.' And sublime and awe-inspiring is this art!"[27] "The departmental *interpreters* of the law in Washington," he wrote in an unsent letter in 1887, "can always be depended on to take any reasonably good law and interpret the common sense out of it. They can be depended on, every time, to defeat a good law, and make it inoperative—yes, and utterly grotesque, too, mere matter for laughter and derision."[28] His faith in Washington did not increase through the years. When his nephew, Samuel Moffett, sent him *Suggestions on Government* in 1894, proposing a progressive agenda, Clemens wrote back: "There is no good government at all & none is possible."[29]

With Theodore Roosevelt's ascendancy to the presidency in 1901, Clemens became exceedingly anxious about the accretion of executive power. The "White House commands are not under restraint of law or custom," he dictated in his unpublished auto-biography. The White House "can ride down the Congress as the Czar cannot ride down the Duma. It can concentrate and augment power in the Capital by despoiling the States of their reserved rights...It can pack the Supreme Court with judges friendly to its ambition."[30]

While leery of the expanding federal bureaucracy, Clemens did not spurn all federal programs. He supported increased funding for US Army Corps of Engineers projects to build dams and levees to develop the Mississippi River for commerce. In 1882 the rupture and collapse of a levee had resulted in untold destruction. In *Life on the Mississippi*, he predicted that the river communities would be devastated by future spring floods—a prophecy that has too often come true.[31] This was one area where Clemens and Roosevelt had a common interest. Because he supported these internal improvements, Clemens thought that Ethan Hitchcock, Roosevelt's secretary of the interior, was his best appointment.[32] Nineteenth century liberals like Clemens supported government programs that facilitated industrialization and private sector growth such as an efficient transportation infrastructure. He wrote admiringly of the transportation systems built by Napoleon III and Alexander II, noting that "one can tell what a nation is if he can only see its roads."

When government restricted individual choices, however, Clemens retained his frontier-bred libertarian streak. He believed that citizens in a democracy must fight bureaucratic intrusions that arbitrarily restrain individual liberty. As a concerned citizen, he believed in protesting all forms of exploitation, no matter how trivial. "We allow our commonest rights to be trampled underfoot every day and everywhere," he wrote, and he thought "every citizen of the republic ought to consider himself an unofficial policeman...that the only effective way of preserving or protecting public rights was for each citizen to do his share in preventing or punishing such infringements of them as came under his personal notice."[33]

In *The Gilded Age*, Philip Sterling speaks for Twain (and Warner), opining that "no country can be well governed unless its citizens as a body keep religiously before their minds that they are the guardians of the law, and that the law officers are only the machinery for its execution, nothing more."[34] Commenting on her father's libertarian streak, Clara Clemens noted that he "did not easily or meekly succumb to rules and regulations imposed on the public."[35] Clemens wondered "if we shall have any liberties left, by and by if we keep up our American habit of meekly submitting to every imposition that is put upon us."[36] He especially fought the discourtesies and restrictions imposed upon him by the railroads.[37]

In a July Fourth speech to Americans in London, Clemens referred "with effusion to our railway system, which consents to let us live, though it might do the opposite being our owners."[38] The railroads, he noted, had only run "over heedless and unnecessary people at crossings." They "seriously regretted the killings of these thirty thousand people, and went so far as to pay for some of them—voluntarily, of course, for the meanest of us would not claim that we possess a court treacherous enough to enforce a law against a railroad company." Clemens was especially touched by one incident. "After an accident, the company sent home the remains of a dear and distant old relative of mine in a basket with the remark, 'please state what figure you hold him at—and return the basket.'"[39]

Clemens was a one-man vigilante squad, hell-bent on improving the quality of life in the nation he loved. He took on the corrupt inspection of ocean liners docking at US ports. He went to court against a cab driver who overcharged one of his household workers. He claimed that the conductors of the New York Railway Company had robbed his daughters. He mailed scathing letters to the telephone, telegraph, and light companies when their service did not meet his expectations.[40]

In his novels Twain championed individual freedom and conscience freed from the constraints of oppressive government, Old World caste systems, and ingrained prejudice. In the economic and political spheres, he thought that hard work, innovation, risk-taking, courage, and integrity should be rewarded, and persons with superior talent and work ethic would be rewarded more generously. In contrast to European society, he believed that in the United States "inequalities are measured by degrees & shades of difference in capacity, not by accidental differences in birth."[41] Government owes every citizen *only* the same "legal right and privilege."[42]

Clemens summed up his views on the ideal political system in a speech to foreign critics: "Let us then say in broad terms, that any system which has...human slavery, despotic government, inequality, numerous and brutal punishments for crime, superstition almost universal, and dirt and poverty almost universal—is not a real civilization, and any system which has none of them is."[43]

Having witnessed the crushing effect of economic cycles on his father's fortunes, and having seen thousands thrown out of work during periodic recessions, Clemens was not unsympathetic to the temporary plight of the unemployed. He gave benefit lectures and participated in other charitable events, although he was concerned that money did not go to "professional paupers" but instead to "worthy and honest poor families and individuals who have fallen into poverty through stress of circumstances but endured their miseries in silence and concealment." He complained that some charitable groups wasted their money and did more harm than good.[44]

A Tale of Today

Clemens's concern about how Congress politicized the nation's first social safety system— Civil War pensions— seems relevant to the current debate about subsequent and far more substantial federal safety-net programs. While Social Security, Medicare, Medicaid, comprehensive health care, veterans' benefits, and public assistance programs serve honorable and necessary purposes, can Congress exercise the discipline to ensure that future revenues will cover projected costs and to render proper oversight to deter overutilization, inefficiency, fraud and abuse? Few elected leaders appear willing to take the political risk of placing entitlement programs on a sustainable path.

Clemens's concerns about America drifting into European-style bureaucratic paternalism, crushing individual initiative, remain central to the current political debate. The president of the American Enterprise Institute, a conservative Washington think tank, poses the question in today's terms. We are facing "a new struggle between two competing visions," Arthur Brooks writes. Will America "continue to be an exceptional nation organized around principles of free enterprise—limited government, reliance upon entrepreneurship, and rewards determined by market forces?" Or will America "move toward European-style statism, grounded in expanding bureaucracies, a managed economy, and large scale income redistribution?" Brooks argued that the "visions are not reconcilable. We must choose."[45]

The accretion of federal power criticized by Clemens pales in comparison to the proliferation of federal programs and

---

mountains of federal law and regulation that have arisen in the century since his death. Clemens warned that once laws are enacted and entitlements created, like the post-Civil War pensions, they assume a life of their own. As President Reagan was fond of saying, the closest thing to eternal life on earth is a temporary government program. Laws enacted during the Great Depression to rescue failing family farmers now provide $15 billion annually to large corporate farms. Between 2003 and 2005, seventy-three percent of farm subsidies went to 10 percent of the recipients, among the largest of them John Hancock Life Insurance, International Paper, Chevron, and several prominent members of Congress, although some incremental reforms to the farm bill have subsequently been enacted.[46]

Most troubling is the redundancy and overlap in federal programs. Are twenty separate federal programs aiding the homeless really necessary? The stovepipe nature of categorical programs, reflecting the fragmented congressional committee structure, imposes duplicative burdens on state and local governments and the private sector and wastes time and resources in bureaucratic in-fighting and coordination.

Nonetheless, like so many voters and politicians today, Clemens thought that federal programs that benefited his pet projects and places were exemplary government, while other appropriations were "pork" and a waste of the taxpayers' money. He supported government programs that build transportation infrastructure to facilitate commerce and that prepare skilled workers for productive jobs through practical education.

Given Clemens's strong conviction that citizen activists can and should fight unjust, unfair and insensitive laws, rules and regulatory intrusions by government and the private sector, it would be interesting to hear his commentary on the 1960's civil rights movement which demonstrated the power of citizen action to bring about revolutionary change in discriminatory laws and cultural practices through peaceful protest. Citizen movements today from the Tea Party to Occupy Wall Street reflect an engaged citizenry highlighting in the public conscience such challenges as the unsustainable federal debt and growing income disparity.

All Politics is Local

Clemens's skepticism of government extended to all levels. He once defined "public servants" as "persons chosen by the people to distribute the graft."[47] He had observed political corruption in Hannibal, St. Louis, Carson City and San Francisco. But during his long stays in New York City, he had witnessed corruption as a high art. Boss William Tweed's Tammany Hall tentacles reached into almost every public office and institution—governor, mayor, the courts, the district attorney, and the police. For the right price, the Tweed Ring political machine immunized from prosecution gamblers, houses of prostitution, saloons, and ordinary businessmen who skirted the law. The Tweed Ring doled out patronage, city contracts, and other favors to their comrades in graft. Tammany Hall bilked the city budget for some $200 million for the rental of nonexistent armories, repairs never made to city streets and buildings, and bills for phantom plumbing and carpentry. The city machine paid four times the actual cost of constructing new court houses, paid $7500 for thermometers, purchased $400,000 safes, and subcontracted for electricians who did no work. It spewed forth innovative renditions of such timeworn products as blackmail, graft, extortion, and fraud.[48]

Closely associated with Tweed—and similarly immortalized by Thomas Nast's cartoons—railroad and finance tycoons Jay Gould and James Fisk Jr. became the archetypical robber barons of the Gilded Age. By bribing judges and legislators, the "most hated man in America" Gould and "Diamond Jim" Fisk conspired with Daniel Drew to gain control of the Erie Railroad. Gould allegedly spent a million dollars to bribe New York State legislators to legalize eight million dollars in stock watering for the Erie Railroad.* In return for favorable legislation, Tweed became a director of the Erie and shared in its monopoly profits. Gould once explained to a state legislative committee how a corporate leader uses political contributions to maximize profits: "It was the custom when men received nominations to come to me for contributions, and I made them, and considered them good paying investments for the [railroad]. In a Republican district, I was a strong Republican; in a Democratic district, I was Democratic; and in doubtful districts I was doubtful. In politics I was an Erie Railroad man every time."[49]

While living in Buffalo, Clemens fearlessly took on the robber barons and their influence in New York state and local politics. In a series of articles published in *The Galaxy* in 1870, Twain satirized the political corruption and patronage of the Democratic political machine. In the illustrations to *A Burlesque Autobiography* (unrelated to the text), Gould, Fisk, and New York governor John Hoffman are depicted in "The House that Jack Built"—the Erie Railroad headquarters—where they colluded to swindle the public and purchase the legislature.[50] In "Running for Governor," Twain parodies Governor Hoffman in a state election in which two political machines sling mud at each other. Hoffman wins the election because his opponent was "insufficiently schooled in corrupt politics."[51] On September 17, 1871, the intrepid Twain published "The Revised Catechism" in *The New York Tribune,* a burlesque based on the shorter Westminster catechism, consisting of questions and answers in a modern moral philosophy class:

Q: What is the chief end of man?
A: To get rich.

---

* Stock watering was a method of increasing the weight of cows before sale. When cattle driver Daniel Drew became a financier, the term was applied to inflating artificially the value of stock, a form of securities fraud that was common under older corporate laws that focused on the par value of stock.

Q: In what way?

A: Dishonestly, if we can. Honestly, if we must.

Q: Who is God, the one and only true?

A: Money is God. Gold and Greenbacks and Stock—Father and Son and the Ghost of the same—three persons in one; these are the true and only God, mighty and supreme; and William Tweed is his prophet.

Q: How shall a man attain the chief end of life?

A: By furnishing imaginary carpets to the Court House; apocryphal chairs to the armories, and invisible printing to the city.

Q: Who were the models the young men were taught to emulate in former days?

A: Washington and Franklin,

Q: Whom do they and should they emulate now in this era of enlightenment?

A: Tweed, Hall...Fisk, Gould....

Q: What books were chiefly prized for the training of the young in former days?

A: Poor Richard's Almanac, the Pilgrim's Progress, and the Declaration of Independence.

Q: What are the best Sunday-School books in this more enlightened age?

A: St. Fisk's Ingenious Robberies...St. Gould on the Watering of Stock...St. Tweed's Handbook of Morals, and the Court-House edition of the Holy Crusade of the Forty Thieves."[52]

Clemens's hometown of Buffalo did not escape his satiric pen. In "A Curious Dream," he mocks the run-down city cemetery in a story about corpses who move their coffins to a better neighborhood.[53] In "A Mysterious Visit," he describes an interview by a tax collector, admitting that he "swore to lie after lie, fraud after fraud, villainy after villainy...But what of it? It is nothing more than thousands of the richest, and proudest, and most respected, honored and courted men in America do every year."[54]

On Valentine's Day in 1892, the Reverend Charles Henry Parkhurst of the Madison Square Presbyterian Church gave a blistering sermon, exposing the Tammany machine's collaboration with prostitution and gambling rings. Undercover investigators had provided the district attorney with a list of 284 gambling joints, brothels, and saloons operating illegally. In 1894 the Lexow investigation disclosed police extortion, ballot box contamination, and blackmail. Twain depicted Tammany's new boss, Richard Croker, with his arms in the city treasury up to his elbows. In 1895 a reform-minded 36-year-old police commissioner– Theodore Roosevelt– was appointed. Despite his much-publicized, aggressive anti-vice campaign, Roosevelt was no match for the dark forces of organized crime. He soon left to become Assistant Secretary of the Navy and thereafter for the green hills of San Juan.[55]

After living in Germany in 1892, Clemens cited Berlin as a model for local governance. There, "the most illustrious citizens" considered it an honor to serve gratis on the Board of Aldermen. They presided over a just and fair system of tax collection, police enforcement, building codes, advertising restrictions, and cleanliness in a "thoroughly well-governed city."[56] He liked the way Berlin prohibited public begging but provided social security for the poor. Clemens thought it doubtful that the best people could be persuaded to run for municipal office in New York or, if they ran, whether they could be elected. He was motivated to try because he believed that engaged, informed citizens could be most effective at the local level where the actions of public officials directly affected their lives.

In 1900 and 1901, reform groups enlisted Clemens's help in battling Tammany Hall corruption. In a 1901 speech to the City Club, entitled "Municipal Corruption," Clemens was accompanied by the social activist Henry Codman Potter, Episcopal bishop of the Diocese of New York. Clemens spoke out for reform. He declared that but one of fifty men in public life was corrupt, but the corrupt 2 percent prevail because they are better organized. The corrupt man contaminates politics because he is organized.

He urged the clean minded forty-nine to "organize, organize, organize."[57]

Clemens got organized. He actively campaigned for the election of a reform candidate—Columbia College president Seth Low—for mayor of New York. In a campaign speech on October 7, 1901, Twain described the fusion candidate Low not as a Republican, but as an "Acorn," a third party interested only in selecting the best candidates for public office.[58] Low won the election. Tammany was defeated. Twain was given much of the credit for the victory. One newspaper reported:

> Who killed Croker?
> I, said Mark Twain,
> I killed Croker
> I, the Jolly Joker.[59]

In a postelection meeting with the Acorns, Clemens declared Tammany dead: "There was no use in blackguarding a corpse." The election of Low was Clemens's last active political campaign at any level. While some might suggest it was a pyrrhic victory—Tammany came back in full force in the next election and dominated New York politics for another three decades—the transitory success of the Acorn/Fusion Party shows how passionate reformers can organize to effectuate change albeit fleeting change without a continuing, sustained organization.

Clemens's advice that reformers must "organize, organize, organize" has been recently echoed by Hacker and Pierson in their book *Winner Take All Politics*, where they postulate that wealthy interests have organized to co-opt democracy, frustrating efforts to translate lofty campaign promises to change the way Washington works into meaningful reform. They write: "Political reformers will need to mobilize for the long haul, appreciating that it is not electoral competitions alone that are decisive, but also the creation of organized capacity to cement a meaningful middle-class democracy by turning electoral victories into substantive and sustainable triumphs."[60]

CHAPTER FIFTEEN

Mark Twain: Defender Of Free Enterprise

"Whenever you find you are on the side of the majority, it is time for reform."

— MARK TWAIN

The historical turning point, Clemens thought, when the lust for money became America's dominant cultural value, was the 1849 California Gold Rush. "Judge" Clemens and "Uncle" James Lampton (Colonel Sellers) epitomized the speculative instincts engrained in the American character, but for the most part, until the mid-nineteenth century, American families worked the farms, passed on core values to their children and stoically accepted life's hardships and blessings. Then, in Clemens's view, Americans in droves abandoned their Puritan values of hard work, family, and a disciplined lifestyle and went west in search of riches in gold and silver. Clemens himself was caught up in the infectious impulse to get rich when he boarded the Overland Stage for the Nevada territories.

Several factors converged to elevate money as the central objective and measurement of success in American society. By using their political influence and engaging in unscrupulous practices, the railroad promoters created a national commerce. By financing the Union victory in the Civil War, the Wall Street bankers gained huge economic and political power, which they retain to this day. Mechanized labor replaced the pride of crafts-manship, and the rise of urban industrialization demanded a compliant workforce. Festering resentments and economic dis-placement after the Civil War, including unemployed veterans and wandering freedmen cut loose from the plantations, tore many Americans from their cultural roots. Immigrants from many countries brought diverse centuries-old traditions, but in the grand melting pot, money was the common language.

Clemens was acutely aware of these trends and the widening gap between rich and poor. He unabashedly targeted the "wor-shippers of the Almighty Dollar," which included the robber bar-ons, the Wall Street bankers, and the industrial tycoons—among them John D. Rockefeller, John Wanamaker, Daniel Drew, and Cornelius Vanderbilt—and their interlocking relationships.[1] J. P. Morgan served on forty-eight corporate boards, Rockefeller on thirty-seven. Most of all, Clemens singled out the secretive, dimin-utive Jay Gould, "the mightiest disaster which has ever befallen this country" for creating the new gospel, "Money is God."* He wrote: "The people had *desired* money before his day, but *he* taught them to fall down and worship it. They had respected men of means before his day, but along with this respect was joined the respect due to the character and industry which had accumulated it. But Jay Gould taught the entire nation to make a god of money and the man, no matter how the money might have been acquired."[2]

---

* Twain wrote in his *Autobiography*, "Jay Gould had just reversed the commer-cial morals of the United States. He had put blight on them from which they have never recovered, and from which they will not recover for as much as a century to come" (MT *Autobiography* 1, 364).

The gospel of Gould was to "get money," he wrote, "Get it quickly. Get it in abundance. Get it in prodigious abundance." Indeed, "like all other nations, we worship money and the possessors of it—they being our aristocracy."[3] Clemens scribbled in his *Notebook*, "Some men worship rank, some worship heroes, some worship power, some worship God, & over these ideals they dispute & cannot unite—but they all worship money."[4] In "The Man That Corrupted Hadleyburg," he wrote allegorically about the corrupting influences of money on a superficially pious community.[5] He ridiculed the elevated social status of people who *appear* to have wealth in the "Million Pound Bank Note."[6] A 1906 sequel, "The $30,000 Bequest," expanded on the effect of money and greed on human behavior. Falsely believing they were to receive a large bequest, a close-knit family is destroyed as they gamble away their imaginary fortune—a metaphor for the cultural destruction caused by Gilded Age tycoons, or, perhaps, by Clemens's own failed investments of Livy's inheritance. Twain wrote in words echoed by more than a few lottery winners over the decades: "Vast wealth, acquired by sudden and unwholesome means, is a snare. It did us no good, transient were its feverish pleasures; yet for its sake we threw away our sweet and simple and happy life."[7]

In his *Notebook* Clemens jotted down a Gilded Age revision of a biblical proverb: "The lack of money is the root of all evil."[8] Clemens satirized the corrupt practices of specialized industries. In "An Inquiry about Insurance," he exposed insurance industry practices that cheated the insured.[9] In "Daniel in the Lion's Den," he targeted unscrupulous stock brokers, calling the San Francisco Board of Brokers the "Den of Forty Thieves" whose floor trading on the exchange was "respectable stealing."[10]

In "An Open Letter to Commodore Vanderbilt," Clemens took on a powerful and ruthless tycoon who built a hundred-million-dollar fortune by stock watering, flaunting rail and steamboat safety standards, and bribing public officials. Vanderbilt was praised by preachers and politicians. He was compared to Lincoln as a "humbly born boy" who had risen to "national eminence."[11] Clemens dissented. In his open letter, he recited anecdotally Vanderbilt's various nefarious acts and concluded: "I don't remember ever reading anything about which you oughtn't be ashamed...Go and surprise the whole country by doing something right."[12]

While Clemens spoke out against the crushing effect of the robber barons and their political servants on immigrant populations festering in tenements and slums, he was not a major player in the rising progressive movement. He was intrigued by Henry George's *Progress and Poverty*, which proposed a single tax on the value of land that George considered a common heritage, and he found "fascinating" Edward Bellamy's utopian nationalism in *Looking Backwards*, but he embraced neither doctrine. He referred to Bellamy as "the man who made the accepted heaven paltry by inventing a better one on earth," but concluded that "the Bellamy boom" promoting socialism was a passing fad.[13]

When Ida Tarbell wrote her series of articles on Standard Oil in *McClure's Magazine*, Clemens arranged an interview for her with Standard Oil vice president Rogers. Her 1904 *History of the Standard Oil Company* painted a devastating portrait of Rockefeller and his strong-arm tactics against rivals and railroads that led to the breakup of Standard Oil. Though not unscathed, Rogers came out looking better than Rockefeller. Tarbell called Rogers "as fine a pirate as ever flew his flag on Wall Street."[14] Clemens was not a fan of Rockefeller, of whom he said: "We gave to the world the spirit of liberty...and now we are giving the world the spirit of graft," but he thought Tarbell's scathing attack was over the top.[15] Clemens gave Rogers a complete pass, recognizing that his friend was as generous in his philanthropy as he was ruthless in business. Rogers paid for Helen Keller's college education and gave her a lifetime annuity. He funded sixty schools in the South for African American farm children. Booker T. Washington called him "one of the best and greatest men I have ever met."[16]

In the 1907 Panic, Clemens suffered from the collapse of the corrupt Knickerbocker Trust, in which he had placed a modest investment. He had witnessed the humiliation of his friend Ulysses Grant, who lost all his savings in what today would be known as the Ponzi scheme of his son's Wall Street partner, Ferdinand Ward. "People are always seeking investments that pay illegitimately large sums; and they never, or seldom, stop to inquire into the nature of the business," Twain wrote in his *Autobiography*.[17] Muckraker Upton Sinclair hoped that Twain, "the uncrowned King of America," would join him in denouncing "capitalist greed and knavery." To Sinclair's disappointment, Clemens demurred.[18] Instead, in unpublished dictations, Twain privately defended J. P. Morgan and the Wall Street bankers for acting to avoid an economic collapse despite President Roosevelt's claim that he had thwarted a depression: "This has been a strange Panic. It has not strongly resembled any Panic in the history of the country...It is as if the business activities of our eighty million people had suddenly come to a standstill, leaving everyone idle, frightened, wondering...The phrase 'laying off' has become common, almost wearisomely so."[19] Clemens concluded, "Last week a prodigious and universal crash was impending and but for one thing would have happened: the millionaire 'bandits' whom the President is so fond of abusing in order to get the applause of the galleries, stepped in and saved the desolation. Mr. Roosevelt promptly claimed the credit of it, and there is much evidence that this inebriated nation thinks he is entitled to it."[20]

Despite the abuses of the Gilded Age– the corporate corruption of the political process and the crony capitalism of the robber barons– Clemens retained his faith in free enterprise, praising technological innovation as the spark of a dynamic economy. The American system was potentially the strongest "if you scrape off our...crust of shabby politicians."[21] It was a period of "great births," he said, when self-educated men invented "the steam press, the steamship, the steel ship, the railroad, the perfected cotton gin, the telegraph, the telephone, the phonograph, the photogravure, the electrotype, the gas light, the electric light, the sewing machine."[22] A handful of self-made geniuses in invention, the arts, exploration, and high finance accounted for civilization's progress, while the conforming masses and their elected politicians followed in herd-like fashion, seeking to capitalize on the brilliance of the few. For this reason Clemens was a strong advocate for patent and copyright protection to encourage and reward innovation and creativity.*[23] He believed that risk-taking that generated useful products and services and enhanced productivity and economic growth should be justly rewarded. He condemned the use of capital to manipulate financial markets, engage in monopolistic abuses, and enrich the wealthy at the expense of the working Americans.

A Tale of Today

Clemens's idealized free-enterprise economy rewards invention and innovation and does not squeeze "every ounce of profit, no matter how much blood is mixed in it," as he wrote in "Letter from the Recording Angel."[24] Such an economy would not incentivize companies to maximize quarterly profits, stock prices, and executive bonuses by deferring research and development, laying off workers, or moving factories offshore.

In **A Connecticut Yankee**, Hank Morgan proposes eliminating the royal grants to nobility that perpetuate a wealthy class of incompetents.[25] Whether in the form of congressional subsidies to railroad tycoons in the Gilded Age or "royal grants" to nobles in King Arthur's court, Twain criticized government favors to the powerful and well-connected. Yet today there are government subsidies and tax breaks for large corporate farms and global oil companies, and bailouts for automobile manufacturers, insurance conglomerates, financial institutions, and investment firms that are "too big to fail." A trillion dollars in annual "tax expenditures" includes special tax breaks

---

* In *The Innocents Abroad*, Twain writes that man's "noblest delight" is the discovery of a new idea, a planet, a hinge, the telegraph, the steamboat, the sewing machine, inoculation against smallpox, etc. "These are the men who have really lived" (IA, 266–67).

for pension plans, premium health insurance, capital gains, vacation homes, and corporate aircraft, which disproportionately perpetuate a special status for America's free-enterprise "nobles."

And while the Gilded Age was characterized by the growing gap between the very rich and working classes, according to the 2010 census, income disparity in the United States is the highest in a hundred years. The share of income going to the top 1 percent of Americans more than doubled between 1980 and 2008, rising from 8 percent to 18 percent. Including capital gains, the top tenth of 1 percent earn 10 percent of all income, having quadrupled their share of the national income since 1975. The wealthiest fifteen thousand families average $27 million in annual income. Clemens was a harsh critic of European class stratification, but today US income disparity far exceeds that of most European and other developed countries. Among the thirty-four member states of the Organization for Economic Cooperation and Development, the United States ranks thirty-first in income equality rankings.[26] Despite the conventional wisdom that America's classless society facilitates upward mobility for the talented, hard worker— "a government which gives each man a fair chance and no favor" as Twain put it—the reality is that government policy perpetuates the wealthy class, and upward mobility is no greater here than in most European countries. As Hacker and Pierson write, citing a study by the Pew Charitable Trusts:

"Compared with other rich nations, moreover, US intergenerational mobility is surprisingly low, in part, because the gap between income groups is so much bigger. The American Dream portrays the United States as a classless society where anyone can rise to the top, regardless of family background. Yet there is more intergenerational upward mobility

in Australia, Sweden, Norway, Finland, Germany, Spain, France, and Canada. In fact, of affluent countries studied, only Britain and Italy have lower intergenerational mobility than the United States does (and they are basically even with the United States)."[27]

Working Men and Women

Clemens's assault on capitalist greed and the ostentatious display of wealth was a bit ironic. His lavish mansion in Nook Farm, his hobnobbing with the rich and powerful, and his reckless pursuit of get-rich schemes subject him to charges of hypocrisy. In addressing a working class audience at the pinnacle of his Hartford success, he referred to the working poor *like himself* who were the backbone of the nation's wealth. This may have sounded off-key, but Clemens had known poverty. Having supported himself since age twelve, he provided financial assistance to his mother and brother throughout their lives. He could empathize with the working person.[28]

The antidote to the excesses of capitalism, in Clemens's opinion, was organized labor. In *Life on the Mississippi*, he described how the river pilots had organized to obtain higher wages and better working conditions despite management's fierce opposition. Their guild was "indestructible," the "strongest commercial organization ever formed among men," and the "tightest monopoly in the world."[29] Citing this story, the Knights of Labor enlisted Clemens's active support for their organizational efforts. Clemens applauded their success in unionizing Jay Gould's southwestern railroads in 1885. In the Great Upheaval of 1886, precipitated by the Knights, fourteen hundred strikes were launched against 11,562 businesses, leading to a national campaign for an eight-hour day.[30]

In *Following the Equator*, Twain praises the Province of South Australia, where "the working man is sovereign; his vote is the desire of the politicians—indeed, it is the very breadth of the politician's being; the parliament exists to deliver the will of the working man, and the government exists to execute it." In Clemens's view Australia's sophisticated political system and tolerant society were attributable to the "great power" of the working man, especially in South Australia, which is "his paradise."[31]

Clemens's strongest statement in support of organized labor came in a March 22, 1886, speech to the Hartford Monday Evening Club, entitled, "Knights of Labor—The New Dynasty." Clemens declared that:

> When *all* the bricklayers, and all the machinists, and all the miners, and blacksmiths, and printers, and hod-carriers, and stevedores, and house-painters, and brakemen, and engineers, and conductors, and factory hands, and horse-car drivers, and all the shop girls, and all the sewing women, and all the telegraph operators; in a word, all the myriads of toilers in whom is slumbering the reality of that thing which you call *Power*, not its age-worn sham and substanceless spectre—when these rise, call the vast spectacle by any deluding name that will please your ear, but the fact remains a *Nation* has arisen.[32]

Clemens urged his colleagues to study carefully the "Manifesto of Wrongs and Demands of the Knights of Labor" and "to secure the toilers a proper share of the wealth they create."[33] The manifesto called for the prohibition of child employment under age fourteen, equal pay for equal work for both sexes, safety laws for mining and manufacturing, and an eight-hour work day, enabling workers to have more time for social enjoyment and intellectual improvement. Clemens asked his well-to-do club members: "Is it possible that so plain and manifest a piece of justice as this is actually lacking to these men, and must be asked for?"[34] The Knights's social platform eventually was mostly enacted into federal law, despite an occasional setback from the Supreme Court. Clemens's early advocacy for these reforms reflected his conviction that through effective organization, working people, who generated wealth in a free economy, could counter the tyranny of a few and offset the power of the industrial tycoons.

In *A Connecticut Yankee*, Hank Morgan predicts to his sixth-century hosts that a couple of thousand years hence workers will rise up and take a hand at fixing their own wages. Touted by the unions, the novel generated popular support for the labor movement. In the *American Claimant*, Twain again highlighted the value of organizing the workforce as Siberian miners were encouraged to strike.

Clemens did not hesitate to criticize organized labor. He complained that trade unions were too insular, limiting their advocacy to immediate self-interests instead of challenging legislative policies that promoted the economic power of the wealthy few. He condemned the closing of craft unions to unskilled workers. He argued that unions should be open to foreign-born workers, helping them develop skills and obtain jobs. He denounced union racism and especially condemned the Knights's anti-Chinese policies. He criticized the unions' objections to technological, labor-saving innovations. He believed that increased productivity would create manifold new jobs in the economy. Technology is, he said, "Labor's savior, benefactor; but Labor doesn't know it & would ignorantly crucify it…Every great invention takes a livelihood away from fifty thousand men—& within ten years *creates* a livelihood for *half a million*… But you can't make Labor appreciate that; he is laboring for *himself*, not for the breadless half million that are issuing from his loins."[35]

Unlike many of his intellectual compatriots, such as William Dean Howells, Clemens did not believe in socialism—government ownership of industry—as an answer to worker oppression. Clemens had seen too much of the corrosive influence of politicians to place trust in government ownership. At heart, he remained an economic conservative, more enamored with Adam Smith's "invisible hand" than Karl Marx's heavy hand of revolutionary socialism. As disgusted as he was with the abuses of monopoly power, he remained committed to responsible free enterprise, contrasting his father-in-law's entrepreneurial capitalism with the piracy of Gould and Fisk. When Jervis Langdon's mining companies were accused of price fixing, he rushed to their defense in an editorial in the *Buffalo Express*, explaining that market demand was driving up prices as the winter approached.[36]

In an 1867 article for *The New York Evening Mail*, Clemens wrote that "there is *nothing* in conservatism antagonistic to progress, on the contrary, resistance to progress is antagonistic to conservatism. Political conservatism seeks the health and longevity of the political body it desires to conserve."[37] In Clemens's view, "progress does not mean radicalism or baneful transformation, or political paralysis." Rather, progress is to the state what "exercise is to man"; the effect of a robust, healthy democracy "must necessarily be progress."[38]

Clemens viewed organized labor as the best path to social reform and revitalized democracy. Like Franklin D. Roosevelt a half century later, Clemens thought effective participation by unions was critical to the preservation of American democracy. Clemens argued that organized labor is "our permanent shield and defence" against socialist agitation and more egregious government intrusion.[39]

A Tale of Today

Organized labor has not been as successful in strengthening the middle class as Clemens would have hoped. In 2011, 93 percent of the American workforce was nonunion, the highest level of nonunion employment since such records have been kept. Workers' wages declined in real dollars, and pension and health care benefits were cut. Job-creating investment in the domestic economy declined as US corporations sat on over two trillion dollars in cash, repurchased shares, or acquired their competitors. "Productivity enhancements" spurred layoffs, and companies moved their operations offshore to benefit from lower wage workers and lower taxes. Over the past decade, US-based multinational corporations cut almost two million jobs in the United States while adding over two million overseas.[40]

In contrast executive compensation has quadrupled since 1975. The United States ranks first in the world in the ratio of corporate CEO compensation to the pay of production manufacturing workers. According to a 2011 Institute for Policy Studies report, the CEOs of the largest corporations received 325 times the compensation of the average American worker.[41] Top corporate executives constitute 60 percent of the richest one-tenth of 1 percent of all Americans.

In contrast, the net worth of American families plummeted after the 2008 financial crisis. A June 2012 Federal Reserve survey found that from 2007 to 2010 the median net worth of families fell 39 percent (from $126,400 to $77,300), roughly to the level of 1992.[42] As the wealth of working men and women declined, poverty levels rose. Between 1996 and 2009, the number of Americans in poverty rose from thirty-six million to forty-four million, constituting 22 percent of the population. The number of people in severe poverty rose thirty-six percent, from fourteen million to nineteen million, the highest number in decades.[43] Krugman warns that "High inequality, which has turned us into a nation of a much weakened middle class, has a corrosive effect on social relations and politics, one that has become ever more apparent as America has moved deeper into a new Gilded Age."[44]

If working men and women are unsuccessful in mitigating the downward spiral of the middle class—encouraging job-creating investment in the domestic economy and increasing their purchasing power as the driver of economic growth—then sooner or later calls for increased government intervention will likely be reflected in the voting booths or on the streets. This is the lesson of the Gilded Age as labor violence broke out in New York, Pittsburgh, Milwaukee, Chicago (Haymarket Square), and other cities, setting the conditions for intervention by the federal government and the creation of the social safety nets during the progressive administrations of the twentieth century.[45]

The creation of good paying jobs was a key issue in the 2016 presidential campaign, and will likely be a high priority *for the Trump administration as it pursues tax reform that incentivizes investment in domestic manufacturing, more equitable trade relationships, and less "job-killing" regulation.*

Copyright

No public policy stirred more of the mature Clemens's passion, persistence, and promotional skill than copyright protection. His views on copyright struck deeply to his core—his pocketbook. With his popularity as a writer established after the publication of *The Innocents Abroad*, he took extraordinary—and often unsuccessful—measures to protect his books from foreign pirated editions that would eat into his profits. Over thirty years he spent more time in Washington, DC, lobbying for copyright protection legislation and testifying before congressional committees on copyright than on all other issues combined. Noting that copyright protection is mandated by the US Constitution, he vented his frustration with congressional inaction in an 1880 letter to Rollin Daggett, a Nevada newspaper colleague who later served in Congress. Communicating in the comfortable language to which they were accustomed, Clemens wrote: "What a silly son-of-a-bitch of a law the present law against book piracy is. I believe it was framed by a (goddamnd) idiot & passed by a Congress of (goddamnd) muttonheads."[46]

Clemens advocated for extension of the copyright term, which was forty-two years when he started writing books. Although he would have preferred a copyright in perpetuity, he supported legislation that would extend it to the life of the author plus fifty years. Clemens also lobbied for international copyright protection, urging the government to negotiate treaties to protect American authors from foreign publishers who pirated their works and flooded the US market.

Clemens argued that since unprotected foreign writers received no royalties in the United States, their books were underpriced, giving them an unfair competitive advantage. Second, as American authors became more popular abroad, their works were pirated by unscrupulous foreign publishers.

Third, American booksellers were handicapped as pirated publications flowed across the borders, undercutting their prices. Fourth, because American writers were not adequately protected, American readers were deprived of great American literature.[47]

Clemens's passion for copyright reform was fueled by his frustration with the inconvenience, costly international travel, and diminished income that the hodgepodge and lax enforcement of copyright laws produced. At the time when he hit his stride as a writer, securing a British copyright required that a book be published in England before it came out in any other country. During an 1873 trip to London, Clemens arranged for the publication of *The Gilded Age* by Routledge & Sons. It was published in London on December 23, 1873, and in Hartford on Christmas Eve, fulfilling English law.[48]

Clemens joined the American Copyright League to seek congressional action.[49] On November 19, 1885, he met for an hour with President Cleveland who agreed to include copyright protection in his annual message to Congress, and in January 1886, Clemens testified on Senator Hawley's copyright bill before the US Senate Committee on Patents.[50] Along with several other distinguished authors, Clemens held several readings in a Washington church on March 16, 1888, to rally support for copyright reform. The First Lady, Frances Folsom Cleveland, attended the first reading and her husband joined her for the second, after which the visiting author-lobbyists had tea at the White House.

In January 1889 Clemens, alerted by Hawley that the legislation was scheduled for a floor vote, rushed to Washington to lobby the House members. Once again his hopes were dashed when a filibuster on another bill derailed the vote and killed the legislation for the session.[51] Having urged passage of the legislation, President Cleveland wrote Clemens on February 15 that another floor vote was scheduled for February 20. Clemens scurried down to Washington again, but the legislation was defeated. A frustrated Clemens thanked Cleveland for his support: "Although a most worthy cause has failed once more we who are interested have one large consolation: that the country has at last had a President who appreciated its importance and did everything…to…carry it to a successful issue."[52]

"This Thomas Nast cartoon lampoons Twain forgoing to Canada to secure a copyright for the Prince and the Pauper."
Courtesy: The Mark Twain House & Museum, Hartford. CT

An international copyright protection bill finally passed in the last hour of the last day of the Fifty-First Congress. It was signed into law by President Benjamin Harrison, Cleveland's successor, on March 4, 1891 and a series of treaties were negotiated, most importantly, with the United Kingdom. Even with this success after so many years of effort, Clemens and the American Copyright League continued to lobby for strengthening copyright protections.

On a cold, windy Friday afternoon on December 7, 1906, Mark Twain made a grand appearance at the Great Hall of the Library of Congress, inaugurating his white flannel suit, white cravat, white shoes, and now completely white, unruly hair. He was appearing before the Senate Committee on Patents. All eyes diverted to Twain as he entered the Senate reading room packed with lobbyists and lawyers. He was there to bat clean-up in support of legislation that would lengthen the term of copyright protection for "creative endeavors" to the life of the author plus fifty years, testifying after a panel of distinguished authors, artists, and musicians that included Howells and John Phillip Sousa.[53] The clarity, logic, and underlying philosophy of Clemens's presentation made a strong impression on the senators and his humor sent them into gales of laughter. Clemens said he supported the bill, at least such portions "as he could understand," legislative language being an art form uniquely within the province of legislators. Clemens thought the copyright extension would "satisfy any reasonable author," taking "care of his children," and letting the "grandchildren take care of themselves."[54]

The day after his appearance, Clemens stopped by the White House and told the doorkeeper, "I want the usual thing—I want to see the president." Roosevelt clenched his teeth and granted an immediate audience to the popular celebrity. Strolling onto the White House lawn a few minutes later, Clemens brazenly informed the accompanying paparazzi, "The president is one with us on the copyright matter."[55]

Clemens followed up his testimony with a "Dear Uncle Joseph" letter to Speaker of the House Joe Cannon. He asked for the privilege of going onto the House floor to lobby the members one by one on the copyright bill.[56] He said he had "the arguments" with him and "also a barrel. With liquid in it."[57] The speaker gave him a private room in the Capitol and sent for members to come and meet with Clemens individually.[58] Clemens wrote a friend that face to face meetings were necessary because members would not read the "deluge of printed documents" instructing them on the legislation—"Congress can't and won't commit suicide in that way." It took another three years, and Clemens did not get everything he wanted. On March 3, 1909, Congress passed a new copyright act, extending the term of protection to fifty-six years. While short of perpetuity, this was sufficient to protect Twain's early works, and, most importantly for him, it was better than the law in Great Britain.* Missouri congressman Champ Clark, who soon was to become speaker of the House, had championed the bill. He credited Twain's white-suited testimony for its success. "Your ideas and wishes in the matter constitute the best guide we have as to what should be done in this case," he wrote to Clemens.[59] In 1976 it was extended to the life of the author plus fifty years, and in 1998, it was extended to the life of the author plus seventy years.

In his seminal work, *Copyright and Copywrongs*, Siva Vaidhyanathan credits Clemens with defining the terms of the copyright debate which continues to this day. In Vaidhyanathan's view, Clemens tilted the balance too far in favor of the author's property rights, diminishing the importance of securing wide and easy access to information in a democratic society.[60]

---

* To provide for his family, Clemens had schemed to extend his copyrights by issuing new editions of his most popular works with portions of his autobiography included as footnotes. After all *Tom Sawyer* was mostly autobiographical. But with congressional enactment of a fourteen-year extension, Jean's death, and Clara's prosperous marriage, a disheartened Clemens admitted at the conclusion of his *Autobiography* that he had no more use for the project (MT *Autobiography* 1, 24).

A Tale of Today

Clemens's faith in America's potential was premised on a free society that nurtured creativity and innovation. He lived in an era of unparalleled invention that was encouraged and protected by patent laws and he marshaled his celebrity status to become the driving force for copyright reform that would inspire great art and literature from the young nation.

Some critics today charge that patents are too easily obtained for questionable purposes, inciting a flurry of lawsuits and substituting the courtroom for the marketplace as the epicenter of competitive technologies. Despite challenging structural changes in the economy today, the United States continues to be a leader in innovation and imagination, and, in part due to Clemens's efforts, the federal government has become a more vigilant protector of American creativity. In the age of the US-government-inspired Internet, the opportunities for innovation and creativity expand into unchartered territory. E-books and online reading challenge traditional publishing and journalism. The internet has turned the music industry upside down. Intellectual piracy and competition from emerging powers who do not play by the same rules—such as China—threaten the traditional protections that enable American innovation to flourish. According to Lessig, since 1995, Congress has enacted thirty-two statutes as it struggles to adapt copyright protections to changing technologies in the age of digital architecture.[61] As Clemens sought to provide the international and domestic legal framework that would enable innovation to thrive, so today leadership is urgently needed to protect and encourage the quality that has most uniquely characterized America's greatness—unfettered imagination. The critical issue is how to balance the conflicting values of rewarding innovation and encouraging creativity with the need to protect the free flow of information in the internet age.

Free Trade and Protectionism

Prior to his conversion to the Mugwumps in 1884, Clemens generally supported Republican candidates who advocated high tariffs to protect northern industries and workers from low-wage foreign competition and generate revenues to fund internal improvements and an expanding federal government. Democrats advocated free trade and complained about the unexpended surpluses generated by excessive tariffs. Even during severe recessions, it did not occur to the pre-Keynesian politicians of either party to spend the surpluses to stimulate the economy.

In his 1880 Hartford campaign speech for Garfield, Clemens attacked the Democrats for proposing to lower protective tariffs. He argued in burlesque fashion that the Democrats were "courting industrial disaster." Their policies would create extensive unemployment and widespread poverty, generating a population of tramps. He accused the Democratic Party of favoring the British and southern economies at the expense of the industrial North, whose factory smoke would be stilled.[62]

In 1884 Clemens diametrically shifted his position and unleashed his fiery advocacy in support of Cleveland's opposition to the Republican high-tariff plank. The Republican *Hartford Courant* gleefully ran parallel columns contrasting Clemens's earlier views with his newfound enlightenment.[63] Cleveland devoted his entire second State of the Union address to reducing the tariffs. Protective tariffs constituted a tax on consumer goods and generated government surpluses that should be returned to the people. Cleveland Democrats favored reducing taxes and the size of government.

When Clemens swung to a new point of view, he did not equivocate. He complained that Republican policies were to protect "the interest of a few rich men," and he attacked the high tariff tax on consumers, quipping that the only nontaxed foreign product was "the answer to prayer."[64] In *Tom Sawyer Abroad*, published in 1894, Tom and Huck plan to ship Sahara Desert sand to the United States to sell as souvenirs, but are blocked by the import duty. Tom complains that it is the government's "duty to bust you if they can."[65] He predicts that the Lord's blessing will be taxed by the next Congress because "there wan't nothing foreign that wan't taxed."[66] In his *Notebook* Clemens wrote: "The man who invented protection belongs in hell."[67]

Clemens argued that the high tariff discriminated against western businesses. If the tariff were eliminated, the West Coast manufacturers could import iron ore from Asia. Instead, these businesses paid high transportation costs to ship products from eastern manufacturers "as if there were several rows of custom-fences between the coast and the East."[68] Clemens also complained about business uncertainty caused by constant shifting in import tax rates and duty-free goods.[69] Clemens's biggest problem with the high tariff, however, was that it cushioned the huge trusts in oil, steel, glass, sugar and beef from competition. No fan of monopolies, Clemens was always suspicious of Roosevelt's "trust-busting" exhortations because the president also championed the high tariffs that fertilized the monopolies. "We swept [out] slavery and substituted Protection," Clemens grumbled.[70] In unpublished dictations, he wrote: "By a system of extraordinary tariffs, [the White House] has created a number of giant corporations in the interest of a few rich men, and by most ingenious and persuasive reasoning has convinced the multitudinous and grateful unrich that the tariffs were instituted in *their* interest."[71]

The Dollar

At Alexander Hamilton's urging, the new nation got off to a good start in the international community when the federal government assumed the debt of the Revolutionary War. The Coinage Act of 1792 created the nation's monetary policy based on the dollar backed by gold and silver. To finance the Civil War, Congress enacted a series of legal tender acts, authorizing the printing of paper currency, "greenbacks," which at the time of General Lee's surrender at Appomattox totaled $431 million plus $236 million in federal notes.[72] After the war there was a national political debate over how to redeem the greenbacks and reestablish the dollar's value. Borrowers, farmers, and small businesses preferred an inflationary dollar, greenbacks, or silver-backed currency, enabling them to pay off their debt more cheaply. Wall Street, creditors, industrialists, banks, and wage earners favored a stable currency, backed by the more precious and stable metal, gold. Generally the West, the plains states, and the South favored an inflationary currency, and the populist movement championed by William Jennings Bryan captured the issue and a large segment of the Democratic Party. The Northeast supported a return to the gold standard, but the parties were not always predictable. The gold standard was embraced by eastern but not western Republicans, who favored bimetallism—silver and gold at a defined ratio. Although a Democrat, Cleveland ran on a return to the gold standard, whereas the Republican Benjamin Harrison signed the Sherman Silver Purchase Act of 1890, committing the Treasury Department to buy 4.5 million ounces of silver a month (the nation's output). This created inflationary pressures that—along with the McKinley Tariff Act—contributed to the Panic of 1893, which was marked by bank and railroad failures, a spike in unemployment, home foreclosures, and a run on the gold supply, followed by a severe recession.[73] In his second term, Cleveland convinced Congress to repeal the Sherman Silver Purchase Act.

As success in America was measured by the almighty dollar, the stability and value of the currency was a central political and economic issue during the nineteenth century. Clemens supported a strong dollar but vacillated in how this was to be achieved. His eastern establishment friends were proponents of the gold standard, but his Nevada friends promoted the silver alternative. In 1896 he drafted a satire mocking the dire consequences predicted by the Republican "gold bugs" if Bryan's "free silver" platform were adopted. It would "paralyze all industries, strike prosperity dead & bring upon the country a blight of poverty, disaster and desolation." He compared the hysterical cries to the warnings of the slaveholders that abolishing slavery would destroy the southern economy; "it didn't do it." Clemens queried: "Half our people are for silver—are all the fools on that side?" In his draft essay, Clemens argued that, whether based on gold or silver, the dollar would keep its value because US industry would bloom and Americans would become less dependent on imports. An inflationary dollar would encourage exports and the development of domestic business to replace imported products. American currency would become "stable, trustworthy, & emancipated from caprice and uncertainty. When a man got his coin, now, whether of gold or silver, it would keep its value."[74] Not wanting to offend friends like Rogers, he never published the article.

A Tale of Today

With the creation of the Federal Reserve three years after Clemens's death and the unilateral termination by the United States of the dollar's convertibility to gold in 1971, the dollar became a fiat currency, backed only by the government's promise. As Clemens predicted, the dollar has gained in strength and credibility. Backed only by the US economy, it has become the world's premier currency, and it probably will remain so because there is no viable competitor. Today, despite the efforts of some Libertarian and Tea Party enthusiasts who advocate abolishing the Federal Reserve and returning to the gold standard, currency issues and monetary policy rarely dominate political campaigns.[75] Nonetheless, the dollar is not invincible. Foreign complaints about sustained US trade deficits, mounting federal debt, and political gridlock have occasionally threatened the dollar's value in international markets; it has been sustained in part because its principal rivals, the Euro and the Yuan and the economies they serve, have faced even greater challenges.

Taxes

Clemens railed against taxes, though often in jest. Former Internal Revenue Service commissioner Mortimer Caplan was fond of quoting Twain: "What is the difference between a taxidermist and a tax collector? The taxidermist takes only your skin."[76] Clemens said that he was pleased when a judge found "something that was not taxable"—his "patience."[77] He said he would abstain from profanity except in discussing taxes. Taxes could not be discussed without it.[78] In *The Innocents Abroad*, Twain had written that if like the Italians, Americans had to pay one out of three dollars in taxes, "they would have the law altered." Americans are curious people, he wrote; they protest if they have to pay 7 percent in taxes.[79]

Clemens complained that "the minority are required to furnish the taxes, & the majority are required to say how the money will be spent" because the majority elects Congress. And "in this country, *any*body can go to Congress—& as a general thing that's just the kind that *do* go."[80] Clemens lauded regimes from London to Hawaii which limited the franchise to property-owning taxpayers, denying "useless idlers the privilege of dispensing public moneys purchased by other people." He feared that universal suffrage would grant "all power into the hands of the ignorant non-taxpaying classes." If taxpayers elect the majority, Clemens thought that Congress would spend money more wisely. On the other hand, Twain understood that when the wealthy control the purse strings, they can shape the tax code for their benefit. As he wrote in *Connecticut Yankee*, "there were taxes, and taxes, and taxes, and more taxes, and taxes again, and yet other taxes—upon this free and independent pauper, but none upon his lord the baron or the bishop, none upon the wasteful nobility or the all-devouring Church."[81]

A Tale of Today

Today about half the US population does not pay federal income taxes. Do nontaxpaying voters elect representatives who spend tax revenues too freely? If the vast majority of working men and women paid some federal income tax, as they now pay in payroll taxes, would Congress be held more accountable in spending taxpayer money? A simple, fair, and progressive tax *system in which all working Americans have a stake could result in the election to Congress of representatives who manage the federal purse responsibly. A fair and simple tax system would also eliminate tax loopholes that benefit the wealthy and pick winners and losers among industries and economic sectors. As Twain quipped that Congress can tax anything except patience and prayer, he would likely chuckle when in June 2012 the Supreme Court held that Congress can even tax doing nothing, like failing to purchase health insurance.*[82]

Part IV

Foreign Policy

Staining the flag

CHAPTER SIXTEEN

Mark Twain's Anti-Imperialist Roots

"I am opposed to having the eagle
put its talons on any other land."
— MARK TWAIN

The roots of Clemens's conversion to anti-imperialism lay in his transformative trip to the Sandwich Islands (Hawaii) in 1866. It was his first exposure to a foreign culture, and his views about different societies and America's role in the world evolved as he delivered more than one hundred lectures on Hawaii throughout the United States and England. Later, as he traveled extensively and lived abroad, his outlook became increasingly global: he became a citizen of the world and an international celebrity.

Clemens's views on American influence in Hawaii changed 180 degrees over time.[1] Responding to the drumbeat of San

Francisco business leaders for the annexation of the Hawaiian Islands, Clemens proclaimed in his first public lecture in San Francisco on October 2, 1866: "The property has got to fall to some heir, and why not the United States?"[2] West Coast businessmen had warned him of the fierce competition from the British and the French to develop the islands' sugar, cotton, and rice fields. A self-described "red-hot imperialist," he advocated annexation of Hawaii by the United States.

Clemens estimated that Hawaii could meet a third of the world's sugar demand. He promoted San Francisco as the "Golden Gate" to the Orient, the "depot" and "distribution house." To open up trade relationships with China, he proposed a direct steamship line from the West Coast to China with Hawaii as a "half-way house on the Pacific highway."[3]

When Clemens arrived in New York in 1867, he continued writing and lecturing about Hawaii, culminating in a successful lecture at the Cooper Institute.[4] During his brief tenure as a senate aide later that year, he worked unsuccessfully with West Coast sugar processors to secure ratification of a treaty with Hawaii.

After Clemens moved to Hartford, he began to rework his lecture. He dropped references to annexation.[5] With the death of King Kamehameha V in 1872, the business community began a vigorous campaign for the annexation of Hawaii. *The New York Tribune* editorialized against annexation and invited Clemens to express his views. In January 1873, Clemens wrote to the *Tribune*: "The traders brought labor and fancy diseases—in other words, long, deliberate, infallible, destruction; and the missionaries brought the means of grace and got them ready. So the two forces are working along harmoniously, and anybody who knows anything about figures, can tell you exactly when the last Kanaka will be in Abraham's bosom and his islands in the hands of the whites."[6]

In a follow-up letter, he employed his trademark technique of making outrageous and indefensible arguments in support of the advocates of annexation: "We *must* annex those people. We can afflict them with our wise and beneficent government." Enumerating the various forms of corruption that could be inflicted upon Hawaii, such as that practiced by Tammany's Boss Tweed, he suggested that "we can give them railway corporations who will buy their Legislatures like old clothes, and run over their best citizens," and "we can furnish them some Jay Goulds who will do away with their old time notion that stealing is not respectable."[7]

The *Tribune* explained in an editorial note: "Mr. Clemens, as those who know him will testify, is not only a wit, but a shrewd and accurate observer, and so our readers will find, in the pithy communication published today, not merely food for laughter, but subjects for reflection."[8]

Now firmly opposed to annexation, Clemens supported the claim of William Lunalilo—known as "Prince Bill"—to the vacated throne. He criticized the sugar planters' unscrupulous tactics as they lobbied for annexation that would eliminate the sugar duty and reap them enormous profits. Lunalilo became king, and the *Tribune* credited Twain with the initial failure of the annexation effort, bestowing upon him the title of "Pacific Warwick"—an allusion to the Duke of Warwick's role in Prince Harry's ascendancy to the British throne in Shakespeare's *Henry V.*[9]

Clemens often titled his lecture "Our Fellow Savages of the Sandwich Islands." Absorbing the lessons of Hawaii as he experienced other cultures, Clemens increasingly recognized that American-style democracy, especially when infused with Christian missionary zeal, could not be imposed on other cultures by force or coercion. Americans were still learning how to make it work for themselves. Other cultures would have to find their own way in the context of their own traditions and values. Years later he wrote: "Shall we go on conferring our Civilization upon those peoples that sit in darkness, or shall we give those poor things a rest?"[10]

Clemens foreshadowed his anti-imperialist views in an 1867 satire, "Information Wanted," about US government plans to purchase St. Thomas from Denmark.[11] Twain requested information on behalf of a fictitious uncle about any islands the United States planned to acquire. The uncle was looking for a quiet place to live and work, having been chased out of Alaska by bears and St. Thomas by robbers, disease, and hurricanes. (Clemens had derided the recent purchase of Alaska from Russia, calling it "Walrussia" as he plotted the course of an Alaska iceberg floating though several continents as it melted away.) Attacking the commercial justifications for annexing St. Thomas, Twain posed the broader question: Why was the United States in the territorial expansion business? He concluded (quite prophetically) by asking whether Puerto Rico was next: "He has heard that government is thinking about buying Porto Rico. If that is true, he wishes to try Porto Rico, if it is a quiet place."[12]

The sketch caused a stir. There was a backlash against the proposed annexation of St. Thomas. (During World War I, the military again urged Congress to acquire St. Thomas to protect the Panama Canal, and it was purchased in 1917 and became part of the US Virgin Islands.)

In 1868 the Cubans revolted against colonial Spain. American business interests urged US intervention on the side of the revolutionaries. Clemens opposed US intervention. He argued that both the Spanish and the "Cuba Libre" patriots engaged in similar acts of "murder, theft, burglary, arson, assassination, rape, poison, treachery, mendacity, fratricide, matricide, homicide, parricide, and all cides but suicide"; that both parties to the conflict "stand ready...to sell out body soul and boots, politics, religion and principles, to anybody that will buy"; and that "both sides massacre their prisoners." He suspected the US movement to intervene was merely a subterfuge for Cuban annexation. He wrote a letter to the *Buffalo Express*, of which he was then part owner, that "I don't love the Cuban patriot or the Cuban oppressor either, and never want to see our government 'recognize' anything of theirs but their respective corpses. If the *Buffalo Express* thinks differently, let it say it in its editorials, but not over the signature of yours, with emotion, Mark Twain."[13]

In 1895–96 Clemens again confronted the cultural impact of Western influence on indigenous populations. Accompanied by Livy and Clara on his global lecture tour to pay off his debts, he visited British colonial possessions in the South Pacific, Asia and

Africa. Always an Anglophile, he noted in *Following the Equator* in 1897 that "we Americans are...English in the essentials of our civilization,"[14] He commended the British civil service in India, in contrast to competing colonial powers: the French, the Germans, and "the Land-Robber-in-Chief," the Russians. He wrote: "When one considers what India was under her Hindoo and Mohammedan rulers and what she is now; when one remembers the miseries of her millions then and the protections and humanities which they enjoy now, he must concede that the most fortunate thing that has ever befallen that empire was the establishment of British supremacy there."[15]

Clemens, however, was no longer the innocent amused *Quaker City* voyager, describing new sites and vistas with witty wonder. He had seen too much of the corrupting influence of corporate greed and the arrogance of unrestrained power. He documented in his *Notebooks* the oppression and brutality of colonial domination. His message was becoming more ambiguous, signaling the strident anti-imperialism that was yet to come. In Australia he had observed the British emigrants' cruelty to the aboriginals. He had seen the bravery of the New Zealand Maoris and Tasmanian aboriginals who fought for their way of life with primitive weapons, preferring death to submission.[16] He had witnessed Cecil B. Rhodes's exploitation of South Africa for its mineral and agricultural wealth.[17] Colonialism had only one overriding motivation, he was coming to believe—profit and greed. The large western monopoly corporations of the Gilded Age had exhausted the wealth they could extract from the working classes at home, and set their sights on the abundant untapped resources and cheap labor in undeveloped countries. As he wrote in *Following the Equator*, "No tribe, howsoever insignificant, and no nation, howsoever mighty, occupies a foot of land that was not stolen...In Europe and Asia and Africa every acre of ground has been stolen several millions of times...Africa has been coolly divided up and portioned out among the gang as if they had bought it and paid for it. And now straight away they are beginning the old game again—to steal each other's grabbings."[18]

Clemens rejected the high-sounding hypocrisies that rationalized the colonialists' plunder: "bringing civilization to the natives," "the white man's burden" to care for their "brown-skinned brothers," "civilizing the savages," and "saving the souls of the heathen." As he had mocked the Widow Douglas's attempt to civilize Huck Finn, so he castigated the colonialist's attempt to "shut up those poor natives in the unimaginable perdition of his civilization, committing his crime with the very best intentions" not knowing that "his own civilization is a hell to the savage."[19]After enumerating the horrors that had been committed against native people in the interest of civilizing them, Twain concluded: "There are many humorous things in the world; among them the white man's notion that he is less savage than the other savages."[20]

During most of the decade between 1891 and 1901, Clemens lived in Europe or traveled abroad where his criticism of European colonialism was not met with enthusiasm. The English loved his humor, but resented his caustic commentary on subjects they thought he knew nothing about. He was chastised by the British Journal *Academy*: "When they wish to be instructed concerning Great Britain, they prefer that it should be done by an Englishman."[21]As the Clemens family prepared to return to America at the new century's dawn, they would find that their colony-free country was not without its own imperialist ambitions.

*****

On February 15, 1898, the US battleship *Maine* was patrolling Havana Harbor in solidarity with the Cuban rebels protesting Spain's colonial administration when it suffered a mysterious explosion. Was the explosion caused by combustion of the vessel's coal bunkers, as the Navy found? Or was it caused by a Spanish torpedo as the yellow presses of Hearst and Pulitzer reported, fueling the flames of American outrage? Monitoring the American public's reaction, Spain escalated the hostilities. America went to war against Spain. Lieutenant Colonel Theodore Roosevelt and the Rough Riders charged up San Juan Hill to media star acclaim. Commodore Dewey decimated the Spanish fleet in Manila Bay. In four months the war was over. Or was it? Under the December 10 Treaty of Paris, partially negotiated by Secretary of State John Hay, Spain turned Cuba over to the Americans to prepare it for independence. The United States also paid $20 million to acquire Puerto Rico, the Philippines, and Guam. Hawaii was quietly annexed during the war.[22]

At the time of the *Maine* explosion, the Clemens family was living in Vienna. Responding to press inquiries, Clemens departed from his anti-interventionist stance in 1868 and initially supported the liberation of Cuba from Spanish exploitation. He reasoned: What was more beneficent than America's fighting for another people's freedom? The war was "the worthiest one that was ever fought." Such selflessness was a rare occurrence in civilized history. "I think this is the first time that it has been done," he wrote to Twichell.[23] Colorado senator Henry M. Teller had sponsored an amendment prohibiting the annexation of Cuba. It passed Congress, but was silent on the Philippines and other territorial acquisitions.

The United States was ostensibly in the Philippines to liberate the Filipino revolutionaries from their Spanish tyrants. But the Filipinos did not welcome their white American brothers with garlands and dancing in the streets. They declared war on the United States in February 1899. Emilio Aguinaldo, the Filipino leader who had resisted Spanish rule, led the struggle against American occupation. By July 1902, twenty thousand Filipino soldiers and two hundred thousand civilians would be dead. A total of forty-two hundred Americans would die in securing the nation's newest territorial acquisition, seven thousand miles west of San Francisco.[24]

American culture has often brewed an unsavory mix of religious and military fervor sparked by a grandiose view of the nation's moral role in the world. Indiana senator Albert J. Beveridge referred to America "as God's arbiters, appointed to mediate the destinies of mankind."[25] Pandering to the pulpits, who were proclaiming our duty to Christianize the inferior races, leading senators like Blaine and Beveridge called for the

American military to civilize and liberate the masses. Beveridge proclaimed on the Senate floor:[26]

> The Philippines are ours forever...And just beyond the Philippines are China's illimitable markets. We will not retreat from either. We will not remove our part in the mission of our race, trustee, under God, in the civilization of the world...The Pacific is our ocean. Where shall we turn for consumers of our surpluses? Geography answers the question. China is our natural customer...* It has been charged that our conduct of the war has been cruel [but] Senators must remember that we are not dealing with Americans or Europeans. We are dealing with Orientals.*

President McKinley explained to a group of Methodist ministers that we were acquiring the Philippines "to educate the Filipinos, and uplift and civilize and Christianize them, and by God's grace do the very best we could by them, as our fellow men for whom Christ also died."[27] Under Spanish rule since 1561, the Dominican Friars had long since converted most Filipinos to Catholicism, but this apparently was not true Christianity for a nation whose exceptionalism was rooted in the Protestant ethic of rugged individualism. A minority of leaders like Massachusetts senator George F. Hoar warned of the dangers of the "expansionist alloy of Christian and commercial interests,"[28] but their voices were drowned out in the rising crescendo of patriotic fervor.

Although Clemens supported US intervention on behalf of suppressed peoples seeking freedom from brutal regimes, he understood that the motives underlying such interventions were complex. Between 1798 and 1895, US armed forces had intervened abroad 103 times. In Nicaragua alone, the United States had sent troops to "protect American interests" in 1853,

---

* Beveridge, an historian and Pulitzer Prize-winning author of multivolume biographies of John Marshall and Abraham Lincoln, badly misread the future: The United States would become China's biggest customer in the twentieth century, leading the US-China trade deficit to surge to $273 billion in 2010. Susan Harris draws on Beveridge's quote above for the title to her new book on the US occupation of the Philippines: *God's Arbiters.*

1854, and 1894.[29] There were many factors at play: support for human rights and the democratic aspirations of people rising up against autocracies; humanitarian interests in preventing genocide, massacres, oppression, and hopeless poverty; geopolitical interests in protecting America's national security and defense; support for leaders friendly to the United States who would help advance US foreign policy objectives; defeat of hostile dictators, pirates, insurgents, or terrorists;[30] the expansion of economic spheres of interests (in competition with Europe) in securing natural resources, markets for US goods, and cheap labor; and domestic political benefits that flow from missionary and patriotic zeal, jingoism, and the global exercise of military power.

As Clemens watched Philippine liberation transformed into the suppression of an indigenous insurrection, he was indignant. "When America snatched the Philippines," he later told Paine, "she stained the flag."[31] Boarding the steamship *Minnehaha* for his return to the United States, he told London reporters that America should let the Philippine people be "free, and let them deal with their own domestic questions in their own way." He declared: "We have gone there to conquer, not redeem. I am an anti-imperialist. I am opposed to having the eagle put its talons on any other land."[32] He spoke about the occupation of the Philippines with a chilling practical wisdom that would resonate in future times:

> We were to relieve them from Spanish tyranny to enable them to set up a government of their own, and we were to stand by and see that it got a fair trial. It was not to be a government according to our ideas, but a government that represented the feeling of the majority of the Filipinos, a government according to Filipino ideas. That would have been a worthy mission for the United States.
>
> But now—why have we got into a mess, a quagmire from which each fresh step renders the difficulty of extrication immensely greater. I'm sure I wish I could see what we were getting out of it, and all it means to us as a nation.[33]

Clemens wrote Laurence Hutton, an associate in the Author's Club and the International Copyright League, urging him to solicit former President Cleveland's advice on seeking Supreme Court review of the constitutionality of the Treaty of Paris. Clemens argued that the Constitution does not authorize the forceful acquisition of foreign sovereign territory.[34]

In the Philippines, American soldiers, trained in conventional warfare, confronted an enemy conducting guerilla warfare. General Arthur MacArthur—his son Douglas would later return to the Philippines as a five-star general—described this new kind of evasive adversary: "At one time they are in the ranks as soldiers and immediately thereafter are within the American lines in the attitude of peaceful natives, absorbed in a dense mass of sympathetic people."[35] Responding to an unconventional threat, the Americans were brutal. When a troop ship was scheduled to arrive, the local population was ordered to relocate to remove the threat of a terrorist attack. Those who did not comply were shot.

The *Philadelphia Public Ledger* reported:

> Our men have been relentless; have killed to exterminate men, women, children, prisoners and captives, active insurgents and suspected people, from lads of ten up, an idea prevailing that the Filipino, as such, was little better than a dog... Our soldiers have pumped salt water into men to "make them talk," have taken prisoners people who held up their hands and peacefully surrendered, and an hour later, without an atom of evidence to show that they were even insurrectos, stood them on a bridge and shot them down one by one, to drop them into the water below and float down, as examples to those who found their bullet-loaded corpses.[36]

In 1900 Brigadier General Frederick Funston, US commander in the Philippines, captured Aguinaldo. In an unpublished biography of the Philippine revolutionary, Twain compared Aguinaldo to America's independence fighters. As the war in the Philippines intensified, anti-imperialist organizations coalesced.

Their calm, rational voice was muted by the shrill charge that those who failed to support American soldiers fighting and dying on foreign soil were traitors. Returning to a hero's welcome in the United States, Funston addressed the New York Lotos Club, calling Aguinaldo a "cold blooded murderer," "assassin," and the "dictator of a drunken uncontrollable mob." To raucous applause, the general declared he would rather see the anti-imperialists "hanged for treason—hanged for giving aid and comfort to the enemy—than see the humblest soldier in the United States Army lying dead in the field of battle."[37] Clemens read press reports of the speech, fuming. He decided to break his silence and publish an article about the war.

In "A Defence of General Funston," published in the May 1902 issue of *The North American Review,* Twain describes the atrocities and brutality of the war. He cites General Jake Smith's orders to his men: "Kill and burn—the more you kill and burn the better—Kill all above the age of ten—make Samar a howling wilderness." After describing Funston's treachery and use of bribery in the capture of Aguinaldo, Twain comes to the general's defense with heavy sarcasm. The general was simply a "weak-headed, weak-principled" lackey of the imperialists. Twain urged that Aguinaldo be freed as a great leader of his people.[38]

Twain became the public voice of anti-imperialism. In plain speech and a flurry of essays, he invoked his public celebrity status to dissent from the prevailing view of American expansionism. He reported on the water torture that the US military applied to the Filipino priest Father Augustine, who was accused of raising funds for the resistance. This version of water torture was different from water boarding, or simulated drowning, which was used more recently to extract information from captured terrorists and insurgents. Under the method used in the Philippines, the victim was forced to drink gallons of salt water. A soldier would then jump on the man's stomach until he confessed or died.[39]

In a 1901 July Fourth Address, Twain called for Philippine independence and urged "all lovers of freedom to organize in defense of human rights, now threatened by the greatest government in history."[40] In January 1902 he and Howells joined a group of eminent Americans in a petition to the Senate to end hostilities in the Philippines and negotiate with the leaders of the insurgency. Quoting McKinley's condemnation of the Spanish concentration camps, the petition documented through press reports, letters from returning soldiers and official records that the United States was engaging in the same "inhumane methods" as the Spanish.[41] The petition requested a Senate Committee investigation of alleged army atrocities in the Philippines and, if true, steps taken to stop "the killing of prisoners, the shooting without trial of suspected persons, the use of torture, the employment of savage allies, the wanton destruction of private property, and every other barbarous method of waging war, which this nation from its infancy has ever condemned." [42]

The US-Philippine Commission's Treason Act made advocacy by Filipinos of Philippine independence a crime punishable by a two-thousand-dollar fine and a year in prison. An outraged Clemens wrote in the margin of the Funston speech as it was printed in the *New York Sun*: "If I were in the Philippines, I could be imprisoned a year for publicly expressing the opinion that we ought to withdraw and give those people their independence—an opinion that I desire to express now." Clemens argued that if such a statement is treason in one part of the United States, it doubtless would be treason in another part. He continued, "If so, I am now committing treason—by the provisions of that infernal act—and if I were out there I would hire a hall and do it again."[43]

CHAPTER SEVENTEEN

Twain And Roosevelt's Love-Hate Relationship

The likes of Mark
Twain should be skinned alive.
— THEODORE ROOSEVELT

On September 6, 1901, Leon Czolgosz evaded fifty bodyguards at the Pan American Exposition in Buffalo and fired two bullets into President McKinley. The president died eight days later and was succeeded by his forty-three-year-old vice president, Theodore Roosevelt, the ebullient champion of imperialism. Five weeks later Roosevelt and Clemens attended Yale University's Bicentennial ceremonies, in which they both were to receive honorary degrees. Cheers arose as the celebrity Mark Twain strolled into the auditorium. Roosevelt refused to join him on the platform, muttering just loud enough for his nemesis to hear: "When I hear what Mark Twain and others have said in criticism of the missionaries, I feel like skinning them alive."[1] Roosevelt was elected president in his own right in 1904, and their private schmoozing and public sparing on the issues continued. Clemens wrote in 1907 somewhat naively that "I am against the [president] politically, but this has not affected the friendship existing between us these twenty years."[2] Although he refrained from criticizing the president personally in public, he was vitriolic in his assessment of Roosevelt the president in his autobiographical dictations and correspondence with friends.

Clemens and Roosevelt had much in common. As young men they had ventured out west and experienced frontier freedom from which they drew strength and confidence throughout their lives. They shared an insatiable intellectual curiosity; a love of reading, writing, travel, and nature; gregarious and loquacious personalities; a penchant for publicity; and a desire to fill center stage. Perhaps they were too much alike and recognized in each other their own flaws as masters of hyperbole. "Teedie" (his family nickname), and his younger brother, Elliott (Eleanor Roosevelt's father), shared a laugh as they read *A Tramp Abroad* aloud to each other around the kitchen table.

Indeed, Roosevelt thought Clemens was a "real genius" and that *Huckleberry Finn, Tom Sawyer,* and *Life on the Mississippi* were American classics, but he was offended by *A Connecticut Yankee* because it ridiculed the chivalrous Camelot of which Roosevelt no doubt thought he would have been a charter member.[3] In public he called Twain "not only a great humorist, but a great philosopher."[4] The men apparently enjoyed each other's company, dining together at the White House. Understandably the president was offended when Clemens attacked his policies.[5]

"Every time, in twenty-five years, that I have met Roosevelt the man," Clemens wrote to Twichell, "a wave of welcome has streaked through me with the hand-grip; but whenever (as a rule) I meet Roosevelt the statesman & politician I find him destitute of morals & not respectworthy. It is plain that where his political self & his party are concerned he has nothing resembling a conscience."[6] As president, Roosevelt was "naively indifferent to the restraints of duty & even unaware of them," Clemens complained, he was always ready to "kick the Constitution into the back yard whenever it gets in the way."[7]

On the exercise of military power and what constitutes a "just war," Clemens and Roosevelt were polar opposites. In Clemens's view a war was not "just" simply because the president initiated it, Congress declared it, or the majority of the people supported it. War was justified only to defend the American people from harm (as in the War of 1812), to overthrow brutal regimes (such as czarist Russia), to revolt against colonial subjugation (as Americans had done in the Revolutionary War), or to help liberate oppressed people from foreign domination (such as Cuba from Spain in 1898). In a speech to the New York Lotos Club in 1900, he said that "a righteous war is so rare that it is almost unknown in history."[8] Asked by his friends whether he would be willing to serve in a war launched by his country, he replied:

> If I thought it an unrighteous war I would say so. If I were invited to shoulder a musket and march under that flag, I would decline. I would not voluntarily march under this country's flag nor any other, when it was my private judgment that the country was wrong. If the country *obliged* me to shoulder the musket, I could not help myself, but I would never volunteer. To volunteer would be the act of a traitor to myself, and consequently traitor to my country. If I refused to volunteer, I should be *called* a traitor, I am well aware of that—but that would not make me a traitor. The unanimous vote of sixty millions could not make me a traitor. I should still be a patriot, and in my opinion, the only one in the whole country.[9]

Clemens preferred a gentler diplomacy to the display and exercise of raw power. He counseled "a little concession, now and then, where it can do no harm, is the wiser policy," for a "statesman gains little by the arbitrary exercise of iron-clad authority."[10] In Clemens's time, American diplomats were notoriously underpaid. Conflicting views about America's role in the world generated a vigorous debate about the value of diplomacy versus military power. In 1879 Georgia Democratic senator James H. Blount proposed firing all the diplomats and closing consular offices on the grounds that the transatlantic cable had made them obsolete. Diplomacy was a royal relic of archaic monarchies. Washington could conduct its foreign affairs by telegraph. In the opposite pole, Maine Republican congressman Eugene Hale proposed an appropriations amendment to raise the salaries of underpaid diplomats. He was supported by the erudite house speaker Thomas Reed, who privately shared Clemens's anti-imperialist sentiments. Noting that Americans are "a noble and magnificent people," Reed suggested in his sardonic manner, "yet there is some wisdom outside the United States," and to obtain such knowledge, our honorable diplomats should receive credible salaries comparable to their peers from other nations.[11] Clemens agreed with Reed and Hale and blasted the "trifling salaries" of diplomats:[12] "A country which cannot afford ambassadors' wages should be ashamed to have ambassadors."[13] In private letters to Twichell, Clemens expressed his growing anger over Roosevelt's foreign policies. He berated the president's heavy-handed diplomacy with "little helpless Colombia" and the "little feeble Nicaraguan president" in deciding to construct a canal in Panama. He condemned Roosevelt's firing of the ambassador to Venezuela, Herbert Bowen, who had publicly criticized his predecessor, Francis Loomis ("Bowen was indiscreet, but not dishonest, Theodore and Secretary of War William Howard Taft were *both*"). He was upset by Roosevelt's appointment of his nemesis, Whitelaw Reid,* to the Court of St. James.[14] In an unpublished letter to the editor in 1909, Twain wrote: "We have never had a president before who was destitute of self-respect & of respect for his high office...who was intended for a butcher, a time-keeper or a bully, & missed his mission by compulsion of circumstances over which he had no control."[15]

---

* Clemens had never forgiven Reid, editor of *The New York Tribune*, for the paper's negative review of *The Gilded Age*, and he had campaigned against the Republican ticket of Benjamin Harrison with Reid as the vice presidential candidate in 1892. Reid acknowledged Twain's growing celebrity but thought his writing lowbrow. Awkwardly, they were both scheduled to receive honorary degrees from Oxford on the same day in 1907, and Ambassador Reid felt obligated to host a special tribute to Twain (Shelden, 108–09).

Under Roosevelt the Philippine occupation continued to deteriorate. Faced with a northern insurgency for which the US military was unprepared and untrained, the volunteer army resorted to practices that would never have been condoned in conventional warfare, including the killing and maiming of thousands of innocent civilians and bystanders in what today would be called "collateral damage." At the urging of Clemens and others, Congress conducted an inquiry into the Philippine atrocities. Concerned about losing public support for the war, President Roosevelt simply declared it over in 1902. The US-Philippine Commission passed the Bandolerismo Statute (the Brigandage Act), which *redefined* the continuing armed resistance as "banditry." The last Filipino officers who held out on the northern front were hanged as bandits in 1907.[16]

Focusing on the northern resistance, the United States had negotiated the Bates Agreement in 1898, promising the southern Filipino Muslims autonomy. Nonetheless, in 1903 the US military unilaterally abrogated the Bates Agreement and opened up a second front against the Muslims in the southern islands.[17] Although the American public celebrated its four-month triumph over Spain, assuming the war was over, Clemens continued to write about it until his death in 1910—because the war in the Philippines continued! Arguably the war continues to this day as US-armed Filipino forces seek to quell the southern insurgents now reformulated as the Maoist New People's Army.

In "Grief and Mourning for the Night," Twain describes the horrific 1906 massacre of the Moro Muslims in the crater of an extinct volcano on Mount Dajo led by American war hero General Leonard Wood.* A force of 540 American soldiers,

---

* A graduate of Harvard Medical School, Major General Wood had a long military career in which his role in the Moro massacre has become a footnote. He commanded the "Rough Riders" charge up San Juan Hill; his second-in-command was Roosevelt. Wood was military governor of Cuba from 1900–1902 and governor general of the Philippines from 1921–27. He served as personal physician to President McKinley. Later, as Army chief of staff, he was credited with many reforms that modernized the training and preparedness of the Army, creating the first combined armored divisions that fought in World War I. Wood ran for the Republican nomination for President in 1920 but lost in a deadlocked convention to the dark horse, Warren G. Harding.

aided by native constabularies, circled the rim of the crater in which more than six hundred Muslim men, women, and children were clustered fifty feet below. According to General Wood, the "battle" lasted a day and a half as the US troops fired their artillery and rifles into the crater against fierce opposition from the enemy. (It is unclear what form the opposition took, as the insurgents fought mainly with daggers, cudgels, and old muskets they had captured.) Twain summarized General Wood's report of "a complete victory for the American armies":

> The completeness of the victory is established by this fact: that of the six hundred Moros, not one of them was left alive...Of our six hundred heroes only fifteen lost their lives.
> General Wood was present, looking on. His order had been "kill *or* capture those savages." Apparently our little army considered that the "*or*" left them authorized to kill *or* capture according to taste, and that taste had remained what it has been for eight years, in our army out there—the taste of Christian butchers.[18]

President Roosevelt congratulated General Wood for his "brilliant feat of arms wherein you and [your troops] so well upheld the honor of the American flag."[19] Twain reacted viscerally to Roosevelt's message:

> His whole utterance is merely a convention. Not a word of what he said came out of his heart. He knew perfectly well that to pen six hundred helpless and weaponless savages in a hole like rats in a trap and massacre them in detail during a stretch of a day and a half, from a safe position on the heights above, was no brilliant feat of arms—and would not have been a brilliant feat of arms even if Christian America represented by its salaried soldiers had shot them down with Bibles and the Golden Rule instead of bullets. He knew perfectly well that our uniformed assassins had *not* upheld the honor of the American flag, but had done as they had been

doing continuously for eight years in the Philippines—that is to say, they dishonored it.[20]

In 1906 Twain lectured at Princeton University. Helen Keller and Woodrow Wilson were in the audience. Keller reported that Twain "poured out a volume of invective and ridicule" on US "military exploits" in the Philippines, paid tribute to the Moro Moslems, and cautioned that a nation with so little regard for the liberties of others might soon lose its own freedom.[21]

Helen Keller visits Samuel Clemens in Redding, Connecticut in January 1909, photo taken by Isabel Lyons. Courtesy: Mark Twain Project, The Bancroft Library University of California, Berkeley

In "As Regards Patriotism," Twain rejects the shibboleth that patriotism requires the support of the American troops in the Philippines. "The Patriot did not know just how or when he got his opinions, neither did he care, so long as he was with what seemed to be the majority—which was the main thing, the safe thing, the comfortable thing."[22] Over his lifetime of experience, Clemens had reluctantly concluded that "in any civic crisis of a great and dangerous sort, the common herd is not privately anxious about the rights and wrongs of the matter, it is only anxious to be on the winning side."[23] For Americans, occupation of an Asian country was "an entirely new and untried political project," and when such a project, Twain wrote in 1905, "is sprung upon the people, they are startled, anxious, timid, and for a time they are mute, reserved, non-committal. The great majority of them are not studying the new doctrine and making up their minds about it, they are waiting to see which is going to be the popular side."[24]

Given the atrocities performed in the name of the American flag in the Philippines, Clemens was "quite willing to be called a traitor—quite willing to wear that honorable badge—and not willing to be affronted with the title of Patriot and classed with the Funstons."[25] "Patriotism is being carried to insane excess," he wrote. "I know men who do not love God because He is a foreigner."[26]

Having little faith in his own generation, Clemens urged mothers to raise their children with a different kind of patriotism: "Remember this, take it to heart, live by it, die for it if necessary; that our patriotism is medieval, outworn, obsolete; that the modern patriotism, the true patriotism, the only rational patriotism, *is loyalty to the Nation* ALL the time, loyalty to Government when it deserves it."[27]

In April 1907 Clemens joined Henry Rogers on his yacht, the *Kanawha*, on a cruise to Norfolk, Virginia, to attend the opening of the Exposition celebrating the three hundredth anniversary of the English settlement of Jamestown. Rogers also wanted to visit the terminus of his secretly constructed Virginia Railway, which would transport West Virginia coal to the Atlantic port. Roosevelt, who was on the warpath against Standard Oil and Rogers, was sailing down the Chesapeake on the presidential yacht, the *Mayflower*, toward Norfolk to lead the opening-day ceremonies.

He was greeted with a three-hundred-gun salute from an armada of sixteen battleships painted white. Later in the year this "Great White Fleet" would sail around the world, brandishing America's might as the new global naval power. Clemens had no objection to a "whacking big navy," but feared that "Roosevelt and the politicians were too eager to unleash the martial canines." Roosevelt, the showman, tended to do "insanely spectacular things."[28]

In his *Autobiography* Twain summed up his views about Roosevelt. He conceded that as a private citizen, Theodore was "one of the most likeable men with whom he had been acquainted." He also declared that due to his joyous ebullitions and excited sincerity, Roosevelt "is the most popular human being that ever existed in the United States." The people "see themselves reflected in him." Roosevelt's problem, Clemens thought, was his impulsiveness and inconsistency. "He flies from one thing to another with incredible dispatch—throws a somersault and is straightaway back again where he was last week."[29] Roosevelt lacked the steady, consistent, independent leadership of a Grover Cleveland, who was willing to take an unpopular stand if it was right for the country. Roosevelt failed to ask what was "the right way to do anything." He was too susceptible to the whims and tides of public opinion, too eager to be loved by the public, and too quick to formulate policy to win the media's accolades. As he burnished the image of riding horseback up San Juan Hill so he rode the crest of patriotic hysteria into an era of American imperialism—exposing the fundamental weakness of American democracy where unprincipled leadership interacts with an unthinking public fed by media frenzy.

"Mr. Roosevelt is the most formidable disaster that has befallen the county," Twain dictated for his yet-unpublished autobiography, "but the vast mass of the nation loves him, is frantically fond of him, even idolizes him; this is the simple truth. It sounds like libel upon the intelligence of the human race, but it isn't; there isn't any way to libel the intelligence of the human race."[30]

In the 1908 presidential election, Roosevelt persuaded the Republican Party to nominate his close friend William Howard Taft, the secretary of war—who Clemens said "runs to him daily with the docility of a spaniel to get his permission to do things."[31]

The Democrats turned again to William Jennings Bryan, who had been twice defeated by McKinley. Clemens advised his daughter, Jean, not to "be fooled by the immense noise & racket the Presidential election is making—there is no substance to it & no great interest in it—it is just make believe."[32] Clemens thought that "no sane person wanted Mr. Roosevelt's shadow elected," and what a shadow he cast, as Clemens had earlier described the 335-pound Taft to Twichell as that "great big Secretary of War... oozing fetid pus."[33] Yet he voted for Taft as the lesser evil than the populist-spouting Bryan, and Taft won by a comfortable margin. Once elected, Clemens warmed up to Taft—as he was prone to do with people in power. During Taft's administration, more anti-trust lawsuits were launched than under trust-busting Roosevelt, and the Sixteenth and Seventeenth Amendments were ratified, authorizing respectively a progressive income tax and the direct election of senators.

In letters to his twenty-two-year-old friend Margery Clinton,[*] who was on her way to Washington, Clemens wrote: "You must shake hands with Mr. Taft for me, that able & lovely man."[34] When Miss Clinton returned to Redding after meeting with the president, Clemens wrote her again that "you can't help but like Mr. Taft. The country likes him & respects him." That some disapprove of him was "sure proof, in a public servant, that he is doing his whole duty, as he sees it, regardless of personal consequences." Clemens heaped on the praise: "He has the natural gifts, the culture, the experience, the training, the sanity, the right-mindedness, the honesty, the truthfulness, the modesty, & the dignity properly requisite in a president of the United States, the most responsible post on the planet." In contrast to his predecessor, Taft "possesses every qualification the other one was destitute of."[35]

---

[*] The widower Clemens, living in Stormfield, befriended a number of young girls who were essentially surrogate grandchildren. He called them his "Angel-Fish." Among them was Margery Clinton, the daughter of New York architect Charles William Clinton, who lived next door to the daughter of Henry Rogers in New York City. When Clara returned from a European concert tour, she sought to dismantle her father's club of young girls, fearing it might be misinterpreted.

Clemens died during the Taft administration, but he became acquainted with the man who would succeed him—Woodrow Wilson. Although he had met Wilson a couple times previously, Clemens got to know the fifty-six-year-old president of Princeton University on one of his trips to Bermuda through a mutual friend, Mary Peck. A married woman in her forties, with a neglectful husband addicted to business affairs in Massachusetts, Peck was the belle of Bermuda's social life. She took a shine to the respected author. When Wilson started visiting the island alone in 1907 to decompress from Ivy League pressures, he became infatuated with Peck and a bit jealous of the attention she showered on Clemens. When it became apparent that her romantic intentions were not directed at the author but toward the suave university president, Wilson and Clemens became good friends, billiard partners, and golfing companions. In their last nine-hole match, Clemens's many hours in the billiard room of his Hartford home paid off. He beat Wilson by sinking a long putt. They joined forces to petition the legislature to prohibit the importation of automobiles, which they believed would despoil the island's beauty and character. Of Clemens, Wilson said: "He is certainly the most human of men." Wilson understood how great men, like former President Cleveland, had "learned to love him."[36]

A Tale of Today

An advocate of an enlarged diplomatic corps to pursue alternatives to war, Clemens was engaged in a national debate that continues to this day. In the Bush and Obama administrations, the strongest advocate of increasing the size and responsibilities of the diplomatic corps was Defense Secretary Robert Gates, who understood the horrors of war as an alternative to peaceful dispute resolution. Gates also worried about the nation-building responsibilities thrust upon the shoulders of young volunteer soldiers who were asked to win the hearts of peoples plagued by terrorist insurgencies. Gates complained to

Congress that the entire diplomatic corps could not man a single aircraft carrier, and there are more members of military bands than US foreign service officers.

Until his death, Clemens continued to speak out against the Philippine occupation, raising fundamental questions. The same kinds of questions are asked today about US foreign military interventions. When is it necessary and appropriate for the United States to intervene militarily? Have all means of peaceful resolution been exhausted? What are the US objectives (e.g., to defend against an imminent threat to national security, to assist an oppressed people gain freedom from a brutal dictator, to impose American-style democracy or cultural or religious values on an indigenous population, or to protect or expand US economic spheres of influence—such as access to energy supplies)? The questions Twain asked remain pertinent: "What are we getting out of it, and what it means to us as a nation."[37] To what extent does patriotic fervor, the inertia of the military-industrial complex or domestic political pressures and strategies obscure a thoughtful analysis of US options? Is US intervention supported by the indigenous population, by US allies, and by the international community? What are the possible long term outcomes of US intervention in a foreign land: democratic self-government, civil war among ethnic populations, geopolitical realignment, anti-US sentiment?

There are many lessons that Twain thought Americans should learn from the interminable Philippine occupation. If the United States decides to intervene, what is the end-goal and how will success be measured, what is the exit strategy, what plans have been made for the occupation and transition of the invaded country, and how can the United States avoid being bogged down, as Twain put it, in "a quagmire from which each fresh step renders the difficulty of extraction immensely greater"?[38] How should the United States protect its soldiers and citizens from unconventional methods of warfare by insurgents or terrorists? Under what circumstances is "collateral damage," the killing or harming of civilians, justified? To what extent should the United States depart from the rules of conventional warfare when the enemy consists of insurgents who do not follow conventional rules, do not wear uniforms, use civilians as shields, and engage in terrorist tactics? These questions continue to haunt American foreign policy. The tactical issues may differ—the use of predator drones, the types of enhanced interrogation techniques to obtain intelligence, the indeterminate detention of prisoners outside the United States, defending against embedded explosive devices and suicide bombers—but the underlying questions are the same that Clemens asked about the Philippines occupation. The issues have continued to shape the US foreign policy debate through the ensuing decades as successive administrations attempt to explain—and the public seeks to understand—US missions and objectives in such far-flung places as Vietnam, Grenada, Somalia, Afghanistan, Iraq, Libya, Syria, and Yemen.

CHAPTER EIGHTEEN

The Many Facets Of Imperialism

"I have filled the position—with some credit, I trust, of self-appointed ambassador-at-large of the United States of America—without salary."

— MARK TWAIN

The Anti-Imperialist League was formed in Boston in November 1898 after the Treaty of Paris ended the Spanish-American War. Local leagues were established throughout the country. Clemens was an active vice president of the Anti-Imperialist League of New York. At a convention of the local organizations in Chicago in October 1899, the American Anti-Imperialist League was founded and headquartered there. The League's platform declared that "imperialism is hostile to liberty and tends toward militarism, an evil from which it has been our glory to be free." The platform reaffirmed that "all men, of whatever race or color, are entitled to life, liberty and the pursuit of happiness" and that "the subjugation of any people is 'criminal aggression' and open disloyalty to the distinctive principles of our government."[1]

In a July 4, 1901, message to the American people, endorsed by Clemens, the League urged the people who had reelected President McKinley to voice their disapproval of his policies of imperialism, urged Congress "to insist that the principles of freedom must be recognized and applied wherever our country holds sway," and called on the Supreme Court to uphold the rights of all human beings under our control. The manifesto quoted the great Supreme Court dissenter, Justice John Marshall Harlan:[*] "The idea that this country may acquire territories anywhere upon the earth, by conquest or treaty, and hold them as mere colonies or provinces, and the people inhabiting them to enjoy only such rights as Congress chooses to accord them, is wholly inconsistent with the spirit and genius as well as the words of the Constitution."[2]

While the anti-imperialist movement was focused on the US annexation of the Philippines, Clemens viewed the issue in a broader context. Imperialism was the autocratic abuse of power to subjugate ordinary citizens. Clemens knitted together many diverse, interrelated issues, such as the suppression of labor, the corruption and greed of politicians, global corporate exploitation, racial oppression, and the exercise of unconstrained executive power by kings, dictators, presidents, and local political machines. In speaking and writing about the interconnectedness of these issues, Clemens stood almost alone. His vision was rooted in his diverse experience. As a newsman he exposed and fought political corruption at all levels of government, from Tammany Hall to Congress. Having traveled and lived extensively abroad, he became an acute observer of global conflicts and atrocities such as the South African wars, the Boxer rebellion, the anti-Semitic trials of Captain Dreyfus, and the brutality

---

[*] Justice John Marshall Harlan dissented 316 times, often foreshadowing the position the Supreme Court would take many years later. His dissent in *Plessey v. Ferguson* became the law of the land in *Brown v. Board of Education*.

of Tsarist Russia. He became a passionate advocate of responsible American participation in the world community.[3]

Tammany Hall

To the chagrin of his anti-imperialist colleagues, Twain kept bringing the Tammany Hall political machine into the public debate on imperialism. He sought to establish two critical points: First, he noted that a corrupt, big-city political machine deprived ordinary people of their natural rights as citizens. The evils of the machine were local and tangible and therefore easier for the public to grasp than the evils perpetrated by sending troops to a foreign land accompanied by patriotic trumpets. Second, America still had a lot of work to do to perfect democracy at home before it could forcefully export it to the rest of the world. Condemning the "loud, pious way" we export our civilization to "the people that sit in darkness," Twain offered up Boss Tammany Hall and Jay Gould as examples of American exceptionalism. It was time, he said, to "sober up and sit down, and think it over first" before seeking to impose our model on other peoples.[4]

South Africa

In 1896 Sam, Livy, and Clara Clemens arrived in South Africa on their world lecture tour. Tensions were mounting between the British and Dutch settlers—Afrikaners or Boers—who occupied adjacent areas. Clemens condemned both groups for their brutal treatment of the native populations. The British envied the valuable mines and productive farmland held by the Afrikaners, but attempts by the English adventurer Sir Leander Starr Jameson to seize the Boer republics had failed. Spurred by the ambitious industrialist Cecil B. Rhodes, the British contemplated a war that would unify South Africa as a British colony. On October 11, 1899, when war finally broke out, Clemens considered the British to be the aggressors, motivated by Rhodes's hunger for natural resources and cheap labor. He wrote in his *Notebook*: "Be he Boer or be he Briton, it is murder, & England committed it by the hand of [secretary of state for the colonies Joseph] Chamberlain & the Cabinet, the lackeys of Cecil Rhodes & his Forty Thieves, the South Africa Company."[5] Although he sympathized with the Boers, he remained silent for geopolitical reasons. "Every day I write (in my head) bitter magazine articles about it," he confessed, "but I have to stop with that. For England must not fail." He valued the longstanding cultural affinity and shared democratic traditions between the United States and the United Kingdom, which he feared, prophetically, might be called upon to confront the rise of German and Russian nationalism whose "political degradations...would envelop the globe and steep it in a sort of Middle-Age night and slavery."[6]

On December 12, 1900, twenty-six-year-old Winston Churchill spoke at the Waldorf-Astoria in New York. It was his first stop on a tour promoting a book about his capture by the Boers in South Africa and rationalizing British support for the war. Most of the anti-imperialists—including Clemens's friend Howells—boycotted the event, but Clemens could never turn down access to a podium. Besides, he had rather admired Churchill's brash, cocky style when he met him in 1899 at a London party.[7] He introduced Churchill at the Waldorf dinner and used the occasion to condemn US and UK imperialism: "I think England sinned when she got herself into a war in South Africa which she could have avoided, just as we have sinned in getting into a similar war in the Philippines. Mr. Churchill by his father is an Englishman; by his mother he is an American; no doubt a blend that makes the perfect man. England and America; yes, we are kin. And now that we are also kin in sin, there is nothing more to be desired. The harmony is complete, the blend is perfect."[8]

Churchill was so honored by the opportunity to meet Mark Twain that he ignored the insult. He asked for an autographed set of the author's works. Twain inscribed them: "To do good is noble, to teach others to do good is nobler, and no trouble." Many years later, Churchill wrote about the occasion: "Of course we argued about the war. After some interchanges I found myself beaten back to the citadel, 'My country right or wrong.' 'Ah,' said the old gentleman, 'when the poor country is fighting for its life, I agree. But that was not your case.'"[9]

China

Clemens respect for Chinese culture and his disdain for the condescending and discriminatory attitude of Westerners toward the Chinese were rooted in his days as a San Francisco reporter. He warily watched as the British, French, and Germans staked out "concessions" in China, applying their own laws and governing authorities and ignoring the local Chinese—except when it came to taxing them. In 1868 Clemens had warned that unless the Chinese were treated with dignity and respect, they would rise up and expel the foreigners.[10] In the Boxer Rebellion in 1900, they attempted just that. The united Western powers sent troops, including American soldiers, to quash the rebellion. On August 15, 1900, Clemens wrote to Twichell that all his "sympathies are with the Chinese. They have been villainously dealt with by the sceptered thieves of Europe, and I hope they will drive all foreigners out and keep them out for good. I only wish it; of course I do not expect it."[11] The rebellion was crushed, and exorbitant compensation was exacted from the Chinese. Any defeat of China, Clemens predicted, would be temporary, for China eventually would be free of foreign influence and "save herself."

In 1900 he addressed the Public Education Association, foreshadowing John Kennedy's "Ich bin ein Berliner" speech more than six decades later. "I am a Boxer," he declared.

Why should not China be free from the foreigners who are only making trouble on her soil? If they would only all go home, what a pleasant place China would be for the Chinese! We do not allow Chinamen to come here, and I would say in all seriousness that it would be a graceful thing to let China decide who shall go there.

China never wanted foreigners any more than foreigners wanted Chinamen, and on this question, I am with the Boxers every time. The Boxer is a patriot... I wish him success.[12]

The Dreyfus Affair

In December 1894 Captain Alfred Dreyfus, a French Army officer, was convicted of treason on trumped-up evidence and sentenced to life imprisonment. Three years later another army officer was acquitted of spying on evidence that would have proved Dreyfus's innocence. But Dreyfus was Jewish. Because his conviction was based on the prosecutor's false evidence, Clemens found it "irregular," anti-Semitic, and culturally arrogant. "It is un-English; it is un-American; it is French,"[13] Clemens praised Emile Zola's essay "J'accuse" charging France with persecuting Dreyfus, for which Zola was arrested and convicted of libel. In Dreyfus's retrial in 1899, the French court found that the evidence used to convict him had been forged. It nevertheless found him guilty for the second time, which ignited international media condemnation of French anti-Semitism. Under international pressure Dreyfus was pardoned but removed from the military. He was tried a third time in 1904–05, found innocent, and reinstated in the army.

Living in Europe at the time, Clemens wisely warned of rising militarism and anti-Semitism on the continent. In Twain's essay "The Stupendous Procession," French anti-Semitism was equated with English, German, Russian, and American imperialism. He saw how governments could invoke anti-Semitism to rally jingoistic crowds in support of nationalistic expansionism. He considered Zola a hero, writing to him that "ecclesiastical and military courts made up of cowards…can be bred at the rate of a million a year, but it takes five centuries to breed a Joan of Arc or a Zola."[14]

Russia

In 1890 Clemens attended a lecture on czarist Russia's oppression of Siberian miners. He stood up in the audience in an uncontrolled fury, declaring in the voice of a premodern terrorist, "If such a government cannot be overthrown otherwise than by dynamite, then thank God for dynamite!"[15] In April 1891 Clemens became a founding member of the American Society of Friends of Russian Freedom. Other founding members included Julia Ward Howe, James Russell Lowell and William

Lloyd Garrison Jr. Its manifesto was "to aid by all moral and legal means the Russian patriots in their effort to obtain for their country Political freedom and Self Government."[16] The Society issued a monthly publication entitled *Free Russia*, to which Twain promised an article, which he belatedly provided in 1905 with the publication of "The Czar's Soliloquy."

In his little-known 1892 novel *The American Claimant*, Twain merges his stock character Colonel Sellers's penchant for exuberant speculation with the czar's penchant for brutal suppression. Sellers proposes to "buy Siberia and start a republic." The czar has been exporting all the brightest, most industrious minds in Russia to Siberia, so Sellers concludes that Siberia has "more manhood, pluck, true heroism, unselfishness, devotion to high and noble ideals, adoration of liberty, wide education, and *brains*...than any other domain in the whole world." The exiled free thinkers will populate the new Siberian Republic,[17] which would begin a mass exodus from Russia, leaving the czar with "a vacant throne in an empty land!"[18] Grand on scheming but deficient on implementation, the Siberian proposal—like all of Sellers's other schemes—comes to naught, but only after Twain takes aim at czarist Russia.

A few years later, Clemens's disgust with the czar's internal oppression turned to anger at Russia's external aggression. In the Russo-Japanese war of 1904–05, Russia invaded Manchuria and seized Port Arthur, massacring the Chinese peasants along the way. Twain attacked Russian imperialism in his essays "To a Person Sitting in Darkness," "The Stupendous Procession," "Flies and Russians," and "The Fable of the Yellow Peril." Twain even criticized Theodore Roosevelt for his successful mediation of the September 1905 peace treaty between the warring parties at Portsmouth, New Hampshire. Russia, which had lost several battles and seen its naval fleet decimated, was forced to recognize Korea, and Japan emerged as Asia's strongest power. Roosevelt's mediation was widely applauded. Cardinal Joseph Gibbons, the ranking Catholic prelate in the United States, called him "the angel of peace to the world," and the president won the Nobel Peace Prize—the first American to win a Nobel

Prize in any category. But Clemens dissented. He called the peace treaty "the most conspicuous disaster in political history" because, in his judgment, it rescued imperial Russia from a devastating defeat. He wrote to the *Boston Globe*: "One more battle would have abolished the waiting chains of billions upon billions of unborn Russians," but now the czar would "resume his medieval barbarisms with a relieved spirit and an immeasurable joy."[19]

Roosevelt invited Clemens to lunch in November 1905, but failed to charm him. On leaving the White House, Twain handed out his own less than salutary Thanksgiving statement to reporters, suggesting that the deity did not have much to be grateful for given "the year's results in Russia." There, the czar's agents had "killed and wounded fifty thousand Jews by unusual and unpleasant methods, butchering the men and women with knife and bayonet; flinging them out of windows; saturating them with kerosene and setting fire to them; shutting them up in cellars and smothering them with smoke; drenching their children with boiling water; tearing other children asunder by methods of the Middle Ages."[20]

In March 1906 the grizzled but volcanic Nikolai Tchaikovsky, the father of the Russian revolutionary movement and younger brother of the composer Pyotr Ilyich Tchaikovsky, toured the United States, raising funds for a free Russia. Due to a conflict, Clemens was unable to speak at the fund-raising event, but he sent a message: "My sympathies are with the Russian revolution...I hope it will succeed." He wrote that "Government by falsified promises, by lies, by treachery, and by the butcher-knife, for the aggrandizement of a single family of drones and its idle and vicious kin has been borne quite long enough in Russia... Some of us, even the white-headed, may live to see the blessed day when Czars and Grand Dukes will be as scarce [in Russia] as I trust they are in heaven."[21]

When the writer Maxim Gorky arrived in New York in April 1906 to generate support for a free Russia, he received a hero's welcome. Clemens introduced Gorky at a dinner sponsored by the A Club, a group of progressive writers. He drew a parallel with the American Revolution: "Anybody whose ancestors were in this country when we were trying to free ourselves from oppression must sympathize with those who now are trying to do the same in Russia."[22] The next morning *The New York Times* headline screamed: "Gorky and Twain plead for Revolution." *The New York World* ran a cartoon showing Mark Twain "toppling the Russian throne with a pen."[23]

Gorky's triumphant visit to America came to a screeching halt when the newspapers revealed that he was accompanied by a Russian actress who was not his wife. This was the Victorian age. Gorky and friend were evicted from their hotel, and events in his honor were canceled. Clemens was one of the last holdouts. He finally succumbed and reluctantly withdrew as a host of a literary dinner for the Russian novelist when he felt Gorky "had lost his efficiency as a persuader."[24] The dinner was canceled. Clemens later mused that "laws can be evaded and punishment escaped, but an openly transgressed custom brings sure punishment," for "Custom is custom…facts, reasonings, arguments have no more effect upon it than the idle winds have on Gibraltar."[25] Clemens nonetheless defended his efforts to assist Gorky and the Russian Revolution.[26] He argued that the United States had accepted aid from France during the Revolutionary War. He declared: "I am a revolutionist by birth, breeding and principle, and I am therefore in sympathy with any kind of revolution anywhere. There never is a revolution unless there is oppression to instigate the people."[27] Paine wrote after Clemens's death at the time of the 1917 Russian Revolution that "few things would have given him more comfort than to have known that a little more than ten years would see the downfall of Russian Imperialism."[28]

Twain's widely read, acclaimed, and condemned masterpiece on imperialism was published in the *North American Review* in 1901, entitled "To the Person Sitting in Darkness."[29] The title was taken from the book of Matthew in the New Testament when Jesus is about to preach the Sermon on the Mount in fulfillment of Isaiah's prophecy that "the people who have sat in darkness have seen a great light." Presumably the title is an ironic reference to the enlightenment that imperialism brings to heathen savages.

Twain suggested that the indigenous peoples were getting weary of the "Blessings-of-Civilization Trust," the Western powers' proclamation that they were exporting "LOVE, JUSTICE, GENTLENESS, CHRISTIANITY, PROTECTION OF THE WEAK, TEMPERANCE, LAW AND ORDER, LIBERTY, EQUALITY, HONORABLE DEALING, MERCY, EDUCATION—and so on." These were the brands advertised on the cover, Twain wrote. Inside, "the Actual Thing that the Customer Sitting in Darkness buys with his blood and tears and land and liberty" is economic exploitation of his resources and labor—"a private raid for cash."[30]

In "To the Person Sitting in Darkness," Twain explores the mixed motivations underlying imperialism: "There must be two Americas: one that sets the captive free, and one that...kills him to get his land."[31] At its core, is imperialism simply a belief in white supremacy?[32] Is imperialism extraterritorial greed, the unrestrained expansion of capitalism that has exhausted its domestic markets? ("It will give Business a splendid new start.")[33] Is imperialism missionary zeal in which Christians commit to save the ignorant masses from a fiery hell? ("The missionaries braved a thousand privations to come and make the [natives] permanently miserable in telling them how beautiful and how blissful a place heaven is and how nearly impossible it is to get there.")[34] Is imperialism a reflection of America's European colonial heritage? Can America divorce itself from the belligerent nationalism of European monarchies and dictatorships that compete for colonial territories? (On US liberation of the Philippines: "we were only playing the American game in public—in private it was the European.")[35] Is imperialism justified by the misguided notion that it is essential to progress and civilization in the undeveloped world?[36]

Having compared and condemned in his essay German, Russian, and English imperialism, as well as missionaries and political machines,[37] Twain then excoriates the US intervention in the Philippines:

There have been lies; yes, but they were told in a good cause. We have been treacherous; but that was only in order that real good might come out of apparent evil. True, we have crushed a deceived and confiding people; we have turned against the weak and friendless who have trusted us; we have stamped out a just and intelligent and well-ordered republic; we have stabbed an ally in the back and slapped the face of a guest...We have robbed a trusting friend of his land and his liberty...we have debauched America's honor and blackened her face before the world.[38]

Publication of the article sent shockwaves through the populace, but Twain's references to missionaries and Tammany Hall drew the harshest criticism. He acknowledged that by ridiculing the Christian missionaries he had gotten himself "into hot water with the clergy and the other goody-goody people."[39] Clemens was skeptical of "do-gooders." He thought "there was no such thing as a good deed," at least not one which did not have both good and evil consequences.[40] When the New York Anti-Imperialist League reprinted 125,000 copies of "To the Person Sitting in Darkness" for distribution throughout the country, the League's secretary, Edward Ordway, proclaimed: "These burning words of Mark Twain will do as much to stir the sluggish conscience of the American people as anything that has yet appeared on the subject."[41] Ordway, however, had removed the references to the missionaries and Tammany Hall from the essay.

In "A Salutation Speech from the Nineteenth Century to the Twentieth" to the New England League, Twain offered an anti-imperialist manifesto that was widely reprinted and circulated throughout the country. In an oft-quoted passage, Twain again tied together German, Russian, English, and American imperialism: "I bring you the stately matron called CHRISTENDOM, returning bedraggled, besmirched and dishonored from pirate raids in Kiao-Chow, Manchuria, South Africa, and the Philippines, with her soul full of meanness, her pocket full of boodle and her mouth full of pious hypocrisies."[42]

Publishing the "Salutation," the Chicago-based weekly *The Public* featured a debate on imperialism by four prominent national leaders: McKinley, Roosevelt, Bryan, and Twain; the latter held no office and aspired to none.[43]

In 1902 moderate anti-imperialists applauded when Cuba was granted independence, albeit under stringent conditions, which Twain referred to as "a new set of leg-irons and hand-cuffs."[44] Its constitution was subject to US congressional approval, international alliances were prohibited, and US military intervention was authorized to quell political unrest and force the payment of international debts. It was over the Philippines in 1904, however, that the anti-imperialist movement fractured. Some members sympathized with business leaders who viewed investment in the Philippines as an alternative to governing the archipelago. By creating commercial ties and trade, the United States would foster economic development that would lay the foundation for democratic self-government over time. Some of the Filipino leaders, who were the beneficiaries of such investment, signaled to Congress their support for a slower, more phased-in approach to independence. Even Clemens's resistance hero, Emilio Aguinaldo, supported the slower path to independence. The national Anti-Imperialist organization and Clemens's New York branch were disbanded. The New England branch was reconstituted as a national organization of purists who advocated immediate and unconditional independence for the Philippines. Twain was listed as a vice president.

In his later writings, Twain's viewed imperialism as simply another manifestation of the human condition in which brutality and violence were inherent, hereditary characteristics that made conflict, expansionism, and war inevitable. Traces of his passionate anti-imperialism permeate his later deterministic works: "No. 44, The Mysterious Stranger," "The Recurrent Major and Minor Compliment," "The Refuge of the Derelicts," "Three Thousand Years Among the Microbes," "What is Man?" "Extract from Captain Stormfield's Visit to Heaven," and "The War Prayer."

In the "Chronicles of Young Satan," Twain describes the visit of Satan to a rural Austrian village in 1702. Satan recounts the progress of the human race in terms that make Dr. Howard

Zinn's *A People's History of the United States* seem like a children's bedtime story. Civilization progresses from Cain's murder of Abel through Sodom and Gomorrah and countless tribal wars to the birth of Christianity, "which greatly improved the deadly effectiveness of weapons of slaughter." Twain writes in the words of Satan: "Cain did his murder with a club; the Hebrews did their murders with javelins and swords; the Greeks and Romans added protective armor and the fine arts of military organization and generalship; the Christian has added guns and gunpowder; two centuries from now he will have so greatly improved the deadly effectiveness of his weapons of slaughter that all men will confess that without the Christian civilization war must have remained a poor and trifling thing to the end of time."[45]

In the story, Satan even anticipates and addresses the often heard rationalization of "just wars": "There has never been a just one, never an honorable one—on the part of the instigator of the war. I can see a million years ahead, and this rule will never change in so many as a half a dozen instances." Twain starkly describes the way a nation gets into an unjust war:

The loud little handful—as usual—will shout for the war. The pulpit will—warily and cautiously—object—at first.... 'It is unjust and dishonorable, and there is no necessity for it.'

Then the handful will shout louder...and presently the anti-war audience will thin out and lose popularity.

Before long you will see...the whole nation—pulpit and all—will take up the war-cry, and shout itself hoarse, and mob any honest man who ventures to open his mouth; and presently such mouths will cease to be open.

Next the statesmen will invent cheap lies, putting the blame upon the nation that is attacked, and every man will be glad of these conscience-smoothing falsities, and will diligently study them, and refuse to examine any refutations of them; and thus he will by and by convince himself that the war is just, and will thank God for the better sleep he enjoys after this process of grotesque self-deception.[46]

Despite his deepening pessimism, Twain, buoyed by what he saw on his trips to Australia and India, advocated international arbitration as a means of resolving disputes between nations.[47] He supported disarmament, proposing to get "the four great powers to agree to reduce their strength 10 percent a year and thrash the others into doing likewise."[48] Twain argued that with modern weaponry, the great powers had multiples of the manpower required "to accomplish all necessary war work," and that in their military buildup, they were wasting their money and their prosperity. He was resigned that "perpetual peace" cannot be achieved on any terms, but he hoped "we can gradually reduce the war strength of Europe till we get it down to where it ought to be—twenty thousand men, properly armed." Then, he added, "when we want a war, anybody can afford it."[49]

Despite his antiwar rhetoric, Clemens was not a pacifist. In *A Connecticut Yankee*, he wrote that no people ever achieved freedom by "goody-goody talk and moral suasion." History teaches that all successful revolutions "must *begin* in blood."[50]

Nonetheless, as he grew older he became increasingly pessimistic about mankind's propensity to initiate unjust and unnecessary wars. In his darkening disillusionment, he wrote "The War Prayer." Paine argued against publication and Clemens agreed: "I have told the whole truth in that, and only dead men can tell the truth in this world. It can be published after I am dead."[51] It was not published in full until 1923.

"The War Prayer" opens with a display of exalted patriotism as the nation goes to war. A "half dozen rash spirits that ventured to disapprove of the war and cast a doubt upon its righteousness straightaway got such a stern and angry warning that for their personal safety's sake they quickly shrank out of sight and offended no more in that light."[52] Sunday prayers are said for the departing troops, asking God to grant them victory. A stranger enters the church and beckons the Minister to step aside. He describes himself as a messenger of God. He says that God will grant their prayer if they first will listen to the "full import." A prayer, he says is both uttered and unuttered. God has heard both, and now they must hear the silent prayer—the consequences of their patriotic prayer. The Messenger from God speaks the silent prayer:

> O Lord, our Father, our young patriots, idols of our hearts, go forth to battle—be Thou near them!...O Lord, our God, help us to tear their soldiers to bloody shreds with our shells; help us to cover their smiling fields with pale forms of their patriot dead; help us to drown the thunder of the guns with the shrieks of their wounded, writhing in pain; help us to lay waste their humble homes with a hurricane of fire; help us to wring the hearts of their unoffending widows with unavailing grief; help us to turn them out roofless with their little children to wander unfriended in the wastes of their desolated lands in rags and hunger and thirst...We ask it, in the spirit of love, of Him Who is the Source of Love...Amen.[53]

Clemens concludes: "The Messenger awaited a response from the congregation. There was none since they considered him a lunatic."[54]

Increasingly concerned that a nation that deprived others of their liberty was destined to lose its own, Twain wrote a few years before his death two unpublished chapters of an unfinished work: *Glances at History* or *Outlines of History*. The chapters describe a great republic about to invade a small country. A wise man counsels the people not to support a preemptive and unjust war, but his words are ignored. The politicians chant: "Our Country, right or wrong." The wise man responds: "Only when a republic's *life* is in danger should a man uphold his government when it is wrong. There is no other time. This republic's life is not in peril. The nation has sold its honor for a phrase."[55]

Ignoring the wise man, the government stirs up a fury of patriotism and goes to war. The small country is crushed. The great republic is "irrevocably in the hands of the prodigiously rich." "Suffrage had become a mere machine" and there is "no principle but commercialism, no patriotism but of the pocket."[56]

In his unfinished allegory, Twain illustrates the dangers of a combustible collaboration among commercial imperialism, the military establishment and unrestrained executive power, sustained by a complacent public that can be stirred to patriotic fervor by the media, the pulpit, and government propaganda. As the fictional King Edward VI says to Miles Hendon in *The Prince and the Pauper*, "Peace! What are thy paltry domains, thy trivial interests, contrasted with matters which concern the weal of a nation and the integrity of a throne?"[57]

Sam Clemens liked to read and write in bed, smoking cigars and often burning the sheets. Courtesy: Mark Twain Project, The Bancroft Library University of California, Berkeley

Clemens wrote Clara in 1905 that he was reading Suetonius again—having first been introduced to the Roman historian as a Mississippi pilot apprentice—and he had concluded that "while this country is not Rome in-the-days-of-early-Caesars, but there are resemblances and they are increasing. In a hundred years there'll be a king roosting here." Clemens wrote that he knew "*monarchy's* ancestor," and it was "Mr. Roosevelt." Then he crossed out "Mr. Roosevelt" and wrote: "the Republican Party, after which comes the Labor Party & after it the Monarchy."[58]

In a letter to the *London Times* in 1900, captioned "Missionaries in World Politics," Twain argued that, "the source of religion and of patriotism is one and the same—the heart and not the head."[59] In America, Clemens wrote in his *Notebook*, we have adopted the gospel of monarchial patriotism—"The King can do no wrong"—with one unimportant change in the wording—"Our country right *or* wrong!" In doing so, "We have thrown away the most valuable asset we have—the individual right to oppose both flag and country when he (just *he* by himself) believes them to be in the wrong."[60] To constrain mounting imperialist pressures, voters must use their heads as well as their hearts. Only an intelligent and involved electorate could prevent unjust wars, preserve freedom for Americans and protect and promote liberty for other nations.

In his anti-imperialism writings, Twain liked the symbolism of the theatrical soliloquy. The actor steps forward, apart from the ongoing play, and speaks directly to the audience. By adopting this device, Twain emphasizes the separateness and aloofness of an autocratic ruler from the ongoing play of life—the rules by which ordinary people act out their lives.

His first soliloquy was inspired by Czar Nicholas II on January 22, 1905. The czar ordered his troops to fire on striking workers in St. Petersburg. Twain then took aim at the czar in "On the Russian Revolution: The Czar's Soliloquy," which was published in the *North American Review*.[61] Each morning after his bath, Nicholas II meditates, reflecting on the source of his authority. As he stares at his scrawny naked body in the mirror, he realizes that without his uniform, medals, and titles, he is a rather pathetic person. Yet despite the massacres and atrocities he has ordered, his people remain loyal to him. They support his imperialist ventures into Poland and Finland. He wonders why their patriotism is directed to him and not to the nation and the

Russian people. Brushing aside such troublesome reflections, he dons his clothes and assumes his authority.*

Nicholas's authority is absolute. He does not preside over a civilized country where the laws "restrain all persons, and restrain them alike, which is fair and righteous." In a democratic society, no man is above the law, but the autocrat considers himself not simply above the law—he is the law itself. Twain believed that the more autocratic the ruler, the more invidious the oppression. He equated absolute sovereignty with unvarnished, unrestrained, and uncompromising imperialism.

Twain's second, more searing use of the soliloquy was an indictment so explosive that it was rejected by the *North American Review*. In 1876 King Leopold II of Belgium organized "the International Association for the Exploration and Civilization of Central Africa," a region then called the Belgian Congo (now The Democratic Republic of the Congo). After explorer Henry M. Stanley had failed to interest the British in developing the lower Congo, he approached Leopold who sent him to the region to stake out claims for the Association. The Congo free state was established as Leopold's suzerainty. The Belgian parliament approved his exclusive, personal ownership of over one million square miles of territory inhabited by twenty million people. At an 1884 Berlin conference, thirteen European nations endorsed the legitimacy of his private empire. Twain mistakenly suggested that the United States had supported the Berlin Resolution. It had not, but Chester Arthur's administration was the first to recognize Leopold's claim to the Congo.

The British investigative reporter E. D. Morel, whose life passion was to reveal to the world the atrocities of King Leopold's

---

* Twain liked the metaphor of clothes. As he said upon returning from the Sandwich Islands: "Clothes make the man; naked people have little or no influence in society." In *The Prince and the Pauper* and *Pudd'nhead Wilson*, he illustrates how the external trappings of class have nothing to do with the character. He once wrote in his *Notebook*: "Strip the human race, absolutely naked, and it would be a real democracy. But the introduction of even a rag of tiger skin, or a cowtail, could make a bag of distinction and be the beginning of a monarchy."

brutal regime, established the Congo Reform Association to lobby for change in the Congo's status. Morel told Clemens how Leopold expropriated native lands and used slave labor to extract rubber and ivory for export. The laborers' meager pay was recaptured by Leopold through iniquitous taxes. To maintain discipline, villages were burned, women tortured and raped, and children mutilated. Missionaries reported how conscripted Congo soldiers from unfriendly tribes cut off the hands of laborers who failed to meet their rubber quotas. An African American Presbyterian missionary, Reverend W. H. Sheppard, had discovered eighty-one severed hands being smoked over a fire. Petty theft of ivory was punished by tying the accused to a stake to die in the blazing tropical sun. At first the missionaries' accounts were met with disbelief, but they were substantiated by a courageous British consul, Roger Casement, whose collaborating reports were issued by the British Foreign Office in February 1904.[62]

In a 1904 "Thanksgiving Sentiment," Twain sardonically praised the United States government as the "official Godfather of the Congo graveyard, first of the Powers to recognize its pirate flag and become responsible through silence for the prodigious depravations and multitudinous murders committed under it upon its helpless natives by King Leopold of Belgium in these past twenty years."[63] By 1905 Leopold's rule had cost some five to eight million Congolese lives. In September 1905 an outraged Twain published a fifty-page pamphlet, "King Leopold's Soliloquy: A Defense of His Congo Rule."[64] All proceeds went to Morel's Reform Association of which Twain, Booker T. Washington and several missionaries served as vice presidents.[65]

In his soliloquy Leopold angrily rejects the mounting criticism of his "Free Congo State." After all, he is bringing the gospel to the savages. His infliction of barbarities and atrocities is merely an adaptation of native customs. His ransoming of prisoners is necessary for the repayment of debts. Leopold quotes disdainfully from his critics, who fail to appreciate how he has lifted up "twenty-five million of the gentle and harmless blacks out of darkness and into light, the light of our blessed Redeemer, the light that streams from his holy Word, the light that makes glorious our noble civilization."[66] Twain reaches the heights of hyperbole reminiscent of the early Nevada satires that caused him so much grief.[67]

With Mark Twain's name attached, the pamphlet went through several printings. A second edition was embellished with photographs of natives with severed hands provided by the "incorruptible Kodak," as Twain called it, the "only witness" Leopold could "not bribe."[68] In one picture, a grieving father sits quietly on a mat staring at the severed hand and foot of his child. That single horrifying picture spoke more poignantly than Twain's burlesque soliloquy.

Leopold launched an all-out public relations response. He produced a forty-seven-page "Answer to Mark Twain."[69] His agents also garnered the support of powerful US senators like Henry Cabot Lodge and Nelson W. Aldrich, chairman of the Senate Finance Committee and father-in law of John D. Rockefeller Jr. Having been promised substantial Congo concession rights, Aldrich blocked Secretary of State Elihu Root's appointment of a US counsel general to the Congo to report on the situation. Leopold threw a lot of money and Congo concession opportunities at wealthy supporters such as J. P. Morgan, John D. Rockefeller Jr., the Guggenheims, and Bernard Baruch. The propaganda machine generated a series of media articles praising Leopold's civilizing and development activities in the Congo.[70]

Clemens traveled to Washington three times to lobby Roosevelt, Root, and the Senate Foreign Relations Committee, urging them to speak out against the Congo atrocities. Of Clemens's passion, Booker T. Washington wrote: "I have never known him to be so stirred up on any one question as he was on that of the cruel treatment of the natives in the Congo free state...He never seemed to tire of talking on the subject."[71] Clemens believed that Leopold's "crimes are the concern of every one, of every man who feels that it is his duty as a man to prevent murder, no matter who is the murderer or how far away he seeks to commit his sordid crime." Advances in communication and transportation have made "the whole world one neighborhood."[72]

Leopold's propaganda machine made a huge mistake: his agents attempted to bribe a Senate Foreign Relations Committee staff member, Thomas G. Garrett. When the incident became public, Garrett was fired and the Reform Association was able to persuade Congress to pass a resolution (albeit watered down by Aldrich) reversing the "hands-off US policy" and calling for cooperation with the British in ending Leopold's private rule of the Congo. Roosevelt even suggested an international conference to address the issue. In a defensive maneuver, Leopold proposed establishing an investigative commission. The proposal backfired as the commission incorporated evidence of atrocities in its report.

After two years of intense negotiations, Leopold's personal rule of the Congo was formally ended in November 1908. The Congo became a Belgian colony. It was a tepid victory for the Reform Association, as the subsequent century of Congo turmoil would all too vividly demonstrate.[73]

Yet something important had happened. A grassroots organization had taken on the most powerful financial and political interests of the developed world on behalf of the rights of exploited people in an underdeveloped country.

A Tale of Today

The Anti-Imperialism League was one of the first issue-based organizations to launch a major grassroots campaign to inform the public and engage citizens in influencing national policies and election outcomes—a model replicated many times in the ensuing decades by environmental, civil rights, Tea Party, and Occupy Wall Street movements. Clemens brought to the movement a public voice who commanded press attention and a forceful writing style that conveyed a message with reason and fierce satire.

Clemens's passionate involvement in the Congo Reform Association was the beginning of human rights activism that would find legitimacy in international law, in the United

Nations Charter, and in international conventions. It was also the beginning of a parallel phenomenon: the power of a charismatic celebrity to rally support for a worthy cause—to address the exploitation of the powerless—an issue that governments and corporations had every reason to ignore, if not cover up. It is a model that subsequently has often been invoked by actors, writers, and rock stars from George Clooney to U2's Bono.

Twain's condemnation of Western imperialism in China and domestic discrimination against the Chinese provides a backdrop for assessing modern relations with China. If such relations today are subject to tension and strain over Chinese aggression in the South China Sea, the dispute over the Senkaku and Diaoyu islands, military exports to Taiwan or a congratulatory phone call from its leader, the valuation of the Renminbi, the pirating of intellectual property, cybersecurity, and the trade imbalance, it would behoove the US government to remember that culturally the Chinese take a long view of history, and the West's record of relations with China is not without blemish.

On Russia, Clemens did not live to celebrate the transient democratic Kerensky government, which was followed by the rise of Lenin and Communism, the Stalin era of gulags and genocide, and the post-World War II Soviet expansion to the Iron Curtain. In the denouement of **Connecticut Yankee***, Twain illustrates how difficult it is for a people unaccustomed to self-government to repel autocratic rule and establish a working democracy. With the collapse of the Soviet Union in 1991, the process began in Russia, even if the fulfillment of Clemens's hopeful vision is not yet in sight.*

Clemens's empathy for oppressed peoples and aversion to dictators represents a persistent but lesser strand in US foreign policy, even as billions of dollars of military aid and security support have been given to shore up autocratic rulers including the Shah of Iran, Marcos, Pinochet, Sukarno/Suharto, Musharraf, and Mubarak, to name but a few. Despite occasional imperialist tendencies, America has selflessly—if sometimes arrogantly—promoted self-government abroad through assistance programs to build democratic institutions, promote the rule of law, and assure free and fair elections. With the advent of the Arab Spring in 2011, the United States has lent support in varying degrees to freedom-seeking peoples in oppressed lands, not always with good results. If such support is cautiously rendered at times, it is well to remember another lesson from the **Connecticut Yankee**. However noble at their inception, protest movements and revolutions do not always turn out well. They may produce brutal dictatorships, from Stalin to Fidel Castro to Robert Mugabe. They may be co-opted by fanatical extremists like Al Qaeda and ISIS or unfriendly movements like Hamas or Hezbollah. As Clemens witnessed personally, the French Revolution detoured through the Second Empire under Napoleon III.

Twain's writings on unjust and preemptive wars retain a contemporary vitality. His skepticism about the unsavory mix of religion, patriotism, and militarism remain noteworthy. He wrote that "the poor have been taxed in some nations to the starvation point to support giant armaments which Christian governments have built up."[74] Foreshadowing President Eisenhower's warning of an military-industrial complex a half century later, Clemens feared that profit-hungry commercial interests with global designs would impel an ambitious and charismatic president to enlarge the military and exert its power to extend American economic influence into foreign territories, rallying a patriotic public to the cause, in the long tradition of European monarchies.

Twain condemned the advances in weaponry and the escalating arms race among the "Christian" developed nations, enhancing the brutality and destructiveness of war, but he did not live to see how prophetic his vision would become with the development of nuclear weapons and predator drones.

EPILOGUE

Halley's Comet returns

CHAPTER NINETEEN

A Man For All Seasons

"He's a walking contradiction,
partly truth and partly fiction."

— KRIS KRISTOPHERSON

Clemens grew up during a time of conflict and change. He was pulled and tugged between his empathy for the low life and his aspiration for the high life, his disdain for imperfect democracy and his contempt for despotic autocracy, and his ear for the vernacular and his yearning to be accepted by literary society. Through it all he was able to see through the rags or robes that clothed the human vessel and perceive the values, wisdom, knavery, or deceit that defined character.

His opinions evolved and changed—sometimes 180 degrees. The irony of Twain's inconsistency is not so much the contradiction between his youthful and more mature views on slavery, race, women's suffrage, tariffs and protectionism, the death penalty, and other economic and social issues as he abandoned his southern roots and became a nineteenth century liberal. Rather, the irony is in the apparent inconsistency between his public pronouncements and private practices:

The coauthor of *The Gilded Age*, who condemned the culture of greed and speculation, the robber barons, and the tyranny of the almighty dollar, built a lavish mansion monument to himself and was forced into bankruptcy because of his insatiable pursuit of wealth through speculative ventures.

The brilliant satirist of the influence of the lobby on the legislative process was a frequent visitor to Washington to lobby for legislation that served his financial self-interest.

The voice of grassroots American culture, who mocked the mimicry of English literature, was a devout Anglophile, proudly wearing his Oxford robes as authentication of his literary merit.

The religious skeptic who ultimately rejected Christianity frequently attended church, counted among his closest friends ministers of the gospel, and was a passionate moralist.

The antiwar skeptic (author of "The War Prayer") who deserted the Marion Rangers after two weeks of retreating *revered* war hero General Grant, published the memoirs of several military leaders, cherished his visits to West Point, and advocated the violent overthrow of czarist Russia.

The Mugwump who argued that character was more important than political affiliation never voted for Lincoln or Theodore Roosevelt but embraced the ineffectual President Grant and campaigned for Garfield and Hayes.

The staunch opponent of bigotry and prejudice ridiculed American Indians, Mormons, and the Irish.

The vigorous advocate of democracy argued that only the educated elite should vote, or, at a minimum, their votes should be more heavily weighted.

These inconsistencies are integral to the genius of Mark Twain. Rejecting adherence to any dogma—religious, patriotic, economic, academic, or political—he fearlessly reacted with wit and wisdom to the changing circumstances that confronted him. For Clemens consistency was a straightjacket for small minds; a seemingly precipitous shift in opinion reflected a supple intellect open to new ideas. Absorbing the wisdom of practical experience along the way, the school dropout Sam Clemens evolved into Mark Twain, the white-suited global celebrity whose sparkling insights were untethered to any conventional wisdom. In a lifetime of diverse experience—punctuated by pinnacles of public acclaim and troughs of personal tragedy—he trusted only his common sense instincts.

Amid all the conflict and contradiction, a remarkably clear and simple message comes through. The *potential* greatness of the American Republic is its unique blend of representative democracy and responsible free enterprise that—freed of oppressive autocracy, class stratification, established religion, European-style paternalistic bureaucracy, monopolistic practices, and racial and gender prejudice—rewards individual initiative, intelligence, invention, innovation, and intellect. In pursuit of this potential, however, Clemens became a vigorous advocate for the rights of minorities and women, honest and competent government, and social justice. About "our greatest social critic," Foner states, "*he speaks to us with an immediacy that surmounts the barriers of time.*"[1] Eschewing false patriotism, party platitudes, and grandiose views of American exceptionalism, he applies his homegrown sense of morality to the nation's foreign policy. He evolves, in Maxwell Geismar's words, into "*his mature role as America's conscience before the face of the world.*"[2]

In storytelling, lectures, satire, essays, correspondence, and interviews, Clemens urged his readers and listeners to think for themselves, challenging the conventional wisdom of religious, political, corporate, and academic leaders. Twain's candid commentary continues to challenge current conventions.

On Democracy

Democracy is imperfect, Clemens readily acknowledged, but superior to monarchy, aristocracy, and autocracy. The foundation of a vibrant democracy is an educated and engaged electorate who understands how a constitutional Republic is supposed to work and elects representatives of experience and integrity who will advance the "general good." Learning to be a good citizen begins on the mother's knee and in nursery school and continues in civic education throughout the school years. It requires an informed citizenry to elect representatives of character at all levels of government who put the public interest ahead of personal aggrandizement—citizens who are able to pierce through the slogans and platitudes that pass for patriotism and actively engage in the electoral process, lobby for policies that advance the community's interest, and challenge the abuse of authority in government and business.

A democracy co-opted by an ignorant or apathetic majority is undisciplined, unaccountable, and inevitably corrupt. Having observed democracy in many venues, Clemens concluded that corruption is its greatest threat. While he believed that only a small percentage of federal, state, and local officials engage in illegal conduct, he contends that they are better organized. He urged the overwhelming majority of honest politicians and the electorate to organize, fight corruption, and hold public officials accountable. As monarchy is in human nature's "blood and bones" (in today's terms their genes), Twain urged Americans to resist the accretion of presidential power, the expansion of federal bureaucracy, or the perpetuation of a political dynasty. In a democracy the people can make a difference. As he once wrote Livy, democracy works because, "When we are not satisfied, we can *change* things."[3] Or, more to the point, he said to *The New York Herald* in 1905: "*At any election the people, if they choose, may turn out the whole crowd.*"[4]

Yet today our elementary and secondary educational system is failing in its essential role of citizen education. Schools are dropping courses in civics, and surveys show that a large majority of Americans are woefully ignorant about their own history, the separation of powers among the three branches of government, and the protections of the Bill of Rights.[5] Even the world's most respected university system is in jeopardy as tuition skyrockets and state support declines. Over the last two decades, state support for Jefferson's University of Virginia has declined from 26 percent to 7 percent of the state's budget, and at the prestigious University of Michigan, state support has declined from 48 percent to 17 percent.[6] Falling SAT scores and the declining percentage of students who finish college are other indications of a deteriorating educational foundation that is critical if the electorate is to keep up with the growing complexity of government in an increasingly integrated and competitive global environment.[7]

Heeding Clemens's admonition, civics courses—teaching responsible participation in a democratic society—ought to be an essential part of the curriculum, starting as early as pre-school or Head Start. Progressive curricula should be designed for each grade that prepares the student for the responsibility of self-government that democracy demands of her or him. An informed, involved citizenry will not only improve the quality of representational government, it will reduce the need for regulatory supervision. A properly educated populace will assume greater personal responsibility for protecting the environment, ensuring the safety of the workplace, and cultivating a healthy life-style. An activist citizenry will protest unjust laws, excessive regulations and unresponsive bureaucracy in government and the private sector.

Patriotism

To the vast majority of people, "Patriotism is merely a religion—love of country, worship of country, devotion to the country's flag." In monarchies, Twain contended, patriotism is "furnished from the throne, cut and dried, to the subject," and in "America it is furnished, cut and dried, to the citizen by the politician and the newspaper." It is procured second hand. The patriot does not know or care "just how or when or where he got his opinions...so long as he was with the majority—which was the main thing, the safe thing, the comfortable thing."[8]

But not for Clemens. True patriotism is not loyalty to the nation's leaders or even to the country, right or wrong.[9] Patriotism is not to be confused with missionary zeal, jingoistic nationalism, or self-righteous proclamations of America's superiority and exceptionalism. It is not expressed in symbols and slogans. True patriotism is loyalty to country when it is right, and speaking out courageously when the country is wrong. Fundamental to Twain's conception of a working democracy is that each person *"must speak. And it is a solemn and mighty responsibility, and not lightly to be flung aside at the bullying of the pulpit, press, government, or the empty-catch phrases of politicians."*[10] True patriotism is tolerance and respect for other points of view. True patriotism is acting on one's conscience in matters of public affairs and not simply following the herd—"Patriotism reasoned out in the man's own head and fire-assayed and tested and proved in his own conscience."[11]

In today's world of pledges, platitudes, and party-distributed talking points, it would be wise to rethink the meaning of true patriotism and loyalty to country that Clemens espoused.

Church and State

As Hank Morgan says in *Connecticut Yankee*, *"an Established Church is only a political machine; it was invented for that; it is nursed, cradled, preserved for that; it is an enemy to human liberty and it does no good that it could not better do in a split-up and scattered condition."*[12] Clemens believed that the separation of the state from organized religion distinguished America from its European ancestors. Neither a government of laws nor the conscience of the people is sanctioned by any particular version of divine authority. The people are free to believe or not believe what they choose. But he worried that *"the mania for giving the Government power to meddle with the private affairs of… citizens is likely to cause endless trouble… and there is great danger that our people will lose their independence of thought and action, which is the cause of much of our greatness."*[13] He objected to the infusion of religious symbolism into secular activity, such as the inclusion of "In God We Trust" on coins, Sunday blue laws, and tax exemptions for church property. He understood that the protection of religious diversity and expression is a critical value in a free society and that religious communities can make important

412

contributions to uplifting the human condition and providing support for the less fortunate. Government policy that protects free expression, prohibits religious discrimination, and prevents state support for religion requires a citizenry that is tolerant, open-minded, and respectful of the nation's constitutional legacy.

Clemens cautioned, however, that constant vigilance is required to guard against the entanglement of church and state and the encroachment of religion into the affairs of state. Powerful lobbies today seek to incorporate theological tenets into public policy, provide backdoor funding for religious schools, mandate government intrusion into personal liberty, and constrain individual freedom, health care treatments, and lifestyles choices.

Congress

In his first visit to the Capitol in 1854, the teenage Clemens showed a sophisticated understanding of the framers' vision of the first branch of government—Congress. The founders foresaw a great deliberative body in which elite, educated, propertied men would represent sovereign states and the people in debating consequential issues facing the nation. Through their shared wisdom, Congress would take into account the varied philosophies of its members and the economic conditions of the states and steer the nation on a proper course. Senators selected by the state legislators would constrain precipitous action by the people's House, and the cumbersome system of checks and balances would ensure that progress was measured and incremental.

To be faithful to the framers' vision, Clemens thought, Congress should again become, as in the days of Clay and Webster, the great debating society on issues of national import. This vision did not anticipate partisan gamesmanship, hours of wasted time in parliamentary maneuvers, or two-minute diatribes before C-SPAN cameras. It did not envision that elected representatives would make myriad pledges to special-interest groups, thereby forfeiting their ability to think and act independently and forge compromises in the national interest. The founders did not take into account the demands of the costly perpetual election cycle that would compel career politicians to spend the majority of their time raising money for reelection, delegating to staff and lobbyists the legislative work they were hired to do. The framers did not plan for three-day legislative workweeks and thousand-page bills festooned with special-interest provisions drafted by lobbyists that senators and representatives have no time to read, much less understand. As members of Congress increasingly proclaim the importance of basing their legislative action on the Constitution, they would be wise to consider the kind of Congress the framers intended.

Party Rivalry in Congress

The Constitution is silent on the formation of political parties. It is not self-evident that the constitutional system of separation of powers (in contrast to a parliamentary system) functions efficiently when dominated by political party rivalry—at least that was the concern of George Washington and, a century later, Mark Twain. On his first visit to the nation's capital, 18-year old Sam Clemens worried that Congress failed to live up to the founders' vision of thoughtful independent representatives of diverse economic and cultural interests seeking common ground after a vigorous, healthy debate of ideas. As he observed members of Congress over the years wrangling over petty, inconsequential matters, he wrote that "such conduct is neither royal, republican, nor democratic; it is simply boy's play." Clemens concluded that the nation was not well served by elected representatives who put loyalty to political parties and platforms ahead of the public interest. "In the interest of party expediency, they give solemn pledges; they make solemn compacts," he wrote, delivering "political conscience into someone else's keeping."[14] Political parties tend to polarize the country, promote partisan competition instead of cooperative action in the public interest, and discourage compromise in developing sound public policy. Twain said it less tactfully: "Look at the tyranny of party—at what is called party allegiance, party loyalty—a snare invented by designing men for selfish purposes—and which turns voters into chattels, slaves, rabbits, and all the while their masters, and they themselves are shouting rubbish about liberty, independence, freedom of opinion, freedom of speech, honestly unconscious of the fantastic contradiction."[15] Defenders of partisanship argue that party divisions in Congress simply reflect the nation's wider cultural divide. A June 2012 Pew Research Center survey of American values found a sharp division along political lines with an increasing gap between Republicans and Democrats on the role of government and the importance of a safety-net.[16] The new media– cable TV and the internet– reflect and reinforce these differences. As politicians, voters and the media intensify the partisan divide, the unanswered question is whether the US non-parliamentary constitutional system can accommodate the increasing intolerance, lack of civility, and stalemate. Has government become dysfunctional? Echoes of Clemens's statement that "there isn't any wisdom in this kind of warfare"[17] can be heard today in the growing number of independents, voter dissatisfaction with politicians and the status quo, and the declining approval ratings of a Congress stalemated by partisan gridlock.

The Lobby

Clemens understood that the right to petition the government, embraced by the First Amendment, is essential to a workable democracy. In lobbying for copyright protection, Clemens shared his experience and expertise with legislators bereft of knowledge in this field. There were no writers or artists in Congress, Clemens complained.

The problem, skillfully identified by Twain in *The Gilded Age*, is that the Washington lobby's greatest expertise is too often in raising money to buy access and influence. If lobbying were divorced from fund-raising and campaign contributions, then the public might appreciate the constructive, essential expertise lobbyists bring to fashioning good legislation, as Clemens demonstrated in his work for copyright reform.

In today's complex universe of federal statutes, regulations, and programs—where the federal government has penetrated every corner of the US economy—people with experience in finance, health care, the environment, energy, consumer protection, and other sectors provide indispensable expertise in the legislative process. They help lawmakers understand the consequences—intended and unintended—of federal initiatives and help them analyze alternatives; balance competing interests; minimize market distortions; prepare, modify, amend, or repeal legislation; and evaluate, recalibrate, or terminate federal programs. If congressional hearings were again to become open-minded fact-finding inquiries instead of vehicles to advance a partisan agenda and capture precious camera time, then experts could provide invaluable information on the public record that would enlighten the debate and improve the legislative product.

In the aftermath of the Abramoff scandals, Congress has taken modest steps to curtail lobbying abuses. Reflecting a political calculus that demonizing Washington lobbyists is good campaign strategy, some proposals overreach and intrude upon First Amendment-protected values of citizen participation in the legislative process, discouraging, for example, forums in which public officials and experts can share information. The real problem, identified by Twain, is the use of money to obtain access and influence. A temporary moratorium on earmarks limited the members' ability to reward lobbyists for their fund-raising, but much more can be done. Lobbyists could be barred from contributing to campaigns or fund-raising for members and committees they lobby. There could be a system of credentialing lobbyists that would require adherence to a code of ethics and an enforcement mechanism for those who violate it. In addition, Congress could pass shorter, simpler laws that are not Christmas tree targets for lobbyists' ornamentation, beginning by simplifying the Internal Revenue Code, closing loopholes and abolishing two-year tax extenders.

The Perpetual Election Cycle

Clemens found little value in political campaigns. They generated sham issues to wrap the party's candidate in the flag and fatally damage the opposition with slurs and unsubstantiated allegations. Campaign promises have little relevance to governing and tend to be forgotten after Election Day. In 1906 he wrote: *"If we would learn what the human race really is at bottom, we need only observe it at election times."*[18]

In 1876 Clemens campaigned for Republican Rutherford B. Hayes who advocated civil service reform, a one-term presidency, and fiscally responsible government. Hayes, as was the custom of the day, let his surrogates campaign for him. Engaging in the political fray was beneath the dignity of a prospective president. Hayes kept on officeholders where they were performing well and shunned nepotism and the appointment of inexperienced political loyalists. Resisting efforts to draft him for a second term, he stood by his promise and returned to Ohio. He advocated a single nonrenewable six-year term for the presidency. He believed that a president cannot govern responsibly when he or she is in the midst of campaigning for reelection. How would the people know whether his or her proposals were those of a partisan seeking reelection or a statesman setting forth policies in the best interest of the entire nation? Today the need to raise huge amounts of money and campaign for reelection over many months inevitably diverts the incumbent president from the extraordinary challenges of governing in today's dangerous and complex global environment.

By 1884, disillusioned with political parties, Clemens decided that a candidate's character should be the overriding consideration. Joining the Mugwumps, Twain wrote in his *Autobiography*, "When voting, it was our duty to vote for the best man, regardless of party name. We had no other creed. Vote for the best man—that was creed enough."[19] The Democratic candidate Cleveland had a record of fighting corrupt political machines, vetoing special-interest legislation, and appointing competent officials from both political parties. In his first term, he bucked the headwinds of public opinion and the political and business establishments—fighting protectionism, inflation, and wasteful government spending.

In today's continuous campaign cycle, there is much to be said for Cleveland's dignified approach to elections. Americans might ask whether, in Twain's words, "the empty catch phrases of politicians" during election campaigns shield the voters from the real issues that need to be confronted by an accountable government. Does the perpetual campaign—reinforced by a media hungry for the advertising revenues that controversy generates—polarize the nation and obstruct the cooperation and compromise that are the lubricant of a workable democracy? Does the deluge of money into campaigns—the emergence of the super PAC and 501(c)4s—dilute the efficacy of the one-person-one-vote premise of democracy and promote growing income inequality in America by buying access for the wealthy few? Does the ability of a handful of billionaires to expend unlimited funds in support of a presidential candidate enlarge the field of potential nominees or distort the election process by flooding the airways with negative advertising, generating voter cynicism and mistrust of politicians generally? If an airline were to air a graphic commercial depicting how a flyer on one of its competitors would die in a fiery crash, would anyone choose to fly—on any airline? Yet this is essentially the nature of political advertising—demonizing the competitors, mischaracterizing their positions, and spreading half-truths or lies about their record. Given the proliferation of fake news on the internet, Twain's satires "Running for Governor" and "Mark Twain, Presidential Candidate," illustrating how false news can destroy a candidate, are remarkably prophetic and relevant.

If the yet-unknown effect of opening the sluices of unlimited campaign funding actually destroys candidates, fosters voter cynicism, and buys access and influence for the wealthy few, the public may rise up and demand a more sensible alternative. With so much money flowing into campaigns and so many cottage industries with vested interests, campaigning becomes all-consuming, and politics overwhelms the less theatrical and more subtle task of actually governing. It seems that with each election cycle the discourse becomes cruder, the facts less truthful, and the promises more surreal. Contrary to searching for common ground– the premise of workable democratic self-government– candidates thrive on setting up straw men that they can vehemently oppose. Mark Twain once wrote: *"if you would work the multiplication table into the Democratic platform, the Republicans will vote it down at the election."*[20]

The continuous campaign adversely affects the allocation of the incumbents' time and distorts her or his view of the issues. In most other civilized nations, elections are limited to a reasonably short period of time, but in the United States election madness is perpetual. Does the constant assault of well-financed campaigns inhibit office-holders from taking courageous but unpopular action in the national interest? For example, Republican presidents Eisenhower, Reagan, and George H. W. Bush raised the tax on gasoline to fund transportation improvements; many economists agree that increasing the gas tax, instituting a carbon tax, or changing the way travel is taxed would decrease demand for imported petroleum, create market incentives to develop more environmentally beneficial fuel sources, provide critical funding for the nation's deteriorating infrastructure, and reduce the pressure on the federal debt. But can politicians today take such a stance amid the perpetual campaign? More troubling is the tendency to display a belligerent, blustering toughness against perceived threats to the national interest, undercutting efforts at quiet diplomacy. How can incumbents campaigning for reelection demonize the opposition on Monday and seek common ground on Tuesday to address compelling national needs?

Selection of Candidates—Primaries

Clemens repeatedly complained that Americans sit at home while the ward heelers and corrupt political machines select candidates for political office behind closed doors in smoke-filled rooms. Why then, he asked, should voters be surprised on Election Day when they are offered a choice of two unsatisfactory candidates?

The modern primary system was an attempt at reform. It hasn't worked. Why? Most state legislatures gerrymander (reshape, sometimes in contorted fashion) congressional districts after each census to ensure safe districts for the majority party's incumbents. This has minimized competition for congressional seats, created enclaves for ideological purists, and punished open-minded legislators who vote their conscience instead of adhering to the party line. Party heretics face a primary challenge. Further, only a small percentage of citizens vote in primaries, and they tend to be the most ideologically motivated. Closed primaries in which only registered party members may vote offer no incentive for candidates to reach out to independents (now the largest voting bloc) or a broader spectrum

419

of constituents. Presidential primaries in thirty-one states are closed, in most cases for both parties. The long-term effect of gerrymandering and closed primaries has been to reduce the number of centrists or moderates in Congress who are the linchpins of compromise and bipartisan cooperation.

These deficiencies can be remedied if there is the political will. Legislative reapportionment can be based on nonpartisan or bipartisan commissions as several states are now doing. When California turned to a Citizen Redistricting Commission after the 2010 census, a number of competitive races resulted, causing some veterans in previously uncontested seats to grumble that the loss of congressional seniority could cost the state federal dollars.

Some states are experimenting with alternatives to the party primary. California, Washington, Alaska, and Louisiana are experimenting with a general open primary for nonpresidential elections in which the top two candidates, regardless of political affiliation, face each other in a general election runoff. At a minimum, party primaries could be open to independent voters, encouraging candidates to broaden their appeal to a larger cross-section of voters in their districts. And there is always the option of bringing back the Mugwumps—or some alternative third party of organized independents, such as Americans Elect or No Labels.

Thoughtful observers like Mann, Ornstein, Kaiser, Krugman, Lessig, Hacker and Pierson, among many others cited in this tale of today, have diagnosed the cancer in the nation's politics, analyzed alternative treatments and proposed an array of possible fixes that deserve the serious attention of the engaged citizen-voter.

The Executive Branch

From Clemens's perspective the post-Civil War federal bureaucracy had mushroomed to preposterous proportions. Clemens worried that the federal accretion of power increased the opportunity for abuse. As Congress raised revenues, its members allocated funds to programs and projects that advanced their personal financial interests and reelection prospects. Well-intended programs were transformed into vote-buying entitlements as legislators abandoned discipline and curried favor with their supporters.[21]

Clemens complained that federal bureaucrats, then appointed mostly by patronage, will "take any reasonably good law and interpret the common sense out of it."[22] He argued that there are no measures of success and accountability—like profits or bankruptcy in the private sector—that constrain bureaucratic expansion and reward efficiency. Clemens worried that "circumstances will gradually take away the powers of the States and concentrate them in the central government," advocating that citizens "obstruct these encroachments and steadily resist them."[23]

Over the past century, Congress has created a plethora of programs, usually requiring new bureaucracies to implement at both the federal and state levels. Programs are created to serve specific needs of older Americans; provide job training and employment opportunities; promote economic development; ensure food safety; combat drug abuse and addiction; fund roads, airports, busses, and bike paths; and enhance all kinds of educational opportunities, to cite but a few examples. Such well-intended initiatives have created a sprawling, compartmentalized, and fragmented federal bureaucracy that addresses important issues on a piecemeal basis rather than serving the needs of families and communities in an integrated fashion.[24] Today there are fifteen federal programs involved in food safety, twenty programs dealing with the homeless, and eighty programs addressing economic development. As these categorical, single-purpose programs proliferate, so do conflict, overlap, inconsistency, and the need for coordination among bureaucratic offices and levels of government.[25]

As federal programs proliferate like a kudzu invasion, objective observers have recommended ways to streamline the bureaucracy along functional lines. Notable examples include the Ash Commission, appointed by President Nixon in 1969, and most recently President Obama's proposal in his 2012 State of the Union address for authority to consolidate and reorganize the federal bureaucracy to eliminate redundancy. The president cited the twelve agencies that deal with exports and the five that deal with housing policy. He claimed that over the past two years he had requested to no avail the elimination of two hundred nonperforming federal programs. Obama offered his "favorite example: the Interior Department is in charge of salmon, while they are in fresh water, but the Commerce Department handles them when they are in salt water. And I hear that it gets even more complicated when they are smoked."[26] With widespread recognition of the problem, why has so little been done? Are members of Congress reluctant to lose funding and oversight control of programs within their purview? Are they too busy campaigning and engaging in partisan maneuvering to take the time to dig into the kudzu weeds? Probably all of the above. Party politics appears to impede rather than achieve common-sense solutions. Twain's wandering through the federal bureaucratic maze in the "Great Beef Contract" was way ahead of its time.

Although the size of today's federal bureaucracy is beyond the imagination of America's most imaginative author, Clemens's common-sense views are worthy of consideration as the nation's leaders and would-be leaders struggle with decades of rising citizen contempt for the federal government, flamed by candidates for public office who like to run against Washington bureaucrats. What might Americans today take from this Gilded Age observer?

At a time when federal deficit spending is under attack, substantial savings and improved effectiveness could be achieved if similar programs are consolidated, levels of hierarchy reduced, lines of authority simplified, and ineffective programs terminated. The federal government should not undertake responsibilities that can be more efficiently managed by the states or in the private sector. Like successful companies, the federal bureaucracy needs continually to reinvent itself, constantly evaluating programs, terminating regulations that either have served their purpose or failed to do so, and subjecting new regulations to a rigorous test of cost-effectiveness and an analysis of unintended consequences beyond the purview of a specific agency's statutory mandate, such as such as the effect of an environmental regulation or licensing requirement on jobs and competition. Private-sector efficiencies and incentives should be applied to government where feasible, including compensation and pro-motion based on successful results. Senior government positions should be filled by expert, experienced personnel regardless of political party. Civil servants should have the opportunity and incentive to rise to top-tier positions provided they have dem-onstrated efficient management skills. The number of political appointees should be limited to avoid padding the bureaucracy with extra layers of government and insulating policy makers from institutional expertise. Too many senior management posi-tions are filled by inexperienced political appointees who stay only long enough to develop contacts that can be exploited in higher paying private sector jobs. Political operatives should not be on the federal payroll.

Fiscal Responsibility

Clemens was a consistent advocate for fiscally responsible government. In describing how the well-intentioned Civil War pension system "degenerated into a wider and more offensive system of vote-purchasing," Twain astutely captured a funda-mental weakness of the legislative process, the tendency to cre-ate open-ended entitlements that curry favor with an important voting bloc, like veterans or seniors, deferring the mushrooming costs to future generations– "robbing a younger son to fatten an elder," as Twain put it.[27] He identified the phenomenon, but he could not have predicted its consequences a century after his death.

At the end of 2011, the Government Accountability Office [GAO] calculated the net present value of future promises to Social Security and Medicare recipients as $33.8 trillion. This is more than twice the $13.1 trillion value of all compa-nies traded on the New York Stock Exchange and more than five times the $6.2 trillion equity value of US taxpayer homes. According to GAO "there is not enough wealth in America to meet these promises."[28] In this century entitlement programs (*e.g.*, Social Security, Medicare, and Medicaid) and the inter-est on the federal debt are projected to consume more than

90 percent of the federal budget, leaving less than 10 percent to fund national defense; homeland security; education; infrastructure; environmental protection; food, drug, occupational, transportation, and product safety; and all other discretionary programs. The longer Congress defers correcting the problem it has created, the more painful the solution will be.[29] Recent political campaigns have avoided a thoughtful discussion of these issues, preferring instead to invoke them as weapons against the opposition. Sadly, political institutions have mostly frustrated—rather than facilitated—the resolution of fiscal challenges that are solvable.

Government and the Private Sector

The source of America's greatness—the free-enterprise system—encourages and rewards innovation and productivity. Clemens warned that too much government may cause the people to "sink into the helplessness of the Frenchman and German who expects his government" to meet his every need.[30]

Clemens survived boom and bust cycles (1837, 1857, 1973, 1893, and 1907), and experienced financial success and failure. He knew that risky speculation often caused economic and personal depression. He believed that speculation is good where it serves the purposes of innovation, invention, and increased productivity, and that risk-taking should be amply rewarded where it adds value to the economy. He recognized that reckless financial speculation and unconstrained greed have a corrosive effect on a free economy, widening the gap between the rich and poor, oppressing the working class, defiling the environment, and creating cycles of economic panic.

In performing its limited role in regulating the economy, Clemens believed that government should foster fair competition, avoid distortions and unnecessary burdens on the private sector, empower the working class and consumers to protect themselves from unscrupulous practices, and undertake only those functions that cannot be performed efficiently by private enterprise. He warned that constantly changing government policies create uncertainty and inhibit investment and economic growth—a theme repeatedly echoed by the US Chamber of

Commerce. Twain complained that "*a man invests years of work and a vast sum of money in a worthy enterprise, upon the faith of existing laws; then the law is changed, and the man is robbed by his own government.*"[31]

Civil Rights

Clemens believed that every American is entitled to equal treatment under the law and an equal opportunity to succeed based on his or her intelligence, drive, and talent. Unlike the royal grants to King Arthur's nobles, who were sustained by a "gigantic system of out-door relief," government should not bestow favors based on class or wealth. Irrelevant characteristics such as race, gender, ethnicity, or religion should not be barriers to opportunity—nor should they be an entitlement. Government should enforce laws against discrimination, but government cannot create equality in an economic or social sense. Americans are not equal—some are smarter, more diligent, and more charming. People have different skills and aptitudes, and they should be rewarded in accordance with the value the economy places on their contributions. Twain wrote that the phrase "free and equal" was not intended to "set aside the law of Nature." The Constitution only guarantees to "*each an equal right with his neighbor to exercise his talent.*"[32] Freed of European class stratification, Americans should be able to move up the economic ladder as fast as skill and hard work propel them.

The story of the 2010 census presents a very different picture: a declining middle class, growing numbers in poverty (especially among minority populations and children), and the amassing of great wealth by the top 1 percent—reminiscent of the Gilded Age. Income disparity today exceeds that in Europe (where it is also growing), and there is less upward mobility in America's purportedly classless society. In funding over a trillion dollars in annual "tax expenditures," Congress—fueled by fund-raising lobbyists—not only adds to the federal debt but distorts the free market, picks winners and losers, and benefits the wealthy few with premium health insurance, golden retirement plans, fancy vacation homes, and private aircraft.

The Criminal Justice System

Twain believed that capital punishment is unjust. While the poor go to the gallows, the wealthy hire silver-tongued lawyers to persuade vulnerable juries that they are temporarily insane or otherwise not guilty. In practice the death penalty is administered unequally and unjustly. He also believed that incarceration, especially of juveniles, is often counterproductive, and that the jury system is a sham.

Many thoughtful Americans today question the fairness of capital punishment and worry about the overcrowded prison population. Nineteen states have abolished the death penalty. With 5 percent of the world's population, the United States has 25 percent of the world's prisoners—2.3 million—more than any other country. The jury system debate continues as prosecutors plea bargain to avoid trials and litigants explore alternative methods of dispute resolution such as mediated settlements, arbitration, bench trials (before a judge only), or mini-trials.

Foreign Policy

Clemens believed that American democracy cannot be imposed by force on other nations. Each nation has to embrace democracy in the context of its own culture. The United States should not initiate wars, and responsible citizens should oppose "unjust wars" even if in so doing they are labeled unpatriotic or traitorous.

Clemens also advocated increasing the responsibilities and pay of the diplomatic corps. He argued that through diplomacy America should be willing to give ground on lesser priorities and compromise with other states to foster international cooperation and peace. Nations must agree to reduce arms and armed forces and seek arbitration to resolve international conflicts. Free trade and the elimination of tariffs promote economic growth and global interdependence. International cooperation is essential to secure protections for copyrights and patents. Ahead of his time, America's most peripatetic writer urged respect for different cultures, traditions, and religions. He understood that ultimately we are all global citizens.

"I came in with Halley's Comet in 1835, and I expect to go out with it."
Courtesy; The Mark Twain House & Museum, Hartford CT

The Return of Halley's Comet

If a white-suited celebrity commentator were to descend on the American political scene today, untethered to any political party, religion, corporate entity, or economic ideology, but applying the same sort of bold, practical, empirical common-sense approach that characterized Clemens's outlook, what might she or he advise? Perhaps the following:

- *Effective representative democracy depends upon educated, informed, and engaged voters demanding accountability from their elected leaders, and to achieve this result over the long term, civic education—imparting the knowledge and sense of personal responsibility and participation required for*

427

democratic self-government—should be emphasized through-
out the educational spectrum.

- *Congress should amend its procedures and ways of doing business to reflect the framers' constitutional vision of accomplished senators and representatives debating the great issues of the day as they seek to advance the common good after taking into account the different perspectives and interests of their constituents.*
- *In the election of candidates for public office, Americans need to place greater emphasis on character, relevant experience, the courage of one's convictions, and the capacity to govern effectively, and less emphasis on party politics and winning at all costs.*
- *Instead of endless campaigning, Americans should insist on short campaigns, insisting that candidates address the critical issues facing the nation's future.* *
- *Americans and their elected representatives should reject the partisan politics that floods the airways with negative ads, abuses the legislative process, and forces lawmakers into uncompromising corners.*
- *Campaign contributors and fundraisers should not be rewarded with targeted appropriations, legislative amendments, tax loopholes, tariff reductions, or patronage.*
- *Elections should be decided by informed voters, not by the amount of campaign contributions.*

---

* For example, candidates' debates could be scheduled to address specific sujects in depth, such as tax reform, a secure retirement (addressing Social Securty, Medicare, and pension reform), church and state, infrastructure, fighting terorism, etc. Finding media outlets for such debates would not be as difficult as getting the candidates to agree.

These changes would require a monumental cultural shift. As Twain wrote, voters "think they think upon the great political questions, and they do, but they think with their party, not independently; they read its literature, but not that of the other side."³³

Instead of viewing issues through a partisan political prism, voters would demand common-sense solutions to practical problems. Instead of seeking rhetorical reinforcement of preexisting biases, voters would listen with open minds to new ideas. Instead of cheering on combative candidates who demonize their opponents with negative advertising, voters would save their cheerleading for sports teams and demand that candidates address the issues in a tolerant, civil, and rational way. Instead of being obsessed with winning political contests, voters would elect experienced representatives who are able to think and act independently and courageously in the overall public interest. Instead of expecting instant grandiose solutions, voters would encourage steady, incremental consensus-based progress. In lieu of gridlock and stalemate, voters would demand bipartisan cooperation and compromise in forging responsible public policy. Creating a culture of responsible voter participation begins with training the next generation of voters. There are numerous organizations dedicated to this purpose, and, judging by opinion polls, the voters are ahead of the politicians. Americans can also look to periods of their own history for guidance.

With such a cultural change, voters might find that there is far more common ground than difference. Wall Street occupiers and Tea Party activists, along with Wall Street CEOs and the main-street middle class, might find more areas of agreement than difference. Who can argue with a lean and efficient federal government that manages its budget responsibly and generates the revenues necessary to pay for essential services? Who can argue with the urgent need to reform entitlements, the tax code, and state mandates? Who can argue with cost-effective federal regulation that provides a consistent framework for a just, fair, safe, environmentally sensitive, dynamic, growing, and job-creating private sector? Who can argue that the sprawling bureaucracy needs to be streamlined, redundant programs consolidated, ineffective programs terminated, and essential programs adequately and timely funded? Who can argue that the vitality of America's innovative free-market economy requires substantial improvements in education and infrastructure, along with a skilled workforce and manufacturing base? Who can argue that sustained economic growth requires a vibrant middle class that is productively employed and unburdened by excessive debt? Who can argue that international trade agreements must be balanced, just and fair to American workers? Who can argue that America's foreign policy in the post-Cold War era must be flexible, engaged, and cooperative? Meeting these challenges requires leaders who will discard polarizing platitudes and listen to each other and expert advice, who will analyze specific policies and programs with open minds, and who have the courage to act in the public interest, even against the prevailing puffs of public opinion.

Ideological differences are important in a vibrant democracy, but ceaseless partisanship and nonstop electioneering leaves no time for civil discourse and consensus problem-solving, which is what governing in a democracy is all about. In an election campaign, a challenger attacks the incumbent on many fronts, but if elected, the challenger may find that his or her policies do not differ that much in practice. That is because there is little similarity between a polarizing campaign and consensus-building governing. Today, American politics seems way out of balance. Far too much weight is placed on campaigning and not enough on responsible governing. It behooves Americans to remember the advice of Hank Morgan to feudal England: democracy's ultimate safeguard is that "all political power is inherent in the people [who] have at all times an undeniable and indefeasible right to alter their form of government in such a manner as they think expedient."[34]

A politically savvy but disillusioned Mark Twain warned that **"it cannot be well or safe to let the present political conditions continue indefinitely."** He urged American citizenship to **"rise up from its disheartenment and see that it is done."**[35]

After the most unconventional election in recent decades, when many voters expressed their discontent with the responsiveness of government to their needs and aspirations, Mark Twain's conviction that American democracy only works when informed and engaged citizens hold their elected representatives accountable has never been more relevant. Citizens of all persuasions must rise up from their "disheartenment" and insist that our leaders and political institutions work for the benefit of all Americans.

Acknowledgments

The story of Samuel Langhorne Clemens, who became Mark Twain, has been told often and well. Extraordinary scholars have detailed and dissected his remarkable life.[1] They have described the career of the first truly American author,[2] the rise of America's first global celebrity,[3] a fearless commentator on American culture,[4] the anguished conscience of a nation torn by racial divide,[5] or the world's most famous schizophrene.[6] There are many interpretations and many spins on this truly American phenomenon. There is the loving, loyal firsthand account of Albert Bigelow Paine[7]and the comprehensive account—perhaps one of the least reliable—by Twain himself, the full text of which he prohibited from publication until a hundred years after his death. Often lying in bed clad in a Persian silk dressing gown, propped up against snowy white pillows, the aging Twain furiously dictated five thousand pages of rambling thoughts, jumping around spontaneously in time and place, quipping that "when I was young, I could remember anything whether it happened or not, but I am getting old and soon will remember only the latter."[8] In October 2010 the Mark Twain Papers & Project in Berkeley published the first of three volumes of unexpurgated autobiography as Twain planned it.[9] The third and final volume was published in 2015. In 1924 Paine published a heavily edited two-volume autobiography,[10] and in 1959 a readable, single-volume chronological abridgement by Charles Neider became available.[11]

In addition to Clemens's many letters, speeches, essays, books, and unpublished dictations, the writings of Budd, Camfield, Carter, Fears, Foner, French, Fulton, Geismar, Peterson, Rasmussen, and Zwick—as evidenced by numerous endnote references—have been especially helpful in understanding Clemens's views. An important inspiration was a *Mark*

Twain Tonight! performance by Hal Holbrook in Washington, DC, at the beginning of this century. Using Twain's own words, Holbrook moved the audience from raucous laughter to stunned silence with commentary that was topical and relevant for an audience enmeshed in legislative politics and two foreign wars. I have been privileged to hear Holbrook perform at least once a decade since 1959. He has brought to modern audiences what crowds all over the world experienced in nineteenth-century lecture halls from America's first global celebrity.

I am indebted to Steve Courtney, whose Mark Twain scholarship, wise counsel, and editorial improvements have contributed greatly to this book. The faults, flaws, and factual errors are my responsibility alone. My sister, Dr. Marinka Bliss, was the first to read the manuscript and has provided corrections and an index for this edition. My assistant, Doris Beckett, was a patient and cheerful advisor to this technology-challenged two-finger typist. Robert Hirst, Neda Salem, and the staff of the Mark Twain Papers & Project in Berkeley, California, have opened up their files and provided helpful assistance. Jeffrey Nichols, Beth Miller, and Patti Philippon of the staff of The Mark Twain House & Museum in Hartford, Connecticut; Henry Sweets and the staff of the Mark Twain Boyhood Home & Museum in Hannibal, Missouri; and Barbara Snedecor and Mark Woodhouse of the Center for Mark Twain Studies in Elmira, New York, have all expanded my knowledge and fanned my enthusiasm for this project. I am also grateful for the assistance of Tom Culbertson of the Rutherford B. Hayes Presidential House and Library and Leaky Mathews for their assistance and advice. My thanks also to Bill Coleman, Pat Hass, Ed Harper, Leonard Wainstein, Sandy Shaw, Carl Schenker, Ellen Sandel, Debbie Fisher, Clark Beim-Esche, and Josh of Create-Space for their suggestions and support. My lifelong partner, Nancy, and my sons, Evan and Bion, have offered much valuable advice and, most importantly, tolerated my endless quotations of Mark Twain at the dinner table. I also am grateful to my two wonderful daughters-in-law, Mary and Caitlin, and our grandchildren, Calliope June, Nolan Thomas and Wyatt Emerson, who have helped sustain me during this project.

Chronology

1835	Samuel Langhorne Clemens born in Florida, MO on November 30.
1839	Clemens family moves to Hannibal.
1847	John Marshall Clemens dies; Sam quits school.
1849-52	Printer's Devil. Writes political satires for the Hannibal newspapers.
1853-54	Leaves home for St. Louis, New York and Philadelphia.
2/1854	Sam Clemens visits Washington, DC.
1855-57	Works in Keokuk, IA, St. Louis and Cincinnati.
1858-61	At various times, supports the Whig, Know Nothing, and Constitutional Union parties. Does not vote for Abraham Lincoln. Mississippi River Pilot. At outset of the Civil War joins the Marion Rangers and deserts after two weeks. On July 18, 1861, heads for Nevada Territories with older brother Orion, who is appointed Secretary of the Nevada Territories by President Lincoln. Arrives in Carson on August 14, 1861.
1862	Joins the Virginia City *Territorial Enterprise* staff; covers the Territorial Legislature.
1863	Adopts the pen name "Mark Twain." Covers the first Nevada State constitutional convention.

1864   Lives in San Francisco, with side-trips to Jackass Hill and the Sandwich Islands (Hawaii) as reporter for the *Morning Call, The Californian, Golden Era, Sacramento Union* and *Alta California.* Starts lecturing. Leaves San Francisco for the East Coast.

1867   Arrives in New York City to lecture, publish a book of short stories, and sail on the Quaker City for Europe and the Holy Land.

11/1867   Takes job as a legislative clerk to Republican Senator William Stewart of Nevada and rooms with him a block north of the Willard Hotel in Washington, D.C. Receives a letter from Elisha Bliss, Jr. of the American Publishing Company in Hartford inquiring whether he would like to write a book about the Quaker City tour.

12/1867   Sam Clemens resigns his Senate clerkship and continues as a reporter in the capital while he negotiates a book contract for *Innocents Abroad,* and travels to New York to meet his future wife, Olivia "Livy" Langdon. Writes a series of satires on government and reports on post-Civil War Reconstruction legislation and Andrew Johnson's impeachment.

1868   Travels to San Francisco, New York City, Hartford and Elmira, New York working on *Innocents Abroad* and courting Livy.

1869-70   Becomes engaged to Livy and a part owner and editor of the Republican-oriented *Buffalo Express.* Condemns corruption in New York State and local politics. Starts a lecture tour and marries Livy on February 2, 1870. Livy's father Jervis Langdon dies, and Sam's first child, a son Langdon, is born prematurely in November.

1871   Moves to Nook Farm in Hartford, a staunchly progressive Republican community. Supports mostly Republican candidates over the next decade.

1872   Publishes *Roughing It* and *Sketches*. Daughter Susy is born on March 19 and son, Langdon dies on June 2.

1873   Publishes *The Gilded Age* with co-author, Charles Dudley Warner, which becomes the generic name for the epoch of corruption in politics and the private sector.

1874   His play, *Colonel Sellers*, based on *The Gilded Age*, is a success. Second daughter, Clara, is born on June 8. The Clemens move into their newly constructed home in Hartford.

1875-81   Campaigns for Rutherford B. Hayes in 1876. Continues to publish subscription books with the American Publishing Company, including *Tom Sawyer*, and *Tramp Abroad*. Daughter Jean is born on July 26, 1880. Elisha Bliss dies in 1880 and Twain publishes his next book, *The Prince and the Pauper* with James Osborne, Inc. in 1881. Campaigns for James Garfield in 1880.

1882-91   Frustrated with corruption in politics, Twain becomes a MUGWUMP, voting for character over political party. To the dismay of his Nook Farm neighbors, he supports Democrat Grover Cleveland for President over Republican James Blaine. Founds Charles L. Webster Publishing Company, lectures, publishes *Life on the Mississippi* (1883); *Huckleberry Finn* (1885); General Grant's *Personal Memoirs* (1885) and *A Connecticut Yankee in King Arthur's Court* (1889). His mother dies on October 27, 1890. Clemens makes a series of unwise investments, including the Paige Compositor.

1892-95   Lives mostly in Europe, writing and struggling with bad investments. Webster Company declares bankruptcy. Henry Huttleston Rogers offers financial advice. Publishes *Pudd'nhead Wilson* (1894).

1895-96   To pay off debts, he does a world lecture tour to Australia, New Zealand, India and South Africa.

1896   Daughter Susy dies of meningitis on August 18. Publishes *Joan of Arc*.

1897   Brother Orion dies. Publishes *Following the Equator*.

1898-1907   Pays off all his debts. Lives mostly in New York; works on darker stories, many of which are not published until after his death; becomes active in the Anti-Imperialism movement. Campaigns for a reform candidate for Mayor of New York in 1901, Seth Low, and is credited with throwing Tammy Hall out of office. Livy dies in Florence on June 5, 1904. Becomes increasingly disillusioned with presidential candidates of both political parties, McKinley and Roosevelt for the Republicans and William Jennings Bryan for the Democrats. Receives honorary degree from Oxford in 1907.

1908-1910   Moves to "Stormfield" home in Redding, Connecticut. Jean drowns in the bathtub after an epileptic seizure on Christmas Eve, 1909. Clemens dies on April 21, 1910 as Halley's Comet returns 75 years after his birth, as he predicted he would.

BIBLIOGRAPHY

Writings By Mark Twain

(Unless otherwise specified, references to Mark Twain's books are to The Oxford Mark Twain; Edited by Shelly Fisher Fishkin, 29 Volumes. New York: Oxford University Press, 1996; consisting of facsimiles of first editions.)

Adventures of Huckleberry Finn.

The Adventures of Tom Sawyer.

The American Claimant.

The Autobiography of Mark Twain. ed. Charles Neider, New York: Harper & Row, 1959.

Autobiography of Mark Twain, Volume I, ed. Harriet Elinor Smith, Berkeley: University of California Press, 2010.

Autobiography of Mark Twain, Volume II, ed. Benjamin Griffin and Harriet Elinor Smith, Berkeley: University of California Press, 2013.

Autobiography of Mark Twain, Volume III, ed. Benjamin Griffin and Harriet Elinor Smith, Berkeley: University of California Press, 2015.

Mark Twain's Autobiography, ed. Albert Bigalow Paine, 2 Vols. New York: Harper & Bros., 1924.

Autobiographical Dictations, Mark Twain Project, Bancroft Library, Berkeley.

The Bible According to Mark Twain: Irreverent Writings on Eden, Heaven, and the Flood by America's Master Satirist, ed. Howard G. Baetzhold and Joseph B. McCullough, New York: Simon & Schuster, 1995.

The Celebrated Frog of Calaveras County, and Other Sketches,

Chapters from My Autobiography.

Christian Science.

Clemens of the "Call": Mark Twain in San Francisco, ed. Edgar Marquess Branch, Berkeley: University of California Press, 1969.

The Complete Essays of Mark Twain, ed. Charles Neider, New York: De Capo Press, Perseus Book Group, 1963.

Collected Tales, Sketches, Speeches, & Essays, 1891-1910. ed. Louis J. Budd, New York: Library of America, 1992.

A Connecticut Yankee in King Arthur's Court.

The Curious Republic of Gondour and Other Whimsical Sketches, New York: Boni & Liveright, 1919.

The Diaries of Adam and Eve.

Early Tales & Sketches. Vol. 1, 1851-1864. Vol. 2, 1864-1865, ed. Edgar Marquess Branch and Robert H. Hirst, Berkeley: University of California Press, 1979-81.

Europe and Elsewhere, New York: Harper & Brothers, 1923.

Extract from Captain Stormfield's Visit to Heaven.

Following the Equator and Anti-Imperialist Essays.

The Gilded Age, A Tale of Today.

Heretical Fictions, ed. L. Berklove and J. Csicsila, Iowa City: University of Iowa Press, 2010.

How to Tell a Story and Other Essays.

Huck Finn and Tom Sawyer Among the Indians: And Other Unfinished Stories, Berkeley: University of California Press, 1989.

The Innocents Abroad.

The Literary Apprenticeship of Mark 'Twain. ed. Edgar Marquess Branch, Iowa City: University of Iowa Press, 1950.

The Love Letters of Mark Twain, ed. Dixon Wecter, New York: Harper & Bros., 1949.

Letters from the Earth, ed. Bernard DeVoto, New York: Perennial Library, 1974.

Letters from the Sandwich Islands, Palo Alto: Stanford University Press, 1938.

Letters in the Muscatine Journal, ed., Edgar M. Branch, Chicago: Mark Twain Association of America, 1942.

Life on the Mississippi.

Mark Twain's Mysterious Stranger Manuscripts, ed. William Gibson, Mark Twain Project, Berkeley, 1969.

Mark Twain-Howells Letters: The Correspondence of Samuel L. Clemens and William Dean Howells, ed. Henry Nash Smith and William M. Gibson. 2 Vols. Cambridge: Harvard University Press, 1960.

Mark Twain in Eruption, ed. Bernard DeVoto, New York: Harper & Bros., 1940.

Mark Twain in Hawaii: Roughing It in the Sandwich Islands, ed. A Grove Day, Honolulu: Mutual Publishing Company, 1990.

Mark Twain in Virginia City, ed. Paul Fatout. Bloomington: Indiana University Press, 1964.

Mark Twain of the Enterprise: Newspaper Articles and Other Documents, 1862-1864. ed. Henry Nash Smith. Berkeley: University of California Press, 1957.

Mark Twain and the Buffalo Express, ed. J. McCullough and J. McIntire-Strasburg, DeKalb: Northern University Press, 1999.

Mark Twain on the Damned Human Race, ed. Janet Smith., New York: Hill & Wang, 1962.

Mark Twain on the Lecture Circuit. ed. Paul Fatout, Bloomington: Indiana University Press, 1960.

Mark Twain: The Complete Interviews, ed. Gary Scharnhorst, Tuscaloosa: University of Alabama Press, 2006.

Mark Twain on Potholes and Politics, Letters to the Editor, ed. Gary Scharnhorst, Columbia: University of Missouri Press, 2014.

Mark Twain's Correspondence with Henry Huttleston Rogers, 1893-1909, ed. Lewis Leary, Berkeley: University of California Press, 1969.

Mark Twain Letters, Mark Twain Papers, California Digital Library, Mark Twain Project, Bancroft Library, University of California, on-line <http//www.marktwainproject.org/xtf/view?docId=letters.

Mark Twain's Letters, ed. Albert Bigalow Paine. 2 vols., New York: Harper & Bros., 1917.

Mark Twain's Letters, Vol. 1, 1853-1866, ed. Edgar Marquess Branch, Michael B. Frank, and Kenneth Anderson, Vol. 2, 1867-1868, ed. Harriet Elinor Smith and Richard Bucci. Vol. 3, 1869, ed. Victor Fischer and Michael B. Frank. Vol. 4, 1870-1871, edited by Victor Fischer and Michael B. Frank. Vol. 5, 1872-1873, ed. Lin Salamo and Harriet Elinor Smith. Vol. 6, 1874-1875, ed. Michael B. Frank and Harriet Elinor Smith. Berkeley: University of California Press, 1988-2002.

Mark Twain Letters from Hawaii, ed. A Grove Day, Honolulu: University of Hawaii Press, 1975.

Mark Twain's Letters to His Publishers, 1867-1894. ed. Hamlin Hill, Berkeley: University of California Press, 1967.

Mark Twain: Collected Tales, Sketches, Speeches & Essays, 1852-1890, New American Library Edition, ed. Louis Budd, Ann Arbor, University of Michigan Press, 1992

Mark Twain's Notebook, ed. Albert Bigelow Paine, New York: Harper & Bros., 1935.

Mark Twain's Notebooks & Journals, Vol. 1, 1855-1873, ed. Frederick Anderson, Michael B. Frank, and Kenneth M. Sanderson, Vol. 2, 1877-1883, ed. Frederick Anderson; Lin Salamo, and Bernard L. Stein, Vol. 3, 1883-1891, ed. Robert Pack Browning, Michael B. Frank, and Lin Salamo, Berkeley: University of California Press, 1979.

Mark Twain Speaking, ed. Paul Fatout. Iowa City: University of Iowa Press, 1976.

Mark Twain Speaks of Himself, ed. Paul Fatout, West Lafayette, Ind.: Purdue University Press, 1978.

Mark Twain's Satires and Burlesques, ed. Franklin R. Rogers, Berkeley: University of California Press, 1967.

Mark Twain's Weapons of Satire: Anti-Imperialist Writings on the Philippine-American War, ed. Jim Zwick, Syracuse: Syracuse University Press, 1992.

The Man That Corrupted Hadleyburg and Other Stories and Essays.

Merry Tales.

No. 44, The Mysterious Stranger, Berkeley: University of California Press, 1982.

Personal Recollections of Joan of Arc.

The Prince and the Pauper.

Republican Letters, ed. Cyril Clemens, Webster Groves, Mo., International Mark Twain Society, 1941.

Roughing It.

Selected Mark Twain-Howells Letters, ed. Frederick Anderson, William Gibson, and Henry Nash Smith, Cambridge: Belknap Press of Harvard University Press, 1967.

Sketches, New and Old.

Speeches.

The Stolen White Elephant and Other Detective Stories.

Tom Sawyer Abroad.

The Tragedy of Pudd'nhead Wilson and the Comedy of Those Extraordinary Twins.

A Tramp Abroad.

The £1,000,000 Bank-Note and Other New Stories.

The $30,000 Bequest and Other Stories.

1601, and Is Shakespeare Dead?

The Letters of Quintus Curtius Snodgrass, ed. Ernest E. Leisy, Dallas: Southern Methodist University Press, 1946.

The Political Tales and Truth of Mark Twain, ed. David Hodge and Stacy Freeman, San Rafael, CA: New World Library, 1992.

The Portable Mark Twain, ed. Thomas Quirk, New York: Penguin, 2004.

The Prince and the Pauper, ed. Victor Fischer and Lin Salamo, Berkeley: University of California Press, 1979.

Washington in 1868, ed. Cyril Clemens, Webster Groves, Mo: International Mark Twain Society, 1943.

What Is Man? And Other Philosophical Writings, ed. Paul Bender, Berkeley: University of California Press, 1973.

OTHER SOURCES

Abramoff, Jack, *Capitol Punishment: The Hard Truth About Corruption From America's Most Notorious Lobbyist*, New York: Midpoint Trade Books, 2011.

Anderson, Frederick, ed., *Mark Twain: The Critical Heritage*, London: Routledge & Kegan Paul, 1971.

Andrews, Kenneth, *Nook Farm: Mark Twain's Hartford Circle*, Cambridge: Harvard University Press, 1950.

Berge, William H., "Voices for Imperialism: Josiah Strong and the Protestant Clergy,"Border States, no. 1 (1973). http://spider.georgetowncollege.edu/htallant/border/bs1/berge.htm.

Bliss, Walter, *Twainiana Notes of Walter Bliss*, Hartford: The Hobby Shop, 1930.

Branch, Edgar Marquess, *The Literary Apprenticeship of Mark Twain*, Urbana: University of Illinois, 1950.

Brashear, Minnie, *Mark Twain, Son of Missouri*, Chapel Hill: University of North Carolina Press, 1934.

Brinkley, Douglas, *The Wilderness Warrior*, New York: Harper Collins, 2009.

Brooks, Van Wyck, *The Ordeal of Mark Twain*, New York: Dutton, 1920.

Budd, Louis J., *Mark Twain, Social Philosopher*, Bloomington: Indiana University Press, 1962.

Budd, Louis J., and Edwin H. Cady, ed. *On Mark Twain: The Best from American Literature*, Durham: Duke University Press, 1987.

Carter, Paul Jefferson Jr., *The Social and Political Ideas of Mark Twain*, Ph.D Thesis, University of Kentucky, 1939.

Camfield, Gregg, *Sentimental Twain: Samuel Clemens in the Maze of Moral Philosophy*, Philadelphia: University of Pennsylvania Press, 1994.

Camfield, Gregg, ed., *The Oxford Companion to Mark Twain*, Oxford: Oxford University Press, 2003.

Chamberlain, Fred C., *The Blow from Behind: A Defense of the Flag in the Philippines*, Boston: Lee & Shepard, 1903. Chapter 9 republished in

"Anti-Imperialism in the United States, 1898-1935," ed. Jim Zwick. www. boondocksnet.com/ai/ reaction/bfb_09.html.

Clemens, Clara, *My Father Mark Twain*, New York: Harper & Bros., 1931.

Clemens, Susy, *Papa: An Intimate Biography of Mark Twain*, ed. Charles Neider. Garden City, NY: Doubleday, 1985.

Conway, Moncure Daniel, *Autobiography: Memories and Experiences of Moncure Daniel Conway*, Boston: Houghton Mifflin, 1904.

Cooper, Robert, *Around the World With Mark Twain*, New York: Arcade Publishing, 2000.

Courtney, Steve, *Joseph Hopkins Twichell: The Life and Times of Mark Twain's Closest Friend*, Athens: University of Georgia Press, 2008.

Cox, James M, *Mark Twain: The Fate of Humor*, Princeton: Princeton University Press, 1966.

Dempsey, Terrell, *Searching for Jim: Slavery in Sam Clemens's World*, Columbia: University of Missouri Press, 2003.

Deneen, Patrick J. and Romance, Joseph, *Democracy's Literature: Politics and Fiction in America*, Lanham, MD, Rowman & Littlefield Publishers, Inc., 2005.

DeVoto, Bernard, *Mark Twain's America*, Cambridge: Houghton Mifflin, 1932.

Dionne, E.J., Jr., *Our Divided Political Heart, the Battle for the American Ideal in an Age of Discontent*, New York: Bloomsbury (2012)

Duckett, Margaret, *Mark Twain and Bret Harte*, Norman: University of Oklahoma Press, 1964.

Fears, David H., *Mark Twain Day by Day*, Volumes I, I-2, II, and III, Banks, OR: Horizon Micro, 2009.

Fishkin, Shelley Fisher, ed., *A Historical Guide to Mark Twain*, Oxford: Oxford University Press, 2002.

Fishkin, Shelley Fisher, *Lighting Out for the Territory: Reflections on Mark Twain and American Culture*, Oxford: Oxford University Press, 1997.

Fishkin, Shelley Fisher, *Was Huck Black? Mark Twain and African-American Voices*, Oxford: Oxford University Press, 1993.

Foner, Philip S., *Mark Twain, Social Critic*, New York: International Publishers, 1958.

Fulton, Joe B., *The Reconstruction of Mark Twain– How a Confederate Bushwhacker Became the Lincoln of Our Literature*, Baton Rouge: Louisiana State University Press, 2010.

French, Bryant Morey, *Mark Twain and The Gilded Age*, Dallas: Southern Methodist University Press, 1965.

Geismar, Maxwell, *Mark Twain, An American Prophet,* Boston: Houghton Mifflin Company, 1970.

Gibson, William H., "Mark Twain and Howells: Anti-Imperialists," *New England Quarterly,* vol. 20 (December 1947).

Gillman, Susan, *Dark Twins: Imposture and Identity in Mark Twain's America,* Chicago: University of Chicago Press, 1989.

Gillman, Susan and Robinson, Forrest G., *Mark Twain's Pudd'nhead Wilson, Race Conflict and Culture,* Durham: Duke University Press, 1990

Graff, Henry F., *Grover Cleveland,* New York: Henry Holt & Co., 2002.

Grant, Ulysses S., *The Personal Memoirs of U. S. Grant,* New York: Webster & Company, 1885.

Grant, James, *Mr. Speaker, The Life and Times of Thomas B. Reed, The Man Who Broke the Filibuster,* New York: Simon & Schuster, 2011.

Green, Constance, *Washington: A History of the Capital 1800-1950,* Princeton: Princeton University Press, 1962, Volume I, 21, 179-80.

Gribben, Alan, *Mark Twain's Library: A Reconstruction,* 2 vols., Boston: G. K. Hall, 1980.

Harris, Susan K., *God's Arbiters, Americans and the Philippines, 1898-1902, The War that Sparked Mark Twain's Conflict with America,* New York: Oxford Press, 2011.

Hill, Hamlin, *Mark Twain: God's Fool.* New York: Harper & Row, 1973.

Hill, Hamlin, *Mark Twain and Elisha Bliss,* Colombia: University of Missouri Press, 1964.

Hirst, Robert H., "The Making of *The Innocents Abroad.*" Ph.D. dissertation, University of California, Berkeley, 1975.

Hirst, Robert H., "Sinners and Pilgrims," *Bancroftiana,* no. 113 (Fall 1998).

Hirst, Robert H., "What Paine Left Out," *Bancroftiana,* no. 125 (Fall 2004).

Hochschild, Adam, *King Leopold's Ghost, A Story of Greed, Terror, and Heroism in Colonial Africa,* Boston: Houghton Mifflin Company, 1999.

Hoffman, Andrew, *Inventing Mark Twain: The Lives of Samuel Langhorne Clemens,* New York: William Morrow & Co., 1997.

Hoogenboom, Ari, *The Presidency of Rutherford B. Hayes,* Lawrence: University of Kansas Press, 1988.

Howells, William Dean, *My Mark Twain: Reminiscences and Criticisms,* ed. Marilyn Austin Baldwin, Baton Rouge: Louisiana State University Press, 1967.

Jacob, Kathryn Allamong, *King of the Lobby,* Baltimore: Johns Hopkins University Press, 2010.

Jonnes, Jill, *Conquering Gotham, A Gilded Age Epic: The Construction of Penn Station and its Tunnels,* New York: Viking 2007.

Kaiser, Robert G., *So Damn Much Money, The Triumph of Lobbying and the Corrosion of American Government*, New York: Vintage Books, 2009.

Kaplan, Fred, *The Singular Mark Twain*, New York: Doubleday, 2003.

Kaplan, Justin, *Mr. Clemens and Mark Twain*, New York: Simon & Schuster, 1966.

Krause, Sydney J., *Mark Twain as Critic*, Baltimore: Johns Hopkins University Press, 1967.

Krugman, Paul, *The Conscience of a Liberal*, New York: W.W. Norton & Company, 2007.

Lauber, John, *The Making of Mark Twain: A Biography*, New York: Noonday Press, 1985.

LeMaster, J. R. and Wilson, James D., *The Mark Twain Encyclopedia*, New York: Garland Pub., 1993.

Leonard, James, et al., ed. *Satire or Evasion? Black Perspectives on Huckleberry Finn*, Durham: Duke University Press, 1992.

Leonard, James, "Mark Twain and Politics," *A Companion to Mark Twain*, ed. Peter Messent and Louis J. Budd, Oxford: Blackwell, 2005, 94.

Lorch, Fred W., "The American Vandal Abroad," *The Trouble Begins at Eight: Mark Twain's Lecture Tours*, Ames: Iowa State University Press, 1966.

Loving, Jerome, *Mark Twain: The Adventures of Samuel L. Clemens*, Berkeley: University of California Press, 2010.

Madrick, Jeff, *Age of Greed, The Triumph of Finance and the Decline of America, 1970 to the Present*, New York: Alfred A Knopf, 2011.

Mann, Thomas E. and Ornstein, Norman J., *The Broken Branch, How Congress is Failing America and How to Get it Back on Track*, New York: Oxford University Press, 2006.

Mann, Thomas E. and Ornstein, Norman J., *It's Even Worse Than It Looks, How the American Constitutional System Collided with the New Politics of Extremism*, New York: Basic Books, 2012.

Masters, Edgar Lee, *Mark Twain: A Portrait*, New York: Charles Scribner's Sons, 1938.

McFarland, Philip, *Mark Twain and the Colonel: Samuel L. Clemens, Theodore Roosevelt and the Arrival of the New Century*, Lanham, MD: Rowman & Littlefield, 2012.

Menand, Louis, *The Metaphysical Club: A Story of Ideas in America*, New York: Farrar, Strauss, and Giroux, 2001.

Michelson, Bruce, *Printer's Devil*, Berkeley: University of California Press, 2006.

Muller, John, *Mark Twain in Washington D.C.*, Charleston: History press, 2013.

Ober, K. Patrick, *Mark Twain and Medicine*, Columbia: University of Missouri Press, 2003.

Oppenheimer, Danny and Edwards, Mike, *Democracy Despite Itself, Why A System That Shouldn't Work at All, Works So Well*, Cambridge, MA, MIT Press, 2012.

Paine, Albert Bigelow, *Mark Twain: A Biography*, 4 vols., New York: Harper & Bros., 1912.

Paine, Thomas, *Collected Writings*, ed. Eric Foner, New York: Library of America, 1995.

Pemberton, T Edgar, *The Life of Bret Harte*, New York: Dodd, Mead & Co., 1903.

Perry, Mark, *Grant and Twain: The Story of a Friendship That Changed America*, New York: Random House, 2004.

Peters, Charles, *How Washington Really Works*, New York: Basic Books. 1980.

Peterson, Svend, *Mark Twain and The Government*, Idaho: Caxton, 1962.

Phipps, William E., *Mark Twain's Religion*, Macon, GA.: Mercer University Press, 2003.

Powers, Ron, *Mark Twain: A Life*, New York: Free Press, 2005.

Powers, Ron, *Dangerous Water: A Biography of the Boy Who Became Mark Twain*, New York: Basic Books, 1999.

Quinn, Arthur H., *American Fiction, A Historical and Critical Survey*, New York: Hubbard Bros., 1936.

Quirk, Thomas, *Mark Twain and Human Nature*, Columbia: University of Missouri Press, 2007.

Railton, Stephen, "Jim and Mark Twain: What Do Dey Stan' For?" *Virginia Quarterly Review*, vol. 63, Summer 1987.

Rasmussen, R. Kent, *Mark Twain A to Z: The Essential Reference to His Life and Writings*, New York: Facts on File, 1995.

Reich, Robert B., *After Shock, The Next Economy and America's Future*, New York: Alfred A. Knopf, 2010.

Richardson, Robert D. Jr., *Emerson: The Mind on Fire*, Berkeley: University of California Press, 1995.

Samuel, Terrence, *The Upper House, A Journey Behind the Closed Doors of the U.S. Senate*, New York: Palgrave Macmillan, 2011.

Sanborn, Margaret, *Mark Twain: The Bachelor Years*, New York: Doubleday, 1990.

Shapiro, Ira, *The Last Great Senate, Courage and Statesmanship in Times of Crisis*, New York: Public Affairs, 2012.

Shelden, Michael, *Mark Twain: Man in White, the Grand Adventure of His Final Years*, New York: Random House, 2010.

Stewart, William, *Reminiscences of Senator William M. Stewart of Nevada,* ed. George Rathwell Brown, New York: Neale Publishing Co., 1908.

Stewart, David, *Impeached: The Trial of President Andrew Johnson and The Fight for Lincoln's Legacy,* New York: Simon & Schuster, 2009.

Sundquist, Eric, *Mark Twain: A Collection of Critical Essays,* Englewood Cliffs, NJ: Prentice Hall, 1994.

Sundquist, Eric, "Mark Twain and Homer Plessey," in Gillman and Robinson, 46.

Taper, Bernard, *Mark Twain's San Francisco,* New York: McGraw-Hill, 1963.

Tarnoff, Ben, *The Bohemians,* New York: Penguin Press, 2014.

Townsend, George Alfred, *Washington Outside and Inside,* Hartford, CT: Betts & Co., 1873.

Trachtenberg, Alan, *Democratic Vistas,* 1860-1880, New York: G. Braziller, 1970.

Trachtenberg, Alan, *The Incorporation of America: Culture and Society in the Gilded Age,* New York: Hill and Wang, 1882.

Trombley, Laura Skandera, *Mark Twain's Other Woman,* New York: Knopf, 2010.

Twichell, Joseph, *Personal Journal,* Joseph Twichell Collection, Beinecke Rare Book and Manuscript Library, Yale University, New Haven, Connecticut.

Vaidhyanathan, Siva, *Copyrights and Copywrongs: The Rise of Intellectual Property and How It Threatens Creativity,* New York: New York University Press, 2001.

Walker, Franklin, ed., *The Washoe Giant in San Francisco,* Los Angeles: Ward Ritchie Press 1938.

Ward, Geoffrey C., et al., *Mark Twain: An Illustrated Biography,* New York: Alfred A. Knopf, 2001.

Webster, Samuel Charles, ed., *Mark Twain, Business Man,* Boston: Little, Brown & Co., 1946.

Wecter, Dixon, *Sam Clemens of Hannibal,* Cambridge: Riverside Press, 1952.

Willis, Resa, *Mark and Livy: The Love Story of Mark Twain and the Woman Who Almost Tamed Him,* New York: Atheneum, 1992.

White, Richard, *Railroaded, The Transcontinentals and the Making of Modern America,* New York: W.W. Norton & Company, 2011.

Zacks, Richard, *Island of Vice: Theodore Roosevelt's Doomed Quest to Clean Up Sin-Loving New York,* New York: Doubleday, 2012.

Zinn, Howard, *A People's History of the United States, 1492-Present,* New York: HarperCollins, 2003.

Zuckert, Catherine H., *Natural Right and the American Imagination, Political Philosophy in Novel Form*, Savage, MD, Rowman & Littlefield Publishers, Inc., 1990.

Zwick, Jim, *Confronting Imperialism, Essays on Mark Twain and the Anti-Imperialist League*, West Conshohocken, PA: Infinity Publishers, 2007.

Zwick, Jim, "Mark Twain and Imperialism," *Historical Guide*; "Anti-Imperialism in The United States, 1898-1935."

End Notes

REFERENCES

Abbreviations

[Citations to Mark Twain's writings (unless otherwise specified) are to *The Oxford Mark Twain*, edited by Shelly Fisher Fishkin, 29 volumes. New York: Oxford University Press, 1996] [For complete citations to other sources, see the Bibliography.]

AD	*Unpublished autobiographical dictations, Mark Twain Project, Berkeley.*
MT Autobiography	*Autobiography of Mark Twain, Volumes 1-3, Mark Twain Project, University of California, Berkeley, 2010.*
AC	*The American Claimant.*
CY	*A Connecticut Yankee in King Arthur's Court.*
FE	*Following the Equator and Anti-Imperialist Essays.*
GA	*The Gilded Age, A Tale of Today.*
HF	*The Adventures of Huckleberry Finn.*
Twain-Howells Letters	*Selected Mark Twain -Howells Letters.*
IA	*Innocents Abroad.*

JA	*The Personal Recollections of Joan of Arc.*
LM	*Life on the Mississippi.*
MTA-P	*Mark Twain's Autobiography, ed. Albert Bigelow Paine, 2 Vols. (1924)*
MTB	*Albert Bigelow Paine, Mark Twain, A Biography, 4 Vols. (1912).*
MTL	*Mark Twain's Letters, Mark Twain Papers, Mark Twain Project, University of California at Berkeley; on-line and in five published volumes. http://www.marktwainproject.org/xtf/view?docId=letters. On-line citations (#UCCCL); published volumes (Letters I-V).*
MTP	*Mark Twain Papers, Mark Twain Project, Bancroft Library, University of California, Berkeley.*
MTNJ	*Mark Twain's Notebooks & Journals, Vols. 1-3, Mark Twain Project/Papers, Bancroft Library, University of California, Berkeley.*
MT Eruption	*Mark Twain in Eruption, ed. DeVoto.*
44 MS	*44 Mysterious Stranger*
PW	*The Tragedy of Pudd'nhead Wilson and the Comedy of Those Extraordinary Twains.*
RBHL	*President Rutherford B. Hayes Presidential Library and Museum, Fremont, Ohio.*
RBHJ	*President Hayes' Journal.*
RI	*Roughing It.*
Sketches	*Sketches, New and Old.*
Speeches	*Speeches.*

TA   *The Tramp Abroad.*

TS   *The Adventures of Tom Sawyer.*

END NOTES
PREFACE
Chapter quote from MTB, 1511.

1. Mark Twain, *The Mysterious Stranger,* ed. William M. Gibson, *Berkeley: University of California Press, 1969, 25.*
2. *Foner, 400.*
3. *Budd, 210-15.*
4. *MTNJ, Ch xxxi, quoted in Peterson 37.*
5. *MT Speeches (1910 ed.), 415 quoted in Peterson 46.*
6. *MT Autobiography 3, 259; MT Autobiography 2, 371; MT Eruption (entry July 16, 1908), 2; Peterson, 48-49. "It is not worthwhile to try to keep history from repeating itself," Twain wrote, "for man's character will always make the preventing of the repetitions impossible." MT Eruption (January 15, 1907) quoted in Political Tales, 99.*
7. *"Passage from a Lecture," The Bible According to Mark Twain, 78.*
8. *See, e.g., Don Peck, "Can the Middle Class be Saved?" Atlantic Monthly, September 2011, 60, 62; Paul Krugman, "Gilded Once More," New York Times, April 27, 2007, Op-ed; Paul Krugman, "We are the 99.9%," New York Times, November 24, 2011, Op-ed ("The big winners in this new Gilded Age have been a handful of very wealthy people.")*
9. *Dionne, 187.*
10. *Krugman, 39.*
11. *White, 17-38, 93-118, 155-58, 456-57, 507-17. Stanford Professor Richard White's excellent book, Railroaded, The Transcontinentals and the Making of Modern America, describes how the building of the transcontinental railroads created the modern political-economic structure. See also Trachtenberg, Incorporation of America, who quotes Charles Francis Adams, Jr: "The system of corporate life is a new power, for which our language contains no name. We have no word to express government by moneyed corporations." Id. at 3.*
12. *MT Autobiography 1, 464; White, 88-92, 102-109.*
13. *Nicolas Barreyre, The Politics of Economic Crisis: The Panic of 1873, The End of Reconstruction and the Realignment of American Politics, Journal of the Gilded Age and Progressive Era, 2011, 403-23; White, 83-84.*

14. Reich, 56-57; According to Simon Johnson, formerly chief economist of the International Monetary Fund, between 1973 and 1985, US banks never earned more that 16 percent of domestic corporate profits. In the mid-2000s that figure rose to 44 percent. Harold Myerson, "Rescuing America from Wall Street," Washington Post, October 5, 2011, op-ed.

15. Congressional Budget Office, "Trends in the Distribution of Household Income Between 1979 and 2007," October 2011. The study found that between 1970 and 2007, the after-tax income of the wealthiest one percent of the population increased by 275 percent compared to only 18 percent for the poorest 20 per cent; see also Reich, 6-7, 19-20; Ylan Q. Mui, "Families see their wealth sapped," Washington Post, June 12, 2012, A1c6; Atlantic Monthly, July-August, 2011, 60.

16. Connor Dougherty, "Income Slides to 1996 Levels," Wall Street Journal, September 14, 2011, A1cs3-6; Michael A. Fletcher, "Census Shows Impact of Recession," Washington Post, September 14, 2011, A1cs2-5.

17. Peck, Atlantic Monthly, 60, 62.

18. Steven Pearlstein, Harold Gortner Lecture, George Mason University, April 16, 2012.

19. Interview, New York Herald, August 28, 1876; Peterson, 96.

20. FE (PW's New Calendar), 99.

21. SLC Letter to Helene Picard, February 22, 1902, Letters 2:719 (UCLC 33404), quoted in Quirk, 245.

22. Interview, New York Herald, August 28, 1876.

23. Mark Twain Letters from Hawaii, 109; Letters to the Sacramento Weekly Union quoted in "Letters from the Sandwich Islands," 80.

24. FE (PW's New Calendar), 119.

25. Mark Twain: Collected Tales, Sketches, Speeches & Essays, 1852-1890, vol. 3., 577-583.

26. "Skeleton Plan of a Proposed Casting Vote Party," quoted in MTB, 1148.

PROLOGUE: A FLYING TRIP TO WASHINGTON
Chapter quote from GA, 224.

1. MTL: SLC to Muscatine Journal, February 17-18, 1854 (UCCL 00007); see also Letters in the Muscatine Journal, 20-22.

2. MTP: Mark Twain Letter from Washington No. 1 to the Virginia City Territorial Enterprise, December 4, 1867 (hereafter "MT Letter from Washington No. –")

3. Constance Green, Washington: A History of the Capital 1800 - 1950, Vol. I, 21, 179-80.

4.   *MTL: SLC to Muscatine Journal, February 17-18, 1854 (UCCL 00007); see also GA, 222.*

5.   *Id.(UCCL 00007) n7.*

6.   *Jacob, 10.*

7.   *MTL: SLC to Muscatine Journal, February 17-18, 1854 (UCCL 00007).*

8.   *LM, 476; MTB, 581.*

9.   *Four years later Mathew Brady set up a photography studio on the north side of Pennsylvania Avenue above Gilman's Drug Store. Jacob, 10. See Jacqueline Trescott, "The photographer who went to war," Washington Post, November 7, 2010, R6cs1-4.*

10. *MTP: MT Letter from Washington No. 1, December 4, 1867; GA, 221.*

11. *MTL: SLC to Muscatine Journal, February 17-18, 1854 (UCCL 00007).*

12. *Id.*

13. *Id.*

14. *Id.*

15. *Id.*

16. *MTP: MT Letter from Washington No. 1, December 4, 1867.*

17. *TS, 178; Wecter, 195.*

18. *MTL: SLC to Muscatine Journal, February 17-18, 1854 (UCCL 00007); Hoffman, 38.*

19. *GA, 409.*

20. *Id., 221.*

21. *GA, 221-22; French, 179.*

22. *MTL: SLC to Muscatine Journal, February 17-18, 1854 (UCCL 00007).*

23. *Id.; Hoffman, 38.*

24. *GA, 225.*

25. *What Is Man? 106.*

26. *FE, 645; MT Autobiography 2, 290.*

CHAPTER ONE
SHAPING SAM'S VIEWS OF DEMOCRACY
Chapter quote from Lincoln in His
Own Words, ed. Milton Meltzer, New York: Harcourt, 1993.

1.   *MT Autobiography 1, 217, 212; Neider, 9.*

2.   *J.R. LeMaster, 589.*

3.   *Speeches, 290.*

4.   MT Autobiography 1, 206, 208, 469. The land was in Fentress County between the Cumberland and Tennessee rivers, a few hundred miles from Knoxville. John Clemens and later his oldest son, Orion, turned down several decent offers to purchase the land. The only money the Clemens family ever made from the Tennessee land was from Twain's fictionalized account in The Gilded Age.

5   French, 152; Neider, 23; Powers, 10; GA, 26 (In Twain's fictionalized account in The Gilded Age, Colonel Sellers (a stand-in for Cousin James Lampton) wrote to (John Clemens) encouraging him to come to Missouri: "I've got the biggest scheme on earth. Mum's the word."); MT Autobiography 1, 215-16.

6.   Fears I, 2; Rasmussen, 78.

7.   Carter, 21-22; Rasmussen, 78-79.

8.   Fears I, 6.

9.   MTB, 5; Foner, 16.

10.   MT Autobiography 1, 454, 470.

11.   Doris and Samuel Webster, "Whitewashing Jane Clemens," Bookman, LXI (July 1925).

12.   MT Autobiography 1, 212; Neider, 8.

13.   See HF, 125-28.

14.   MT Autobiography 1, 274-76; Neider, 130-33.

15.   Interview quoted in Loving, 360.

16.   MT Autobiography 1, 204; MTB, 1545. According to family legend, Clemens' mother was a descendant of British royalty but his father was descended from Judge Gregory Clement who signed the death warrant for Charles I.

17.   Twain once wrote, "Truth is stranger than fiction but it is because Fiction is obliged to stick to possibilities; Truth isn't." FE (PW's New Calendar), 156.

CHAPTER TWO
THE EDUCATION OF A PRINTER, PILOT AND POLITICAL REPORTER

Chapter quote attributed to Lincoln by William Dean Howells.

1.   RI, 292.

2.   Powers, 45- 61.

3.   Returning home from work, Sam picked up a page fragment skirting along the street in a puff of wind, a page torn from a book about Joan of Arc. Recalling

his mother's royal pretensions, he became an ardent reader of history, fascinated by the struggle of the oppressed against the tyranny of kings and dictators. This lifelong obsession would fuel several books and, in his later years, shocking commentary condemning European colonialism and American imperialism.

4. *Powers, 60.*

5. *Letter to Hannibal Western Union quoted in Wecter, Sam Clemens of Hannibal, 239; Fears I, 18; Edgar M. Branch, 7 (Sam's first known published story, "The Dandy Frightening the Squatter" (June 27, 1850) displays his fine-tuned ear for the vernacular. This humorous tale is about a "dandy" on a riverboat who spies a "squatter" on the riverbank and decides to frighten him with a show of bravado that will impress the young ladies on board. Brandishing two fancy pistols and a bowie knife, he verbally threatens the rustic woodsman who plants his fist between the dandy's eyes and sends him sprawling into the Mississippi. Sam's ridicule of the dandy's showmanship foreshadows a lifetime of satirizing pretentious politicians whose actions belie their lofty rhetoric.) Tom Quirk, 32; In another early story, "Connubial Bliss," Sam probably reflected his parent's marital relations as he contrasted the romance of courtship to the drudgery of marriage. Branch, 7.*

6. *"Blabbing Government Secrets" quoted in Branch, 14-15, 219.*

7. *"Editorial Agility" quoted in Branch, 13; Muscatine Letters, ed. Branch, 7 (Sam ridiculed the editor of the Democratic paper by depicting him jumping over nine pews when terrified by a small fire. In "Local" he satirized a crude town opponent.).*

8. *"Assistant's Column" quoted in Branch, 18.*

9. *Michelson, 28-30.*

10. *MTB, 95; MT Autobiography 1, 460.*

11. *MTL: Letter to Muscatine Journal, December 24, 1853 (UCCL 00006); Muscatine Journal, ed. Branch, 13.*

12. *Id.*

13. *MTNJ entry 1877-78 quoted in Peterson, 33.*

14. *Leonard, 96. Fillmore had previously succeeded to the Presidency after Zachary Taylor's death and worked with Senator Stephen Douglas to secure passage of the unfortunate Kansas-Nebraska Act of 1850. When the Whigs denied Fillmore the nomination in 1852, he decided to join the American Party – the Know-Nothings' political arm.*

15. *LM, 166.*

16. *Id., 217; Powers, 780.*

17.   *Scott v. Sanford, 60 U.S. 576 (1857).*

18   *"Citizenship," 10 Op. Att'y Gen., 382-413 (opinion of Edward Bates).*

19.   *LM, 320-21.*

20.   *Fulton, 26-27.*

21.   *LM, 320-21 ("The South has not yet recovered from the debilitating influence" of Sir Walter Scott and his "grotesque chivalry and romantic juvenilities.").*

22.   *Neider, 134.*

23.   *"The Private History of a Campaign that Failed," Merry Tales, 9, 50.*

24.   *Neider, 133.*

25.   *"The Private History of a Campaign that Failed," Merry Tales, 9, 44-45.*

CHAPTER THREE
FRONTIER POLITICS
Chapter quote from MTP: MTNJ #32, 72.

1.   *MT Autobiography 2, 4-5 ("By the time he had been Governor a year, he had shaken hands with every human in the Territory of Nevada and after that he instantly knew these people by sight and could call them by name."); Neider, 135.*

2.   *RI, 302-03.*

3.   *The Washoe Giant in San Francisco, ed. Franklin Walker, 1938, 57; Carter, 62.*

4.   *RI, 303.*

5.   *MTB, 206; RI, 296; Carter, 54.*

6.   *Clemens supplemented his meager income with additional assignments such as recording secretary for the Washoe Agricultural, Mining and Mechanical Association Fair. Budd, 8.*

7.   *MTL: SLC Letter to Orion and Mollie Clemens, October 21, 1862 (UCCL 00060).*

8.   *Mark Twain of the Enterprise, ed. Henry Nash Smith ("Smith"), 63.*

9.   *Clemens told his editor Joe Goodman that he wanted to sign his articles Mark Twain. MTB, 220-27 (Clemens quickly became a favorite with the members, who enjoyed his sharp letters with their amusing turn of phrase and valued his sincerity and general friendship. Jack Simmons, Speaker of the House, and Billy Clagget, leader of the Humboldt delegation, were his special cronies who kept him inside the political machine. Clagget would eventually be elected to Congress.).*

10.   *Smith, 9-13.*

11.   *RI, 192; Smith, 34.*

12.   *MTA-P, 307-08; Neider, 137.*

13. *MTL: SLC to Jane Clemens, August 19, 1863 (UCCL 00071).*

14. *MTB, 224 (Paine wrote: "The Enterprise was a powerful organ... and Mark Twain had become its chief tribune. That he was fearless, merciless, and incorruptible without doubt had a salutary influence on that legislative session. He reveled in his power, but it is not recorded that he ever abused it." Id., 224).*

15. *Smith, 162-67. In an unsigned article he singled out Stewart's bill to appropriate $1,800 to Sheriff D.J. Gasherie for the maintenance of Ormsby County paupers, a $20,000 appropriation to fund a seminary in Carson City for forty students, and various other funding measures that would benefit specific legislators – precursors to the modern day congressional earmark.*

16. *Budd, 11.*

17. *MT Autobiography 2, 5; Neider, 137.*

18. *MTL: SLC to Jane Clemens and Pamela Moffett, April 11 and 12, 1863 (UCCL 00063); MTB, 229.*

19. *MT Letter of December 12, 1863 quoted in Smith, 97-98. Twain charged Stewart with "eternally distorting facts and principles," and called him a "long-legged, bull-headed, whopper-jawed, constructionary monomaniac" who "would climb out of his coffin and construe the burial service."*

20. *MTL: SLC to Jane Clemens, January 2, 1864 (UCCL 00072), n1. A state created by such a constitution "would be a fraudulent and impotent institution," and as a result Nevada would be "kicked back into territorial condition again on account of it." Id. For his opposition to the constitution, Clemens received a gold watch from Alexander Baldwin (Stewart's law partner) and Theodore Winters, the major shareholder of the Ophir Silver Mining Company. Nye also gave him a coveted Notary Public appointment, bypassing a long list of applicants. Clemens was definitely a journalist to be reckoned with.*

21. *W. Stewart, Reminiscences of Senator William M. Stewart of Nevada ("W. Stewart"), 167.*

22. *MT Autobiography 2, 20; Neider, 139. Clemens later wrote William Dean Howells that Orion "belonged to as many as five different religious denominations." MTL: SLC to Howells, February 9, 1879, Howells Letters, 123. Twain joked in his autobiography that every time Orion changed his religion his new church would make him treasurer because he would stop the graft. He also "exhibited a facility in changing his political complexion." One morning when Orion was a Republican, he was invited to give a political dinner speech, but after lunch he became a Democrat and wrote a score of anti-Republican slogans to be carried in a torchlight parade. By evening he had converted back to Republican. His speech went well, except for the slogans that were paraded "in front of him, to the joy of*

every witness present." MT Autobiography 2, 26; Neider, 292-93. Clemens once told Howells that he could always predict a "party's funeral" when he learned how his "brother had made up his mind to vote. For some inscrutable reason God never allows him to vote right." Orion was "simply hell on political sagacity." MTL: SLC to Howells, September 21, 1876 (UCCL 01367).

23.   Smith, 144-45.

24.   Branch, 89-90.

25.   Twain's address is quoted in Smith, 105.

26.   Quoted in Branch, 92.

27.   Id., 93. The Third House passed legislation barring women from preaching or operating a business and barring sheriffs from arresting criminals despite strong evidence unless the "criminal shall insist on the privilege of being arrested."

28.   Id.

29.   MTL: SLC to Jane and Mollie Clemens, August 19, 1863 (UCCL 00071).

30.   W. Stewart, 220. Born in 1827. Bill Stewart descended from Scotch ancestry who migrated to Massachusetts before the Revolution. His maternal grandfather fought in the American Revolution, and his father served in the War of 1812. His mother, Miranda Morris, was a descendant of a signer of the Declaration of Independence. Stewart dropped out of Yale University in 1850 to join the California Gold Rush. After working as a successful lawyer in San Francisco, and serving briefly as California Attorney General, Stewart again caught the fever– this time for silver– and headed for Nevada, then part of the Utah Territories. He made his fortune as a mining lawyer. In one trial Stewart snapped at the opposition lawyer (who later became his partner): "You little shrimp, if you don't stop those tactics, I'll eat you." Baldwin replied: If you do, you will have more brains in your belly than you have in your head." Effie Mona Mock, "William Morris Stewart 1827-1909, "Nevada Historical Society Quarterly Vo. VII, No. 1-2, 1964, 54-56.

31.   Branch, 101.

32.   Id., 97.

33.   MTL: SLC to unidentified recipient, February, 1891, quoted in Foner, 86.

34.   "Story of the Bad Little Boy," Sketches, 51.

35.   Clemens, "A Stage Robber Among Us," Call, July 20, 1864; Clemens, "More Stage Robbers and their Confederates Captured," Call, August 3, 1864; "A Confederate Caged," Call, August 26, 1864; Mark Twain, Clemens of the Call, 259-64;276-77.

36.   MT Autobiography 2, 115; Taper, 218-20. Believing that only property owners should vote, Clemens had even denigrated his own right to vote on the Nevada

constitution, "having no taxable property," and "no tangible right to take an interest." Budd, 15.

37.　Twain, "An Unbiased Criticism," in Democratic Vistas 1860-1880, 314; "The Great Prize Fight" in Branch, 86.

38.　MT Autobiography 2, 120. Harte would give Clemens a helping hand in crafting his first successful book, The Innocents Abroad, but the roller-coaster relationship between Clemens and Harte went through many phases. In sequence, Clemens treated him as a contemporary, colleague, competitor, co-author and cast-off. In the early years his praise was exuberant; in later years his criticism was caustic and condescending. Forgetting in later life the early helping hand, Clemens felt his fading frontier friend had let him down on a playwriting project and had become an insufferable freeloader.

39.　"Lucretia Smith's Soldier," Californian quoted in Fulton, 113..

40.　Alta California, April 17, 1867, quoted in Fulton, 127-29..

41.　Fulton, 124.

42.　"Mark Twain and the Colored Man," Territorial Enterprise quoted in Fulton, 126. Racism was prevalent in the territories and it was not limited to southern ex-patriots. Like other white observers, Twain admitted at first that he resented allowing the "damned naygurs" to march at all, but then he noted, foreshadowing his evolving views on race, that white people "have got to sing with them in heaven or scorch with them in hell someday, in the most familiar and sociable way, and on a footing of most perfect equality." Fears I, 136.

43.　The Celebrated Jumping Frog of Calaveras County and Other Sketches, 1.

44.　Budd, 14.

45.　Foner, 31.

46.　Branch, 142.

47.　Id.; MT Letters, December 20-22, 1865 and February 15, 1866 cited in Budd, 15-16.

48.　MT Autobiography 3, 78; Foner, 30.

49.　Phipps, 54.

50.　"Chief Burke's Star Chamber Board of Police Commissioners," Territorial Enterprise, February 15, 1866, quoted in Taper, 218-20; Fears I, 153; Quirk, 21-22.

51.　"What have the police been doing," quoted in Branch, 144.

52.　New York Tribune, March 11, 1868, 2cl.

53.　"My Debut as a Literary Person,"; MT Autobiography, 1, 502-03; W. Bliss, Twainiana, Notes, 5 (Twain's first magazine article).

54. *MTP: Sacramento Weekly Union, June 23, 1866; Letters from Hawaii,109.*

55. *Id., 112.*

56. *Letters from the Sandwich Islands, 42.*

57. *Id.*

58. *Id. Twain described a visit to an ancient temple, where human sacrifices had been made. "A simple child of nature, yielding momentarily to sin when sorely tempted, acknowledged his error . . . and offered up his grandmother as an atoning sacrifice... the luckless sinner could keep on cleansing his conscience . . . as long as the relations held out."*

59. *Id. When friends thought a sick person was going to die, a couple of dozen neighbors surrounded his hut "and kept up a deafening wailing night and day" until he died or recovered: "No doubt this arrangement has helped many a subject to a shroud before his appointed time." He further noted the Hawaiians generous hospitality: "They freely offer their houses, food, beds," adding gratuitously in 1866, "and often their wives and daughters." Loving, 115.*

60. *Zwick, 88; Letters from Hawaii, 116-19; Loving, 115. He mocked the excessive use of titles, a harbinger of his days to come in Washington. Budd, 21.*

61. *Taper, 247. He was critical of the obsequious American Finance Minister, C.C. Harris, and the arrogant Anglican Bishop T.N. Snead for the "culture" they brought to the native people.*

62. *See Menand, 116.*

63. *Powers, 164.*

64. *IA, 268.*

65. *Id., 258.*

CHAPTER FOUR
SAM CLEMENS' SHORT GOVERNMENT CAREER
Chapter quote from FE (PW's New Calendar), 99.

1. *Cong. Globe, 40th Cong., 2d Sess. app 2-3, December 3, 1867; see David Stewart, Impeached, 16 ("D. Stewart") (Johnson frequently made disparaging comments about blacks, whom he considered "inferior to the white man in point of intellect– better calculated in physical structure to undergo drudgery and hardship.").*

2. *Charles Dickens, A Tale of Two Cities, Philadelphia: T.B. Peterson & Brothers, 1859, 1.*

3. *"Unless you can get the ear of a Senator, or a Congressman, or a Chief of a Bureau or Department, and persuade him to use his 'influence' in your behalf, you cannot get an employment of the most trivial nature in Washington."* GA, 223; Jacob, 72.

4. MTL: SLC to Jane Clemens and family, August 9, 1867 (UCCL 00144).

5. GA, 218.

6. W. Stewart, 219-20.

7. Id., 220. *In his memoirs, Stewart was getting even for Twain's references to the senator in Roughing It where Stewart is accused of cheating and depicted in an illustration as a villain with a patch over one eye. Twain claims to have given him "a sound thrashing."* RI, 309; MTB, 247n, 347n1.

8. Id., 220. *Contrast Senator Stewart's comment that Twain was an unpopular scamp with Paine's recollection that he "became a favorite with the members."* MTB, 220. *As Twain once said, "the very ink with which all history is written is merely fluid prejudice."* FE (PW's New Calendar), 699.

9. Id., 222.

10. W. Stewart, 222.

11. MTP: *MT Letters from Washington 1, 2, 4 ("more vim and spirit than any other senator"), 5 (floor speech on mining "by far the best and ablest of its kind"), 8, 9 ("about the hardest working man in Congress");* Budd, 29.

12. Loving, 148; Washington in 1868, 6

13. W. Stewart, 219-20; MTA-P, 109; Washington in 1868, 6.

14. Townsend, 75; Jacob, 5, 163, Dictionary of American Politics, 1892, 315. *According to Robert Kaiser's excellent book, So Damned Much Money, wealthy New York merchants lobbied the first Congress in New York City in March, 1789, hosting a dinner lubricated with wine and spirits as they argued against a tariff bill that would increase the cost of their imports. But even they were not the first. Within two weeks after the colonialists arrived at Jamestown on June 6, 1607, a petition seeking "Reformatyon" of certain preposterous proceedings was filed with the governing council and was approved four days later.* Kaiser, 82, 96.

15. W. Stewart, 168.

16. Id. *Stewart was also the recipient of the last words ever written by Abraham Lincoln. At the request of a friend, Judge Niles Searls, Stewart had sent a calling card to Lincoln requesting a meeting in the evening of April 14, 1865, and Lincoln replied: "I am engaged to go to the theatre with Mrs. Lincoln. It is the kind of engagement I never break. Come with your friend tomorrow at 10:00 and I shall be glad to see you. A. Lincoln."* Nevada Historical Society Quarterly, 37.

17. *W. Stewart, 170 (Stewart also said of Lincoln: "Without schooling, he wrote the best English; . . . without education in rhetoric or logic, he was the most conclusive reasoner; without the slightest pretense to oratory, he was the most persuasive speaker of his time. He was the kindest most benevolent and humane man of his generation.")*

18. *Id., 201; See also Nevada Historical Society Quarterly, 51-53.*

19. *White, 24.*

20. *White, 101; quotation is from a letter from Huntington to Crocker, May 17, 1869, Huntington Letters 1:429 quoted in White, 116, 560n89. White documents in excruciating detail the competition and corruption of the railroad lobbies in seeking congressional favors. See, e.g., id., 93-130, 347-55; Kaiser, 85.*

21. *W. Stewart, 17.*

22. *MTL: SLC to Emily A. Severance, December 24, 1867 (UCCL 0278), n4; SLC to Frank Fuller, November 24, 1867 (UCCL 00158), n5.*

23. *MTP: MT Letter from Washington No. 1, December 4, 1867.*

24. *Id.*

25. *Id.*

26. *MTP: MTNJ 1, 492.*

27. *Id, 494; Powers, 24.*

28. *MTP: MTNJ 1, 491-94.*

29. *Benjamin B. French to Johnson, February 8, 1866 in Johnson Papers 10:57; Cong. Globe, 40th Cong., 2d sess., app. 2-3 (December 3, 1867) quoted in D. Stewart, 16.*

30. *Id.*

31. *MTP: MTNJ 1, 487-90.*

32. *Id., 490.*

33. *Id., 487.*

34. *Id., 492.*

35. *MTP: MT Letter from Washington No. 3, January 11, 1868.*

36. *MTP: MT Letter from Washington No. 1, December 4, 1867; Fulton, 136.*

37. *MTL: SLC to Jane Clemens and Family, November 25, 1867 (UCCL 00162).*

38. *Carter, 280. Clemens wrote to Orion in February 21, 1868 about the "pitiful intellects in this Congress... There are few of them I find pleasant enough company to visit.... I am infernally tired of Wash. & its 'attractions.'" SLC to Orion, February 21, 1868 (UCCL 00198). He wrote to the New York Tribune, "To my mind Judas Iscariot was nothing but a low, mean, premature Congressman" quoted in Peterson, 31.*

39.   SLC to Frank Fuller, December 5, 1867 (UCCL 00170), n 2.

40.   W. Stewart, 223-24; F. Kaplan, 58.

41.   MTL: SLC to Severance, December 24, 1867 (UCCL 02780), n 4.

42.   Id.

43.   MTP: "The Facts Concerning The Recent Resignation," New York Tribune, December 27, 1867; MTB, 361; Sketches, 264.

44.   Id; Sketches, 264, 268-69.

45.   Id.

46.   Interview, New York Tribune, February 13, 1868 quoted in Budd, 34; MTB, 361.

47.   New York Citizen, December 21, 1867 described in Lauber, 222.

48.   Budd, 34. In "General Spinner as a Religious Enthusiast," written during this period, Twain commended the honest U.S. Treasurer for not cashing a fraudulent voucher.

49.   "The Facts Concerning the Great Beef Contract," Sketches, 432.

50.   MTP: Alta California, January 21, 1868.

51.   MTP: MTNJ 1, 489; GA, 223-25.

52.   MTP: San Francisco Alta, January 21, 1868. Today, no doubt, there is a surplus of employees, both political and career, in some departments that neither the authorizing congressional committee nor the executive program manager has an incentive to address since they are too often motivated by "preserving their turf" and "expanding their empire" rather than promoting government-wide efficiency.

53.   "The Facts Concerning the Case of George Fisher," Sketches, 109, 116.

54.   Rasmussen, 328-2 (In another letter drafted for the senator, Clemens called an alderman's inquiry about water lots "atrocious nonsense," and in response to a request to change a postal route, he wrote a "complex tangle harping on Indian atrocities along the routes.").

55.   Sketches, 287, 290-91.

56.   Id, 292.

57.   AC, 30-31.

58.   GA, 217.

59.   Id., 341.

60.   MTP: New York Herald, February 3, 1868, 5c4.

61.   MT Autobiography 2, 37.

62.   Id.

63.   CY, 98.

64. *Id.: See also GA, 304 "Being now wealthy and distinguished, Mr. O'Riley, still bearing the legislative "Hon." attached to his name (for titles never die in America, although we do take a republican pride in poking fun at such trifles)."*

65. *Quote from Foner, 86.*

66. *MTP: Chicago Republican, February 8, 1868.*

67. *MTB, 1472-73; French, 191.*

68. *SLC letter to unidentified recipient in 1891 quoted in Peterson, 26 ("the smallest minds and the selfishest souls and the cowardliest hearts that God makes.").*

69. *Washington Post, December 12, 1906. Over the years, Clemens continued to take potshots at Congress. In A Tramp Abroad, Jim Baker described the character of a blue jay, "a jay hasn't got any more principal [sic] than a Congressman. A jay will lie, a jay will steal, a jay will deceive, a jay will betray; and four times out of five, a jay will go back on his solemnest promise. The sacredness of an obligation is a thing which you can't cram into no blue-jay's head." A Tramp Abroad, 37.*

70. *Paul Kane, "In Congress partisanship is no longer something to hide," Washington Post, December 7, 2011.*

71. *MTL: SLC to Laurence Hutton, February 4, 1884 (UCCL 02905).*

72. *As a result of federal legislation, most Americans breathe purer air, drink and swim in cleaner water, work, play, live, eat and save under safer conditions, travel more efficiently and safely, receive decent health care, are protected from foreign and domestic threats, and benefit from a stronger safety net.*

73. *"A Hidden World Growing Beyond Control," Washington Post, July 7, 2010, 1c1.*

74. *Kaiser, 213.*

CHAPTER FIVE
A CAPITOL REPORTER

Chapter quote is from "On Postage Rates on
Author's Manuscript," September 1882, Who Is Mark Twain?, 95.

1. *MTP: New York Evening Post, January 20, 1883. "There are more boarding houses to the square acre in Washington than there are in any other city in the land," Clemens wrote, and that is because "the population of Washington consists pretty much entirely of government employees and the people who board them." GA, 222-23.*

2. *MTP: "On Riley– Newspaper Correspondent," Buffalo Express, October 19, 1870, 244; New York Herald, May 19, 1889.*

3. *Sketches, 155.*

4. *MT Autobiography 1, 281; Neider, 201-02.*

5. *MTL: SLC to John Russell Young, December 4, 1867 (UCCL 00168), n 1. French says it was Secretary of State Seward who intervened on behalf of Swinton. French, 187; see also MT Eruption, 353.*

6. *MT Autobiography 1, 67; MT Autobiography 2, 180; Powers, 226.*

7. *MTL: SLC to Jane Clemens and Pamela Moffett, January 20, 1868 (UCCL 12725); "Concerning Gen. Grant's Intentions," New York Tribune, December 1868. In his excellent book on Mark Twain in Washington D.C., John Muller makes a discovery. He describes a similar humorous fictional interview of General Grant published in the New York Times of November 29, 1867 under the by line Scupper Nong and reprinted in the November 30ᵗʰ Philadelphia Evening Telegraph attributed to Mark Twain.*

8. *MTA-P, 72; Neider, Olivia Letters, March 2, 1868, 275.*

9. *Neider, 229; Lauber, 220.*

10. *Id.*

11. *Washington Evening Star, January 10, 1868, 1c1. According to the Evening Star, Clemens was "of medium size, a cast-iron, inflexibility of feature, frame, face, eyes that lacked expression from their neutral hue and the light color of the brown, a drawling speech, and a general air of being about half-asleep." His "slowness of speech and movement" were not a "stage mannerism;" he was "probably the laziest walker that ever stepped." He has "never been known to disgorge more than ten words per minute; and the saunter of Walt Whitman is a race-horse compared with his snail-like progress over the ground."*

12. *To the Editors of the Washington Chronicle, January 10, 1868 (UCCL 00127); MTL: SLC to Jane Clemens and Family, December 10, 1867 (UCCL 00171), n 2.*

13. *MTL: SLC to Frank Fuller, November 24, 1867 (UCCL 00158).*

14. *MTL: SLC to Orion Clemens, February 21, 1868 (UCCL 00198).*

15. *Sketches, 233, 238; see also "Journalism in Tennessee," Sketches, 44, 46.*

16. *Sketch Book, November, 1870, The Twainian, May, 1940 quoted in Peterson, 103.*

17. *"The License of the Press," ed., Neider, The Complete Essays of Mark Twain, 10-11.*

18. *Fleischman, The Trouble Begins at 8: A Life of Mark Twain in the Wild, Wild West, New York: HarperCollins, 2008, 180.*

19. *Fatout, Mark Twain Speaking, 20-21; Washington National Intelligence, January 13, 1868, (Twain suggested that he was asked to speak because he was "a trifle less homely than the other members of the Club.").*

20. *Id. Twain kept the reporters laughing with comments like: "What, sir, would the people of the earth be without women?" (The quintessential pause with a quizzical glance at the audience before providing the obvious answer in his trademark Missouri drawl.) "They would be scarce, sir, almighty scarce."*

21. *MTL: SLC to Jane Clemens & Family, January 14, 1868 (UCCL 00179).*

22. *MTB I, 359; MTP: MTNJ 1, 123-24; MTL: SLC to Jane Clemens and Pamela Moffett, February 6, 1868 (UCCL 00177) and n2. Clemens initially turned down the postmaster job when he heard that an old friend, Matthias Gilbert Upton, editor of the Alta, wanted it. Then a "complacent idiot," according to Clemens, "suddenly turned up on the inside track." Clemens got a dozen senators pledged against the "idiot", apparently a San Francisco merchant and party functionary named Charles A. Kennedy, and even persuaded Supreme Court Justice Stephen J. Field to get out of his sickbed and lobby President Johnson against Kennedy. ("It was jolly. In just no time at all I knocked that complacent idiot's kite so high that it will never come down. Then Judge Field said that if I wanted the place he could pledge me as the President's appointment – & Senator Conness said he could guarantee me the Senate's confirmation. It was a great temptation, but it would render it impossible to fill my book contract & I had to drop the idea."); SLC to Jane Clemens & Family, December 10, 1867 (UCCL 00171), n 3.*

23. *MTP: MT Letter from Washington No. 3, January 11, 1868, 2c4.*

24. *Id.*

25. *MTP: MT Letter from Washington No. 8, March 1, 1868, 2cs4-5; New York Herald, May 19, 1868, 19; Hoffman, 136.*

26. *MTL: SLC Letter to Jane Clemens, December 10, 1867 (UCCL 00171); San Francisco Alta, September 29, 1867 (MT 00568).*

27. *MTP: Washington Evening Star, November 26, 1867; see IA, 315-36.*

28. *MTP: MT Letter from Washington No. 3, January 11, 1868, 2c4.*

29. *MTP: San Francisco Alta California, February 11, 1868.*

30. *Justice Field is best remembered for his ruling for the Southern Pacific Railroad that corporations are "persons" within the meaning of the Fourteenth Amendment and therefore entitled to constitutional protections. The doctrine was recently applied in the Citizens United case to allow corporations to exercise of their Free Speech rights through unlimited funding of campaign ads.*

31. *MTP: Alta California, February 19, 1868.*

32. *Alta California, February 19, 1868 quoted in Peterson, 121-22.*

33. *MTP: MT Letter from Washington No. 2, January 7, 1868, 1 (Twain commended Senator Nye's sponsorship of a Nevada township law that he thought should be applied to all states.).*

34.   MTP: MT Letter from Washington No. 5, February 18, 1868, 2cs 5-6.

35.   MTP: MT Letter from Washington No. 4, January 30, 1868, 2c4 (Twain's Washington reports included gossip, society news and entertainment. Clemens applauded the performance of Broadway's Worrell sisters, who had started their stage career in San Francisco and toured the Nevada mining towns. Id. He mocked "the best dressed man" in Washington, Abe Curry, a real estate developer known as "the father of Carson City," who lobbied the Nevada congressional delegation to support his many investments. Curry was the stereotype of a capital phenomenon, the dandy self-promoter. Clemens had carried a grudge against Curry, who had made trouble for him over the Hopkins massacre story.).

36.   MTP: MT Letter from Washington No. 3, January 11, 1868, 2c4 (Clemens told a story of the aborted marriage between one of General Grant's staff officers, Colonel Ely Parker, the chief of six Indian nations, to a Caucasian woman. Grant had planned to give away the bride, but the marriage was called off when the tribal leaders objected to an interracial marriage.).

37.   Id.; MTL: SLC to Emily A. Severance, December 24, 1867 (UCCL 02780), n3. Clemens argued that the treaty's $150,000 cost to the Treasury paled by comparison to federal grants of a hundred million dollars to the Pacific railroads and a half-million dollars to the steamship company, the China Mail.

38.   MTP: MT Letter from Washington No. 4, January 30, 1868, 2c4.

39.   Id.

40.   MTP: New York Tribune, February 13, 1868, 2cs1-2.

41.   MTP: MT Letter from Washington No. 2, January 7, 1861, 1.

42.   Fulton, 154-55.

43.   MTP: New York Tribune, February 13, 1868.

44.   Id.

45.   MTP: New York Tribune, February 15, 1868. All Democrats voted against the bill.

46.   MTP: MT Letter from Washington No. 5, February 18, 1868, 2cs 5-6.

47.   The Lincoln Republicans established the "National Union Party" ticket in 1864, replacing the anti-slavery Vice President Hannibal Hamlin from Maine with a southern Democrat, who as a senator from Tennessee had not joined in the rebellion and who became the state's military governor during the war. Johnson, however, did not share the views of the congressional Republican majority on the reconstruction of the South.

48.   MTP: MT Letter from Washington No. 7, February 27, 1868, 2c5.

49.   MTP: Chicago Republican, February 19, 1868, 2; Washington in 1868, 23-34.

50. MTP: *Chicago Republican*, March 1,1868, 2.

51. *Id.*

52. *A New Cabinet Regulator,"* Washington Evening Star, December 14, 1867.

53. MTP: *MT Letter from Washington No. 10*, March 13, 1868, 1cs1-2.

54. MTP: *Washington Morning Chronicle*, February 22, 1868.

55. MTP: *MT Letter from Washington No. 10*, March 13, 1868, 1cs1-2.

56. MTP: *MT Letter from Washington No. 9*, March 7, 1868; Budd, 35.

57. Budd, 35.

58. MTP: *MT Letter from Washington No. 8*, March 1, 1868, 2cs4-5; Washington in 1868, 8.

59. MTP: *MT Letter from Washington No. 9*, March 7, 1868, 1cs1-3,6.

60. *Id.*

61. *Id.*

62. See D. Stewart, 240-99.

63. Clemens' journalistic assault on government corruption was not limited to Congress. In a letter to the Enterprise, Twain described an honest but lowly federal clerk who had "no rules of action for his guidance except some effete maxims of integrity picked up in Sunday school." His co-workers observed that "he never stole anything" and that "people who came to bribe him went away with a disappointed expression of disapproval in their faces." When the clerk informed the secretary of the department in which he worked that his co-workers were planning a gigantic swindle, the secretary fired him. When he informed Congress, the senators told him he had "ruined himself," and he remained unemployed to that very day. The clerk was thought to be very odd. He did not live by the creed that the "whole city was polluted with peculation and all other forms of rascality– debauched and demoralized by the wholesale dishonesty that prevails in every single department of the Washington Government, great and small." Such was the destiny of the whistle blower – then and now. MT Letter from Washington No. 9, March 7, 1868, 1cs1-3. In his continuing reports to the Enterprise, Twain criticized legislative schemes to benefit railroads and confer a monopoly on the Branch Mint. He reported on rumors of an attempt to blow up the Capitol with 180 pounds of glycerin – terrorism is not a new phenomenon. MTP: *MT Letter from Washington No. 11*, April 17, 1868, 1cs1-2.

64. MTP: *New York Tribune*, March 4, 1869; Budd, 36.

65. MTL: SLC to Orion Clemens, February 21, 1868 (UCCL 00198).

66. GA, 397.

67. Fulton, 120; MTP: *MT Letter from Washington No. 9*, March 7, 1868, 1cs1-3; MTP: *MT Letter from Washington No. 11*, April 17, 18681cs1-2.; see MT

Eruption (entry January 30, 1907), 81; Christian Science, 361:("there are Christian Private Morals, but there are no Christian Public Morals, at the polls or in Congress or anywhere else– except here and there scattered around like lost comets in the solar system. ").

68.   *MTP: New York Herald, May 19, 1889, 19.*

69.   *The Wit and Wisdom of Mark Twain, 35 (attributed).*

70.   *"Interviewing the Interviewer," January 1870, Who Is Mark Twain?, 159-63 (Twain mocked the lazy journalistic practice of making up falsehoods– a practice in which he was personally skilled. He concocted a fictitious interview with General Grant in 1870: "There is a report that Gen. Grant was drunk yesterday." "Is there any truth to it? "No, sir." "Then publish it by all means– say it is true– . make a sensation of it– invent affidavits.") When the New York Sun found it difficult to get access to important people, Twain wrote: "it matters little what people actually said anyhow, so we can get up the interview just as well in the office." Id., 162.*

71.   *Clemens had no compulsion, however, about asking Justice Field to recommend a Nevada silver mine friend, Harvey Beckwith, for the position of special revenue agent in San Francisco. Such agents were needed to catch illicit whiskey makers who evaded the two-dollar-per-gallon federal whiskey tax imposed in 1863. Johnson instead nominated Beckwith as superintendent of the U.S. Mint in San Francisco, but the Senate (in constant battle with the President) refused to confirm him. MTL: SLC to Justice Stephen Field, January 9, 1868 (UCCL 00177) and n1.*

72.   *Editorial, "Undiplomatic Senate Hold-Ups," Wall Street Journal, December 15, 2011, 18cs1-2.*

73.   *Robert Pear, "In House, Many Spoke with One Voice: Lobbyists," New York Times, November 14, 2009.*

CHAPTER SIX
A BLISSFUL ENCOUNTER
Quote from Hamlin Hill,
Mark Twain and Elisha Bliss, title of Chapter II.

1.   *MTL: E. Bliss, Jr. to SLC, November 21, 1867 (UCCL 00165) n1, (MTL:1,140); SLC to Jane Clemens and Pamela Moffett, January 24, 1868 (UCCL 00182) n3 (UCCL 48578).*

2   *MTP: "Hartford," Chicago Republican, August 17, 1868; Fears I, 256. Later, Clemens playfully commented on Hartford's full-service industries: "A city whose*

fame as an insurance center has extended to all lands and given us the name of being a quadruple band of brothers working sweetly hand in hand – the Colt's Arms Company making the destruction of our race easy and convenient, our life insurance citizens paying for the victims when they pass away, Mr. Batterson [owner of a nationally known ornamental stone business] perpetuating their memory with stately monuments, and our fire insurance companies taking care of their hereafter." "Speech on Accident Insurance," 1875, Sketches, 229.

3. *Hill, 4; Michelson, 17-18, 80-81.*

4. *Elisha Bliss responded to the criticism in a letter to the New York Tribune: "In the little towns where there are no bookstores the book agent induces people to buy. One book thus sold is read with avidity by the whole household, and when another agent comes, it is ready to buy another book. In that way, a nucleus is formed for hundreds of thousands of little libraries throughout the country, which never would have existed except for the book agent. After a few books are bought by subscription the people go to the bookstores, if there are any in their neighborhood.... There is a large field covered with people that have no opportunity to buy books except in the way we sell them." MTP: E. Bliss, New York Tribune, October 28, 1874; Hill, 10.*

5. *Albert Deane Richardson (1833-1869) was the chief war correspondent for the New York Tribune in 1860. He was captured at Vicksburg while attempting to evade confederate batteries. Eighteen months later he escaped from a confederate prison in Salisbury, North Carolina and wrote a best-selling book about his experiences. The American Publishing Company had just published another Richardson book, Beyond the Mississippi, which sold about 75,000 copies by 1869.*

6. *MTL: SLC to E. Bliss, December 2, 1867 (UCCL 00165).*

7. *MTL: SLC to E. Bliss, January 27, 1868 (UCCL 00185).*

8. *Lauber, 256.*

9. *MTL: SLC to Jane Clemens and Pamela Moffett, January 24, 1868 (UCCL 00182) n11 (SLC 1868 MT 00642).*

10. *MTL: SLC to William Bowen, January 25, 1868 (UCCL 00184); Lauber, 223.*

11. *Lauber, 256.*

12. *MTL: SLC to E. Bliss, January 28, 1870 (UCCL 00418) ("I am so satisfied in the way you are running the book. You are running it in a tip-top, first class style."); Loving, 159 (impressed with the immense success of Innocents Abroad, Twain continued writing for Bliss for more than ten years.).*

13. *Hill, 40-43, 64-67, 114-22, 152-53; W. Bliss, 2. Elisha Bliss was not a literary person. Born in Springfield, Massachusetts, in 1821, he worked in the retail dry goods business, pursuing a similar trade in New Jersey and New York City before moving to Hartford, where he worked in dry goods and then lumber. In 1867, he was appointed Secretary of the American Publishing Company, which up to that point had published only three books. In 1870, Bliss became president, reverting to secretary in 1871, and then reassuming the presidency in 1873 until his death. Under his leadership, the company became the most respected and successful subscription house. Bliss greatly expanded the number and kinds of books published– more than 50 in the first ten years. He had an instinct for popular taste, was willing to take a risk on new ventures, and, most important, recognized the value of humor in entertaining his customers. Hill, 15-16. In his obituary, the Hartford Courant wrote that Bliss was "a man of great business energy, a thorough master of the subscription book business and an excellent organizer of agencies. He was a good judge of what would suit the popular mind, and his quick perception well fitted him to select the proper agents to bring his publications before the public." The Bliss Family in America, Vol. 1, Midland, Michigan, 1982, 411 ("Genealogy").*

14. *Hill, 28.*

15. *"Mystic Man's Grandfather Published Mark Twain's Books," The Compass, May 6, 1981, 2.*

16. *Courtney, 20-25, 60-62, 102-04, 120-22. Chaplain Twichell was assigned to the New York Zoaves, decked out in turbans, fezzes and scarlet pantaloons. His commanding officer was General Daniel E. Sickles whom Twichell helped restrain as a combat surgeon amputated his leg without anesthesia at the battle of Gettysburg. Before the war Sickles had been acquitted, on a plea of insanity, for killing near the White House the son of Francis Scott Key who was having an affair with his wife.*

17. *Id.; Andrews, 25-41.*

18. *IA, 274-75.*

19. *MT Autobiography 2, 48; Powers, 269; MTB, 371.*

20. *MTL: Bliss to SLC, December 24, 1867 (UCCL 48578).*

21. *French, 8 (Innocents Abroad was Twain's best-selling book during his lifetime.); W. Bliss, 6*

22. *Rasmussen, 213.*

23. *W.D. Howells, 101.*

24. *IA, 270.*

25. *Lauber, 229.*

26. *MTL: SLC to Olivia Langdon, February 13, 14, 1869 (UCCL 00250).*

27. *Powers, 274, 282.*

28. *Buffalo Express, August 21, 1869, xxxviii.*

29. *Powers, 278.*

30. *MTL: SLC to Olivia Clemens, July 6, 1870 (UCCL 00487); SLC to Olivia Clemens, July 8, 1870 (UCCL 00488); Fears I, 323. On July 4, 1870, Clemens accompanied several New York Congressmen on a quick trip to Washington to lobby for the passage of Senate Bill 1025. The bill would have restructured the Tennessee judicial system, facilitating a lawsuit by Brown and Company against the City of Memphis for a half a million dollars owed for paving the city streets. The suit had been stalled in the crowded docket of a single judge riding the circuit among three districts. The bill would have added additional judges assigned to each district, expediting pending cases. Clemens' father-in-law had invested in the company which was headed by a nephew.*

31. *"At the President's Reception," Buffalo Express, October 1, 1870, 229, 232; MT Autobiography 2, 180.*

32. *FE, 38, 41; MT Autobiography 1, 67-68; MTL: SLC to Olivia Clemens, July 8, 1870 & n5 (UCCL 00488).*

33. *Id. at n3. Brady's portrait of Lincoln still graces the five dollar bill. After being photographed, Clemens spent a half a day in the House gallery and met with a former territorial colleague, Congressman Thomas Fitch of Nevada, encouraging him to lecture about his frontier experiences. Fitch had been editor of the Virginia City Union and had been wounded in a duel with Joe Goodman, Clemens' boss and editor of the rival Enterprise. Later Fitch became Washoe County district attorney, a member of the Nevada constitutional convention and a Republican congressman from the new state.*

34. *MTL 4, 167 quoted in Fears I, 323.*

35. *MTL: SLC to Olivia Clemens, July 8, 1870 (UCCL 00488).*

36. *MTL 4:328 quoted in Fears I, 344.*

37. *Washington National Republican, September 21, 1871; MTL 4: 454n2 quoted in Fears I, 359. "Mark Twain Takes Out a Patent– Why He Did It," He was interviewed about the invention by the Washington National Republican.*

38. *Fatout, MT Speaking, 41-48.*

39. *Andrews, 3-7.*

40. *MT Autobiography 1, 433 (Clemens "confesses" [wrongly] for the first time in his unpublished autobiography that he "was the cause of [Langdon's] illness," having suppressed for decades his "shame for that treacherous morning's work.")*

41. *MTL: SLC to Pamela Moffett, April 28, 1873 (UCCL 12784).*

42. *French, 8.*

43. *MT Autobiography 2, 50-52; Neider, 210-11.*

44. *MT Autobiography 2, 50-52; Neider, 297.*

45. *MT Autobiography 1, 370.*

46. *Id., 372.*

47. *Neider, 298.*

48. *MTB, 697. Bliss offered Clemens a seven and a half percent royalty on his second book, Roughing It, and Clemens asked for half the profits. For the first 100,000 in sales, Bliss told Clemens that he would do better with the royalty; after 200,000 the company would fare better. The contract signed by Clemens did not include language on half the profits. MT Autobiography 1, 371. "Though Bliss and Twain disagreed at times on business contracts, there is little doubt that Bliss contributed greatly to Twain's success and popularity." Genealogy, 412.*

49. *MTL: SLC to George Washington Cable, June 4, 1883 (UCCL 08821); MT Autobiography 1, 477. MTL: SLC to Pamela Moffett, April 28, 1873 (UCCL 12784).*

CHAPTER SEVEN
AN AMERICAN NOVELIST IS BORN
Chapter quote from Henry Claridge, William Faulkner, 275.

1. *MTB, 476-77; Powers, 328-29; French, 25-30 (French questions Paine's version of the inception of the novel during the winter dinner party and suggests that the idea may have been suggested by Warner on a walk to church. Another version is that Clemens said to Warner as they returned from a walk in Hartford: "let us write a burlesque on the modern novel.").*

2. *MT Autobiography 1, 206-209.*

3. *Kansas state senator Noble asked that the bribe money be used to educate the children of Kansas. A state investigation later found Pomeroy guilty of bribery. But the U.S. government, ever unable to throw stones at its own, found the evidence insufficient. As the Nation's E. L. Godkin commented: "All being corrupt together, what is the use of investigating each other." F. Kaplan, 162. Pomeroy was not re-elected and moved to Washington and then Massachusetts where he ran for President on the Prohibition Party ticket in 1884. Pomeroy's attempt to buy his re-election was not an aberration. Of the charge that Senator Guggenheim had paid the Colorado legislature to elect him, Clemens later*

conceded that this "is almost the customary way, now." Senator Guggenheim "is not aware that he has been guilty of an indelicacy, let alone a gross crime." MT Eruption, 82; French, 95; MT Autobiography 2, 410.

4. *MTL: SLC to Olivia Clemens, July 8, 1870 (UCCL 00488).*

5. *Treasury Secretary Benjamin H. Bristow launched a massive investigation. Among those not convicted was Grant's private secretary, Orville E. Babcock. The president intervened on his behalf. Much to Grant's chagrin, Bristow resigned his post and became a leader of the reformist wing of the Republican Party.*

6. *Secretary Belknap was impeached by the House, but, after his tearful resignation, acquitted by the Senate.*

7. *Enlisting the aide of the president's brother-in-law to keep the White House from intervening, Fisk and Gould purchased massive amounts of gold and gold futures sending the price into the stratosphere. To his credit, Grant, sensing a public catastrophe, ignored his brother-in-law's advice and ordered the immediate sale of four million dollars of government gold, sending the price plummeting.*

8. *MTP: MTNJ 1, 492, 494.*

9. *French, 119.*

10. *Id., 88.*

11. *Id., 85; Rudyard Kipling, Letters of Travel, Garden City: Doubleday, Page & Co., 1913, II, 180.*

12. *French, 88.*

13. *Id.; Albert R. Kitzhaber, "Mark Twain's use of the Pomeroy Case in The Gilded Age," Modern Language Quarterly, XV, March, 1954, 42-56.*

14. *Id.; Other characters are also drawn from real political and business figures. Barely disguising the names, Chairman Buckstone was Congressman Ralph P. Buckland of Ohio or Charles W. Buckley of Alabama or a composite of the two. Mr. Bigler was the former senator and governor of Pennsylvania credited with chartering Credit Mobilier, General Sutter was Ben "the Beast" Butler of Massachusetts, and Fairoaks was Congressman Oakes Ames of Credit Mobilier. Other characters were modeled on political bosses, judges and financial actors, like Boss Tweed of the New York City political machine (Wm. Weed). The fictional Wall Street financiers Duff Brown and Rodney Schaick were probably John Duff and Sidney Dillon, director and chairman of the Union Pacific respectively. Others, like Congressman Trollop, were probably composites. Id., 136; see MTP: MTNBJ 1, 492 ("large, bald" Buckland "never says anything," his "clothes hang ungainly on his shapeless body."); Congressman Hufty was*

Thomas A. Jencks of Rhode Island or John Taffee of Nebraska, Senator Simon was Senator Cameron of Pennsylvania, Spatters was Cong. James W. Patterson of New Hampshire, Hopperson was Cong. Benjamin H. Epperson of New York.

15. *GA, 323, 327-28; French, 92, 135.*

16. *GA, 533. Dilworthy was acquitted of any wrongdoing by the Senate and cast his last vote as a senator to pay every member of Congress a bonus for past work done. In this way, Twain worked into the novel a satire of the infamous Salary Grab Act.*

17. *French, 89-90.*

18. *Id., 85.*

19. *GA, 29; see also MT Autobiography 1, 206-09.*

20. *GA, 52.*

21. *Id., 62.*

22. *Id., 184.*

23. *Id., 243.*

24. *Id., 150.*

25. *Id., 183.*

26. *Id. 295-312.*

27. *French, 96.*

28. *Id., 97.*

29. *Speeches, 414.*

30. *Roughing It, 343.*

31. *French, 102; MTB, 438-40.*

32. *Roughing It, 343.*

33. *North American Review quoted in French, 98.*

34. *French, 98-99.*

35. *GA, 303.*

36. *Id., v. Chapter 62, in which Philip's perseverance pays off when he strikes a coal vein is preceded by a Rabinal-Achi, a West African proverb: La xalog, la xamaih mi-x-ul-nu qiza u quial gay, u quial agab. Id., 560. Readers could not understand this not-so-subtle attempt to satirize pretentious authors who invoke foreign phrases without explaining them. In 1899, translations were added in an appendix. The above quote reads: Is it in vain, is it without profit, that I am come here to lose so many days, so many nights?"; see W. Bliss, 18.*

37. *New York Tribune, April 23, 1873 quoted in French, 13.*

38. *Boston Evening Transcript and Hartford Times reviews quoted in Fears I, 437.*

39. *Chicago Tribune review quoted in French, 15-18.*

40. *MTP: New York Herald, December 22, 1873.*

41.   *Quoted in French, 21.*

42.   *MTP: New York Herald, December 22, 1873.*

43.   *Boston Transcript review quoted in French, 20.*

44.   *DeVoto, 286.*

45.   *Geismar, 35.*

46.   *Quinn, American Fiction: An Historical and Critical Survey, New York: Hubbard Bros, 1936, 246-47.*

47.   *Foner, 113, 93-94 (Clemens presents a "truer history than appears in many textbooks in American history.").*

48.   *Garry Wills, "Mark Twain has been gone 100 years but his Political Wisdom Endures," New York Times, 1976.*

49.   *Henry Adams, Democracy, An American Novel, New York: Henry Holt and Company, 1908; see Kaiser, 83, 90.*

50.   *Shelley Fisher Fishkin, "Mark Twain and the Stage," A Companion to Mark Twain, 259 (2005).*

51.   *Id., 264; Fears I, 467.*

52.   *Clemens was not satisfied with Raymond's performance of Colonel Sellers. Clemens thought Raymond played the role for laughs and missed the character's subtle pathos; he had called Raymond "empty and selfish and vulgar and silly." See MT Autobiography 1, 206-07; Neider, 25-26; Fears I, 467.*

53.   *In 1882, elated after completing Life on the Mississippi, Twain conspired with Howells to exploit once again the larger-than-life persona of Colonel Sellers in a new stage play: Colonel Sellers as Scientist. The two friends thoroughly enjoyed taking the eccentric speculator to new heights– as a mad scientist, drunken temperance advocate and spiritualist. John Raymond read the play but turned down the role of Colonel Sellers, no doubt recalling his rancorous relationship with Clemens during the first "Colonel Sellers" production. Alfred P. Burbank, a stand-up comedian, was recruited for the impossible task of assuming a part so clearly identified with Raymond. Renamed "The American Claimant (Colonel Sellers as a Scientist)," the new play was published in 1887. It received poor reviews at trial runs before small audiences in Rochester and Syracuse. Panned by New York City critics, it closed on its September 23, 1887 opening night at the Lyceum Theater. "Mr. Clemens lacks something, perhaps it is talent, that a playwright should possess," wrote the New York Times critic, the play "has neither plot nor action." Clemens bought out Howell's share and financed a tour of one-night stands. MTP: New York Times, September 24, 1887.*

54.   *Krugman, 17.*

CHAPTER EIGHT
THE GILDED AGE: A TALE OF CONGRESS TODAY?
Chapter quote from GA, 456-66.

1. *GA, 372-76; 378-88; French 122-23.*

2. *GA, 386-87.*

3. *French, in his study of The Gilded Age, suggests two female lobbyists who could have been the prototype for Laura: a Mrs. Straitor, the effervescent young widow of a general, who lobbied the Interior Department on Indian contracts, and a lobbyist for Jay Gould known as "the Queen," who allegedly wrote a lengthy speech for Georgia Senator Benjamin Hill in support of railroad appropriations. Mrs. Straitor's lobbying bills were paid by the notoriously corrupt Perry Fuller, whose bribery of senators during Andrew Johnson's impeachment trial facilitated Johnson's acquittal. French, 111.*

4. *Letter from Grenville M. Dodge to Anne Dodge, March 30, 1867, quoted in Jacob, 108; Emily Edson Briggs, The Olivia Letters, New York: Neal Publishing, 1906, 91-92.*

5. *Townsend, 455-57; John B. Ellis, Sights and Secrets of the National Capital, 183-84; Jacob, 109.*

6. *French, 113; Townsend, 456; Jacob, 109.*

7. *White, 103-09.*

8. *Jacob, 118-22; Kaiser, 85-86.*

9. *Jacob, 134-35.*

10. *See William T. Coleman, Jr. and Donald T. Bliss, Counsel for the Situation, Shaping the Law to Realize America's Promise, Washington D.C.: Brookings Institution Press, 2010: "In the Washington context, the counsel for the situation acts as a mediator between the private sector and government, a bridge between law and public policy. Effective counsel is able to explain to government officials how the government's statutory obligations can be met in the most efficient way and how sometimes conflicting public interest considerations can be reconciled. To function effectively government requires substantial information from the private sector and a full understanding of the consequences (intended and unintended) of the exercise of its regulatory and fiscal powers. Counsel can marshal and present complex information in a credible, skillful way that facilitates good policymaking." Id., 366-67.*

11. *OpenSecrets.org; Brill, 28; American League of Lobbyist's website (www.alldc. org); Jacob, 163 (Jacob counts 31,193 registered lobbyists in 2007).*

12. *OpenSecrets.org; Kaiser, 361-367. Presidential aspirants have promised to change Washington, campaigning against "special interests" that have "bought and sold the legislative process." President Woodrow Wilson railed against the "insidious" royally-financed lobby for high tariffs "calculated to mislead the judgments of public men." Having campaigned on a promise to change the way Washington works (and having refused to accept campaign contributions from lobbyists), President Barack Obama issued an executive order on his first full day in office affecting appointments to his administration: (1) former lobbyists were barred from working in any agency or on any subject which they had lobbied over the prior two years, and (2) every appointee was required to sign a pledge that they would not lobby the Obama administration after they leave government service. Obama further prohibited federal employees from receiving gifts from lobbyists and required lobbyists seeking to influence executive decision-making to communicate in writing for the public record. The effect of these provisions was mixed. The president granted waivers in several high profile cases, appointed former lobbyists to senior White House positions that did not require Senate confirmation, and suffered through some embarrassing set-backs, including the withdrawal of his choice of former Senate majority leader, Thomas Daschle, for secretary of health and human services. Having raised the bar, the process of appointing key officials became bogged down in lengthy back-ground checks and a number of talented prospective nominees withdrew from consideration, causing many senior level vacancies to linger on for many months into his administration. Proposals by the Obama Administration's Office of Government Ethics to eliminate exceptions for de minimis gifts ($20) and "widely attended gatherings" have drawn criticism for creating barriers that block the exchange of useful information between civil servants and the private sector.*

13. *Robert Pear, "In House, Many Spoke with One Voice: Lobbyists," New York Times, November 14, 2009.*

14. *"Puppets in Congress," Editorial, New York Times, November 17, 2009.*

15. *Dan Eggen, "Report finds blurry line between Hill and Wall Street," Washington Post, June 4, 2010, A14; see also OpenSecrets.org.*

16. *Id.; see www.citizen.org.*

17. *Financial Crisis Inquiry Commission, Financial Crisis Inquiry Report, (2011), xviii; Lessig, 83.*

18. *Eggen, supra, note 15.*

19. *Id. Despite the onslaught of lobbyists for the financial services industry, Congress passed the Dodd-Frank Financial Reform and Consumer Protection*

Act, intended to strengthen the regulation of financial institutions, although lobbyists today are busy at work seeking its repeal, which has been proposed by the president-elect and the incoming majority in both houses of Congress. Is history repeating itself?

20. Dan Eggen and Kimberly Kindy, "Most in oil, gas lobbies worked for government," *Washington Post*, July 22, 2010, A1cs1-6; see also Davis S. Hilzenrath, "Concerns about the SEC's revolving door," *Washington Post*, May 13, 2011, A12cs5-6 (219 former Securities and Exchange Commission employees filed almost 800 disclosure statements of their representation of clients or employers in dealings with the agency); See Lessig, 223 (congressional staff tenure is declining as Hill aides see government as a pathway to lucrative lobbying. From 1998 to 2004, 3,600 congressional aides have passed through the revolving door.); Kaiser, 343-44.

21. R. Jeffrey Smith and Dan Eggen, "More former lobbyists flowing to jobs on Hill," *Washington Post*, March 18, 2011, A11cs4-6; Dan Eggen "Rhetoric Aside, many incoming Republicans hiring lobbyists," *Washington Post*, December 9, 2010, A25cs1-4.

22. Brody Mullins and Danny Yardron, "Government Jobs, Outside Income," *Wall Street Journal*, June 22, 2011, A1cs3-4.

23. Love Letters, 221; MTNJ, 189, quoted in Budd, 110.

24. GA, 328. In an earlier draft of Seller's comments, Clemens had written that a great many Congressmen "have bought their seats...with money, & the whole country recognizes that as a right & legitimate; so why should anyone complain if they try to get back some of the money they have spent?" French, 67.

25. Id., 254-55.

26. Id., 143.

27. Mark Twain Speeches, 414 (1910 edition)(prepared but not delivered) quoted in Peterson, 38; best government quote is attributed..

28. MT Eruption (entry November 24, 1906), 375.

29. Kaiser, 116; http:www.fecgov/pages/fecrecord/october2011/2011pacmidyear. shtml.

30. Kaiser, 115; Lessig, 91.

31. Kaiser, 53; Lessig, 91 (quoting Cong. Tim Roemer, D-Ind, members "spend too much of their time dialing for dollars, rather than sitting in a committee room and protecting the dollars of their constituents.)

32. Kaiser, 297.

33. Id., 144-47.

34. Susan Schmidt, "Abramoff to begin sentence today," Washington Post, November 15, 2006.

35. Kaiser, 18.

36. CBS Worldwide, Inc, 60 Minutes News transcript, November 6, 2011, 5.

37. See R. Jeffrey Smith, "Lobbying for redemption," Washington Post, December 11, 2011, B1; Jack Abramoff, Capitol Punishment, New York: WND Books (2011).

38. Kaiser, 19; see also Lessig, 8 (Russell B. Long, former Chair of the Senate Finance Committee said: "Almost a hairlines difference separates bribes and contributions"; Judge Richard Posner: "the legislative system [is] one of quasi-bribery.").

39. Kaiser, 148, 356; Lessig, 125.

40. Steven Brill, "On Sale: Your Government. Why Lobbying is Washington's Best Bargain," Time Magazine, July 12, 2010, 28, 35. In 2010, Senator Evan Bayh cited as one of his reasons for not seeking reelection was that "when candidates for public office are spending 90 percent of their time raising money, that's time not spent with constituents or with public policy experts." And increasingly, money these days does not come from constituents but from well-funded out of state individuals or advocacy organizations. Ezra Klein, "In Congress, Fundraising's Steep Price," Washington Post, October 31, 2010, B3c5.

41. American Bar Association Section on Administrative Law and Regulatory Policy Task Force on Federal Lobbying Laws, "Lobbying Law in the Spotlight: Challenges and Proposed Improvements," January 3, 2011.

42. President Barack Obama, State of the Union Address to Congress, January 24, 2012, www.whitehouse.gov/blog/2012/01/24/remarks/president-obama-state-union; Editorial, "So Who is a Lobbyist?" New York Times, January 27, 2012, A20cs1-2.

43. Abramoff, 273-75.

44. "Leadership PACs: PAC Contributions to federal Candidates," Center for Responsive Politics, April 25, 2011; R. Jeffrey Smith, "Following the PAC" Washington Post, June 2, 2010, A3cs1-6.

45. Citizens United v. Federal Election Commission, 558 US 50 (2010)(The case involved an unflattering movie about Democratic presidential candidate, Hillary Clinton, aired before the primaries.) The ability of an individual to make unlimited independent expenditures on behalf of a candidate was established in 1976 in Buckley v. Valeo. In a March 2010 decision by the U.S. Circuit Court for the District of Columbia, SpeechNow.org v. Federal Election Commission, the ability of individuals to pool their resources to make independent expenditures not coordinated with a campaign was established. Citizens United extended the principle to corporations, unions, and associations, including 501c (4) tax

exempt non-profit organizations, which are not required to disclose their sources of funding.

46. *See Editorial, New York Times, April 19, 2010; American Tradition Partnership v. Bullock, 567 US____ (June 25, 2012); see Robert Barnes and Dan Eggen, "Justices reject state law, uphold Citizens United ruling," Washington Post, June 26, 2012, A7cs1-6.*

47. *Fredreka Schouten, Christopher Schnaars, and Gregory Korte, "Individuals, not corporations, drive lion's share of super PAC financing," USA Today, February 2, 2012, 7Acs2-5; Fredreka Schouten, Gregory Korte, and Christopher Schnaars, "A quarter of super PAC dough is from 5 donors," USA Today, February 22, 2012, 6Acs1-6; see also Trevor Potter, "Myths about Super PACs," Washington Post, April 15, 2012, B2cs4-5.A.*

48. *T.W. Farnam, "Mystery donor gives $10 million for attack ads," Washington Post, April 14, 2012, A6cs1-3; Dan Eggen, "The candidate Super PAC: just a branch of the campaign?" Washington Post, August 25, 2011, A13cs1-3; see also Fred Wertheimer, "How to stop super PACS," Washington Post, April 4, 2012, A17cs5-6; Dan Eggen, "Super PACs are often a friends and family plan," Washington Post, June 11, 2012, A1c1; Ezra Klein, "Disclosing the deeper ills of campaign finance," Washington Post, July 28, 2012, A2cs3-6.*

49. *GA, 399.*

50. *Tom Colburn, "Just say no to earmarks," Wall Street Journal, February 10, 2006, quoted in Lessig, 125.*

51. *"OMB Guidance to Agencies on Definition of Earmarks," www.earmarks.omb. gov.*

52. *OMB Reports on Earmarks. www.earmarks.omb.gov.; Citizens against Government Waste, www.cagw.org./reports/pig-book/2010; see also www. OpenSecrets.org/earmarks/index.php.*

53. *www.washingtonpost.com/investigations/congressional-earmarmarks-some- times-used-to..., February 15, 2012.*

54. *Matt Taibbi, "Four Amendments and a Funeral," Rollingstone.com, August 10, 2005. Senator Jeff Flake, a vociferous opponent of earmarks, who was punished by the Republican leadership until they came around to his position, once considered proposing a Pork Hall of Fame, but feared Congress would actually fund it. David M. Herszenhorn, "Earmarks Ban Exposes Rifts Within Both Parties," New York Times, November 16, 2010, A20.*

55. *Ellen Nakashima and Paul Kane, "Dozens in Congress under Ethics Inquiry," Washington Post, October 30, 2009, A1cs3-6. A staff memorandum from the House Ethics Committee, "one of the most secretive panels in Congress," was*

leaked to the newspaper. The embarrassed committee chair quickly reassured the public that "no inference should be made as to any Member." Even though several lawmakers have been under investigation for their earmarking practices, they nonetheless managed to steer a half a billion dollars of federal funding to four projects where the recipients were facing criminal probes. A leading house Democrat earmarked $2.4 million for a local company that was being investigated for diverting federal funds. The New York Sun reported in 2005 that the two New York senators had earmarked $123 million of the special wartime supplemental appropriations for New York-sited projects that the defense department had not requested in its budget proposal. In many of these cases, the recipients had made significant contributions to the senators' campaigns. Brian McGuire, "Schumer, Clinton Earmark Funds for Contributors," New York Sun, December 27, 2005; John D. McKinnon and Brody Mullins, "Defense Bill Earmarks Total $4 Billion," Wall Street Journal," December 22, 2009, A4.

56. Id. "In emails, lobbyists perceive ties between campaign cash, earmarks," R. Jeffrey Smith, "Thin wall separates lobbyist contributions, earmarks," Washington Post, March 7, 2010, A6; Washington Post, March 6, 2010, A3; Carol D. Leonnig and T.W. Farnam, "In Congress, Checks, Votes, Often Overlap," Washington Post, December 26, 2010, A1cs4-5; see also Lessig, 223-24.

57. T.W. Farnam, "Report: Ex-lawmakers lobbied for groups that got earmarks," Washington Post, January 28, 2012, A16cs1-6.

58. Kimberly Kindy, "McCaskell-led report blasts earmarks," Washington Post, December 11, 2011, A3cs3-6.

59. Lori Montgomery, "Report: 1 in 4 millionaires pays lower tax rate," Washington Post, October 13, 2011, A6cs5-6. According to the Hamilton Project at the Brookings Institute, the major annual individual tax expenditures that benefit mostly the wealthy in descending order are preferential rates on capital gains and dividends ($91 billion), state and local income, property and sales taxes ($84 billion), retirement savings ($206 billion), and employer-provided health care and other health care expenditures ($214 billion). Even the mortgage interest deduction favors the wealthy who are likely to have larger mortgages and second homes ($113 billion). Only earned income and child and dependent care tax benefits primarily benefit the poor and middle class ($76 billion). The figures are 2015 projections based on the 2012 Code. See Lori Montgomery, "Changes to tax breaks on retirement savings weighed," Washington Post, April 18, 2012, A3cs1-5.

60. Brian Kelleher Richter, Krislert Samphan Tharak, and Jeffrey F. Timmons, "Lobbying and Taxes," American Journal of Political Science 53 (2009), 893, 896, cited in Lessig, 202.

61.   Lessig, 205.

62.   GA, 322.

63.   French, 127; W. Stewart, 198-200.

64.   GA, 377-78.

65.   French, 129.

66.   White, 25, 60-62.

67   GA, 327-28.

68.   Id., 326.

69.   Id., 327.

70.   White, 66.

71.   David S. Fallis, Scott Higham, and Kimberly Kindy, "Public Projects, Private Interests," Washington Post, February 7, 2012, A1cs3-4.

72.   Scott Higham, Kimberly Kindy, and David Fallis, "Capitol Assets: Some legislators send millions to groups connected to their relatives," Washington Post, February 9, 2012, A1.

73.   Robert O'Harrow Jr. and Dan Keating, "When public duties and private investments intersect," Washington Post, June 14, 2010, A1cs1-4; Robert O'Harrow, Jr. and Dan Keating, "Moran portfolio shows Congress' leeway in trading," Washington Post, May 25, 2010, A1,18; Paul Kane and Karen Yourish, "Lawmakers held oil, gas stock," Washington Post, June 17, 2010, A3cs1-6; Washington Post, November 23, 2009, A1; Tom McGinty, Jason Zweig and Brody Mullins, "Congress Has Active Investors," Wall Street Journal, November 6-7, 1010, B1cs2-5 ("86 legislators and congressional aides on both sides of the aisle reported frequent trades of securities.").

74.   Id.; See Dennis F. Thompson, Political Ethics and Public Office, Cambridge: Harvard University Press, 1990; Dennis F. Thompson, Ethics in Congress from Individual to Institutional Corruption, Washington D.C.: Brookings Institution Press, 1995.

75.   Dan Keating, David S, Fallis, Kimberly Kindy, and Scott Higham, "Legislators traded millions in stocks they could impact," Washington Post, June 24, 2012, A1cs5-6; Kimberly Kindy, Scott Higham, David S. Fallis, and Dan Keating, Washington Post, June 25, 2012, A1c1.

76.   Lessig, 216.

77.   CBS Worldwide Inc., CBS 60 Minutes News Transcripts, November 13, 2011, 2-6.

78.   Jonathan Macey, "Congress's Phony Insider-Trading Reform," Wall Street Journal, December 13, 2011, A21cs1-3. See Letter to WSJ from Robert Khuzami, Director, SEC Enforcement Division, "Our insider trading laws already apply to Congress," December 16, 2011, 18cs3-5.

79. *GA, xxxvi.*

80. *GA, 410; GA, 409-13.*

81. *GA, 417.In his excellent book on lobbying, Robert Kaiser describes how senators help each other out with projects that are important to their home state constituents. When President George H.W. Bush and his Secretary of Defense Dick Cheney decided to terminate the nuclear attack submarine project, the Seawolf, after the collapse of the Soviet Union, the four Senators of the affected states– Connecticut and Rhode Island– exchanged favors with fellow senators to defeat the rescission. At $2 billion a copy the Seawolf had been designed to attack Soviet submarines. Pennsylvania Arlen Specter agreed to vote against the rescission if Senators Dodd, Lieberman, Chaffee and Pell would vote to save the Philadelphia Navy Yard which also was scheduled for closing. As Arkansas Senator David Pryor conceded, perhaps explaining why the federal deficit keeps growing (and why representatives of urban areas vote for farm subsidies and those from the farm belt vote for mass transit subsidies), "We all have our Seawolfs." Kaiser, 236-37.*

82. *Mann and Ornstein, Broken Branch, 19; see also Hacker & Pierson, 237, 264-71, 280-300.*

83. *Id., 36-37.*

84. *Alexander Hamilton, Federalist #22, The Federalist Papers, Oxford University Press (2008) quoted in Hacker & Pierson, 242.*

85. *Sarah Binder, Politics or Principle: Filibustering in the United States Senate, Washington D.C.: Brookings Institution, 1997; Joann Indiana Rigdon, "Filibuster Reform," Washington Lawyer, September 2012, 24 et seq.*

86. *Barbara Sinclair, "The 60-vote Senate: Strategies, Process and Outcomes," U.S. Senate Exceptionalism, ed., Bruce Openheimer, Columbus: Ohio State Press,(2002), cited in Hacker & Pierson, 242.*

87. *Mann and Ornstein, It's Even Worse, 87-91.*

88. *See Hacker & Pierson, 241-43. Incredibly, in 2010 one senator put a blanket hold on all 70 presidential nominees pending confirmation until funding was approved for a facility in his state; Al Kamen, "In the Loop," Washington Post, May 10, 2010, A16; Editorial, "A Senate in the Thrall of Secrecy," Washington Post, May 24, 2010; editorial, "The Recess Mess," Washington Post, April 3, 2010; editorial, "Secret holds - will Congress finally end them? Washington Post, May 10, 2010A1cs1-3; Scott Wilson, "Obama uses recess to fill posts." Washington Post, March 28, 2010, A4. Editorial, "Pssst, Over to You," New York Times, May 12, 2010.*

89. *E.J. Dionne and William A. Galston, "A Half-Empty Government Can't Govern, Why Everyone Wants To Fix the Appointments Process, Why It Never Happens, and How To Get It Done," Brookings Institution, December 14, 2010, cited in Mann and Ornstein, It's Even Worse, 95, 213n16.*

90. *George Packer, "The Empty Chamber," New Yorker, August 9, 2010, 38, 47; Paul Kane, "Newer Members aim to fix a broken Senate," Washington Post, March 26, 2010; Ezra Klein, After health care, we need Senate reform," Washington Post, December 27, 2009, B1cs1-2; Ed O'Keefe, "Transition Measure on way to Obama," Washington Post, October 1, 2010, B3cs5-6 (encouraging effective transition planning). See "Budget Office Held Hostage," editorial, Washington Post, October 3, 2010, A18. See also editorial, "Advise, Consent or Ignore– the broken Senate Confirmation Process gets worse," Washington Post, June 11, 2011, A14cs1-3.*

91. *In early 2011 three factors compelled the Senate leadership to modify its rules: persistent reporting on how the Senate rules were used to obstruct legislation and executive and judicial appointments, led by the press; voter frustration with Congress in the midterm 2010 elections, resulting in the defeat of many incumbents; and plummeting opinion polls registering disapproval of Congress. In June 2011 the Senate passed a reform bill 79–20 initiated by several junior senators exempting from full Senate confirmation about 200 presidential appointments out of the 1400 that currently require it and exempting another 270 positions from committee hearings before a floor vote unless a senator objects. The bill was enacted in 2012. The Senate also barred "secret" holds for more than two days by which a single senator can anonymously block appointments and legislation. After two days, the hold continues but the name of the senator placing the hold is disclosed. In his January 2012 State of the Union address, President Obama urged Congress to eliminate the filibuster on nominees to federal agencies and the judiciary and guarantee an up or down vote within ninety days. Majority Leader Harry Reid stipulated that the sixty-vote rule would continue to apply to Supreme Court nominees.*

. *The Senate also eliminated the stalling tactic by which amendments must be read in their entirety on the Senate floor when the language has been available for 72 hours and proposed to simplify on a single form the information required of a nominee. The Presidential Appointment Efficiency and Streamlining Act passed the Senate on June 29, 2011. See Carl Levin and Lamar Alexander, "Fighting Senate gridlock through self-restraint," Washington Post, April 27, 2012.*

92. Mann and Ornstein, *Broken Branch*, 21.

93. *Washington in 1868*, 34.

94. *The Leader's Lecture Series*, May 23, 2001, quoted in Terence Samuel, *The Upper House*, New York: Palgrave, Macmillan (2010), 12-13.

95. "A Little Note to Paul Bourget," *The Writings of Mark Twain*, Vol. 22, New York: Harper & Brothers, 1899, 172-73; Peterson, 100.

96. See Editorial, "California shows way on drawing new lines for Congress," *USA Today*, February, 2012, A8cs1-2; Paul Kane, "GOP Rep. Drier says he'll retire," *Washington Post*, March 1, 2012, A8cs1-2.

97. David M. Kennedy, "Throwing the Bums Out for 140 Years," *New York Times*, November 6, 2010, op-ed..

98. "Polarization is the dominant political theme of our time," William A. Galston and Thomas E. Mann, "Republicans Slide Right," *Washington Post*, May 16, 2010, A13cs1-4; Joel Achenbach, "Bipartisan? Ha. Congress Created a Desert Aisle," *Washington Post*, September 5, 2009, C1c6. Terence Samuel quotes Tennessee Senator Bob Corker: "About half of what we do in the Senate is absolutely useless…It's like an arms race. We send all these messaging votes, and then they have to send messaging votes. They are a waste of time. We take so many votes that do not matter." Samuel, 153-54. Corker found that party members are "together all the time" in strategy meetings on how to counter "the other side."; Mann and Ornstein, *It's Even Worse*, 6, 18, 23-24, 29, 36, 44-51, 51-58, 102, 136-37; Krugman, 4-7, 37, 73-74.

99. Kaiser, 261-62.

100. John Dingell, "Congress need a fresh, bipartisan start," *Washington Post*, September 9, 2011, Op-ed.

101. Id.

102. Ronald Brownstein, "The Four Quadrants of Congress," *National Journal*, January 30, 2011, cited in Mann and Ornstein *It's Even Worse*, 45; Pew Research Center, "Partisan Polarization Surges in Bush, Obama Years: Trends in American Values: 1987-2012," June 4, 2012; Dan Balz, "Politics, the Great American Divider," *Washington Post*, June 5, 2012, A2cs3-6.

103. Evan Bayh, "Why I'm Leaving the Senate," *New York Times*, February 20, 2010.

104. Olympia J. Snowe, "How the public can save the Senate," *Washington Post*, March 4, 2012, A23cs1-2.

CHAPTER NINE
A GILDED TALE OF HUMAN NATURE IN
POLITICS, THE MEDIA AND BUSINESS

Chapter quote is from
"Extracts From the Discourse of Reginald Selkirk, the Mad Philosopher,
To Her Grandeur, The Acting Head of the Human Race,"
The Bible According to Mark Twain, 76.

1.   *More Maxims of Mark, 10 quoted in Peterson, 64.*

2.   *MT Autobiography 2,409; MT Eruption, 81, January 30, 1907.*

3.   *Christian Science, 360-61.*

4.   *Id.*

5.   *GA, 478.*

6.   *Id., 397.*

7.   *See, e.g., Dana Milbank, "House Republicans' Class(lessness) of '94,"*
Washington Post, May 19, 2010, A-2, (describing the scandals involving fif-
teen Republican congressional members of the class of '94.); Paul Kane and
Carol Leonnig, "Ensign broke law, panel finds: Senate committee will refer case
involving affair cover-up to Justice for possible charges," Washington Post, May
13, 2011, A1c1; see also French, 91.

8.   *GA, 531.*

9.   *Id., 465-66.*

10. *Id., 465-69.*

11. *French, 124.*

12. *Report of the House Committee on Standards of Official Conduct, February 26,*
2010; Paul Kane and Carol D. Leonnig, "Ethics panel clears 7 in earmark
grants," Washington Post, February 27, 2010; see also Dana Milbank, "A
House Full of Rangels," Washington Post, December 6, 2010, A21c1.

13. *Editorial, "Resolution threatens power of the Office of Congressional ethics,"*
Washington Post, June 4, 2020, A18. Regrettably, twenty members of the congres-
sional black caucus introduced a resolution in 2010 that would substantially cur-
tail its powers, prohibiting the disclosure of its findings when the House committee
dismisses the complaint and restricting the initiation of investigations. In 2011,
the House pressed charges against former Ways and Means Committee Chairman
Charles Rangel and the Senate referred its findings against Senator Ensign to the
Justice Department, suggesting a somewhat tougher stance on ethics violations.

14.   *"The License of the Press," The Complete Essays of Mark Twain, ed., Neider, 10.*

15.   *"The American Press," 1888, Who Is Mark Twain?, 200.*

16.   *GA, 392-95.*

17.   *"The American Press,"1888, Who is Mark Twain? 202-05.*

18.   *Europe & Elsewhere, 96-97; MTP: "Personal Sketches," New York Evening Mail, November 21, 1867, 3. One journalist Clemens admired was William Cowper Prime, editor-in-chief of the Journal of Commerce, "one of the most respectable, useful and commercial papers," because it had "no connection with Wall Street speculations and abominations," "shares," "pools," or "stocks." Prime had decided to move to New York because he "wisely made up his mind that the best part of him can never perfectly develop into ripe bloom and fruit in the atmosphere of capitals." Id.*

19.   *Paul Kane and Scott Clement, "Poll finds congressional approval rating is lowest in two decades," Washington Post, October 5, 2011. According to one Gallop poll, the approval rating hit a low of 8 percent during 2011, settling at 11 percent at the end of the year.*

20.   *See study by Adam Thierer for the American Enterprise Institute, cited by Mann and Ornstein, It's Worse Than You Think, 59.*

21.   *"The Dervish and the Offensive Stranger," The Complete Essays of Mark Twain, 587.*

22.   *"The American Press,"1888, Who Is Mark Twain 202-05.*

23.   *Dionne, 3.*

24.   *GA, 81-82, 110-11 (Twain's first draft referred to "dried apples" instead of turnips.); see photograph of manuscript.*

25.   *FE (PW's New Calendar), 535.*

26   *GA, 456.*

27.   *See Steven Pearlstein, "This Wall Street fairy tale doesn't have a happy ending," Washington Post, October 30, 2009.*

28.   *GA, 457-58.*

29.   *Id, 565-66.*

30.   *Budd, 52-53; French, 82.*

31.   *While Clemens admired Andrew Carnegie's steel processing innovations, he was frustrated with Carnegie's overblown ego, predatory business practices, and unwillingness to support Clemens' pet projects (like the children's theatre), Clemens became disdainful of him, claiming that Carnegie "had bought fame and paid cash for it," and mocking his diminutive stature physically and morally– "he looks incredibly small, almost unthinkably small." MT Autobiography 3, 181; Shelden, 162.*

32. *SLC to Pamela Moffett, June 12, 1870 (UCCL 00479).*

33. *CY, 107.*

34. *Rasmussen, 424-25.*

35. *CY, 234.*

36. *Camfield, Sentimental Twain, 177.*

37. *During the past twenty-five years, the free market economy has misallocated trillions of dollars in speculation in housing, telecom, energy derivatives, fantasy dot.com companies, and risky investment vehicles on the theory that there are easier ways to accumulate wealth than by inventing and marketing new products. Madrick, 79, 95, 223-242, 307-389, 395.*

38. *Lessig, 76-77; Frank Portnoy, Infectious Greed: How Deceit and Risk Corrupted the Financial Markets, New York: Times Books, 2003.*

39. *Madrick, 396.*

CHAPTER TEN
MARK TWAIN AMONG THE REPUBLICANS
Chapter quote from
MTL: SLC to Miss Helene Ricard, St. Die, France, February 22, 1902.

1. *MT Autobiography 1, 452.*

2. *Branch, 287n89; May 11, 1863, Letters I, 73-76.*

3. *Branch, 78.*

4. *Id., 79; San Francisco Call, August 30, 1863: RI, 241-47.*

5. *GA, 326-28.*

6. *Powers, 192.*

7. *MTP: MTNJ 1, 130.*

8. *MTP: MTNJ 1, 143*

9. *"Adventures in Hayti," Buffalo Express; Budd, 43.*

10. *MTP: New York Times, February 12, 1901; MT, "A Lincoln Memorial," New York Times, January 134, 1907, 1; Fulton, 192-94.*

11. *Speeches, 411.*

12. *MT Autobiography 1, 316.*

13. *Id., 315, 576.*

14. *Id., 315-16.*

15. *Id., 316*

16. *MT Autobiography 1, 145; "The Private Habits of Horace Greeley" quoted in Leonard, 98-99; see Twain, "Champion of chirography of the modern*

Cincinnatus," in F. G. Welch, That Convention, or, Five Days a Politician, New York, F. G. Welch, 1872, 146, 149.

17. *Twain, "Rights of Women," December 16, 1867.*

18. *"The Secret of Dr. Livingstone's Continued Voluntary Exile," Hartford Courant, July 20, 1872, 2; MTL: Letters 5: 249-50, n4.*

19. *MTL: SLC to Thomas Nast, December 10, 1872 (UCCL 00843).*

20. *White, 84; Flood, 76.*

21. *"Running for Governor," Sketches, 311, 315.*

22. *New York Evening Post, May 9, 1879.*

23. *Hoogenboom, 1-3.*

24. *Id., 3.*

25. *MTL: SLC to Howells, September 14, 1876 (UCCL 02505). Howells wrote Clemens on August 5, 1876, that he was "about to begin a campaign life of Hayes," claiming that he "wrote the Life of Lincoln, which elected him." Howells Letters, 74. Clemens' southern cousin, Sherrard, wrote Sam a blistering letter when he learned of his support for Hayes, "who is the mere, representative, of wall street brokers, three ball men, Lombardy Jews, European Sioux, class legislation, special privileges to the few, and denial of equality of taxation, to the many– the mere convenient pimp of the bondholders and office holders."; MTL: Sherrard Clemens to SLC, September 2, 1876 (CU MARK); see also MT Autobiography 1, 528; MTL: SLC to Howells, May 1, 1877 (UCCL 01422).*

26. *"Political Views of a Humorist," New York Herald, August 28, 1876, 3; Gary Scharmhorst, Mark Twain: The Complete Interviews. Clemens found Tilden "purposefully vague" on the issues no doubt because the Democratic Party was so divided. See also Howells Letters, 76; MTP: 76 Nominations for President Hayes and Tilden (MTDP 00227). Having read Hayes' letter accepting the Republican nomination, Clemens wrote that Hayes "expresses my own political convictions." MTL: SLC to Hugh McDermott, August 6 or 7, 1876 (UCCL 05983).*

27. *Hartford quotations from Budd, 66.*

28. *Hartford speech recorded in New York Times, October 2, 1876.*

29. *GA, 223.*

30. *Hartford speech recorded in New York Times, October 2, 1876; MTP: n1 (UCCL 01371); see also Fatout, 98 (Twain:"we hope to make worth and capacity the sole requirements of the civil service"); see also MT Autobiography 2, 4,5.*

31. *Reference to "The Coming Man" in Budd, 44 ("a superbly witty warning against making some ward-heeler our new minister to England.").*

32. *New York Times, October 19, 1879; Howells Letters. 419.*

33. *MTL: SLC to Howells, Letters I, 112.*

34. *MT Autobiography 2, 424; Neider, 397.*

35. *Id.*

36. *RBHJ, 52-53 (entry December, 1876).*

37. *Hoogenboom, 53.*

38. *Id.*

39. *Id., 54.*

40. *RBHL: Illinois State Testimonial to Mrs. President Hayes, January 24, 1881.*

41. *RBHL: SLC to C.W. Stoddard, September 20, 1876.*

42. *MTL: SLC to Howells, May 1, 1877 (UCCL 01422).*

43. *RBHL: SLC to Howells, February 22, 1877.*

44. *Hoogenboom, 113; RBHL: Howells to President Hayes, February 29, 1877. Clemens also involved Howells as a conduit in seeking the appointment of a friend to head the Indian Bureau, writing that Lt. Colonel Richard Irvin Dodge (author of "The Great Plains and Their Inhabitants") "knows all about Indians and yet has some humanity"– qualities "seldom found in the same individual." Howells sent along the letter with the note: "Here's Mark Twain's contribution to your cabinet." The President telegraphed Clemens: "Dispatch received. Please communicate with the Sec'y of Treasury at Washington and proper course will be taken." RBHL: Hayes to SLC, September 20, 1877.*

45. *RBHL: President Hayes to Howells, April 5, 1878; Birchard A. Hayes to Elinor Howells, July 9, 1877.*

46. *RBHL; Hayes wrote his wife Lucy "Had a good talk with Mark Twain and like him." RBHL: RBH to Lucy, August 8, 1885.*

47. *RBHJ, 546 (entry February 14, 1890).*

48. *In April 1882, Hayes wrote Clemens that "the children of all ages in my numerous households have enjoyed your new book so much that I thank you on their and my behalf. The child in his eighth year and the child in his sixtieth and all in between them in age and of both sexes were equally hearty in the applause and delight. The Prince and the Pauper is as entertaining as Robinson Crusoe to the young Folks and the older ones see in it a most effective presentation of the inhuman criminal laws, hardly yet wiped out, of English jurisprudence, and the only defense or explanation rather, of the Puritan Codes of our ancestor." RBHL: Hayes to Mr. Clements [sic] April 6, 1882. Clemens replied promptly, claiming that due to mental telepathy (of which Clemens was then a devotee), he was in the process of writing Hayes about a dinner discussion with old friends who had rendered a "verdict" on his administration "that its quiet unostentatious, but real and substantial greatness would steadily rise into higher and*

higher prominence, as time and distance give it a right perspective, until at last it would stand out against the horizon of history in its true proportions."
RBHL: SLC to RB Hayes, April 6, 1882.

49. *RBHJ, 556, (entry March 18, 1890): Hayes described Connecticut Yankee as "another of the list of nihilistic novels," by which he meant no disparagement. He wrote that he called a "nihilist" a man who is opposed to government by the rich. The political definition of "nihilism" in vogue at the time was "a doctrine that existing social, political and economic institutions must be completely destroyed to make way for new institutions." Noah Webster, An American Dictionary of the English Language.*

50. *Hoogenboom, 92.*

51. *C.R. William, Life of Rutherford B. Hayes, Columbus: Ohio State Archeological and Historical Society, 1928, 382-84.*

52. *MTL: SLC to Howells, November 17, 1879 (UCCL 01718); Howells Letters, 139.*

53. *MTL: SLC to Howells, June 15, 1880 (UCCL 01812).*

54. *Budd, 82.*

55. *MTL: SLC to James A. Garfield, January 12, 1881 (UCCL 01891); MTB, 702.*

56. *MTB, 710.*

57. *MTNJ quote from Budd, 157.*

58. *MTB, 711.*

59. *Hoogenboom, 129-43.*

60. *Fears I, 979.*

61. *MTL: SLC to Howells, February 27, 1885 (UCCL 02605); Fears I, 1017. Cable's faith-based advocacy for African- American rights may have influenced Twain's poignant portrait of Huck Finn's troubled conscience as Huck weighed his loyalty to the slave Jim against eternal damnation. Twain was struggling with the novel at the time. But Cable's sanctimony began to wear a bit thin. During the trip to Washington, Clemens wrote to Howells that he was tiring of Cable's religiosity: "He is pleasant company. . . We do not quarrel. . . but in him & his person I have learned to hate all religions. He has taught me to detest the Sabbath-day & hunt up new and troublesome ways to dishonor it."*

62. *MTL: SLC to Livy, March 2, 1885n (UCCL 03180).*

63. *MTL: SLC to Livy, March 4, 1885 (UCCL 03183); MT Autobiography 2, 70; Flood, 135-36; Perry, 159; MTNJ 3, 168.*

64. *MT Autobiography 2, 71-73; Neider, 330; MT Autobiography 1, 66-98.*

65.   Perry, 232. Perry suggests that Twain's reference in the Notice per order of GG in the preface of Huckleberry Finn is a tribute to Grant. Other scholars believe that the tribute is to Twain's longtime butler and a former slave, George Griffin. See also Flood, 245.

66.   Mark Twain, The Mysterious Stranger, ed. William M. Gibson, Berkeley: University of California Press, 1969 quoted in Budd, 208.

CHAPTER ELEVEN
MARK TWAIN THE MUGWUMP
Chapter quote from
Interview, New York Herald, August 28, 1876;Mark Twain:
The Complete Interviews, 6.

1.   Fatout, 182-83.

2.   MT Autobiography 1, 315-319.

3.   Zachary Karabell, Chester Alan Arthur, New York: Henry Holt & Co. (2004), 132.

4.   MT Autobiography 1, 316-17; See also Albert Bigelow Paine's version of the billiard room conversations. MTB, 778-80.

5.   MTL: SLC to Charles Erskine Scott Wood, November 5, 1884 (UCCL 11996).

6.   From MTNJ, 202-03 quoted in Carter, 250.

7.   MT Autobiography 1, 316-17.

8.   Id., 317.

9.   MTL: SLC to Howells, September 17, 1884 (UCCL 02587).

10.   MTL: SLC to Pierce, October 22, 1884 (UCCL 03011).

11.   CY, 158-59.

12.   From "A Tribute" quoted in Carter, 251.

13.   MT Autobiography 1, 317. Warner's resignation from the Courant is disputed in Andrews, Nook Farm, 115; Clemens later chastised him for continuing to work for the Courant. MT Autobiography 1, 577.

14.   Id., 316-18.

15.   Fulton, 191.

16.   MT Autobiography 1, 315.

17.   Christian Science, 360. At Carnegie Hall on January 22, 1906, Twain spoke in honor of the 25th anniversary of the Tuskegee Institute: Twain argued, "There are Christian Private Morals, but there are no Christian Public Morals." According

to Twain, "every born American ... let his creed or destitution of creed be what it may, is indisputably a Christian to this degree– that his moral constitution is Christian." Clemens continued, "For 363 days a year, the American observes these Christian private morals in domestic and commercial life, keeping "undefiled the Nation's character at its best and highest; then in the other two days of the year he leaves his Christian private morals at home, and carries his Christian public morals to the tax office and the polls and does his best to damage and undo his whole year's faithful and righteous worth." At the polls, "he will vote against the best man in the whole land if he is on the wrong ticket." It is undisputed "that there are two kinds of Christian morals, so unrelated that they are no more kin to each other than are the archangels and politicians." MT Autobiography 1, 306.

18.   MT Eruption, 2.

19.   Municipal Corruption," Speeches, 121; see also James S. Leonard and James Wharton Leonard, "Mark Twain and the Anti-Doughnut Party," Mark Twain Annual No. 9 (2011), 10.

20.   "Proposed Casting Vote Party," Europe and Elsewhere, 236-37; MTB, 1147.

21.   MTB, 779-80; "Christian Citizenship," Colliers (1950); See also Harris, 38.

22.   MT Autobiography 1, 389.

23.   From "Consistency," Speeches, 130, quoted in Carter, 252.

24.   George Washington, Farewell Address, 1796, http://avalon.law.yale.edu/18th_century/washing.asp.

25.   GA, 530-31.

26.   Edmund H. Yates, Celebrities at Home (London, 1879, Third. Ser.), 141; Budd, 80.

27.   Interview, New York Herald, November 12, 1905.

28.   MT Autobiography 1, 318.

29.   Late one frosty night, shortly before the 1884 election, Clemens, his friend the Rev. Joseph Twichell and the Rev. Francis Goodwin were "tramping home through the deserted streets in the face of a wintery gale." They had just attended a meeting of the Monday Evening Club at which, during a heated political debate, the three had been identified as traitors for vowing not to vote for Blaine. Goodwin, a highly respected Episcopalian minister and civic leader, suggested that instead of simply pocketing three votes, they should cast them for Cleveland, thereby marshaling six votes for the defeat of Blaine. They agreed to do so. Twichell probably voted for the Prohibition candidate, and according to Clemens, it nearly cost him his ministry, as a group of staunchly Republican elders narrowly failed to convince the congregation to remove him from the pulpit. Clemens never faulted Twichell for reverting to the safe Republicanism of Hartford society. "He sacrificed his

political independence, and saved his family by it," which Clemens thought was *"the highest loyalty and the best." Id., 318-19, 577.*

30. *Graff, 37-40, 72-77.*

31. *Twain-Howells Letters, 237. .*

32. *Robert McNamara, "The Election of 1884 Between Cleveland and Blaine was Marked by Scandals," http://history1800s.about.com/od/presidentialcampaigns/a/election of 1884.htm.*

33. *Graff, 96.*

34. *MTL: SLC to President Cleveland, September 23, 1885 (UCCL 03290).*

35. *MTL: Letter from President Cleveland to Mark Twain, September 24, 1885.*

36. *MTP: MTNJ 3, 211.*

37. *Budd, 80. For men he admired and personally liked, Clemens was incredibly forgiving when their policies and practices were diametrically opposed to his principles: Hay (an expansionist secretary of state), Grant (presiding over a corrupt administration), and Henry Rogers (a Standard Oil tycoon).*

38. *MTL: SLC to Twichell, November 4, 1904 (UCCL 06945). At Secretary State John Hay's 67th birthday celebration, Twain praised the man who rose from rural Illinois to national prominence, declaring that "It could not have happened in any other country. Our institutions give men the positions that of right belong to them through merit… not by heredities, and not by family influences or extraneous help." "Sixty-Seventh Birthday," Speeches, 363, 371-72. (To make his point, Clemens overlooked the facts that Hay was the beneficiary of a private school education who at 22 through a classmate contact was appointed a private secretary to the revered Lincoln, that he had married into a wealthy Cleveland family, and that as Secretary of State he had advanced the imperialist policies of McKinley and Theodore Roosevelt.)*

39. *MTL: SLC to Livy, January 28, 1886 (UCCL 03361).*

40. *"Books Reviewed," New York Times, December 6, 1886, 3.*

41. *In a return trip to Washington on October 24, 1886, Clemens met with General Philip H. Sheridan. They signed a contract in early November, and the general's Personal Memoirs was published in 1888. Webster & Co. also published books by the widows of General Winfield Scott Hancock and General George A. Custer of Little Big Horn fame, and a book by General Samuel Wylie Crawford, Genesis of the Civil War: The Story of Sumter. In 1890 Webster published a later edition of the Memoirs of Gen. W.T. Sherman. MTP: Letter of Introduction, October 26, 1886; Fears II, 94; Brooklyn Eagle, May 11, 1891, 6.*

42. *"Banquet Hall Orators," New York Times, December 5, 1886, 2 (may be apocryphal.).*

43. *"Mark Twain's Speech," Washington Post, February 4, 1889, 2.*

44. *Clemens hung around Washington until the Senator would see him, but Jones kept brushing him off. To pass the time, he spoke to the national wholesale druggist association. He returned again to Washington on October 1 seeking to persuade Jones to bring additional investors into his failing enterprise. On January 15, 1891, Clemens finally secured a meeting with Jones, which lasted about two minutes, before being interrupted by urgent Senate business.*

45. *On February 13, 1891, the senator wrote Clemens, declining to invest in the Paige contraption because the smart money was now being invested in Mergenthaler's Linotype. Clemens wrote back desperately that if Jones had given him a half hour of his time "instead of two minutes," he would have convinced the senator that his investment would be "fully protected." Jones, who represented Nevada, had profited greatly from the Comstock Silver Lode and was a cohort of Stewart. He had been president of the Hartford Accident Insurance Company and had guaranteed Clemens' investment in that company. When the company failed in March 1878, Clemens received full restitution of $23,000. F. Kaplan, 306. How could Clemens reconcile his frequent lobbying visits to the capital with his satire of the Washington lobby in The Gilded Age? There is no indication that Clemens acted unscrupulously in his contacts with members of Congress. His celebrity stature granted him access, but he had to make his case on the merits. He explained to Livy that lobbying for a good cause was exercising responsible citizenship. That is why he tirelessly answered the call of his fellow authors to lobby for copyright reform.*

46. *MT Autobiography 2, 79-80. Always fascinated with science and technology, Clemens spent much time in Nikola Tesla's laboratory and had patented three inventions: an adjustable garment strap, a history trivia game and his financially successful self-pasting scrapbook. As a former printer's devil, he was intrigued by the Paige typesetter's technology, which he believed would replace the slow process of loading a composing stick. When it worked, the Paige machine was a marvel to observe: 18,000 parts typing more accurately and at seven times the speed of human typesetters. But it was prone to breakdowns. Clemens poured $300,000 into it (about seven million in today's dollars), losing most of his books' profits and much of his wife's inheritance. Before the Paige machine could be perfected, the Linotype made it obsolete. Fears II, 583. The Paige compositor was not his only dry hole. His friendship with a Quaker City pal, Dan Slote, took a bad turn when photoengraving made obsolete their investment in the Kaolatype chalk-plate picture printing process. He invested in a steam pulley*

and an insurance scheme. Clemens' bad investments and his publishing company's failure (after overreaching on a biography of Pope Leo XIII and a compendium of literary humor) led to his bankruptcy. A Washington Post columnist caustically commented: "One good way to locate an unsafe investment is to find out whether Mark Twain has been permitted to get in on the ground floor." Clemens confided to a reporter that he had been "swindled out of more money than there is on the planet." Columnist, Washington Post, January 27, 1908 quoted in Shelden, 155.

47. *MTL: SLC to Livy, November 10, 1893 (UCCL 04495).*

48. *MTL: SLC to Grover Cleveland, February 23, 1886 (MS: DLC,# 03371); MT Autobiography 1, 390-91; MTL: SLC to Ruth Cleveland, November 3, 1892 (MS: DLC # 02398).*

49. *Neider, 422.*

50. *"Municipal Corruption," Speeches, 122.*

51. *MTL: SLC to John Y. MacAlister, December 12, 1900 (#05943).*

52. *"The Privilege of the Grave," September 1905, Who Is Mark Twain?, 57-58.*

53. *Christian Science, 41; Leonard, 108.*

54. *Chicago Times, January 27, 1876, quoted in Budd, 62.*

55. *MTP: Introduction 1876-80 (MTDP 00213); MTL: SLC to Mary Fairbanks, February 6, 1880 (UCCL 01758).*

56. *Phipps, 160; MT Eruption, January 28, 1907, 71-72.*

57. *"Mark Twain in White Greets 1907," New York Tribune, January 1, 1907; Shelden, 5.*

58. *New York Herald, March 11, 1906.*

59. *MT Eruption, January 28, 1907, 71-72.*

60. *GA, 532.*

61. *MT Autobiography 2, 387-90; see also Shelden, 15-19.*

62. *Speeches, 121.*

63. *MT Autobiography 1, 314; "Votes for Women," Speech to the Hebrew Industrial School for Girls, Speeches, 101-03.*

64. *Mark Twain's Speeches (1884) quoted in Political Tales and Truth, 19-20; Peterson, 74.*

65. *Phil Keisling, "To Reduce Partisanship, Get Rid of Partisans," New York Times, March 22, 2010, op-ed.*

66. *Matt Miller, a senior fellow at the Center for American Progress, has urged a wealthy individual to fund a ballot access drive for the 2012 election that would enable a third party candidate to emerge who would be a centrist problem-solver,*

unconstrained by party ideology. Frustrated independents may gravitate toward a third party, but a third party may have unintended consequences. It may capture centrists' votes and tilt the election to the most extreme of the two party candidates. It may result in no candidate securing a majority of the Electoral College which would throw the election into the House of Representatives, where each state has one vote and smaller states a disproportionate advantage. Even if an independent candidate is elected president, she or he would have no support from her or his party in Congress. Third Party candidates often take courageous stands on issues that the major candidates are too timid to tackle. John Anderson opposed ethanol subsidies in the Iowa debate, and Ross Perot was among the first to raise concerns about the rising federal debt. Americans Elect has written electoral rules so that if there is a three-way plurality, it would pledge to vote for the most reasonable and centrist candidate. See Matt Miller, "How billionaires could save the country," Washington Post, September 1, 2011, Op-ed.

CHAPTER TWELVE
THE SEEDS OF DEMOCRACY
Chapter quote from
The Complete Essays of Mark Twain, ed., Charles Neider, 583.

1. *MTL: SLC to Jane Clemens and Family, June 1, 1867 (UCCL 00132).*
2. *The Celebrated Jumping Frog of Calaveras County, and Other Sketches, 127.*
3. *"The Late Benjamin Franklin," Sketches, 275.*
4. *"Americans and the English," Speeches, 413-14.*
5. *"Plymouth Rock and the Pilgrims," Speeches, 17, 21.*
6. *"Americans and the English," Speeches, 413-14; Randall Knoper, "Mark Twain and Nation," A Companion to Mark Twain, 5-6.*
7. *CY, 540, 565, 569-71. Some scholars have suggested that the real satire of Connecticut Yankee is not the evils of feudalism but the evils of technology in the hands of flawed human beings with "superstition" in their "blood and bones." Industry and the economy were obliterated, foreshadowing the evil consequences of a totally technology-driven materialistic society, ultimately leading to nuclear annihilation. For thoughtful commentary on the political message of Connecticut Yankee, see Patrick Deneen and Joseph Romance, Democracy's Literature: Politics and Fiction in America, and Catherine H. Zuckhert, Natural Right and the American Imagination: Political Philosophy in Novel Form.*

8.   *MTL: SLC to Mary Fairbanks, August 6, 1877 (UCCL 01467).*

9.   *Letter from SLC to Howells, August 5, 1889 (UCCL 03924); Twain- Howells Letters, 276; Carter, 144-45; Geismar, 108, 214; Foner, 138.*

10.   *GA, 530-31; see also 302.*

11.   *CY, 387; Geismar, 121.*

12.   *Carter, 356.*

13.   *MTL: Letters I, 289 quoted in Carter, 358.*

14.   *Quote from Geismar, 202-03.*

15.   *FE, 195 (PW's New Calendar); MTP: MTNJ # 32b (entry June 22, 1897), 72.*

16.   *"The Privilege of the Grave," September 1905, Who Is Mark Twain?, 55.*

17.   *"The American Vandal," Mark Twain Speeches, 29-30; Carter, 304.*

18.   *Id.*

19.   *IA, 650.*

20.   *MTP: MTNJ #32b, 70.*

21.   *Loving, 308.*

22.   *Address to the Young Men's Christian Association at the Majestic Theatre, New York, March 4, 1905, MT Speeches, 136.*

23.   *"Education and Citizenship," Speeches, 147-48.*

24.   *Id., 147.*

25.   *JA, 7.*

26.   *1601, and Is Shakespeare Dead?, 127-28.*

27.   *GA, 60.*

28.   *FE, 598.*

29.   *AC, 94-107.*

30.   *"Public Education Association," Speeches, 144, 146.*

31.   *"As Regards Patriotism," A Pen Warmed Up, 44-46.*

32.   *Id.*

33.   *Id.*

34.   *Id.*

35.   *New York Times, March 17, 1901.*

36.   *MTNJ, ch 25 quoted in Peterson, 83-84.*

37.   *Quoted in Budd, 184.*

38.   *"Educating Theatre-Goers," Speeches, 71-73; "The Educational Theater," Speeches, 74-76.*

39.   *Id.*

40.   *Id.*

41.   *Editorial, "Students of History, How to Make Civics a National Priority Again," Washington Post, June 6, 2011, A14.*

42. *Id. Former Supreme Court Justice Sandra Day O'Connor has launched an initiative involving colorful virtual games to empower students with knowledge about how their government works. Not surprisingly, Supreme Court Justices like O'Connor, Kennedy and Breyer are among those most active in promoting school programs to increase public understanding of how our government works. As representatives of the judicial branch, which has no power to enforce its decisions and which depends upon public acceptance of time-tested adversarial procedures and reasoned decision-making, the Justices should be concerned.*

43. *The Curious Republic of Gondour and Other Whimsical Sketches; Leonard, 100; Carter, 356. How did Clemens reconcile his views on the voting rights of women and minorities and his elitist, Whig-inspired skepticism of universal suffrage? As his views matured, he recognized that smart, educated and informed women and minorities should vote – and democracy would be better off for it. Race, ethnicity or gender should not restrict the participation of informed citizens in democratic self-government. Freed of artificial constraints of class, race and gender, American democracy would thrive if informed voters wisely exercised their citizenship responsibilities.*

44. *HF, 49-50; Budd, 96.*

45. *"The Quarrel in a Strong Box," November 1897, Who Is Mark Twain?, 71, 74-75.*

46. *MTNJ, 400-01.*

47. *AC, 22.*

48. *Id., 230-31.*

49. *CY, 159; Geismar, 118.*

50. *MTL: SLC to Livy, November 10, 1893 (UCCL 04495); see also Oppenheimer and Edwards, Democracy Despite Itself.*

CHAPTER THIRTEEN
MARK TWAIN SOCIAL ACTIVIST
Chapter quote from
"Concerning the Jews,"
The Complete Essays of Mark Twain, ed. Charles Neider, 236.

1. *MTB, 371. In the West, Clemens befriended Unitarian Ministers like Henry Bellows of San Francisco, founder of the precursor to the American Red Cross, The United States Sanitary Commission, which provided battlefield medical relief during the Civil War. He also enjoyed the company of Virginia City Episcopal*

Minister Frank Rising, who joined him on the trip to the Sandwich Islands and was tragically killed in the Ohio River steamboat explosion on December 19, 1869 that was fictionalized in The Gilded Age. As he moved East, Clemens sincerely tried to adopt Livy's progressive Protestantism, the "social gospel" espoused by the Langdon family's Elmira Park Street Church led by the eccentric Thomas K. Beecher, brother of Henry Ward Beecher of Plymouth Church in Brooklyn. See Debby Applegate, The Most Famous Man in America: The Biography of Henry Ward Beecher. Clemens' closest adult friend was Joseph Twichell, a disciple of Horace Bushnell's liberal Congregationalism. In their long walks in the woods, they were often joined by Episcopal Minister Frances Goodwin. New England was in the thralls of Emerson's Transcendentalism, influenced by eastern religions, its "oversoul" a New England adaptation of the Hindu Brahman. In his later years, Twain became very close to Unitarian Henry Huddleston Rogers who helped him through his financial difficulties. See Lewis Gaston Leary, Mark Twain's Correspondence with Henry Huttleston Rogers 1893-1909, 468 n1. His English literary agent, Moncure D. Conway started out as a Methodist Minister, studied under Emerson and became a Unitarian Minister and then founded a London ethical society.

2.   *Neider, 125-27.*

3.   *Foner, 170.*

4.   *Id.; MTP: MTNJ 1, 110.*

5.   *Clara Clemens, Awake to a Perfect Day My Experience with Christian Science, New York, 1956.*

6.   *Dwayne Eutsey, "Following the Equator to the Horizon Rim of Consciousness: Mark Twain en route to India and Beyond," presentation at Elmira College Center for Mark Twain Studies, October 16, 2010.*

7.   *Philip S. Foner in 1958, Maxwell Geismar in 1973, Louis J. Budd in 2001, among others, have thoughtfully addressed many of these issues in scholarly works that are commended to the reader.*

8.   *FE (PW's New Calendar), 132. Clemens often recorded pithy aphorisms in his Notebook, which he later included in speeches or publications, such as this one in PW's New Calendar.*

9.   *MTP: AD, "Creed" 1880; Foner, 174; Shelden, 192; AD, January 13, 1908, June 25, 1906.*

10. *Clemens did not define the "other immoralities." What were they? Some faiths prohibit smoking, drinking, homosexuality, pre-marital sex and adultery. Were these universal moral values or simply pious strictures of particular sects? Clemens didn't delve too deeply into this quagmire.*

11. *1601 and Is Shakespeare Dead?, ii.*

12. *Geismar, 470.*

13. *MTP: AD, January 13, 1908; MT Eruption, 315; June 25, 1906.*

14. *Geismar, 380. In his visit to heaven, Captain Stormfield expressed surprise that with all the psalm singing, praying and halos, heaven has "left entirely out it, the supremest of all his delights, the one ecstasy that stands first and foremost in the heart of every individual of his race – and of ours– sexual intercourse." Id., 514.*

15. *MTB, 1357, 63.*

16. *FE, 476-77.*

17. *For Twain, "The Being who is to me the real God is the One who created this majestic universe and rules it.... His real character is written in the plain words in His real Bible, which is Nature and her history..." Nature is not a consoling God. "The Book of Nature tells us that His laws inflict pain and suffering and sorrow." This is not because he is the vengeful, anthropomorphic God of the Old Testament, bringing floods, earthquakes, and epidemics as punishment. Rather, the laws of Nature are indifferent to human experience, getting no pleasure out of misery and showing an "entire absence of sentimental justice." MTB, 1583; Carter, 149: see also FE, 132; MTB, 1355-57. Twain's evolving concept of God embraced western and eastern religious concepts, tempered by evolution and scientific pragmatism. According to Paine, Twain thought that the stories and themes of the Bible were rooted in Chinese, Hindu, Egyptian, Greek and Roman traditions– the "Golden Rule" was borrowed from Confucius. "Human beings" need to "revise" their conception of God. "Most of the scientists have done so already but most dare not say so." MTB, 1357; LeMaster, 324.*

18. *Geismar, 534. Integrating his views about evolution and morality, Twain wrote in his Autobiography that physiologically, man is inferior to the animals in strength, speed, eyesight, and endurance, but he excels in "one great and shining gift– intellectuality." No beast or fowl can outrun the locomotive; no condor could out see the telescope or microscope. The strength of the tiger or elephant pales next to the force of the gun. In the evolutionary chain, man is a pauper, but "by grace of his intellect, he is incomparably the richest of all the animals now." But he is still "a pauper in morals– incomparably the poorest of creatures.... The gods value morals alone...If intellect is welcome anywhere in the other world, it is hell, not heaven." MT Autobiography 1, 186-87.*

19. *Letters from Hawaii, 175-76; Mark Twain in Hawaii, 24; Foner, 192.*

20. *IA, 261; Foner, 194-95.*

21. *Powers, 243.*

22. *"The International Lightning Trust," Mark Twain Fables of Man, ed. John Tuckley, 1972.*

23. *MTNJ, 313 quoted in Carter, 177.*

24. *Garry Wills, Under God, The Classic Work on Religion and American Politics, New York: Simon & Schuster, 1990.*

25. *IA, 258; Foner, 194.*

26. *MTP: MTNJ #32(b)(II), 38 quoted in Foner, 196.*

27. *MTP: Editorial, Alta California, November 29, 1867, 2c2. An 1867 editorial in the Alta California referred to the accounts given by Twain and other travelers in Italy of "the vast amount of wealth locked up in the treasury of the Papal Church." "The time will come," the editorial naively predicted, when "this useless hoard will pass into the general wealth of the country, and impoverished Italy will gain something of value."*

28. *CY, 191; Europe and Elsewhere, 128; Carter, 178.*

29. *CY, 118; Foner, 197-98. In The Mysterious Stranger, his 1898 allegory masterpiece, Twain explains that established religion is simply a means by which oppressive minorities dominate the majority of the people who are "secretly kindhearted" and passive, capitalizing on a "large defect" in the human race who, like sheep, "don't dare to assert themselves." Democracy fails because "monarchies, aristocracies, and religions are all based on that large defect." The Mysterious Stranger, 117-18 quoted in Carter, 179. In his last major work, Following the Equator, Twain referred to his first experience with an established church– his visit to the Sandwich Islands. He praised Liholiho, who was both a King and a reformer (which is like "mixing fire and gunpowder"). Liholiho destroyed the native "Established Church, root and branch," eliminating both the royal power emanating from the divine right, "the best friend a King could have," and the instrument that had oppressed, terrorized and enslaved his people. FE, 53-54. In abolishing the indigenous religion, Liholiho created a vacuum into which the Christian missionaries moved with dubious consequences.*

30. *CY, 118.*

31. *Quote from Shelden, 77.*

32. *CY, 118.*

33. *Id., 216*

34. *Id., 158. In Following the Equator, Twain singled out for special praise the Province of South Australia as a "hospitable home" for "every religion," listing some 65 different denominations and sects flourishing in a "healthy religious atmosphere." FE, 181-83.*

35. *MTNJ, ch 21 quoted in Peterson, 23.*

36.   *Shelden, 228.*

37.   *"Education and Citizenship," Speeches, 147-49; See also MT Eruption, 50.*

38.   *Shelden, 227,*

39.   *"Tammany and Croker," Speeches, 114, 117.*

40.   *"Extract from Captain Stormfields Visit to Heaven."*

41.   *Quote from Foner, 170.*

42.   *MTB 2, 764.*

43.   *MTP: MTNJ #32 b, 63.*

44.   *FE, 507. In a visit to Benares, Clemens met a Hindu ascetic, Sri 108 Swami Bhaskarananda Sarawati (for his 108 names) who sat naked on a rug in a garden to meditate and read the sacred scriptures. The people considered him a god. His disciple, Mina Bahadur Rana, had given up a high government position and all his worldly wealth to study religion under him. Twain noted that Christians, who revere priests and ministers who heed Christ's calling, scoffed at the Hindu calling him a crank. Reverence for one's own sacred beliefs and its followers, Twain contended, is without special merit. "The reverence which is difficult, and which has personal merit in it, is the respect which you pay, without compulsion, to the political or religious attitude of a man, whose beliefs are not yours." Although one is not expected to revere his gods or his politics, Twain said, "you can respect him...But it is very, very difficult...So we hardly ever try." FE, 514; see also Washington Post, July 15, 2011, A8cs1-6.*

45.   *MT Autobiography 1, 212.*

46   *Id, 211.*

47.   *MTL: SLC to Jane Clemens, August 24, 1853 (UCCL 02711); SLC to Orion Clemens, November 28, 1853 (UCCL 00003) (As a teenager, Sam shared with Orion his prejudice against immigrants as well: "so many abominable foreigners here...who hate everything American, and they are whiskey-swilling, God-despising heathens.").*

48.   *Dred Scott v. Sandford, 19 Howard 393 (March 6, 1857). For only the second time in the nation's history, the Supreme Court declared an act of Congress unconstitutional – the Missouri Compromise –ruling that Congress had no authority to abolish slavery in the territories because slaves were property protected by the Fifth Amendment. That anchor of the Bill of Rights, intended to accord "due process of law" for all Americans, was turned on its head and invoked to protect the "property rights" of slave owners and deny due process and liberty to one-third of all Americans. In North and South, the nation's great universities, scientists, ministers, statesmen and educators, with very few exceptions, accepted Negro inferiority as a scientific fact. Menand, 8, 87, 97, 116.*

49. *George Frederickson, Big Enough to be Inconsistent, Abraham Lincoln Confronts Slavery and Race, Cambridge, MA: Harvard University Press, 2008,109-114; See also Eric Foner, Our Lincoln, New Perspectives on Lincoln and his World, New York: W. W. Norton, 2010. Lincoln felt powerless to abolish constitutionally protected slavery in the South. He opposed its extension to the territories. When the southern states seceded, he invoked his constitutional war powers to emancipate the slaves in the states of secession. He did not live to see the ratification of the Thirteenth Amendment.*

50. *See generally Fulton and Richard Kluger, Simple Justice, New York: Knopf, 1975.*

51. *Kluger, Simple Justice; John Hope Franklin, From Slavery to Freedom: A History of Negro Americans, New York: Knopf, 1947.*

52. *"A True Story," Sketches, 202.*

53. *Howells, "Review of Sketches New and Old," Atlantic Monthly, December 1875, quoted in Foner, 262.*

54. *HF, 272.*

55. *PW, Hartford: American Publishing Company, 1894.*

56. *Id. Although Pudd'nhead Wilson was published in 1894, Clemens had long been fascinated by racial classifications. See Fears I, 136. In an article for the Territorial Enterprise in 1865, he crudely satirized a July 4th parade in which the white men marched first, followed by the light-skinned "colored" men, in "nicely graduated shades of darkness." Bringing up the rear were the dark-skinned Negros "so that no man could tell where the white folks left off and the niggers began." Fears 1, 136.*

57. *Id. Three years after the publication of Pudd'nhead Wilson, the Supreme Court issued the infamous decision of Plessy v. Ferguson, 163 U.S. 537 (1896), upholding state segregation laws and establishing the "separate but equal" doctrine that sanctified the practice of racial apartheid in the United States until it was overruled by a unanimous Supreme Court in Brown v. Board of Education in 1954, 347 U.S. 483 (1954). At issue was a Louisiana law requiring separate rail cars for blacks and whites. Mr. Plessy, who purchased a first-class rail ticket in New Orleans and attempted to sit in a white-only car, was one-eighth Negro and easily passed for white. The suit was brought as a test case in conjunction with the railroads which objected to the extra cost of adding additional rail cars. The stipulated facts stated that skin color was not an issue. The Supreme Court held that states could separate the races for reasons of public order, culture and tradition as long as equal facilities were provided. Equal facilities rarely ever were. Clemens could hardly have predicted that more than a half century of racial*

segregation would be sanctioned by a Supreme Court decision that rested on the fallacious racial premise he had satirized in Pudd'nhead Wilson.

58. *Twain foreshadowed the argument that would be made in the Brown v. Board of Education cases challenging the laws of public school racial segregation. Expert witness sociologist Kenneth Clark's doll studies (which recently have been updated with similar effect) showed that when little black children in segregated schools were shown white and black dolls, they preferred the white dolls because they were conditioned to see them as prettier and smarter. See Kurland and Casper, Landmark Briefs and Arguments of the Supreme Court, Bethesda, MD: University Publications of America, 1975, 33-43.*

59. *MT Autobiography 1, 302-09 (Booker T. Washington stated in his address: "No two groups can live side by side where one is in ignorance and poverty, without its condition affecting the other. The black man must be lifted or the white man will be injured in his moral and spiritual life. The degradation of one will mean the degradation of the other." Id., 309.)*

60. *Fears II, 89.*

61. *Editorial "Only a Nigger," Buffalo Express, August 1869, 22.*

62. *HF, 190-91.*

63. *"The United States of Lyncherdom," A Pen Warmed Up, 180.*

64. *Id., 187-88.*

65. *MT Autobiography 2, 115; Foner, 239-40.*

66. *"Disgraceful Persecution of a Boy," Sketches, 117, 119.*

67. *"Goldsmith's Friend Abroad Again," Galaxy, November 1870.*

68. *"John Chinaman in New York," Sketches, 231-32.*

69. *Foner, 250.*

70. *"Treaty with China: Its Provisions Explained; The Treaty Wins China," New York Tribune, August 4, 1868; Foner, 240-41.*

71. *Id.*

72. *MTB, 361.*

73. *"Anson Burlingame," Buffalo Express, February 2, 1870, 153.*

74. *Foner, 234, 238; See, e.g., "Extract from Captain Stormfield's Visit to Heaven;" Budd, 189.*

75. *Arizona v. United States, 567 US___ (June 25, 2012).*

76. *MT Autobiography 1, 420; MTNJ, # 14, 11 quoted in Foner, 293-307.*

77. *Quote from Shelden, 95.*

78. *Twain, "Stirring Times in Austria," Harper's Magazine, March 1888. The dispute involved the substitution of Czech for German as the official language of Bohemia.*

79. *"Concerning The Jews," Harper's Monthly, September 1899.*

80. *"The American Jew as a Soldier," 1895; Foner, 303.*

81. *Cooper, 49.*

82. *RI, 149. See also Kelly Driscoll, "So much for the Aboriginals: The Politics of Selective Racial Sympathy in Following the Equator," Elmira College Center for Mark Twain Studies, October 16, 2010.*

83. *"Fenimore Cooper's Literary Offenses," The Complete Humorous Sketches and Tales of Mark Twain, ed., Neider, 631-42. Twain's attention-getting language would probably make him unemployable today. Stark shock-inducing satire was his trademark.*

84. *Geismar, 72.*

85. *MTL: SLC to President Cleveland, February 23, 1885 (MS: DLCm#03371) quoted in Foner, 308.*

86. *Robert McElroy, Grover Cleveland, The Man and the Statesman, New York: Harper & Brothers, 1923, 229-30.*

87. *MTP: MTNJ, # 35 (1895).*

88. *FE, 208.*

89. *"Grief and Mourning for the Night," A Pen Warmed Up, 97, 98. Scholars have criticized Clemens for ignoring atrocities against the Indians at home lest he offend his American readers as he condemned atrocities in the Philippines, South Africa, the Congo and other foreign places. The Moro massacre has often been compared to Wounded Knee when in December 1890 over 150 Lakota Sioux braves, squaws and children were slaughtered by the U.S. Seventh Calvary Regiment. Clemens became an outspoken critic of slavery and advocate of rights for blacks only after slavery was outlawed, and it became fashionable to associate with African American leaders like Frederick Douglass and Booker T. Washington. In the late nineteenth century, the Indian wars continued out West and Clemens' associations were with the generals who waged them.*

90. *Perhaps Twain subtly addressed the issue in Following the Equator when he wrote: "In more than one country we have hunted the savage and his little children and their mother with dogs and guns through the woods and swamps for an afternoon's sport, and filled the region with happy laughter over their sprawling and stumbling flight...... In many countries we have taken the savage's land from him, and made him our slave, and lashed him every day, and broken his pride, and made death his only friend, and overworked him till he dropped in his tracks; and this we do not care for, because custom has inured us to it." FE, 212.*

91. *RI, 482; Mark Twain in Hawaii, 28.*

92. *RI, 482; Mark Twain in Hawaii, 27.*

93. *SLC to St. Louis Democrat, March 12, 13, 15, 1867; Budd, 23.*

94. *Budd, 34. The flamboyant entrepreneur, George Francis Train, who helped launch Credit Mobilier, partnered with Susan B. Anthony in promoting women's suffrage.*

95. *(Unfinished lecture) Loving, 212; Fred Kaplan, 271; Budd, 55.*

96. *SLC to St. Louis Missouri Democrat, March 1867; Fears I, 193; Fears, I-2, 244..*

97. *SLC letter to the San Francisco Alta quoted in Foner, 116.*

98. *Quote from article on "Common School System" in Foner, 116.*

99. *Id.*

100. *Id., 117.*

101. *American Publisher, July 1871, 4.*

102. *Quote from Budd, 23-24.*

103. *Quote from Foner, 117.*

104. *MTL: SLC to London Standard, March 12, 1874 (UCCL 11880); In Connecticut Yankee, Twain took a transitional position. Hank Morgan proposed giving voting rights to "men and women alike– at any rate to all men, wise or unwise, and to all mothers who at middle age shall be found to know nearly as much as their sons at twenty-one." CY, 514.*

105. *1901 speech on women's suffrage quoted in Foner, 118. Clemens considered Joan of Arc his masterpiece, although many critics would rank it near the bottom of his prodigious output. The book was a tribute to feminine intelligence, ability, courage and leadership, describing Joan as "the only person, of either sex, who has ever held supreme command of the military forces of a nation at the age of seventeen." He became an honorary member of the Joan of Arc Suffrage League. Budd, 165.*

106. *Quote from Foner, 118-19.*

107. *FE, 299.*

108. *"Votes for Women," Speeches, 101, 103.*

109. *MT Autobiography 3, 4; AD quote in Foner, 117.*

110. *FE, 300.*

111. *Foner, 119. Women received the right to vote a half century after the Fifteenth Amendment had prohibited the denial of voting rights to persons on "account of race, color, or previous condition of servitude." Women apparently did not qualify under the "condition of servitude" clause. By the year of Clemens' death, however, several states had enfranchised women: New Jersey (partially), Wyoming (the first to grant full voting rights to women), Colorado, Utah, Idaho, and Washington. Theodore Roosevelt's Bull Moose Party was the first political party to endorse woman's suffrage. Within a few years after Clemens' death,*

California, Oregon, Kansas, Arizona, Montana, Nevada, South Dakota, and Oklahoma granted voting rights to women. In 1916, Jeannette Rankin was elected to Congress from Montana.

112. *MTNJ, 258 quoted in Carter, 171 (recording remarks in an 1895 interview with a reporter of the New South Wales Licensing Guardian.) Clemens' views on temperance reflected his common sense approach to social policy and philosophy. He would take from philosophers ideas that made sense in the practical world of his experience, record them as observations in his Notebook and use them in his essays and fiction.*

113. *PW, 27.*

114. *TS, 32*

115. *John P. Holms and Karin Baji, Bite-size Twain: Wit and Wisdom from the Literary Legend, 68.*

116. *"The Man That Corrupted Hadleyburg, and Other Stories and Essays."*

117. *Budd, 201-02. See Severance Johnson, "Capitol Jokes at the Legislative Session of 1902," (Albany, 1901), 49-56 (Clemens testified before a committee of the state legislature: the "state should not fetter a man's freedom" to treat his body as he likes "to his peril or the peril of anyone else.").*

118. *"Bible Teaching and Religious Practice" in Europe and Elsewhere quoted in Political Tales, 62.*

119. *MT Autobiography 1, 189, 215. When Sam was a boy, the family doctor, a Dr. Meredith, treated the entire family for $25 a year and supplied the drugs, which usually consisted of castor oil with some molasses to wash it down. As an older man suffering from carbuncles, Clemens complained about a physician with a limited practice who made incessant social calls and charged him a premium for each visit.*

120. *Budd, 202.*

121. *Brinkley, 702-03; MT Autobiography, 3, 64 ("The precious slaughter of game which, as Roosevelt claimed, develops heroism and manly virtue, was in reality a sort of brutal thoughtlessness."; see also MT Autobiography 3, 174-76..*

CHAPTER FOURTEEN
MARK TWAIN GOVERNMENT SKEPTIC
Chapter quote from
"Official Physic," The Twainian, November 1943.

1. *Osgood had just published The Prince and the Pauper and was about to accompany Clemens on a voyage down the Mississippi River to retrace Sam's roots to prepare for his book Life on the Mississippi. After Elisha Bliss' death in 1880,*

Clemens left the American Publishing Company and engaged Osgood as his publisher. Although Clemens' book sales had plummeted because of Osgood's unfamiliarity with the subscription publishing business, he defended his new publisher from the district attorney's attack. See Loving, 252. In the unfinished letter, Clemens referred to "Whitman's noble work." Clemens and Whitman were both school drop-outs and outliers from the established literary circles, reflecting the vernacular roots of the young nation rather than British pretensions. Like Leaves of Grass, Huckleberry Finn was banned in Massachusetts— by the Concord Library. Clemens predicted that this act alone would sell an additional 25,000 copies. Clemens and Whitman had lived and worked for the federal government in Washington after the Civil War, and both were fired. Although Clemens included Whitman's works in Webster & Co.'s Library of American Literature and contributed to his charity, they were not close. Nor were they great admirers of each other's creative work.

2. *Loving, 254.*

3. *MTB, Appendix K (Letter to New York Tribune). Clemens was not always against capital punishment. He refused to sign a petition endorsed by Longfellow, Whittier and others, noting on the envelope, "From that inextinguishable dead beat who has infested legislatures for 20 years trying to put an end to capital punishment. No answer." In Tom Sawyer, he mocked the "sappy" women who sought leniency for the killer Injun Joe. See Budd, 61.*

4. *MTNJ, 347; MTNJ, 288-89 quoted in Carter, 315-16.*

5. *Sketches, 187, 190-91.*

6. *Buffalo Express, May 7, 1870, 194-95; In 1870, he published three sketches attacking the insanity defense, "The New Crime," "Our Precious Lunatic," and "Unburlesqueable Things," Quirk, 75.*

7. *Shelden, 193-96 (elaborating on other connections between Clemens, Nesbit and Littleton).*

8. *"Murder and Insanity," Buffalo Express, May 7, 1870, 194-95; MTNJ 3, 346-47. In Tom Sawyer, Injun Joe is publically humiliated when he is horsewhipped with the whole town looking on." TS, 208; Quirk, 94.*

9. *Sketches, 182, 186. When a fortune-teller predicted that Twain would be hanged for his crimes as an editor and lecturer, he asked only for assurance that he would be hanged in New Hampshire. This was an allusion to the 1869 Pike-Brown case, which generated a lot of national publicity. Although Pike had brutally murdered Brown with an ax in a robbery attempt, the defense attorney put sympathetic lay witnesses on the stand who claimed he suffered from a form of temporary insanity called dipsomania. "To be hanged in New Hampshire is*

happiness," Twain wrote, "it leaves an honored name behind a man, and intro-duces him at once to the best New Hampshire society in the other world." Carter, 309 et seq.

10. *What is Man?, 62; Carter, 313-14.*

11. *http://naacpldf.org/category/criminal-justice.*

12. *"Death penalty ends," Washington Post, July 2, 2011.*

13. *See "Two Words: Wasteful and Ineffective," editorial, New York Times, October 11, 2010.*

14. *National Urban League, State of Black America (2010).*

15. *See Marc Mauer and David Cole, "Myths about Americans in prison," Washington Post, June 19, 2011, B2 cs5-6.*

16. *MTB, 942.*

17. *"Dinner to Mr. Jerome," Speeches, 160, 161.*

18. *MT Eruption, January 15, 1907, 67-68; Peterson, 17-21.*

19. *MT Eruption, 61-66; "Official Physic, The Twainian quoted in Peterson, 17-18.*

20. *Id.; MTL: SLC to unidentified addressee date unknown (# 02880).*

21. *MT Eruption, 67-68; Peterson, 18.*

22. *MT Autobiography 2, 314; MT Eruption, 67-70.*

23. *MT Autobiography 2, 313-14; MT Eruption, 64-66.*

24. *MT Autobiography 2, 313-14; MT Eruption, 64-66.*

25. *MT Autobiography 2, 313-14; MT Eruption, 64.*

26. *MT Eruption, Id., 26; Peterson, 57-58. As America expanded westward, there was popular sentiment to move the capital to a more central location. Clemens demurred, pointing out that the revolution in communications and transporta-tion had made a change in location less compelling. "Jealous rivalries" among the "contending western cities" likely would negate any specific proposal, he wrote in 1869."Removal of the Capital," Buffalo Express, August 17, 1869, 7-8. He did regret that St. Louis, with its mix of southern tradition and immi-grant ferment, could not be chosen. Id.*

27. *"On Postage Rates on Author's Manuscripts," September 1882, Who Is Mark Twain?, 95-96.*

28. *Unsent letter addressed to H.C. Christiancy quoted in Peterson 57-58.*

29. *MTL: SLC to Samuel E. Moffett, April 9, 1895 (UCCL 04864).*

30. *MT Eruption, 3. Roosevelt appointed three justices to the Supreme Court, among them the venerable Oliver Wendell Holmes in 1902. But it would be the President's cousin Franklin who would try, but fail, to pack the Supreme Court. And in the end, the FDR Court did as Clemens had predicted it would: It*

reversed its laissez-faire precedents and interpreted the Constitution to allow an expansion of federal legislative authority. The debate continues to this day.

31. *LM, 605-08("perfectly obvious that the control of the Mississippi River must be undertaken by the national government, and cannot be composed by States.");*
     Brinkley, 693.

32. *MTL: SLC to Mary B. Rogers, August 25, 26, and 27, 1906 (#07504).*

33. *Literary Essays, 78-79 quoted in Carter, 295-96.*

34. *GA, 269.*

35. *Clara Clemens, 54-56.*

36. *Id.*

37. *Carter, 297. Clemens denounced the railroads' cost-saving measures that undermined safety, killing twelve hundred persons and injuring sixty thousand in one year. He wrote letters to the victims, conveying the dismal statistics and urging them to sue the railroads. If the railroads were dangerous to passengers and pedestrians, they were even more dangerous to their employees. In 1893, when Congress first enacted railroad safety legislation, 1,567 trainmen had died, and 18,877 were injured. White, 286.*

38. *Speeches, 413, 414-15. Clemens was not alone in his criticism of the railroads. Even Charles Francis Adams, the grandson and great-grandson of U.S. presidents who became president of the Union Pacific after Credit Mobilier and Jay Gould's ravaging of the company, conceded that "the railroad situation in my opinion is as bad as it can be. I think we are all going to the devil together....It is so devoid of all that basis of good faith by which only the business of civilized communities can be successfully conducted... [It] is plunging to destruction just as fast as it can go." White, 212.*

39. *Speeches, 415; see also MT Autobiography 2, 361.*

40. *Carter, 297-98.*

41. *My Twain, 80-81, quoted in Budd, 138.*

42. *Quote from Budd, 138.*

43. *"On Foreign Critics," Speeches quoted in Budd, 139.*

44. *AD quoted in Budd, 69-70.*

45. *Arthur C. Brooks, "America's New Culture War: Free enterprise vs. government control," Washington Post, May 23, 2010, 1301.*

46. *Lessig, 47.*

47. *Ayres, The Wit and Wisdom of Mark Twain, 90; More Maxims of Mark, 12;*
     Peterson, 38.

48. *Foner, 88.*

49.   *Id.; see also MT Autobiography 1, 364.*

50.   *"(Burlesque) Autobiography," The $30,000 Bequest and other Stories.*

51.   *"Running for Governor," Sketches, 311. Reflecting the staunchly Republican bias of his newspaper, The Buffalo Express, Twain, in "Inspired Humor," lampoons the New York World which had urged citizens to "redeem the State" from "Republican corruption, extravagance and misrule" by electing "an honest and incorruptible Democratic legislature." Of the pious Democratic legislators, Clemens wrote, their "religion is to war against all morals and material progress." They were never "known to divert to the erection of a school house, moneys that would suffice to build a distillery." Budd, 43 (quoting from "Inspired Humor," August 19, 1869). Apparently gridlock, partisanship and corruption have continued to infest the New York State legislature, inspiring a 2009 New York Times editorial to recommend throwing out the incumbents regardless of party. "Failed State," Editorial, New York Times, December 30, 2009; "A Broken Legislature," Editorial, New York Times, June 25, 2003; "Albany's Madhouse," Editorial, New York Times, June 9, 2009; "The Fog of Ethics in Albany," Editorial, New York Times, October 27, 2009; "Meanwhile in Albany," Editorial, New York Times, November 4, 2010.*

52.   *"The Revised Catechism," New York Tribune, September 27, 1871; Foner, 90.*

53.   *"A Curious Dream," August 30, 1870, Sketches, 192.*

54.   *"A Mysterious Visit," Sketches, 316,320.*

55.   *See Zacks, Island of Vice.*

56.   *"The German Chicago," Literary Essays, 262 quoted in Carter, 294.*

57.   *"Municipal Corruption," Speeches, 118, 119. Over the years, Tammany Hall remained his primary target. In The Gilded Age, Twain launched an assault on Boss Tweed for his plundering of the City. In an 1873 essay condemning the annexation of the Hawaiian Islands, he cited Boss Tweed as a sterling example of the political corruption that the U.S. would bring to its administration of the new territory. Similarly, in his seminal piece on anti-imperialism targeting the U.S. annexation of the Philippines, "A Person Sitting in Darkness," he cites the Tammany Machine again to illustrate what America could teach the Filipinos about self-government.*

58.   *Foner, 132; MTB, 1145-46. Twain compared Tammany to the British colonial administration of India under Governor-General Warren Hastings. Even the powerful India Company was subservient to his autocratic whims. Like Tammany, Hastings' colonial rule "had but one principle, but one policy, one moving spring of action– avarice, money-lust. So that it got money it cared not*

515

a rap about the means and the methods. It was always ready to lie, forge, betray, steal, swindle, cheat, rob, and no promise, no engagement, no contract, no treaty made by the Boss was worth the paper it was written on or the polluted breath that uttered it." Hastings and Tammany were "twins." The eminent Eighteenth century philosopher and statesman, Edmund Burke, prosecuted the impeachment of Warren Hastings for misfeasance in office in a long trial in which the "the credit and honor of the British Empire" was redeemed.

59.   *MTB, 1147 quoted in Carter, 295.*

60.   *Hacker & Pierson, 305.*

CHAPTER FIFTEEN
MARK TWAIN:
DEFENDER OF FREE ENTERPRISE
Chapter Quote is from MTNJ, ch XVI quoted in Peterson, 62

1.   *Foner, 211-12.*

2.   *MT Autobiography 1, 364.*

3.   *Id.; MT Eruption (December 13, 1906) quoted in Political Tales, 98.*

4.   *MTP: MTNJ, #32b, 58.*

5.   *The Man That Corrupted Hadleyburg and Other Stories and Essays.*

6.   *The £1,000,000 Bank-Note and Other New Stories. In The Innocents Abroad, Twain took note of the honor bestowed on the rich regardless of how they acquired their wealth because "if a man be rich, he is greatly honored, and can be a legislator, a governor, a general, a senator, no matter how ignorant an ass he is." IA, 268.*

7.   *The $30,000 Bequest and Other Stories, 1, 49.*

8.   *MTP: MTNJ, #32(b) (II), 1899, 632. In a "Letter From the Recording Angel," Twain bluntly declared that the chief aim of life is getting rich "dishonestly if we can and honestly if we must;" MT Autobiography 1, 364.*

9.   *"An Inquiry about Insurance," The Celebrated Frog of Calaveras County and Other Sketches," 76; see also "Accident Insurance," Speeches, 249.*

10.   *Foner, 202-03.*

11.   *Quotes from Id., 205.*

12.   *"Open Letter to Commodore Vanderbilt," Packard's Monthly, March 1869 quoted in Foner, 205-06.*

13.   *Howells Letters, 291; Cooper, 280.*

14.   *MTL: SLC to Rogers, December 19 1908; Shelden, 53.*

15. *1905 interview, Boston Transcript quoted in Shelden, 51. Clemens' criticism of Rockefeller was muted by his affection for his chief lieutenant Rogers and his contempt for Roosevelt's brandishing of federal power against the poster child of Standard Oil. When the Hepburn Act prohibited railroad price discrimination and kickbacks on freight costs, the libertarian Clemens dictated to his autobiography: "I would like to know what kind of a goddam govment (sic) this is that ... makes a goddam railroad charge everybody equal & and lets a goddam man charge any goddam price he wants for his goddamn opera box." MTL: SLC to Howells, October 4, 1907, Howells Letters, 394..*

16. *Shelden, 51; Keller, Selected Writings, 62; The Booker T. Washington Papers 10:126.*

17. *MT Autobiography 1, 84*

18. *Shelden, 153; but see MT Autobiography 2 116.*

19. *MT Eruption, 4-5. Clemens was all too familiar with the periodic panics that plagued the American economy. Growing up, his family moved every time a panic decimated his father's business. During his lifetime, he witnessed financial crises in 1837, 1857, 1873, and 1893 and 1907.*

20. *MT Eruption, 6.*

21. *Quotes from Budd, 119.*

22. *Camden's Compliment to Walt Whitman, ed. Traubel, Philadelphia: David McKay, 1889, 64-65; Loving, 308.*

23. *MTNJ, 520-21.*

24. *"Letter from a Recording Angel," cited in Budd, 114.*

25. *CY, 328-30.*

26. *On a world-wide basis, the U.S. ranks just behind Cameroon and the Ivory Coast in the gap between the rich and poor. Peter Whoriskey, "Income gap widens as executives prosper," Washington Post, ," June 19, 2011, A1cs 5-6. Of the top one percent of earners, 41 percent are corporate executives and 18 percent are financial professionals such as hedge fund managers.; 6.2 percent are lawyers; real estate professionals constitute 4.7 percent, and media and sports figures constitute 3 percent. See also Steven Pearlstein, "CEO Pay: Why they're winning," Washington Post, June 26, 2011, G1c1; Editorial, "When the rich get richer," Washington Post, June 26, 2011, A20 cs1-3.*

27. *Miles Corak, "Chasing the Same Dream; Climbing Different Ladders: Economic Mobility in the United States and Canada," Economic Mobility Initiative: An Initiative of the Pew Charitable Trusts (January 2009), 7, cited in Hacker & Pierson, 29.*

28. *Clemens defended the working class, upon whose backs the wealth of the few had been generated. Invoking satire reminiscent of Jonathan Swift's "A Modest Proposal," he suggested that the poor working man should be stuffed into sausage: "Cut up and properly canned, he might be made useful to fatten the natives of the Cannibal Islands and to improve our export trade with that region." He took issue with the Spenserian philosophers who blamed poverty on laziness and lack of initiative. He objected to arguments by the Temperance Movement that excessive drinking caused poverty, rather than the converse. Foner, 214-15. Clemens dined with the philosopher Herbert Spencer in London on July 2, 1873, at the London home of George Washburn Smalley, the Tribune's European correspondent. Spencer applied the theory of "survival of the fittest" to free market economies. MT Autobiography 1, 434, 635.*

29. *LM, 176, 189.*

30. *White, 341; see also Trachtenberg, Incorporation of America, 71.*

31. *FE, 189.*

32. *"Knights of Labor– the New Dynasty," Speeches, quoted in Foner, 222.*

33. *Id., 223.*

34. *Id.. 224.*

35. *SLC to Howells, March 31, 1888, Twain-Howells Letters, 278.*

36. *"Monopoly Speaks, "Buffalo Express, August 20, 186, 11; Budd, 42.*

37. *New York Evening Mail, November 21, 1867, 3.*

38. *Id.*

39. *Budd, 137; Foner, 216-36.*

40. *Don Peck, "Can the Middle Class be Saved?" The Atlantic, September 2011, 60, 62, 68; Jia Lynn Yang, "In companies' job numbers, a key figure is missing," Washington Post, August 22, 2011, A1c1.*

41. *Sarah Anderson, Chuck Collins, Scott Klinger, and Sam Pizzigati, "Executive Excess 2011: the Massive CEO Rewards for Tax Dodging," Institute for Policy Studies. August 31, 2011, 2, www.ips-dc.org/reports/executive-excess-2011. Among the nation's top corporations, the S&P 500 CEO pay in 2010 averaged $10,762,304, up 27.8 percent over 2009. Average worker pay in 2010 was up to $33,121, 3.3 percent over the year before. In 2010, 25 major corporations paid their CEOs more than they paid in federal income taxes.*

42. *Ylan Q. Mui, "Families see their wealth sapped, Middle Class is Hit Hardest, Measure of net worth falls to early -90s level," Washington Post, June 12, 2012, A1c6.*

43. *Joel Berg, "Welfare reform's forgotten goals," Washington Post, August 19, 2011, A25cs2-5.*

44. *Krugman, 245.*

45. *From the ashes of a corrupt government paralyzed by corporate competition for legislative favors, powerful reform movements were spawned. The people elected new leaders who brought change to Washington– Theodore Roosevelt's "Square Deal," Woodrow Wilson's "New Freedom," Franklin Roosevelt's "New Deal," Harry Truman's "Fair Deal," Dwight Eisenhower's "Peace and Prosperity," John Kennedy's "New Frontier," Lyndon Johnson's "The Great Society" and "War on Poverty," and Richard Nixon's "Pragmatic Idealism." Over time, a system of laws and regulations constrained unfettered capitalism and created a safety net for workers, the elderly and the poor. Satirists (like Mark Twain) and historians are quick to identify the substantial flaws in each administration since Lincoln; yet, their lasting legacies constitute the progress of the nation toward that more perfect union: Lincoln (land grant colleges, a national railroad system, emancipation); Theodore Roosevelt-Taft (trust-busting, conservation, safety regulation); Wilson (federal reserve); Franklin Roosevelt (social security, market regulation); Eisenhower (interstate highway system, aid to education); Johnson (Medicare, Medicaid, civil rights); Nixon (clean air, clean water, occupational and consumer safety), to cite but a few examples.*

46. *MTL: SLC to Daggett, May 1, 1880 (UCCL 01798). Twain typed a line through "goddamnd" (sic) twice, as he was prone to do, fully intending that the words be visible to the reader.*

47. *Fears II, 249. As a young writer Clemens enjoyed the benefits of buying inexpensive British books. As in many other areas, his views on copyright evolved as he became a successful author.*

48. *MTL: SLC to Elisha Bliss, July 27, 1873&n2 (UCCL 00956); SLC to Elisha Bliss and n1, July 16, 1873 (UCCL 00953); SLC to T.B. Pugh, July 27, 1873 (UCCL 00957). Publication in England gave only partial protection in other countries in the British Empire. Clemens failed to secure a Canadian copyright for The Prince and the Pauper, but succeeded for Life on the Mississippi after he traveled to Ottawa and remained for the requisite period of time to qualify. In 1883 the New York Times reported on his anger with the State Department's lethargy in protecting American literary products, quoting Clemens: "I am in favor of an international copyright law. So was my great grandfather . . . It is my hope and prayer that . . . the voice of that old man will go down ringing in the interest of that eternal cause for which he struggled and died." "Mark Twain's Copyright Struggles," New York Times, May 30, 1883. When Twain completed his second novel, Tom Sawyer, he turned down an offer from Routledge & Sons in favor of publication by Chatto & Windus a full six months before the U.S.*

publication by the American Publishing Company. MTL: SLC to Elisha Bliss, November 5, 1875, n4 (UCCL 01280). To obtain protection in Canada, he had to pay a 12 and one half percent royalty on each volume sold there. Canadian pirated editions of Tom Sawyer by Belford Publishers had cut deeply into Twain's profits as the books flowed across the northern border during the six month hiatus. Canada required a book to be registered 60 days before publication, but the law was laxly enforced by small fines. "Mark Twain on Copyright Law," New York Times, November 11, 1883.

49.   *MT Autobiography 1, 601 (At a meeting of the Copyright League in New York, Clemens read "A Trying Situation" from Chapter 25 of A Tramp Abroad). In January 1888, a public spat broke out between Mark Twain and Brander Mathews over British copyright law, which Clemens had defended. If an author was willing to publish first in the U.K. and travel to Canada, he would be protected. Mathews thought that was fine for a rich author from Hartford, but what about the struggling writer from Florida? Mathews, later a Columbia University Professor of Literature who served as Chairman of the National Institute of Arts and Letters and The Modern Language Association of America, also took issue with Twain's laying the blame solely on the U. S. government. Fears II, 243. Clemens and Mathews also disagreed on the literary merit of James Fennimore Cooper. Twain wrote: "Mathews tells us Cooper's books 'reveal an extraordinary fullness of invention.' As a rule I am quite willing to accept Brander Mathews literary judgments... but that particular statement needs to be taken with a few tons of salt." Twain suggested that it would be "more decorous for Mathews to keep silent and let persons talk who have read Cooper," who "hadn't any more invention than a horse." See MT, "Fennimore Cooper's Literary Offenses;" MTP: MTNJ 3, 211. On February 4, 1888, the American Copyright League ran an ad in the New York Times urging support for international copyright legislation; Fears II, 249. At the League's urging, New York Congressman William Dorsheimer introduced an international copyright bill in the House, which failed to get a hearing. Clemens' Hartford friend, then Senator Joseph Hawley, introduced a bill in the Senate with a similar fate. Several publishers had quietly opposed the bills because they did not require foreign books sold in the U.S. to use U.S. paper makers, type founders, printers or binders.*

50.   *Fears I, 1074; Fears II, 12-14. Hawley's bill was the eleventh copyright bill in forty years that failed to reach the Senate floor. Authors and publishers had urged Congress to pass this legislation. Clemens' testimony was equivocal, probably because he did not think the bill was strong enough. But in a second day of testimony, Clemens was blunter. He accused Congress of colluding with the foreign*

book "pirates" preying on American writers. Fears II, 13. He urged the lawmakers
to protect American authors and nurture homegrown literature. He supported
Hawley's proposal to "require that books by a foreign author when copyrighted
here shall be printed on this soil." MTNJ 3, 211. In 1886, John Wanamaker,
whose Philadelphia department store was the first to have electricity, a telephone
and an elevator, decided to discount the popular Personal Memoirs of Ulysses S.
Grant, published by Charles W. Webster & Co., as a loss leader to bring customers into the store. An infuriated Clemens sued that "pious son of a dog" on behalf
of his publishing company to enjoin the discount sales. As Clemens dictated to
his autobiography, he wanted to stop "the uncopious, bitter-mouthed, Sunday
School-slabbering sneak-thief, John Wannemaker (sic)" from undercutting his
subscription sales. The federal district court denied the injunction, and after a
full hearing, Clemens' suit was dismissed. MT Eruption, 346-49; Fears II, 60.

51. Fears II, 345-46; see also MT Eruption, 348-49.

52. MTL: SLC Letter to President Cleveland, February 20, 1889 (# 08136); Fears
II, 350.

53. Shelden, xviii.

54. "Copyright," Speeches, 314, 315. Clemens referred to testimony he had given
the House of Lords on copyright protection. When the pompous chairman had
asked him how long copyrights should last, Clemens had replied, "perpetuity."
The annoyed chairman responded that such a proposal was "illogical" because
it had long ago been decided that there is "no such thing as property in ideas."
Clemens challenged the chairman to identify "any property on this planet that
had a pecuniary value which was not derived from an idea or ideas."
The chairman retorted: "Real estate!"
Clemens argued with the chairman that the real value of real estate is not in
the land itself but in the ideas about how it can be used and improved. "The
skyscraper is [an] idea; the railroad is another. The telephone and all those
things are merely symbols which represent ideas." Id., 319-20; see also MT
Autobiography 2, 318-24; MT Autobiography 3, 279-80.

55. "Too Bleak for Mark," Washington Herald, December 9, 1906; "Mark Twain
Demands Thanks of Congress, and Right Away, Too," Washington Times,
December 8, 1906; Shelden, xxxiv.

56. In his autobiographical dictations, Clemens unleashed his frustration with
the copyright laws. He complained that because members of Congress and
Parliament consisted of lawyers, merchants, and bankers but nary an author
or publisher, the laws were "uncompromisingly and hopelessly idiotic." MT
Eruption, 373-75; Neider, 366. Clemens argued that neither England nor

America had produced more than twenty authors whose books outlived the copyright limit of 42 years. Yet, legislators "intensely, pathetically" believe "by some kind of insane reasoning that somebody is in some way benefited by this trivial robbery inflicted upon the families of twenty authors in the course of one hundred years." Of the 220,000 books produced in that century, Clemens claimed, there was not a "bathtub-full of them . . . still alive and marketable." Neider, 368. See Twain-Howells Letters, 392.

57. *MTL: SLC to Joseph G. Cannon, December 7, 1906 (UCCL 07586).*

58. *MTL: SLC to Kate Douglas Wiggin, December 7, 1906, (UCCL 08271); See also MTB, 1341-51 (Twain met with about 80 members of Congress).*

59. *MTL: SLC to Champ Clark, December 13, 1907 (UCCL 12368); Shelden, 326-27; MTB, 1494.*

60. *Siva Vaidhynathan, Copyrights and Copywrongs: The Rise of Intellectual Property and How It Threatens Creativity.*

61. *Copyright Office, Copyright Laws of the United States and Related Laws, Contained in Title 17 of the United States Code, cited in Lessig, 56.*

62. *In 1878, New York Congressman Fernando Wood introduced legislation to reduce tariffs by as much as 40 percent on some goods, but the Wood Tariff bill was essentially killed two years earlier by the Republican opposition led by Congressman William McKinley. Twain, "Campaign Speech," October 26, 1880, quoted in Budd, 82.*

63. *Budd., 112-13.*

64. *Mark Twain's Speeches, 1910, 398 quoted in Peterson, 125.*

65. *Tom Sawyer Abroad, 174; Budd, 157.*

66. *Tom Sawyer Abroad, 178-79; Foner, 128.*

67. *MTP: MTNJ, No. 28, October 19, 1885, 117; Foner, 128; Budd, 157.*

68. *FE, 153; Cooper, 82.*

69. *AD quoted in Foner, 128.*

70. *Quote from Id., 128-29.*

71. *MT Eruption, 3.*

72. *Grant, 102.*

73. *Graff, 100-10; Grant, 293-97, 303-05.*

74. *Foner 129-30.*

75. *When partisan gridlock prevented the people's Congress from taking steps to address high unemployment and the failure of financial markets in 2008 through sound fiscal policy, it is the undemocratic and secretive Federal Reserve that took bold and extraordinary action. Bradley Keoun and Phil Kuntz, "Analysis: $1.2 trillion in loans to Wall Street, Washington Post, August 23, 2011, A13cs1-4.*

76. MTNJ, ch 33 quoted in Peterson, 123.

77. *Dinner of Freundschaft Society, Mark Twain's Speeches, 298, quoted in Peterson, 125.*

78. *"Salutary," Buffalo Express, August 21, 1869, quoted in Peterson, 125.*

79. *IA, 270.*

80. *MTL: Letter to an unidentified recipient, unknown date (MS:CU-MARK, #02880). From his experience with Civil War pensions, Clemens understood how an undisciplined Congress can turn well-intended social programs into vote-getting, out-of-control entitlements.*

81. *CY, 156.*

82. *National Federation of Independent Business v. Sebelius, 567 US ___ (2012); 132 S. Ct. 2566 (2012).*

CHAPTER SIXTEEN
MARK TWAIN'S ANTI-IMPERIALIST ROOTS
Chapter quote is from MT Autobiography 1, 310.

1. *Initially, Clemens reported favorably on the missionaries, whom he considered "pious, hard-working, hard-praying, self-sacrificing . . . devoted to the well being of the people." MTP: MTNJ 1, 154. In Roughing It, he wrote that "the missionaries have clothed them, educated them, broken up the tyrannous authority of their chiefs, and given them freedom and the right to enjoy whatever their hands and brains produce with equal laws for all, and punishment for all alike who transgress them." RI, 464, 477. He found the Catholic missionaries especially "honest, straightforward, frank and open, they are industrious and devoted to their religion and their work; they never meddle, whatever they do can be relied on as being prompted by a good and worthy motive." Foner, 192; "All the natives are Christian, now," Twain wrote, "but many of them still desert to the great God Shark for temporary succor in times of trouble," such as a volcanic eruption. RI, 483; Mark Twain in Hawaii, 29. The missionaries had given the Hawaiians a written language and many books. After the age of eight, he claimed, they could all read and write– the most literate nonwhite race outside of China. The native women were eager church goers and had developed "a profound respect for chastity– in other people." The missionaries had taught them to wear clothes to church, although the transitional period was amusing. At first, some of the women would arrive wearing nothing but "a stovepipe hat and a pair of cheap gloves," followed by a male attired only in a woman's*

bonnet." *Id.,* 24; MTP:MTNJ 1, 154 ("*Missionaries have made honest men out of thieves; instituted marriage; created homes; lifted women to same rights & privileges enjoyed elsewhere; abolished infanticide,*" *etc.*); *Foner,* 191; *Letters from Hawaii,* 274.

2. Lecture on "*The Sandwich Islands,*" *October 2, 1886 quoted in Foner, 311.*

3. MTP: MTNJ, 19; Zwick, 80; *Letters from Hawaii,* 274.

4. Clemens tried to persuade the editor Charles Henry Webb to publish a book on the Sandwich Islands, but Webb was more interested in a collection of short stories anchored by the celebrated jumping frog.

5. Zwick, 83, 86. In 1873, Clemens condemned the Hawaiian hierarchy, the absolute power of the King, the priests, "the chiefs who held the lands by feudal tenure– as they do in England today," and the "common men" who were treated as slaves and "cruelly treated and often killed upon any little, trifling provocation." He concluded: "After all this, at the bottom of the hideous pyramid of brutality, and superstition, and slavery– came the women, the abject slaves of the whole combination." *Mark Twain in Hawaii,* 30. He also began to talk about the harms caused by the missionaries and white business interests to the native populations. He predicted that the introduction of smallpox would lead to their extinction within fifty years. *New York Tribune, January, 1873; Zwick,* 85. Contact with Western civilization had decimated the indigenous population, which Captain Cook had estimated to be around 400,000 eighty years before Clemens arrived in 1866 – when, it was down to 55,000.

6. *New York Tribune, January 1873; Zwick,* 85.

7. *Id.,* 86-87; *New York Tribune, January 1873 quoted in Foner,* 313.

8. *Editorial, New York Tribune, January 1873, quoted in Foner,* 312.

9 *Id.,* 313.

10. "*To a Person Sitting in Darkness,*" *A Pen Warmed Up,* 79. Twain essay quoted in Jim Zwick, *Confronting Imperialism,* 88 & n38. In January 1884, Clemens wrote Howells that he was working on a novel set in the Hawaiian Islands. Only 17 pages of the unfinished manuscript survive, *Id.,* 87-88. but many of the novel's projected concepts were incorporated in Twain's description of English feudal society in *A Connecticut Yankee in King Arthur's Court.* In that book, Twain expresses the futility– indeed the devastation– of imposing American democracy, however well-intended, on a culture unprepared to accept it.

11. "*Information Wanted,*" *Sketches,* 123, 125.

12. *Id.,* 125.

13. "*Ye Cuban Patriot,*" *Buffalo Express, December 25, 1869,* 117, 119.

14. *FE, 321.*

15. *FE, 626.*

16. *Id., 206-13, 256-67, 318-23.*

17. *Id., 660-66.*

18. *Id., 623-24.*

19. *Id., 267.*

20. *Id., 213.*

21. *British Journal Academy quoted in Foner, 318.*

22. *Treaty of Paris (1898).*

23. *MTL: SLC to Twichell, September 13, 1898 (UCCL 05432); Foner, 331; Michaelson, 114.*

24. *Powers, 602.*

25. *Susan Harris' recent book on the U.S. occupation of the Philippines, God's Arbiters, draws parallels to the occupation of Iraq and Afghanistan.*

26. *"The March of the Flag," campaign speech, September 16, 1898, quoted in Howard Zinn, 314; Harris, 204.*

27. *Zinn, 313.*

28. *Harris, 57.*

29. *Zinn, 298 (1962 Report to Congress by Secretary of State Dean Rusk). In more recent years, the Reagan Administration invaded Grenada and, more controversially, secretly sold arms to Iran to fund the Contras in revolt against the Nicaraguan government.*

30. *In more recent decades, U.S. foreign policy objectives have included stopping the spread of communism (the falling domino theory), fighting Al-Qaeda and other international terrorist groups, and constraining nuclear proliferation in countries like Iran and North Korea.*

31. *MTB, 1149-65.*

32. *Interview, New York Herald quoted in Powers, 603.*

33. *MTA-P, 766; Harris, 201-04.*

34. *MTL: SLC to Laurence Hutton, December 3, 1900 (UCCL 05925).*

35. *"Military Situation in the Philippines," Literary Digest 21, November 24, 1909, 605 quoted in Zwick, 122.*

36. *Philadelphia Public Ledger quoted in Zwick, 122-23.*

37. *Speech by General Frederick Funston at the Lotos Club on March 8, 1902 quoted in Foner, 376-77.*

38. *"A Defence of General Funston," North American Review, May, 1902; Zwick, 123; Foner, 375-79 (General Funston had engineered Aguinaldo's capture through trickery. U.S. soldiers entered his compound disguised as prisoners*

accompanied by pro-American Filipino guards. As the American soldiers were near starvation, they gladly accepted nourishment from the revolutionaries before capturing their leader.)

39.   *Zwick, xiii, 122-23; After a congressional investigation, water torture was prohibited, creating a precedent that has been cited to rebut more recent claims that water boarding is not torture.*

40.   *MTP: "The American Anti-Imperialist League, et. al. to the American People", July 4. 1901, New York City, (#11648); "A Liberty Day Statement," Springfield Republican, July 4, 1901.*

41.   *"A Petition from Sundry Citizens of the United States Favoring the Suspension of Hostilities in the Philippine Islands and a Discussion of the Situation between the Government and the Filipino Leaders," quoted in Foner, 367.*

42.   *The Petition was published in the New York Evening Post, accompanied by a bar graph depicting the rising cost in lives and funds of the war against the Filipino revolutionaries. Congress took no action on the petition, but the Administration mildly reprimanded General Smith for his "kill and burn" instructions," Id.*

43.   *Clemens' hand-written notes on Funston's speech quoted in Zwick, 122; Foner, 377-78.*

CHAPTER SEVENTEEN
MARK TWAIN & THEODORE ROOSEVELT
Chapter paraphrase of quote attributed to
Theodore Roosevelt at the 1901 Yale Bicentennial Celebration,
Powers, 611, Fred Kaplan, 585, Justin Kaplan, 364.

1.   *Fred Kaplan, 585; Powers, 610-11.*

2.   *MTL: SLC to J.E. Edmonds, September 27, 1907 (#10377); MT Autobiography 1, 259 ("Mr. Roosevelt is one of the most likeable men that I am acquainted with. I have known him, and have occasionally met him, dined in his company, lunched in his company, for certainly twenty years. I always enjoy his society, he is so hearty, so straightforward, outspoken, and so absolutely sincere. These qualities endear him to me when he is acting in his capacity as a private citizen."); MT Autobiography 2, 9; MT Autobiography 3, 22, 62-63, 134-37, 143, 177-79, 230, 254-58, 297-98, 475-78.*

3.   *Letter from Theodore Roosevelt to George Otto Trevelyan, January 22, 1906, cited in Brinkley, 703.*

4.   *Shelden, 58.*

5.   *MTA-P, 766 ("Theodore the man is sane; in fairness we ought to keep in mind that Theodore, as a statesman and politician, is insane and irresponsible.");* James S. Leonard, "Mark Twain and Politics," A Companion to Mark Twain, 94, 107.

6.   *MTL: SLC to Twichell, February 16, 1905 (#07001) ("I have loved Roosevelt the man & hated Roosevelt the statesman & politician.")*

7.   *MT Eruption, May 30, 1907, 22 (when Collier Magazine praised the President "who gave up power, kept his word, and set a high example," Twain took exception, calling this "the poorest compliment that has ever been fired at a President of the United States.") Id. Viewers of Gutzon Borglum's Mount Rushmore sculpture would rank Roosevelt a greater president than Grover Cleveland or Ulysses S. Grant, Clemens' two personal favorites. McKinley and Roosevelt, Clemens wrote to Twichell were "in private life spotless, in character, honorable, honest, just, humane, generous; scorning trickeries, treacheries, suppressions of the truth, mistranslations of the meaning of facts, the filching of credit earned by another, the condoning of crime, the glorifying of base acts," but their morality was distorted by politics, in which they were the "reverse of all this." MTL: SLC to Twichell, November 4, 1904 (#06945). As President, Roosevelt was the antithesis of the honest, independent, courageous Cleveland. They were as different as "an archangel and the Missing Link." MT Eruption, 347 (Cleveland "was a very great president, a man who not only properly appreciated the dignity of his high office but added to its dignity. The contrast between President Cleveland and the present occupant of the White House is extraordinary."); MT Autobiography 1, 390 (Cleveland "was a Gibraltar against whose solid bulk a whole Atlantic of assaulting politicians would dash itself in vain.").*

8.   *Lotos Club speech, November 10, 1900, quoted in Peterson, 130.*

9.   *MT Autobiography 1, 317.*

10.   *CY, 206.*

11.   *Grant, 71-72.*

12.   *"Diplomatic Pay and Clothes, Forum, March 1899, quoted in Peterson, 42 ("Ours is the only country of first importance that pays our representatives trifling salaries.").*

13.   *Id., 43.*

14.   *MTL: SLC to Twichell, June 24, 1905 (#07069) ("Our Theodore is at it again, you notice. You've considered his irruption of day before yesterday which emptied his crater of that most unvolcanic of material– whitewash. Whitewash & slumgullion." (See Roughing It.). Clemens unloaded his most venomous attacks on the president in private letters to Twichell because he had no other alternative.*

He could not "risk" emptying his "bile" into the North American Review. He had a family to support. He couldn't burden the "good natured" Henry Rogers, who was busy rescuing him from his "leather-headed business snarls." Howells was "too busy& old & lazy & won't stand it," and Clara, his "very dear little ashcat" with "claws," would not put up with it. And so, Clemens unloaded his frustrations on Twichell. "You're It!" he told him. MTL: SLC to Twichell (#07069).

15. *MTL: SLC to unidentified addressee, January 5, 1909 (#09813).*

16. *Zwick, 156;see McFarland, 201-04.*

17. *Id., 157.*

18. *"Grief and Mourning for the Night," A Pen Warmed Up, 97, 98. As reports of the "battle" continued to filter in, the number of slain Moros rose to 900, and it was disclosed that at least some of the American casualties had been struck by "friendly fire" from the exuberant shooters on the crater's rim. Many women and children were killed, but as one headline explained: "Impossible to Tell Sexes Apart in Fierce Battle on Top of Mount Dajo." Despite the headlines, the newspaper editorials were at first eerily silent about this "great victory."*

19. *Id., 101. The New York Post editorialized: "Congress would make no mistake if it should rigidly inquire into the latest 'battle' in the Philippines. What possible military excuse was there charging up a mountain cone?" As more information began to come out, the New York World commented: "There will be many Americans who will regret that so crushing a blow should fall by our arms upon a people who never appealed to us to extend to them the 'blessings of civilization,'" but the New York Times defended the action: "Lamentable as it is to hear of the enforced slaughter of 600 inhabitants of the islands there is yet consolation in the knowledge that these last rebels against our undoubtedly beneficent rule are men who, if nothing except extermination can reduce them to order, can be exterminated with exceptional facility." MT Autobiography 1, 616-18.*

20. *A Pen Warmed Up, 101-02; see McFarland, 206-07.*

21. *The American Magazine, vol 1, August 1929 quoted in Foner, 394; Twain's affection for and special relationship with Helen Keller is recorded in MT Autobiography 1, 464-67,531 ("this wonder of all ages."). Between November 1905 and April 1906, Twain spoke on at least 25 occasions, including speeches before Washington journalists (the Gridiron Club), New York artists and actors (the Players' Club), and various benefits and causes, addressing such topics as*

Roosevelt's Panama policies, Russian oppression, the funding of black colleges, and copyright. MT Autobiography 1, 546.

22. *"As Regards Patriotism," A Pen Warmed Up, 45.*

23. *Fulton, 187. In his Notebook, Clemens lamented the mix of religion and patriotism: "A man ... can't legally be a Christian and a patriot– except in the usual way: one of the two with the mouth, and the other with the heart.... The spirit of Christianity proclaims the brotherhood of the race... The Christian man must forgive his brother man of all crimes he can imagine and commit... Patriotism has its law... It commands that the brother over the border shall be sharply watched and brought to book every time he does us a hurt or offends us with an insult." MTNJ, 332-33 quoted in Carter, 250 et seq.*

24. *"The Privilege of the Grave," September 1905, Who Is Mark Twain?, 57.*

25. *Zwick, 124.*

26. *MTNJ, 295-96 (1896), quoted in Budd, 182-83.*

27. *MTP: AD, 7.*

28. *Shelden, 59-60; MT Eruption, 18.*

29. *Id. In her January 7, 1906 diary entry, Clemens' secretary Isabel Lyon recorded his description of Roosevelt's blustering: "he is magnificent when his ears are pricked up & his tail is in the air & and he attacks a lightening express, only to be lost in the dust the express creates." MT Autobiography 1, 551-52 (quoting Lyon, 1906, 7). In 1907, Twain altered the title page in his volume of Roosevelt's speeches, crossing out "A Square Deal" and substituting "BANALITIES." Id., 552 By this time, however, Clemens was avoiding public criticism of Roosevelt, confining his vitriol to private communications. He explained to Clara that Roosevelt had done him a favor and he had not "been able to say a venomous thing about him in print since." Id.*

30. *MT Eruption, 18.*

31. *Id., 28.*

32. *MTL: SLC to Jean Clemens, October 12, 1908 (# 08136).*

33. *MTL: SCL to Twichell, June 24, 1905 (#07069); see also MT Autobiography 3, 255-58.*

34. *MTL: SLC to Margery Clinton, February 28, 1909 (#11283).*

35. *MTL: SLC to Margery Clinton, March 8, 1909 (#11285).*

36. *Shelden, 208-12, 401; The Papers of Woodrow Wilson 20:133.*

37. *"Sharnhorst," 35 quoted in Harris, 204.*

38. *Id.*

CHAPTER EIGHTEEN
THE MANY FACETS OF IMPERIALISM
Chapter quote from MTB, 1072.

1.   *"Platform of the American Anti-Imperialist League," in Carl Schurz, "Policy of Imperialism," Zwick, 125.*

2.   *MTP: "The American Anti-Imperialist League et al. to the American people," endorsed by Samuel L. Clemens, July 4, 1901, (TS: DLC, #11648).*

3.   *The full range of Twain's writings and activities in support of the anti-imperialist movement was suppressed for several decades after his death. Clemens' literary executor, Paine, and his daughter Clara expunged "anti-American" and "anti-religion" rhetoric from his writings and statements that, in their judgment, would tarnish Twain's reputation as the quintessential American author and humorist. Zwick, 166-67. Upon Paine's death in 1937, Clara continued in the role of chief censor. When Clara died in 1962, Clemens' papers went to the University of California at Berkeley, which established the Mark Twain Project and provided scholarly access to reams of unpublished material. As Twain's suppressed writings were published and his activities disclosed through scholarly research, the breadth of his passion and activism against imperialism was revealed.*

4.   *"To a Person Sitting in Darkness,"("Darkness"), A Pen Warmed Up, 80, 96; Zwick, 87*

5.   *MTB, 1095; Carter, 228.*

6.   *MTL: Letters II, 693 quoted in Carter, 228.*

7.   *Shelden, 107. After his triumphant 1907 trip to England to receive an honorary degree from Oxford, Twain noted in his autobiographical dictations a previous meeting during a visit to the House of Commons with "that soaring and brilliant young statesman, Winston Churchill." Id., 108; Twain-Howells Letters, 346.*

8.   *"China and the Philippines," Speeches, 128, 129; Zwick, 152; Zwick, Weapons of Satire, xxxiv; Springfield Republican, December 14, 1900, 6; New York Evening Post, December 13, 1900, 8.*

9.   *Zwick, 152; Winston S. Churchill, A Roving Commission: My Early Life, New York: Charles Scribner's Sons, 1930, 360.*

10. *Foner, 335; "Treaty with China," New York Tribune, August 4, 1868.*

11. *MTL: SLC to Twichell, August 12, 1900 (UCCL 05849); Foner, 336 (Twichell to SLC, June 1, 1898, August 24, 1900).*

12. *"Public Education Association," Speeches, 144-45.*

13. *"Concerning the Jews" quoted in Zwick, 106-07. Clemens wrote in his Notebook, "There is nothing lower than the human race except the French." MTP: MTNJ, #32b, 57.*

14. *Zwick, 108.*

15. *Quoted in Zwick, 93-94.*

16. *"The Russian Cause in America," Free Russia 1, June 1891, 7, quoted in Zwick, 94.*

17. *AC, 185-86; Zwick, 95.*

18. *AC, 187; Zwick, 95-96; MT Autobiography 1, 462-63.*

19. *MTB, 1243; Carter, 235-36; MT Autobiography 1, 462-63.*

20. *"Less Cause for Thanks Than Man Has His God," Washington Times, November 27, 1905, 1 quoted in Zwick, 98.*

21. *MT Autobiography 1, 463-64; MTB, 1283; Carter 237.*

22. *"Russian Republic," Speeches, 286-87.*

23. *Cartoon, New York World, April 13, 1906; Zwick, 102.*

24. *Zwick, 103.*

25. *MTB, 1285; Carter 238.*

26. *Twain believed that the 130 million "miserable" Russians were worse off than the poor who lived in the Middle Ages. In his autobiographical dictations, he wrote, "the vast population has been ground under the heels, and for the sole and sordid advantage of a procession of crowned assassins and robbers who have all deserved the gallows." Neider, 356.*

27. *New York Sun, April 15, 1906; Zwick, 102.*

28 *Mark Twain's Letters, ed., Paine, 794, quoted in Zwick, 99.*

29. *"Darkness," 74.*

30. *Id, 81. (The essay begins with two quotes. The first is a New York Sun description of New York City's East Side tenements "where naked women dance by night on the streets, . . . where the education of the infants begins with the knowledge of prostitution." The second quote is from a letter reporting that the Reverend William Ament of the American Board of Foreign Missions had returned to China to collect indemnities for damages to mission property by the Boxer rebellion and fines totaling thirteen times the indemnity. The amount of the fine actually paid was substantially less.).*

31. *Id., 88.*

32. *Id., 79.*

33. *Id., 95.*

34. *Letters from Hawaii, 53; Loving, 111; Mark Twain in Hawaii, 10.*

35.   *"Darkness," 90; Michelson, 113.*

36.   *FE, 623-25.*

37.   *The essay covered many manifestations of imperialism: the partitioning of China by the European powers "looting like bandits;" the Christian missionaries' punitive extraction of reparations after the Boxer Rebellion; the "brutalities and inhumanities" of the Boer War; the brutal occupation of the Philippines; the Czar's suppression of labor and invasion of Manchuria; German military expansionism in Shantung; and again linking local machine politics with imperialism ("the most awful forms of Vice is the Profit of the politicians.") "Darkness," 74- 88.*

38.   *Id., 94.*

39.   *SLC to Rudolph Lindau, April 24, 1901 quoted in Susan K. Harris, "Twain and America's Christian Mission Abroad," A Companion to Mark Twain, 40.*

40.   *In 1902, he wrote "The Dervish and the Offensive Stranger." He argues in this dialogue, like a scene from a play, that well-intended actions usually have both good and bad (unintended) consequences. His concluding colloquy revisited the missionaries in China:*
"The Offensive Stranger: Take yet one more instance. With the best intentions the missionary has been laboring in China for eighty years.
"The Dervish: The evil result is–
"The Offensive Stranger: That nearly a hundred thousand Chinamen have acquired our Civilization.
"The Dervish: And the good result is—
"The Offensive Stranger: That by the compassion of God four hundred millions have escaped it." "The Dervish and the Offensive Stranger," A Pen Warmed Up, 197, 200-201.

41.   *City and State, 10, March 21, 1901, 182 cited in Zwick, 116 .*

42.   *Id., 114. The salutation was initially prepared as a toast for the Red Cross Society. It was to be combined with greetings from other famous people. When the other famous people were not forthcoming, Clemens felt used. The Salutation was returned to him and instead published in the New York Herald as "taken down in short-hand by Mark Twain."*

43.   *Zwick, 113-14. In his 1901 unpublished story "The Stupendous Procession," Twain portrayed the human consequences of the Philippines occupation, an empathy that drew deeply from his experiences with the treatment of African-Americans. The article painted a crude portrait of a procession of assorted imperial powers– monarchies, religious leaders, political bosses and criminals– each clothed in appropriate attire and bearing symbols of their treachery.*

Christendom's matron was dressed in flowing robes drenched with blood with a golden crown of thorns on her head. She held a sling shot in one hand and a Bible in the other and she carried a banner with the motto: "Love your Neighbors' Goods as yourself." The English were led by Prime Minister Chamberlain and Cecil Rhodes; followed by Spain, bearing the torture tools of the Inquisition; Russia with floats piled high with massacred Manchurian peasants; France carrying the guillotine with Zola under the axe; and Germany carrying a chained and mutilated Chinese man from Shantung. The largest float was the imperial U.S.. Each float carried a flag. For the U.S., it was the Jolly Roger– the skull and crossbones. The insult to the flag offended Mrs. Clemens and she and Paine conspired to persuade Twain not to publish the article. Twain agreed the article was too strong and since only dead men speak the truth agreed that it should not be published until after his death. "The Stupendous Procession;" Michaelson, 109, 114; Zwick, 127-28. The story's efficacy was not so much in the crude cartoonish images, but in the way Twain tied together the many manifestations of imperialism, Christian missionaries and corporate exploiters, European colonialists, and suppressors of African-Americans in the South and immigrants in the North. The story also describes a Band of Filipinos marching in a parade carrying the banner "Unclassifiable." Living in an occupied territory, they were neither enemies nor citizens. They were without rights or status under U.S. or international law. Some were peaceful villagers by day and rebels by night. George Washington, a spectator at the parade, asks a stranger "Who are those brown people marked "Unclassifiable"? The Stranger answers: "They do not resist our Government, therefore they are not rebels; they do not acknowledge the authority of our Government; therefore in a sense they are not subjects; they are not saleable, therefore in a sense they are not slaves; they are part of the population of the United States, but they are not citizens; they belong to America, but they are not Americans. Politically, they are mongrels– the only ones on the planet, Sir." Id.

44.   *Letter from SLC to Erving Winslow, February, 1905, quoted in Zwick, 119.*

45.   *"The Chronicle of Young Satan," A Pen Warmed Up, 52, 55, which Twain wrote in 1900 as part of the original manuscript of The Mysterious Stranger. Twain narrates the visit of Satan to a rural Austrian village in 1702. The narrative referred to military aggression in South Africa, China and the Philippines, but these references were excluded from the initial publication in 1916. The complete manuscript was not published until 1969. The story continues: "In five or six thousand years five or six high civilizations have risen, flourished, commanded the wonder of the world, then faded out and disappeared; and not one of them*

except the latest, ever invented any sweeping and adequate way to kill people. They all did their best, to kill being the chiefest ambition of the human race and the earliest incident in its history, but only the Christian Civilization has scored a triumph to be proud of. Two centuries from now it will be recognized that all the competent killers are Christian; then the pagan world will go to school [with] the Christian: not to acquire his religion but his guns. The Turk and the Chinamen will buy those, to kill missionaries and converts with." Id., 57.

46. *Id., 60-61. In The Mysterious Stranger, Twain had written that "in the history of the race," there "was never a war started by an aggressor for any clean purpose," quoted in Foner, 380.*

47. *FE, 167-68.*

48. *Letter from SLC to William T. Snead, January 9, 1890, quoted in A Pen Warmed, 71.*

49. *Id., 73.*

50. *CY, 242.*

51. *Foner, 382; Zwick, 166.*

52. *"The War Prayer," A Pen Warmed Up, 107.*

53. *Id., 110-11.*

54. *Id.*

55. *"Glances at History," The Bible According to Mark Twain, 87-88.*

56. *The wise man counsels the people not to support the war. As a world-wide symbol of freedom, "the Republic is safe, her greatness is secure." If the Republic launches a preemptive war, then the perception will change because "against our traditions, we are entering upon an unjust and trivial war, a war against a helpless people for a base object— robbery." The wise man argues: "In a republic, who is 'the country?' Is it the Government which is for the moment is in the saddle? Why, the Government is merely a servant – merely a temporary servant; it cannot be its prerogative to determine what is right and what is wrong, and decide who is patriotic and who isn't. Its function is to obey orders, not originate them. Who, then, is 'the country?' Is it the newspapers? Is it the pulpit? Is it the school superintendent? Why, these are mere parts of the country, not the whole of it; they have not command; they have only their little share in the command. They are but one in the thousands; it is the thousand that command is lodged; they must determine what is right and what is wrong; they must decide who is a patriot and who isn't. "Who are the thousand— that is to say, who are 'the country?' In a monarchy, the King and his family are the country; in a republic, it is the common voice of the people. Each of you, for himself, by himself and on his own responsibility, must speak. And it is a solemn and weighty responsibility, and*

not lightly to be flung aside at the bullying of the pulpit, press, government, or the empty catch-phrases of politicians. Each man must for himself alone decide what is right and what is wrong, which course is patriotic and which isn't. You cannot shirk this and be a man. To decide it against your convictions is to be an unqualified and inexcusable traitor, both to yourself and to your country, let men label you as they may." Foner, 395-96.

57.   *The Prince and the Pauper, 310.*

58.   *MTL: SLC to Clara Clemens, June 18, 1905 (UCCL 07063).*

59.   *SLC to the Editor of the London Times, "The Missionary in World Politics," July 1900, Who is Mark Twain?, 103.*

60.   *MTNJ, ch 35 quoted in Peterson, 83-84.*

61.   *Twain, "On the Russian Revolution: The Czar's Soliloquy," Collected Tales, Speeches and Essays: 1891-1910, 642.*

62.   *Hochschild, 164-75, 195-208; Foner, 384. In the soliloquy, Twain describes the acts of the "unfriendly" tribes who have been conscripted to enforce the natives' rubber collection, quoting the British consul: "Each time the corporal goes out to get rubber, cartridges are given him. He must bring back all not used, and for every one used he must bring back a right hand. M.P told me that sometimes they shot a cartridge at an animal in hunting; they then cut off a hand from a living man... In six months, the State on the Mambogo River [a small region in the Congo] had used 6,000 cartridges, which means that 6,000 people are killed or mutilated. It means more than 6,000, for the people have told me repeatedly that the soldiers kill the children with the butt of their guns." Twain, "King Leopold's Soliloquy: A Defense of His Congo Rule," 2nd ed. (1905) ("King Leopold's Soliloquy").*

63.   *Unpublished article, "Thanksgiving Sentiment," 1904, quoted in Foner, 385; see also MT Autobiography 2, 307.*

64.   *King Leopold's Soliloquy, Boston: P. R. Warren, 1905.*

65.   *Hochschild, 241-42. In the Introduction, Leopold's absolute authority is established: Leopold II is the absolute Master of the whole of the internal and external activity of the Independent State of the Congo. The organization of justice, the army, the industry and commercial regimes are established freely by himself. He would say, and with greater accuracy than did Louis XIX, "The State, it is I." King Leopold's Soliloquy, 2-3.*

66.   *Id., 6. Leopold complains: "These meddlesome American missionaries! These frank British consuls! These blabbingblabbing Belgian-born traitor officials!– those tiresome parrots are always talking, always telling. They have told how for twenty years I have ruled the Congo State, ... a fruitful domain four times as large as the German Empire– claiming and holding its millions of people as*

my private property, my serfs, my slaves; their labor mine, with or without wage; the food they raise not their property but mine; the rubber, the ivory and all the other riches of the land mine– mine solely– and gathered for me by the men, the women and the little children under compulsion of lash and bullet, fire, starvation, mutilation and the halter." Id., 7-8.

67. *Leopold satirizes his own legacy: "Another madman wants to construct a memorial for the perpetuation of my name, out of my 15,000,000 skulls and skeletons, and is so full of vindictive enthusiasm over his strange project. . . . Out of the skulls he will build a combined monument and mausoleum to me which shall exactly duplicate the Great Pyramid of Cheops.... He desires to stuff me and stand me up in the sky ... robed and crowned, with a "pirate flag" in one hand and a butcher- knife and pendant handcuffs in the other." Id., 27-28.*

68. *Id., 39-40.*

69. *Hochschild, 242-45.*

70. *Id., 243-49.*

71. *Id., 241-42.*

72. *Quirk, 281.*

73. *Hochschild, 259, 275-306.*

74. *MT Biography quoted in Political Tales, 40.*

CHAPTER NINETEEN
A MAN FOR ALL SEASONS
Chapter quote from song
"The Pilgrim, chapter 33" by Kris Kristopherson.

1   *Foner, 405.*

2. *Geismar, 426, 502; see Paul Roazen, Cultural Foundations of Political Philosophy, New Brunswick, NJ: Transaction Publishers, 2003, 22.*

3. *MTL: SLC to Livy, November 10, 1893 (UCCL 04495).*

4. *New York Herald, November 12, 1905.*

5   *Sam Dillon, "Failing Grade on Civics Exam Called a 'Crisis,'" New York Times, May 4, 2011.*

6. *Daniel de Vise, "Investment in public ivory towers is eroding," Washington Post, December 27, 2011,1cs1-4.*

7. *Justin Pope, "National SAT reading scores fall to record low," Seattle Times, September 16, 2011; Stephanie Banchero, "SAT Reading, Writing Scores Hit Low," September 15, 2011, Wall Street Journal, A2cs5-6.*

8.   *"As Regards Patriotism," A Pen Warmed Up, 44-45.*

9.   *"To the Male Teachers' Association of the City of New York," New York Times, March 17, 1901.*

10.   *"Glances in History" quoted in Foner, 395-96.*

11.   *"As Regards Patriotism," 45.*

12.   *CY, 216.*

13.   *"Optical Physic," The Twainian, November, 1943, quoted in Peterson, 18-19.*

14.   *Washington in 1868, 33; Christian Science, 361; Europe and Elsewhere, 302-03.*

15.   *MTA-P II, "The Character of Man" (entry January 23, 1906), 10-11 quoted in Peterson, 73.*

16.   *Pew Research Center, "Partisan Polarization Surges in Bush, Obama Years: Trends in American Values: 1987-2012," June 4, 2012; Dan Balz, "Politics, the Great American Divider," Washington Post, June 5, 2012, A2cs3-6.*

17.   *Washington in 1868, 34.*

18.   *MTA-P II, January 23, 1906 quoted in Peterson, 43.*

19   *MTA-P, March 6, 1906 quoted in Peterson, 52.*

20.   *MTNJ, No. 33, August 29, 1900, 23, quoted in Foner, 127-28; Ayres, The Wit and Wisdom of Mark Twain, 125.89; Kaiser, 261-62; Dana Milbank, "Newtonian Nastiness," Washington Post, December 11, 2011, Op-ed.*

21.   *MT Eruption (entry January 15, 1907), 67-69; MTB, 179;MT Autobiography 2, 371-72.*

22.   *Unsent letter to H.C. Christiancy, December 18, 1887 quoted in Peterson, 57-58.*

23.   *MT Eruption, 64-65 (entry December 13, 1906); MT Autobiography 2, 313-14.*

24.   *Former Secretary of Health, Education and Welfare, Elliot Richardson, used to complain facetiously about Congress' "disease of the month club," creating a new program and bureaucracy dedicated to curing whatever illness was in fashion that month.*

25.   *For example, an office devoted to clean air attracts dedicated environmentalists; whereas an office devoted to auto safety attracts safety advocates. The former seeks to reduce automobile emissions, the latter traffic fatalities. Who will ensure a consistent government regulatory policy that enables private manufacturers and their employees to build safe, fuel-efficient, emission-controlled automobiles that consumers will buy?*

26.   *President Barack Obama, State of the Union Address to Congress, January 24, 2012, www.whitehouse.gov/blog/2012/01/24/remarks/president-obama-state-union.*

27. *On February 20, 1891, Clemens was a guest of honor seated next to Kaiser Wilhelm II of Germany, who praised America's generous soldiers' pensions. Clemens responded by saying that the pensions began as a "praiseworthy" program for "soldiers who earned them," but "degenerated " into a "wider system of vote-purchasing,." from MTP, 179 quoted in Peterson, 93.*

28. *Bryan T. Lawrence, "The dirty secret in Uncle Sam's Friday trash dump," Washington Post, December 29, 2011, Op-ed.*

29. *Lori Montgomery, "So much drama, so little debt reduction," Washington Post, December 28, 2011, 1 c1.*

30. *"Optical Physic" quoted in Peterson, 18.*

31. *FE, 228 (reference is to the effect on local wine growers of the government's reduction of wine import duties in Stawell region in Victoria).*

32. *The Quarrel in a Strongbox," 1897, Who Is Mark Twain?, 71, 74-75.*

33. *Europe and Elsewhere (1900) quoted in Political Tales, 96-97.*

34. *CY, 159.*

35. *"Skeleton Plan of a Proposed Casting Vote Party" quoted in MTA-P, 1148.*

Acknowledgments

1. *Greg Camfield, Bernard DeVoto, Paul Fatout, Shelley Fisher Fishkin, Philip Foner, Hamlin Hill, Robert H. Hirst, Andrew Hoffman, William Dean Howells, Fred Kaplan, Justin Kaplan, John Lauber, Jerome Loving, Charles Neider, Albert Bigelow Paine, Ron Powers, Thomas Quirk, Kent Rasmussen, Michael Shelden, Henry Nash Smith, Dixon Wecter, James Zwick and many others. In recreating Mark Twain's Washington experience and political views, the following sources have been especially helpful: Philip S. Foner, Mark Twain Social Critic; Louis J. Budd, Mark Twain Social Philosopher; Tom Quirk, Mark Twain and Human Nature; Bryant Morey French, Mark Twain and The Gilded Age; Paul Jefferson Carter, Jr., The Social and Political Ideas of Mark Twain; Joe Fulton, The Reconstruction of Mark Twain; Robert H. Hirst and the Mark Twain Project at the University of California; Maxwell Geismar, Mark Twain: Prophet; David H. Fears, Mark Twain Day By Day; Joe Fulton, The Reconstruction of Mark Twain; Edgar Lee Masters, Mark Twain: A Portrait; Svend Peterson, Mark Twain and the Government; See Bibliography for full citations.*

2. *Frederick Anderson, Mark Twain: The Critical Heritage; Bernard DeVoto, Mark Twain's America.*

3. *Andrew Hoffman, Inventing Mark Twain.*

4. *Foner, Budd, Carter, Jim Zwick, Anti-Imperialism in the United States, 1898-1935.*

5. *Fulton; Shelley Fisher Fishkin, Lighting Out for the Territory: Reflections on Mark Twain and American Culture.*

6. *G. VanWyck Brooks, The Ordeal of Mark Twain.*

7. *Albert Bigelow Paine, Mark Twain: A Biography, 4 Vols.*

8. *MTB, 1269 (Paine wrote: "I do not wish to say by any means, that his so-called autobiography is a mere fairy tale. It is far from that. It is amazingly truthful in the character picture it represents of the man himself. It is only not reliable– and it sometimes even unjust– as detailed history.")*

9.   *MT Autobiography 1, 25 (Twain said "he would like to wander about, picking up this point and that, as memory or fancy prompted, without any particular biographical order.... It was his purpose... that his dictations should not be published until he had been dead a hundred years or more....") Twain did permit partial (censored) publication of portions of his dictations in a series of articles for the North American Review; see MT Autobiography 2 (2013) and 3 (2015).*

10.   *Albert Bigelow Paine's expurgated two-volume autobiography was censored, containing revisions to language Paine thought offensive. MTA-P.*

11.   *Charles Neider, ed., The Autobiography of Mark Twain.*

Index

41920730R00350

Made in the USA
Middletown, DE
27 March 2017